Case Studies in Intelligent Computing

Achievements and Trends

Case Studies in Intelligent Computing

Achievements and Trends

Edited by Biju Issac and Nauman Israr

CRC Press
Taylor & Francis Group
Boca Raton   London   New York

CRC Press is an imprint of the
Taylor & Francis Group, an **informa** business
AN AUERBACH BOOK

CRC Press
Taylor & Francis Group
6000 Broken Sound Parkway NW, Suite 300
Boca Raton, FL 33487-2742

First issued in paperback 2016

Version Date: 20140508

ISBN 13: 978-1-138-03412-9 (pbk)
ISBN 13: 978-1-4822-0703-3 (hbk)

Library of Congress Cataloging-in-Publication Data

Case studies in intelligent computing : achievements and trends / editors, Biju Issac, Nauman Israr.
    pages cm
    Includes bibliographical references and index.
    ISBN 978-1-4822-0703-3 (hardback)
    1. Artificial intelligence--Industrial applications--Case studies. 2. Artificial
intelligence--Research--Case studies. 3. Computational intelligence--Industrial applications--Case
studies. 4. Computational intelligence--Research--Case studies. 5. Intelligent agents (Computer
software)--Case studies. I. Issac, Biju, editor of compilation. II. Israr, Nauman, editor of compilation.

TA347.A78C37 2014
006.3--dc23   2014008394

Visit the Taylor & Francis Web site at
http://www.taylorandfrancis.com

and the CRC Press Web site at
http://www.crcpress.com

Contents

Preface

Intelligent software can come to decisions on its own, based on the training on a data set—which makes artificial intelligence (AI) a primary area of research these days. AI is the study and design of a system that comprehends its environment and makes decisions that maximize its chances of success. In most cases, it is an application intelligence that evolves over time and gets better with fewer errors. In others, it can be an intelligence derived out of a set of options or constraints. Software that can intelligently find solutions to tough problems is always growing in relevance. AI thus has implications in most areas of applied computing. How can we better understand such intelligent applications and scenarios?

The objective of this book is to capture the recent work and achievements in intelligent computing research through case studies, where the success of machine learning and AI-based application in different scenarios would be dealt with. It will assemble various applications of AI in different fields. The challenges faced and solutions proposed by different researchers in this area will be discussed.

The following is a brief summary extracted from the respective chapters and their abstracts.

Chapter 1, by Kuruvilla Mathew and Biju Issac, surveys the concepts underlying AI and its applications through active implementation or as research work.

Chapter 2, by Amit Laddi and Amod Kumar, discusses a case study involving a noninvasive and instant disease detection technique based upon machine vision through image scanning of the eyes of subjects with conjunctivitis (eye flu) and jaundice. Then the neuro-fuzzy–based software that was developed for the prediction of jaundice and conjunctivitis is used.

Chapter 3, by Aya Sedky Adly et al., provides a comprehensive study that investigates the main aspects of applying low-intensity laser irradiation on stem cells and its effect on their proliferation under different parameters and conditions consolidated by an intelligent agent–based model.

Chapter 4, by Basant Agarwal et al., explains various semantic orientation–based approaches for sentiment analysis that have been previously reported. Then the challenges in the sentiment analysis problem are discussed, and a new efficient semantic orientation–based approach is proposed for sentiment analysis.

Chapter 5, by Debi P. Acharjya, elaborates on a rough set on two universal sets employing the notion of lower and upper approximation, as an information system establishes the relation between different universes. In addition to this, a fuzzy rough set and an intuitionistic fuzzy rough set on two universal sets are also discussed.

Chapter 6, by Ryan G. Goss and Geoff S. Nitschke, proposes an efficient and autonomous method for distinguishing application protocols through the use of a dynamic protocol classification system (DPCS), where the burden of signature creation is reduced, while the accuracy achieved in application protocol identification increases.

Chapter 7, by Mantosh Biswas and Hari Om, presents a case study on various nonwavelet and wavelet image denoising methods by using fuzzy logic and other methods.

Chapter 8, by Hong-Bo Xie et al., discusses a multiclass fuzzy relevance vector machine (FRVM) learning mechanism and evaluates its performance to classify multiple hand motions from experiments conducted on seven subjects with six hand motions using surface electromyographic (SEMG) signals.

Chapter 9, by João P. Souza Medeiros et al., addresses the identification of a remote operating system, across a computer network, with the aid of computational intelligence by extracting distinguishable characteristics from reliable data, using procedures to minimize the amount of data necessary for classification.

Chapter 10, by Kumar S. Ray et al., implements an automated surveillance system for public places such as shopping malls or airports. The method of handling event recognition at the entry point is based on vertical and horizontal histogram analysis of the blob identified by which the number of objects present in the blob can be determined. The multiple-object tracking after the entry point is based on the method of linear assignment and Kalman filter.

Chapter 11, by Lavika Goel, discusses a methodology inspired by nature using remote sensing inputs based on swarm intelligence for strategic decision making in modern warfare. It presents a hybrid ant colony–biogeography-based optimization technique (ACO-BBO) for predicting the deployment strategies of enemy troops in the war theater and finding the shortest and the best feasible path for attack on the enemy base station.

Chapter 12, by Chiranjeevi Manike and Hari Om, deals with high-utility pattern mining, and four significant algorithms in this area are presented, namely, GUIDE (LM), HUI-Miner, utility mining using maximal itemset (UMMI), and a two-phase algorithm. The primary contribution of this work is to show how high-utility pattern mining tasks can be applied on transaction databases in order to know how much memory and processing time are consumed.

Chapter 13, by Masoud Faraki and Mehrtash Harandi, elaborates on an intrinsic bag-of-Riemannian-words model (BoRW), which takes into account the true geometry of tensors in obtaining its codebook and histogram with experiments on a challenging virus texture data set—extending the conventional bag-of-words model from Euclidean space to non-Euclidean Riemannian manifolds.

Chapter 14, by Mohammad Hasan Bahari and Hugo Van Hamme, introduces a novel application-independent performance metric for ordinal, probabilistic-ordinal, and partial-ordinal classification problems. The ordinal distance between two arbitrary vectors in Euclidean space is presented along with a new performance metric, namely, normalized ordinal distance, which is proposed based on the introduced ordinal distance.

Chapter 15, by Neha Sharma and Hari Om, presents a case study wherein five data mining models are designed to predict the survival rate of oral cancer patients, where the predictive models are single tree, TreeBoost, decision tree forest, multilayer perceptron, and support vector machine that address the classification problem.

Chapter 16, by Omaima Nomir and Mohamed Abdel-Mottaleb, develops a system for identifying people from dental x-ray images, where the system automatically segments dental x-ray images into individual teeth and extracts representative feature vectors for each tooth, which are later used for retrieval.

Chapter 17, by Patcharaporn Paokanta, proposes a novel hybrid ontology called Multinomial Logistic Regression (Markov Chain Monte Carlo)-C5.0-Classification and Regression Tree for Thalassemia (a kind of genetic disorder). A knowledge-based system is discussed in terms of theory and performance comparison of the proposed algorithms.

Chapter 18, by R. R. Srikant and Ch. Srinivasa Rao, discusses robot kinematics, which is an essential concept in positioning of robotic manipulators. In their work, inverse kinematics is calculated for a serial manipulator and direct kinematics for a parallel manipulator (i.e., the more difficult ones) using backpropagation neural networks.

Chapter 19, by Saad Alqithami et al., presents the methods of agent-based modeling as a means to define specific tools that inherently affect agent behaviors and help them to socially connect with other agents. A case study of a terrorist organization known as Aum Shinrikyo (Aum) is analyzed using a classic bottom-up perspective of influence on autonomous agents through the social structure.

Chapter 20, by Sumit Tokle et al., combines features of many learning algorithms such as offline critic function and real-time learning algorithms to enhance the lifetime of wireless sensor nodes (WSNs). The purpose of the machine learning algorithm is to guess the environmental behavior, where it is deployed and updates the parameters of WSNs.

Chapter 21, by Senthilkumar K and Arunkumar Thangavelu, proposes a model that uses routing attributes to classify the routing nodes based on a fuzzy proximity relation. They use association rules, a Bayesian approach, and formal concepts analysis (FCA) on ordered categorical classes to determine the behaviors and predict the hidden associations and implications and dependencies of routing attributes, respectively.

Chapter 22, by Vahid Nourani et al., describes rainfall runoff modeling using a wavelet-based artificial neural network (WANN) model. Two mathematical concepts (i.e., self-organizing maps and entropy) are used as feature extraction methods for modeling the rainfall runoff process of the Delaney Creek and Payne Creek subbasins located in Florida, with distinct hydrogeomorphological characteristics.

Chapter 23, by Vijay K Mago et al., shows some pointers in the area of gerontology that can improve the quality of life of older people. They discuss five key AI and mathematical modeling techniques, namely, Bayesian networks, compartmental models, multiagent systems, fuzzy logic, and fuzzy cognitive maps, with example scenarios chosen from long-term care (LTC) institutions.

Chapter 24, by Afef Ben Brahim et al., uses ensemble approaches to combine feature selection and data classification for cancer diagnosis and credit scoring. An ensemble of feature selection techniques is used for feature selection, where each member yields a different feature set. Later, it combines these feature sets to obtain a single solution on which a classifier is trained and also trains a classifier on each feature set to obtain a single classification output.

Chapter 25, by Amit Laddi and Neelam R. Prakash, investigates grade estimation of black tea by examining the physical characteristics of produced black CTC (Crushing, Tearing and Curling) tea by machine vision. A quality grade estimation technique was developed by the application of neuro-fuzzy algorithms. Data analysis in the form of principal component analysis (PCA) was performed to extract significant physical attributes.

We hope these different scenarios of case studies and discussions will provide a great eye opener for the curious minds that are looking for applications of intelligent computing. It will help budding researchers to understand how and where intelligent computing can be applied.

The chapters were accepted based on the results of two reviews done on each of them. We thank the reviewers for their great work.

MATLAB® is a registered trademark of The MathWorks, Inc. For product information, please contact:

The MathWorks, Inc.
3 Apple Hill Drive
Natick, MA 01760-2098 USA
Tel: 508 647 7000
Fax: 508-647-7001
E-mail: info@mathworks.com
Web: www.mathworks.com

Editors

Dr. Biju Issac is a senior lecturer at the School of Computing, Teesside University, United Kingdom, and has more than 15 years of academic experience with higher education in India, Malaysia, and the United Kingdom. He earned a PhD in networking and mobile communications, along with an MCA (master of computer applications) and BE (electronics and communications engineering). He is a senior member of the Institute of Electrical and Electronics Engineers (IEEE), a fellow of the Higher Education Academy, a member of the Institution of Engineering and Technology (IET), and a chartered engineer (CEng). Dr. Issac is a CISCO-Certified Network Associate (CCNA) instructor, a Sun-Certified Java instructor, and a Lotus Notes professional. His broad research interests are in computer networks, wireless networks, computer or network security, mobility management in 802.11 networks, intelligent computing, data mining, spam detection, secure online voting, e-learning, and so forth. Dr. Issac has authored more than 60 peer-reviewed research publications, including conference papers, book chapters, and journal papers. He has supervised postgraduate research students to completion. He is in the technical program committee of many international conferences, is on the editorial board of some journals, and has reviewed many research papers.

Dr. Nauman Israr has been a senior lecturer at the School of Computing, Teesside University, United Kingdom, for many years. He earned his PhD in wireless sensor networks at the University of Bradford, United Kingdom. He teaches computer networks–related subjects at the university. His areas of research expertise are wireless sensor networks, wireless networked control systems, fly-by-wireless systems, active aircraft, and wireless embedded systems. Dr. Israr was a research fellow at Queen's University Belfast (Active Aircraft Project). The aim of that project was to design and develop a wireless nervous system for next-generation Airbus aircraft, where the wireless system will be used to reduce turbulence on the aircraft, thus reducing the fuel burned. He has published a number of conference papers, book chapters, and journal papers.

Contributors

Mohamed Abdel-Mottaleb earned a PhD in computer science from the University of Maryland, College Park, in 1993. Currently, he is a professor and the chairman of the Department of Electrical and Computer Engineering, University of Miami, where his research focuses on 3D face recognition, dental biometrics, visual tracking, and human activity recognition. Prior to joining the University of Miami, from 1993 to 2000, he was with Philips Research, Briarcliff Manor, New York. While there, he was a principal member of the research staff and was a project leader, where he led several projects in image processing and content-based multimedia retrieval. He holds 20 US patents and has published many journal and conference papers in the areas of image processing, computer vision, and content-based retrieval. He is an associate editor for the journal *Pattern Recognition*.

Debi P. Acharjya earned a PhD in computer science from Berhampur University, India; MTech in computer science from Utkal University, India, in 2002; an MPhil from Berhampur University; and an MSc from the National Institute of Technology (NIT), Rourkela, India. He was awarded a gold medal while taking his MSc. Currently, he is a full professor at the School of Computing Sciences and Engineering, VIT University, Vellore, India. He has authored many national and international journal papers, chapters, and four books: *Fundamental Approach to Discrete Mathematics, Computer Based on Mathematics, Theory of Computation, and Rough Set in Knowledge Representation and Granular Computing*. In addition, he has edited two books. He is associated with many professional bodies: the Computer Society of India (CSI), Indian Society for Technical Education (ISTE), Indian Mathematical Society (IMS), the Association of Mathematics Teachers of India (AMIT), Indian Society of Industrial and Applied Mathematics (ISIAM), ORISSA Information Technology Society (OITS), the International Association of Computer Science and Information Technology (IACSIT), the Computer Science Teachers Association (CSTA), the International Rough Set Society (IRSS), and the International Association of Engineers (IAENG). He was the founder–secretary of the OITS Rourkela chapter. His current research interests include rough sets, formal concept analysis, knowledge representation, data mining, granular computing, and business intelligence.

Aya Sedky Adly is a teaching assistant of computer science at the Faculty of Computers and Information, Helwan University. She earned her MS in computers and information, computer science specialization. Her major interesting research tracks are biomedical computing, rehabilitation engineering, computer vision systems, computational intelligence, and dynamic modeling.

Basant Agarwal is a doctoral candidate at the Malaviya National Institute of Technology, Jaipur, India. He earned his MS in computer engineering from the Malaviya National Institute of Technology. His research interests are in natural language processing, machine learning, sentiment analysis, and opinion mining.

Saad Alqithami is a PhD candidate at the Department of Computer Science, Southern Illinois University in Carbondale, where he earned his MS with honors in 2012. He is also a faculty member at Albaha University, Saudi Arabia. His main interests are distributed artificial intelligence, multiagent systems, game theory, robotics, computational social science, and cognitive intelligence. Saad is a member of many learned societies such as the Association for the Advancement of Artificial Intelligence (AAAI), the Association for Computing Machinery (ACM), and the Institute of Electrical and Electronics Engineers (IEEE).

Aida Hosseini Baghanam is a PhD candidate in the Faculty of Water Resources Engineering at the University of Tabriz, Iran, where she has been a student since 2003. She earned her MSc at the University of Tabriz, where she also took her undergraduate study. Her research interests lie in the area of the hydroenvironment and application of artificial intelligence methods on hydrology, specifically rainfall runoff modeling. Aida has published four journal papers as well as two book chapters and over ten conference papers.

Mohamad Hasan Bahari is a PhD candidate at the Center for Processing Speech and Images, KU Leuven, Belgium. His main research focuses on identifying speakers' characteristics (gender, age, accent, etc.) from speech signals. In February 2012, he visited Radboud University Nijmegen, Netherlands, and in winter, spring, and fall 2013, he was a visiting PhD student at the Computer Science and Artificial Intelligence Laboratory (CSAIL), Massachusetts Institute of Technology (MIT), United States. Hasan was granted a Marie Curie Fellowship, and his works have been supported by the European Commission under an ITN project, namely, Bayesian Biometrics for Forensics.

Shamantha Rai Bellipady is currently pursuing a PhD at Indian Institute of Information Technology–Allahabad, India, in the Department of Information Technology (IT). He earned an MTech in IT with specialization in wireless communication and computing from Indian Institute of Information Technology–Allahabad. He is also working as an assistant professor in the Department of Computer Science and Engineering at Sahyadri College of Engineering and Management, Mangalore, India. His areas of interest are localization, topology control, and routing in wireless sensor networks, mobile databases, graph theory, etc.

Mantosh Biswas is an assistant professor in the Department of Computer Engineering at the National Institute of Technology, Kurukshetra, India. He has submitted his PhD thesis in the Department of Computer Science and Engineering at Indian School of Mines, Dhanbad, India. He earned his BTech and MTech in computer science and engineering from West Bengal University of Technology and the National Institute of Technology, Durgapur, India, in 2006 and 2008, respectively. From 2008 to 2009, he was a trainee programmer and lecturer in the Department of Information Technology with PISJ India Pvt. Ltd. and R. K. Degree College, India. He was a teaching assistant in the Department of Computer Science and Engineering at the National Institute of Technology, Silchar, India, from 2009 to 2011. During this period, he was also a researcher in the National Institute of Technology, Silchar. He also received an offer as a deputy engineer in DOEACC Society, Mizoram, India, in 2009. His research area includes signal and image processing, pattern recognition, wavelets, and soft computing.

Waad Bouaguel earned a BS in business computer science and an MSc in modeling from the Higher Institute of Management of Tunis, Tunisia, in 2008 and 2010, respectively. She is currently a PhD student and a research assistant in the computer science department at the same institute. She is interested in employing computational and statistical learning theory to analyze specific challenges presented in big data and feature selection. More specifically, her work examines ensemble techniques for feature selection and rank aggregation.

Afef Ben Brahim earned a BS and an MSc in business computer science from the Higher Institute of Management of Tunis, Tunisia, in 2008 and 2010, respectively. She is currently a PhD student at the same institute and a temporary teacher at the Graduate School of Economics and Management of Tunis, Computer Science Department. Her current interests include feature selection for high-dimensional data, pattern recognition, ensemble methods, and data fusion.

Kingshuk Chatterjee was a project-linked scientist at the Electronics and Communication Sciences Unit, Indian Statistical Institute, India. Currently, Chatterjee is a research scholar at the Indian Statistical Institute and is working toward a PhD in computer science. His general areas of research interest include computer vision, theoretical aspects of DNA computing, and quantum computing.

Vahid Dabbaghian is an adjunct professor at the Department of Mathematics and the School of Computer Science, Simon Fraser University. Dr. Dabbaghian was the director of the Modelling of Complex Social Systems (MoCSSy) Program from June 2009 to March 2013. He earned a PhD in 2003 at Carleton University. Following this, he was a postdoctoral fellow with the Department of Computer Science at the University of Calgary and the Department of Mathematics at Simon Fraser University. He was the leader of the Criminal Justice System project at the Interdisciplinary Research in the Mathematical and Computational Sciences (IRMACS) Centre from May 2006 to May 2009.

Socrates Dokos earned a PhD in biomedical engineering in 1996 from the University of New South Wales, Sydney, Australia, where he is currently an associate professor at the Graduate School of Biomedical Engineering. His research interests include the electrical and mechanical properties of cardiac, neural, and musculoskeletal tissues, having published over 100 journal articles and refereed conference proceedings in these areas. His research has been multidisciplinary, involving techniques ranging from computational modeling and large-scale systems identification to electrophysiological measurements and mechanical testing.

Masoud Faraki earned a BSc in computer engineering (software) in 2006 and an MSc in computer engineering (artificial intelligence) in 2009, both from Isfahan University of Technology, Iran. He has recently completed an internship at the University of Queensland (Australia). His research interests are machine learning and computer vision.

Debayan Ganguly is working as a project-linked scientist at the Electronics and Communication Science Unit, Indian Statistical Institute, India. Currently Ganguly is working toward his PhD in computer science. His general areas of research interest include computer vision, theoretical aspects of DNA computing, and quantum computing. He has a total of three publications in international journals.

Lavika Goel is a research scholar at the Department of Computer Engineering at Delhi Technological University (formerly Delhi College of Engineering), Delhi, India. She worked at Oracle India Private Ltd. for 6 months through campus recruitment and then left it to pursue research in the field of nature-inspired intelligence, her interest area. Securing a percentile of 98.7% in the Graduate Aptitude Test in Engineering (GATE), she earned an ME (with Distinction) in computer technology and applications from Delhi College of Engineering, Delhi, and a BTech (with Honours) in computer science and engineering from Jagadguru Sri Shivarathreeswara Academy of Technical Education (JSSATE), Uttar Pradesh Technical University (U.P.T.U.), and has always been among the top rank holders of the university in these courses.

Ryan G. Goss earned an MTech in information technology from the Nelson Mandela Metropolitan University, South Africa, in 2009. His thesis, titled "Enabling e-Learning 2.0 in Information Security Education: A Semantic Web Approach," focused on educating users on information security concepts by merging Web 2.0 and semantic web technologies. He is currently a registered PhD student at the University of Cape Town (UCT) in South Africa, where his focus has shifted to the application of machine learning in solving classification problems within the network domain.

Jennifer Haegele is a PhD student at the Department of Criminology and Criminal Justice at Southern Illinois University, Carbondale, Illinois. In 2013, she earned a double-major MA in criminology and criminal justice and geography and environmental resources from Southern Illinois University. She is also a cartographer and a geography information systems technician at Morris Library Geospatial Resources. Jennifer's main interests include terrorism, natural disasters, the psychological behavior of offenders and police, geospatial analysis, and agent-based modeling.

Mohamed Hassan Haggag is an associate professor of computer science at the Faculty of Computers and Information, Helwan University. He worked as the head of the computer science department until 2012. Currently, he is the vice dean for community service affairs and environmental development. He is also the manager of the Data Center, Network and Infrastructure Development project at Helwan University and the managing director of the Scientific Computing Center, Helwan University.

Mehrtash Harandi earned a PhD from the University of Tehran, Iran, in 2009. In 2010, he joined the National Information and Communications Technology Australia (NICTA) and the University of Queensland (Australia) as a research scientist. He has previously worked on active learning and object recognition at the Institute for Research in Fundamental Sciences. His current research is mainly focused on Riemannian geometry and its applications in machine learning and computer vision.

Henry Hexmoor earned an MS from Georgia Tech, Atlanta, Georgia, and a PhD in computer science from the State University of New York, Buffalo, in 1996. He taught at the University of North Dakota before a stint at the University of Arkansas. Currently, he is an associate professor with the Computer Science Department, Southern Illinois University, Carbondale, Illinois. He has published widely on artificial intelligence and multiagent systems. His research interests include multiagent systems, artificial intelligence, cognitive science, and mobile robotics. Dr. Hexmoor is an IEEE senior member.

Hu Huang earned a BS and an MS in biomedical engineering from Jiangsu University (Jiangsu, China) in 2007 and 2011, respectively. His research interests are signal processing, pattern recognition, and their application to biomedical problems. He earned an MS in biomedical engineering in 2013 from Carnegie Mellon University (Pittsburgh, Pennsylvania), where his study mainly focused on machine learning and medical image analysis. He is currently pursuing his PhD in biomedical informatics and computational biology at the University of Minnesota (Twin Cities, Minnesota).

Biju Issac earned a PhD in networking and mobile communications, along with an MCA (master of computer applications) and a BE (electronics and communications engineering). He is a senior member of the Institute of Electrical and Electronics Engineers (IEEE), a fellow of the Higher Education Academy, a member of the Institution of Engineering and Technology (IET), and a chartered engineer (CEng). His broad research interests are in computer networks, wireless networks, computer or network security, mobility management in 802.11 networks, intelligent computing, data mining, spam detection, secure online voting, e-learning, and so forth. Dr. Issac works at the School of Computing in Teesside University, United Kingdom, and has authored more than 60 peer-reviewed research publications such as conference papers, book chapters, and journal papers. He is an experienced academic staff member with strong skills in teaching and research. He is in the technical program committee of many international conferences and has reviewed many papers.

Senthilkumar K earned an MTech in computer science and engineering. He is currently working as an assistant professor in the School of Information Technology and Engineering and also as a research member of the Centre for Ambient Intelligence and Advanced Networking Research Lab (C-AMIR) at Vellore Institute of Technology (VIT) University, India. His research interests include mobile ad hoc network (MANET) and fuzzy and rough sets.

Tohid Rezapour Khanghah is a PhD candidate in the Faculty of Water Resources Engineering at the University of Tabriz, Iran, with research interests in artificial intelligence applications to water resources engineering and hydroinformatics. He earned a BSc and an MS in civil engineering from Tabriz University in 2010 and 2012, respectively. His MS thesis, supervised by Prof. Vahid Nourani, was about entropy-based rainfall runoff feature extraction methods employed in wavelet-ANN modeling.

Amod Kumar earned a BE (Hons) in electrical and electronics engineering from Birla Institute of Technology and Science, Pilani, India; an ME in electronics from Punjab University, Chandigarh, India; and a PhD in biomedical signal processing from IIT Delhi, India. He has more than 34 years of experience in research and development of different instruments in the areas of process control, environmental monitoring, biomedical engineering, and prosthetics. He is currently working as a chief scientist at the Department of Biomedical Instrumentation at the Central Scientific Instruments Organisation (CSIO), Chandigarh, which is a constituent laboratory of CSIR. Dr. Kumar has more than 40 publications in reputed national and international journals. He worked at the Technical University Berlin for 1 year on a German fellowship in 1987–1988. He is an adjunct professor at Bengal Engineering and Science University and a senior faculty member of the postgraduate program of the academy of CSIR. His areas of interest are digital signal processing, image processing, and soft computing.

Amit Laddi earned a BTech (Hons) in electronics engineering from Kurukshetra University, India in 2004; earned an ME in electronics engineering in 2012; and is pursuing a PhD at PEC University of Technology, Chandigarh, India. He is currently working as a scientist at the Department of Biomedical Instrumentation at the Central Scientific Instruments Organisation (CSIR-CSIO), Chandigarh. He has more than 7 years of experience in research and development on systems based upon applications of machine vision and soft computing. His main research interests include machine vision and its applications, image and signal processing, and soft computing.

Mohamed Limam earned a BE from the National Agronomy Institute of Tunis, Tunisia, in 1976; an MSc in statistics from the College of Sciences, Oregon State University, United States, in 1981; and a PhD in statistics from the same university in 1985. Currently, he is a professor of statistics at the University of Tunis. His research interests include the area of applied and computational statistics, data mining, statistical quality control, and quality management. He is the author of many research studies. He is a member of the editorial board of the *International Journal of Quality and Standards*. He is the head of the Laboratory of Operations Research Decision and Control of Processes (LARODEC), the founder and president of the Tunisian Association of Statistics and its Applications, and a cofounder of the Tunisian Management Science Society.

Vijay K. Mago is an assistant professor with the Department of Computer Science at Troy University, Alabama, United States. Dr. Mago earned a PhD in computer science in 2010 from Panjab University, India. He worked as a postdoctoral research fellow at the Modelling of Complex Social Systems (MoCSSy) Program at Simon Fraser University from January 2011 to December 2012. Later, Dr. Mago joined the University of Memphis on a project funded by the National Science Foundation–National Institute of Health (NSF–NIH). In August 2013, he joined Troy University as a faculty member. Dr. Mago's research leverages medical decision-making systems to help physicians diagnose and deliver timely interventions or treatments. He is an associate editor of the journal *BMC Medical Informatics and Decision Making*.

Chiranjeevi Manike earned a BTech and an MTech in computer science and engineering in 2003 and 2008, respectively, from Jawaharlal Nehru Technological University at Hyderabad. From 2008 to 2012, he served as a faculty member in Computer Science & Engineering, Indur Institute of Engineering & Technology (IIET), Andhra Pradesh, India. He has been a research scholar in the Department of Computer Science & Engineering, Indian School of Mines, Dhanbad, India. His primary research interests include data mining and data warehousing.

Kuruvilla Mathew has been working with a software industry in the modern-day outsourcing scenario, dealing with clients from the United States, Europe, and Middle East. He has worked in different roles such as a business analyst, project and client coordinator, software engineer, systems administrator, and so forth in various domains and verticals ranging from mobile applications, remote function call (RFC) servers, web technologies, database, enterprise resource planning (ERP), logistics warehouse management, etc. He has also been the Management Representative (MR) for the ISO 9001:2008 quality management systems. After earning an MS, he now works with the Swinburne University of Technology, Malaysia, and is pursuing a PhD with the University Malaysia Sarawak (UNIMAS) in the field of wireless networking. His research interests include networks and artificial intelligence.

João P. Souza Medeiros earned a BS in computer engineering in 2007, an MSc in 2009, and a DSc in 2013, all from the Federal University of Rio Grande do Norte (UFRN). Since 2007, he has been a developer of the Umit project and a contributor of the Nmap project. On August 8, 2010, he became a professor at UFRN as a faculty member of the Department of the Exact and Applied Sciences (DCEA), Caicó, RN, Brazil. He is the founder of the Elements of Information Processing Laboratory (LabEPI). Currently, his research interests include complex networks, computer networks, artificial intelligence, signal processing, information theory, and security.

Namita Mittal has been an assistant professor for 18 years at the Department of Computer Engineering, Malaviya National Institute of Technology, Jaipur, India. She is involved in teaching undergraduate and graduate courses such as database management, information retrieval, data mining, natural language processing, semantic web, and so forth. Dr. Mittal has published several research papers in reputed international conferences and journals. She earned a PhD in computer engineering from Malaviya National Institute of Technology, Jaipur, India.

Mostafa-Sami M. Mostafa is a professor of computer science at the Faculty of Computers and Information, Helwan University. Currently, he is the head of the Computer Science Department and a member of the HCI research lab. He graduated in 1967 as a computer engineer from Military Technical College, Cairo, Egypt, and joined the teaching staff in the same institution in 1980 as a teaching assistant. He earned an MS in 1978 and a PhD from the University of Paul Sabatier, Toulouse, France. Dr. Mostafa has supervised and awarded more than 45 MSc and 12 PhD theses. He has more than 52 publications in different conferences and journals. His major interests and research tracks are software engineering, cloud computing, wireless sensor networks, and biomedical computing.

João B. Borges Neto earned a BS in computer science from the State University of Rio Grande do Norte (UERN), Mossoró, Brazil, in 2006. He earned an MS in teleinformatics engineering from the Federal University of Ceara (UFC), Fortaleza, Brazil, in 2009. Since 2010, he has been a professor at the Federal University of Rio Grande do Norte (UFRN), Caicó, Brazil, in the Department of Exact and Applied Sciences (DCEA). He is a founder of the Elements of Information Processing Laboratory (LabEPI) and has experience in computer networks. His research interests are focused on wireless sensor networks, mobile and ubiquitous computing, and communication protocols.

Geoff S. Nitschke earned a PhD in computer science from the Vrije Universiteit of Amsterdam in the Netherlands in 2009. His thesis title was "Neuro-Evolution for Emergent Specialization in Collective Behavior Systems." From 2009 to 2010, he was a postdoctoral researcher at the Computational Intelligence Research Group (CIRG) at the University of Pretoria, South Africa. From 2011 to 2012, he was a postdoctoral researcher at the Artificial Life Laboratory at the University of Tokyo, Japan. Dr. Nitschke is currently a senior lecturer at the Department of Computer Science, University of Cape Town, South Africa. His current research focus is on using neuroevolution methods to simulate complex behaviors in large groups of agents (simulated robots) in order to address a diverse set of problems ranging from automated collective construction of artificial habitats to scientific investigations of unexplored environments.

Omaima Nomir earned a PhD in electrical and computer engineering from the University of Miami, Coral Gables, Florida, in 2006. Currently, she is an assistant professor in the Department of Computer Science, School of Computer and Information Sciences, University of Manosura,

Egypt. Prior to joining the school, she was a systems analyst. Her duties included analyzing and designing systems for banking and some government agencies, and systems supported by the US Agency for International Development (USAID). Her PhD research was automating human identification using dental x-ray radiographs. Dr. Nomir's research interests include human identification, pattern recognition, medical image processing, and neural networks. She has published 30 research papers in fields related to forensic identification, medical image processing, and pattern recognition.

Vahid Nourani earned a BSc and an MS in civil engineering from the University of Tabriz, Iran, in 1998 and 2000, respectively. He then continued his graduate study in civil and environmental engineering in the field of hydrology at Shiraz University, Iran, and Tohoku University, Japan, and graduated in 2005. Nourani was with the Faculty of Civil Engineering, University of Tabriz, Iran, as an assistant professor from 2005 to 2009 and as an associate professor from 2009 to 2012, and with the Department of Civil Engineering, University of Minnesota, USA, in 2011 as a visiting associate professor. During this period, 45 PhD and MSc students graduated under his technical supervision. Dr. Nourani's research interests include rainfall runoff modeling, artificial intelligence applications to water resource engineering, hydroinformatics, and computational hydraulics. His research outcomes have been published in 51 journal articles, 1 book, 4 book chapters, and more than 55 papers presented in international and national conferences.

Hari Om earned an MSc in mathematics from Dr. B.R. Ambedkar University (formerly Agra University), Agra, at U.P.; an MTech in computer science and engineering from Kurukshetra University at Haryana; and a PhD in computer science from Jawaharlal Nehru University at New Delhi. Presently, he is working as an assistant professor at the Computer Science and Engineering Department at the Indian School of Mines, Dhanabd, India. Dr. Om's primary research interests are data mining, image and signal processing, network security, cryptography, and video on demand. He has published more than 60 papers in international and national journals, including various transactions of the IEEE, and international and national conferences of high repute.

Patcharaporn Paokanta has been a lecturer in the areas of data management, e-commerce, rapid application and development, system analysis and design, and information technology at the College of Arts, Media and Technology, Chiang Mai University (CMU), Thailand. She is studying for a PhD in knowledge management and earned an MS in software engineering in 2009 from the College of Arts, Media and Technology, CMU. In addition, she earned a BS in statistics from the Faculty of Science, CMU, in 2006. Paokanta was awarded an Erasmus Mundus scholarship (E-Link Project) to study and perform research at the University of Sannio in Italy for 10 months. Her research interests include soft computing, data and knowledge engineering, knowledge discovery techniques, statistics, biomedical engineering, knowledge and risk management, artificial and computing intelligence, applied mathematics, Ramsey number, and graph theory. She has published articles in international journal and conference proceedings, including *ICIC Express Letter: An International Journal of Research and Surveys, International Journal of Computer Theory and Engineering, International Journal of Intelligent Information Processing (IJIIP), Lecture Notes in Computer Sciences (LNCS)*, the International Symposium on Applied Sciences in Biomedical and Communication Technologies (ISABEL) 2010, and the IEEE-EMBS International Conferences on Biomedical and Health Informatics (BHI) 2012.

Paulo S. Motta Pires earned an electrical engineering degree (BEE) in 1977 from the Federal University of Rio Grande do Norte (UFRN) and an MSEE in 1980 and a PhD in 1986, both from the State University of Campinas (UNICAMP), Campinas, SP, Brazil. From 1978 until 1991, he was a faculty member of the Electrical Engineering Department, UFRN. Since 1991, he has been a faculty member of the Computer Engineering Department, UFRN, where he is continuing his teaching and research activities. Currently, his research interests are focused on information security.

Neelam Rup Prakash earned a BE in electronics and electrical communications engineering (E&EC) in 1987, an ME electronics in 1996, and a PhD in 2002 from Punjab Engineering College (PEC), Punjab University, Chandigarh, India. She has more than 26 years of experience in both industry and academia. She is currently working as a head of the department (HoD) in E&EC, PEC University of Technology. Dr. Prakash has several publications in reputed journals. Her areas of interest are digital design, communications, and computer-aided diagnostics.

Gutto S. Dantas Queiroz is a student in an information systems course at the Federal University of Rio Grande do Norte (UFRN) and a member of the Elements of Information Processing Laboratory (LabEPI). Currently, his research interests are focused on applications of computer vision, object recognition, digital image processing, and artificial neural networks.

Rajeev Ranjan is pursuing a PhD in the area of wireless sensor networks at Indian Institute of Information Technology–Allahabad (IIIT-A), India. His area of work includes wireless sensor networks—coverage and connectivity, sensor deployment and localization, wireless sensor statistical routing, etc.

Ch. Srinivasa Rao earned a PhD from Andhra University, Visakhapatnam, India, and is currently working in the Department of Mechanical Engineering, GITAM University, India. His areas of research include metal cutting, robotics, and manufacturing processes. He is currently guiding 10 PhD scholars.

Kumar S. Ray, PhD, is a professor at the Electronics and Communication Science Unit at Indian Statistical Institute, Kolkata, India. He is an alumnus of the University of Bradford, United Kingdom. He was a visiting faculty member under the UNDP fellowship program at the University of Texas, Austin, United States. Professor Ray was a member of the task force committee of the Government of India, Department of Electronics (DoE/MIT), for the application of artificial intelligence (AI) in power plants. He is a founder–member of the Indian Society for Fuzzy Mathematics and Information Processing (ISFUMIP) and a member of the Indian Unit for Pattern Recognition and Artificial Intelligence (IUPRAI). He serves as a reviewer of several international journals. His current research interests include AI, computer vision, common-sense reasoning, soft computing, nonmonotonic deductive database systems, and DNA computing.

Neha Sharma earned an MCA from the College of Engineering, Bhubaneshwar, under the Orissa University of Agriculture and Technology in 1999. She is currently pursuing a PhD (computer science) at Indian School of Mines, Dhanbad. She has presented five papers in international conferences and has also published three papers in international journals. She has 9 years of teaching experience and 4 years of industrial experience. Her areas of interest include data mining, database design, analysis and design, software engineering, and metadata.

Vijay Kumar Sharma is working at a faculty at the Malaviya National Institute of Technology, Jaipur, India. He earned an MS in computer engineering from Malaviya National Institute of Technology. His research interests are natural language processing and sentiment analysis.

Andrew Sixsmith has been a professor and the director of the Gerontology Research Centre at Simon Fraser University since 2007. Dr. Sixsmith is an executive board member of the International Society of Gerontechnology and was the chair of the 7th World Conference of the Society in 2010. His research interests include development of technologies for independent living, modeling the well-being of seniors, long-term care, and theory and methods in gerontology. He has attracted funding for many prestigious research projects from the European Commission and the Engineering and Physical Sciences Research Council, Department of Health, and Department of Industry, in the United Kingdom and Canadian Institutes of Health Research (CIHR) in Canada. Dr. Sixsmith has substantial teaching experience within gerontology and has been responsible for innovative educational initiatives in the area of technology and aging.

R. R. Srikant earned a PhD from Andhra University, Visakhapatnam, India. He is currently working at the Department of Mechanical Engineering, GITAM University. His areas of research include manufacturing technology and artificial intelligence.

Arunkumar Thangavelu earned a PhD in computer science from PSG College of Technology, Coimbatore, India. He is currently associated with Vellore Institute of Technology (VIT) University as a professor in the School of Computing Sciences and Engineering. He has 20 years of academic and research and development experience in industries and research institutes. Dr. Thangavelu has published many papers in national/international journals. His area of research interest focuses on ad hoc high-performance networking, aspect-based network management (including 4G networks), ambient technologies, and vehicular-based applications. He is one of the cofounders of Net Research Labs (an ad hoc research forum) and the assistant director of the Centre for Ambient Intelligence and Advanced Networking Research Lab (C-AMIR), VIT University, India.

Sumit Tokle earned an MTech in information technology with specialization in wireless communication of computing from the Indian Institute of Information Technology–Allahabad, India. Currently, he is working as a senior network engineer in Extreme Networks, Chennai, India. His areas of expertise includes wireless networking, wireless routing, multiprotocol label switching (MPLS), border gateway protocol (BGP), etc.

Hugo Van Hamme earned a PhD in electrical engineering from Vrije Universiteit Brussel (VUB) in 1992; an MSc from Imperial College, London, in 1988; and an MS in engineering ("burgerlijk ingenieur") from VUB in 1987. Since 2002, he has been a professor at the Department of Electrical Engineering at KU Leuven. His main research interests are applications of speech technology in education and speech therapy, computational models for speech recognition and language acquisition, and noise robust speech recognition.

Shirshu Varma, after earning a PhD, served in many reputed organizations in India, including Birla Institute of Technology, Mesra (BIT Mesra) Ranchi and the Centre for Development of Advanced Computing (C-DAC) Noida in many capacities such as a lecturer, senior lecturer, and principal project engineer, and is presently working as an associate professor in the Indian Institute of Information Technology–Allahabad (IIIT-Allahabad), India. He has 19 years of experience in teaching and research, has published about 70 papers in international and national journals and conferences, and is an author of 3 book chapters. The number of citations of his papers is approximately 25. Dr. Varma has one patent in progress. He has supervised three PhDs, and two are in progress in the areas of wireless sensor networks and distributed sensing. His areas of interest are intelligent sensor networks, wireless sensor network localization, geographical routing, optical wireless communication, and next-generation wireless sensor networks. His group is mainly focused on analysis of statistical routing, geographical routing in heterogeneous networks, localization error, etc. in wireless sensor networks with the help of sensor motes using various simulation tools.

Ryan Woolrych is a postdoctoral research fellow at the Gerontology Research Centre, Simon Fraser University, Canada. Woolrych has acted as a senior researcher on a number of funded research projects in Europe and North America, examining the impact of assistive technologies on the health and well-being of older adults. His research interests include aging and older adults, home and community, visual methods, participatory research, and ambient-assisted living. He is currently the secretary-general of the International Society of Gerontechnology, involved in coordinating research in the application and development of technologies to support older adults living at home.

Hong-Bo Xie earned a PhD in biomedical engineering from Shanghai Jiao Tong University, Shanghai, China, in 2007. He is currently a vice chancellor postdoctoral fellow in the Graduate School of Biomedical Engineering, University of New South Wales. Dr. Xie has published more than 40 peer-reviewed journal papers. His research interests include neuromuscular bioelectronics and biomechanics, human–computer interfaces, biomedical signal processing, and nonlinear time series analysis.

Chapter 1

Survey of Intelligent Computing

Kuruvilla Mathew and Biju Issac

Contents

Intelligent machines are an idea that might have been older than computers and refer to created devices with humanlike intelligence. Artificial intelligence (AI) is a field in computing that tries to create algorithms or systems that can make decisions in situations with multiple possible courses of action. AI generally works in two phases, one a learning phase, in which it learns about the environment it is working in, and the second, a classification phase, in which it can make decisions based on what it has learned in the learning phase. Most AI technologies are also capable of continuously learning and improving. The application of AI in today's computing scenario spans a wide spectrum, ranging from recognition of human behavior to various optimization techniques to computing system defense, including intrusion detection, detection of cyber terrorism, web mining, biometrics, and many more. The application of AI is not limited to any area and can find implementation in almost all fields of computing. This chapter aims to present a noncomprehensive survey of popular AI in active implementation or research.

1.1 Related Works

McCorduck (1979) discusses a personal inquiry into the history and prospects of AI in the book *Machines Who Think*. This explores such questions as "Can machines think?", "What is machine intelligence?", and many more interesting questions in a personal discovery. Mathew et al. (2013) discuss an "Experimental Comparison of Uninformed and Heuristic AI Algorithms for N Puzzle Solution." The paper compares a few AI techniques for solving an *n*-puzzle. Zeng et al. (2009) presented "A Survey of Affect Recognition Methods: Audio, Visual, and Spontaneous Expressions," in which they present various affect recognition methods and how they aid in language processing by recognizing human nonverbal communication for improving communication. Selfridge and Neisser (1960) present "Pattern Recognition by Machine" and discuss more about feature extraction and how learning can be effected.

Levine (1969) presents a survey on feature extraction. This paper discusses a number of feature extraction methods, which is an important step in AI for the learning process and the progress in research in this area. Brooks (1991) presents "Intelligence without Representation," in which he discusses building intelligent systems incrementally. He explores how small individual systems with adequate parallel processing applied can work together to carry out complex functionalities. Bkassiny et al. (2013) carried out a "Survey on Machine-Learning Techniques in Cognitive Radios" that looks at radios or wireless communications as being self-aware and intelligent, being able to sense ambient environments and alter parameters like signal strength for improved effectiveness in managing interference, and so forth. Dorigo and Birattari (2010) discuss "Ant Colony Optimization," discusses the application of the ant colony technique of optimization, which is implemented as an adaptation of some ant colony behaviors that make use of "pheromones" in communication to use group learning to optimize paths. The method employs "digital ants" to achieve optimal solutions to problems like the traveling salesman problem (TSP). Zhang and Zuo (2007) present "Computational Intelligence-Based Biometric Technologies," which discusses the application of AI in effective recognition of biometric patterns, thereby improving its applications. Holambe et al. (2012) present a brief review and survey of feature extraction methods for Devanagari optical character recognition (OCR). They discuss the application of AI for processing natural language, in particular for the Devanagari. They discuss, particularly, OCR for handwritten scripts.

Tyugu (2011) discusses application of AI in cyber defense (CD). He presented that AI has the capability to scan through huge volumes of data and hence can very quickly spot anomalies and take proactive defense measures. The paper discusses the various methods for applying AI in this field. Zamin (2009) presents a survey on information extraction (IE) for counter-terrorism. He shows how AI can very quickly scan large volumes of data and uncover various indicators for terrorist activities, as well as discover suspects through remotely connected links in very good time. Amrouch and Mostefai (2012) present a survey on the literature of ontology mapping, alignment, and merging. Ontologies help in the representation of data for use by AI engines or algorithms. Ontologies can be mapped, merged, transformed, and so forth for use by different applications in various domains, as applicable. Lunt (1993) presents a survey of intrusion detection techniques using AI in computer systems. He shows how AI can be effective in various forms of intrusion detection and how it can quickly converge to detect intrusion using various kinds of detection techniques. Pal et al. (2002) discuss various web mining tools in a soft computing framework, its relevance, the state of the art, and future directions. Web mining as an extension of data mining can be applied to the World Wide Web to scan the massive amounts of data that are available and classify, index, and group them, and so forth. They explore the application of various AI techniques like fuzzy logic, neural networks, genetic algorithms, and so forth in the application of web mining.

1.2 Introduction

1.2.1 Intelligence and the Meaning of Intelligence

The idea of intelligent devices is older than computers. There were notions of mythical creatures with artificially created intelligence long before computers, and perhaps the original idea of computers could have stemmed from this notion. The notion of artificial intelligence in computing started with attempts at replicating the human ways of reasoning in computing. As realization dawned that a full replication may not be approachable at once due to its magnitude and complexity, research now targets the commercialization of aspects of AI toward providing "intelligent" assistive services to human users (Mathew et al. 2013; Zeng et al. 2009; McCorduck 1979).

If we are to expand on the previous statement, the discussion will go beyond the perimeters of computing, into cognitive sciences and some areas of psychology, but it does justice to lay a platform for further understanding. Human intelligence is capable of making decisions in uncertainty, by compensating for the missing information using the individual's own imagination. It is done by human intelligence by creating the missing portions of the paradigm, as required for making the decision, indiscriminate of the possibility of the created information being quite far from "correctness." It is later possible that the decision made, based on this variation in the constructed image, can be hugely off target and incorrect, but it is acceptable in the real world, as "to err is human." However, consider the possibility of a computer doing the same, to create the missing pieces of information based on data that are available to the computer (most probably through training data) and then making a decision based on this picture, and the decision is off target; it is not acceptable because a machine is not "allowed" to make errors. Expanding this thought, it may never happen that a machine can produce acceptable complete replication of human intelligence, just on the fact that in human intelligence, it is acceptable to make flawed decisions, and the same is not acceptable when done by a machine. This idea is contrary to the idea that with the progress of growth of AI, we might create systems more intelligent than humans. This chapter, however, limits its scope to a discussion of the work on the technical advancement of the computational field of AI.

1.2.2 Intelligence in Computing

To classify a device as "intelligent," it should necessarily satisfy the following requirements.

1. **Learning/adapting:** It should be able to learn from the environment it is working in.
2. **Decision making/classification:** It should be able to make decisions relevant to the environment it is deployed in, on new and unknown inputs.

The practical applications of AI can be seen to span the following areas.

1. **Feature extraction:** Extracting specific features of interest for the domain of application
2. **Cognition or understanding:** To make "sense" of unknown data (after training) when presented
3. **Adaptive technologies:** Technologies that can respond to changing environments
4. **Optimization problems:** Optimizing complex problems
5. **Data mining:** Making sense of and identifying trending patterns, interpreting or selecting relevant information from humungous volumes of data

A widely accepted prediction is that computing will move to the background, weaving itself into the fabric of our everyday living spaces and projecting the human user into the foreground. Consequently, the future "ubiquitous computing" environments will need to have human-centered designs instead of computer-centered designs (Brooks 1991). These devices are predicted to provide smaller aspects of assistive services to human intelligence within a limited scope. Cognitive radio (CR), which has been used to refer to radio devices that are capable of learning and adapting to their environment (Bkassiny et al. 2013), is a good example of such services. Intelligent devices like an intelligent temperature control system in a home are components progressing toward what is commonly referred to as "smart homes." Other services target services for people in need, including those with medical conditions, the best example being Stephen Hawking, whose confinement to a wheelchair has not stopped him from making immense contributions to physics, with the aid of technology.

All AI engines need a learning or training phase, also known as feature extraction. This phase looks at extracting key features of interest for the subsystem and making use of this for future decision making. This is similar to human intelligence, as human intelligence is limited to the amount of information an individual has been exposed to and also, during the exposure, how much information and what particular aspects of the information the individual focused on. This brings us to another aspect of AI systems, where, from the available information, the "relevant information" is filtered through and focused, as required by the paradigm. This chapter will take a noncomprehensive look at some areas of AI research and implementations.

1.3 Feature Extraction

Recognition of patterns is a popular AI task, which involves a transducer to read an image and search for areas of interest in the image at the preprocessor stage, and the classifier stage proceeds to classify it. Selfridge and Nessier (1960) state that at present, the machine can get features from human programmers only, and this can be demonstrated only by experiment. Since there is no general theory determining appropriate features, design of feature extractors is empirical and ad hoc, with inspiration from biological prototypes (Levine 1969).

Real data always come with noise, whether generated at the source or in transition. One of the primary tasks is to remove as much noise as possible, and the process is called "smoothing." Since a number of algorithms are available, the choice of algorithm is determined by simplicity and processor efficiency. Line segment filtrations are applicable in many dimensions, especially for character recognition, and involve elimination of noise and sharp variations. Even though this will dampen the source, the assumption is that the thinned line will retain the essential aspects of the source. Tracing contours is another technique, which traces the contours or outline and uses it to identify the source. There is not much literature available for line drawing, sketches, cartoons, and so forth, but there have been a number of works showcasing detection of cartoons or images (Levine 1969).

Sharp changes in contrast or gray scales are detected as edges and can be applied in the classification problem, which is known as edging. This detection can be used to reduce the size of source data and is a good candidate since it is a relatively simple implementation both in terms of algorithm complexity and computational intensity. In considering shapes and curvatures, it is noted that inflection points on a contour are informationally the richest, and an interesting application of this is in detecting overlaps. One of the correlation methods aligns a center of gravity to a reference point and transforms the object until maximum correlation is achieved. A very promising correlation method uses an image intensifier tube to achieve parallel processing of a picture in very short intervals. Connectivity becomes a challenge when noise gaps can cause breaks in continuous lines, which may be addressed by smoothing the data before processing. Moment transformations use the normalized representation, along with some transformations for recognition of shapes. Local topological properties try to describe the features that a human would use to describe or remember the entity. Even as it is best to carefully select features, some techniques can make use of components like "informative fragments" to create an automatic "feature finder." Retinal maps process considerable data but provide little significance unless they are selectively processed. It also has been shown that grayscale discrimination is not as important as noticing the difference in the significant contrasts between the patterns, but this can be important when it comes to multidimensional entities, in the future (Levine 1969).

It is the general consensus that parallel processing results in faster convergence for pattern recognition. Some of the works, like the use of an image intensifier by Hawkins, are notable in this space. Texture, which is structured patterns on images, relatively simple for humans to identify at a glance, is a difficult task for computer programs, and hence, not much research applies texture into images for pattern recognition. The shape description notices that humans identify a shape by reducing it to some basic shape, describing the structure of an object, independent of orientation, translation, or perturbation. Some methods for this include searching "regions of interest" to derive skeletonization. The relatively new articular approach states, "It is characterized by the reproducible investigation of structural properties" (Levine 1969).

1.4 Affect Recognition

A traditional human–computer interface (HCI) makes use of standard devices such as keyboard, mouse displays, and so forth, which rely on capturing explicit information from the user while ignoring a vast amount of implicit data. As computing for future expectations implies that an HCI needs to be anticipatory and human-centered and able to detect and respond to subtle changes in human behavior. Some examples of HCIs include the system of Lisette and Nazos, combining facial expressions with physiological signals for detection of user emotions; the model of embodied cognition, mapping users' active states, learning or adapting to user behavior based on their facial responses; and assistance in computer-aided learning where technology offers an appropriate tutoring strategy based on information from a user's facial expression. These systems can have their application in domains ranging from service call centers, to intelligent automotive systems, to games and entertainment industries as well. It can even be applied in social and emotional development research areas for assistance in gathering information in the fields of psychology, psychiatry, social sciences, and so forth. In all of this, research has shown that using multidimensional sensors for visuals (2-D and 3-D as well as extending beyond facial expressions) combined with audio for advancing the human affect–sensing technology gives better results as the fusion of both can make use of complimentary information from each of the channels (Brooks 1991).

The challenges in this area are multidimensional. Firstly, there is a noted absence of a database of classified affects. Most of what may be available is the absence of natural noise and is very clear, which is not the case in practical scenarios. The emotions in many of these may be either exaggerated or deliberated and can again vary from the spontaneous responses. Hence, existence of data sets with natural spontaneous data sets is a key component for the progress of research in this area (Brooks 1991).

1.4.1 Human Affect

Human affect or emotion and its application in computing is a multidisciplinary field involving psychology, linguistics, vision and speech analysis, and machine learning. The most popular affects include the following emotional categories: happiness, sadness, fear, anger, disgust, and surprise. Interestingly, this description of the basic emotional categories was accepted cross-culturally, indicative of the fact that emotional perception is largely culture-neutral. When the affect is classified into a large number of dimensions, namely, evaluation that measures how a human feels, activation measuring if humans are likely to take action based on the feeling, and so forth, in 2-D space, some emotions like fear and anger may become indistinguishable. The appraisal-based approach extends the dimensional approach and represents emotions through a set of stimulus evaluations (Brooks 1991).

Psychological studies have revealed (Brooks 1991) that there is a close association between affect and audio and visual signals. A Facial Action Coding System can encode each change to the facial expression into action units, which are very useful in studies on human naturalistic facial behavior and can be used for high-level decision-making processes. The paralinguistic and linguistic content in speech is also a good contributor for gathering affect. Findings on research suggest that linguistics alone is unreliable for analyzing human affect and can provide supportive information to improve some results. Another largely unexplored area is the context of the behavior since human affect signals are context dependent (Brooks 1991).

1.5 Cognitive Radios

Cognition can be defined as a process involved in gaining knowledge and comprehension, including thinking, knowing, remembering, judging, and problem solving (Bkassiny et al. 2013). CR discusses "aware" wireless networks that can continue communication with improved use of the electromagnetic spectrum with techniques like dynamic spectrum sharing and focusing on signal processing for dynamic spectrum access networks. Spectrum sensing, which is an important ingredient of CR, listens to the RF environment to become "aware" of the environment. Many sensing techniques, based on matched filter, energy detection, cyclostationary detection, wavelength detection, covariance detection, cooperative spectrum sensing, and so forth, are suggested, developing and improving the methods for sensing. The cognitive engine is responsible for learning from the inputs of the sensors and reasoning, which becomes more challenging with increased degrees of freedom of the wireless systems. Nodes in distributed networks may make use of the concept docitive networks, which teach each other by exchanging knowledge over wireless connections. The objective of docitive networks is to reduce the cognitive complexity, speed up the learning rate, and generate better and more reliable decisions (Bkassiny et al. 2013). Though the term has been differently explained in many studies, a more widely adapted representation might be that CR is a radio that can sense and adapt to its environment, and therefore, CRs need to be autonomous. Hence, three main characteristics need to be considered when designing efficient learning algorithms in order for CRs to operate efficiently, namely, learning in a partially observable environment, multiagent learning in distributed CRNs, and autonomous learning in unknown RF environments (Bkassiny et al. 2013).

The learning paradigms for this may be unsupervised, suited for environments with little prior knowledge, or supervised, where prior information may be available and can be used to train the system for better results. Three categories of learning regimes identified are learning by instruction, learning by reinforcement, and learning by imitation, in which agents can learn from events from other similar agents. An effective CR will be able to adapt to the appropriate learning regimes, depending on the environments and information available (Bkassiny et al. 2013).

Two key learning problems in CR are decision making and feature classification. Supervised learning requires training sets, and methods using support vector machines (SVMs) are shown to deliver better performance than for artificial neural network (ANN) algorithms, especially for cases with very small training data as ANN is seen to suffer from a risk of overfitting. The learning algorithms, in general, help to optimize the CR behavior (Bkassiny et al. 2013).

Decision making in CR employs techniques like centralized policy making under Markov states with reinforcement learning (RL), which permits agents to alter decisions based on their interaction with the environments autonomously and without supervision, making use of a delayed feedback mechanism to identify rewards and thus better decisions. In the presence of uncertainty of the observation model, some learning algorithms can be applied for decision rules. RL may be applied for interference control to derive optimal signal strength that minimizes. While RL algorithms can lead to optimal solutions, their performance in non-Markovian environments may be questionable, leading to the approach of policy search for non-Markovian learning (Bkassiny et al. 2013). The mathematical tool, game theory, implementing the behavior of entities under conflicting environments, is a good tool for decentralized policy making. The two approaches in game theory, the noncooperative approach (making individual decisions) and the cooperative approach (organizing players into groups and evaluating collective trade-offs), can be extended for application in CR based on the context of application. Learning algorithms like no-regret learning allow uninformed players to learn from their environments based on the benefits of each action in relation to the possible alternatives. Threshold learning is a dynamic adaptive technique that evaluates the effect of previous parameter values to determine the current optimum; it may be applied in CR decision rules under uncertainty (Bkassiny et al. 2013).

The lack of knowledge and the environment of operation of the CR, along with the expectation of a minimum operating requirement, encourage the CR to autonomously explore the surroundings to make decisions. Feature classification in CR using nonparametric unsupervised classification with the Dirichlet process mixture model imposes a nonparametric prior to make few assumptions of the data space and data clustering based on the scenario present. The ANNs attempt to solve the supervised classification, which tries to work with a massive amount of parallel processing, in an attempt to mimic the workings of the human brain. However, the disadvantage of an ANN lies in its extensive training requirements. Another category for CR may be in the form of a centralized cooperative system, in which all observations are collected by a central concentrator; a distributed cooperative system with a decentralized system, which communicate and cooperate; or decentralized, disconnected systems, which are individual systems that do not cooperate and work independently of each other (Bkassiny et al. 2013).

1.6 Ant Colony Approaches to Optimization in AI

The swarm intelligence approach uses the biological communication seen in some colonies of ants, where they optimize paths by some stimuli (pheromones) deposited by some other ants in the colony and use it to mark paths to known food sources. The double bridge experiment shows that the ants start with random paths, but as the time progresses, there is an increased pheromone concentration on the shorter path probably due to the higher frequency of traversal, and eventually, it is observed that the ants end up picking the optimal path from the nest to the food source. The ant colony optimization (ACO) technique employs a number of artificial ants that exchange information, building solutions to optimization problems (Dorigo and Birattari 2010).

ACO for the travelling salesman problem (TSP) solution employs artificial ants to travel each edge until every node is visited. In each subsequent step, ants make a decision based on information from a previous ant visit and eventually converge to optimality. Combinatorial optimization problems can be approached using meta-heuristics, evolving continuously as they approach the solution. The first ACO solution called the ant system updates all the pheromone values each time, whereas in the updated min–max ant system, only the most efficient ant/path pheromones are updated. The ant colony system introduced a local pheromone update by each ant to the last traversed node, which helps in generating and diversifying the solutions. Further work on this involved a proof that the ACO method does converge, with a graph-based ant system algorithm. However, these could not predict the rate of convergence. The ACOs, however, suffer from issues like first-order deception and second-order deception; also, the convergence proofs do not give insight for practical implantation of the techniques (Dorigo and Birattari 2010).

The ACO has been applied in various problems, including but not limited to routing (tsp, vehicle routing, etc.); assignment (sequential ordering, quadratic assignment, etc.); scheduling (timetabling, graph coloring, project scheduling, etc.); subset (open shop, set covering, multiple knapsack, etc.); and many others, the majority of which are nondeterministic polynomial-time hard (NP-hard) problems. The application of an adequate local search mechanism is shown to improve effectiveness, especially when working on NP-hard problems. The future research in ACO is expected to focus on richer optimization, including stochastic nature, dynamic data modifications, and multiple objectives, and on a better understanding of the theoretical properties of ACO (Dorigo and Birattari 2010).

1.7 Intelligence-Based Biometric Technologies

The intelligent approach, because of its adaptive, robust, and parallel computational natures, has been proved to be effective and efficient in biometric feature extraction and matching tasks. These tasks find wide application in automatic access control systems for surveillance, computer security, and so forth. Though the biometric techniques measure well against alternative techniques, they also pose issues in the acquisition and preprocessing of biometric data (often noisy, partially occluded, or inaccurately located). This can effectively be addressed using AI, which brings in adaptability, uncertainty modeling, robustness, and parallel computing architecture to the paradigm (Zhang and Zuo 2007).

1.7.1 Feature Extraction

Biometric models are quite complex to represent, and CI-based techniques are up for this task. A multilayer perceptron (MLP) in neural networks (NNs) with a back-propagation training method can adequately approximate nonlinear mappings and hence is a good technique for identification of discriminative features, filtering, and enhancement of biometric signals. Associative memory as an effective single-layer model can deduce and retrieve memorized information from possibly incomplete or corrupt biometric information. A self-organizing NN makes use of a self-organizing man (SOM), which is an unsupervised method that can keep the topological relationship of the data. Adaptive principle component analysis (PCA) and linear discriminative analysis are two methods employed for dimensionality reduction using CI, and independent component analysis (ICA), as an extension of PCA, has been widely applied for blind signal separation and feature extraction. Evolutionary feature extraction employs genetic algorithms (GA) to eventually converge to the fittest solution in optimization problems and kernel dimensionality reduction methods for nonlinear feature extraction problems. The iteratively reweighted least-squares method is another method for solving nonlinear optimality problems, which has been applied to the development of robust PCA (Zhang and Zuo 2007).

1.7.2 Biometric Matching

A feature vector extracted from a biometric system or sensor is matched with the stored data based on a one-to-many comparison. The radial basis function neural network is a three-layer feed-forward NN with an input layer, a hidden layer, and an output layer and is usually trained with a two-step process. The SVM is a powerful classification tool with good performance and that embeds nonlinear decision function via kernel function. SVMs have seen successful application in speaker and face recognition. Fuzzy technology offers a more flexible and efficient method that can be applied into many biometric recognition systems (Zhang and Zuo 2007).

1.8 AI for Language Processing in OCR

AI can be applied to make sense of natural languages to process natural language representations and "understand" the meaning. One of the complex tasks in this is OCR on Devanagari script—the Indian alphabet used to write Sanskrit, Hindi, and many other languages. Efforts in this line started before 1980. Two key classifications of OCR techniques are feature-mapped and image-mapped recognition. The feature-mapped method looks for discriminative information in a set of features for its identification. There are a number of methods applied for Devanagari feature extraction. Some of them are 64-dimension feature vector and directional information from the contour, NNs, structure analysis, modified quadratic discriminate function, visual discriminating methods for separating characters, fuzzy models, and so forth. Some methods made use of component analysis for feature extraction from numerical images, or Gaussian distribution functions with multiclassifier connectionist architecture for increasing recognition reliability. Zernike introduced the Zernike moments, which are the projection of the image function onto a set of complex polynomials, which form a complete orthogonal set over the interior of the unit circle, which was used in a feature-based approach for Devanagari handwritten character recognition. For computing Zernike moments, the points falling outside the circle are not used. K-nearest neighbor (K-NN) classification plots training patterns on a d-dimensional space, where d is the number of features. Unknown patterns are plotted in the same space and classified according to its K most similar patterns, that is, nearest neighbors. SVMs classification uses slack variables that measure the error at each point. Other attempts at developing a bilingual system use global and local features from the left and right projection profiles of numeral images for Devanagari and Roman scripts. Methods of using a decision tree for recognizing constrained hand-printed characters using primitive features or extracting nodal features, and multilayer perception for recognition of handwritten Devanagari numbers. A significant amount of later works toward improving efficiency of recognition have been made by combining different strategies (Holambe et al. 2012).

1.9 AI in CD

The massive size of operations in cyberspace necessitates some amount of automation to make CD a possibility. With the fact that cyberspace has invaded every area in the running of a nation, the network-centric warfare or cyber warfare is also an active area of challenge, calling on the requirement for active CD. There are a number of technologies and tools currently available for CD, which we will look into in this section (Tyugu 2011).

Neural nets began with the invention of the perceptron, by Frank Rosenblatt, in 1957, where a large number of perceptrons combine to provide a massive amount of parallel processing, providing very good speed of operation. With their high speed, they are very popular in CD. Expert systems include a knowledge base and an inference engine and can be applied for finding answers to questions in some application domain presented either by a user or by another software. Intelligent agents are software components that have components of intelligence, like proactiveness, understanding of an agent communication language, reactivity (ability to make some decisions and to act), planning ability, mobility, and reflection ability, and hence should be able to develop a concept of "cyber-police" using agents. To apply a search problem and application of search algorithms, one should be able to generate candidates for solutions and a procedure to be available for evaluating adequacy of a proposed candidate for a solution, and the efficiency can be increased. The learning process for machines is another important aspect of AI, in which the system is able to process new information or rearrange available information in order to extend the knowledge of the system. Two key methods of learning in AI are supervised learning, as in learning with a teacher of some kind, and unsupervised learning. The constraint-solving approach in AI tries to solve problems that are represented as a set of constraints, and the solution of the problem is achieved when the constraints (or requirements) are satisfied. A challenging area in CD is the knowledge management for net-centric warfare, and only automated methods can provide rapid assessment of the situation to provide support to the decision makers. A larger knowledge base will definitely help expert systems to get wider application. The Singularity Institute for Artificial Intelligence, founded in 2000, warns researchers of the danger that exponentially faster development of intelligence in computers may occur. This development may lead to singularity, which is described as the technological creation of smarter-than-human intelligence, and there are several different technologies that, if they reached a threshold level of sophistication, would enable the creation of smarter-than-human intelligence (Tyugu 2011).

1.10 Use of AI in Counterterrorism

As the number of terrorist attacks and threats increases, a number of AI techniques for surveillance have become an active area of research. Counterterrorism refers to all kinds of policies, operations, techniques, tactics, and programs that governments implement to fight terrorism. The ability of AI techniques to be able to scan through a very large amount of data and its application in natural language processing is a great tool for IE. There are concerns of privacy infringement and inconvenience resulting from false positives, and hence, there exist research opportunities on reduction of false positives. There are a lot of technical challenges in extraction of information relevant to counterterrorism from the perspective of the field of computing. One method for IE, described by Norshuhani Zamin (2009), depicts it as a process following from the corpus to a text preprocessing to a name entity recognition, with the reference of a name dictionary, through a coreference resolution, through entity extraction according to some extraction pattern, and link analysis.

Text preprocessing involves cleaning up of the text, by removing unwanted elements like images, white spaces, special characters, and so forth and applying a parser like the link grammar (LG) or the subject–verb–object English parser. Name entity resolution identifies the nouns (names) by classification of the text into predefined categories like names of persons, organizations, locations, dates, times, quantities, monetary values, percentages, and so forth. Auto Slog and PALKA are tools that can learn the patterns extracted into dictionaries. Research has successfully used LG to identify a subject and an object and apply them on a corpus with close to 100% results (Zamin 2009).

Different descriptions of the same entity appearing in different parts of the text are called coreference resolution, interaction, or relation extraction and require deeper analysis. Misspelling, phonetically identical elements, cross-lingual transliteration, title and name permutation, and omission can be hard to match with the names of known matches, for which sources like SecondString, Riddle data set, BART, MUC-6 data set, and so forth come up to predict similar-sounding names with a percentage of resemblance. Data extraction identifies and classifies text according to some predetermined characteristics. This step looks for key words or related words and their single occurrence or semantically connected occurrences to detect target message. KNOWITALL, INEXT, and so forth are approaches that can be used for this cause. Link analysis, though not a part of IE, tries to identify links of interest to the subject under IE and can be a useful tool for the purpose. For example, a manual link analysis process was able to connect all the attackers of the 9/11 incident and create a link graph indicating the involved entities. Investigative data mining can be applied in the context of law enforcement and uses intelligent analysis to automate the link analysis (Zamin 2009).

1.11 Ontology Mapping for AI

An ontology is designed and developed for sharing among multiple applications, preserving their semantics, enabling systems to utilize multiple ontology and the same ontology to be used by multiple applications. This section looks at the three main operations performed on ontologies, namely, *ontology mapping*, *ontology alignment*, and *ontology merging*, which provide a base for other operations like translation, reconciliation, coordination, and negotiation between ontologies. Ontology mapping is defined as formal expression describing a semantic relationship between two (or more) concepts belonging to two (or more) different ontologies. Ontology alignment is defined as a set of matches between two (or more) ontologies in the same domain or in related domains. The mapped ontologies can be merged to form a new ontology. Mapping discovery is a common subprocess, which works by mapping relationships using inference engines and reasoning as an improved technique. Some frameworks like SUMO or DOLCE allow using shared ontologies with the objective of providing a common framework as a reference to the semantic web ontologies that facilitates information sharing between them. Mapping discoveries using heuristics exploits semantics contained in ontologies for matching. Different types of mismatches can happen between different ontologies, namely, *syntactic mismatches*, in which two ontologies may be syntactically heterogeneous if they are represented by different representation languages and can be resolved by transforming them to the same representation; *lexical mismatches*, which describe the heterogeneities between the names of entities, instances, properties, or relations such as synonyms, homonyms, homophones, and so forth; and *semantic mismatches*, which are the conceptual or metaphysical mismatches. The semantic mismatches can be classified as *coverage mismatch* (covering different portions), *granuility mismatch* (mismatch in the amount of details provided by each ontology), and *perspective mismatch* (mismatch in the perspective or viewpoint for the same entity). Some tools for merging ontologies discussed are FCA-Merge, IF-Map, SMART, PROMPT, PROMTP-Diff, CAIMAN, ONION, and so forth (Amrouch and Mostefai 2012).

1.12 Intrusion Detection

Intrusion in information systems may be defined as accessing the system in ways or methods that violate the policies of the system, and intrusion detection is the process of identifying when or after which point an intrusion has occurred. Intrusion detection is therefore the first step in any defense system (Lunt 1993).

Network-based intrusion detection systems (IDSs) are deployed to scan for intrusion on the network layer and are best suited for application for sources outside the perimeter of the LAN, and they may prove very useful when deployed just outside the firewall. Host-based IDSs, on the other hand, work on individual hosts, where "agents" monitor activities, and these can detect both internal (from within the network) and external (outside the network) intrusion attempts. Each of the methods has its strengths and weaknesses, and hence, a combination of both will make the IDS implementation stronger (Lunt 1993).

The different methods for intrusion detection (ID) include *pattern matching*, which looks for known ID patterns or signatures in incoming traffic; *stateful pattern matching*, which includes context-to-pattern matching; *protocol decode–based analysis*, which is an intelligent extension of stateful packet matching and attempts to replicate a client–server communication sequence; *heuristics-based analysis*, which makes use of statistical analysis; and *anomaly-based analysis*, which looks for traffic anomalies, differentiating them from flash crowds, to identify intrusion traffic (Lunt 1993).

The fuzzy clustering approach works on sampling low-level kernel data and makes use of outlier detections to capture anomalous behavior. This technique is based on describing attacks using some semantically rich language like DAML. This intrusion detection works over two phases. The first uses data mining techniques on stream to capture and detect anomalies, and the second phase reasons the anomalies detected with reference to the attacks defined using the DAMLs. More information on data mining is covered in Section 1.13. Data mining discovers anomaly patterns;

data collection modeling collects system information like memory use, CPU load, and so forth; principle component analysis constructs new representations of feature sets in reduced dimensionalities; and then fuzzy set clustering clusters data using fuzzy decisions and detection of intrusion data. Integrated service works on the idea that multiple components of the system should work together for improved detection (Lunt 1993).

1.13 Web Mining

The vast explosion of the Internet and the growth of the World Wide Web have put massive amounts of data accessible over the Internet. The data have also diverged from simple text to the use of multimedia and rich interactive applications, forming a vast collection of uncontrolled, unlabeled, heterogeneous data. As a result, we have an overflow of information, but knowledge takes time and effort to sift through this vast foray of information. This profusion has led to the need for automated "mining" techniques that can scan through this vast foray of information and bring out useful information (Pal et al. 2002). In order to remove the human factor in mining the data, we need to embed AI into web mining. The challenge of the AI is to find, extract, filter, and evaluate relevant information from unlabeled, heterogeneous, and distributed data on the web. The area of soft computing attempts to resolve these challenges (Pal et al. 2002). The principal soft computing tools include fuzzy sets dealing with decision making in situations of uncertainty, ANNs for modeling of complex function, GAs as efficient search methods, and rough set (RS) theory helping with granular knowledge discovery (Pal et al. 2002). Data mining refers to the nontrivial process of identifying valid, novel, potentially useful, and ultimately understandable patterns in data, and web mining takes this to the web. Web mining can be viewed as the use of data mining techniques to automatically retrieve, extract, generalize, and analyze information for knowledge discovery from web documents and services (Pal et al. 2002). Web data may be (1) unlabeled, (2) distributed, (3) heterogeneous (mixed media), (4) semistructured, (5) time varying, or (6) high dimensional. Web mining therefore looks at the large amount of hyperlinked information and processes it under the context of the need for (1) handling context sensitive and imprecise queries, (2) summarization and deduction, and (3) personalization and learning, which, though related to data mining, carves a niche area for itself (Pal et al. 2002).

1.13.1 Mining Components and Methodologies

1. **Resource discovery:** Resource discovery, also referred to as information retrieval (IR), refers to the process of discovering related new content, minimizing the amount of irrelevant information that is fetched. Crawlers and meta-crawlers on the web work systematically and methodologically to make sure that all data on the web are categorized and indexed. Research in this field is along the line of modeling, user interfaces, visualization, and filtering during searches (Pal et al. 2002).
2. **Information selection, extraction, and preprocessing:** The challenge ensuing involves being able to automatically extract knowledge from the information without human intervention, which is called IE. Common methods for extraction include writing wrappers and hunting through a document looking for specific answers (slot fills). Where IR looks at information indiscriminately, IE looks at the document under some structure and context (Pal et al. 2002).

3. **Generalization:** This stage tries to identify patterns from the extracted information. Many data mining techniques, like uncertainty sampling, which reduces the amount of unlabeled data needed, and association rule mining, which extends the association rule into relationship to aid in decision making, are used in web content mining (Pal et al. 2002).

4. **Analysis:** Analysis, which is a data-driven problem, assumes that sufficient data are available. The human role in analysis makes it necessary that tools appropriately visualize, interpret, and represent these patterns to assist in the discovery of information or knowledge on the web (Pal et al. 2002).

1.13.2 Fuzzy Logic, NNs, GAs, and RSs for Web Mining

Under fuzzy logic (FL), the web mining task falls mainly under generalization. The fuzzy set theory works to extend the Boolean theory and apply concepts of least likely, most likely, average, and so forth for its solution, bringing in more flexibility to information representation. FL can be a great option to apply humanlike deductive capabilities to search engines, with the help of fuzzy clustering and association rule mining. NN applies its massive parallelization capabilities for IR, and IE tasks provide excellent adaptive learning capacities. Page ranking application can make good use of the technology. A combination of neural and fuzzy technologies called neuro-fuzzy gives good optimization for including the relevance parameter into the searches. NN can be applied for providing deductive capabilities to web mining. GA, a randomized search and optimization technique, is efficient, adaptive, and robust. It is ideal for searching, finding relevant homepages, query optimization, exploring different areas of the solution space, document representation, automatic web page categorization and updating, distributed mining, using gene expression messy GA or distributed data mining, and so forth. An interesting area of application for GA is in the creation of adaptive websites, which automatically improve the organization and presentation, learning from visitor access patterns. The capability of RS is granular; IR capabilities that provide efficient document retrieval and representations. RS as well as rough-fuzzy sets can be used to handle heterogeneous data very well and also for association/clustering (Pal et al. 2002).

1.14 Conclusion

The idea of AI might have predated computers, but the practical application of this is seen with the advent of its application in computing technologies. Initially, the idea was to completely replicate human intelligence, but this was proving to be a much-larger-than-anticipated task, and hence, further research in this field narrowed down to finding intelligent solutions to smaller subsystems or components, providing assistive services to human decision making. A number of methods exist in this field, and it is growing every day, attracting huge chunks of research in this direction. The application of AI is in diverse fields; almost every domain requires some kind of decision making, and if AI can provide decision making with acceptable error rates, it can be an effective support service for human decision making. It will also remove the need for excessive human intervention and, many times, will provide much faster convergence to optimal solutions. Some of the data-intensive tasks are of mammoth volumes and therefore cannot be effectively executed without some kind of intelligent systems. Different techniques and algorithms for AI are in existence and undergoing active research; each has its own advantages and disadvantages based on the field of application. There is therefore no single solution for all the problem domains, and research opportunities are open toward application and optimization of various AI techniques toward each other.

References

Amrouch, S., & Mostefai, S. (2012, March). Survey on the literature of ontology mapping, alignment and merging. In *Information Technology and e-Services (ICITeS), 2012 International Conference on*. IEEE, 1–5.

Bkassiny, M., Li, Y., & Jayaweera, S. (2013). A survey on machine-learning techniques in cognitive radios. *Communications Surveys & Tutorials, IEEE, 15*(3), 1136–1159.

Brooks, R. A. (1991). Intelligence without representation. *Artificial Intelligence, 47*(1–3), 139–159.

Dorigo, M., & Birattari, M. (2010). Ant colony optimization. In *Encyclopedia of Machine Learning*. Springer US, 36–39.

Holambe, A. N., Thool, R. C., & Jagade, S. M. (2012, January). A brief review and survey of feature extraction methods for Devanagari OCR. In *ICT and Knowledge Engineering (ICT & Knowledge Engineering), 2011 9th International Conference on*. IEEE, 99–104.

Levine, M. D. (1969). Feature extraction: A survey. *Proceedings of the IEEE, 57*(8), 1391–1407.

Lunt, T. F. (1993). A survey of intrusion detection techniques. *Computers & Security, 12*(4), 405–418.

Mathew, K., Tabassum, M., & Ramakrishnan, M. (2013, November). Experimental comparison of uninformed and heuristic AI algorithms for N puzzle solution. *Proceedings of The Second International Conference on Informatics Engineering and Information Science (ICIEI52013)*, Kuala Lumpur, Malaysia, November 12–14, 2013, The Society of Digital Information and Wireless Communications, pp. 51–59.

McCorduck, P. (1979). *Machines Who Think: A Personal Inquiry into the History and Prospects of Artificial Intelligence*. San Francisco: Wh Freeman.

Pal, S. K., Talwar, V., & Mitra, P. (2002). Web mining in soft computing framework: Relevance, state of the art and future directions. *Neural Networks, IEEE Transactions on, 13*(5), 1163–1177.

Selfridge, O. G., & Neisser, U. (1960). Pattern recognition by machine. *Scientific American, 203*, 60–68.

Tyugu, E. (2011, June). Artificial intelligence in cyber defense. In *Cyber Conflict (ICCC), 2011 3rd International Conference on*. IEEE, 1–11.

Zamin, N. (2009, November). Information extraction for counter-terrorism: A survey. In *Future Computing, Service Computation, Cognitive, Adaptive, Content, Patterns, 2009. COMPUTATIONWORLD'09. Computation World*. IEEE, 520–526.

Zeng, Z., Pantic, M., Roisman, G. I., & Huang, T. S. (2009). A survey of affect recognition methods: Audio, visual, and spontaneous expressions. *Pattern Analysis and Machine Intelligence, IEEE Transactions on, 31*(1), 39–58.

Zhang, D., & Zuo, W. (2007). Computational intelligence-based biometric technologies. *Computational Intelligence Magazine, IEEE, 2*(2), 26–36.

Chapter 2

Intelligent Machine Vision Technique for Disease Detection through Eye Scanning

Amit Laddi and Amod Kumar

Contents

2.1 Introduction

This chapter discusses a case study that involved a noninvasive and instant disease detection technique based upon machine vision through the scanning of the eyes of the subjects. The detected diseases involved conjunctivitis (eye flu) and jaundice. In the proposed technique, color images of the sclera region of the subjects' eyes were acquired by using an imaging setup specifically designed for the purpose. The image acquisition setup consists of three separate charge-coupled device (3CCD) digital color camera kept in an aphotic enclosure. The facial region of the patient was lit under controlled illumination, and the images of the targeted region, namely, sclera region of the eyes, were acquired and processed using the algorithms developed in a MATLAB® environment to get the respective color attributes in RGB and La*b* color models. Principal component analysis (PCA)-based discrimination was applied over the color data of the subjects that showed high variance. The results of PCA indicated correlations among patients and the color attributes. The neuro-fuzzy-based software was developed for the prediction of jaundice and conjunctivitis along with the degree of severity and types, respectively. The experimental results showed good performance for the proposed method as compared to the conventional chemical methods with an accuracy level of over 90%.

2.1.1 Conjuctivitis and Its Detection

Conjunctivitis or eye conjunctivitis is a condition characterized by a reddish coloration of the eyes. Conjunctivitis, also known as eye conjunctivitis or red eye, is a common eye condition in which conjunctiva, which is the clear membrane covering the white of the eye and lining the eyelids, becomes inflamed. In other words, it is the inflammation of the conjunctiva, a transparent membrane covering the front of the eye. It is due to viral or bacterial infection or may result from an allergic reaction or irritation of the conjunctiva such as pollution, ultraviolet light, and so forth. Bacterial conjunctivitis may be caused by any of several types of bacteria. Viral conjunctivitis can occur in epidemics caused by one of the viruses responsible for the common cold. Allergic conjunctivitis is a common feature of allergy to dust, pollen, and other airborne substances. The condition may also be triggered by chemicals founds in eyedrops, cosmetics, or contact lens solutions.

This reddish coloration due to the aforementioned three major reasons needs to be explored as diagnosis of the correct problem will allow rapid medication and fast recovery of the patient. Thus, it was a dire need to think about a technique that is easy to use, is cost effective, is noninvasive, is user friendly, and does not require a specially trained person to operate, so that any patient can test himself/herself without any hassle. The proposed technique was based upon measuring the degree of redness of the sclera region of the eyes, which may be difficult to detect with the naked eye, but machine vision can easily discriminate between nearly the same colors. The system works on the principle of image acquisition and processing to detect the conjunctivitis, and then its type can be determined using soft-computing techniques such as adaptive neuro-fuzzy inference system (ANFIS). The proposed work consists of algorithms developed to separate the sclera region from the rest of the image and determine the color values of the targeted region, that is, the sclera region. The color of the sclera region of the eyes was then used for the detection of the conjunctivitis and its type. The authors found very little research work in this direction (Guillon and Shah 1996; Horak et al. 1996). As per the literature available, some algorithms are developed to get the eyeball tracking and color of the iris of the eyes at nonuniform lightening conditions (Khosravi and Safabakhsh 2008; Izadi and Safabakhsh 2009; Davatzikos and Prince 1999; Betke et al. 2000; Van et al. 2010); measuring conjunctiva vessel widths (Owen et al. 2004); and so forth. Several attempts were also reported for noninvasive determination of hemoglobin by digital photography of the eyes of the patients in emergency conditions (Suner et al. 2007).

2.1.2 *Jaundice and Its Prediction*

Jaundice is a type of liver disease that is characterized by yellowish discoloration of the whites of the eyes, skin, and mucous membranes caused by deposition of bile salts in these tissues. It occurs as a symptom of various diseases such as hepatitis or liver cancer. Mild jaundice is common in newborn babies and generally disappears within a few days as the enzymes are formed in the body. Jaundice in adults is more dangerous than in newborn babies and is to be treated within the right time. Traditional chemical and biological procedures of jaundice detection such as urine, serum, and liver function tests are time consuming and result in the severity of disease increasing to harmful levels, which may lead to casualty. Thus, there is a need for a noninvasive, cost-effective, easy-to-use, and user-friendly method for jaundice detection.

Bilirubin is the yellow breakdown product of normal heme catabolism, which is formed by the breakdown of hemoglobin during the destruction of worn-out red blood cells. The pigment is then excreted by the liver into the bile via the bile ducts, resulting in yellowish color in the sclera region of the eyes and face. Literature shows some algorithms to get eyeball tracking (Lin et al. 2006) and the color of the iris of the eyes (Edwards et al. 2012); measurements of conjunctival vessel widths (Owen et al. 2004; Chaudhuri et al. 1989; Rassam et al. 1994); and so forth. Several attempts were reported for noninvasive determination of hemoglobin by digital photography of the eyes of the patients in emergency conditions, but no research work has been reported in this direction for jaundice detection.

As the identification of the color of the sclera region of the patient's eye can be useful in making an accurate decision about his/her suffering from jaundice (Nash and Guha 2011), the authors have developed a system that is based on the image acquisition of both the eyes of the patient. By using image processing, the sclera region of the eyes was detected, and the color of the detected region was analyzed to confirm jaundice. Furthermore, based upon soft computing, the degree of severity of jaundice was calculated. PCA-based discrimination analysis between jaundice patients and healthy subjects was also performed, which showed that color attributes obtained through machine vision can detect jaundice effectively. These results are useful for developing noninvasive and fast jaundice detection instrument. A machine vision-based method to measure the degree of yellowness of the sclera region of the eyes was attributed to the inability of human eyes to detect slight changes in color.

2.2 Materials and Methods

The major work carried out in this experiment is to extract the target region along with the amount of color in the form of RGB and La*b* color values. These color values were analyzed with real patient data to generate the respective models as per the disease data, which can confirm the disease. The complete procedure includes an image acquisition module to acquire the images of the sclera region of the eyes of the subjects under consideration with the light illumination set at an optimum level. The preprocessing steps such as geometric correction and image calibration were done to minimize the errors during image capturing. These images were fed to the image-processing software, which first detects the targeted region, that is, the sclera of the eye, and then calculates the color information of this region. Various experiments were performed over a large number of subjects to get the range of color to detect the disease and its severity or types. The identification of the color of the sclera region of the patient's eyes was found significant in making an accurate decision about his/her suffering from diseases such as conjunctivitis or jaundice and so forth. If the patient is suffering from conjunctivitis, the second step would be to detect its type; in the case of jaundice, its severity needs to be detected.

MATLAB-based programs were developed using the ANFIS function for the two cases discussed in this chapter. The first case deals with the detection of conjunctivitis type among three categories, namely, viral, bacterial, or allergic. The proposed technique provides the output in terms of degree of severity of the conjunctivitis from minimum to maximum levels.

In the second case, the classification of jaundice and nonjaundice patients along with the confirmation of the disease and degree of its severity was determined.

2.3 Data Collection

Data collection of the patients and normal subjects was done on voluntary basis. The data were acquired using a machine vision setup, as shown in Figure 2.1, under fixed conditions with light illumination intensity of a white LED ring light set to 1000 lux intensity along with fixed focus and working distance.

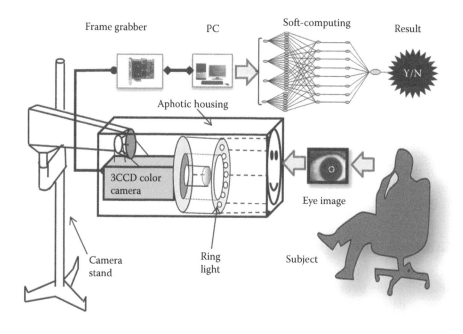

Figure 2.1 Machine vision-based system for disease detection through eye scanning.

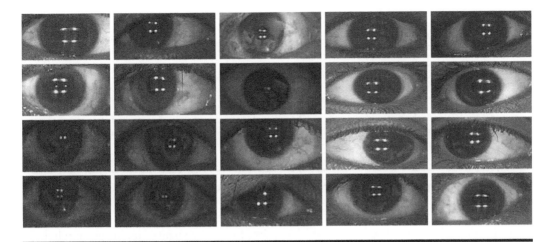

Figure 2.2   Images of sclera region of eyes.

2.4 Machine Vision Setup

The image acquisition setup was designed in order to place the face of the subject in such a manner that the eyes should lie against a camera's field of view inside the aphotic housing and perpendicular to the camera axis. The 3CCD camera (Jai CV m9 CL) was adjusted along the horizontal axis over the boom stand (Edmund Optics). The camera has an effective pixel resolution of 1024 (h) × 768 (v) with pixel cell size of 4.65 (h) × 4.65 (v) μm. It gives a 3 × 8-bit RGB image output via the Camera Link port as an interface medium to the frame grabber card, which was mounted in the PCI express slot of the workstation computer. The lens attached (KOWA LM25NC3) on the C-mount of the camera has 25 mm variable focal length and an aperture of 0.5 inch diameter. After setting the focal length at 25 mm, the distance from the sampler to the camera lens, called the working distance, is 135 mm, and the field of view is 25.5 (h) × 19 (v) mm. The camera is fixed on the interface plate of the boom stand along with white LED ring-light adjustment, which keeps the camera as well as the light source on the same axis but perpendicular to the target image to be acquired. Aphotic housing made up of a black sheet (nonreflective acrylic) is used to block the ambient light. The white LED light's illumination intensity is controlled by an intensity controller (CS100-IC). The suitable level of the intensity of illumination was set as 1000 lux by using calibration tiles (black and white) as above this, the intensity value glare increases (Chaudhuri et al. 1989). The ring light illuminates the target area, and the 3CCD camera acquires images of both eyes of the subjects. The data collected in the form of images of both eyes (Figure 2.2) of the subjects were saved to the database.

2.5 Detection of Conjunctivitis

2.5.1 Image Processing and Data Analysis

One data set of the acquired images of the subjects was analyzed and processed by using image-processing algorithms to get the color information to be used by soft-computing techniques for the detection of conjunctivitis. The color of the sclera region of an eye around the iris is extracted

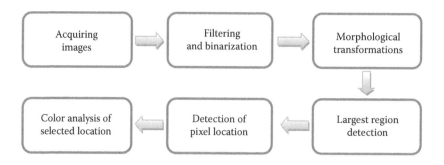

Figure 2.3 Image-processing steps for conjunctivitis detection.

by image-processing steps (Figure 2.3), which consist of image segmentation, image morphology, and color analysis. The images acquired by the 3CCD digital color camera were first filtered using a Gaussian low-pass filter to attenuate variations of the light intensity and smoothening of the images by eliminating details and blurring edges. The applied formula for the low-pass filter is shown for pixel value P (i, j) as follows:

If P (i, j) – $M < S$
Then P (i, j) = $P (i, j)$
Else P (i, j) = M

where M is the mean value of P (i, j) and its neighbors and S is their standard deviation for each pixel P (i, j) set to the mean value M if it falls outside the range $[M - S, M + S]$.

After Gaussian low-pass filtering, the unsharp filtering operation was done over the image, which has the effect of making edges and fine detail in the image crisper. The next step was gray-level morphology to extract the required area from the color image. The grayscale image thresholding operation was performed over the image into background and foreground states. To convert the grayscale image to binary form, binary morphology was applied, which consists of all the zero-valued pixels placed at the background state and all the nonzero-valued pixels placed at the foreground state. The auto thresholding function was used to avoid nonlinearity in detection of the required region, and an algorithm was made to auto detect the largest region of the eye image, that is, the sclera region. The pixel values of this region were used to get the color values in the form of RGB planes.

2.5.2 Conjunctivitis Detection

The RGB color values obtained after image acquisition and processing were analyzed according to real patient data (a total of 50 patients suffering from eye conjunctivitis) to form an algorithm written in MATLAB software as follows:

If $R > 180$
  $G > 0$ AND $G < 60$
  $B > 0$ AND $B < 60$
  Then CONJUNCTIVITIS Yes
  Else CONJUNCTIVITIS No

where *R*, *G*, and *B* are the mean color intensity values for red, green, and blue color planes, respectively. The subject having eye color values between the given ranges for red, green, and blue planes was detected as a conjunctivitis patient.

The conclusion of this algorithm was given in the form of Yes or No. The degree of the severity of the CONJUNCTIVITIS was detected as

$$Degree\% = 350 - (B + A)/2 - R$$

where *R*, *G*, and *B* are the mean color intensity values.

2.5.3 Detection of the Type of Conjunctivitis

To detect viral conjunctivitis, redness along with a watery substance was observed. Bacterial conjunctivitis required detection of a yellow substance inside the eye. Allergic conjunctivitis will not have both these symptoms, and only swelling was detected. The flowchart shown in Figure 2.4 explains the process to detect the type of conjunctivitis. This algorithm had some disadvantages as the symptoms and the severity vary from patient to patient due to which a new approach based upon soft computing was used, which removes all the abnormalities of this technique. As the data

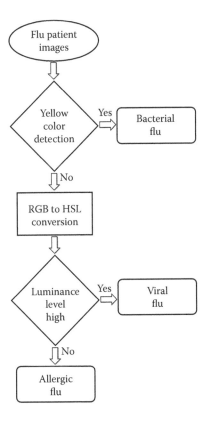

Figure 2.4   Detection of the type of conjunctivitis.

were found to be unfocused due to various factors responsible for the disease and fuzzy logic is a convenient way of mapping an input space to an output space on such data, the advantage of working upon nonlinear data was the reason for choosing fuzzy logic, as it can model nonlinear functions of arbitrary complexity. In the present work, the authors suggested the detection of conjunctivitis by observations based upon the R, G, and B intensity values in terms of numbers, and designing of a fuzzy inference system (FIS) required calculation of the type, value, and number of the membership functions along with the formation of rules. As the number of patients under consideration was very large and the data are complex, it would have required a lot of time and effort to generate rules for each patient. Therefore, to generate the rules for a fuzzy logic system, a new approach was used that could not only generate the rules automatically but also use advanced learning of the artificial neural network (ANN), known as ANFIS. The neuro-adaptive learning of ANFIS works similarly to that of ANN and provides a method for the fuzzy modeling procedure to learn information about any data set. The ANFIS computes and adjusts the membership function parameters associated with input/output data. The procedure of ANFIS is simplistic and efficient for training the large database of patient information with respect to their type of conjunctivitis.

By using a given input/output data set, the ANFIS function constructs a Sugeno-type FIS whose membership function parameters are adjusted using a backpropagation algorithm either alone or in combination with a least-squares type of method. The parameters associated with the membership functions change through the learning process. The ANFIS function generates single output obtained using weighted average defuzzification. Also, all the output membership functions must be of the same type and are either linear or constant. The ANFIS function includes loading of the input/output data set, generation, training, and validation of the FIS. The FIS is trained by loading a training data set that contains the desired input/output data of the system to be modeled, arranged in column vectors with output in the last column, and generates single-output Sugeno-type FIS by different partitioning techniques such as grid partitioning, subtractive clustering, and fuzzy c-means. The backpropagation or hybrid optimization methods are used to train the FIS structure. Finally, the optimization methods train the membership function parameters to emulate the training data by entering the number of training epochs or the training error tolerance to set the stopping criteria for training. The training process stops whenever the maximum epoch number is reached or the training error goal is achieved.

The RGB color intensities were quantified and fed to the ANFIS-based algorithm, which is a combination of the neural network adaptive capabilities and the fuzzy logic qualitative approach, by using the "genfis3" function for rule generation and hybrid learning methodology for training fuzzy membership function parameters, which consist of least-squares estimation with the backpropagation algorithm of ANN. To check and validate the ANFIS model, the training error and checking data error were also calculated. The training error is the difference between the training data output value and the output of the FIS corresponding to the same training data input value and is measured in the form of root mean squared error of the training data set at each epoch.

The ANFIS model was trained with input data as R, G, and B values and three states (type of conjunctivitis) were fed as output (Figure 2.5). If conjunctivitis was detected, then the program would give one of three outputs in the form of bacterial, viral, or allergic conjunctivitis. The program was trained with 70 samples, with 50 cases of conjunctivitis having 20 viral, 25 bacterial, and 5 allergic cases, and provided over 90% accuracy in predicting eye conjunctivitis correctly over the acquired data (doctor's observations).

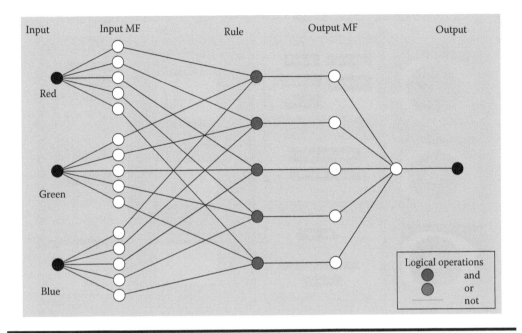

Figure 2.5   ANFIS algorithm for the detection of conjunctivitis.

As the testing or checking data are used for testing the generalization capability of the FIS at each epoch and they have the same format as that of the training data but their elements are different from those of the training data, the checking data were used for testing the generalization capability of the FIS at each epoch. The checking data (20%) have the same format as that of the training data (80%), and their elements are generally distinct from those of the training data. The need for testing data is to avoid overfitting problem as the model structure used for ANFIS is fixed and there is a tendency for such a model to overfit the data on which it is trained. This data set is used to cross-validate the fuzzy inference model by repeated checking. The training and checking error was calculated, which checks and validates the ANFIS model.

This model was further used to create a PC-based system as shown in Figure 2.5 using MATLAB software. The graphical user interface (GUI) of the proposed system is divided into three modules. The first and second modules are used for image acquisition and data analysis. The third module is used for displaying the information in RGB format, and histographs along with the results of testing conjunctivitis count as a percentage, with an option to save it to the database.

The PC-based noninvasive technique for detection of conjunctivitis and identification of its type by machine vision technique was trained and tested on 70 subjects with a high degree of accuracy, as the wrong detection was found in 6 subjects only. The authors have devised an objective method that correlates conjunctiva color with the type of the conjunctivitis of the patient, and also, it is able to predict the severity of the conjunctivitis of the patients, as shown in the GUI (Figure 2.6). The advantages of the proposed system are that it is noninvasive, instant, low cost, and user friendly. The system is also capable of recording data for future use.

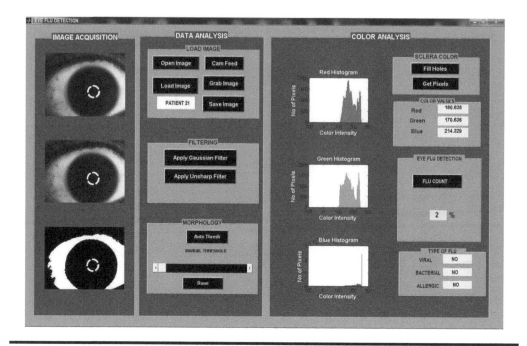

Figure 2.6 Graphical user interface for conjunctivitis detection.

2.6 Detection of Jaundice

2.6.1 Image Analysis

The image-processing algorithm includes image segmentation, image morphology, and color analysis. The image-processing steps for conjunctivitis detection were applied in this case, but the output was detected in terms of the La*b* color format. Based upon the color information, the detection of jaundice was done by using a soft-computing technique.

2.6.2 Classification of Jaundice and Nonjaundice Patients

The color of the sclera region of the eyes of all the patients was subjected to PCA. The output of PCA analysis was the clustered data, which show the variability among various patients based upon color attributes. A PCA score plot of PC1 versus PC2 for the observed eye data plotted using three color variables showed 89% variance (Figure 2.7).

The PCA biplot shows the mapping of jaundice and healthy patients on PC1 and PC2 axes. The healthy subjects were mapped along the negative PC1 axis, whereas the patients suffering from jaundice were mapped along the positive PC1 axis. It was observed that healthy patients were positively correlated to L but negatively correlated to a* and b* values, as the eye color of healthy patients may seldom found to be yellow or reddish. Consequently, the jaundice patients were found to be positively correlated to both a* and b* values. The positive values of a* and b* were related to the redness and yellowness, respectively. The higher values of b* are related to yellowness, which implies the occurrence of jaundice, whereas higher b values denote any eye infection that causes redness of the sclera region. The L value represents the lightness and shows no implications. Therefore, the results of PCA show that color values can clearly discriminate between jaundice patients and healthy subjects.

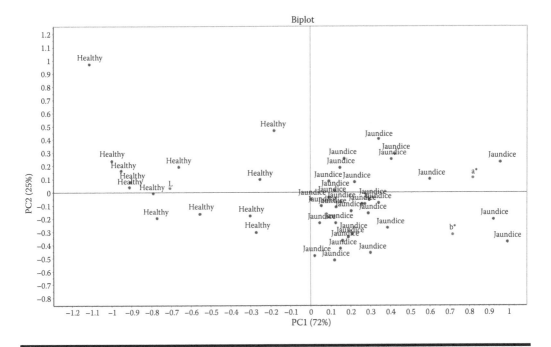

Figure 2.7 PCA-based discrimination analysis between jaundice and nonjaundice subjects.

2.6.3 Detection of Jaundice and Its Degree of Severity

2.6.3.1 Statistical Analysis Using PCA

The classification between jaundice and nonjaundice patients can be done by using PCA, which is a statistical analysis technique and gives an interpretable overview of the significant information in the form of multidimensional data clusters consisting of the principal components (PCs), which are linear functions of the original variables. The higher-order PCs starting from PC1 are more significant and cover the maximum variation in the data in decreasing order. Also, they are orthogonal to each other.

The significant color attributes causing maximum discrimination can be identified by using a PCA biplot, which is the combination of scores and loading weights (relationship between samples and variables). The score vectors plotted against each other determine the variance in the input data, whereas the loading weights show how much each variable out of all variables contributes to explained response variation along any two PCs in a two-dimensional space. The mapping of the loading weights from the origin shows the significance of the corresponding variables (Esbensen 2004).

2.6.3.2 Neuro-Fuzzy-Based Detection of Jaundice and Its Severity

The detection of jaundice based upon color attributes is a nonlinear problem due to the variability of body parameters of different patients, and over such data, fuzzy logic can be applied easily. However, fixation of different ranges for color attributes L, a*, and b* along with development of a rule base is a very tiresome job due to the data obtained from a large number of patients. Again, to generate the rules for a fuzzy logic system, an ANFIS-based approach was used as it generates the rules automatically and has advanced learning of an ANN. This technique is very simple and efficient.

The observed color values were quantified and fed to the ANFIS-based algorithm (combination of the neural network adaptive capabilities and the fuzzy logic qualitative approach) developed in MATLAB software, which consists of three color attributes as inputs to the ANFIS model and a single decision (degree of severity of jaundice), as shown in Figure 2.8. For rule generation, genfis3 function, and training fuzzy membership function parameters, a hybrid learning methodology

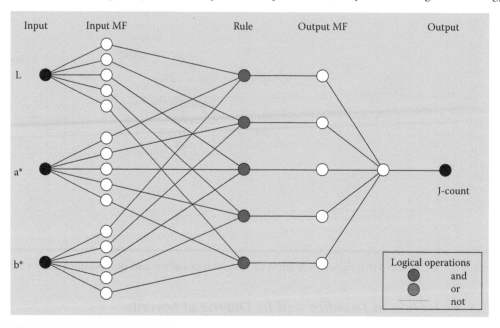

Figure 2.8   ANFIS algorithm for jaundice detection.

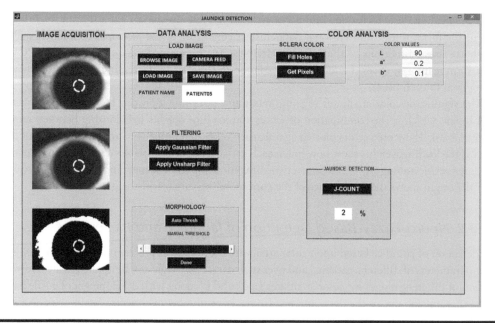

Figure 2.9   Graphical user interface for jaundice detection.

(combination of least-squares estimation with backpropagation algorithm of ANN) was used. The system's accuracy comes out to be over 90% in detecting jaundice correctly.

Further, based upon the ANFIS algorithm, GUI using MATLAB software is designed for jaundice detection (Figure 2.9), which consists of three modules, namely, image acquisition, data analysis, and color analysis. In this study, the color of the sclera region of a patient's eye in terms of L, a*, and b* values was trained by taking 330 subjects suffering from mild jaundice to severe jaundice. The result of the analysis provides the j-count (percentage of jaundice detected), which can be interpreted as per the doctor's recommendations, that is, if the value of j-count is more than 50%, then the patient has severe jaundice; otherwise, he/she may have mild jaundice.

2.7 Conclusion

The intelligent techniques for the detection of eye diseases were used based upon the ANFIS function of MATLAB. The data were obtained using machine vision. The accuracy and user-friendliness of the proposed techniques show their future scope in medical diagnosis. These techniques can be useful for the detection of a number of other diseases with an added advantage of being noninvasive and low cost.

Acknowledgments

The authors are thankful to the Council of Scientific & Industrial Research (CSIR), India, for its funding and cooperation. The authors are also thankful to the subjects who volunteered their data for the required experimentation.

References

Betke M., Mullally W., and Magee J. Active detection of eye scleras in real time. Proceedings of the IEEE CVPR Workshop on Human Modeling, Analysis and Synthesis, HMAS 2000, Hilton Head Island, SC, June 2000.

Chaudhuri S.C.S., Katz N., Nelson M. and Goldbaum M. Detection of blood vessels in retinal images using twodimensional matched filters. *IEEE Trans Med Imag*, vol. 8, pp. 263–269, 1989.

Davatzikos C. and Prince J.L. Convexity analysis of active contour problems. *Image Vision Comput*, vol. 17, pp. 27–36, 1999.

Edwards M., Gozdzik A., Ross K., Miles J. and Parra E.J. Technical note: Quantitative measures of iris color using high resolution photographs. *Am J Phys Anthropol*, vol. 147(1), pp. 141–149, 2012.

Esbensen K.H. *Multivariate Data Analysis in Practice: An Introduction to Multivariate Data Analysis and Experimental Design*, 5th ed. CAMO Process AS, Oslo, Norway, pp. 33–40, 2004.

Guillon M. and Shah D. Objective measurement of contact lens-induced conjunctival redness. *Opt Vis Sci*, vol. 73(9), pp. 595–605, 1996.

Horak F., Berger U., Menapace R. and Schuster N. Quantification of conjunctival vascular reaction by digital imaging. *J Allergy Clin Immunol*, vol. 98(3), pp. 495–500, 1996.

Izadi M. and Safabakhsh R. An improved time-adaptive self-organizing map for high-speed shape modeling. *Pattern Recogn*, vol. 42, pp. 1361–1370, 2009.

Khosravi M.H. and Safabakhsh R. Human eye sclera detection and tracking using a modified time-adaptive self-organizing map. *Pattern Recogn*, vol. 41, pp. 2571–2593, 2008.

Lin C.S., Ho C.W., Chang K.C., Hung S.S., Shei H.J. and Yeh M.S. A novel device for head gesture measurement system in combination with eye-controlled human–machine interface. *Opt Lasers Eng*, vol. 44(6), pp. 597–614, 2006.

Nash K. and Guha I.N. *Hepatology: Clinical Cases Uncovered*. Wiley-Blackwell, pp. 31–32, March 2011.

Owen C.G., Ellis T.J. and Woodward E.G. A comparison of manual and automated methods of measuring conjunctival vessel widths from photographic and digital images. *Ophthalmic Physiol Opt*, vol. 24, pp. 74–81, 2004.

Rassam S.M., Patel V., Brinchmann-Hansen O., Engvold O. and Kohner E.M. Accurate vessel widthmeasurement from fundus photographs: A new concept. *Br J Ophthalmol*, vol. 78, pp. 24–29, 1994.

Suner S., Crawford G., Mcmurdy J. and Jay G. Non-invasive determination of hemoglobin by digital photography of palpebral conjunctiva. *J Emerg Med*, vol. 33, pp. 105–111, 2007.

Van N., Nguyen H., Binh T.H. and Kim H. Eye feature extraction using K-means clustering for low illumination and iris color variety. 11th International Conference on Control Automation Robotics & Vision (ICARCV) Singapore, pp. 633–637, December 7–10, 2010.

Chapter 3

Laser Promotes Proliferation of Stem Cells: A Comprehensive Case Study Consolidated by Intelligent Agent–Based Model Predictions

Aya Sedky Adly, Mohamed Hassan Haggag,
and Mostafa-Sami M. Mostafa

Contents

Understanding stem cells' behavior and improving their proliferation in different situations and cultures are considered among the most challenging aspects in stem cell research. A better understanding of these processes may yield information about how they arise and suggests new strategies for therapy. Low-intensity laser irradiation has been shown to enhance stem cell proliferation when using the appropriate set of parameters and conditions. A critical factor is the correct selection of suitable laser sources and parameters in a manner that enhances the proliferation and adapts the process to the requirements of the stem cell type, nature, state, and properties. The development of a flexible, reproducible, and scalable computer model can play a key role in such systems, as it can be a tool for observing stem cells' characteristics, predicting their behavior, and supporting decisions for selecting their right set of conditions and parameters. This work provides a prospective comprehensive study that investigates the main aspects of applying low-intensity laser irradiation on stem cells and its effect on their proliferation under different parameters and conditions consolidated by an intelligent agent–based model. In this work, several stem cell types were investigated; some were validated and confirmed by clinical and experimental trials including bone marrow mesenchymal stem cells, umbilical cord mesenchymal stem cells, adipose-derived stem cells, cardiac stem cells, periodontal ligament stem cells, dental pulp stem cells, and satellite cells; others still need to be confirmed by clinical trials such as endothelial stem cells, amniotic fluid stem cells, renal stem cells, and epithelial stem cells. This study recommends a wavelength ranging from 530 to 680 nm and an energy density ranging from 0.3 to 6.0 J/cm^2 with short exposure times. Short evaluation periods are preferred since the enhancement extent of proliferation decreases with time as the process of cell differentiation increases.

3.1 Introduction

Recently, there has been a growing awareness of the need to use models to understand and predict the behaviors of stem cells. There have been several attempts to build models that can predict how stem cells behave either individually or in groups. For years, researchers have tried different ways to control stem cell proliferation and differentiation; they have also tried to develop strategies to help them to produce specific cell lines [1–3]. Some of them were theoretical, which have been proposed for description [4,5]. However, these models were limited as they were based on hypothesis without experimental or clinical verification. There are some models that focused on regulatory networks and gene interactions [6]. Other models focused on constituents in the extracellular medium activate signaling pathways involved in the stem cell's decision to replicate or differentiate [7–10]. More recently, Li Shaofan and Zeng Xiaowei [11–13] focused on simulating contact and adhesion of stem cells, while Qiu et al. [14] focused on simulating the stem cell microenvironment in vitro to culture and expand cord and umbilical cord mesenchymal stem cells.

Stem cells are present throughout life, from the fertilized oocyte to the adult. They have a remarkable regenerative ability, an extensive proliferative potential, and an amazing ability to develop into many different cell types. Research on stem cells enables scientists to learn about the cells' essential properties and to advance their knowledge about their characteristics and behaviors in different situations. Stem cell research is one of the most fascinating areas of contemporary biology that rapidly generates new discoveries [15–20].

Effects of low-intensity laser therapy on different fields have been known for over 40 years, since the invention of lasers, and have become a focus of recent research [21–23]. It has become a clinically accepted tool in tissue engineering processes, including healing [24–28], synthesizing collagen [29,30], relieving pain [31–34], decreasing inflammation [25,35,36], reducing edema [37,38], affecting cell proliferation [39–65], facilitating cell differentiation [55,57,59], and promoting cell survival and viability [50–52]. A range of studies on low-intensity laser irradiation and stem cells have reported its ability to affect proliferation of stem cells [45–65]. These studies have shown that it can produce significant and often desirable effects on stem cells' proliferation when choosing the appropriate parameters and conditions.

Today's scientific emerging interest in tissue engineering using stem cells stimulated us to develop a model to estimate, examine, and investigate the effects of low-intensity laser irradiation on proliferation of different types of stem cells, including mesenchymal stem cells, umbilical cord mesenchymal stem cells, adipose-derived stem cells, cardiac stem cells, periodontal ligament stem cells, dental pulp stem cells, satellite cells, endothelial stem cells, amniotic fluid stem cells, renal stem cells, and epithelial stem cells.

3.2 Dynamics of Stem Cells

Man has always known that the human body can heal itself. For thousands of years, people have observed that minor cuts and abrasions go through a process of healing, a process often referred to as regeneration. While it is easy to see that a cut upon the arm heals itself through regeneration, it is less understood that the same regenerative process is continuously ongoing within the body. It is a common belief that the human body completely renews itself every 7 years [66,67].

Stem cells have, since their first description, been recognized as a theoretically endless source of cells capable of differentiation into any somatic cell type. They provide the means for the embryo to diversify, that is, to give rise to all specified functions of every organ in the body and for homeostasis and regeneration in the adult. As somatic development proceeds, stem cells become increasingly restricted in their potential, that is, their fate becomes set for specific tissue. Stem cells are defined by their capacity to self-renew, that is, to divide and create additional stem cells or daughter cells, and also to differentiate along a specified developmental pathway. Other cells of the body, the so-called somatic cells, do not have these abilities [68,69].

Regenerative medicine is the science and technology built around stem cells' regenerative capacity, and it is considered as the application of tissue, sciences, engineering, computations, and related biological and biochemical principles that restore the structure and function of damaged tissues and organs. This revolutionary technology encompasses many novel approaches that help in developing therapies for previously untreatable diseases, including the following:

- Using therapies that prompt the body to autonomously regenerate damaged tissues
- Using tissue-engineered implants to prompt regeneration
- Direct transplantation of healthy tissues into damaged environments
- Testing of new drugs and medications for safety on differentiated cells generated from stem cell lines
- Producing hormones or proteins that are used as medications, such as generating insulin by culturing insulin-producing cells

However, to realize the promise of novel stem cell–based therapies for such diseases, scientists must be able to easily and reproducibly proliferate stem cells to generate sufficient quantities of tissue and manipulate them to possess the necessary characteristics for successful differentiation, transplantation, and engraftment. Due to the fact that stem cells grow and proliferate at slow rates, a therapy that can induce and enhance their proliferation will significantly shorten cells' preparation time and hence increase the number of clinical trials and avoid contamination.

Proliferation is a process involving a sequential pattern of cyclic, repeating changes in gene expression, leading ultimately to the physical division of cells. A stem cell can divide into two identical stem cells (replication) by symmetric division or one replicate and a differentiated daughter cell by asymmetric division [66,68,70–72]. Maintenance means to keep at an existing state or level and, when considered in terms of numbers, the ability to maintain its own numbers. Self-maintenance implies maintenance of a functional ability (e.g., number) irrespective of the identity. Replication means duplication or repetition and is thus a property of proliferative cells. Self-replication implies production of identical twins. Renewal can be defined as "to make like new," which can be considered as an element of rejuvenation. Self-renewal implies the cell's capability of generating populations with the same (or similar) functional ability and composition as the population from which it originated. Regeneration implies "to make again" something that was already preexisting. Successive differentiation processes are often expressed as canalization [66,68,70].

Each specialized cell type in an organism expresses a subset of all the genes that constitute the genome of that species. Each cell type is defined by its particular pattern of regulated gene expression. Cell differentiation is thus a transition of a cell from one cell type to another, and it involves a switch from one pattern of gene expression to another. However, sometimes during differentiation, stem cells lose their unique molecular signature or stemness. Most efforts have been devoted to driving cells down differentiation pathways by natural means. Dedifferentiation is a cellular process in which a partially or terminally differentiated cell reverts to an earlier developmental stage, usually as part of a regenerative process [73–77]. Adult stem cells are often localized to specific locations, so-called niches, which are considered specific anatomic locations that regulate how cells participate in tissue generation, maintenance, and repair [78,79]. The niches are mainly composed of a group of cells in an extracellular matrix that provides services to ensure survival and protection, enticing stem cells to stay put. Inside the niche, stem cells put their genes for specialization on hold as they are generally kept undifferentiated by their niche. In addition, the process of exit from the niche itself can sometimes be enough to cause differentiation. This means that not only regulatory genes from niche cells determine the future path of stem cells, but also both niche and stem cells possess genes that produce proteins that act as a series of on–off switches for their division and differentiation [80,81].

In general, the promise of stem cell therapies is an exciting one, and there are many technical hurdles between this promise and the realization of its uses, which will only be overcome through years of continued intensive stem cell research [3,68,71].

3.3 Model Description

To conduct an experiment, a laser source and a cell proliferation assay (or any suitable techniques to infer cell proliferation) are needed. However, to run the model, genomic sequences of the chromosomes along with their annotation databases are needed. The model may require setting some parameters and defining information on gene expression patterns according to different biological conditions along with gene expression changes measured according to cell type, organism part, developmental stage, disease state, and any other biological/experimental conditions of interest.

The model applies the idea of intelligent agents where its structure is defined as a specific environment in which agents are situated. The behavior of agents is influenced by states and types of agents that are situated in adjacent and at distant sites.

The capabilities of agents include both the ability to adapt and the ability to learn. Adaptation implies sensing the environment and reconfiguring in response. This can be achieved through the choice of alternative problem-solving rules or algorithms, or through the discovery of problem-solving strategies. Learning may proceed through observing actual data, and then it implies a capability of introspection and analysis of behavior and success. Alternatively, learning may proceed by example and generalization, and then it implies a capacity to abstract and generalize. We could group agents used in this work into five classes based on their degree of perceived intelligence and capability: (1) a simple reflex agent (acts only on the basis of the current percept), (2) a model-based reflex agent (keeps track of the current state of its world using an internal model, before choosing an action), (3) a goal-based agent (stores information regarding desirable situations, to select the one that reaches a goal state), (4) a utility-based agent (distinguishes between goal states and non-goal states and can define how desirable a particular state is), and (5) a learning agent (can initially operate in unknown environments and become more competent than its initial knowledge alone might allow). Agents' behavior is nondeterministic. Interactions and responding abilities are governed by a set of rules that define their behavior. Rules will often contradict, and there must be some mechanism for selecting over them. Agents are not aware of the system macroview although they have the capability of responding to local environmental factors as well as external dynamics and signaling under various conditions. In addition, they are not able to know the state and current behavior of every other agent [81–83].

The system development of this model is highly related to time and is considered at discrete time steps $t = \Delta t_m = m \times \Delta t$, $(m = 0, 1, 2,...)$ with a fixed length Δt. The illustrations that follow show how a very simple formula is deduced to calculate the population growth and estimations of proliferation parameters based on the initial number of cells (Table 3.1).

During development of multicellular organisms, cells become different from one another by distinct use of their genetic program where cellular memory mechanisms enable cells to "remember" their chosen fate over many cell divisions. This implies that to grow and maintain a specific

Table 3.1 Nomenclature

$№(t)$	Number of cells at time t in population
$№_o$	The initial number of cells in population
CCT	Average cell cycle time
Δt	Time step
ψ	The average number of divisions occurred during time t
I_{G1}	Checkpoint located at the end of the cell cycle's G_1 phase
I_S	Checkpoint located at the end of the cell cycle's S phase
I_{G2}	Checkpoint located at the end of the cell cycle's G_2 phase
I_M	Checkpoint located at the end of the cell cycle's M phase
I_{G0}	Checkpoint located at the end of the cell cycle's G_0 phase
μ	The mitotic index
D	The differentiation index
$\vec{D}$	The differentiation rate
$\tilde{D}$	The dedifferentiation rate
ρ	The cell death index for normal cells
α	The cell death index for senescent cells
e	Number of available population crypts
E	Tendency matrix for population cells, $№_\psi \times e$ matrix valued functions of t
$E_{ij}(t)$	The tendency of the ith cell to the jth crypt at time t
ε	Number of available energy densities
S	Stimulation rates matrix of proliferation, $\varepsilon \times e$ matrix valued functions of t
$S_{kj}(t)$	Stimulation rate of proliferation at the kth energy intensity on the jth crypt at time t
F	Facilitation rates matrix of differentiation, $\varepsilon \times e$ matrix valued functions of t
$F_{kj}(t)$	Facilitation rate of differentiation at the kth energy intensity on the jth crypt at time t

state, particular configurations of gene expression need to be transmitted to daughter cells. Population growth of cells and estimations of proliferation parameters often are calculated using the exponential equation

$$№(t) = №_o \, 2^{t/CCT} \tag{3.1}$$

where the number of cells $№$, at time t, depends on the initial number of cells, $№_o$, and its average cell cycle time CCT.

A cell cycle is the series of events that take place in a cell between its formation and the moment it replicates itself. The cell cycle consists of four distinct phases: S phase (synthesis), during which DNA is synthesized; M phase (mitosis), during which the actual cell division occurs; and two gap (growth) phases, G_1 and G_2, which fall between M & S and S & M, respectively, as shown in Figure 3.1.

Cells that have temporarily or reversibly stopped dividing are said to have entered a G_0 phase, while cells that have permanently stopped dividing due to age or accumulated DNA damage are said to be senescent [84,85].

So by using $\psi = t/CCT$ for simplicity, where ψ is the average number of divisions that occurred during time t, the equation would be

$$\mathcal{N}(t) = \mathcal{N}_\psi = \mathcal{N}_o \, 2^\psi \tag{3.2}$$

There is a checkpoint l_{G1} located at the end of the cell cycle's G_1 phase, just before entry into S phase, making the key decision of whether the cell should divide, delay division, or enter a resting stage and cease proliferation, that is, become quiescent. Most cells stop at this stage and enter the resting state G_0, in which case a cell does not act as an actual stem cell, but since it can reenter the cycle, it has the potential to act as a stem cell.

With l_{G0} being the time length that a cell resides in G_0 phase, we could reformulate ψ as

$$\psi = t/(CCT + l_{G0}) \tag{3.3}$$

The G_1 phase, S phase, and G_2 phase are collectively known as *interphase* and M phase as *metaphase*. A newborn cell resides either in G_0, the nondividing state, or in G_1 until physiological parameters allow it to enter the S phase and to start replicating its genetic material. Metabolic activity, cell growth, and cell differentiation all occur during interphase, and G_1 phase is considered the major period of cell growth during its lifespan [84,85].

Therefore, a cell differentiation, which is possible only during the interphase, can occur with probability $d = 0$ when the cell is in the metaphase.

The previous equation that describes population growth assumes that all cells are actively dividing to give rise to two daughter cells. In order to describe it more accurately, we could include a parameter that accounts for the presence of senescence, an irreversible state in which the cell no longer divides:

$$\mathcal{N}_\psi = \begin{cases} \mathcal{N}, & \psi - 0 \\ (1-\mu)\mathcal{N}_{\psi-1} + 2\mu \, \mathcal{N}_{\psi-1}, & \psi > 0 \end{cases} \tag{3.4}$$

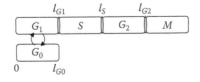

Figure 3.1 Cell cycle phases.

where μ is the mitotic index (the ratio of cells that are undergoing mitosis), $(1 - \mu).N_{\psi-1}$ are senescent cells, and $2\mu.N_{\psi-1}$ are dividing ones. This gives the following equation after simplification:

$$N_{\psi} = \begin{cases} N_{o}, & \psi - 0 \\ (1 + \mu).N_{\psi-1}, & \psi > 0 \end{cases} \tag{3.5}$$

And its closed form would be

$$N_{\psi} = N_{o}(1 + \mu)^{\psi} \tag{3.6}$$

This equation assumes that the ratio of dividing cells μ is independent of previous states. In other words, it neglects the fact that senescence is an irreversible state. So in order to get a better description, permanently nondividing cells of the previous state should not be included in computing the ratio of dividing cells of the current state as they usually cannot reenter the cell cycle again; this gives the equation

$$N_{\psi} = [(1 - \mu).N_{o} + (1 - \mu)(2\mu).N_{o} + (1 - \mu)(2\mu)^{2}.N_{o} + \cdots + (1 - \mu)(2\mu)^{\psi-1}.N_{o}] + (2\mu)^{\psi}N_{o} \tag{3.7}$$

Rearranging the terms gives a geometric series:

$$N_{\psi} = N_{o}\left[(1-\mu)\sum_{i=0}^{\psi-1}(2\mu) + (2\mu)^{\psi}\right] \tag{3.8}$$

And by applying the identity $\sum_{i=0}^{n-1}x^{i} = \left[\dfrac{x^{n}-1}{x-1}\right]$ when $x \neq 1$ provides the following equation:

$$N_{\psi} = N_{o}\left[(1-\mu)\left[\dfrac{(2\mu)^{\psi}-1}{(2\mu)-1}\right] + (2\mu)^{\psi}\right] \tag{3.9}$$

In stem cell population growth, there is a dynamic balance between self-maintenance and differentiation processes. Such populations are rarely homogeneous, as the stem cell has a tendency to response to different signals, giving rise to a precursor and then fully differentiating, while at the same time maintaining its functionality and number [66,68,70–72]. To provide a formula for this cell growth and to understand these processes, we must include a term to account for cells that started the differentiation process as a response to certain stimuli causing them to leave their niche and home to a different medium. And accordingly, as initiating differentiation leads to changes in cell type, which lead to temporary (as it may be capable to dedifferentiate) loss of abilities to maintain its previous state, we could exclude it from its previous population:

$$N_{\psi} = N_{o}\left[(1-\mu)\left[\dfrac{(2\mu)^{\psi}-1}{(2\mu)-1}\right] + (2\mu)^{\psi}\right](1-D)^{\psi} \tag{3.10}$$

where D is the differentiation index (the ratio of cells that are undergoing differentiation).

Of course, it would be also necessary to add those who dedifferentiated to their previous state as well, which would increase the number of cells by considering $D = f(\vec{D}, \bar{D})$, where $\vec{D}$ is the differentiation rate and $\bar{D}$ is the dedifferentiation rate.

This equation still is not accurate, as senescent cells normally do not differentiate as they cannot enter the cell cycle:

$$
\begin{aligned}
\mathcal{N}_\psi &= [(1-\mu)\mathcal{N} + (1-\mu)(2\mu)(1-D)\mathcal{N} + (1-\mu)(2\mu)^2(1-D)^2\mathcal{N} + \cdots \\
&\quad + (1-\mu)(2\mu)^{\psi-1}(1-D)^{\psi-1}\mathcal{N}] + (2\mu)^\psi(1-D)^\psi\,\mathcal{N}
\end{aligned}
\tag{3.11}
$$

This was simplified to

$$
\mathcal{N}_\psi = \mathcal{N}\left[(1-\mu)\left[\frac{(2\mu(1-D))^\psi - 1}{2\mu(1-D)-1}\right] + (2\mu)^\psi(1-D)^\psi\right]
\tag{3.12}
$$

However, due to environmental factors and normal metabolic processes inside the cell, a cell can undergo damage, which can impede a cell's ability to carry out its function. A cell that has accumulated a large amount of damage, or one that no longer effectively repairs its molecules' damage, can commit suicide, which is called apoptosis or programmed cell death [84–86]. Thus, by considering conditions of significant cell death,

$$
\mathcal{N}_\psi = \mathcal{N}\left[(1-\mu)\left[\frac{(2\mu - 2\mu D)^\psi - 1}{(2\mu - 2\mu D) - 1}\right] + (2\mu(1-D))^\psi\right](1-\rho)^\psi
\tag{3.13}
$$

where ρ is the cell death index (the ratio of cells that are undergoing programmed death or apoptosis).

And as the rate of suicide cells in senescent cells is usually different from normal cells (normally higher),

$$
\begin{aligned}
\mathcal{N} = \mathcal{N}\,[(1-\mu)[&(1-\alpha)\psi \\
&+ (1-\alpha)^{\psi-1}(1-\rho)(2\mu)(1-D) \\
&+ (1-\alpha)^{\psi-2}(1-\rho)^2(2\mu)^2(1-D)^2 + \cdots \\
&+ (1-\alpha)(1-\rho)^{\psi-1}(2\mu)^{\psi-1}(1-D)^{\psi-1}]]
\end{aligned}
\tag{3.14}
$$

This was simplified to

$$
\mathcal{N}_\psi = \mathcal{N}\left[(1-\mu)\sum_{i=0}^{\psi-1}[(1-\alpha)^{\psi-1}(2\mu(1-\rho)(1-D))^i] + (2\mu(1-\rho)(1-D))^\psi\right]
\tag{3.15}
$$

where ρ is the cell death index for normal cells and α is the cell death index for senescent cells. Moreover, we could define some of the parameters that are associated with this formula.

Although stem cells normally reside in a specific microenvironmental niche, they are also assumed to be able to reside in more than one environment and migrate from one crypt to another within their system according to their tendency to this crypt. Cell migration is a central process in the development and maintenance of multicellular organisms. Tissue formation during embryonic development, wound healing, and immune responses all require the movement of cells in a particular direction to a specific location [80,81].

We can define the cell migration and cell tendency as

e Number of available population crypts

E Tendency matrix for population cells, $N_\psi^0 \times e$ matrix valued functions of t

where $E_{ij}(t)$ is the tendency of the ith cell to the jth crypt at time t. At every time step, a cell should make a decision whether to reside on its crypt or to migrate. This decision depends mainly on its current position, state, and tendency matrix.

In addition, it is well known that low-intensity laser irradiation significantly stimulates proliferation, which was confirmed by previous studies in this field [45–65].

We can define the effect of low-intensity laser on population growth as

ε Number of available energy densities

S Stimulation rates matrix of proliferation, $\varepsilon \times e$ matrix valued functions of t

F Facilitation rates matrix of differentiation, $\varepsilon \times e$ matrix valued functions of t

where $S_{kj}(t)$ is the stimulation rate of proliferation at the kth energy intensity on the jth crypt at time t, and $F_{kj}(t)$ is the facilitation rate of differentiation at the kth energy intensity on the jth crypt at time t.

Other formulas and parameters can be added to the model as required. This enables flexible programmability in accounting for experimental data through dynamically organized intelligent agents. Thus, the model achieves scalability by partitioning processes between different interacting agents that have different degrees of intelligence and capabilities while adding rules, constraints, equations, functionalities, and environmental factors. However, the model is deeply integrated with the agents' components and intelligence level. Therefore, it takes more effort to add some rules to agents with a lower intelligence level, as it may require some capabilities that should be embedded into the agent's architecture. This problem can be solved by training the model using a variety of real-world experimental data. In fact, training the model with previous experimental data that have the same biological/experimental conditions may yield more accuracy in the model predictions, but it is not a necessity as long as all the required data are available. However, to ensure a meaningful modeling and to validate its utility and performance, we have conducted validation tests of the proposed model. By doing so, we can identify and compare the parameters of the model, according to verified scenarios, by applying it to previously investigated and measured clinical trials and experiments that investigated different stem cell types.

3.4 Results

Numbers of stem cells were calculated over time in different groups. Figures 3.2 through 3.9 demonstrate the effects of low-intensity laser at various energy densities on the proliferation of

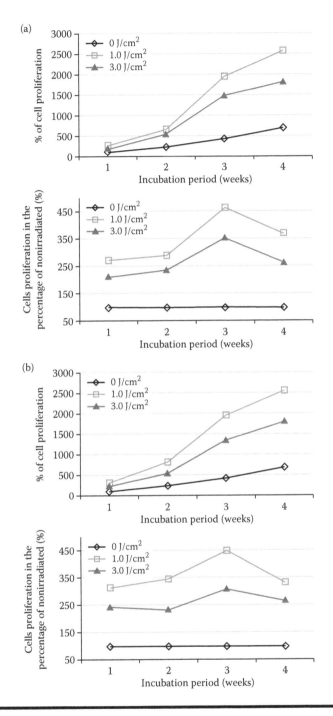

Figure 3.2 Effect of low-intensity laser irradiation on proliferation of mesenchymal stem cells. (a) Curves of the actual experimental results of Hana et al. (From Hana, T. et al., *Lasers Surg. Med.*, 39, 2007.) (b) Curves of the model results for the same experiment.

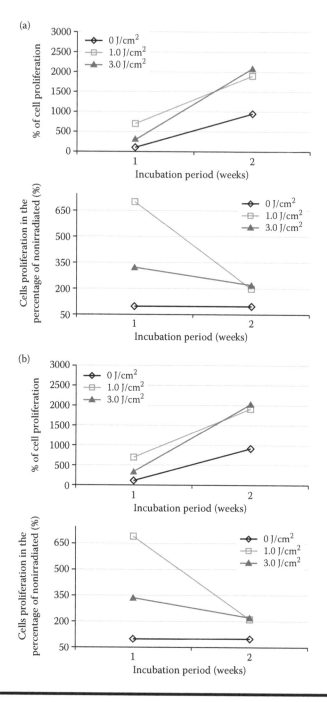

Figure 3.3 Effect of low-intensity laser irradiation on proliferation of cardiac stem cells. (a) Curves of the actual experimental results of Hana et al. (From Hana, T. et al., *Lasers Surg. Med.*, 39, 2007.) (b) Curves of the model results for the same experiment.

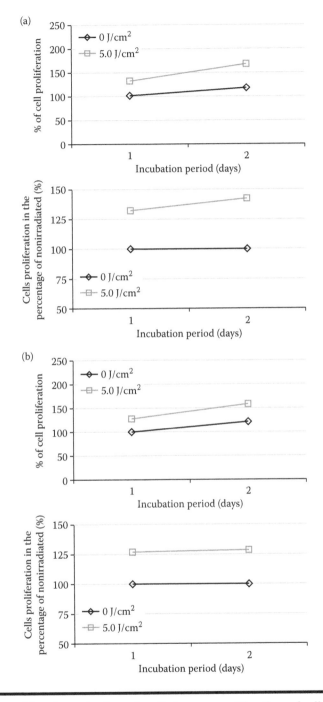

Figure 3.4 Effect of low-intensity laser irradiation on proliferation of adipose-derived stem cells. (a) Curves of the actual experimental results of Mvula et al. (From Mvula, B. et al., *Lasers Med. Sci.*, 23, 2008.) (b) Curves of the model results for the same experiment.

stem cells during different incubation periods. In order to compare the mean number of stem cells between irradiated groups and the nonirradiated group, the figure values were calculated in two ways. The first way was calculating as a percentage in the initial number of cells by dividing the number of cells in all groups by the initial number of cells and then multiplying by 100. The second way was calculating as a percentage of nonirradiated cells by dividing the number of cells in each group by the number of nonirradiated cells that took the same incubation period and then multiplying by 100. The detailed irradiation parameters are reported in Table 3.2.

3.4.1 Effect of Low-Intensity Laser on the Proliferation of Mesenchymal and Cardiac Stem Cells

3.4.1.1 Experimental Results

Hana et al. [45] measured the effect of laser irradiation on proliferation of both mesenchymal and cardiac stem cells. The number of mesenchymal stem cells increased rapidly from the first week to the fourth week after low-intensity laser treatment for both a duration of 20 s at an energy density of 1 J/cm^2 and a duration of 60 s at an energy density of 3 J/cm^2 as compared to nonirradiated cells. Similarly, the number of cardiac stem cells irradiated at 1–2 weeks postculturing increased for both energy densities of 1 and 3 J/cm^2. It would appear that the energy density of 1 J/cm^2 caused

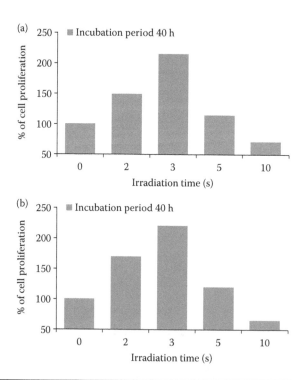

Figure 3.5   Effect of low-intensity laser irradiation on proliferation of satellite cells at various time intervals. (a) Actual experimental results of Nadav et al. (From Nadav, B.D. et al., *Biochim. Biophys. Acta*, 1448, 1999.) (b) Model results for the same experiment.

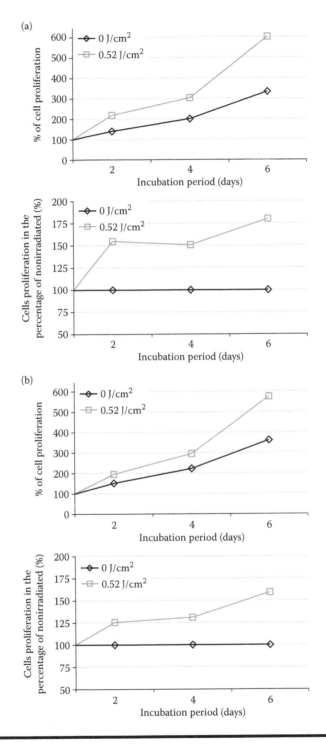

Figure 3.6 **Effect of low-intensity laser irradiation on proliferation of satellite cells. (a) Curves of the actual experimental results of Hou et al. (From Hou, J.F. et al.,** *Lasers Surg. Med.* **40, 2008.) (b) Curves of the model results for the same experiment.**

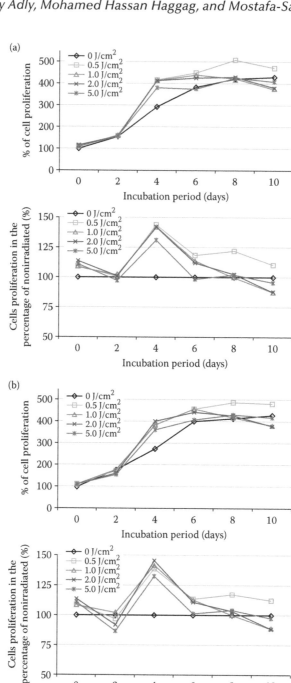

Figure 3.7 **Effect of low-intensity laser irradiation on proliferation of bone marrow–derived mesenchymal stem cells. (a) Curves of the actual experimental results of Hou et al. (From Hou, J.F. et al.,** *Lasers Surg. Med.* **40, 2008.) (b) Curves of the model results for the same experiment.**

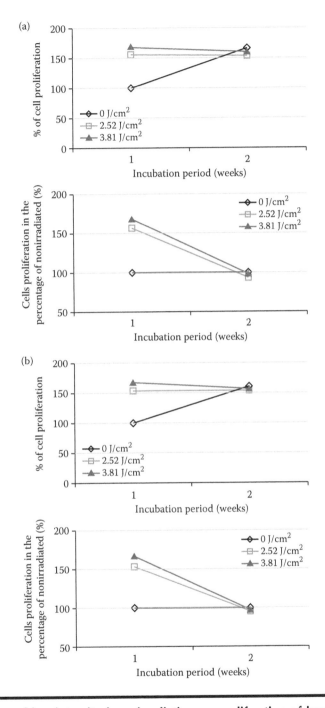

Figure 3.8 Effect of low-intensity laser irradiation on proliferation of human mesenchymal stem cells. (a) Curves of the actual experimental results of Leonida et al. (From Leonida, A. et al., *Lasers Med. Sci.*, 28, 2013.) (b) Curves of the model results for the same experiment.

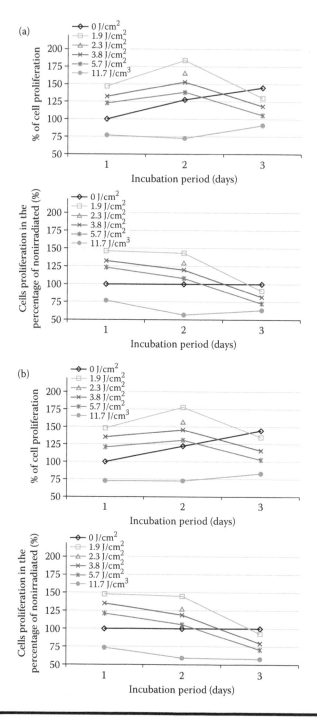

Figure 3.9   Effect of low-intensity laser irradiation on proliferation of human mesenchymal stem cells. (a) Curves of the actual experimental results of Horvát-Karajz et al. (From Horvát-Karajz et al., *Lasers Surg. Med.*, 41, 2009.) (b) Curves of the model results for the same experiment.

Table 3.2   Effect of Low-Intensity Laser on the Proliferation of Different Types of Stem Cells

Cell Type	Species	Mode of Action	Wavelength (nm)	Irradiation Time (s)	Power (mW)	Power Density (mW/cm²)	Energy (J)	Energy Density (J/cm²)	Beam Diameter (cm)	Beam Area (cm²)	Evaluated Incubation Periods Post Irradiation (h)	Compared Experiment Ref. [1]	Observations
Bone marrow mesenchymal stem cells	Charles River rats	Pulsed	804	20, 60	40	50	0.8, 2.4	1, 3	1.0	0.785	168, 336, 504, 672	[45]	The group irradiated with an energy density of 1.0 J/cm² improved in cell proliferation in comparison to other groups. The extent of enhancement of cell proliferation decreased with time (after 504 h).
	Sprague-Dawley rats	Continuous	635	75, 150, 300, 750	60	6.61	4.5, 9, 18, 45	0.5, 1.0, 2.0, 5.0	3.4	9.08	0, 48, 96, 144, 192, 240	[46]	Low and moderate energy densities increased cell proliferation, and 0.5 J/cm² was found to be an optimal energy density.
	Sprague-Dawley rats	Continuous	635	75	60	6.61	4.5	0.5	3.4	9.08	0, 24, 48, 96, 144, 192	[47]	At an energy density of 0.5 J/cm², cell proliferation increased rapidly after 24 h and reached the highest level after 144 h.
	Mice	Continuous	660	25, 50, 75, 25, 75	60	76, 76, 76, 94, 156	1.5, 3, 4.5, 1.5, 4.5	1.9, 3.8, 5.7, 2.35, 11.7	1, 1, 1, 0.9, 0.7	0.785, 0.785, 0.785, 0.636, 0.385	24, 48, 72	[48]	Low and moderate energy densities increased cell proliferation, and high energy densities decreased cell proliferation. The 1.9 J/cm² energy density improved cell proliferation in comparison to other groups. No significant changes in cell proliferation were detected after 72 h incubation compared to the nonirradiated group.
	Mice	Continuous	635	10, 26	89	32.6, 12.6	0.9, 2.3	0.33	1.86, 3	2.73, 7.03	0, 24, 48, 72	[49]	Proliferation of irradiated cells increased compared to nonirradiated cells at 24, 48, and 72 h.

(continued)

Table 3.2 (Continued) Effect of Low-Intensity Laser on the Proliferation of Different Types of Stem Cells

Cell Type	Species	Mode of Action	Wavelength (nm)	Irradiation Time (s)	Power (mW)	Power Density (mW/cm²)	Energy (J)	Energy Density (J/cm²)	Beam Diameter (cm)	Beam Area (cm²)	Evaluated Incubation Periods Post Irradiation (h)	Compared Experiment Ref. []	Observations
	Mice	Continuous	660	100, 200, 400	38	10	3.8, 7.6, 15.2	1, 2, 4	2.2	3.8	24, 72, 120	[50]	No significant differences were found at 24 and 72 h. At 120 h, cell proliferation increased at both energy densities of 2 and 4 J/cm².
	Mice	Continuous	632.8	600	10	0.5	6	0.3	5	20	24, 168, 336	[51]	There was a noticeable enhancement in proliferation after 168 h of irradiation.
	Human	Pulsed	1064	0.135	1500, 2250	18,750, 28,100	0.1, 0.15	2.52, 3.81	0.32, 0.226	0.08, 0.04	168, 336	[52]	There was no statistically significant difference between both power levels of irradiation. The extent of enhancement of cell proliferation decreased with time (after 336 h).
	Human	Continuous	810	12, 18, 24, 36	50	167	6.67, 10, 13.33, 20	2, 3, 4, 6	0.6	0.3	168	[53]	Cell proliferation increased at all energy densities except for 6.0 J/cm² in comparison to control groups after 168 h.
Umbilical cord mesenchymal stem cells	Human	Continuous	940	600	200	6.67	120	4	6.2	30	48	[54]	Proliferation of irradiated cells with an energy density of 4.0 J/cm² increased compared to nonirradiated cells.
Cardiac stem cells	Charles River rats	Pulsed	804	20, 60	40	50	0.8, 2.4	1, 3	1.0	0.785	168, 336	[45]	The group irradiated with an energy density of 1.0 J/cm² improved in cell proliferation in comparison to other groups. The extent of enhancement of cell proliferation decreased with time (after 336 h).

Cell type	Species	Mode	Wavelength								Time (h)	Ref.	Results
Adipose-derived stem cells	Human	Continuous	635	900	50	5.5	45	5	3.3	9	24, 48	[55]	Proliferation of irradiated cells with an energy density of 5.0 J/cm^2 increased compared to nonirradiated cells at both time points.
	Human	Continuous	636	413	110	12.1	45	5	3.3	9	0, 24, 48	[56]	Proliferation of irradiated cells with an energy density of 5.0 J/cm^2 increased compared to nonirradiated cells at 24 and 48 h time points.
	Human	Continuous	6.36	586	78	8.59	45.4	5	3.4	9.08	24, 48, 72	[57]	Irradiated cells with an energy density of 5.0 J/cm^2 increased in numbers compared to nonirradiated cells and reached the highest level at 72 h.
	Human	Continuous	532	30, 45, 60, 180, 300	30	153	1, 1.36, 1.84, 5.6, 9	5, 6.8, 9.2, 28, 45	0.5	0.2	48	[58]	After 48 h of irradiation, shorter exposure times (30, 45, 60 s) led to significantly increased proliferation, while longer exposure times (180, 300 s) decreased cell proliferation.
	Human	Continuous	636	413	110	12.1	45.4	5	3.4	9.08	0, 24, 48	[59]	Cell proliferation increased rapidly in irradiated compared to nonirradiated cells and reached the highest level at 48 h.
	Human	Continuous	680	1276, 2551, 3887	35.6	3.92	45.4, 90.8, 136.2	5, 10, 15	3.4	9.08	24	[60]	After 24 h of irradiation with long exposure times, cells irradiated at 680 nm showed no statistically significant difference in proliferation compared to nonirradiated cells at all energy densities, while irradiation at 830 nm showed a significant decrease in proliferation at 10 and 15 J/cm^2 compared to both the nonirradiated and irradiated cells at 680 nm.
			830	1299, 2597, 3896	35	3.85							
Periodontal ligament stem cells	Human	Continuous	660	16, 33	30	1000	0.015, 0.03	0.5, 1.0	0.2	0.03	0, 24, 48, 72	[61]	After 48 h, the group irradiated with an energy density of 1.0 J/cm^2 improved in cell proliferation in comparison to other groups and reached the highest level after 72 h.

(continued)

Table 3.2 (Continued) Effect of Low-Intensity Laser on the Proliferation of Different Types of Stem Cells

Cell Type	Species	Mode of Action	Wavelength (nm)	Irradiation Time (s)	Power (mW)	Power Density (mW/cm²)	Energy (J)	Energy Density (J/cm²)	Beam Diameter (cm)	Beam Area (cm²)	Evaluated Incubation Periods Post Irradiation (h)	Compared Experiment Ref. [ ]	Observations
	Human	Continuous	660	66, 132, 264	70	15.17	4.61, 9.23, 18.46	1, 2, 4	2.4	4.61	24, 72, 120	[62]	After 72 h, the group irradiated with an energy density of 2.0 J/cm² improved in cell proliferation in comparison to other groups and reached the highest level after 120 h.
	Human	Continuous	660	6, 3	20, 40	500, 1000	0.12	3	5.642	25	20, 24, 48, 72	[63]	Moderate energy densities (3.0 J/cm²) increased proliferation of dental pulp stem cells. The group irradiated with an output power of 20 mW improved in cell proliferation in comparison to other groups.
Dental pulp stem cells	Human	Continuous	660	10, 60	0.2 / 28	5 / 700	0.002, 0.012 / 0.280, 1.680	0.05, 0.3 / 7, 42	0.226	0.04	24, 48, 72, 96	[64]	Very low energy densities (0.05, 0.3 J/cm²) and very high energy densities (7, 42 J/cm²) did not increase the proliferation of dental pulp stem cells.
Satellite cells	Charles River rats	Continuous	632	2, 3, 5, 10	4.5	173	0.009, 0.0135, 0.0225, 0.045	0.35, 0.52, 0.87, 1.73	0.18	0.226	48, 96, 144	[65]	Low energy densities increased proliferation of satellite cells. The group that received 3 s of irradiation at an energy density of 0.52 J/cm² improved in cell proliferation in comparison to other groups and reached the highest level after 144 h.

a higher stimulation of cell proliferation than 3 J/cm² in both cell types. The extent of enhancement of cell proliferation did not increase with time but leveled off or decreased (after 3 weeks in mesenchymal stem cells or 1 week in cardiac stem cells) (Figures 3.2a and 3.3a).

3.4.1.2 Model Predictions

The model results compared to their experiment demonstrate that both numbers of mesenchymal and cardiac stem cells increased nearly the same as the experimental results, although the enhancement increased more smoothly than that of the experimental results, which can be noticed clearly at an energy density of 1 J/cm². From the current findings, it would appear that the model accuracy is higher for short incubation periods than long ones (Figures 3.2b and 3.3b).

3.4.1.3 Observations

Low-level laser irradiation significantly promotes the proliferation of both mesenchymal and cardiac stem cells. Enhancement in cell proliferation was found to be higher at 3 weeks postculturing than at the rest for mesenchymal stem cells and lower at 2 weeks than at 1 week for cardiac stem cells in both experimental results and model predictions.

3.4.2 Effect of Low-Intensity Laser on the Proliferation of Adipose-Derived Stem Cells

3.4.2.1 Experimental Results

Mvula et al. [55] measured the effect of laser irradiation on proliferation of adult human adipose-derived stem cells. Proliferation of irradiated cells resulted in statistically significant increases in values compared to nonirradiated cells at both 24 h/day 0 and 48 h/day 1 (Figure 3.4a).

3.4.2.2 Model Predictions

The results computed after applying the model to their experiment showed no significant difference from the actual experimental results. However, on both day 0 and day 1, numbers in the irradiated groups were slightly lower than the actual experimental results (Figure 3.4b).

3.4.2.3 Observations

Low-level laser irradiation results in a statistically significant increase in proliferation of adipose-derived stem cells in both the experimental results and the model predictions.

3.4.3 Effect of Low-Intensity Laser on the Proliferation of Satellite Cells

3.4.3.1 Experimental Results

Nadav et al. [65] measured the effect of laser irradiation on proliferation of satellite cells. Cells were irradiated for various time intervals (1–10 s) and then incubated for 40 h. Their results showed that laser irradiation increased satellite cell proliferation in a bell-shaped manner, with a maximal and statistically significant effect at 3 s. Ten seconds of irradiation caused a significant inhibitory effect on cell proliferation compared to nonirradiated cells. Cells irradiated for 3 s were monitored in parallel with nonirradiated cells for 6 days, and the number of proliferating cells following irradiation was higher than the control cell number from the second day on. The difference was statistically significant at 2, 4, and 6 days in culture, being highest at 6 days (Figures 3.5a and 3.6a).

3.4.3.2 Model Predictions

Comparing the effect of laser irradiation computed by the model to their experiment, it was noted that satellite cell proliferation increased in a bell-shaped manner for time intervals (1–10 s); however, all the values were slightly lower than those of actual experimental results except the last interval 10 s, which was slightly higher than that of the actual experimental results, but it still caused an inhibitory effect on cell proliferation compared to nonirradiated cells. The maximum value was the same as the actual experimental results, at 3 s. Proliferation of cells irradiated for 3 s was higher than nonirradiated cells; however, all the values were slightly higher than those of the experimental results for nonirradiated cells. On the other hand, all the values were slightly lower than those of the experimental results for irradiated cells (Figures 3.5b and 3.6b).

3.4.3.3 Observations

Low-level laser irradiation results in a statistically significant increase in proliferation of satellite cells, and 3 s was found to be an optimal irradiation time in both the experimental results and the model predictions.

3.4.4 Effect of Low-Intensity Laser on the Proliferation of Bone Marrow–Derived Mesenchymal Stem Cells

3.4.4.1 Experimental Results

Hou et al. [46] measured the effect of laser irradiation on proliferation of bone marrow–derived mesenchymal stem cells. Cell numbers increased rapidly from day 0 to day 4 after low-intensity laser treatment and then reached a stationary phase by day 6. They also observed cell growth curves between the nonirradiated and irradiated groups throughout the cell-culture period. They indicated no significant differences between the nonirradiated and irradiated groups between day 0 and day 10. At day 2, groups irradiated at 0.5, 1.0, and 2.0 J/cm² showed significantly higher numbers than the nonirradiated group. At day 4, numbers in all irradiated groups were higher than those in the nonirradiated group, and there were no significant differences among the irradiated groups. At day 6, numbers in groups irradiated at 0.5, 1.0, and 0.2 J/cm² were significantly higher than those in the nonirradiated group. At day 8, only the group irradiated at 0.5 J/cm² showed significantly higher numbers than those in other groups, including the nonirradiated group (Figure 3.7a).

3.4.4.2 Model Predictions

The results computed after applying the model to their experiment showed no significant difference from the actual experimental results. However, on day 2, numbers in the nonirradiated and irradiated groups were slightly higher than the actual experimental results except for the group irradiated at 5.0 J/cm². At day 4, the model results were nearly the same for all groups except for groups irradiated at 0.5 and 1.0 J/cm², which had a lower number than that of the actual results.

The overall results on all days seemed to change more smoothly in the model results than the actual experimental results (Figure 3.7b).

3.4.4.3 Observations

Low-level laser irradiation results in a statistically significant increase in proliferation of bone marrow–derived mesenchymal stem cells, and 0.5 J/cm² was found to be an optimal energy density in both the experimental results and the model predictions.

3.4.5 Effect of Low-Intensity Laser on the Proliferation of Human Mesenchymal Stem Cells

3.4.5.1 Experimental Results

Leonida et al. [52] measured the effect of laser irradiation on proliferation of human mesenchymal stem cells. After the first week, proliferation of irradiated cells resulted in statistically significant increases in both groups compared to nonirradiated cells. After 2 weeks, irradiated cells showed the first signs of suffering as they did not record any increase in proliferation compared to nonirradiated cells, although there was a significant increase in both nonirradiated cell proliferation and irradiated cell differentiation. These signs are probably not directly related to laser treatment, since the process of cell proliferation decreases with an increase in the process of cell differentiation (Figure 3.8a).

3.4.5.2 Model Predictions

Comparing the effect of laser irradiation computed by the model to their experiment, it was noted that cell proliferation increased in both groups after a week in the actual experiment. After 2 weeks, cell numbers in all groups were somewhat similar. All the values were slightly less than the actual experimental results (Figure 3.8b).

3.4.5.3 Observations

Statistically significant cell proliferation was observed 1 week after irradiation. There was no significant difference in proliferation between the two used power levels of irradiation. After 2 weeks, the number of cells contained in all groups was similar. There was no significant difference between the model results and the actual experimental results.

3.4.6 Effect of Low-Intensity Laser on the Proliferation of Murine Mesenchymal Stem Cells

3.4.6.1 Experimental Results

Horvát-Karajz et al. [48] measured the effect of laser irradiation on proliferation of mesenchymal stem cells. Cells were irradiated at different doses. The 1.9 J/cm² dose resulted in the largest culture growth during the first and second days of incubation. The same effect was observed with a 3.8 J/cm² dose after 1 day of incubation and then with 2.3 and 3.8 J/cm² doses after 2 days of incubation. No significant changes were detected with 1.9 and 3.8 J/cm² after 3 days of incubation compared to the nonirradiated group. Stimulatory activity was seen with 5.7 J/cm^2 after 1 day and inhibition after 3 days of incubation, while a significant effect was not present after 2 days. A higher dose of 11.7 J/cm^2 of laser achieved the inhibition of proliferation at 2 and 3 days of incubation, but 2 days was not enough to present any significant effect with this dose (Figure 3.9a).

3.4.6.2 Model Predictions

The results computed after applying the model to their experiment showed no significant difference from the actual experimental results. However, the higher dose of 11.7 J/cm^2 of laser achieved more inhibition of proliferation than the actual experimental results, especially at 3 days of incubation (Figure 3.9b).

3.4.6.3 Observations

Low-level laser effectively increases proliferation, especially at a dose of 1.9 J/cm^2 at 1 and 2 days of incubation in both model predictions and actual experimental results.

3.4.7 Effect of Low-Intensity Laser on the Proliferation of Different Types of Stem Cells

Several stem cell types were investigated; some were validated and confirmed by clinical and experimental trials, which are summarized in Table 3.2, including mesenchymal stem cells, umbilical cord mesenchymal stem cells, adipose-derived stem cells, cardiac stem cells, periodontal ligament stem cells, dental pulp stem cells, and satellite cells.

Furthermore, this study estimated that low-intensity laser irradiation with a power density ranging from 0.5 to 6.0 J/cm^2 with short exposure times and a wavelength ranging from 630 to 660 nm will increase proliferation in endothelial stem cells, amniotic fluid stem cells, renal stem cells, and epithelial stem cells. However, we could not find any clinical experiments with enough details to compare it to the estimated results; hence, these results still need to be confirmed by clinical trials.

3.5 Conclusions

The present study demonstrates that low-intensity laser can significantly promote the proliferation of stem cells when appropriate laser irradiation parameters are used. However, it can also have opposite effects on stem cell proliferation due to the complexity of rationally choosing among a large number of parameters such as mode of action, wavelength, exposure time, energy density, power density, and beam area. This complexity led to the reporting of some negative studies as well as many positive ones (Table 3.2).

This study recommends a wavelength ranging from 530 to 680 nm and an energy density ranging from 0.3 to 6.0 J/cm^2 with short exposure times. Short evaluation periods are preferred since the enhancement extent of proliferation decreases with time as the process of cell differentiation increases.

Higher wavelengths, ranging from 680 to 950, could be useful if the energy density values range from 0.5 to 4 J/cm^2 or if shorter exposure times are used (20 to 30 s). Long exposure times, very low energy densities, and very high energy densities normally do not increase the proliferation of stem cells; in contrary, they can have a negative effect. Evaluating stem cell proliferation after very long incubation periods normally indicates a negative effect or reduction in the extent of enhancement. These signs are not directly related to laser treatment, since the process of cell proliferation decreases with the increase in the process of cell differentiation.

In this contribution, several stem cell types were investigated; some were validated and confirmed by clinical and experimental trials, including bone marrow mesenchymal stem cells, umbilical cord mesenchymal stem cells, adipose-derived stem cells, cardiac stem cells, periodontal ligament stem cells, dental pulp stem cells, and satellite cells; and others still need to be confirmed by clinical trials, such as endothelial stem cells, amniotic fluid stem cells, renal stem cells, and epithelial stem cells. However, in order to address the effects of all laser parameters, all investigated types still need more clinical and experimental trials.

References

1. Masson S, Harrison DJ, Plevris JN, Newsome PN. 2004. Potential of hematopoietic stem cell therapy in hepatology: A critical review. *Stem Cells* 22:897–907.
2. Heng BC, Cao T, Lee EH. 2004. Directing stem cell differentiation into the chondrogenic lineage in vitro. *Stem Cells* 22:1152–1167.
3. Atala A. 2006. Recent developments in tissue engineering and regenerative medicine. *Curr Opin Pediatr* 18(2):167–171.
4. Theise ND, d'Inverno M. 2004. Understanding cell lineages as complex adaptive systems. *Blood Cells Mol Dis* 32:17–20.
5. Cinquin O, Demongeot J. 2005. High-dimensional switches and the modeling of cellular differentiation. *J Theor Biol* 233:391–411.
6. Chickarmane V, Troein C, Nuber U, Sauro HM, Peterson C. 2006. Transcriptional dynamics of the embryonic stem cell switch. *PLoS Comput Biol* 2(9):e123.
7. Li L, Neaves WB. 2006. Normal stem cells and cancer stem cells: The niche matters. *Cancer Res* 66:4553–4557.
8. Fuchs E, Tumbar T, Guasch G. 2004. Socializing with the neighbors: Stem cells and their niche. *Cell* 116:769–778.
9. Tumbar T, Guasch G, Greco V et al. 2004. Defining the epithelial stem cell niche in skin. *Science* 303:359–363.
10. Rizvi AZ, Wong MH. 2005. Epithelial stem cells and their niche: There is no place like home. *Stem Cells* 23:150–165.
11. Li S, Zeng X. 2010. Modeling and simulation of soft contact and adhesion of stem cells. MRS Proceedings 1274-QQ02-02.
12. Zeng X, Li S. 2011. Modeling and simulation of substrate elasticity sensing in stem cells. *Comput Methods Biomech Biomed Eng* 14(5):447–458.
13. Zeng X, Li S. 2011. Multiscale modeling and simulation of soft adhesion and contact of stem cells. *J Mech Behav Biomed Mater* 4:180–189.
14. Yun Q, Qing Z, Shu-dong X, Zheng W. 2012. Simulation of stem cell microenvironment in vitro to culture and expand cord and umbilical cord mesenchymal stem cells. *Chin J Tissue Eng Res* 16(10): 1756–1760.
15. Siniscalco D, Giordano A, Galderisi U. 2012. Novel insights in basic and applied stem cell therapy. *J Cell Physiol* 227:2283–2286.
16. Chris Mason. 2009. Regenerative medicine glossary. *Regen Med* 4(4 Suppl):S1–S88. doi:10.2217/rme.09.s1. PMID19604041.
17. Mason C, Dunnill P. 2008. A brief definition of regenerative medicine. *Regen Med* 3(1):1–5. doi:10.2217/17460751.3.1.1. PMID18154457.

18. Riazi AM, Kwon SY, Stanford WL. 2009. Stem cell sources for regenerative medicine. *Methods Mol Biol* 482:55–90. doi:10.1007/978-1-59745-060-7_5. PMID19089350.

19. Lysaght MJ, Crager J. 2009. Origins. *Tissue Eng, Part A* 15(7):1449–1450. doi:10.1089/ten.tea .2007.0412. PMID19327019.

20. Placzek MR, Chung IM, Macedo HM et al. 2009. Stem cell bioprocessing: Fundamentals and principles. *J R Soc Interface* 6(32):209–232. doi:10.1098/rsif.2008.0442. PMC2659585. PMID19033137.

21. Splinter R. 2006. *An Introduction to Biomedical Optics.* CRC Press, Boca Raton, FL.

22. Tuner J, Hode L. 2002. *Laser Therapy—Clinical Practice and Scientific Background.* Prima Books, Grängesberg, Sweden.

23. Karu T. 2007. *Ten Lectures on Basic Science of Laser Phototherapy.* Prima Books AB, Grangesberg, Sweden.

24. Arany PR, Nayak RS, Hallikerimath S et al. 2007. Activation of latent TGF-beta1 by low-power laser in vitro correlates with increased TGF-beta1 levels in laser-enhanced oral wound healing. *Wound Repair Regen* 15:866–874. doi:10.1111/j.1524-475x.2007.00306.x.

25. Arora H, Pai KM, Maiya A et al. 2008. Efficacy of He-Ne Laser in the prevention and treatment of radiotherapy-induced oral mucositis in oral cancer patients. *Oral Surg Oral Med Oral Pathol Oral Radiol Endod* 105:180–186.

26. Gal P, Mokry M, Vidinsky B et al. 2009. Effect of equal daily doses achieved by different power densities of low-level laser therapy at 635 nm on open skin wound healing in normal and corticosteroid-treated rats. *Lasers Med Sci* 24:539–547. doi:10.1007/s10103-008-0604-9.

27. Woodruff L, Bounkeo J, Brannon W et al. 2004. The efficacy of laser therapy in wound repair: A meta-analysis of the literature. *Photomed Laser Surg* 22:241–247.

28. Hawkins D, Abrahamse H. 2007. Phototherapy—A treatment modality for wound healing and pain relief. *Afr J Biomed Res* 10:99–109.

29. Lam TS, Abergel RP, Meeker CA et al. 1986. Laser stimulation of collagen synthesis in human skin fibroblast cultures. *Lasers Life Sci* 1:61–77.

30. Yu W, Naim JO, Lanzafame RJ. 1994. The effect of laser irradiation on the release of bFGF from 3T3 fibroblasts. *Photochem Photobiol* 59(2):167–170.

31. Djavid GE, Mehrdad R, Ghasemi M et al. 2007. In chronic low back pain, low level laser therapy combined with exercise is more beneficial than exercise alone in long term: A randomized trial. *Aust J Physiother* 53:155–160.

32. Karu T. 1998. *The Science of Low Power Laser Therapy.* Gordon and Breach Science Publishers, London.

33. Iijima K, Shimoyama N, Shimoyama M et al. 1989. Effect of repeated irradiation of low-power He-Ne laser in pain relief from postherpetic neuralgia. *Clin J Pain* 5:271–274. doi:10.1097/00002508-198909000-00013. CrossRef PubMed/NCBI.

34. Kemmotsu O, Sato K, Furomido H et al. 1991. Efficacy of low reactive-level laser therapy for pain attenuation of postherpetic neuralgia. *Laser Ther* 3:1–75.

35. Qadri T, Bohdanecka P, Tuner J et al. 2007. The importance of coherence length in laser phototherapy of gingival inflammation: A pilot study. *Lasers Med Sci* 22(4):245–251.

36. Martin R. 2003. Laser-accelerated inflammation/pain reduction and healing practical. *Pain Manage* 3:20–25.

37. Stergioulas A. 2004. Low-level laser treatment can reduce edema in second degree ankle sprains. *J Clin Laser Med Surg* 22(2):125–128.

38. Enwemeka CS, Parker JC, Dowdy DS et al. 2004. The efficacy of low power lasers in tissue repair and pain control: A meta analysis study. *Photomed Laser Surg* 22:323–329.

39. Zhang L, Xing D, Gao X, Wu S. 2009. Low-power laser irradiation promotes cell proliferation by activating PI3K/Akt pathway. *J Cell Physiol* 219:553–562.

40. Gao X, Xing D. 2009. Molecular mechanisms of cell proliferation induced by low-power laser irradiation. *J Biomed Sci* 16:4.

41. Hu WP, Wang JJ, Yu CL et al. 2007. Helium-Neon laser irradiation stimulates cell proliferation through photostimulatory effects in mitochondria. *J Invest Dermatol* 127:2048–2057.

42. Moore P, Ridgway TD, Higbee RG et al. 2005. Effect of wavelength on low-intensity laser irradiation stimulated cell proliferation in vitro. *Lasers Surg Med* 36:8–12.

43. Fujihara NA, Hiraki KRN, Marque MM. 2006. Irradiation at 780 nm increases proliferation rate of osteoblasts independently of dexamethasone presence. *Lasers Surg Med* 38:332–336.
44. Taniguchi D, Dai P, Hojo T et al. 2009. Low-energy laser irradiation promotes synovial fibroblast proliferation by modulating p15 subcellular localization. *Lasers Surg Med* 41(3):232–239.
45. Hana T, Maltz L, Oron U. 2007. Low-level laser irradiation (LLLI) promotes proliferation of mesenchymal and cardiac stem cells in culture. *Lasers Surg Med* 39:373–378.
46. Hou JF, Zhang H, Yuan X et al. 2008. In vitro effects of low-level laser irradiation for bone marrow mesenchymal stem cells: Proliferation, growth factors secretion and myogenic differentiation. *Lasers Surg Med* 40(10):726–733.
47. Wu YH, Wang J, Gong DX et al. 2012. Effects of low-level laser irradiation on mesenchymal stem cell proliferation: A microarray analysis. *Lasers Med Sci* 27:509–519.
48. Horvát-Karajz K, Kovács V, Balogh Z et al. 2009. In vitro effect of carboplatin, cytarabine, paclitaxel, vincistine and low power laser irradiation on murine mesenchymal stem cells. *Onkologie* 32/4:216–217, *Lasers Surg Med* 41:463–469.
49. Giannelli M, Chellini F, Sassoli C et al. 2013. Photoactivation of bone marrow mesenchymal stromal cells with diode laser: Effects and mechanisms of action. *J Cell Physiol* 228(1):172–181.
50. Wu JY, Wang YH, Wang GJ et al. 2012. Low-power GaAlAs laser irradiation promotes the proliferation and osteogenic differentiation of stem cells via IGF1 and BMP2. *PLoS One* 7:e44027. doi:10.1371/journal.pone.0044027.
51. Abramovitch-Gottlib L, Gross T, Naveh D et al. 2005. Low-level laser irradiation stimulates osteogenic phenotype of mesenchymal stem cells seeded on a three-dimensional biomatrix. *Lasers Med Sci* 20(3–4):138–146.
52. Leonida A, Paiusco A, Rossi G et al. 2013. Effects of low-level laser irradiation on proliferation and osteoblastic differentiation of human mesenchymal stem cells seeded on a three-dimensional biomatrix: In vitro pilot study. *Lasers Med Sci* 28(1):125–132.
53. Soleimani M, Abbasnia E, Fathi M et al. 2011. The effects of low-level laser irradiation on differentiation and proliferation of human bone marrow mesenchymal stem cells into neurons and osteoblasts—An in vitro study. *Lasers Med Sci* 27(2):423–430. doi:10.1007/s10103-011-0930-1.
54. Akkinepally D, Arif A, Gaffoor E et al. 2012. Laser Irradiation on Human Umbilical Cord Stroma Derived Mesenchymal Stem Cells for Regenerative Medicine Applications in vitro Study. 1:290. doi:10.4172/scientificreports.290.
55. Mvula B, Mathope T, Moore T, Abrahamse H. 2008. The effect of low level laser irradiation on adult human adipose derived stem cells. *Lasers Med Sci* 23:277–282. doi:10.1007/s10103-007-0479-1.
56. Mvula B, Moore TJ, Abrahamse H. 2010. Effect of low-level laser irradiation and epidermal growth factor on adult human adipose-derived stem cells. *Lasers Med Sci* 25(1):33–39.
57. de Villiers JA, Houreld NN, Abrahamse H. 2011. Influence of low intensity laser irradiation on isolated human adipose derived stem cells over 72 hours and their differentiation potential into smooth muscle cells using retinoic acid. *Stem Cell Rev* 7(4):869–882.
58. Anwer AG, Gosnell ME, Perinchery SM et al. 2012. Visible 532nm laser irradiation of human adipose tissue-derived stem cells: Effect on proliferation rates, mitochondria membrane potential and autofluorescence. *Lasers Surg Med* 44(9):769–778. doi:10.1002/lsm.22083.
59. Abrahamse H, de Villiers J, Mvula B. 2007. *The Effect of Laser Irradiation on Adipose Derived Stem Cell Proliferation and Differentiation*. Laser Florence, Firenze.
60. Abrahamse H, Hourled NN, Muller S, Ndlovu L. 2010. Fluence and wavelength of low intensity laser irradiation affect activity and proliferation of human adipose derived stem cells. *Med Technol SA* 24(2):15–20.
61. Soares DM, Ginani F, Henriques AG et al. 2013. Effects of laser therapy on the proliferation of human periodontal ligament stem cells. *Lasers Med Sci.*, Springer, London, doi:10.1007/s10103-013-1436-9.
62. Wu JY, Chen CH, Yeh LY et al. 2013. Low-power laser irradiation promotes the proliferation and osteogenic differentiation of human periodontal ligament cells via cyclic adenosine monophosphate. *Int J Oral Sci* 5:85–91. doi:10.1038/ijos.2013.38.
63. Eduardo Fde P, Bueno DF, de Freitas PM et al. 2008. Stem cell proliferation under low-intensity laser irradiation: A preliminary study. *Lasers Surg Med* 40(6):433–438.

64. Pereira LO, Longo JP, Azevedo RB. 2012. Laser irradiation did not increase the proliferation or the differentiation of stem cells from normal and inflamed dental pulp. *Arch Oral Biol* 57(8):1079–1085.

65. Nadav BD, Gavriella S, Andrey I et al. 1999. Low-energy laser irradiation affects satellite cell proliferation and differentiation in vitro. *Biochim Biophys Acta* 1448:372–380.

66. Atala A, Lanza R, Nerem R, Thomson JA. 2007. *Principles of Regenerative Medicine*. Academic Press, New York. ISBN:9780123694102.

67. Stocum DL. 2012. *Regenerative Biology and Medicine*. Academic Press, 2nd ed., 2012. ISBN: 978-0-12-384860-4.

68. Low WC. 2008. *Stem Cells and Regenerative Medicine*. World Scientific Pub Co Inc. ISBN-10 :9812775765, ISBN-13:978-9812775764.

69. Wobus AM, Boheler KR. 2005. Embryonic stem cells: Prospects for developmental biology and cell therapy. *Physiol Rev* 85:635–678.

70. Meyer U, Meyer T, Handschel J, Wiesmann HP. 2009. *Fundamentals of Tissue Engineering and Regenerative Medicine*. Springer, Verlag Berlin Heidelberg. ISBN:3540777547.

71. Mao JJ, Mikos A, Novakovic GV. 2007. *Translational Approaches in Tissue Engineering and Regenerative Medicine*. Artech House. ISBN-10:1596931116, ISBN-13:978-1596931114.

72. Atala A, Lanza R, Thomson JA, Nerem R, eds. 2011. *Principles of Regenerative Medicine*, 2nd ed. Academic Press, San Diego, CA.

73. Reubinoff BE, Pera MF, Fong CY et al. 2000. Embryonic stem cell lines from human blastocysts: Somatic differentiation in vitro. *Nat Biotechnol* 18:399–404.

74. Collas P. 2007. Dedifferentiation of cells: New approaches. *Cytotherapy* 9(3):236–244.

75. Oliveri RS. 2007. Epigenetic dedifferentiation of somatic cells into pluripotency: Cellular alchemy in the age of regenerative medicine? *Regen Med* 2(5):795–816.

76. Collas P, Taranger CK. 2006. Toward reprogramming cells to pluripotency. *Ernst Schering Res Found Workshop* 60:47–67.

77. Antonio J, Boulaiz H, Peran M. 2009. Therapeutic Potential of Differentiation in Cancer and Normal Stem Cells, Nova Science Publishers Inc. ISBN-13:978-1606929179.

78. Zipori D. 2009. Biology of stem cells and the molecular basis of the stem state. *Anticancer Res* 29(11):277. ISBN:978-1-60761-129-5.

79. Grodzicker T, Stewart D, Stillman B. 2009. *Control and Regulation of Stem Cells*. Cold Spring Harbor Laboratory Press, New York. ISBN:0879698624.

80. Watt FM, Hogan BLM. 2000. Out of Eden: Stem cells and their niches. *Science* 287(5457):1427.

81. AS Adly, MH Haggag, MSM Mostafa. 2014. Applied Methods and Techniques for Mechatronic Systems. Springer. ISBN: 978-3-642-36384-9.

82. Adly AS, Aboutabl AE, Ibrahim MS. 2011. Modeling of gene therapy for regenerative cells using intelligent agents. *Adv Exp Med Biol* 696:317–325. doi:10.1007/978-1-4419-7046-6_32, PMID21431572.

83. Adly AS, Kandil OA, Ibrahim MS et al. 2010. Computational and theoretical concepts for regulating stem cells using viral and physical methods. *Mach Learn Syst Eng* 68:533–546. doi:10.1007/978-90-481-9419-3_41.

84. Qu Z, MacLellan WR, Weiss JN. 2003. Dynamics of the cell cycle: Checkpoints, sizers and timers. *Biophys J* 85(6):3600–11.

85. Burdon T, Smith A, Savatier P. 2002. Signalling, cell cycle and pluripotency in embryonic stem cells. *Trends Cell Biol* 12(9):432–438.

86. Cohen WW. 2007. *A Computer Scientist's Guide to Cell Biology*. Springer, LLC. e-ISBN:978-0-387-48278-1.

Chapter 4

Semantic Orientation–Based Approaches for Sentiment Analysis

Basant Agarwal, Namita Mittal, and Vijay Kumar Sharma

Contents

Sentiment analysis determines the polarity of text, whether it belongs to a positive or negative polarity. One motivation for sentiment analysis research is the need for users and e-commerce companies to know the public opinion from blogs, online forums, reviews about certain products, services, topics, and so forth. Polar words like *good*, *bad*, *excellent*, *boring*, and so forth are key indicators for recognizing the overall polarity of the document as positive or negative orientation. Phrases can convey sentiment information more efficiently than individual words. For example, the word *unpredictable* may have a negative polarity in an automobile review, with the phrase "unpredictable steering," but it could have positive polarity for a movie review with the phrase "unpredictable story." Phrases are very important for sentiment analysis as individual words are incapable of incorporating contextual and syntactic information, which is very important for sentiment analysis. In this chapter, various semantic orientation–based approaches are discussed for sentiment analysis, which is previously reported in the literature. Next, challenges in the sentiment analysis problem are discussed. Further, a new efficient semantic orientation–based approach is proposed for sentiment analysis. The proposed approach works as follows. Initially, various features like unigrams, part-of-speech (POS) pattern–based features, dependency features, and modified dependency features are extracted. Next, supervised and semisupervised methods for the computation of semantic orientation of these features based on mutual information are investigated. Finally, the overall sentiment orientation of the document is determined by aggregating the polarity values of all the phrases in the document. Experimental results show the effectiveness of the proposed methods.

4.1 Introduction

People often take the advice of other people for making everyday decisions. They read consumer reviews before buying appliances or ask friends to recommend a restaurant or movie for the evening. Nowadays, people share their opinion through blogs, reviews, social networking websites, and so forth. With the increase in this online content, there is also an increase in the need for automatic analysis of these opinionated texts. Extraction of sentiments from the text has been getting a lot of attention from the industry, as Internet users' opinions about their products and services may be very useful to improve them. Opinion mining or sentiment analysis is the field of analyzing people's opinions and sentiments toward entities such as products, services, and so forth in the text (Liu 2012). Sentiment analysis research can be categorized into document-level, sentence-level, and aspect/feature-level sentiment analysis. Document-level sentiment analysis classifies a review document as a positive or negative sentiment polar document. It considers a document as a single unit (Agarwal and Mittal 2012). Sentence-level sentiment analysis takes a sentence to extract the opinion or sentiment expressed in that sentence. Aspect-based sentiment analysis deals with the methods that identify the entities in the text about which an opinion is expressed. Further, the sentiments expressed about these entities are identified. Other important tasks in sentiment analysis and opinion mining research are opinion summarization, opinion retrieval, spam review detection, and so forth. Sentiment analysis research challenges and existing solutions are nicely presented in detail in some previous works (Pang and Lee 2008; Liu 2012; Cambria and Hussain 2012).

In the literature, various approaches have been applied for sentiment analysis. Mainly, these approaches may be categorized into machine learning approaches (Pang et al. 2002; Agarwal and Mittal 2013a), knowledge-based approaches (Cambria et al. 2013), and semantic orientation–based approaches (Turney 2002). This chapter focuses on the semantic orientation–based approaches for sentiment analysis. Semantic orientation–based approaches work as follows. Initially, efficient sentiment-rich features are extracted, which carry useful key information for detection of sentiments present in the text. Further, semantic orientation or polarity is computed using various methods. Finally, the overall polarity of the document is determined by aggregating the semantic orientation of all the features in the document.

This chapter discusses the state-of-the-art methods based on the semantic orientation–based approach for sentiment analysis. Next, the issues and challenges faced by sentiment analysis are discussed. Finally, a new semisupervised method is proposed, which tries to handle the problem of scarcity of availability of a labeled data set for every domain. The main objective of this chapter is to propose a system for the domains in which a labeled data set is a problem. As sentiment analysis is a domain-specific problem, a model developed for one domain may not work efficiently for another domain. In addition, this chapter tries to extract efficient features for sentiment analysis and also presents an improved method for computation of the semantic orientation of the features. The proposed system works as follows. Initially, various features like unigrams, past-of-speech (POS) pattern–based features, dependency features, and modified dependency features are extracted. Next, supervised and semisupervised methods are used for computation of the semantic orientation of the features extracted. Mutual information is used for computing the semantic orientation of the features. Then, for the semisupervised method, the mutual information method is improved for better results. Finally, the overall polarity of the document is determined by aggregating the semantic orientations of all the features.

4.2 Related Work

Sentiment analysis research has increased tremendously in recent times with a special interest in the classification of text into positive or negative polarity (Pang and Lee 2008; Poria et al. 2013). It has attracted the attention of companies and politicians due to its importance in knowing the opinion of people about their products, policies, and so forth. Sentiment analysis research can be broadly categorized into machine learning–based approaches (Pang et al. 2002), semantic orientation–based approaches (Turney 2002), and knowledge-based approaches (Cambria et al. 2013). This chapter focuses on the semantic orientation–based approaches for sentiment analysis. Initial work for identifying the semantic orientation of words was done by Vasileios and McKeown (1997). They developed a supervised learning method for calculating the semantic orientation of adjectives. Esuli and Sebastiani (2005) proposed a method to determine the semantic orientation of subjective words based on quantitative analysis of the glosses of these words.

Turney (2002) proposed an unsupervised method for identifying the polarity of a movie review document. Initially, he extracted two-word phrases using fixed POS-based patterns, and then the semantic orientation of those phrases was computed using the pointwise mutual information (PMI) method. Finally, the overall polarity of the document was recognized by aggregating the

semantic orientation of all the phrases. Turney and Littman (2003) introduced a method for inferring the semantic orientation of a word based on the statistical association of a word with a fixed
set of positive and negative words. They experimented with two approaches, namely, PMI and
latent semantic analysis (LSA). Tan et al. (2011) proposed a linguistic approach that combines the
typed dependencies and subjective phrase analysis to identify the sentence-level sentiment polarity. Their proposed method considers the intensity of words and domain terms that may the influence the sentiment polarity. Tan et al. (2012) studied the complex relationships between words
using class sequential rules (CSR) to learn the typed dependency patterns. Further, they considered these polarity pattern rules to detect the sentiment polarity at the phrase level. Ohana and
Tierney (2009) extracted the semantic orientation scores of adjectives, adverbs, verbs, and nouns
from SentiWordNet (Esuli and Sebastiani 2006), and further, overall semantic orientation of a
document was computed by averaging the semantic score of adjectives, adverbs, verbs, and noun.
Mukras et al. (2008) proposed a method for automatic identification of a POS-based pattern for
extraction of polar phrases. They applied various feature selection methods, namely, information gain (IG), chi-squares (CHI), and document frequency (DF), for identification of important
phrase patterns. Further, they applied the PMI method for calculation of the semantic orientation
of phrases. Zhang et al. (2009) proposed a method to determine the polarity of a sentence based
on word dependency rules and then predicted the polarity of the chinese document by summing
up the results from each sentence. Fei et al. (2004) constructed some phrase patterns with adjectives, adverbs, prepositions, conjunctions, noun, and verbs. Further, the semantic orientation of
these phrases was calculated using an unsupervised method, and finally, the overall polarity of the
text was determined by summing up the semantic orientation of all the words. Takamura et al.
(2006) proposed latent variable models for predicting the semantic orientation and classification
of phrases. However, their model was limited for the phrases that were seen in the training corpus.
Further, Takamura et al. (2007) proposed a method for determining the semantic orientation of
adjective–noun pair phrases, which was able to predict the semantic orientation of unseen phrases.

A dependency tree of a sentence produces a syntactic relation among words in the sentence.
Several researchers have investigated the importance of these syntactic relations for sentiment
analysis (Nakagawa et al. 2010; Thet et al. 2009). Thet et al. (2009) generated a dependency tree
of a sentence and split the sentence into clauses. Further, a contextual sentiment score for each
clause was determined. Kaji and Kitsuregawa (2007) extracted polar sentences from the Japanese
HTML documents using language structural clues. Next, phrases were extracted from polar sentences using a dependency parser. Further, the semantic score of each polar phrase was computed
using the CHI and PMI method.

4.3 Issues and Challenges of Sentiment Analysis

There are several challenges and issues in the sentiment analysis research that need to be handled.

4.3.1 Domain Dependency

The same words may be used for expressing different sentiments in a sentence according to the
domain. The meaning of the words changes according to the domain; it creates a problem for
the sentiment analysis model. For example, the word *unpredictable* has a positive orientation in
the movie review domain in the sense of an "unpredictable plot" but may be negatively oriented
for the car review domain in the senses of "unpredictable steering." Another example may be "go

read the book," which may be considered positive for the book review domain but may be used in a negative sense in the movie review domain (Pang and Lee 2008).

4.3.2 Subjectivity Detection

In the reviews, both subjective and objective sentences are written. Objective sentences are those sentences that do not carry any sentiment information, unlike subjective sentences. It is not easy to identify the subjective portion of the text from the overall review because the same words may be used in subjective and objective sentences. For example, "author used very crude language" and "crude oil is extracted from sea beds." In this example, the word *crude* is used for expressing sentiment in the first sentence; however, the second sentence is purely objective (Verma and Bhattacharyya 2009). Movie review sentiment analysis faces the challenge of handling the real facts, which are generally mixed with actual review data. People generally discuss the general traits of actors and the plot of movie and relate the movie to their regular lives. It is very difficult to extract the opinion from the reviews when there is a discussion of good qualities of actors and actress yet, in the end, overall, the movie is disliked. Similarly, in product reviews, people talk about various features of the product; some features are liked and some are disliked. These types of reviews are difficult to classify.

4.3.3 Thwarted Expectation

It is very difficult to extract the correct opinion from reviews having thwarted expectations. In certain reviews, most of the text represents a positive or negative polarity, and suddenly, the polarity of the overall text is reversed (Verma and Bhattacharyya 2009). For example, "This film has a great cast. It has an excellent storyline and nice cinematography. However, it can't hold up the audiences."

4.3.4 Comparative Sentences

Comparative sentences express sentiments based on similarities or differences of more than one object. It is difficult to extract the correct opinion automatically because it is difficult to identify which opinion words are used for which object (Kumar and Sebastian 2012). For example, "car X is better than car Y" expresses a totally different opinion from "car Y is better than car X."

4.3.5 Negation

Negation reverses the polarity of the words present in the sentences. For example, "I do not like this movie very much." The polarity of the sentence reverses due to the presence of negation word "not." Explicit negation in the sentence may be handled by appending "NOT_" to the words nearer to the negation. For example, from the previous sentence, the feature "NOT_like" would be extracted in place of "like" (Pang et al. 2002). However, sometimes it becomes very difficult to extract the correct opinion from such sentences as "No wonder everyone loves it."

4.3.6 Implicit Opinion

The sentiment expressed in the text may be categorized as explicit where opinion is expressed explicitly using opinion words, for example, "This is a wonderful movie." It is easier to identify the opinion expressed in these types of sentences. On the other hand, there are implicit sentiment sentences, in which a whole sentence implies some opinion, for example, "I will definitely watch this movie again and again." This presents a positive opinion. Opinion from these types of sentences is difficult to extract (Kumar and Sebastian 2012).

4.3.7 Opinion Spam

Opinion spam refers to fake and bogus reviews, which try to mislead readers and automated systems by giving positive reviews about some products in order to promote those products and/or by giving negative reviews about some products in order to damage the reputation of the competitor company's product. It is very difficult to identify these fake reviews as they look like legitimate reviews (Pang and Lee 2008).

4.4 Proposed Approach

Semantic orientation–based approaches for sentiment analysis work as follows. Initially, sentiment-rich words/features are extracted. Further, semantic orientations of these sentiment-rich words or phrases are determined using various methods, and overall semantic orientation of the overall document is computed accordingly. The pictorial representation of the sentiment analysis is given in Figure 4.1. All the phases are discussed in detail in subsequent subsections.

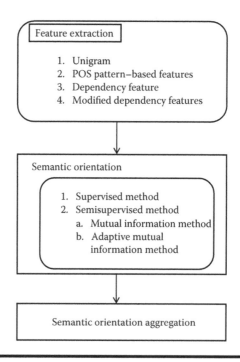

Figure 4.1 Proposed approach.

4.4.1 Feature Extraction

Semantic orientation–based approaches totally rely on the sentiment-rich words like adjectives, adverbs, and so forth extracted from the review document, as it is highly intuitive that such words are used for expressing sentiments in text (Agarwal et al. 2013b). Various types of sentiment-rich words and phrases are extracted in this chapter, as discussed in the subsequent subsections.

4.4.1.1 Unigram

All the unique words in the corpus are considered as features if they conform to a specific POS tag, that is, JJ (adjective), RB (adverb), NN (noun), VB (Verb) and do not conform to other unimportant POS like DT (Determiner). For example sentence, "this was great movie," the POS tagged sentence is "this_DT was_VB great_JJ movie_NN." Here, the word *great* is an adjective and shows positive sentiment; other words *this, was* are not conveying any sentiment in the text.

4.4.1.2 POS Pattern–Based Features

Phrases are very useful for extraction of syntactic, contextual information, which is very important for sentiment analysis.

For example, attaching an adverb like "very" with a polar adjective "good" will increase the intensity of the word "good." This information may be useful for sentiment classification. In addition, phrases are capable of capturing contextual information like "not good," "unpredictable story," "amazing movie," and so forth. Therefore, two-word phrases are extracted that conform to the predefined pattern. These POS pattern are given in Table 4.1.

4.4.1.3 Dependency Features

A deeper linguistic analysis of syntactic relations may be important for sentiment analysis. Several researchers have used syntactic patterns for sentiment analysis. A dependency tree of a sentence produces syntactic relation information from the text. Wiebe and Riloff (2005) investigated that syntactic patterns are very effective for subjective detection, which is a prior step to sentiment classification.

A Stanford dependency parser is used to generate the dependency relation for a given text. For example, all the dependency relations for the sentence "This movie is very nice" are "det(movie,this)," "nsubj(nice_movie)," "cop(nice_is)," and "advmod(nice_very)." Out of these dependency relations, the features "nice_movie," "nice_is," and "nice_very" are selected according to the relations given in Table 4.2 for sentiment classification. Table 4.2 presents the dependency relations that are used to extract the sentiment-rich dependency features from the text.

4.4.1.4 Modified Dependency Features

A dependency relation produces a syntactic relationship between the words of the text; some patterns are identified in the text such that by modifying those phrases, sentiment analysis accuracy may be enhanced (Liu et al. 2012). In this chapter, all the rules are taken from Liu et al. (2012), as their method has shown a significant improvement in the performance of dependency relations–based features.

Table 4.1 POS Patterns

S. No.	First Word	Second Word	Example
1	JJ	NN/NNS	technical_JJ directing_NN, emotional_JJ scene_NN
2	RB/RBR/RBS	JJ	completely_RB hot_JJ, wonderfully_RB underplayed_JJ
3	JJ	JJ	disney_JJ animated_JJ, strong_JJ supporting_JJ
4	NN/NNS	JJ	nothing_JJ unexpected_JJ, story_NN interesting_JJ
5	RB/RBR/RBS	VB/VBD/VBN/VBG	definitely_RB recommend_VB pleasantly_RB surprised_VBN
6	VBN	NN/NNS	haunted_VBN hill_NN, born_VBN killers_NNS
7	VB/VBG/VBP	JJ/JJR/JJS	spend_VBP most_JJS, feel_VB good_JJ
8	JJ	VBN/VBG	good_JJ looking_VBG, absent_JJ minded_VBN
9	RB/RBR/RBS	RB/RBR/RBS	most_RBS likely_RB, probably_RB more_RBR

Table 4.2   Selected Dependency Relations

S. No.	Relation	Meaning	Example
1	Acomp	Adjectival complement	(look, good)
2	Advmod	Adverbial complement	(cool, pretty)
3	Amod	Adjectival modifier	(performance, poor)
4	Dobj	Direct object	(appreciated, actor)
5	Neg	Negation modifier	(happy, not)
6	Nsubj	Nominal subject	(good, actors)
7	Rcmod	Relative clause modifier	(film, exhilarate)
8	Xcomp	Open clause complement	(bored, watching)
9	Cop	Copula	(beautiful, is)
10	Ccomp	Clausal complement	(happens, bored)

1. Implicit negation: Explicit negation may be handled by the relation "neg" due to the explicit negation term, but there is a need to handle implicit negation externally. For example, the explicit negation "This is not a great movie" returns the negation relations "neg(great, not)" and "neg(movie, not)," but the implicit negation "No one like these extra functions" or "This news is too good to be true" does not contain any explicit negation term, so implicit negation handling rules are proposed based on some pattern.
2. Range pattern: Some text containing some patterns talks about a standard. For example, in "The quality of this movie is below average," "below average" indicates the pattern for the standard.
3. Trend pattern: In some cases, the text describes changes in an object. For example, in "The popularity of this product is continuously increased," the term "increase" indicates a trend pattern.

Some terms are identified for handling these patterns. Negative nouns, adverbs, and adjectives are identified for *implicit negation* handling. Negative nouns are given by "no one," "nothing," "none," or "nobody." Negative adverbs are given by "no," "not," "never," "rarely," or "hardly." Negative adjectives are given by "impossible" or "difficult." The terms identified for *range pattern* are "above" and "below," which about some standard. So a WordNet synset of "above" and "below" are extracted for the range pattern. The "above" synset is given by "above," "higher," "supra," or "high." The below synset is given by "below," "lower," "beneath," "infra," "downstairs," "under," or "lack." A *trend pattern* is identified by the terms "increase" and "decrease," so a WordNet synset of "increase" and "decrease" is extracted. The "increase" synset is given by "increase," "addition," "gain," "increment," "growth," "step-up," or "improve." The "decrease" synset is given by "decrease," "lessening," "drop-off," "decrement," "diminution," "reduction," "step-down," "diminish," "lessen," "fall," "minify," or "abate." Some rules are given to handle these patterns in Table 4.3.

Subj relations are given by "nsubj," "nsubjpass," "xsubj," and "agent"; obj relations are "dobj," "iobj," and "xcomp"; and prep relations are "prep" and "prepc."

4.4.2 Semantic Orientation

After extraction of various features, semantic orientation of these is determined using a supervised and semisupervised method, discussed in detail in subsequent subsections.

4.4.2.1 Supervised Method

Computation of semantic orientation of the phrase/feature is based on the assumption that if a phrase is occurring frequently and predominantly in one class (positive or negative), then that phrase would have high polarity. If a phrase has a high positive polarity value, this indicates that the phrase has occurred more with positive sentences, that is, positive words. PMI is generally used to calculate the strength of association between a phrase and positive or negative sentences. It is defined as follows (Kaji and Kitsuregawa 2007).

$$\text{PMI}(c, \text{pos}) = \log_2 \frac{P(c, \text{pos})}{P(c)P(\text{pos})} \tag{4.1}$$

Table 4.3 Modified Dependency Relations

S. No.	Relation	Example	Handling Rules
1	Sub(V, N)	Nobody$_N$ likes$_V$ this movie	If arg2 in negative noun then insert neg(arg1, not)
2	Obj(V, N)	None$_N$ of them support$_V$ him	If arg2 in negative noun then insert neg(arg1, not)
3	Advmod(V, R)	PM2.5 rarely$_R$ decreased$_V$ recently	If arg2 in negative adverb then insert neg(arg1, not)
4	Ccomp(J, V)	It is impossible$_J$ to overrate$_V$ it	If arg1 in negative adjective then insert neg(arg2, not)
5	Xcomp(J, V)	This news is too good$_J$ to believe$_V$	If relation advmod(arg1, too) exist then insert neg(arg2, not)
6	Amod(N, J)	High$_J$ interest rate$_N$	If arg2 in above synset then replace arg2 to 'abv' and if arg2 in below synset then replace arg2 to 'blw'
	Advmod(J, R)	Fall$_J$ below$_R$	
7	Prep(N1, N2)	Lack$_{N1}$ of training$_{N2}$	If arg1 in above synset then replace arg1 to 'abv' and if arg1 in below synset then replace arg1 to 'blw'
8	Obj(V, N)	This accessory can abate$_V$ damage$_N$	If arg2 in increase synset then replace arg2 to 'inc' and if arg2 in decrease synset then replace arg2 to 'dec'

$$\text{PMI}(c, \text{neg}) = \log_2 \frac{P(c, \text{neg})}{P(c)P(\text{neg})} \tag{4.2}$$

Here, $P(c,\text{pos})$ is the probability that a phrase occurs in positive documents, that is, the frequency of the positive documents in which the phrase occurs divided by the total number of positive documents. $P(c,\text{neg})$ is the probability that a phrase occurs in a negative document, that is, the frequency of negative documents in which the phrase occurred divided by the total number of negative documents. The polarity value of the phrase is determined by the PMI value difference (Turney 2002). The semantic orientation of a phrase (p) is computed using Equation 4.4.

$$SO(p) = \text{PMI}(c,\text{pos}) - \text{PMI}(c,\text{neg}) \tag{4.3}$$

$$SO(p) = \log_2 \frac{P(c,\text{pos})/P(\text{pos})}{P(c,\text{neg})/P(\text{neg})} \tag{4.4}$$

4.4.2.2 Semisupervised Method

The main problem with the supervised method is the availability of labeled data for every domain. Therefore, we propose a new semisupervised method that needs a small number of labeled documents. In this method, initially, we create a list of positive and negative seed words from a small number of labeled documents. Then, we compute the semantic orientation value of all the features present in the document based on the list of these positive and negative seed words.

The process to get the list of positive and negative seed words is as follows. Initially, a set of positive and negative words is taken from the General Inquirer and then their frequency. Initially, each word is extracted from labeled documents; further, their positive and negative DF are computed in a small number of labeled documents.

If f_p is the frequency of a word in positive documents and f_n is the frequency in negative documents, then those words are selected as positive and negative seed words that satisfy the given constraint c as given in Equation 4.5.

$$c = \begin{cases} \dfrac{(f_p + 1)}{n * (f_n + 1)} > 1, f_n \neq 0, \text{ for positive seed word} \\ \dfrac{(f_n + 1)}{n * (f_p + 1)} > 1, f_p \neq 0, \text{ for negative seed word} \end{cases} \tag{4.5}$$

The assumption behind the constraint is that more frequently occurring words in one class are strongly related to that class. The value of n in the equation is determined empirically. The semi-supervised method was applied on movie review data; 100 positive and 100 negative documents were selected from corpus. Further, the frequency of positive and negative words was counted in positive and negative documents to further apply the constraint given in Equation 4.6. A list of some examples of positive and negative words given with their frequency is shown in Table 4.4. Based on this, 40 positive and 34 negative words are selected as seed words, and the same process is applied on book review data; then, 10 positive and 11 negative words are selected as seed words.

After determination of seed words, semantic orientations of the features are computed using these seed words. Two methods are used for this purpose, which are discussed separately in subsequent subsections.

Table 4.4   List of Words and Their Frequency

Positive Words			Negative Words		
Word	Positive Count	Negative Count	Word	Positive Count	Negative Count
Memorable	14	2	Worst	3	16
Effective	14	2	Boring	3	16
Powerful	15	4	Waste	3	15
Incredible	7	1	Terrible	3	13
Outstanding	6	1	Ridiculous	2	9
Wonderfully	6	1	Stupid	4	13
Fantastic	5	1	Lame	1	9

4.4.2.2.1 Mutual Information Method

Therefore, semantic orientation of words and phrases is computed using the manually created positive and negative seed word list. A list of positive and negative seed words is given for a movie review data set in Table 4.4.

The basic intuition behind this method is almost the same as for the supervised method: if a feature occurs frequently with positive seed words and also does not occur frequently with negative seed words, then that feature will have a high positive polarity value. Semantic orientation of a feature is computed using Equation 4.6.

$$SO(C) = \log_2 \frac{p(c, \mathrm{pos\_seed\_word})}{p(c, \mathrm{neg\_seed\_word})} \tag{4.6}$$

$p(c, \mathrm{pos\_seed\_word})$ is the probability of feature occurrence with positive seed words, and $p(c, \mathrm{neg\_seed\_word})$ is the probability of feature occurrence with negative seed words in an unlabeled document corpus. $p(c, \mathrm{pos\_seed\_word})$ and $p(c, \mathrm{neg\_seed\_word})$ are computed as given in Equations 4.7 and 4.8.

$$p(c, \mathrm{pos\_seed\_word}) = \frac{f(c, \mathrm{pos\_seed\_word})}{f(\mathrm{pos\_seed\_word})} \tag{4.7}$$

$$p(c, \mathrm{neg\_seed\_word}) = \frac{f(c, \mathrm{neg\_seed\_word})}{f(\mathrm{neg\_seed\_word})} \tag{4.8}$$

$f(c, \mathrm{pos\_seed\_word})$ is the number of documents containing the feature and positive seed words in the same document, and $f(\mathrm{pos\_seed\_word})$ is the number of documents containing positive seed words and the feature.

4.4.2.2.2 Adaptive Mutual Information Method

Performance of the mutual information method depends on the co-occurrence frequency of the features with the positive and negative seed words. Sometimes, semantic orientation of the feature is not computed correctly because negative and positive opinion seed words are used in the same review, or positive seed words in negative reviews and vice versa. That is why actual polarity of a feature is not computed correctly. Therefore, we propose an adaptive method for computation of co-occurrence of a feature with positive or negative seed words. In this adaptive method, a sentence is initially classified as positive or negative based on the number of positive and negative seed words present in that sentence. It is done by labeling the sentence positive if it has more positive seed words and otherwise labeling as negative. For example, consider that a positive opinion sentence, "There is stupid acting by Mr. John but the storyline of the movie is wonderful, and there is amazing direction" has positive seed words (wonderful, amazing) and negative seed word (stupid). In this sentence, for the feature "amazing direction," its co-occurrence frequency with a positive seed word is 1 and is also 1 with a negative seed word, resulting in neutral polarity values using the traditional method of polarity computation. Further, if the adaptive mutual information method is applied, initially, the sentence would be converted as positive, thus discarding the co-occurrence of negative seed words and only considering the co-occurrence frequency of positive seed words, which is 1, resulting in overall positive polarity.

Consider another negative opinion sentence as example: "The movie was ridiculous, although it had nice cinematography, but the story was boring" has positive seed words (nice) and negative seed words (ridiculous, boring). In this sentence, for the feature "boring story," its co-occurrence frequency with positive seed words is 1, and that with negative seed words is also 1, resulting in neutral polarity values using the traditional method of polarity computation. However, with the adaptive mutual information method, it will have a co-occurrence frequency with negative seed words of 1, discarding the frequency with positive seed words, resulting in negative overall polarity of the feature.

4.4.3 Semantic Orientation Aggregation

After computation of semantic orientation of all the features of the training documents, a lexicon of various features with their semantic orientation is developed. Further, for the testing document, initially, features are extracted, and then semantic orientation values of these features are retrieved from the developed lexicon. Finally, summing up the semantic orientations of all the features from the document would give the overall semantic orientation of the document. If the overall semantic orientation is positive, the document is labeled as a positive polar document, or else it is labeled as a negative polar document.

4.5 Experiment Result and Discussion

To evaluate the effectiveness of the proposed methods for sentiment analysis, two publically available standard data sets are used. The first data set is the movie review data set, also known as Cornell's data set (Pang and Lee 2004). Another data set is the book review data set, provided by Amazon product reviews (Blitzer et al. 2007). Both the data sets contain 2000 movie reviews consisting of 1000 positive and 1000 negative reviews. For all the experiments, initially, the training data set is created by randomly selecting 700 positive and 700 negative documents. Then, the remaining 300 positive and 300 negative documents are used for the testing of the proposed approach. Accuracy is used as a performance evaluation measure, which is computed by dividing correctly classified testing documents to the total testing documents.

4.5.1 Result and Discussion

All the experimental results are categorized into supervised and unsupervised methods on the basis of the methods used for computing the semantic orientations of the features extracted.

4.5.1.1 Supervised Method

Accuracies for various features with the supervised method using movie reviews and book reviews are presented in Table 4.5. First of all, POS-based unigram features are investigated. This feature produces an accuracy of 75.33% and 72.17% for movie reviews and book reviews, respectively, as given in Table 4.5. Accuracy with unigram features is considered to be the baseline. Further, POS pattern–based features are investigated for sentiment analysis. These features improve the accuracy

Table 4.5   Accuracy (in %) for Various Features with Supervised
Method

Features	Accuracy	
	Movie Review	*Book Review*
Unigrams	75.33%	72.17%
POS pattern–based features	81.50% (+8.1%)	75.00% (+3.9%)
Dependency features	82.50% (+9.5%)	77.27% (+7.06%)
Modified dependency features	87.50% (+16.1%)	81.91% (+13.4%)

from 75.33% to 81.50% (+8.1%) and 72.17% to 75.00% (+3.9%) for movie review and book review data sets, respectively, as given in Table 4.5. This is due to the fact that POS pattern–based features incorporate the contextual information, which is very important for sentiment analysis. Further, dependency features are considered as features for sentiment analysis. These features further improve the accuracy up to 82.50% (+9.5%) and 77.27% (+7.06%) for movie review and book review data sets, respectively, as shown in Table 4.5. This is due to the fact that POS pattern–based features are very sparse as compared to dependency features, and in addition, dependency features incorporate the syntactic relation present in the sentence, which is important for sentiment analysis. However, sometimes, these dependency features face the problem of overgeneralization; therefore, some modifications are used, as suggested by Liu et al. (2012). The modified features improve the performance significantly up to 87.5% (+16.1%) and 81.91% (+13.4%) for movie review and book review data sets, respectively, as shown in Table 4.5.

4.5.1.2 Semisupervised Classification

The supervised method faces the problem of availability of a labeled data set for every domain. Therefore, the semisupervised method is proposed for sentiment analysis. All the accuracies for various features with both methods of computing the semantic orientation are reported in Table 4.6. Unigram features give an accuracy of 69.67% and 68.67% for the movie review and book review data sets, respectively; however, this performance is much less as compared to the respective supervised method. But it may be improved with efficient features. These unigram accuracies are considered to be baseline accuracy. The performance of the same unigram features are improved up to 72.83% (+4.5%) and 70.17% (+2.1%) for the movie review and book review data sets, respectively, by using the adaptive mutual information method for computing semantic orientation in place of the traditional mutual information method, as given in Table 4.6.

Next, POS pattern–based features produce an accuracy of 72% (+3.34%) and 74.33% (+6.68%) for the mutual information– and adaptive mutual information–based methods, respectively, with the movie review data set.

Next, dependency features give the best accuracy of 78.50% (+12.67%) for the movie review data set, and further, by improving the feature extraction method for dependency features, accuracy is increased up to 84.83% (+21.75) and 79.50 (+15.7%) for the movie review and book review data sets, respectively. However, this accuracy is less than its respective supervised method, but by improving the feature extraction method and polarity calculation method, accuracy for the semisupervised method may be increased. And this method may be very useful for the domain in which a labeled data set is a problem.

Table 4.6 Accuracies (in %) for Various Features with Semisupervised Method

Features	Accuracy			
	Movie Review		Book Review	
	Mutual Information	*Adaptive Mutual Information*	*Mutual Information*	*Adaptive Mutual Information*
Unigrams	69.67%	72.83% (+4.5%)	68.67%	70.17% (+2.1%)
POS pattern–based features	72.00% (+3.34%)	74.33% (+6.68%)	71.17% (+3.6%)	73.83% (+7.5%)
Dependency features	75.83% (+8.84%)	78.50% (+12.67%)	72.17% (+5.0%)	75.17% (+9.4%)
Modified dependency features	79.83% (+14.5%)	84.83% (+21.75%)	76.33% (+11.1%)	79.50% (+15.7%)

4.6 Conclusion

Sentiment analysis research highly depends on the efficient features that carry most of the sentiment information of the text, and further, it is very important to assign accurate polarity values to these features. This chapter initially discusses the work related to this. Next, challenges and issues in sentiment analysis are discussed. Further, an efficient method is proposed for sentiment analysis. Also, a new semisupervised approach is proposed for the semantic orientation–based approach, which may be very useful for the domain in which a labeled data set is a problem. To build the sentiment analysis model as sentiment analysis is a domain-specific problem; a model developed for one domain may not work efficiently for another domain. In addition, this chapter tries to extract efficient features for sentiment analysis and also presents an improved method for computation of the semantic orientation of the features. Experimental results show the effectiveness of the proposed method. In the future, more efficient sentiment-rich features may be extracted. It would also be good if word sense disambiguation (WSD) could be incorporated into the feature extraction process for efficient identification of polarity values. Also, the proposed methods may be applied for non-English languages as well.

References

Agarwal B., Mittal N. (2012). "Categorical probability proportion difference (CPPD): A feature selection method for sentiment classification," in Proceedings of the 2nd Workshop on Sentiment Analysis Where AI Meets Psychology (SAAIP), COLING, pp. 17–26.

Agarwal B., Mittal N. (2013a). "Optimal feature selection for sentiment analysis," in 14th International Conference on Intelligent Text Processing and Computational Linguistics (CICLing 2013), Vol. 7817, pp. 13–24.

Agarwal B., Sharma V., Mittal N. (2013b). "Sentiment classification of review documents using phrases patterns," in the International Conference on Advances in Computing, Communications and Informatics (ICACCI), pp. 1577–1580.

Blitzer J., Dredze M., Pereira F. (2007). "Biographies, Bollywood, boom-boxes and blenders: Domain adaptation for sentiment classification," in Proc. Assoc. Computational Linguistics, ACL Press, pp. 440–447.

Cambria E., Hussain A. (2012). *Sentic Computing: Techniques, Tools, and Applications*. Dordrecht, Netherlands: Springer.

Cambria E., Schuller B., Xia Y., Havasi C. (2013). "New avenues in opinion mining and sentiment analysis," *IEEE Intelligent Systems*, 28(2), pp. 15–21.

Esuli A., Sebastiani F. (2005). "Determining the semantic orientation of terms through gloss analysis," in Proceedings of the ACM Conference on Information and Knowledge Management (CIKM).

Esuli A., Sebastiani F. (2006). "SentiWordNet: A publicly available lexical resource for opinion mining," in Proceedings of Language Resources and Evaluation (LREC).

Fei Z., Liu J., Wu G. (2004). "Sentiment classification using phrase pattern," in Proceedings of the Fourth International Conference on Computer and Information Technology (CIT'04), pp. 1147–1152.

Kaji N., Kitsuregawa M. (2007). "Building lexicon for sentiment analysis from massive collection of HTML documents," in Proceedings of the Joint Conference on Empirical Methods in Natural 35 Language Processing and Computational Natural Language Learning (EMNLP-CoNLL), pp. 1075–1083.

Kumar A., Sebastian T. M. (2012). "Sentiment analysis: A perspective on its past, present and future," *International Journal of Intelligent Systems and Applications*, 10, pp. 1–14.

Liu B. (2012). "Sentiment analysis and opinion mining," *Synthesis Lectures on Human Language Technologies*, Morgan & Claypool Publishers, ISBN 9781608458844, USA.

Liu S., Agam G., Grossman D. G. (2012). "Generalized sentiment-bearing expression features for sentiment analysis," in 24th International Conference on Computational Linguistics (COLING), Posters, pp. 733–744.

Mukras R., Wiratunga N., Lothian R. (2008). "Selecting bi-tags for sentiment analysis of text," in the Proceedings of 27th SGAI International Conference on Innovative Techniques and Applications of Artificial Intelligence, pp. 181–194.

Nakagawa T., Inui K., Kurohashi S. (2010). "Dependency treebased sentiment classification using CRFs with hidden variables," in Human Language Technologies: The 2010 Annual Conference of the North American Chapter of the ACL, pp. 786–794.

Ohana B., Tierney B. (2009). "Sentiment classification of reviews using SentiWordNet," in IT&T Conference.

Pang B., Lee L. (2004). "A sentimental education: Sentiment analysis using subjectivity summarization based on minimum cuts," in Proceedings of the Association for Computational Linguistics (ACL), pp. 271–278.

Pang B., Lee L. (2008). "Opinion mining and sentiment analysis," *Foundations and Trends in Information Retrieval*, 2(1–2), pp. 1–135.

Pang B., Lee L., Vaithyanathan S. (2002). "Thumbs up? Sentiment classification using machine x`learning techniques," in Proceedings of the Conference on Empirical Methods in Natural Language Processing (EMNLP), pp. 79–86.

Poria S., Gelbukh A., Hussain A., Howard N., Das D., Bandyopadhyay S. (2013) "Enhanced SenticNet with affective labels for concept-based Opinion mining," *IEEE Intelligent Systems*, 28(2), pp. 31–38.

Takamura H., Inui T., Okumura M. (2006). "Latent variable models for semantic orientations of phrases," in Proceedings of the European Chapter of the Association for Computational Linguistics (EACL).

Takamura H., Inui T., Okumura M. (2007). "Extracting semantic orientations of phrases from dictionary," in Proceedings of the Joint Human Language Technology/North American Chapter of the ACL Conference (HLT-NAACL).

Tan L. K. W., Na J. C., Theng Y. L., Chang K. Y. (2011). "Sentence-level sentiment polarity classification using a linguistic approach," in Proc. ICADL 2011, pp. 77–87.

Tan L. K. W., Na J. C., Theng Y. L., Chang K. Y. (2012). "Phrase-level sentiment polarity classification using rule based typed dependencies and additional complex phrases consideration," *Journal of Computer Science and Technology*, 27(3), pp. 650–666.

Thet T. T., Na J. C., Khoo C. S. G., Shakthikumar S. (2009). "Sentiment analysis of movie reviews on discussion boards using a linguistic approach," in Proceedings of the 1st International CIKM Workshop on Topic-Sentiment Analysis for Mass Opinion, pp. 81–84.

Turney P. D. (2002). "Thumbs up or thumbs down? Semantic orientation applied to unsupervised classification of reviews," in ACL, pp. 417–424.

Turney P., Littman M. L. (2003). "Measuring praise and criticism: Inference of semantic orientation from association," *ACM Transactions on Information Systems*, 21(4), pp. 315–346.

Vasileios H., McKeown K. R. (1997). "Predicting the semantic orientation of adjectives," in ACL, pp. 174–181.

Verma S., Bhattacharyya P. (2009). "Incorporating semantic knowledge for sentiment analysis," in Proceedings of ICON.

Wiebe J., Riloff E. (2005). "Creating subjective and objective sentence classifiers from unannotated texts," in 6th International Conference, CICLing 2005, pp. 486–497.

Zhang C., Zeng D., Li J., Wang F. Y., Zuo W. (2009). "Sentiment analysis of Chinese documents: From sentence to document level," *Journal of the American Society for Information Science and Technology*, 60(12), pp. 2474–2487.

Chapter 5

Rough Set on Two Universal Sets and Knowledge Representation

Debi P. Acharjya

Contents

The amount of data being collected across a wide variety of fields today far exceeds our ability to reduce and analyze without the use of automated analysis techniques. Also, the whole data may not be of user interest and may be imperfect. So, it is very challenging to organize these data in a formal system that provides outputs in a more relevant, useful, and structured manner. There are many techniques available to retrieve knowledge from this voluminous amount of data. Rough sets are one among them. The notion of rough sets captures the indiscernibility of elements in a set. But in many real-life situations, an information system establishes the relation between different universes. This led to the extension of a rough set on a single universal set to a rough set on two universal sets. In this chapter, rough sets on two universal sets employing the notion of the lower and upper approximation are discussed. In addition to this, fuzzy rough sets and intuitionistic fuzzy rough sets on two universal sets are also discussed. Finally, a real-life example for the depth classification of the concept is provided.

5.1 Introduction

At the present age of the Internet, a huge repository of data is available across various domains. Therefore, it is very hard to extract useful information from the voluminous amount of data available in the universe. So, information retrieval and knowledge representation have become among the most popular areas of recent research. Information retrieval and acquisition of knowledge are among the important components of an information system. In order to transform the processed data intelligently and automatically into useful information and knowledge, there is a need for techniques and tools. Classical tools can be used to some extent to deal with problems arising in economics, social science, medical service, and engineering when the data are crisp, deterministic, and precise in character. However, these tools fail to solve problems when the data are inconsistent, ambiguous, and precise in character. In order to overcome this, the fuzzy set by Zadeh (1965), the rough set by Pawlak (1982, 1991), and the soft set by Molodtsov (1999) were developed. Development of these techniques and tools are studied under different domains like knowledge discovery in database, computational intelligence, knowledge engineering, granular computing, and so forth (Kryszkiewlcz 1998; Lin 1998, 2005; Pawlak 2004; Zhong and Skowron 2001).

The rough set (Pawlak 1982, 1991) philosophy is based on the concept that there is some information associated with each object of the universe. So, there is a need to classify objects of the universe based on the indiscernibility relation between them. The basic idea of the rough set is based upon the approximation of sets by a pair of sets known as lower and upper approximation. Here, the lower and upper approximation operators are based on an equivalence relation. However, the requirement of an equivalence relation is a failure in many real-life problems. In order to overcome this, the rough set is generalized to some extent. For instance, the equivalence relation is generalized to binary relations (Bonikowski 1994; Kondo 2005, 2006; Pawlak and Skowron 2007a; Yao 1998; Zhu 2007), neighborhood systems (Lin 1989), coverings (Zhu and Wang 2007; Zhu 2006a, 2006b, 2006c), Boolean algebras (Liu 2005; Pawlak and Skowron 2007b), fuzzy lattices (Liu 2008), and completely distributive lattices (Chen et al. 2006).

On the contrary, the rough set is generalized to a fuzzy environment, such as a fuzzy rough set (Dubois and Prade 1990) and a rough fuzzy set (Dubois and Prade 1990). Further, the indiscernibility relation is generalized to almost indiscernibility relation to study many real-life problems. Based on a fuzzy proximity relation, the concept of a rough set on fuzzy approximation spaces and its applications were studied by Tripathy and Acharjya (Tripathy and Acharjya

2010; Acharjya 2013). This fuzzy proximity relation is further generalized to intuitionistic fuzzy proximity relation, and the concept of a rough set on intuitionistic fuzzy approximation space and its applications were studied (Acharjya 2013). The different applications and hybrid models that consist of formal concept analysis and ordering rules are also studied (Acharjya 2009; Acharjya and Ezhilarasi 2011; Tripathy et al. 2011a; Tripathy and Acharjya 2011). Further, rough set models on two universal sets are generalized with generalized approximation spaces and interval structure (Wong et al. 1993). A further study in the same direction is continued in this chapter.

The rest of the chapter is organized as follows: Section 5.2 presents the foundations of the rough set based on two universal sets. In addition, topological characterization of a rough set on two universal sets and basic operations such as union and intersection on it are discussed. The knowledge obtained in this section is further validated by a real-life example. Section 5.3 discusses the approximation of classifications and measures of uncertainty of a rough set on two universal sets. Fuzzy rough sets on two universal sets and its algebraic properties that are defined with the help of a solitary set with respect to a fuzzy relation are studied in Section 5.4. In addition, topological characterization of a fuzzy rough set on two universal sets is discussed. Fuzzy sets are intuitionistic fuzzy sets, but the converse is not necessarily true. Therefore, intuitionistic fuzzy approximation space is a generalization of fuzzy approximation space. Thus, the concept of a fuzzy rough set on two universal sets is generalized to an intuitionistic fuzzy rough set based on two universal sets in Section 5.5. This section also provides an insight to the algebraic properties of an intuitionistic fuzzy rough set on two universal sets. The chapter ends with a conclusion in Section 5.6.

5.2 Rough Set Based on Two Universal Sets

The rough set model is generalized using two distinct but related universal sets by Wong et al. (1993). Let U and V be two universal sets and $R \subseteq (U \times V)$ be a binary relation. By a knowledge base, one understands the relational system (U, V, R), an approximation space. For an element $x \in U$, the right neighborhood or the R-relative set of x in U, $r(x)$ is defined as $r(x) = \cup\{y \in V : (x, y) \in R\}$. Similarly, for an element $y \in V$, the left neighborhood or the R-relative set of y in V, $l(y)$ is defined as $l(y) = \cup\{x \in U : (x, y) \in R\}$.

For any two elements $x_1, x_2 \in U$, x_1 and x_2 are equivalent if $r(x_1) = r(x_2)$. Therefore, $(x_1, x_2) \in E_U$ if and only if $r(x_1) = r(x_2)$, where E_U denotes the equivalence relation on U. Hence, E_U partitions the universal set U into disjoint subsets and is denoted as U/E_U. Similarly, for any two elements $y_1, y_2 \in V$, y_1 and y_2 are equivalent if $l(y_1) = l(y_2)$. Thus, $(y_1, y_2) \in E_V$ if and only if $l(y_1) = l(y_2)$, where E_V denotes the equivalence relation on V and partitions the universal set V into disjoint subsets. Therefore, for the approximation space (U, V, R), $E_V \circ R = R = R \circ E_U$, where $E_V \circ R$ is the composition of R and E_V.

For any $Y \subseteq V$ and the binary relation R, two subsets $\underline{R}Y$ and $\overline{R}Y$, called the R-lower and R-upper approximations of Y, respectively, are associated, which are given by

$$\underline{R}Y = \bigcup\{x \in U : r(x) \subseteq Y\} \tag{5.1}$$

$$\overline{R}Y = \bigcup\{x \in U : r(x) \cap Y \neq \phi\} \tag{5.2}$$

The R-boundary of Y is denoted as $BN_R(Y)$ and is given as $BN_R(Y) = \overline{R}Y - \underline{R}Y$. The pair $(\underline{R}Y, \overline{R}Y)$ is called the rough set of $Y \subseteq V$ if $\underline{R}Y \neq \overline{R}Y$ or, equivalently, $BN_R(Y) \neq \phi$. The lower and upper approximations can also be presented in an equivalent form by equivalence class $[x]_E$ as follows:

$$\underline{R}Y = \bigcup_{r(x) \subseteq Y} [x]_E \tag{5.3}$$

$$\overline{R}Y = \bigcup_{r(x) \cap Y \neq \phi} [x]_E \tag{5.4}$$

Further, if U and V are finite sets, then the binary relation R from U to V can be represented as $R(x, y)$, where

$$R(x, y) = \begin{cases} 1 & \text{if } (x, y) \in R \\ 0 & \text{if } (x, y) \notin R \end{cases}$$

The characteristic function of $X \subseteq U$ is defined for each $x \in U$ as follows:

$$X(x) = \begin{cases} 1 & \text{if } x \in X \\ 0 & \text{if } x \notin X \end{cases}$$

Therefore, the R-lower and R-upper approximations can be also presented in an equivalent form as shown by the following, where $\wedge$ and $\vee$ denote minimum and maximum operators, respectively:

$$(\underline{R}Y)x = \bigwedge_{y \in V} ((1 - R(x, y)) \vee Y(y)) \tag{5.5}$$

$$(\overline{R}Y)x = \bigvee_{y \in V} (R(x, y) \wedge Y(y)) \tag{5.6}$$

Example 5.1

Let $U = \{x_1, x_2, x_3, x_4, x_5\}$ and $V = \{y_1, y_2, y_3, y_4, y_5, y_6\}$. Consider the relation R given by its Boolean matrix:

$$R = \begin{pmatrix} 1 & 1 & 0 & 0 & 1 & 0 \\ 0 & 0 & 1 & 0 & 0 & 1 \\ 0 & 1 & 0 & 1 & 0 & 0 \\ 1 & 0 & 1 & 1 & 1 & 1 \\ 1 & 1 & 0 & 0 & 1 & 0 \end{pmatrix}$$

From the relation R, it is clear that $r(x_1) = \{y_1, y_2, y_5\}$; $r(x_2) = \{y_3, y_6\}$; $r(x_3) = \{y_2, y_4\}$; $r(x_4) = \{y_1, y_3, y_4, y_5, y_6\}$ and $r(x_5) = \{y_1, y_2, y_5\}$. Therefore, $U/E_U = \{\{x_1, x_5\}, \{x_2\}, \{x_3\}, \{x_4\}\}$. Similarly, $V/E_V = \{\{y_1, y_5\}, \{y_3, y_6\}, \{y_2\}, \{y_4\}\}$.

Let us consider the target set $Y = \{y_1, y_2, y_4, y_5\}$. Therefore, the R-lower approximation, $\underline{R}Y$, is given as $\underline{R}Y = \{x_1, x_3, x_5\}$, whereas the R-upper approximation, $\bar{R}Y$, is given as $\bar{R}Y = \{x_1, x_3, x_4, x_5\}$. The R-boundary elements of Y are given as $BN_R(Y) = \bar{R}Y - \underline{R}Y = \{x_4\}$.

Definition 5.1

Let U and V be two universal sets. Let R be a binary relation from U to V. If $x \in U$ and $r(x) = \phi$, then x is a solitary element with respect to R. The set of all solitary elements with respect to the relation R is called a solitary set and is denoted as S. Mathematically,

$$S = \{x \in U : r(x) = \phi\} \tag{5.7}$$

■

5.2.1 Algebraic Properties of Rough Set Based on Two Universal Sets

The algebraic properties as established by Guilong Liu (2010) that are interesting and valuable in the theory of rough sets are listed as follows. Let R be an arbitrary binary relation from U to V. Let S be a solitary set with respect to the relation R. For subsets X, Y in V

1. $\bar{R}Y = \underset{y \in Y}{\cup} l(y)$.
2. $\underline{R}\phi = S, \bar{R}\phi = \phi, \underline{R}V = U$ and $\bar{R}V = S'$, where S' denotes the complement of S in U.
3. $S \subseteq \underline{R}X$ and $\bar{R}X \subseteq S'$.
4. $\underline{R}X - S \subseteq \bar{R}X$.
5. $\underline{R}X = U$ iff $\underset{x \in U}{\cup} r(x) \subseteq X$; $\bar{R}X = \phi$ iff $X \subseteq (\underset{x \in U}{\cup} r(x))'$.
6. If $S \neq \phi$, then $\underline{R}X \neq \bar{R}X$ for all $X \in P(V)$, where $P(V)$ denotes the power set of V.
7. For any given index set I, $X_i \in P(V)$, $\underline{R}(\cap_{i \in I} X_i) = \cap_{i \in I} \underline{R}X_i$ and $\bar{R}(\cup_{i \in I} X_i) = \cup_{i \in I} \bar{R}X_i$.
8. If $X \subseteq Y$, then $\underline{R}X \subseteq \underline{R}Y$ and $\bar{R}X \subseteq \bar{R}Y$.
9. $\underline{R}X \cup \underline{R}Y \subseteq \underline{R}(X \cup Y)$, and $\bar{R}(X \cap Y) \subseteq \bar{R}X \cap \bar{R}Y$.
10. $(\underline{R}X)' = \bar{R}X'$, and $(\bar{R}X)' = \underline{R}X'$.
11. There exists some $X \in P(U)$ such that $\underline{R}X = \bar{R}X$ if and only if R is serial.
12. If G is another binary relation from U to V and $\bar{R}X = \bar{G}X$ for all $x \in P(V)$, then $R = G$.
13. If G is another binary relation from U to V and $\underline{R}X = \underline{G}X$ for all $x \in P(V)$, then $R = G$.

5.2.2 Topological Characterization of Rough Set Based on Two Universal Sets

An interesting characterization of a rough set on two universal sets employing the notion of the lower and upper approximation as established by Tripathy et al. (2011b) is discussed in this section.

It results in four important and different types of rough sets on two universal sets as shown in the following, whereas the basic operations such as union and intersection on these types of rough sets are discussed in Section 5.2.3. These are more important while studying approximation of classifications and rule induction.

Type 1: If $\underline{R}Y \neq \phi$ and $\overline{R}Y \neq U$, then Y is *roughly R-definable* on two universal sets.
Type 2: If $\underline{R}Y = \phi$ and $\overline{R}Y \neq U$, then Y is *internally R-undefinable* on two universal sets.
Type 3: If $\underline{R}Y \neq \phi$ and $\overline{R}Y = U$, then Y is *externally R-undefinable* on two universal sets.
Type 4: If $\underline{R}Y = \phi$ and $\overline{R}Y = U$, then Y is *totally R-undefinable* on two universal sets.

Example 5.2

The following example will depict the aforementioned classification of rough sets on two universal sets in more detail. Let us consider two universes U and V as $U = \{x_1, x_2, x_3, x_4, x_5\}$ and $V = \{y_1, y_2, y_3, y_4, y_5, y_6\}$. Consider the binary relation R from $U \rightarrow V$ as $R = \{(x_1, y_1), (x_1, y_2), (x_1, y_5), (x_2, y_1), (x_2, y_2), (x_2, y_3), (x_3, y_4), (x_3, y_5), (x_4, y_1), (x_4, y_2), (x_4, y_3), (x_5, y_4), (x_5, y_6)\}$. Therefore, the relational system $K = (U, V, R)$ is an approximation space. The previous relation can be represented by its Boolean matrix as

$$R = \begin{pmatrix} 1 & 1 & 0 & 0 & 1 & 0 \\ 1 & 1 & 1 & 0 & 0 & 0 \\ 0 & 0 & 0 & 1 & 1 & 0 \\ 1 & 1 & 1 & 0 & 0 & 0 \\ 0 & 0 & 0 & 1 & 0 & 1 \end{pmatrix}$$

From the previous relation R, it is clear that $r(x_1) = \{y_1, y_2, y_5\}$; $r(x_2) = \{y_1, y_2, y_3\}$; $r(x_3) = \{y_4, y_5\}$; $r(x_4) = \{y_1, y_2, y_3\}$; $r(x_5) = \{y_4, y_6\}$. Therefore, $U/E_U = \{\{x_1\}, \{x_3\}, \{x_2, x_4\}, \{x_5\}\}$. Similarly, on employing left neighborhood as discussed earlier, $V/E_V = \{\{y_1, y_2\}, \{y_3\}, \{y_4\}, \{y_5\}, \{y_6\}\}$. The sets Y_1, Y_2, Y_3, Y_4 are examples of different types of rough sets on two universal sets, where

$$Y_1 = \{y_1, y_2, y_5\}, \ Y_2 = \{y_1, y_2\},$$

$$Y_3 = \{y_1, y_2, y_4, y_5\} \text{ and } Y_4 = \{y_3, y_5, y_6\}.$$

The corresponding lower and upper approximations are given as follows:

$$\underline{R}Y_1 = \{x_1\} \neq \phi; \quad \overline{R}Y_1 = \{x_1, x_2, x_3, x_4\} \neq U \qquad \text{(type 1)}$$

$$\underline{R}Y_2 = \phi; \quad \overline{R}Y_2 = \{x_1, x_2, x_4\} \neq U \qquad \text{(type 2)}$$

$$\underline{R}Y_3 = \{x_1, x_3\} \neq \phi; \quad \overline{R}Y_3 = \{x_1, x_2, x_3, x_4, x_5\} = U \qquad \text{(type 3)}$$

$$\underline{R}Y_4 = \phi; \quad \overline{R}Y_4 = \{x_1, x_2, x_3, x_4, x_5\} = U \qquad \text{(type 4)}$$

5.2.3 Basic Operations on Topological Characterization

This section discusses the basic operations such as union and intersection of two rough sets of any one of the four types. The tables corresponding to union and intersection are presented in the following. Both the operations contain ambiguity cases. Proofs and detailed discussion on these ambiguity cases can be found in the work of Tripathy et al. (2011b).

Table of Union

In case of union as given in Table 5.1, out of 16 cases, as many as 9 are unambiguous, whereas 7 cases consist of ambiguity. In one case, it can be any one of the four types. These ambiguities are due to the inclusion $\underline{R}X \cup \underline{R}Y \subseteq \underline{R}(X \cup Y)$. Here, the entry in the ith row and jth column of the table is denoted as (i,j). In the following table, $\underline{R}X \cup \underline{R}Y \subseteq \underline{R}(X \cup Y)$ and $\overline{R}(\cup_{i \in I} X_i) = \cup_{i \in I} \overline{R}X_i$ are used to deduce the different possible cases.

Table of Intersection

It is interesting to see from Table 5.2 that out of 16 cases for intersection, 7 cases are ambiguous, whereas 9 cases are unambiguous. Also, it is observed that in one case, it can be any one of the four types. Here, the entry in the ith row and jth column of the table is denoted by the notation (i,j). In the following table, $\underline{R}(\cap_{i \in I} X_i) = \cap_{i \in I} \underline{R}X_i$ and $\overline{R}(X \cap Y) \subseteq \overline{R}X \cap \overline{R}Y$ are used to deduce the possible cases.

Table 5.1 Table of Union

∪	Type 1	Type 2	Type 3	Type 4
Type 1	Type 1/type 3	Type 1/type 3	Type 3	Type 3
Type 2	Type 1/type 3	Type 1/type 2/ type 3/type 4	Type 3	Type 3/type 4
Type 3	Type 3	Type 3	Type 3	Type 3
Type 4	Type 3	Type 3/type 4	Type 3	Type 3/type 4

Table 5.2 Table of Intersection

∩	Type 1	Type 2	Type 3	Type 4
Type 1	Type 1/type 2	Type 2	Type 1/type 2	Type 2
Type 2	Type 2	Type 2	Type 2	Type 2
Type 3	Type 1/type 2	Type 2	Type 1/type 2/ type 3/type 4	Type 2/type 4
Type 4	Type 2	Type 2	Type 2/type 4	Type 2/type 4

5.2.4 A Real-Life Application between Customers and the Supermarkets

This section demonstrates how the aforementioned concepts can be applied to real-life problems. Consider an example in which the relation between customers and the supermarkets in a particular metropolitan city is studied. In general, a supermarket takes care of a customer's everyday household needs and more. Therefore, it spreads across a wide range of products of food and nonfood items, ranging from basic necessities such as fruits and vegetables, staples, personal care, home care, household care products, general merchandise, and dairy products. Hence, it is a one-stop solution for customers to fulfill daily shopping needs at a convenient location close to the customer. Apart from this, the best possible value for customer's money, quality of the product, style, and the behavior of supporting staff play a vital role in choosing a supermarket. However, there exist many other factors in choosing a supermarket. For this reason, in general, a customer has to depend on more than one supermarket in a city. Therefore, it is essential to establish the relation between the customers and the supermarkets in a city. To make analysis simple and clear, a small universe U of 7 customers and another small universe V of 10 supermarkets in a particular city are considered. The relation R between U and V is defined by the following Boolean matrix. In the following, the ambiguity results obtained in Tables 5.1 and 5.2 are verified.

$$R = \begin{pmatrix} 1 & 1 & 0 & 0 & 1 & 1 & 0 & 1 & 1 & 0 \\ 1 & 1 & 1 & 0 & 0 & 1 & 1 & 1 & 0 & 0 \\ 0 & 0 & 0 & 1 & 0 & 0 & 1 & 0 & 0 & 1 \\ 1 & 1 & 1 & 0 & 0 & 1 & 1 & 1 & 0 & 0 \\ 1 & 0 & 0 & 1 & 1 & 0 & 1 & 1 & 1 & 1 \\ 1 & 1 & 0 & 0 & 1 & 1 & 0 & 1 & 1 & 0 \\ 1 & 1 & 1 & 0 & 0 & 0 & 1 & 1 & 0 & 0 \end{pmatrix}$$

Therefore, $r(x_1) = \{y_1, y_2, y_5, y_6, y_8, y_9\}$; $r(x_2) = \{y_1, y_2, y_3, y_6, y_7, y_8\}$; $r(x_3) = \{y_4, y_7, y_{10}\}$; $r(x_4) = \{y_1, y_2, y_3, y_6, y_7, y_8\}$; $r(x_5) = \{y_1, y_4, y_5, y_7, y_8, y_9, y_{10}\}$; $r(x_6) = \{y_1, y_2, y_5, y_6, y_8, y_9\}$ and $r(x_7) = \{y_1, y_2, y_3, y_7, y_8\}$. $U/E_U = \{\{x_1, x_6\}, \{x_2, x_4\}, \{x_3\}, \{x_5\}, \{x_7\}\}$ and $V/E_V = \{\{y_1, y_8\}, \{y_2\}, \{y_3\}, \{y_4, y_{10}\}, \{y_5, y_9\}, \{y_6\}, \{y_7\}\}$.

Let $Y_1 = \{y_3, y_4\}$ and $Y_2 = \{y_3, y_7, y_{10}\}$. Therefore, $\underline{R}Y_1 = \underline{R}Y_2 = \phi$, and $\overline{R}Y_1 = \overline{R}Y_2 = \{x_2, x_3, x_4, x_5, x_7\} \neq U$. This depicts that Y_1 and Y_2 both are of type 2. Now, $\underline{R}(Y_1 \cup Y_2) = \{x_3\} \neq \phi$, and $\overline{R}(Y_1 \cup Y_2) = \{x_2, x_3, x_4, x_5, x_7\} \neq U$. Therefore, $(Y_1 \cup Y_2)$ is of type 1.

On taking $Y_1 = \{y_3, y_{10}\}$ and $Y_2 = \{y_3, y_4\}$, it is obtained as $\underline{R}Y_1 = \underline{R}Y_2 = \phi$, and $\overline{R}Y_1 = \overline{R}Y_2 = \{x_2, x_3, x_4, x_5, x_7\} \neq U$. This depicts that Y_1 and Y_2 both are of type 2. Now, $\underline{R}(Y_1 \cup Y_2) = \phi$, and $\overline{R}(Y_1 \cup Y_2) = \{x_2, x_3, x_4, x_5, x_7\} \neq U$. Thus, $(Y_1 \cup Y_2)$ is of type 2.

Again, on taking $Y_1 = \{y_3, y_7, y_{10}\}$ and $Y_2 = \{y_4, y_5, y_6\}$, the lower and upper approximation are obtained as $\underline{R}Y_1 = \underline{R}Y_2 = \phi$, $\overline{R}Y_1 = \{x_2, x_3, x_4, x_5, x_7\} \neq U$, and $\overline{R}Y_2 = \{x_1, x_2, x_3, x_4, x_5, x_6\} \neq U$. It states that Y_1 and Y_2 both are of type 2. Now, $\underline{R}(Y_1 \cup Y_2) = \{x_3\} \neq \phi$, and $\overline{R}(Y_1 \cup Y_2) = \{x_1, x_2, x_3, x_4, x_5, x_6, x_7\} = U$. Thus, $(Y_1 \cup Y_2)$ is of type 3.

Further, on taking $Y_1 = \{y_3, y_{10}\}$ and $Y_2 = \{y_5\}$, the lower and upper approximations are obtained as $\underline{R}Y_1 = \underline{R}Y_2 = \phi$, $\overline{R}Y_1 = \{x_2, x_3, x_4, x_5, x_7\} \neq U$, and $\overline{R}Y_2 = \{x_1, x_5, x_6\} \neq U$. This depicts that both Y_1 and Y_2 are of type 2. Now, $\underline{R}(Y_1 \cup Y_2) = \phi$, and $\overline{R}(Y_1 \cup Y_2) = \{x_1, x_2, x_3, x_4, x_5, x_6, x_7\} = U$. Thus, $(Y_1 \cup Y_2)$ is of type 4. The previous example verifies the (2, 2) case of the table of union.

Similarly, the following example verifies the (3, 3) case of the table of intersection.

On taking $Y_1 = \{y_1, y_2, y_3, y_4, y_6, y_7, y_8, y_{10}\}$ and $Y_2 = \{y_4, y_5, y_7 y_{10}\}$, the lower and upper approximation are obtained as $\underline{R}Y_1 = \{x_2, x_3, x_4, x_7\} \neq \phi$, $\underline{R}Y_2 = \{x_3\} \neq \phi$ and $\overline{R}Y_1 = \overline{R}Y_2 = U$. This indicates that Y_1 and Y_2 both are of type 3. Now, $\underline{R}(Y_1 \cap Y_2) = \{x_3\} \neq \phi$, and $\overline{R}(Y_1 \cap Y_2) = \{x_2, x_3, x_4, x_5, x_7\} \neq U$. Therefore, $(Y_1 \cap Y_2)$ is of type 1.

On considering $Y_1 = \{y_1, y_2, y_3, y_7, y_8\}$ and $Y_2 = \{y_3, y_4, y_5, y_7 y_{10}\}$; $\underline{R}Y_1 = \{x_7\} \neq \phi$, $\underline{R}Y_2 = \{x_3\} \neq \phi$, and $\overline{R}Y_1 = \overline{R}Y_2 = U$. It states that Y_1 and Y_2 both are of type 3. Now, $\underline{R}(Y_1 \cap Y_2) = \phi$, and $\overline{R}(Y_1 \cap Y_2) = \{x_2, x_3, x_4, x_5, x_7\} \neq U$. Hence, $(Y_1 \cap Y_2)$ is of type 2.

Again, on taking $Y_1 = \{y_2, y_4, y_7, y_{10}\}$ and $Y_2 = \{y_2, y_4, y_6, y_7 y_{10}\}$, it is obtained as $\underline{R}Y_1 = \underline{R}Y_2 = \{x_3\} \neq \phi$, and $\overline{R}Y_1 = \overline{R}Y_2 = U$. It depicts that both Y_1 and Y_2 are of type 3. Now, $\underline{R}(Y_1 \cap Y_2) = \{x_3\} \neq \phi$, and $\overline{R}(Y_1 \cap Y_2) = U$. Thus, $(Y_1 \cap Y_2)$ is of type 3.

Further, on taking $Y_1 = \{y_4, y_7, y_8, y_{10}\}$ and $Y_2 = \{y_1, y_2, y_3, y_4, y_7, y_8\}$, it can be obtained as $\underline{R}Y_1 = \{x_3\} \neq \phi$, $\underline{R}Y_2 = \{x_7\} \neq \phi$ and $\overline{R}Y_1 = \overline{R}Y_2 = U$. This depicts that Y_1 and Y_2 both are of type 3. Now, $\underline{R}(Y_1 \cap Y_2) = \phi$, and $\overline{R}(Y_1 \cap Y_2) = U$. Thus, $(Y_1 \cap Y_2)$ is of type 4.

5.3 Approximation of Classifications

The rough set (Pawlak 1982, 1991) philosophy specifies the depth of understanding of the object and its attributes influencing the object with a depicted value. Therefore, there is a need to classify objects of the universe based on the indiscernibility relation between them. The basic idea of a rough set is based upon the approximation of sets by a pair of sets known as lower and upper approximation. Here, the lower and upper approximation operators are based on an equivalence relation. However, the requirement of equivalence relation is a restrictive condition that may limit the application of the rough set model. Therefore, the rough set is generalized by Guilong Liu (2010) to a rough set on two universal sets. Because we are interested in classifications based on binary relation, it is interesting to have the idea of approximation of classifications. It is because classifications of universes play central roles in rough set theory. This section formally discusses the classification and important result that are important in the study of knowledge discovery databases (Tripathy and Acharjya 2012).

Definition 5.2

Let $F = \{Y_1, Y_2, \ldots, Y_n\}$, where $n > 1$ is a family of nonempty sets defined over V. The family F is said to be a classification of V if and only if $(Y_i \cap Y_j) = \phi$ for $i \neq j$ and $\sum_{k=1}^{n} Y_k = V$. ■

Definition 5.3

Let $F = \{Y_1, Y_2, \ldots, Y_n\}$ be a family of nonempty classification of V, and let R be a binary relation from $U \to V$. Then the R-lower and R-upper approximation of the family $F = \{Y_1, Y_2, \ldots, Y_n\}$ are given as

$$\underline{R}F = \{\underline{R}Y_1, \underline{R}Y_2, \underline{R}Y_3, \ldots, \underline{R}Y_n\} \text{ and}$$

$$\overline{R}F = \{\overline{R}Y_1, \overline{R}Y_2, \overline{R}Y_3, \ldots, \overline{R}Y_n\},$$

respectively. ■

This section establishes two theorems that are important in the context of knowledge representation, from which many corollaries can be derived including the four theorems established by Grzymala-Busse (1988). Examples are provided to illustrate the results obtained.

Theorem 5.1

Let R be a binary relation from $U \rightarrow V$ and let $F = \{Y_1, Y_2, \ldots, Y_n\}$, where $n > 1$ is a classification of V. For any $i \in \{1, 2, 3, \ldots, n\}$, $\bar{R}(\bigcup_i Y_i) = U$ if and only if $\underline{R}(\bigcup_j Y_j) = \phi$ for $j \neq i$ and $j \in \{1, 2, 3, \ldots, n\}$. ■

Proof

If $\bar{R}(\bigcup_i Y_i) = U$, then for every $x \in U$ such that $r(x) \cap (\bigcup_i Y_i) \neq \phi$. This implies that $r(x) \subseteq Y_j$ does not hold for each $j \neq i$ and $j \in \{1, 2, 3, \ldots, n\}$. Therefore, $\underline{R}Y_j = \phi$ for all $j \neq i$ and $j \in \{1, 2, 3, \ldots, n\}$. Consequently, $\underline{R}(\bigcup_j Y_j) = \phi$ for $j \neq i$ and $j \in \{1, 2, 3, \ldots, n\}$.

Conversely, if $\underline{R}(\bigcup_j Y_j) = \phi$ for $j \in \{1, 2, 3, \ldots, n\}$, then for each $x \in U$, $r(x) \subseteq Y_j$ does not hold for each $j \in \{1, 2, 3, \ldots, n\}$. It implies that for every $x \in U$, $r(x) \cap (\bigcup_i Y_i) \neq \phi$ for $i \neq j$ and $i \in \{1, 2, 3, \ldots, n\}$. Therefore, $\bar{R}(\bigcup_i Y_i) = U$. ■

Corollary 5.1

Let R be a binary relation from $U \rightarrow V$ and let $F = \{Y_1, Y_2, \ldots, Y_n\}$, where $n > 1$ is a classification of V. For any $i \in \{1, 2, 3, \ldots, n\}$, if $\bar{R}(\bigcup_i Y_i) = U$, then $\underline{R}Y_j = \phi$ for each $j \neq i$ and $j \in \{1, 2, 3, \ldots, n\}$. ■

Corollary 5.2

Let R be a binary relation from $U \rightarrow V$ and let $F = \{Y_1, Y_2, \ldots, Y_n\}$, where $n > 1$ is a classification of V. For each $i \in \{1, 2, 3, \ldots, n\}$, $\bar{R}Y_i = U$ if and only if $\underline{R}(\bigcup_j Y_j) = \phi$ for each $j \neq i$ and $j \in \{1, 2, 3, \ldots, n\}$. ■

Corollary 5.3

Let R be a binary relation from $U \rightarrow V$ and let $F = \{Y_1, Y_2, \ldots, Y_n\}$, where $n > 1$ is a classification of V. For each $i \in \{1, 2, 3, \ldots, n\}$, $\underline{R}Y_i = \phi$ if and only if $\bar{R}(\bigcup_j Y_j) = U$, for each $j \neq i$ and $j \in \{1, 2, 3, \ldots, n\}$. ■

Corollary 5.4

Let R be a binary relation from $U \rightarrow V$ and let $F = \{Y_1, Y_2, \ldots, Y_n\}$, where $n > 1$ is a classification of V. If there exists $i \in \{1, 2, 3, \ldots, n\}$ such that $\bar{R}Y_i = U$, then for each $j \neq i$ and $j \in \{1, 2, 3, \ldots, n\}$, $\underline{R}Y_j = \phi$. ■

Corollary 5.5

Let R be a binary relation from $U \to V$ and let $F = \{Y_1, Y_2,..., Y_n\}$, where $n > 1$ is a classification of V. If $\overline{R}Y_i = U$ for all $i \in \{1, 2, 3,..., n\}$, then $\underline{R}Y_i = \phi$ for all $i \in \{1, 2, 3,..., n\}$. ■

Example 5.3

Let $U = \{x_1, x_2, x_3, x_4, x_5\}$ and $V = \{y_1, y_2, y_3, y_4, y_5, y_6\}$. Consider the relation R given by its Boolean matrix as defined in the following.

$$R = \begin{pmatrix} 1 & 1 & 0 & 0 & 1 & 0 \\ 0 & 0 & 1 & 0 & 0 & 1 \\ 0 & 1 & 0 & 1 & 0 & 0 \\ 1 & 0 & 1 & 1 & 1 & 1 \\ 1 & 1 & 0 & 0 & 1 & 0 \end{pmatrix}$$

From the relation R, it is clear that $r(x_1) = \{y_1, y_2, y_5\}$; $r(x_2) = \{y_3, y_6\}$; $r(x_3) = \{y_2, y_4\}$; $r(x_4) = \{y_1, y_3, y_4, y_5, y_6\}$ and $r(x_5) = \{y_1, y_2, y_5\}$. Therefore, $U/E_U = \{\{x_1, x_5\}, \{x_2\}, \{x_3\}, \{x_4\}\}$. Similarly, $V/E_V = \{\{y_1, y_5\}, \{y_3, y_6\}, \{y_2\}, \{y_4\}\}$.

Let the classification $C = \{Y_1, Y_2\}$ be given, where $Y_1 = \{y_1, y_2, y_6\}$ and $Y_2 = \{y_3, y_4, y_5\}$. Because $\overline{R}Y_1 = U = \overline{R}Y_2$, $\underline{R}Y_1 = \phi = \underline{R}Y_2$. This verifies Corollary 5.5.

Let the classification $C = \{Y_1, Y_2, Y_3\}$ be given, where $Y_1 = \{y_2, y_3, y_5\}$; $Y_2 = \{y_1, y_4\}$ and $Y_3 = \{y_6\}$. Because $\overline{R}Y_1 = \{x_1, x_2, x_3, x_4, x_5\} = U$, $\underline{R}Y_2 = \phi$ and $\underline{R}Y_3 = \phi$. This verifies Corollary 5.4. Similarly, the other corollaries of Theorem 5.1 mentioned previously can also be verified through examples by taking a different classification C.

Theorem 5.2

Let R be a binary relation from $U \to V$ and let $F = \{Y_1, Y_2,..., Y_n\}$, where $n > 1$ is a classification of V. For any $i \in \{1, 2, 3,..., n\}$, $\underline{R}(\bigcup_i Y_i) \neq \phi$ if and only if $\bigcup_j \overline{R}Y_j \neq U$ for $j \neq i$ and $j \in \{1, 2, 3,..., n\}$. ■

Proof

(Necessary Part)

Suppose that $\underline{R}(\bigcup_i Y_i) \neq \phi$. Then there exists $x \in U$ such that $r(x) \subseteq (\bigcup_i Y_i)$. This implies that $r(x) \cap Y_j = \phi$ for all $j \neq i$ and $j \in \{1, 2, 3,..., n\}$. It indicates that $x \notin \overline{R}Y_j$ for all $j \neq i$ and $j \in \{1, 2, 3,..., n\}$. Consequently, $\bigcup_j \overline{R}Y_j \neq U$ for $j \neq i$ and $j \in \{1, 2, 3,..., n\}$.

(Sufficiency Part)

Let $i \in \{1, 2, 3,..., n\}$. Suppose that $\bigcup_j \overline{R}Y_j \neq U$ for $j \neq i$ and $j \in \{1, 2, 3,..., n\}$. By property of upper approximation, $\overline{R}(\bigcup_j Y_j) = \bigcup_j \overline{R}Y_j \neq U$. So there exists $r(x)$ for some $x \in U$ such that $r(x) \cap (\bigcup_j Y_j) = \phi$. It indicates that $r(x) \subseteq (\bigcup_i Y_i)$. Consequently, $\underline{R}(\bigcup_i Y_i) \neq \phi$. ■

Corollary 5.6

Let R be a binary relation from $U \to V$ and let $F = \{Y_1, Y_2, \ldots, Y_n\}$, where $n > 1$ is a classification of V. For any $i \in \{1, 2, 3, \ldots, n\}$, if $\underline{R}(\bigcup_i Y_i) \neq \phi$, then $\overline{R}Y_j \neq U$ for each $j \neq i$ and $j \in \{1, 2, 3, \ldots, n\}$. ■

Corollary 5.7

Let R be a binary relation from $U \to V$ and let $F = \{Y_1, Y_2, \ldots, Y_n\}$, where $n > 1$ is a classification of V. For any $i \in \{1, 2, 3, \ldots, n\}$, $\underline{R}Y_i \neq \phi$ if and only if $\bigcup_j \overline{R}Y_j \neq U$ for $j \neq i$ and $j \in \{1, 2, 3, \ldots, n\}$. ■

Corollary 5.8

Let R be a binary relation from $U \to V$ and let $F = \{Y_1, Y_2, \ldots, Y_n\}$, where $n > 1$ is a classification of V. For all i, $i \in \{1, 2, 3, \ldots, n\}$, $\overline{R}Y_i \neq U$ if and only if $\underline{R}(\bigcup_j Y_j) \neq \phi$ for $j \neq i$ and $j \in \{1, 2, 3, \ldots, n\}$. ■

Corollary 5.9

Let R be a binary relation from $U \to V$ and let $F = \{Y_1, Y_2, \ldots, Y_n\}$, where $n > 1$ is a classification of V. If there exists $i \in \{1, 2, 3, \ldots, n\}$ such that $\underline{R}Y_i \neq \phi$, then $\overline{R}Y_j \neq U$ for each $j \neq i$ and $j \in \{1, 2, 3, \ldots, n\}$. ■

Corollary 5.10

Let R be a binary relation from $U \to V$ and let $F = \{Y_1, Y_2, \ldots, Y_n\}$, where $n > 1$ is a classification of V. If for all $i \in \{1, 2, 3, \ldots, n\}$, $\underline{R}Y_i \neq \phi$ holds, then $\overline{R}Y_j \neq U$ for all $i \in \{1, 2, 3, \ldots, n\}$. ■

Example 5.4

Let $U = \{x_1, x_2, x_3, x_4, x_5\}$ and $V = \{y_1, y_2, y_3, y_4, y_5, y_6\}$. Consider the relation R given by its Boolean matrix:

$$R = \begin{pmatrix} 1 & 1 & 0 & 0 & 1 & 0 \\ 0 & 0 & 1 & 0 & 0 & 1 \\ 0 & 1 & 0 & 1 & 0 & 0 \\ 1 & 0 & 1 & 1 & 1 & 1 \\ 1 & 1 & 0 & 0 & 1 & 0 \end{pmatrix}$$

From the relation R it is clear that $r(x_1) = \{y_1, y_2, y_5\}$; $r(x_2) = \{y_3, y_6\}$; $r(x_3) = \{y_2, y_4\}$; $r(x_4) = \{y_1, y_3, y_4, y_5, y_6\}$ and $r(x_5) = \{y_1, y_2, y_5\}$. Therefore, $U/E_U = \{\{x_1, x_5\}, \{x_2\}, \{x_3\}, \{x_4\}\}$. Similarly, $V/E_V = \{\{y_1, y_5\}, \{y_3, y_6\}, \{y_2\}, \{y_4\}\}$. Let us consider the classification $C = \{Y_1, Y_2\}$ where $Y_1 = \{y_1, y_2, y_4\}$ and $Y_2 = \{y_3, y_5, y_6\}$. Because $\underline{R}Y_1 = \{x_3\} \neq \phi$, $\underline{R}Y_2 = \{x_2\} \neq \phi$, $\overline{R}Y_1 = \{x_1, x_3, x_4, x_5\} \neq U$ and $\overline{R}Y_2 = \{x_1, x_2, x_4, x_5\} \neq U$. This verifies Corollary 5.9.

Let the classification $C = \{Y_1, Y_2, Y_3\}$ be given, where $Y_1 = \{y_1, y_2, y_4\}$; $Y_2 = \{y_3, y_6\}$ and $Y_3 = \{y_5\}$. Because $\underline{R}Y_2 = \{x_2\} \neq \phi$, $\overline{R}Y_1 = \{x_1, x_3, x_4, x_5\} \neq U$ and $\overline{R}Y_3 = \{x_1, x_4, x_5\} \neq U$. Similarly, $\underline{R}Y_1 = \{x_3\} \neq \phi$ with $\overline{R}Y_2 = \{x_2, x_4\} \neq U$ and $\overline{R}Y_3 = \{x_1, x_4, x_5\} \neq U$. This verifies Corollary 5.9. Similarly, the other corollaries of Theorem 5.2 mentioned prior can also be verified through examples by taking a different classification C.

5.3.1 Measures of Uncertainty

In this section, some properties of measures of uncertainty such as accuracy and quality of approximation employing the binary relation R are established. The number of elements in a set V is denoted by $card(V)$. Let $F = \{Y_1, Y_2, ..., Y_n\}$ be a family of nonempty classifications. Then the R-lower and R-upper approximation of the family F are given as $\underline{R}F = \{\underline{R}Y_1, \underline{R}Y_2, \underline{R}Y_3, ..., \underline{R}Y_n\}$ and $\overline{R}F = \{\overline{R}Y_1, \overline{R}Y_2, \overline{R}Y_3, ..., \overline{R}Y_n\}$, respectively. Therefore, accuracy of approximation and quality of approximation of the family F employing the binary relation R are defined as follows:

Definition 5.4

The accuracy of approximation of the family of classification F that expresses the percentage of possible correct decisions when classifying objects employing the binary relation R is defined as

$$\alpha_R(F) = \frac{\sum_{i=1}^{n} card(\underline{R}Y_i)}{\sum_{i=1}^{n} card(\overline{R}Y_i)} \tag{5.8}$$

■

Definition 5.5

The quality of approximation of F that expresses the percentage of objects that can be correctly classified to classes of F by the binary relation R is defined as

$$v_R(F) = \frac{\sum card(\underline{R}Y_i)}{card(V)} \text{ for } i = 1, 2, 3, ..., n \tag{5.9}$$

■

Definition 5.6

The family $F = \{Y_1, Y_2, ..., Y_n\}$ is said to be R-definable if and only if $\underline{R}F = \overline{R}F$; that is, $\underline{R}Y_i = \overline{R}Y_i$ for $i = 1, 2, 3, ..., n$.

■

Theorem 5.3

Let R be a binary relation from $U \to V$ and let $F = \{Y_1, Y_2,...,Y_n\}$, where $n > 1$ is a classification of V. For any R-definable classification F in V, $\alpha_R(F) = \nu_R(F) = 1$. Hence, if a classification F is R-definable, then it is totally independent on R. ■

Proof

For any R-definable classification F, $\underline{R}F = \overline{R}F$; that, is $\underline{R}Y_i = \overline{R}Y_i$ for $i = 1, 2, 3,..., n$. Therefore, by definition,

$$\alpha_R(F) = \frac{\sum_{i=1}^{n} card(\underline{R}Y_i)}{\sum_{i=1}^{n} card(\overline{R}Y_i)} = 1$$

Again, by property of upper and lower approximation and as F is a classification of V,

$$\sum_{i=1}^{n} card(\overline{R}Y_i) \geq \sum_{i=1}^{n} card(Y_i) = card\left(\bigcup_{i=1}^{n} Y_i\right) = card(V) \text{ and}$$

$$\sum_{i=1}^{n} card(\underline{R}Y_i) \leq \sum_{i=1}^{n} card(Y_i) = card\left(\bigcup_{i=1}^{n} Y_i\right) = card(V)$$

But for R-definable classifications, $\sum_{i=1}^{n} card(\underline{R}Y_i) = \sum_{i=1}^{n} card(\overline{R}Y_i)$, and hence, $\sum_{i=1}^{n} card(\underline{R}Y_i) = card(V)$. Therefore, by definition,

$$\nu_R(F) = \frac{\sum card(\underline{R}Y_i)}{card(V)} = 1$$

■

Theorem 5.4

Let R be a binary relation from $U \to V$ and let $F = \{Y_1, Y_2,..., Y_n\}$, where $n > 1$ is a classification of V. If $\alpha_R(F) = \nu_R(F) = 1$, then F is R-definable V. ■

Proof

If $\alpha_R(F) = 1$, then by definition, $\sum_{i=1}^{n} card(\underline{R}Y_i) = \sum_{i=1}^{n} card(\overline{R}Y_i)$. Again by definition of lower and upper approximation, $card(\underline{R}Y_i) \leq card(\overline{R}Y_i)$. It indicates that $\underline{R}Y_i = \overline{R}Y_i$ for $i = 1, 2, 3,\ldots, n$. Therefore, F is R-definable V. ■

Theorem 5.5

Let R be a binary relation from $U \rightarrow V$ and for any classification $F = \{Y_1, Y_2,\ldots, Y_n\}$, $n > 1$ in V, $0 \leq \alpha_R(F) \leq \nu_R(F) \leq 1$. ■

Proof

By property of lower approximation and as F is a classification of V,

$$\sum_{i=1}^{n} card(\underline{R}Y_i) \leq \sum_{i=1}^{n} card(Y_i) = card\left(\bigcup_{i=1}^{n} Y_i\right) = card(V)$$

Therefore, by definition, $\nu_R(F) = \dfrac{\sum card(\underline{R}Y_i)}{card(V)} \leq \dfrac{card(V)}{card(V)} = 1$.

Again, $\sum_{i=1}^{n} card(\overline{R}Y_i) \geq \sum_{i=1}^{n} card(Y_i) = card\left(\bigcup_{i=1}^{n} Y_i\right) = card(V)$. Hence, by definition,

$\alpha_R(F) = \dfrac{\sum card(\underline{R}Y_i)}{\sum card(\overline{R}Y_i)} \leq \dfrac{\sum card(\underline{R}Y_i)}{card(V)} = \nu_R(F)$; that is, $\alpha_R(F) \leq \nu_R(F)$, and consequently, $0 \leq$

$\alpha_R(F) \leq \nu_R(F) \leq 1$. ■

5.3.2 *Rough Equality of Sets on Two Universal Sets*

The concept of the rough set differs essentially from the ordinary concept of the set in that for the rough sets, we are unable to define uniquely the membership relation. In set theory, two sets are said to be equal if they have the same elements. However, this is not true in the case of rough sets. Therefore, the concept of rough (approximate) equality was introduced by Novotny and Pawlak (1985). Thus, two sets can be unequal in set theory but can be approximately equal. This is an important feature, and according to our state of knowledge, the sets have close features that are enough to be assumed approximately equal. This is due to the indiscernibility relation between the objects of the universe. But the indiscernibility relation is a restrictive relation that may limit the application of the rough set. Therefore, the rough set has extended to the settings of the rough set on two universal sets based on binary relation. Hence, the aforementioned concept of rough equality of sets can be extended to the settings of rough equality of sets on two universal sets. In fact, three kinds of rough equality of sets on two universal sets are introduced (Acharjya and Tripathy 2013). The formal definitions are presented as follows.

Definition 5.7

Let U and V be two universal sets and $R \subseteq (U \times V)$ be a binary relation. Let the relational system (U, V, R) be a knowledge base, and $Y_1, Y_2 \subseteq V$. We say that

1. Sets Y_1 and Y_2 are bottom R-equal in V if $\underline{R}Y_1 = \underline{R}Y_2$. We write it as $Y_1 \approx_B Y_2$.
2. Sets Y_1 and Y_2 are top R-equal in V if $\overline{R}Y_1 = \overline{R}Y_2$. We write it as $Y_1 \approx_T Y_2$.
3. Sets Y_1 and Y_2 are R-equal in V if $Y_1 \approx_B Y_2$ and $Y_1 \approx_T Y_2$. We write it as $Y_1 \approx Y_2$.

The following physical interpretations with the aforementioned notion of rough equality of sets on two universal sets are associated. If $Y_1 \approx_B Y_2$, this means that positive examples of the sets Y_1 and Y_2 in V are equal. If $Y_1 \approx_T Y_2$, then the negative examples of the sets Y_1 and Y_2 in V are equal. If $Y_1 \approx Y_2$, this means that both positive and negative examples of the sets Y_1 and Y_2 in V are the same. ■

Example 5.5

Let $U = \{x_1, x_2, x_3, x_4, x_5\}$ and $V = \{y_1, y_2, y_3, y_4, y_5, y_6, y_7, y_8\}$. Consider the binary relation R as $R = \{(x_1, y_2), (x_1, y_3), (x_2, y_1), (x_2, y_4), (x_2, y_5), (x_3, y_3), (x_3, y_6), (x_3, y_7), (x_4, y_1), (x_4, y_7), (x_4, y_8), (x_5, y_2), (x_5, y_3)\}$. Therefore, R can be written in its Boolean matrix form as

$$
R = \begin{pmatrix}
0 & 1 & 1 & 0 & 0 & 0 & 0 & 0 \\
1 & 0 & 0 & 1 & 1 & 0 & 0 & 0 \\
0 & 0 & 1 & 0 & 0 & 1 & 1 & 0 \\
1 & 0 & 0 & 0 & 0 & 0 & 1 & 1 \\
0 & 1 & 1 & 0 & 0 & 0 & 0 & 0
\end{pmatrix}
$$

From the relation R, it is clear that $r(x_1) = \{y_2, y_3\}$; $r(x_2) = \{y_1, y_4, y_5\}$; $r(x_3) = \{y_3, y_6, y_7\}$; $r(x_4) = \{y_1, y_4, y_5\}$; and $r(x_5) = \{y_2, y_3\}$. Therefore, $U|E_U = \{\{x_1, x_5\}, \{x_2\}, \{x_3\}, \{x_4\}\}$.

For sets $Y_1 = \{y_1, y_2, y_3\}$ and $Y_2 = \{y_2, y_3, y_7\}$, it is obtained as $\underline{R}Y_1 = \{x_1, x_5\} = \underline{R}Y_2$; therefore, $Y_1 \approx_B Y_2$. Hence, Y_1 and Y_2 are bottom R-equal in V. Again, on considering $Y_1 = \{y_1, y_2, y_7\}$ and $Y_2 = \{y_2, y_3, y_4, y_8\}$, it is obtained as $\overline{R}Y_1 = \{x_1, x_2, x_3, x_4, x_5\} = \overline{R}Y_2$; therefore $Y_1 \approx_T Y_2$. Hence Y_1 and Y_2 are top R-equal in V. Similarly on taking $Y_1 = \{y_2, y_4, y_6\}$ and $Y_2 = \{y_3, y_4, y_6\}$ it can be obtained as $\underline{R}Y_1 = \phi = \underline{R}Y_2$, and $\overline{R}Y_1 = \{x_1, x_2, x_3, x_5\} = \overline{R}Y_2$; therefore, $Y_1 \approx Y_2$. Hence, Y_1 and Y_2 are R-equal in V.

Proposition 5.1

The following properties of relations $\approx_B$, $\approx_T$, and $\approx$ are immediate consequences of the definitions. Let U and V be two universal sets and $R \subseteq (U \times V)$ be a binary relation. Then for $Y_1, Y_2 \subseteq V$, the following properties hold. ■

1. $Y_1 \approx_B Y_2$ if and only if $(Y_1 \cap Y_2) \approx_B Y_1$ and $(Y_1 \cap Y_2) \approx_B Y_2$.
2. $Y_1 \approx_T Y_2$ if and only if $(Y_1 \cup Y_2) \approx_T Y_1$ and $(Y_1 \cup Y_2) \approx_T Y_2$.
3. If $Y_1 \approx_T Y_1'$ and $Y_2 \approx_T Y_2'$, then $(Y_1 \cup Y_2) \approx_T (Y_1' \cup Y_2')$.
4. If $Y_1 \approx_B Y_1'$ and $Y_2 \approx_B Y_2'$, then $(Y_1 \cap Y_2) \approx_B (Y_1' \cap Y_2')$.
5. If $Y_1 \subseteq Y_2$ and $Y_2 \approx_T \phi$, then $Y_1 \approx_T \phi$.
6. If $Y_1 \subseteq Y_2$ and $Y_1 \approx_T V$, then $Y_2 \approx_T V$.
7. If $Y_1 \approx_B \phi$ or $Y_2 \approx_B \phi$, then $(Y_1 \cap Y_2) \approx_B \phi$.
8. If $Y_1 \approx_T V$ or $Y_2 \approx_T V$, then $(Y_1 \cup Y_2) \approx_T V$.

5.3.3 Rough Inclusion of Sets on Two Universal Sets

Inclusion relation is one of the fundamental concepts in set theory. An analogous notion in the rough set is introduced by Pawlak (1991). Hence, rough inclusion of sets can be extended to the settings of rough inclusion of sets on two universal sets. This section defines the rough inclusion of sets on two universal sets in the same way as rough equality of sets on two universal sets. The formal definition of rough inclusion of sets on two universal sets is as follows.

Definition 5.8

Let U and V be two universal sets and $R \subseteq (U \times V)$ be a binary relation. Let the relational system (U, V, R) be a knowledge base, and $Y_1, Y_2 \subseteq V$. We say that

1. Set Y_1 is bottom R-included in Y_2 if and only if $\underline{R}Y_1 \subseteq \underline{R}Y_2$. We denote it as $Y_1 [\![_B Y_2$.
2. Set Y_1 is top R-included in Y_2 if and only if $\overline{R}Y_1 \subseteq \overline{R}Y_2$. We denote it as $Y_1 [\![_T Y_2$.
3. Set Y_1 is said to be R-included in Y_2 if and only if $Y_1 [\![_B Y_2$ and $Y_1 [\![_T Y_2$. We denote it as $Y_1 [\![Y_2$. ■

Example 5.6

Let us consider the knowledge base as in Example 5.5. In this knowledge base for sets $Y_1 = \{y_2, y_3, y_4\}$ and $Y_2 = \{y_2, y_3, y_6, y_7\}$, the lower approximation is given as $\underline{R}Y_1 = \{x_1, x_5\}$ and $\underline{R}Y_2 = \{x_1, x_3, x_5\}$. Therefore, $\underline{R}Y_1 \subseteq \underline{R}Y_2$. It implies that Y_1 is bottom R-included in the set Y_2. Again, on taking $Y_1 = \{y_2, y_3, y_6\}$ and $Y_2 = \{y_2, y_7\}$, it can be seen as $\overline{R}Y_1 = \{x_1, x_3, x_5\}$ and $\overline{R}Y_2 = \{x_1, x_3, x_4, x_5\}$. Thus, $\overline{R}Y_1 \subseteq \overline{R}Y_2$. It indicates that Y_1 is top R-included in the set Y_2. Similarly, on taking $Y_1 = \{y_2, y_3\}$ and $Y_2 = \{y_2, y_3, y_6, y_7\}$, one can obtain lower and upper approximation as $\underline{R}Y_1 = \{x_1, x_5\}$; $\underline{R}Y_2 = \{x_1, x_3, x_5\}$; $\overline{R}Y_1 = \{x_1, x_5\}$; and $\overline{R}Y_2 = \{x_1, x_3, x_4, x_5\}$. Therefore, $\underline{R}Y_1 \subseteq \underline{R}Y_2$ and $\overline{R}Y_1 \subseteq \overline{R}Y_2$. It indicates that Y_1 is R-included in the set Y_2.

Proposition 5.2

The following properties of relations $[\![_B$, $[\![_T$, and $[\![$ are immediate consequences of the definitions. Let U and V be two universal sets and $R \subseteq (U \times V)$ be a binary relation. Then for $Y_1, Y_2 \subseteq V$, the following properties hold. ■

1. If $Y_1 \subseteq Y_2$, then $Y_1 [\![_B Y_2$, $Y_1 [\![_T Y_2$, and $Y_1 [\![Y_2$.
2. If $Y_1 [\![_B Y_2$ and $Y_2 [\![_B Y_1$, then $Y_1 \approx_B Y_2$.
3. If $Y_1 [\![_T Y_2$ and $Y_2 [\![_T Y_1$, then $Y_1 \approx_T Y_2$.
4. If $Y_1 [\![Y_2$ and $Y_2 [\![Y_1$, then $Y_1 \approx Y_2$.
5. $Y_1 [\![_T Y_2$ if and only if $(Y_1 \cup Y_2) \approx_T Y_2$.
6. $Y_1 [\![_B Y_2$ if and only if $(Y_1 \cap Y_2) \approx_B Y_1$.
7. If $Y_1 \subseteq Y_2$, $Y_1 \approx_B Y_1'$ and $Y_2 \approx_B Y_2'$, then $Y_1' [\![_B Y_2'$.
8. If $Y_1 \subseteq Y_2$, $Y_1 \approx_T Y_1'$ and $Y_2 \approx_T Y_2'$, then $Y_1' [\![_T Y_2'$.
9. If $Y_1 \subseteq Y_2$, $Y_1 \approx Y_1'$ and $Y_2 \approx Y_2'$, then $Y_1' [\![Y_2'$.
10. If $Y_1' [\![_T Y_1$ and $Y_2' [\![_T Y_2$, then $(Y_1' \cup Y_2') [\![_T (Y_1 \cup Y_2)$.
11. If $Y_1' [\![_B Y_1$ and $Y_2' [\![_B Y_2$, then $(Y_1' \cap Y_2') [\![_B (Y_1 \cap Y_2)$.
12. $(Y_1 \cap Y_2) [\![_B Y_1 [\![_T (Y_1 \cup Y_2)$.
13. If $Y_1 [\![_B Y_2$ and $Y_1 \approx_B Y_3$, then $Y_3 [\![_B Y_2$.
14. If $Y_1 [\![_T Y_2$ and $Y_1 \approx_T Y_3$, then $Y_3 [\![_T Y_2$.
15. If $Y_1 [\![Y_2$ and $Y_1 \approx Y_3$, then $Y_3 [\![Y_2$.

5.4 Fuzzy Rough Set Based on Two Universal Sets

The basic idea of rough sets, introduced by Pawlak (1982, 1991), depends upon the notion of equivalence relations defined over a universe U. However, equivalence relations in real-life problems are relatively rare in practice. Therefore, efforts have been made to make the relations less significant by removing one or more of the three requirements of an equivalence relation. A fuzzy relation is an extension of the concept of a relation on any set U. Therefore, fuzzy rough sets by Dubois and Prade (1990) generalize the concepts of Pawlak rough sets. Further, it is generalized to fuzzy rough sets in two universal sets by Guilong Liu (2010). However, for completeness of the chapter, the definitions and basic concepts of fuzzy rough sets on two universal sets are stated in this section.

Let U be a universe of discourse and x be a particular element of U. A fuzzy set X of U is defined as a collection of ordered pairs $(x, \mu_X(x))$, where $\mu_X(x)$: $U \rightarrow [0, 1]$ is a mapping known as the membership function of X. The family of all fuzzy sets in U is denoted as $F(U)$.

Let U and V be two nonempty universal sets. Let R_F be a fuzzy binary relation from $U \rightarrow V$. Therefore, (U, V, R_F) is called a fuzzy approximation space. For any $Y \in F(V)$ and the fuzzy binary relation R_F, we associate two subsets $\underline{R_F} Y$ and $\overline{R_F} Y$, called the R_F-lower and R_F-upper approximations of Y, respectively. A fuzzy rough set (Liu 2010) is a pair $(\underline{R_F} Y, \overline{R_F} Y)$ of fuzzy sets on U such that for every $x \in U$,

$$(\underline{R_F} Y)x = \bigwedge_{y \in V} ((1 - \mu_{R_F}(x, y)) \vee Y(y)) \tag{5.10}$$

$$(\overline{R_F} Y)x = \bigvee_{y \in V} (\mu_{R_F}(x, y) \wedge Y(y)) \tag{5.11}$$

Definition 5.9

Let U and V be two universal sets and R_F be a fuzzy relation from $U \to V$. If $x \in U$ and $\mu_{R_F}(x, y) = 0$ for all $y \in V$, then x is called a solitary element with respect to R_F. The set of all solitary elements with respect to the fuzzy relation R_F is called a solitary set and is denoted as S, where

$$S = \{x : x \in U, \mu_{R_F}(x, y) = 0 \quad \forall \ y \in V\} \text{ and } \mu_{R_F}(x, y) = \text{Minimum } (\mu_U(x), \mu_V(y)). \quad ■$$

5.4.1 Algebraic Properties of Fuzzy Rough Set Based on Two Universal Sets

The algebraic properties of fuzzy rough sets on two universal sets as established by Guilong Liu (2010) and important in the context of rough sets are stated in the following. Let U and V be two universal sets. Let R_F be a fuzzy relation from U to V, and S the solitary set with respect to R_F. Then for $X, Y \in F(V)$, the following properties hold:

1. $\overline{R_F}\phi \subseteq S$, $\underline{R_F}\phi = \phi$, $\underline{R_F}V = U$ and $\overline{R_F}V = S'$, where S' denotes the complement of S in U.
2. $S \subseteq \overline{R_F}X$ and $\underline{R_F}X \subseteq S'$.
3. If $S \neq \phi$, then $\underline{R_F}X \neq \overline{R_F}X$.
4. For any given index set I, $X_i \in F(V)$, $\underline{R_F}(\bigcap_{i \in I} X_i) = \bigcap_{i \in I} \underline{R_F}X_i$ and $\overline{R_F}(\bigcup_{i \in I} X_i) = \bigcup_{i \in I} \overline{R_F}X_i$.
5. If $X \subseteq Y$, then $\underline{R_F}X \subseteq \underline{R_F}Y$ and $\overline{R_F}X \subseteq \overline{R_F}Y$.
6. $\underline{R_F}X \cup \underline{R_F}Y \subseteq \underline{R_F}(X \cup Y)$, and $\overline{R_F}(X \cap Y) \subseteq \overline{R_F}X \cap \overline{R_F}Y$.
7. $(\underline{R_F}X)' = \overline{R_F}X'$ and $(\overline{R_F}X)' = \underline{R_F}X'$.

5.4.2 Topological Characterization of Fuzzy Rough Set Based on Two Universal Sets

This section introduces an interesting topological characterization of fuzzy rough set on two universal sets employing the notion of the lower and upper approximation. It results in four important and different types of fuzzy rough sets on two universal sets, shown as follows. Here, $A > 0$ represents those elements of A having positive membership value.

Type 1: If $(\underline{R_F}Y)_{>0} \neq \phi$ and $(\overline{R_F}Y)_{>0} \neq U$, then Y is *roughly R_F-definable* on two universal sets.

Type 2: If $(\underline{R_F}Y)_{>0} = \phi$ and $(\overline{R_F}Y)_{>0} \neq U$, then Y is *internally R_F-undefinable* on two universal sets.

Type 3: If $(\underline{R_F}Y)_{>0} \neq \phi$ and $(\overline{R_F}Y)_{>0} = U$, then Y is *externally R_F-undefinable* on two universal sets.

Type 4: If $(\underline{R_F}Y)_{>0} = \phi$ and $\overline{R_F}Y = U$, then Y is *totally R_F-undefinable* on two universal sets.

5.4.3 Real-Life Application of Fuzzy Multicriteria Decision Making

This section depicts a real-life application such as fuzzy multicriteria decision making of a fuzzy rough set on two universal sets. The model application is explained as fuzzy rough set upper approximation. Let us consider multicriteria decision making in the case of supermarkets in a particular territory. Let us set the criteria $V = \{v_1, v_2, v_3, v_4, v_5, v_6\}$, in which v_1 denotes the best possible value for a customer's money; v_2 denotes the quality of the product; v_3 denotes the behavior of supporting staff; v_4 denotes the location of the supermarket; v_5 denotes availability of items; and v_6 denotes offers. Let us consider the decisions $U = \{d_1, d_2, d_3, d_4, d_5\}$, in which d_1 denotes outstanding; d_2 denotes most welcome; d_3 denotes welcome; d_4 denotes least welcome; and d_5 denotes not welcome. Several varieties of customers and professionals are invited to a survey that only focuses on the criterion of best possible value for customers' money in a supermarket. If 15% of people select "outstanding," 25% select "most welcome," 35% select "welcome," 10% select "least welcome," and 15% select "not welcome," then the vector can be obtained as $(0.15, 0.25, 0.35, 0.1, 0.15)^t$, where t represents the transpose. Similarly, the decisions based on other criteria are obtained as follows: $(0, 0.35, 0.45, 0.1, 0.1)^t$, $(0.55, 0.15, 0.2, 0, 0.1)^t$, $(0.1, 0.1, 0.45, 0.2, 0.2)^t$, $(0, 0, 0.15, 0.35, 0.5)^t$, and $(0.25, 0.25, 0.2, 0.1, 0.2)^t$. Based on the aforementioned decision vectors, the fuzzy relation R_F from U to V is presented by the following matrix:

$$R_F = \begin{pmatrix} 0.15 & 0.1 & 0.55 & 0.1 & 0 & 0.25 \\ 0.25 & 0.35 & 0.15 & 0.1 & 0 & 0.25 \\ 0.35 & 0.25 & 0.2 & 0.4 & 0.15 & 0.2 \\ 0.1 & 0.1 & 0 & 0.2 & 0.35 & 0.1 \\ 0.15 & 0.2 & 0.1 & 0.2 & 0.5 & 0.2 \end{pmatrix}$$

It is assumed that there are two categories of customers, where right weights for each criterion in V are $Y_1 = (0.35, 0.15, 0.2, 0.1, 0.1, 0.01)$ and $Y_2 = (0.2, 0.4, 0.15, 0.1, 0.1, 0.05)$, respectively. By using upper approximation, they are obtained as

$$\bar{R}Y_1 = (0.2, 0.25, 0.35, 0.1, 0.15)^t$$

$$\bar{R}Y_2 = (0.15, 0.35, 0.25, 0.1, 0.2)^t$$

From this analysis, according to the principle of maximum membership, the decision for the first category of customers is "welcome," whereas the decision for the second category of customers is "most welcome."

5.5 Intuitionistic Fuzzy Rough Set Based on Two Universal Sets

In the previous section, Guilong Liu's (2010) fuzzy rough set based on two universal sets is discussed. In fuzzy set theory, the nonmembership values are not considered, and we assume that membership values of all elements exist. However, it is not true in many real-life problems, due to the presence of hesitation. In fuzzy set theory, if $\mu(x)$ is the degree of membership of an element x, then the degree of nonmembership of x is calculated using the mathematical formula $(1 - \mu(x))$, with the assumption that the full part of the degree of membership is determinism and the indeterministic part is zero. This is not always applicable in real life, and hence, intuitionistic fuzzy set theory is better. At the same time, intuitionistic fuzzy set theory reduces to fuzzy set theory if the indeterministic part is zero. It indicates that the intuitionistic fuzzy set model is a generalized model over the fuzzy set model. Therefore, an intuitionistic fuzzy rough set on two universal sets is a better model than a fuzzy rough set on two universal sets. To unfold the chapter, the definitions, notations, and results of the intuitionistic fuzzy rough set on two universal sets are discussed (Acharjya and Tripathy 2012). The chapter uses the standard notation μ for membership and v for nonmembership functions that are associated with an intuitionistic fuzzy set.

Definition 5.10 (Atanasov 1986)

Let U be a universe of discourse and x be a particular element of U. An intuitionistic fuzzy set X of U is defined as $<x, \mu_X(x), v_X(x)>$, where the functions $\mu_X: U \rightarrow [0,1]$ and $v_X: U \rightarrow [0,1]$ define the degree of membership and degree of nonmembership, respectively, of the element $x \in U$ to the set X, and for every $x \in U$, $0 \le \mu_X(x) + v_X(x) \le 1$. The amount $\pi_X(x) = 1 - (\mu_X(x) + v_X(x))$ is called the hesitation part, which may cater to either a membership value or nonmembership value or both. For simplicity, the notation (μ_X, v_X) is used to denote the intuitionistic fuzzy set X. The family of all intuitionistic fuzzy subsets of U is denoted by $IF(U)$. The complement of an intuitionistic fuzzy set X is denoted by

$$X' = \{< x, v_X(x), \mu_X(x) >|x \in U\}.$$

Definition 5.11 (Atanasov 1986)

Let U and V be two nonempty universal sets. An intuitionistic fuzzy relation R_{IF} from $U \rightarrow V$ is an intuitionistic fuzzy set of $(U \times V)$ characterized by the membership function μ_R and nonmembership function v_R, where

$$R_{IF} = \{< (x, y), \mu_{R_{IF}} (x, y), v_{R_{IF}} (x, y) >\,|\,x \in U, y \in V\}$$

with $0 \le \mu_{R_{IF}} (x, y) + v_{R_{IF}} (x, y) \le 1$ for every $(x, y) \in U \times V$. ■

Definition 5.12

Let U and V be two universal sets and R_{IF} be an intuitionistic fuzzy relation from U to V. If $x \in U$, $\mu_{R_{IF}} (x, y) = 0$, and $v_{R_{IF}} (x, y) = 1$ for all $y \in V$, then x is said to be a solitary element with respect to R_{IF}. The set of all solitary elements with respect to the relation R_{IF} is called the solitary set S. That is,

$$S = \{x \mid x \in U, \mu_{R_{IF}}(x,y) = 0, \nu_{R_{IF}}(x,y) = 1 \; \forall \; y \in V\}. \qquad ■$$

Definition 5.13

Let U and V be two nonempty universal sets and R_{IF} be an intuitionistic fuzzy relation from U to V. Therefore, (U, V, R_{IF}) is called an intuitionistic fuzzy approximation space. For $Y \in IF(V)$, an intuitionistic fuzzy rough set is a pair $(\underline{R_{IF}Y}, \overline{R_{IF}Y})$ of intuitionistic fuzzy sets on U such that for every $x \in U$,

$$\underline{R_{IF}Y} = \{< x, \mu_{\underline{R_{IF}(Y)}}(x), \nu_{\underline{R_{IF}(Y)}}(x) > \mid x \in U\} \qquad (5.12)$$

$$\overline{R_{IF}Y} = \{< x, \mu_{\overline{R_{IF}(Y)}}(x), \nu_{\overline{R_{IF}(Y)}}(x) > \mid x \in U\} \qquad (5.13)$$

where

$\mu_{\underline{R_{IF}(Y)}}(x) = \bigwedge\limits_{y \in V} [\nu_{R_{IF}}(x,y) \vee \mu_Y(y)];$

$\nu_{\underline{R_{IF}(Y)}}(x) = \bigvee\limits_{y \in V} [\mu_{R_{IF}}(x,y) \wedge \nu_Y(y)]$

$\mu_{\overline{R_{IF}(Y)}}(x) = \bigvee\limits_{y \in V} [\mu_{R_{IF}}(x,y) \wedge \mu_Y(y)]$ and

$\nu_{\overline{R_{IF}(Y)}}(x) = \bigwedge\limits_{y \in V} [\nu_{R_{IF}}(x,y) \vee \nu_Y(y)]$

The pair $(\underline{R_{IF}Y}, \overline{R_{IF}Y})$ is called the intuitionistic fuzzy rough set of Y with respect to (U, V, R_{IF}), where $\underline{R_{IF}}, \overline{R_{IF}} : IF(U) \rightarrow IF(V)$ are referred to as lower and upper intuitionistic fuzzy rough approximation operators on two universal sets, respectively. ■

5.5.1 Algebraic Properties of Intuitionistic Fuzzy Rough Set Based on Two Universal Sets

This section discusses the algebraic properties of an intuitionistic fuzzy rough set on two universal sets through a solitary set that are interesting and valuable in the study of intuitionistic fuzzy rough sets on two universal sets. These properties are useful in finding knowledge from the universe.

Proposition 5.3

Let U and V be two universal sets. Let R_{IF} be an intuitionistic fuzzy relation from U to V, and further, let S be the solitary set with respect to R_{IF}. Then for $X, Y \in F(V)$, the following properties hold:

1. $R_{IF}(V) = U$ and $\overline{R_{IF}}(\phi) = \phi$.
2. If $X \subseteq Y$, then $\underline{R_{IF}}(X) \subseteq \underline{R_{IF}}(Y)$ and $\overline{R_{IF}}(X) \subseteq \overline{R_{IF}}(Y)$.
3. $\underline{R_{IF}}(X) = (\overline{R_{IF}}(X'))'$ and $\overline{R_{IF}}(X) = (\underline{R_{IF}}(X'))'$.
4. $\underline{R_{IF}}\phi \supseteq S$ and $\overline{R_{IF}}V \subseteq S'$, where S' denotes the complement of S in U.
5. For any given index set J, $X_i \in IF(V)$, $\underline{R_{IF}}(\bigcup\limits_{i \in J} X_i) \supseteq \bigcup\limits_{i \in J} \underline{R_{IF}}X_i$ and $\overline{R_{IF}}(\bigcap\limits_{i \in J} X_i) \subseteq \bigcap\limits_{i \in J} \overline{R_{IF}}X_i$.
6. For any given index set J, $X_i \in IF(V)$, $\underline{R_{IF}}(\bigcap\limits_{i \in J} X_i) = \bigcap\limits_{i \in J} \underline{R_{IF}}X_i$ and $\overline{R_{IF}}(\bigcup\limits_{i \in J} X_i) = \bigcup\limits_{i \in J} \overline{R_{IF}}X_i$. ■

5.5.2 *Knowledge Representation*

In Section 5.2.4, a real-life problem is discussed in which the relation between customers and the supermarkets in a particular metropolitan city is studied. However, it is observed that due to several factors such as best possible value for the customer's money, quality of the product, style, and the behavior of the supporting staff, customers depend on more than one supermarket. Therefore, from customer behavior, it is clear that they are not happy with one supermarket. Hence, an intuitionistic fuzzy relation better depicts the relation between the customers and supermarkets. To make our analysis simple, a small universe U of five customers and another small universe V of six supermarkets are considered in a particular city. Therefore, (U, V, R_{IF}) is an intuitionistic fuzzy approximation space, where $U = \{c_1, c_2, c_3, c_4, c_5\}$ and $V = \{m_1, m_2, m_3, m_4, m_5, m_6\}$. We define the intuitionistic fuzzy relation $R_{IF} \in IF(U \times V)$ by the following matrix:

$$R_{IF} = \begin{array}{c} \\ c_1 \\ c_2 \\ c_3 \\ c_4 \\ c_5 \end{array} \begin{bmatrix} m_1 & m_2 & m_3 & m_4 & m_5 & m_6 \\ 0.8,0.1 & 0.2,0.5 & 0.6,0.2 & 0.4,0.4 & 0,1 & 0.4,0.2 \\ 0.7,0.3 & 0.9,0.1 & 0.5,0.4 & 1,0 & 0.4,0.5 & 0.5,0.4 \\ 0.3,0.6 & 0.6,0.2 & 0.4,0.5 & 0.3,0.4 & 0.2,0.4 & 0.3,0.3 \\ 0.5,0.5 & 0.3,0.6 & 0.7,0.2 & 0.6,0.3 & 0.2,0.4 & 0.6,0.4 \\ 0.7,0.2 & 0.1,0.8 & 0.4,0.3 & 0.5,0.4 & 0,0.6 & 0.5,0.2 \end{bmatrix}$$

Let us consider an intuitionistic fuzzy set $Y = \{<m_1, 0.6, 0.2>, <m_2, 0.5, 0.4>, <m_3, 0.3, 0.5>, <m_4, 0.8, 0.1>, <m_5, 1, 0>, <m_6, 0.7, 0.2>$. Thus, by Definition 5.13,

$$\mu_{\underline{R_{IF}}(Y)}(c_1) = \bigwedge_{y \in V}[\nu_{R_{IF}}(c_1, y) \vee \mu_Y(y)]$$

$$= [0.1 \vee 0.6] \wedge [0.5 \vee 0.5] \wedge [0.2 \vee 0.3] \wedge [0.4 \vee 0.8] \wedge [1 \vee 1] \wedge [0.2 \vee 0.7]$$

$$= 0.6 \wedge 0.5 \wedge 0.3 \wedge 0.8 \wedge 1 \wedge 0.7$$

$$= 0.3$$

$$\nu_{\underline{R_{IF}}(Y)}(c_1) = \bigvee_{y \in V} [\mu_{R_{IF}}(c_1, y) \wedge \nu_Y(y)]$$

$$= [0.8 \wedge 0.2] \vee [0.2 \wedge 0.4] \vee [0.6 \wedge 0.5] \vee [0.4 \wedge 0.1] \vee [0 \wedge 0] \vee [0.4 \wedge 0.2]$$

$$= 0.2 \vee 0.2 \vee 0.5 \vee 0.1 \vee 0 \vee 0.2$$

$$= 0.5$$

$$\mu_{\underline{R_{IF}}(Y)}(c_2) = \bigwedge_{y \in V} [\nu_{R_{IF}}(c_2, y) \vee \mu_Y(y)]$$

$$= [0.3 \vee 0.6] \wedge [0.1 \vee 0.5] \wedge [0.4 \vee 0.3] \wedge [0 \vee 0.8] \wedge [0.5 \vee 1] \wedge [0.4 \vee 0.7]$$

$$= 0.6 \wedge 0.5 \wedge 0.4 \wedge 0.8 \wedge 1 \wedge 0.7$$

$$= 0.4$$

$$\nu_{\underline{R_{IF}}(Y)}(c_2) = \bigvee_{y \in V} [\mu_{R_{IF}}(c_2, y) \wedge \nu_Y(y)]$$

$$= [0.7 \wedge 0.2] \vee [0.9 \wedge 0.4] \vee [0.5 \wedge 0.5] \vee [1 \wedge 0.1] \vee [0.4 \wedge 0] \vee [0.5 \wedge 0.2]$$

$$= 0.2 \vee 0.4 \vee 0.5 \vee 0.1 \vee 0 \vee 0.2$$

$$= 0.5$$

$$\mu_{\underline{R_{IF}}(Y)}(c_3) = \bigwedge_{y \in V} [\nu_{R_{IF}}(c_3, y) \vee \mu_Y(y)]$$

$$= [0.6 \vee 0.6] \wedge [0.2 \vee 0.5] \wedge [0.5 \vee 0.3] \wedge [0.4 \vee 0.8] \wedge [0.4 \vee 1] \wedge [0.3 \vee 0.7]$$

$$= 0.6 \wedge 0.5 \wedge 0.5 \wedge 0.8 \wedge 1 \wedge 0.7$$

$$= 0.5$$

$$\nu_{\underline{R_{IF}}(Y)}(c_3) = \bigvee_{y \in V} [\mu_{R_{IF}}(c_3, y) \wedge \nu_Y(y)]$$

$$= [0.3 \wedge 0.2] \vee [0.6 \wedge 0.4] \vee [0.4 \wedge 0.5] \vee [0.3 \wedge 0.1] \vee [0.2 \wedge 0] \vee [0.3 \wedge 0.2]$$

$$= 0.2 \vee 0.4 \vee 0.4 \vee 0.1 \vee 0 \vee 0.2$$

$$= 0.4$$

$$\mu_{\underline{R_{IF}(Y)}}(c_4) = \underset{y \in V}{\wedge} [\nu_{R_{IF}}(c_4, y) \vee \mu_Y(y)]$$

$$= [0.5 \vee 0.6] \wedge [0.6 \vee 0.5] \wedge [0.2 \vee 0.3] \wedge [0.3 \vee 0.8] \wedge [0.4 \vee 1] \wedge [0.4 \vee 0.7]$$

$$= 0.6 \wedge 0.6 \wedge 0.3 \wedge 0.8 \wedge 1 \wedge 0.7$$

$$= 0.3$$

$$\nu_{\underline{R_{IF}(Y)}}(c_4) = \underset{y \in V}{\vee} [\mu_{R_{IF}}(c_4, y) \wedge \nu_Y(y)]$$

$$= [0.5 \wedge 0.2] \vee [0.3 \wedge 0.4] \vee [0.7 \wedge 0.5] \vee [0.6 \wedge 0.1] \vee [0.2 \wedge 0] \vee [0.6 \wedge 0.2]$$

$$= 0.2 \vee 0.3 \vee 0.5 \vee 0.1 \vee 0 \vee 0.2$$

$$= 0.5$$

$$\mu_{\underline{R_{IF}(Y)}}(c_5) = \underset{y \in V}{\wedge} [\nu_{R_{IF}}(c_5, y) \vee \mu_Y(y)]$$

$$= [0.2 \vee 0.6] \wedge [0.8 \vee 0.5] \wedge [0.3 \vee 0.3] \wedge [0.4 \vee 0.8] \wedge [0.6 \vee 1] \wedge [0.2 \vee 0.7]$$

$$= 0.6 \wedge 0.8 \wedge 0.3 \wedge 0.8 \wedge 1 \wedge 0.7$$

$$= 0.3$$

$$\nu_{\underline{R_{IF}(Y)}}(c_5) = \underset{y \in V}{\vee} [\mu_{R_{IF}}(c_5, y) \wedge \nu_Y(y)]$$

$$= [0.7 \wedge 0.2] \vee [0.1 \wedge 0.4] \vee [0.4 \wedge 0.5] \vee [0.5 \wedge 0.1] \vee [0 \wedge 0] \vee [0.5 \wedge 0.2]$$

$$= 0.2 \vee 0.1 \vee 0.4 \vee 0.1 \vee 0 \vee 0.2$$

$$= 0.4$$

Hence, the lower approximation is given as

$$\underline{R_{IF}}Y = \{< c_1, 0.3, 0.5 >, < c_2, 0.4, 0.5 >, < c_3, 0.5, 0.4 >, < c_4, 0.3, 0.5 >, < c_5, 0.3, 0.4 >\}$$

Similarly,

$$\mu_{\overline{R_{IF}(Y)}}(c_1) = \underset{y \in V}{\vee} [\mu_{R_{IF}}(c_1, y) \wedge \mu_Y(y)]$$

$$= [0.8 \wedge 0.6] \vee [0.2 \wedge 0.5] \vee [0.6 \wedge 0.3] \vee [0.4 \wedge 0.8] \vee [0 \wedge 1] \vee [0.4 \wedge 0.7]$$

$$= 0.6 \vee 0.2 \vee 0.3 \vee 0.4 \vee 0 \vee 0.4$$

$$= 0.6$$

$$\nu_{\overline{R_{IF}(Y)}}(c_1) = \bigwedge_{y \in V} [\nu_{R_{IF}}(c_1, y) \vee \nu_Y(y)]$$

$$= [0.1 \vee 0.2] \wedge [0.5 \vee 0.4] \wedge [0.2 \vee 0.5] \wedge [0.4 \vee 0.1] \wedge [1 \vee 0] \wedge [0.2 \vee 0.2]$$

$$= 0.2 \wedge 0.5 \wedge 0.5 \wedge 0.4 \wedge 1 \wedge 0.2$$

$$= 0.2$$

$$\mu_{\overline{R_{IF}(Y)}}(c_2) = \bigvee_{y \in V} [\mu_{R_{IF}}(c_2, y) \wedge \mu_Y(y)]$$

$$= [0.7 \wedge 0.6] \vee [0.9 \wedge 0.5] \vee [0.5 \wedge 0.3] \vee [1 \wedge 0.8] \vee [0.4 \wedge 1] \vee [0.5 \wedge 0.7]$$

$$= 0.6 \vee 0.5 \vee 0.3 \vee 0.8 \vee 0.4 \vee 0.5$$

$$= 0.8$$

$$\nu_{\overline{R_{IF}(Y)}}(c_2) = \bigwedge_{y \in V} [\nu_{R_{IF}}(c_2, y) \vee \nu_Y(y)]$$

$$= [0.3 \vee 0.2] \wedge [0.1 \vee 0.4] \wedge [0.4 \vee 0.5] \wedge [0 \vee 0.1] \wedge [0.5 \vee 0] \wedge [0.4 \vee 0.2]$$

$$= 0.3 \wedge 0.4 \wedge 0.5 \wedge 0.1 \wedge 0.5 \wedge 0.4$$

$$= 0.1$$

$$\mu_{\overline{R_{IF}(Y)}}(c_3) = \bigvee_{y \in V} [\mu_{R_{IF}}(c_3, y) \wedge \mu_Y(y)]$$

$$= [0.3 \wedge 0.6] \vee [0.6 \wedge 0.5] \vee [0.4 \wedge 0.3] \vee [0.3 \wedge 0.8] \vee [0.2 \wedge 1] \vee [0.3 \wedge 0.7]$$

$$= 0.3 \vee 0.5 \vee 0.3 \vee 0.3 \vee 0.2 \vee 0.3$$

$$= 0.5$$

$$\nu_{\overline{R_{IF}(Y)}}(c_3) = \bigwedge_{y \in V} [\nu_{R_{IF}}(c_3, y) \vee \nu_Y(y)]$$

$$= [0.6 \vee 0.2] \wedge [0.2 \vee 0.4] \wedge [0.5 \vee 0.5] \wedge [0.4 \vee 0.1] \wedge [0.4 \vee 0] \wedge [0.3 \vee 0.2]$$

$$= 0.6 \wedge 0.4 \wedge 0.5 \wedge 0.4 \wedge 0.4 \wedge 0.3$$

$$= 0.3$$

$$\mu_{\overline{R_{IF}(Y)}}(c_4) = \underset{y \in V}{\vee} [\mu_{R_{IF}}(c_4, y) \wedge \mu_Y(y)]$$

$$= [0.5 \wedge 0.6] \vee [0.3 \wedge 0.5] \vee [0.7 \wedge 0.3] \vee [0.6 \wedge 0.8] \vee [0.2 \wedge 1] \vee [0.6 \wedge 0.7]$$

$$= 0.5 \vee 0.3 \vee 0.3 \vee 0.6 \vee 0.2 \vee 0.6$$

$$= 0.6$$

$$\nu_{\overline{R_{IF}(Y)}}(c_4) = \underset{y \in V}{\wedge} [\nu_{R_{IF}}(c_4, y) \vee \nu_Y(y)]$$

$$= [0.5 \vee 0.2] \wedge [0.6 \vee 0.4] \wedge [0.2 \vee 0.5] \wedge [0.3 \vee 0.1] \wedge [0.4 \vee 0] \wedge [0.4 \vee 0.2]$$

$$= 0.5 \wedge 0.6 \wedge 0.5 \wedge 0.3 \wedge 0.4 \wedge 0.4$$

$$= 0.3$$

$$\mu_{\overline{R_{IF}(Y)}}(c_5) = \underset{y \in V}{\vee} [\mu_{R_{IF}}(c_5, y) \wedge \mu_Y(y)]$$

$$= [0.7 \wedge 0.6] \vee [0.1 \wedge 0.5] \vee [0.4 \wedge 0.3] \vee [0.5 \wedge 0.8] \vee [0 \wedge 1] \vee [0.5 \wedge 0.7]$$

$$= 0.6 \vee 0.1 \vee 0.3 \vee 0.5 \vee 0 \vee 0.5$$

$$= 0.6$$

$$\nu_{\overline{R_{IF}(Y)}}(c_5) = \underset{y \in V}{\wedge} [\nu_{R_{IF}}(c_5, y) \vee \nu_Y(y)]$$

$$= [0.2 \vee 0.2] \wedge [0.8 \vee 0.4] \wedge [0.3 \vee 0.5] \wedge [0.4 \vee 0.1] \wedge [0.6 \vee 0] \wedge [0.2 \vee 0.2]$$

$$= 0.2 \wedge 0.8 \wedge 0.5 \wedge 0.4 \wedge 0.6 \wedge 0.2$$

$$= 0.2$$

Hence, the lower approximation is given as

$$\overline{R_{IF}Y} = \{< c_1, 0.6, 0.2 >, < c_2, 0.8, 0.1 >, < c_3, 0.5, 0.3 >, < c_4, 0.6, 0.3 >, < c_5, 0.6, 0.2 >\}$$

5.6 Conclusion

This chapter extends the study of rough sets on two universal sets further by defining their topological characterization and establishing results on intersection or union of any two elements of any topological characterization. Also, the study has extended further by defining approximation of classifications, rough equality, and rough inclusion in the context of a rough set on two universal sets. The accuracy and quality of approximation of classification are also defined. Also, through propositions, the inexactness of classification using topological means as in the case of sets is described. The different types of fuzzy rough sets on two universal sets and their application to multicriteria decision making are defined. Finally, an intuitionistic fuzzy rough set on two universal sets and its properties are studied. A real-life example to verify the concepts developed for application in knowledge extraction and design of knowledge bases is provided. Further research is planned to evaluate the model in the context of multigranulation, where more than one binary relation is used to study real-life problems.

References

Acharjya, D. P. 2009. Comparative study of rough sets on fuzzy approximation spaces and intuitionistic fuzzy approximation spaces. *International Journal of Computational and Applied Mathematics* 4:95–106.

Acharjya, D. P. 2013. Rough computing based information retrieval in knowledge discovery databases. In *Information and Knowledge Management-Tools, Techniques and Practices*, ed. Roy, A. K., 123–153. New-India Publishing Company, New Delhi, India.

Acharjya, D. P. and Ezhilarasi, L. 2011. A knowledge mining model for ranking institutions using rough computing with ordering rules and formal concept analysis. *International Journal of Computer Science Issues* 8:417–425.

Acharjya, D. P. and Tripathy, B. K. 2012. Intuitionistic fuzzy rough set on two universal sets and knowledge representation. *Mathematical Sciences-International Research Journal* 1:584–598.

Acharjya, D. P. and Tripathy, B. K. 2013. Topological characterization, measures of uncertainty and rough equality of sets on two universal sets. *International Journal of Intelligent Systems and Applications* 5:16–24.

Atanasov, K. T. 1986. Intuitionistic fuzzy sets. *Fuzzy Sets and Systems* 20:87–96.

Bonikowski, Z. 1994. Aggebraic structure of rough sets. In *Rough Sets, Fuzzy Sets and Knowledge Discovery*, ed. Ziarko, W. P., 242–247. Springer-Verlag, USA.

Chen, D., Zhang, W., Yeung, D. and Tsang, E. C. C. 2006. Rough approximations on a complete completely distributive lattice with applications to generalized rough sets. *Information Sciences* 176:1829–1848.

Dubois, D. and Prade, H. 1990. Rough fuzzy sets and fuzzy rough sets. *International Journal of General System* 17:191–209.

Grzymala-Busse, J. W. 1988. Knowledge acquisition under uncertainty—A rough set approach. *Journal of Intelligent and Robotic System* 1:3–16.

Kondo, M. 2005. Algebraic approach to generalized rough sets. *Lecture Notes in Artificial Intelligence* 3641:132–140.

Kondo, M. 2006. On the structure of generalized rough sets. *Information Sciences* 176:589–600.

Kryszkiewlcz, M. 1998. Rough set approach to incomplete information systems. *Information Sciences* 112: 39–49.

Lin, T. Y. 1989. Neighborhood systems and approximation in database and knowledge base systems. In *Proceedings of the Fourth International Symposium on Methodologies of Intelligent Systems*, 75–86.

Lin, T. Y. 1998. Granular computing on binary relations I: Data mining and neighborhood systems. In *Rough Sets in Knowledge Discovery*, eds. Skoworn, A. and Polkowski, L., 107–121. Springer-Verlag, USA.

Lin, T. Y. 2005. Granular computing: Examples, intuitions and modeling. In *Proceeding of the IEEE International Conference on Granular Computing*, Beijing, China, 40–44.

Liu, G. L. 2005. Rough sets over the Boolean algebras. *Lecture Notes in Artificial Intelligence* 3641:24–31.

Liu, G. L. 2008. Generalized rough sets over fuzzy lattices. *Information Sciences* 178:1651–1662.

Liu, G. 2010. Rough set theory based on two universal sets and its applications. *Knowledge Based Systems* 23:110–115.

Molodtsov, D. 1999. Soft set theory-first results. *Computers and Mathematics with Applications* 37:19–31.

Novotny, M. and Pawlak, Z. 1985. Characterization of rough top equalities and rough bottom equalities. *Bulletin Polish Academy of Science and Mathematics* 33:91–97.

Pawlak, Z. 1982. Rough sets. *International Journal of Computer Information Science* 11:341–356.

Pawlak, Z. 1991. *Rough Sets: Theoretical Aspects of Reasoning about Data*. Kluwer Academic Publishers.

Pawlak, Z. 2004. Decision rules and flow networks. *European Journal of Operational Research* 154:184–190.

Pawlak, Z. and Skowron, A. 2007a. Rough sets: Some extensions. *Information Sciences* 177:28–40.

Pawlak, Z. and Skowron, A. 2007b. Rough sets and Boolean reasoning. *Information Sciences* 177:41–73.

Tripathy, B. K. and Acharjya, D. P. 2010. Knowledge mining using ordering rules and rough sets on fuzzy approximation spaces. *International Journal of Advances in Science and Technology* 1:41–50.

Tripathy, B. K. and Acharjya, D. P. 2011. Association rule granulation using rough sets on intuitionistic fuzzy approximation spaces and granular computing. *Annals. Computer Science Series* 9:125–144.

Tripathy, B. K. and Acharjya, D. P. 2012. Approximation of classification and measures of uncertainty in rough set on two universal sets. *International Journal of Advanced Science and Technology* 40:77–90.

Tripathy, B. K., Acharjya, D. P. and Cynthya, V. 2011a. A framework for intelligent medical diagnosis using rough set with formal concept analysis. *International Journal of Artificial Intelligence & Applications* 2:45–66.

Tripathy, B. K., Acharjya, D. P. and Ezhilarsi, L. 2011b. Topological characterization of rough set on two universal sets and knowledge representation. In *Global Trends in Information Systems and Software Applications*, eds. Krishna, P., Babu, M. and Ariwa, E., 68–81. Springer, Berlin, Heidelberg.

Wong, S. K. M., Wang, L. S. and Yao, Y. Y. 1993. Interval structure: A framework for representing uncertain information. In *Proceedings of the 8th Conference on Uncertainty in Artificial Intelligence*, 336–343.

Yao, Y. Y. 1998. Constructive and algebraic methods of the theory of rough sets. *Information Sciences* 109:21–47.

Zadeh, L. A. 1965. Fuzzy sets. *Information and Control* 8:338–353.

Zhong, N. and Skowron, A. 2001. A rough set-based knowledge discovery process. *International Journal of Applied Mathematics Computer Science* 11:603–619.

Zhu, W. 2006a. Properties of the first type of covering based rough sets. In *Proceedings of the Sixth IEEE International Conference on Data Mining*, 407–411.

Zhu, W. 2006b. Properties of the fourth type of covering based rough sets. In *Proceedings of the Sixth IEEE International Conference on Hybrid Intelligent Systems*, 43.

Zhu, W. 2006c. Properties of the second type of covering based rough sets. In *Proceedings of the IEEE International Conference on Web Intelligence and Intelligent Agent Technology*, 494–497.

Zhu, W. 2007. Generalized rough sets based on relations. *Information Sciences* 177:4997–5011.

Zhu, W. and Wang, F. Y. 2007. On three types of covering rough sets. *IEEE Transactions on Knowledge and Data Engineering* 19:1131–1144.

Chapter 6

Automating Network Protocol Identification

Ryan G. Goss and Geoff S. Nitschke

Contents

The proliferation of computer network users has, in recent years, placed a strain on network resources, such as bandwidth and number allocations. This issue is more apparent where connectivity is limited, such as in developing countries. The provisioning of services over these congested resources needs to be managed, ensuring a fair *quality of experience* (QoE) to consumers and producers alike. *Quality of service* (QoS) techniques used to manage such resources require constant revision, catering for new application protocols introduced to the network on a daily basis. This research proposes an efficient, autonomous method for distinguishing application protocols through the use of a *dynamic protocol classification system* (DPCS). Using this method, the burden of signature creation is reduced, while the accuracy achieved in application protocol identification increases.

6.1 Introduction

Computer networks have grown substantially in recent years, due in part to the increasing global reach of the Internet, network access speeds, and content availability. This growth continues to spur the development of numerous applications using both client–server and *peer-to-peer* (P2P) communication architectures. Each application uses a specific application protocol, generating a number of flows in order to exchange data. In computer networks, a flow describes a sequence of packet exchanges between hosts, uniquely identified by its 5-tuple identifier: *source IP address, destination IP address, source port, destination port*, and *protocol identifier*. In order to identify the underlying application protocol of a flow, a unique signature is required.

Network administrators traditionally used packet header information, such as source and destination ports and protocol, to formulate signatures and classify flows on a network. As this information is configured by the two communicating hosts, alternative port and protocol information can be negotiated, effectively negating the effect of port-based filters and restrictions (Alshammari and Zincir-Heywood 2008). This issue is problematic, since an increasing number of application developers seek to evade classification. P2P application protocols exacerbate this problem by operating in a decentralized manner, dynamically selecting the ports and protocols on which they communicate (Auld et al. 2007). The inefficiencies associated with classic port-based classification forced industry and researchers alike to consider a number of alternatives, such as *deep packet inspection* (DPI) and statistical analysis.

DPI has become an essential tool for network engineers, enabling them to search both packet header and payload (content) for predefined application protocol signatures (Huang and Zhang 2008). These signature matches are often performed using regular expressions in software or through the use of specialized hardware, such as a *field-programmable gate array* (FPGA) (Huang and Zhang 2008). While DPI yields excellent results in identifying plaintext flows, encryption renders the content of packets opaque and thus the use of DPI inept. Statistical analysis addresses the problem of opaque, encrypted flows by inferring the application (Gebski et al. 2006) or application class (Auld et al. 2007; Li et al. 2007; Moore and Papagiannaki 2005) of a flow by examining statistical information over a number of packet exchanges. The advantage of statistical analysis is that regardless of how applications attempt to disguise themselves, through encryption or port randomization, the characteristics exhibited over their packet exchanges remain intact.

The definition and provisioning of signatures are often a service provided by the vendors of traffic management devices through the supply of updated signature packs. These signature packs need to be regularly updated in order to keep up with advances in application protocol development. According to Szabo et al. (2007), this is one of the most significant problems associated with signature-based systems, since each vendor is responsible for the creation of their own proprietary signature packs, compatible with their systems. Furthermore, the attributes, or discriminators, extracted to describe a network flow and the mechanism employed to distinctly identify them are often a closely guarded secret. For these reasons, accuracy and performance variances between vendor equipment are not uncommon. The process of creating and deploying signatures in this manner is suboptimal, as the development of new application protocols far exceeds signature production by vendors. This results in a significant amount of network flows remaining unclassified or inaccurately classified until an update is released. This, in turn, results in network administrators being unable to manage the network resources at their disposal.

Given these issues, this research proposes a *dynamic protocol classifier* (DPC) method to address the two major issues pertinent in flow classification, *accuracy* and *automation*. Automation refers to methods that automate input from a user (manual annotation for new applications) or vendor (signature packs written for new classifiers). Using the proposed DPC method, new application protocols are automatically discovered in a training data set using a select set of discriminators. These discovered protocols are subsequently used to train artificial neural network (ANN) classifiers, in order to identify future instances of the protocols. Accuracy refers to the ability of such an automated method to discriminate between different application protocols and noise in training and test data, as well as the ability for trained ANN classifiers to correctly identify future instances of the protocol.

In order to increase the efficacy of clustered training data, the DPC method includes the *density-bases spatial clustering of applications with noise* (DBSCAN) method as its unsupervised learning component. DBSCAN is capable of forming arbitrarily shaped clusters to deal with noise in the data. We thus hypothesize that the DPC method will outperform (with statistical significance), for this case study, the accuracy achieved by a *hierarchical self-organizing map* (HSOM) (Goss and Nitschke 2013a) and *k*-means (Goss and Nitschke 2013b) method.

6.2 Related Work

Machine learning (ML) has been the subject of much research in classifying network traffic using flow statistics inferred from a network (Alshammari and Zincir-Heywood 2009; Auld et al. 2007; Bernaille et al. 2006). These statistical features, or discriminators, are calculated over multiple packet exchanges. ML classifiers are trained to associate particular discriminator sets, or patterns, with known traffic classes. The classifiers are then able to identify and differentiate future unclassified flows using previously learned rules (Nguyen and Armitage 2008). Hu and Shen (2012) compare the efficiency of several ML techniques, providing an overview of recent advances in this area. Hu and Shen (2012) present algorithms for the creation of specific feature sets and classification models, comparing the efficiency of each. The authors considered a number of classification methods, including *genetic algorithms* (GA) and Bayesian classification, as well as unsupervised clustering methods including *expectation maximum* (EM) clustering (Dempster et al. 1977) and *k*-means clustering (MacQueen 1967).

Two key metrics for measuring the performance of a traffic classification system are accuracy and completeness (Szabo et al. 2007). As such, the discriminators used to train classifiers and those used to test existing classifiers are significant. The quality of the discriminators used to describe a flow is crucial to the performance of an ML method (Nguyen and Armitage 2008) and has thus been the topic of research, including that of Auld et al. (2007), Bernaille et al. (2006), Este et al. (2008), Gargiulo et al. (2009), Moore and Papagiannaki (2005), Moore et al. (2005), McGregor et al. (2004), Huang and Zhang (2008), Alshammari and Zincir-Heywood (2007), and Li et al. (2007). As the number of applications encrypting their communications rises (Nascimento et al. 2013), the dependency on DPI wanes. Instead, the focus has shifted toward discriminators that remain effective through plaintext and encrypted flows. For example, McGregor et al. (2004) examine plots of packet size against packet *interarrival times* (IATs) for a number of flows. The authors concluded that the results of these plots were indicative of the application type. In addition to these discriminators, the authors described the flows through the extraction of byte counts, connection duration, number of transitions between transaction and bulk transfer modes, and the amount of time spent in the idle state. These characteristics were used by an EM algorithm, which grouped them into a small number of clusters.

Bernaille et al. (2005) dispute the use of discriminators such as IAT due to the influence of network load and *transport control protocol* (TCP) acknowledgements. Instead, the authors use the direction and size of each packet, recorded over a number of packet exchanges. Each flow record was transformed into a *hidden Markov model* (HMM). Thereafter, *spectral clustering* (Von Luxburg

2007) was used to find clusters in the likelihood space. The results of this work demonstrated a system capable of recognizing behavioral characteristics of a flow, with an accuracy performance of 90%, given observation of as little as the first several packets.

Li et al. (2007) demonstrate the classification of Internet traffic using a *support vector machine* (SVM) (Cortes and Vapnik 1995). The authors do so using 19 distinct discriminators, including the total number of packets in the flow, average packet size, duration of the flow, packet and byte ratios, and the average window size. Results showed a 99.41% degree of accuracy.

Alshammari and Zincir-Heywood (2009) focused on identifying the *Secure Shell* (SSH) and *Skype* application protocols. They do so by comparing five different ML techniques, including *AdaBoost* (Freund and Schapire 1995), SVM, naive Bayesian (Devroye 1996), RIPPER (Cohen 1995), and C4.5 (Quinlan 1993). Using discriminators such as various packet IAT measurements, forward and backward packet size information, and the duration of the flow, the authors were able to highlight C4.5 as the highest-performing algorithm, scoring approximately 97% in the best-case test scenario.

Goss and Botha (2012) demonstrate the utility of a generic discriminator set that is suitable for identifying distinct application protocols at an early stage of their existence. In this work, ANN classifiers were trained using manually annotated data sets to identify application protocols with a 99% degree of accuracy. Goss and Nitschke (2013a) extend this work using an HSOM to automate the manual annotation process. Each cluster identified by the HSOM corresponds to a specific application protocol within the data set. Features of each cluster were subsequently used to train an ANN classifier to identify future instances of the protocol. Testing these classifiers resulted in a 98% degree of accuracy.

Goss and Nitschke (2013b) use k-means to cluster the recorded data sets. Dissimilar to k-means implementation described by Hu and Shen (2012), where the number of clusters, k, is preset, Goss and Nitschke (2013b) use an *evolutionary algorithm* (EA) (Eiben and Smith 2003) to approximate the best value of k. The EA uses the *silhouette cluster evaluation* method (Rousseeuw 1987) as part of the fitness function for evaluating each k value. Although a high degree of accuracy was demonstrated, the k-means algorithm is still not the most appropriate clustering method due to its inability to find nonlinearly separable clusters (Jain 2010).

However, both the k-means and HSOM algorithms suffer from this problem and are thus susceptible to outlying points skewing the clustering results. The inability to detect and manage outliers renders the HSOM and k-means algorithms unsuitable for operation in noisy data sets, such as those describing live network traffic. The emergent spherical clusters indicative of k-means and HSOM clustering are highly susceptible to noise in the data. Furthermore, multiple passes on each datum are required by each of these algorithms as part of their clustering process, reducing the overall efficiency of these methods. Classifier efficiency is important to ensure completeness of the system and to ensure that the system is always up-to-date. Thus, an alternative solution is needed, where nonspherical clusters with the ability to counteract the effect of noise emerge.

6.3 Method

To address the problematic issues associated with the HSOM and k-means methods, we propose a DPC method for automating the identification of application protocols as they traverse the network. The DPC method also used an EA to automate the tuning of clustering parameters as well as to determine the optimal structure of each ANN classifier. The research objective was to demonstrate increased efficiency of the DPC method comparative to related methods applied to the same task. For data sets of fabricated network traffic, the accuracy and efficiency of the

DPC method were compared to the HSOM (Goss and Nitschke 2013a) and *k*-means (Goss and Nitschke 2013b) methods. For clustering data sets describing live network traffic, DBSCAN (Ester et al. 1996) was tested as an alternative to the HSOM and *k*-means methods.

Figure 6.1 delineates a method for automated network flow classification via automatically training ANN classifiers to identify application protocols traversing the network. ANNs were

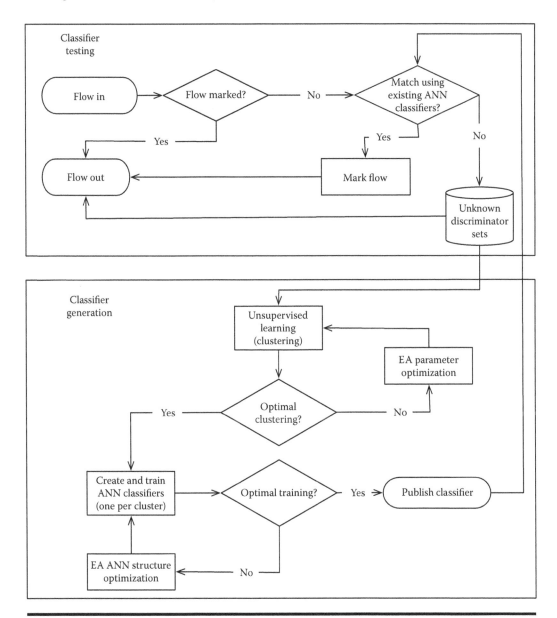

Figure 6.1 Bottom: An unsupervised clustering method is used to identify new protocols as clusters in the training data. An *artificial neural network* (ANN) classifier is trained to identify future instances of each cluster (application protocol). Top: Unknown protocols are broken down into their defining discriminator sets and placed in the training data, upon which the clustering method operates in subsequent iterations.

selected in favor of alternative supervised learning methods, such as decision trees, due to their ability to operate both as independent classifiers or in an ensemble. This allows a single classifier to be transported from one system to another without requiring all supporting classifiers to follow suit. The classifiers created by this method were subsequently used to test and mark each flow as it switched through a network. Critical to the method's success was the ability to describe a flow by its underlying application protocol. As each application communicates with a remote host using a unique pattern of byte exchanges, inferring the underlying application protocol of a flow is accomplished by examining certain statistical and payload characteristics. These characteristics, or discriminators, are common to both the training and testing data used by the method.

This research used a generic set of discriminators, capable of identifying new and previously observed application protocols, proposed and tested by Goss and Botha (2012). These discriminators were able to uniquely fingerprint the underlying application protocol of a flow early upon it entering the network. Early identification allows prompt prioritization of the flow and management of its resources as it transits the network. Resources refer to the amount of bandwidth (speed) and priority (order of preference when arriving at a router) allocated to a given application.

The discriminators included the *direction of the first four payload-bearing packets*, the *average size of these packets*, and the *numeric value of the first three bytes of payload in each direction*. The directionality of the flow was determined through observation of the *synchronization* (SYN) packet. A SYN packet is the first packet sent in a TCP communication when a new session is requested. The requirement for observation of a SYN packet therefore dictates that only flows utilizing the TCP were considered.

It is envisaged that via modification of the base discriminator set, this method will also support user *datagram protocol* (UDP)–based flows. However, demonstration of this is outside the scope of this chapter.

After a predefined number of packet exchanges, the recorded discriminator sets for each flow were tested against existing classifiers. The order in which the classifiers were tested was based on previous results, with the most popular classifiers tested first. The popularity of each classifier was determined by the function $P(x) = f/t$ where x denotes the event of a successful match, f the number of previously successful matches, and t the number of trials. Evaluating a flow using the most probable classifiers reduces the number of tests required for classification, improving the overall efficiency of the system.

Discriminator sets belonging to unidentified flows were added to a database and the flow marked as *unknown*. These data were then clustered by the DBSCAN algorithm:

```
DBSCAN(D, eps, minPTS)
C = 0
for each unvisited point P in dataset D
mark P as visited
NeighborPts = regionQuery(P, eps)
if sizeof(NeighborPts) < minPTS
      mark P as NOISE
else
      C = next cluster
      expandCluster(P, NeighborPts, C, eps, minPTS)

expandCluster(P, NeighborPts, C, eps, minPTS)
add P to cluster C
for each point P' in NeighborPts
```

```
if P' is not visited
     mark P' as visited
     NeighborPts' = regionQuery(P', eps)
     if sizeof(NeighborPts') > = minPTS
     NeighborPts = NeighborPts joined with NeighborPts'
if P' is not yet member of any cluster
     add P' to cluster C
regionQuery(P, eps)
return all points within P's eps-neighborhood (including P)
```

DBSCAN requires two parameters for clustering, namely, the maximal distance between neighbors, *epsilon* (ε), and the minimum points per cluster (*minPTS*). The value for ε was restricted to $min(knn) < \varepsilon < max(knn)$, where *knn* was the distance of each datum to its nearest neighbor. The value of *minPTS* was in the range $D + 1 < minPTS < (|db|)/2$, where D denotes the number of dimensions of the input vector and *db* is the database of unknown discriminator sets.

A GA (Eiben and Smith 2003) tuned this clustering process, adjusting the values of ε and *minPTS* over a number of iterations. The GA's genotype was a bit-string that encoded the value of ε and *minPTS*. The initial genotype population consisted of randomly generated values. Using *silhouette cluster analysis* (Rousseeuw 1987), the GA's fitness function scored each genotype with a value in the range [–1, 1], according to how well DBSCAN clustered the training data with the given (encoded) ε and *minPTS* values. This score measured how tightly grouped the members of each cluster are and was thus a measure of the success of the clustering process. A score toward the value of 1 indicated more optimal clustering, while a lower score, the converse.

At each generation of the GA, *fitness proportionate selection* was used to select pairs of parents, where each pair of parents was recombined using one-point crossover (Eiben and Smith 2003) to produce one child genotype. This process was repeated until enough child genotypes had been produced to replace the previous population. *Elitism* was also applied such that the highest-scoring genotype was transferred to the next generation. *Bit-string mutation* was then applied to flip one bit of each child genotype with a 0.5 degree of probability (Table 6.1). The GA was run for 1000 generations (Table 6.1), after which time the fittest genotype was selected for the optimal ε and *minPTS*.

Each cluster within the optimized clustered data set describes a unique application protocol. As such, a classifier was required to identify future instances of the application. A separate ANN classifier was created for each cluster, with the data of the cluster used as the training set. Initially,

Table 6.1 EA Parameters

Parameter	Initial Value	Start Range	End Range
Generations	1000	–	–
Mutation Rate	0.5	–	–
Number of Genes	20	–	–
Crossover Point	Random	0	20
Epsilon (ε)	0.00002	0.00001	0.0001
minPTS	645	12	711

the number input nodes of each classifier ANN equals the magnitude of the discriminator set. The output of each classifier was a single node that returned the probability of a supplied input vector being a match.

The number of hidden layer nodes and the number of hidden layers were optimized by a GA. Each genotype was encoded as a bit-string, and the number of hidden layer nodes was set in the range [1, 5]. The fitness function was the classification accuracy of an ANN with *n* hidden nodes. The GA also employed fitness proportionate selection, generational replacement, one-point crossover, and bit-flip mutation in the same method as used to evolve the ε and *minPTS* parameters for the DBSCAN method.

6.4 Experiments

Three experiment sets were conducted to evaluate the classification of network traffic flows. The first experiment tested the capability of the unsupervised learning component (DBSCAN-based clustering) on a training data set. The second experiment set evaluated the EA optimization method that tunes DBSCAN clustering parameters and ANN topology of the ANN assigned to classify each cluster. The third experiment set verified the learnt classification behaviors of each of the ANN classifiers using a manually annotated data set recorded in a real-world network environment.

6.4.1 Experiment Set 1: Unsupervised Learning

Flow inspector software* was developed for recording discriminators from passing flows. This software observes and records information about traffic flows passing through the interfaces of the device on which it is deployed. The software made use of iptables and specifically the libipq module to pipe this information through a user-space daemon for analysis.

The software was configured to record 11 discriminators (determined by Goss and Botha 2012) for each flow, including the direction and average size of the first payload-bearing packets as well as the value of the first three bytes of payload in either direction. The software was deployed at a midsized corporate establishment, set to record flow information for a period of 1 h on a normal business day. At the outset, no predefined classifiers were made available, and therefore, all flows were sampled, with their discriminator sets appended to the training data set. In total, 1421 TCP flows were sampled and appended to the database for evaluation by DBSCAN.

A GA was applied to tune the DBSCAN clustering parameters ε and *minPTS* (Section 6.3), where the search space for ε was determined by plotting the distance to the nearest neighbor of each datum on a histogram (Figure 6.2). Figure 6.2 shows the average distance of each datum to its nearest neighbor, with the *knee* of the graph at an approximate value of 0.00005. The knee of the graph is indicative of the most likely value of ε, the point at which the distance between neighbors increases exponentially, due to the presence of outliers (noise). The search space for ε was therefore constrained to values between 0.00001 and 0.0001. Similarly, the search space for the *minPTS* parameter was configured such that $D + 1 < = minPTS < = (|db|)/2$, between 12 and 711. The GA parameters, their initial values, and the search space for each are listed in Table 6.1. This GA was executed for 1000 generations, where optimal ε and *minPTS* values of 0.00004 and 61, respectively, were found. The clustered data set consisted of six distinct clusters, with a silhouette

---

* Custom-designed by Ryan Goss. Details can be found at http://goo.gl/80BQE.

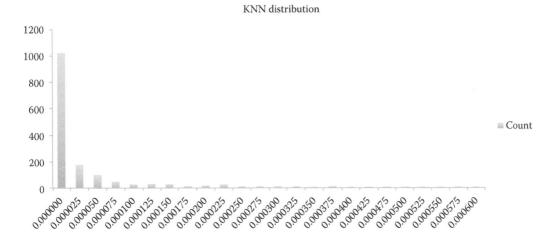

Figure 6.2   Histogram depicting nearest neighbors.

Table 6.2   Clustering Results

Cluster	Datum	Silhouette
1	127	0.993615
2	319	0.989984
3	101	0.997174
4	61	0.999032
5	175	0.996352
6	74	0.991109

value of 0.993615. The clusters, with their associated datum and silhouette values, are summarized in Table 6.2. The clusters were then saved for the second experiment set (Section 6.4.2).

6.4.2 Experiment Set 2: ANN Classifiers

Each of the six clusters identified by experiment set 1 (Section 6.4.1) were used as training sets by an ANN that attempted to classify the protocol represented by each cluster. The following pseudo-code describes the ANN classification process, given the clustered data.

```
For each cluster c in [identified clusters]
1. Mark data linked to c with "1"
2. Mark data external to c with "0"
3. For i = 1 to EA_max_generations
        For each s genome in EA_population
                Create ANN a to identify c using structure s
                Train: 1000 iterations using marked datum
                If accuracy(a) > current_best_for_c
```

Table 6.3   EA Optimization Results

Cluster	Hidden Layers	Neurons per Hidden Layer	Accuracy
1	4	10	99.897%
2	4	11	99.983%
3	2	4	99.996%
4	2	11	99.992%
5	3	11	99.948%
6	4	11	99.970%

```
            current_best_for_c = a
            Fitness(s) = accuracy(a)
        Next s
Next i
4. Set c_ann = current_best_for_c
Next cluster
```

Each ANN was a fully connected feed-forward network with one hidden layer of log-sigmoidal nodes. The ANN has one output code (indicating the accuracy of classification within the range [0.0, 1.0]) that also uses a log-sigmoid activation function. The input layer consisted of 11 input neurons corresponding to the 11 discriminators used for classification (Section 6.4.1). A GA was used in order to determine an appropriate number of hidden layer nodes as well as number of hidden layers (Section 6.3) for each cluster in the clustered data.

The GA was run for each cluster, resulting in six different ANN topologies (Table 6.3). At the end of each GA run for each cluster, the ANN topology resulting in the highest score was retained as the classifier that is most suitable. Table 6.3 presents the ANN topology for each cluster classification that yielded the highest accuracy. These results were gained from training each ANN on each cluster of the clustered data set (Section 6.4.1) for 1000 iterations.

6.4.3 Experiment Set 3: Classifier Testing

The flow inspector software (Section 6.4.1) was once again deployed for the purpose of capturing discriminators in each passing TCP flow over a 15 min period. Concurrently, a separate instance of the flow inspector software was connected to a *wide area network* (WAN) of a home broadband user, recording TCP flows over a 1 h period. The flow inspector recorded for 1 h since the traffic volumes of the home user were significantly less than those of the corporate network. Each of the data recorded during this process was manually annotated by experts, identifying them by their underlying application protocol (for verification).

In order to adequately test the trained ANN classifiers, five randomly selected samples for each protocol were presented to the ANN classifiers trained in experiment set 2 (Section 6.4.2). The highest-scoring (classification accuracy) ANN classifier and the average output scores are presented in Table 6.4 for a given set of protocols. These results are presented with those attained by a heuristic annotation method (Goss and Botha 2012), an HSOM method (Goss and Nitschke 2013a), and a *k*-means method (Goss and Nitschke 2013b) for the same protocols. In Table 6.4, – indicates that the protocol was not tested, and DPC refers to the classification accuracy of the *DPC* method

Table 6.4   Classification Results on Test Data

Protocol	Classifier Number	DPC	Heuristic	HSOM	K-means
POP3	2	99.96%	99.06%	99.88%	–
Simple Mail Transfer Protocol (SMTP)	3	99.90%	99.92%	99.86%	99.94%
Internet Message Access Protocol (IMAP)	–	–	–	99.77%	99.86%
HyperText Transfer Protocol (HTTP)	1	100.00%	99.93%	69.60%	99.88%
HyperText Transfer Protocol Secure (HTTPS)	5	99.92%	99.95%	99.95%	99.89%
Soulseek	–	–	–	99.83%	–
BitTorrent	6	99.82%	–	99.70%	98.78%
PPTP	4	99.41%	–	–	–

proposed in this chapter. Heuristic refers to the manual annotation method for protocol identification described by Goss and Botha (2012).

6.5 Discussion

Results indicate the degree of accuracy (close to% 100) for the evolved ANN classifiers. The topology of each of the six ANN classifiers was evolved specifically to maximize the classification accuracy of each with respect to clustered training data. Six ANN classifiers were evolved since there were six clusters (where each cluster corresponded to a detected application protocol) in the training data set. The high classification accuracy was verified for both training and test data. To properly test the capability of trained classifiers to accurately classify any given protocol, a set of application protocols were randomly selected from a given protocol set. Furthermore, fabricated *test* protocols were randomly generated from an existing discriminator set.

Trained ANN classifier accuracy is comparable to that yielded by an HSOM (Goss and Nitschke 2013a) and *k*-means (Goss and Nitschke 2013b) method for the same application protocol classification task. New flows were captured on corporate and a home Asymmetric Digital Subscriber Line (ADSL) network and were used as the test data for the trained ANN classifiers. This was done so the authors could ascertain how well the trained ANN classifiers are able to dynamically classify the most popular application protocols (such as HTTP and SMTP) from *live* network flows of corporate versus home networks. In order to ensure that the ANN classifiers were properly trained, that is, generalizing such that newly observed protocols were properly classified, only classifications yielding a 95% or higher degree of accuracy were considered. Classifications with a lower degree of accuracy were considered to have an unknown classification.

Table 6.4 indicates that all classifiers yielded a degree of accuracy of 99% or higher when given the task of identifying eight given application protocols in live traffic flows. The DPC method yielded comparable classification results (no statistically significant difference) to the HSOM and *k*-means methods. The exception was that the DPC and *k*-means methods both significantly outperformed

HSOM for accurately classifying the HTTP protocol. In the HSOM method, HTTP transactions using the HTTP 1.1 protocol (pipe-lining) spread the HTTP protocol over a number of clusters and, subsequently, a number of classifiers. Testing the discriminator sets manually annotated HTTP by experts against each individual classifier subsequently resulted in the low score being produced. The *k*-means method was able to overcome this problem; however, the specifics of this are not mentioned in the work. In the DPC method, these HTTP 1.1 requests were, upon further investigation, discarded by DBSCAN as "noise" due to the lack of samples during the clustering process.

Another key difference among the DPC, HSOM, and *k*-means methods that affected overall classification accuracy in this comparative study was the efficacy of the clustering of training data. The capability of unsupervised learning (clustering) data to correctly cluster traffic flow data according to identified application protocols impacted the ANN backpropagation training process and, thus, ANN classification accuracy.

For this clustering process, both the *k*-means and HSOM methods required many iterations before clusters emerged in the final layer of the SOM (Goss and Nitschke 2013a). Both the HSOM and *k*-means methods worked with a data set of 1973 data points with 11 dimensions (discriminators). In the first layer of the HSOM, clustering occurred after 300 iterations. Each iteration equated to the evaluation of 1973 discriminators for each of the 400 neurons in the first layer. Clustering at the first layer of the HSOM resulted in each of 50 *best matching unit* (BMU) clusters being evaluated against 100 neurons in the second layer for additional 100 iterations.

The final layer of the HSOM identified 14 clusters; however, only 11 data sets were considered and used in training ANN classifiers due to the lack of datum samples in three of the clusters. The *k*-means method (Goss and Nitschke 2013b) was similarly inefficient in that multiple iterations of the method were required for each datum within the traffic flow data set that was being clustered. Given randomly selected centroids, *k* = 16 clusters were derived, with a calculated silhouette value of 0.916821. For the DBSCAN method, a data set of 1421 data points with 11 dimensions (discriminators) was recorded. The DBSCAN method evaluates each data point only once for each run of the algorithm. In contrast to the HSOM and *k*-means methods, this resulted in increased efficiency when clustering data sets of recorded network traffic.

Also, the DBSCAN method did not produce clusters with an insufficient number of sample data points, as was the case for both the HSOM and *k*-means methods. In the case of both HSOM and *k*-means, clusters that contained an insufficient number of data points had to be manually removed. This meant that, dissimilar to the DPC method, the HSOM and *k*-means methods could not be fully automated. For example, in the HSOM clustering, three clusters emerged, which DBSCAN would have considered noise. This result is attributed to the capability of DBSCAN to form arbitrarily shaped clusters and its robustness toward outlier detection (noise), elements that skew both the HSOM and *k*-means methods.

Furthermore, the DPC method was advantageous in that the ε and *minPTS* parameters were evolved to values that worked well for the clustering of recorded traffic flow training data that were clustered by the DBSCAN component of DPC. The DPC method also had the advantage that the DBSCAN component was able to form complex shapes in its clustering process and thus cluster nonlinearly separable data.

6.6 Conclusion

This chapter presented the DPC method for a case study of automated application protocol identification on computer networks. This study extended previous work (Goss and Botha 2012; Goss and Nitschke 2013a,b) that showed the benefit of unsupervised clustering methods (HSOM and *k*-means) for dynamic application protocol identification on recorded traffic flows. Such automation is beneficial since it alleviates for network administrators the delays experienced waiting for new signatures to be created by the vendor. Methods that automate the classification of new protocols must thus work with the data of live traffic flows and be able to dynamically ascertain the defining features of new protocols that traverse the network (Szabo et al. 2007).

This case study demonstrated that the DPC method was appropriate for dynamically identifying new protocols and generating signatures ad hoc. The clustering component (DBSCAN) of DPC was found to be more efficient and appropriate for the given protocol classification and identification task. *Efficient* refers to the lower number of evaluations per data point required for DBSCAN to cluster the training data. *Appropriate* refers to the capability of DBSCAN to more effectively (comparative to the HSOM and *k*-means methods) exclude noise from clustered data via forming nonspherical clusters, and to cluster nonlinearly separable data. Also, DBSCAN (more generally the DPC method) did not require the number of clusters to be specified *a priori*, as was necessitated by *k*-means.

The DPC method demonstrated an average classification accuracy of 99% given the task of dynamically identifying eight application protocols. The overall classification accuracy of the DPC method was comparable to that achieved by HSOM and *k*-means. Hence, the hypothesis that the DPC method would outperform (with statistical significance) the HSOM and *k*-means methods (Section 6.1) was refuted. However, these latter two methods are still to be tested for the Point-to-Point Tunnelling Protocol (PPTP), Soulseek, and Post Office Protocol v3 (POP3) protocols. While the average accuracy achieved was favorable (in excess of 99%), it is still to be determined whether such accuracy would persist with an increased sample set with additional protocols observed by the flow inspector software.

Future work will address the issue of clustering high-dimensional data, which has been elucidated as problematic for nonparametric density-based methods, such as DBSCAN (Jain 2010). Whereas this work used data sets defined by 11 discriminators (dimensions), future studies will compare the capability of *k*-means, HSOM, and the DPC method to work with significantly higher-dimensional data. Future work will also address extensions to the DBSCAN component of the DPC method, such as allowing for an ε value to be dynamically set for emerging clusters, after initially being set for the entire clustering process. Furthermore, the DBSCAN component will be compared with the Ordering Points To Identify the Clustering Structure (OPTICS) (Ankerst et al. 1999) and DeLiClu algorithms (Achtert et al. 2006) to investigate the possibility of overcoming DBSCAN's limitation in performing optimally within large density distributions.

References

Achtert, E., Böhm, C., & Kröger, P. (2006). DeLi-Clu: Boosting Robustness, Completeness, Usability, and Efficiency of Hierarchical Clustering by a Closest Pair Ranking. In *Advances in Knowledge Discovery and Data Mining* (pp. 119–128). Springer, Berlin, Heidelberg.

Alshammari, R., & Zincir-Heywood, A. (2007). A Flow Based Approach for SSH Traffic Detection. In *Proceedings of the IEEE International Conference on System, Man and Cybernetics* (pp. 296–301). IEEE Computer Society, Montreal, Que.

Alshammari, R., & Zincir-Heywood, A. (2008). Investigating Two Different Approaches for Encrypted Traffic Classification. In *Proceedings of the Sixth Annual Conference on Privacy, Security and Trust* (pp. 156–166). IEEE Computer Society.

Alshammari, R., & Zincir-Heywood, A. (2009). Machine Learning Based Encrypted Traffic Classification: Identifying SSH and Skype. In *Computational Intelligence for Security and Defence Applications* (pp. 1–8). IEEE, Ottawa, ON.

Ankerst, M., Breunig, M., Kriegel, H., & Sander, J. (1999). OPTICS: Ordering Points to Identify the Clustering Structure. *ACM SIGMOD Record, 28*(2), 49–60.

Auld, T., Moore, A., & Gull, S. (2007). Bayesian Neural Networks for Internet Traffic Classification. *IEEE Transactions on Neural Networks, 18*(1), 223–239.

Bernaille, L., Soule, A., Akodjenou, I., & Salamatian, K. (2005). Blind Application Recognition through Behavioral Classification. *CNRS LIP6, Technical Report.*

Bernaille, L., Teixeira, R., & Salamatian, K. (2006). Early Application Identification. In *Proceedings of the 2006 ACM CoNEXT Conference* (p. 6).

Cohen, W. (1995). Fast Effective Rule Induction. In *Proceedings of the Twelfth International Conference on Machine Learning* (Vol. 95, pp. 115–123).

Cortes, C., & Vapnik, V. (1995). Support-Vector Networks. *Machine Learning, 20*(3), 273–297.

Dempster, A., Laird, N., & Rubin, D. (1977). Maximum Likelihood from Incomplete Data via the EM Algorithm. *Journal of the Royal Statistical Society, Series B (Methodological), 39*(1), 1–38.

Devroye, L. (1996). *A Probabilistic Theory of Pattern Recognition* (Vol. 31). Springer Verlag, Germany.

Eiben, A., & Smith, J. (2003). *Introduction to Evolutionary Computing.* Springer.

Este, A., Gargiulo, F., Gringoli, F., Salgarelli, L., & Sansone, C. (2008). Pattern Recognition Approaches for Classifying IP Flows. In *Proceedings of the 2008 Joint IAPR International Workshop on Structural, Syntactic and Statistical Pattern Recognition* (pp. 885–895). Springer-Verlag, Berlin, Heidelberg. doi: 10.1007/978-3-540-89689-0_92.

Ester, M., Kriegel, H., Sander, J., & Xu, X. (1996). A Density-based Algorithm for Discovering Clusters in Large Spatial Databases with Noise. In *Knowledge Discovery in Databases* (Vol. 96, pp. 226–231). AAAI, Portland, Oregon.

Freund, Y., & Schapire, R. E. (1995). A Decision-Theoretic Generalization of On-line Learning and an Application to Boosting. In *Computational Learning Theory* (pp. 23–37). *Journal of Computer and System Sciences, 55*(1), 119–139. Elsevier.

Gargiulo, F., Kuncheva, L., & Sansone, C. (2009). Network Protocol Verification by a Classifier Selection Ensemble. In *Multiple Classifier Systems* (pp. 314–323). Springer-Verlag, Berlin, Heidelberg.

Gebski, M., Penev, A., & Wong, R. (2006). Protocol Identification of Encrypted Network Traffic. In *Proceedings of the 2006 IEEE/WIC/ACM International Conference on Web Intelligence* (pp. 957–960). IEEE Computer Society.

Goss, R., & Botha, R. (2012). Establishing Discernible Flow Characteristics for Accurate, Real-time Network Protocol Identification. In *Proceedings of the 2012 International Network Conference (INC2012)* (pp. 25–34). IEEE Computer Society, Port Elizabeth, South Africa.

Goss, R., & Nitschke, G. (2013a). Automated Network Application Classification: A Competitive Learning Approach. In *Proceedings of the IEEE Symposium Series on Computational Intelligence (IEEE SSCI 2013)* (pp. 45–52). IEEE Press, Singapore.

Goss, R., & Nitschke, G. (2013b). Network Protocol Identification Ensemble with EA Optimization. In *Proceedings of the Genetic and Evolutionary Computation Conference (GECCO2013)* (pp. 1735–1736). ACM Press, Amsterdam, Netherlands.

Hu, B., & Shen, Y. (2012). Machine Learning Based Network Traffic Classification: A Survey. *Journal of Information and Computational Science, 9*(11), 3161–3170.

Huang, K., & Zhang, D. (2008). A Byte-Filtered String Matching Algorithm for Fast Deep Packet Inspection. In *Proceedings of the Ninth International Conference for Young Computer Scientists* (pp. 2073–2078). IEEE Computer Society.

Jain, A. (2010). Data Clustering: 50 Years beyond K-means. *Pattern Recognition Letters, 31*(8), 651–666. doi: 10.1016/j.patrec.2009.09.011.

Li, Z., Yuan, R., & Guan, X. (2007). Traffic Classification—Towards Accurate Real Time Network Applications. In *Proceedings of the Twelfth International Conference on Human-Computer Interaction: Applications and Services* (pp. 67–76). Springer-Verlag, Berlin, Heidelberg.

MacQueen, J. (1967). Some Methods for Classification and Analysis of Multivariate Observations. In *Proceedings of the Fifth Berkeley Symposium on Mathematical Statistics and Probability* (Vol. 1, p. 14).

McGregor, A., Hall, M., Lorier, P., & Brunskill, J. (2004). Flow Clustering Using Machine Learning Techniques. *Passive and Active Network Measurement*, 3015, 205–214.

Moore, A., & Papagiannaki, K. (2005). Toward the Accurate Identification of Network Applications. In *Passive and Active Network Measurement* (Vol. 3431, pp. 41–54). Springer, Berlin, Germany.

Moore, A., Zuev, D., Crogan, M., & Mary, Q. (2005). *Discriminators for Use in Flow-based Classification*. Queen Mary and Westfield College, Department of Computer Science, London.

Nascimento, Z., Sadok, D., & Fernandes, S. (2013). A Hybrid Model for Network Traffic Identification Based on Association Rules and Self-Organizing Maps (SOM). In *Proceedings of the Ninth International Conference on Networking and Services (ICNS2013)* (pp. 213–219).

Nguyen, T., & Armitage, G. (2008). A Survey of Techniques for Internet Traffic Classification using Machine Learning. *IEEE Communications Surveys & Tutorials*, 10(4), 56–76.

Quinlan, J. (1993). C4. 5: Programs for Machine Learning. *Morgan Kaufmann Series in Machine Learning*, vol. 1.

Rousseeuw, P. (1987). Silhouettes: A Graphical Aid to the Interpretation and Validation of Cluster Analysis. *Journal of Computational and Applied Mathematics*, 20, 53–65.

Szabo, G., Szabo, I., & Orincsay, D. (2007, June). Accurate Traffic Classification. In *IEEE International Symposium on a World of Wireless, Mobile and Multimedia Networks* (pp. 1–8).

Von Luxburg, U. (2007). A tutorial on Spectral Clustering. *Statistics and Computing*, 17(4), 395–416.

Chapter 7

Intelligent and Non-Intelligent Approaches in Image Denoising: A Comparative Study

Mantosh Biswas and Hari Om

Contents

The images in creating, transmitting, and decoding processes generally get distorted by different types of noise. It becomes very necessary to reduce or remove the noise from the image in order to get its actual contents. Noise reduction has become a required step for any sophisticated algorithm in image processing. It is an open problem that has received considerable attention in literature for several decades. To make a balance between denoising and blurring and obtain clean images is a challenging issue in image processing. Though this issue has existed for a long time, there is no completely satisfactory solution. Over the last two decades, the wavelet-based denoising methods have been applied to the problem of noise reduction, and they have been shown to outperform the traditional nonwavelet-based denoising methods with or without intelligence approach. This chapter presents a case study on various image denoising methods by considering intelligence approach, that is, fuzzy logic. The denoising methods may be classified as nonwavelet and wavelet methods. In nonwavelet methods, the pixel values are modified in their original form, whereas in wavelet methods, the pixel values are first transformed into wavelet (time and frequency) domain, and then these values are modified in order to reduce the noise. In a denoising method, the pixels (or wavelet coefficients) are processed with or without using the information from its neighboring pixels (or neighboring wavelet coefficients), which are called term-by-term and block-by-block approaches, respectively. The state-of-the-art denoising methods assume that the images are corrupted with the additive white Gaussian noise (AWGN). A quantitative comparison between the denoising methods for both objective and subjective qualities of the images is considered as these two parameters are widely used for statistical computations in terms of peak signal-to-noise ratio and structural similarity index measure. The experimental results demonstrate that (i) the wavelet-based denoising methods using block-by-block approach give better results than the term-by-term ones for all noise levels; (ii) the wavelet-based denoising methods using intelligence approach, especially fuzzy logic, give better results than the nonwavelet without using fuzzy logic; and (iii) the wavelet-based denoising methods using fuzzy logic give better results for higher noise levels than the nonwavelet with fuzzy logic in terms of visual quality of the image.

7.1 Introduction

A digital image consists of basic units called pixels. In digital image processing, various fundamental steps are performed to represent it, improve its visual quality, select its important features, etc. as shown in Figure 7.1 [1–3]. First, the image is acquired, which is called image acquisition step, and then other processing steps are performed. While acquiring an image or performing processing steps, the image is embedded with unwanted data that degrade its visual quality, leading to sometimes misinterpretation of the image. We discuss about these unwanted data called noise.

Noise is an unwanted signal that interferes with the original signal and degrades the visual quality of the digital image signal. The main sources of noise in digital images are imperfect instruments, problems during their acquisition process, interference of natural phenomena, etc. [1]. Image denoising is the preprocessing or enhancement step in the field of photography, research, technology, and medical science, where somehow an image has been degraded and needs to be

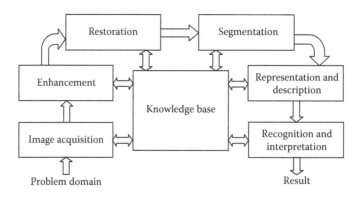

Figure 7.1   Fundamental steps in digital image processing.

restored before further processing [3]. It is still a challenging problem for researchers as image denoising causes blurring and introduces artifacts. Different types of images inherit different types of noise, and accordingly, different noise models are used to represent them. Denoising methods are problem specific and depend upon the type of image and the noise model used [1–3]. The Gaussian noise (white noise), salt-and-pepper noise, and speckle noise are some types of noise generally found in images. Denoising an image using different techniques with intelligence, that is, fuzzy logic, and without intelligence is the main discussion of this chapter.

Image denoising has become an active research area in image processing. It stands out uniquely with its own recognition despite several researches that have gone in a number of different fields. Many noise reduction methods have been developed for removing the noise and retaining the image features such as edge details. The choice of a denoising method depends on the application and on the type of noise present in the image. Each method has its own assumptions, advantages, and limitations. The basic idea behind these methods is to acquire better results in terms of visual quality after removing the noise. We can find many traditional noise reduction methods that are either in spatial or frequency domain or hybrid [1–5]. The spatial low-pass filters not only smooth away the noise but also blur the edges in images. The spatial high-pass filters make edges sharper and improve the spatial resolution but at the same time amplify the noisy background. The conventional fast Fourier transform (FFT) based image denoising methods are essentially a low-pass filtering technique in which edges are not as sharp in the reconstructed image as they were in the original image. The edge information is spread across the frequencies because of the basis functions of the FFT, which are not localized in time or space [6–8]. The linear and nonlinear filters are the nonwavelet-based filters having good image detail preservation properties, for example, edges/texts, and hence, they are highly desirable for image filtering [1–5]. Linear filters, for example, low- and high-pass filters, and nonlinear filters, such as Weiner and median, work well with noise and at the same time retain the sharp edges in the reconstructed images. These filters can achieve reasonably good performance for low corrupted images and not highly corrupted images. Another disadvantage of these filters is the extra computational time needed to sort the intensity values of each mask in a noisy image. Therefore, these types of filters are not generally suitable for filtering of different parts of a noisy image. The filtering mechanisms should ideally vary from pixel to pixel depending upon the local context. The spatial filters have long been used as the traditional means for removing the noise from the signals. These filters usually smooth the data to reduce the noise and also to blur the data. In recent years, researchers have discussed artificial intelligence-based denoising methods as some soft computing tools, such as fuzzy logic, neural networks, genetic algorithms, etc., have the capabilities of learning and describing uncertainties that overcome the limitation of linear and nonlinear filtering methods [9–16]. The filtering approach has been proved to be the best when the image is corrupted with salt-and-pepper noise [4,5]. The wavelet-based approaches find applications in denoising the images corrupted with the Gaussian noise [17–20]. A different class of methods exploits the decomposition of the data into wavelet basis, that is, thresholding and shrinking the wavelet coefficients in order to denoise the data. The wavelet-based image denoising is an important class of noise reduction methods [21–23]. The wavelets have a natural ability to represent the images in a very sparse form, which is the foundation of wavelet-based denoising using thresholding.

In this chapter, several representations of thresholding and shrinking methods are discussed. These thresholding methods are either based on term by term [17–20,24–32] such as VisuShrink, SureShrink, BayesShrink, and their variants; or block by block [33–41] such as NeighBlock, NeighShrink, ModiNeighShrink, and their variants. The term-by-term methods use individual pixels (or wavelet coefficients) for denoising without considering the neighboring pixels (or wavelet coefficients), and the block-by-block methods consider the neighboring pixels (or wavelet coefficients) for the desired pixel (or wavelet coefficients) to be denoised. The denoising methods may roughly be classified as nonwavelet- and wavelet-based methods as the wavelet-based methods have overtaken the other methods. We also consider fuzzy logic implementation of these methods as one of the soft computing tools [42–49] because the fuzzy logic exploits attractive features of several existing methods [4,5], provides adaptation to natural images with different textures, and ensures an appropriate trade-off between the noise suppression and detail preservation in a noisy image. Although fuzzy techniques have already been applied in several domains of image processing, namely, filtering, interpolation, and morphology, they have numerous practical applications in industrial and medical image processing [42,43]. Nevertheless, most of the fuzzy logic-based techniques are not specifically designed for noises especially the Gaussian one, which do not produce convincing results to handle this type of noise. The fuzzy rule–based systems solve this problem trivially and efficiently by combining the consequence of the rules. In other words, a fuzzy rule–based system makes "soft" decisions based on each condition, aggregates the decisions made, and finally makes the decision based on aggregation [9,42]. The noise considered in this chapter is the AWGN, which is mutually uncorrelated. The performance of thresholding and shrinking methods for denoising in the wavelet domain has been evaluated using the peak signal-to-noise ratio (PSNR) and structural similarity index measure (SSIM). The rest of the chapter is organized as follows. The mathematical formulation of image denoising for wavelet-based methods is given in Section 7.2. Section 7.3 discusses various denoising methods. The experiment results and discussions are given in Section 7.5. Finally, the conclusion is given in Section 7.6.

7.2 Mathematical Formulation

Generally the mathematical formulation of image denoising can be written as

$$y_{m,n} = x_{m,n} + n_{m,n}, \ 1 \le m, \ n \le M; \quad M \text{ is the original image dimension} \tag{7.1}$$

where $y \{y_{m,n}, \ 1 \le m, \ n \le M\}$ is the noisy image of the original image $x \{x_{m,n}, \ 1 \le m, \ n \le M\}$ that is corrupted by independent and identically distributed (i.i.d.) AWGN n with zero-valued mean and variance σ^2. Here, $y_{m,n}$, $x_{m,n}$, and $n_{m,n}$ denote the intensity values at the (m,n)th position in the noisy image, the original image, and the noise, respectively.

Here, the main goal is to minimize the mean square error (MSE) between the noisy image pixels $y_{m,n}$ and original image pixels $x_{m,n}$. Let $W(\cdot)$ and $W^{-1}(\cdot)$ denote the forward and backward wavelet transform operators, respectively, and $D(\cdot, T)$ denote the denoising operator with threshold T [23]. We denoise y to recover $\hat{X}$ as an estimate of the original image x in the following steps:

   i. Apply forward operator $W(\cdot)$ to noisy image y, that is, $F = W(y)$.
  ii. Apply denoising operator D to F, that is, $\bar{X} = D(F,T)$.
 iii. Apply inverse wavelet transform $W^{-1}(\cdot)$ to reconstruct image $\hat{X}$ from $\bar{X}$, that is, $\hat{X} = W^{-1}(\bar{X})$.

These image denoising steps are illustrated graphically in Figure 7.2.

To carry out the above steps, we need to derive threshold that helps in evaluating the shrinkage factor and then apply the denoising procedure. The thresholding is a simple nonlinear technique that operates on the wavelet coefficients. In its most basic form, each wavelet coefficient is thresholded by comparing against the selected threshold. If the coefficient is smaller than the selected threshold, it is set to zero; otherwise, it is kept as it is. The threshold is generally of two types: hard

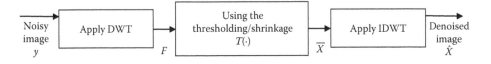

Figure 7.2   Image denoising process.

and soft threshold [24,26] (see Figure 7.3). The hard threshold is discontinuous and yields abrupt artifacts in the recovered image, whereas the soft threshold does not. Therefore, the soft thresholding is preferred over the hard one. In hard thresholding, all values having magnitude greater than the selected threshold value, say T, remain unchanged, and those less than T are set to zero. This process creates a region around zero, where the values are considered negligible. Mathematically, the hard and soft thresholds may be defined as follows:

Hard threshold

$$\bar{X} = \begin{cases} P, & |P| \geq T \\ 0, & \text{otherwise} \end{cases} \tag{7.2}$$

Soft threshold

$$\bar{X} = \begin{cases} sign(P)(P-T), & |P| > T \\ 0, & |P| \leq T \end{cases} \tag{7.3}$$

$$\text{where, } sign(P) = \begin{cases} 1 & \text{for } P > 0 \\ -1 & \text{for } P < 0 \\ 0 & \text{for } P = 0 \end{cases}$$

Here, P denotes the pixel value or the wavelet coefficient in the image, and $\bar{X}$ is the thresholded pixel value in the image.

Graphically, the hard and soft threshold functions are shown in Figure 7.3a and b, respectively.

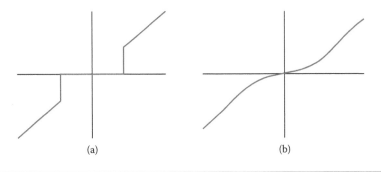

(a)   (b)

Figure 7.3   Thresholding with (a) hard threshold and (b) soft threshold.

7.3 Denoising Methods

The nonwavelet-based denoising methods, that is, filtering, are an essential part of any signal processing system [4,5]. This involves estimation of a signal/image, which is degraded in most cases by additive random noise. Several filtering techniques have been discussed in refs. [1–5]. Among them, the linear or nonlinear techniques have been the methods of choice for many years because of their simplicity. Most of these techniques, however, assume a Gaussian model for statistical characteristics of the underlying process and try to optimize the parameters of the system for this model. The classical versions of the filter based on artificial intelligence (AI) techniques include fuzzy logic, neural networks, genetic algorithms, etc. [10–16]. Here, we discuss fuzzy-based noise removal filters, namely, ATMED, ATMAB, and FPS, whose performance is compared with that of the nonwavelet denoising methods: Weiner and median filters [44,45]. The Weiner filter requires information about the spectra of the noisy and original signal [1–3]. It works well only for smooth signals and the Gaussian noise. In the Fourier domain, it is defined as follows:

$$\hat{X}(m,n) = \frac{h^*(m,n)\,y_s(m,n)}{\left|h(m,n)\right|^2 y_s(m,n) + y_n(m,n)} \tag{7.4}$$

where $h(m,n)$ and $h^*(m,n)$ denote the degradation function and its complex conjugate, and $y_n(m,n)$ and $y_s(m,n)$ denote the power spectral density of the noisy and nondegraded image, respectively, at position (m,n).

A median filter follows the moving window principle like mean filter [1–3]. A 3×3, 5×5, or 7×7 kernel of pixels, also called the neighboring window, is moved over the entire image. The central pixel in the window is replaced by the median of the pixel values in that window. The median is more robust than the mean because one of the neighboring pixels is used as a median. It does not create a new pixel value when straddled with an edge and, thus, preserves sharp edges unlike in the case of a mean.

The fuzzy logic is a promising approach to remove the noise from a noisy image [42–49]. We discuss image denoising methods based on a soft computing tool especially fuzzy logic. In these techniques, a fuzzy shrinkage factor expresses how likely a coefficient is of interest, and the process is accomplished by using the appropriate fuzzy rules. Some of the important shrinkage methods based on soft thresholding by considering the fuzzy rules are discussed below.

The asymmetrical triangular fuzzy filter with median center (ATMED) is the neighborhood filter that considers the deviation of a noisy pixel value with the median value of the neighboring window in order to replace that noisy pixel with a fitting output based on the fuzzy triangular membership function (MF), which is given as follows [44,45]:

$$\hat{X}(m,n) = \begin{cases} 1 - \dfrac{y_{\text{med}}(m,n) - y(m+i,n+j)}{y_{\text{med}}(m,n) - y_{\min}(m,n)}, & \text{for } y_{\min}(m,n) \le y(m+i,n+j) \le y_{\text{med}}(m,n) \\[4mm] 1 - \dfrac{y(m+i,n+j) - y_{\text{med}}(m,n)}{y_{\max}(m,n) - y_{\text{med}}(m,n)}, & \text{for } y_{\text{med}}(m,n) \le y(m+i,n+j) \le y_{\max}(m,n) \\[4mm] 1, & \begin{aligned} &\text{for } y_{\text{med}}(m,n) - y_{\min}(m,n) = 0 \quad \text{or} \\ &y_{\max}(m,n) - y_{\text{med}}(m,n) = 0 \end{aligned} \end{cases}$$

$$\tag{7.5}$$

where $y_{\max}$, $y_{\min}$, and y_{med} are the maximum, minimum, and median values, respectively, in the neighborhood window of size $i \times j$ centered at (m,n); $i, j \geq 1$ are real positive odd integers.

The asymmetrical triangular fuzzy filter with moving average center (ATMAV) is a neighborhood filter that considers the deviation of a noisy pixel with the mean value for replacing that noisy pixel with a fitting output based on the fuzzy triangular MF that is given by [44,45]

$$
\hat{X}(m,n) = \begin{cases}
1 - \dfrac{y_{\text{avg}}(m,n) - y(m+i,n+j)}{y_{\text{avg}}(m,n) - y_{\min}(m,n)}, & \text{for } y_{\min}(m,n) \leq y(m+i,n+j) \leq y_{\text{avg}}(m,n) \\[3mm]
1 - \dfrac{y(m+i,n+j) - y_{\text{agv}}(m,n)}{y_{\max}(m,n) - y_{\text{avg}}(m,n)}, & \text{for } y_{\text{avg}}(m,n) \leq y(m+i,n+j) \leq y_{\max}(m,n) \\[3mm]
1, & \begin{aligned} &\text{for } y_{\text{avg}}(m,n) - y_{\min}(m,n) = 0 \quad \text{or} \\ &y_{\max}(m,n) - y_{\text{avg}}(m,n) = 0 \end{aligned}
\end{cases}
$$

$$(7.6)$$

where y_{avg} is the moving average value or the mean of $(m+i, n+j)$ pixels in the window at index (i,j).

The Fuzzy Tri State (FTS) filter, proposed by Arunkumar et al. [45], performs averaging operations by incorporating the following: ATMED, ATMAV, and median filters (MED). This filter takes into account the important image characteristics such as edges/textures and makes tri-state decision in order to replace the central pixel based on its comparison with the outputs from the ATMED, ATMAV, and MED filters. The filter uses the following rules to get the output:

$$
\hat{X}(m,n) = \begin{cases}
\text{ATMED}(m,n), & \text{if } T \geq \text{abs}(y(m,n) - \text{ATMED}(m,n)) \\[2mm]
\text{MED}(m,n), & \text{if } \text{abs}(y(m,n) - \text{ATMED}(m,n)) \leq T \leq \text{abs}(y(m,n) - \text{ATMAV}(m,n)) \\[2mm]
\text{ATMAV}(m,n), & \text{if } T \leq \text{abs}(y(m,n) - \text{ATMAV}(m,n))
\end{cases}
$$

$$(7.7)$$

Here, T, ATMED(m,n), ATMAV(m,n), and MED(m,n) are the threshold values calculated by using the fuzzy rules in the range $[0,1]$ at the (m,n) location and the noiseless image value using ATMED, ATMAV, and MED, respectively.

The nonwavelet-based techniques generally blur the sharp edges and destroy lines and other fine details in a noisy image; thus, they fail to produce satisfactory results for a broad range of low contrast images. Also, they are computationally expensive. To overcome these shortcomings, the researchers use wavelet-based techniques such as VisuShrink, SureShrink, BayesShrink, NeighShrink, and intelligence-based wavelet shrinkage methods [46–49]. These techniques are superior due to good energy compaction, sparsity, multiresolution structures, etc. We now discuss these methods briefly.

The state-of-the-art-denoising methods for selecting threshold in order to denoise a noisy image using wavelet transforms are discussed in refs. [17–20,24–41]. The choice of a threshold, an important point of interest, plays a major role in noise removal from the noisy images because denoising produces smoothed images and reduces the image sharpness. Donoho and Johnstone [20,24–26] have done good works on finding the thresholds; however, a few have been designed specifically for images. The VisuShrink uses a threshold value T_{Visu} that is proportional to the standard deviation of the noise [24,26]. It is also probably the most popular global thresholding approach. The threshold used in the VisuShrink, also referred to as the universal threshold, is defined as follows:

$$T_{\text{Visu}} = \sigma\sqrt{2\log M} \tag{7.8}$$

where σ^2 is the noise variance present in the signal, and M is the signal size or the number of samples.

An estimation of the noise variance σ^2 is obtained based on the median absolute deviation that is given by (see Figure 7.4):

$$\sigma^2 = \left[\frac{\text{median}\left|HH_1\right|}{0.6745}\right]^2 \tag{7.9}$$

This threshold produces a denoised image, which loses many of the detailed coefficients due to its large threshold value. Here, HH_1 refers to the approximate image at the first decomposition level using the wavelet transform.

The SureShrink developed by Donoho and Johnstone [25] overcomes this drawback of the VisuShrink as it has a different threshold for each subband. The name "SureShrink" has been derived from Stein's unbiased risk estimator (SURE), and it is optimally smoothness-adaptive by the statistics of the input data. It is a combination of the universal threshold and the SURE threshold. This threshold yields much better image quality and lower MSE than the VisuShrink as the SureShrink suppresses the noise by thresholding the empirical wavelet coefficients. The SureShrink threshold T_{Sure} is defined as follows:

$$T_{\text{Sure}} = \left(t_J, \sigma\sqrt{2\log M}\right) \tag{7.10}$$

where t_J denotes the value that minimizes the SURE from the noisy coefficients at the Jth decomposition level in the wavelet domain.

The BayesShrink minimizes the Bayesian risk, hence its name [27]. The Bayesian risk, using probabilistic approach, helps decision making (e.g., classification) to minimize the risk (cost). It uses soft thresholding and is subband-dependent, which means that the thresholding is done at

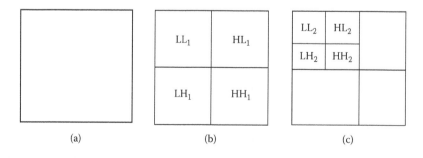

Figure 7.4 **2D-DWT image decomposition: (a) original; (b) 1-level; and (c) 2-level.**

each band of resolution, that is, each subband in the wavelet decomposition. This threshold T_{Bayes} is defined as follows:

$$T_{\text{Bayes}} = \frac{\sigma^2}{\sigma_s} \tag{7.11}$$

where σ^2 is the noise variance given in Equation 7.9, and σ_s^2 is the original signal variance that is given by

$$\sigma_s^2 = \max\left(0, \frac{1}{M^2}\sum_{m,n=1}^{M} F_{m,n}^2 - \sigma^2\right) \tag{7.12}$$

Here, $F_{m,n}$ denotes the wavelet coefficient at location (m,n). The BayesShrink is simple and effective, and outperforms the SureShrink.

The above denoising methods, that is, VisuShrink, SureShrink, and BayesShrink, sometimes blur the image and lose some details as the constructed wavelet coefficients are smaller than their threshold values. Finding the optimal value of the threshold is a major problem. A small threshold surpasses all the noisy coefficients, and the resultant denoised signal is still noisy. A large threshold value makes more number of coefficients as zero that leads to a smooth signal. It destroys the details that may cause blurs and artifacts. Therefore, we discuss other related denoising methods by analyzing the parameters of the wavelet coefficients in each subband in order to have an optimal value. In these methods, the threshold is decided based on the noisy coefficients in each subband and variance of these noisy coefficients. In ref. [28], we modify the VisuShrink threshold by including the decomposition level. The modified threshold T_{EI} is defined as follows:

$$T_{\text{EI}} = \sigma\sqrt{2\log \bar{M} - k} \tag{7.13}$$

Here, $\bar{M} (= M \times M)$ represents the original image size, and σ^2 is the noise variance that is given in Equation 7.9, $k = 1, 2, \ldots, J$, where J is the number of decomposition levels.

This method outperforms the VisuShrink denoising method. In other methods [29,30], the new threshold functions T_{NI} and T_{NS} have been developed to improve the VisuShrink method as in ref. [29]. The threshold function T_{NI} is defined as follows:

$$T_{\text{NI}} = 2\sigma + \left(\frac{\left(\sigma\sqrt{2\log\dfrac{M}{2^k} - k}\right) - \text{I}}{\left(\sigma\sqrt{2\log\dfrac{M}{2^k} - k}\right) + \text{I}}\right) \tag{7.14}$$

where I is calculated as

$$I = \frac{\sum_{q=0}^{2} A(q)}{\hat{M}} \tag{7.15}$$

Here, $A(q) = \sum |F_{m,n}|$, for $q = 0, 1, 2$; $F_{m,n}$ represents the horizontal, vertical, and diagonal wavelet coefficients at position (m,n), respectively.

The threshold function T_{NS} is adaptive to different subband characteristics, and it is obtained by analyzing the parameters of the wavelet coefficients as follows [30]:

$$T_{NS} = \sigma e^{\left(\frac{T_{Visu}-I}{T_{Visu}+I}\right)}; \quad T_{Visu} \text{ and } I \text{ are defined in Equations 7.8 and 7.15, respectively.} \quad (7.16)$$

In another method, new threshold T that can keep more information of the noisy image is defined as follows [31,32]:

$$T = \left(1 - e^{-\frac{F_{m,n}^2}{H_C}}\right); \quad 1 \le c \le 2 \quad (7.17)$$

The parameter H_1 is computed once for each subband at each decomposition level using the following expression [31]:

$$H_1 = \sigma \left(\frac{\sum F_{m,n} - \sigma}{\sum F_{m,n} + \sigma}\right)\left(\sqrt{\frac{\log \hat{M}}{k}}\right) \quad (7.18)$$

Here, $k = 1, 2, \ldots, J$, where J signifies the number of decomposition levels, $\hat{M} = \dfrac{M}{2^k}$, and σ^2 is the noise variance that is defined in Equation 7.9.

Another adaptive parameter H_2 is defined for each subband at each decomposition level k as follows [32]:

$$H_2 = \sigma \left(2^{-\frac{V_s}{\sigma}}\right)\left(\sqrt{f(n)\left(\frac{\log \hat{M}}{k}\right)}\right) \quad (7.19)$$

where $f(n) = \left(\dfrac{2n}{2n+1}\right)$, which is called the noise reduction factor; n is a positive integer, that is, $n > 0$.

The choice of n is not dependent on scale, subband, noise, and image. It has, however, been observed that the reconstructed image has good quality, that is, a high PSNR for higher values of n in case of a high noise level on average, as the new threshold function given in Equation 7.17 increases for all values of n and hence the method performs significantly better for higher noise values.

Another parameter V_s is defined as follows:

$$V_s = \max\left(0, \frac{\sum\limits_{m,n=0}^{M-1} F_{m,n}}{\hat{M}} - \sigma\right); \quad F \in \text{details subband coefficients in } HH_k, HL_k, \text{ and } LH_k. \quad (7.20)$$

The experimental results show that these methods outperform the VisuShrink, SureShrink, and BayesShrink denoising methods.

Cai and Silverman [33] have discussed a simple effective approach for 1-D signals by incorporating the neighboring coefficients, which is named as NeighBlock. It consists of the following steps:

a. Decompose the noisy signal into the orthogonal wavelet domain.
b. Define a small block D of length $l_0 = \log(M/2)$ for each decomposition level with each coefficient.
c. Block is extended in each direction by $l_1 = \max(1, (l_0/2))$, and new block length is $l = l_0 + 2l_1$.
   New block D with block length l consists of thresholded noisy coefficients and its neighbors.
d. Desired noise free image $\bar{X}$ of F is obtained as follows:

$$\bar{X} = F\left(\left(1 - \frac{lT^2}{S^2}\right)_+\right) \tag{7.21}$$

Here, threshold $T = 4.50525$, and S^2 denotes the sum of squares of wavelet coefficients $d(p,q)$ in the neighboring window $D(m,n)$ (see Figure 7.5), that is,

$$S^2 = \sum_{p,q \in D(m,n)} d^2(p,q) \tag{7.22}$$

e. Reconstruct denoised data using inverse discrete wavelet transform (IDWT) from thresholded coefficients.

The above denoising method NeighBlock [33] was meant for 1-D signals. Its variant for 2-D signals, called NeighShrink, incorporates the neighboring coefficients in the thresholding process by considering a local (square) window of length L (a positive odd integer) and uses the VisuShrink threshold [34–37]. The coefficients in different subbands are thresholded independently; however, the threshold value and the neighboring window size are kept unchanged in all subbands. Shrinking of wavelet coefficients is done according to the James–Stein (JS) rule, which is given as follows:

$$\bar{X} = F\left(\left(1 - \frac{T_{\text{Visu}}^2}{S^2}\right)_+\right) \tag{7.23}$$

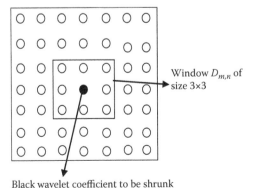

Window $D_{m,n}$ of size 3×3

Black wavelet coefficient to be shrunk

Figure 7.5 **Neighborhood window centered at wavelet coefficient to be shrunk.**

After applying the above shrinkage factor to wavelet coefficients, it has been observed that some details in the image are lost and sometimes the reconstructed image becomes blurred due to a large value of the shrinkage factor. This problem has been overcome by using the ModiNeighShrink shrinkage factor [37], which is given as follows:

$$\bar{X} = F\left(\left(1 - \frac{3}{4}\frac{T_{\text{Visu}}^2}{S^2}\right)_+\right) \tag{7.24}$$

Another denoising method, namely, IAWDMBNC [38], that improves the NeighShrink [34–37] considers the adaptive threshold T_{IA} that is defined as follows:

$$T_{\text{IA}} = T_{\text{Visu}}\left(\frac{Sq_{\max} - S^2}{Sq_{\max} - Sq_{\min}}\right) \tag{7.25}$$

Here, T_{Visu} is the VisuShrink threshold defined in Equation 7.8. $Sq_{\max}$ and $Sq_{\min}$ represent the maximum and minimum summation square of wavelet coefficients, S^2, defined in Equation 7.22 at the same level, respectively.

Shrinking of the noisy wavelet coefficients is done using the following relation:

$$\bar{X} = F\left(1 - \left(\frac{T_{\text{IA}}^2}{S^2}\right)^k\right)_+; \quad 1 \le k \le J, \tag{7.26}$$

where J denotes the number of decomposition levels.

NeighShrink [33–37] and ModiNeighShrink [37] are important methods to remove the noise from a corrupted image based on the universal threshold. These methods have disadvantages: (a) they use suboptimal universal threshold, and (b) they use identical neighboring window size in all subbands. We now discuss an improved method [39–41] that determines a threshold as well as neighboring window size for every subband using its length. This threshold value, denoted by T_{II}, is defined as follows [39]:

$$T_{\text{II}} = \sigma\sqrt{2\log \hat{M}} \tag{7.27}$$

where $\hat{M} = \dfrac{M}{2^k}$, $k = 1, 2, \ldots, J$, where J denotes decomposition levels, and σ^2 is the noise variance defined in Equation 7.9.

Shrinking of the noisy wavelet coefficients is done as follows [37]:

$$\bar{X} = F\lambda \tag{7.28}$$

Here, λ is defined in terms of S^2 as follows:

$$\lambda = \left(1 - \frac{3}{4}\frac{T_{\text{II}}^2}{S^2}\right)_+ \tag{7.29}$$

The + sign in this relation means to keep the positive value and discard negative values, that is, set them to zero.

In the methods discussed in refs. [33–37], some image details are lost and sometimes the reconstructed image becomes blurred due to suboptimal universal threshold. These shortcomings can be overcome by modifying all the details of the noisy coefficients using the exponential function, which leads to exponential decay of the wavelet coefficients across scales. Therefore, an adaptive image denoising method has been developed to remove the noise efficiently [40]. It follows the threshold T_{AW} as defined below:

$$T_{AW} = f(t)\sigma\sqrt{2\log \hat{M}} - k \tag{7.30}$$

Here, $f(t)$ is an improving factor that is given as $f(t) = e^{-\frac{t}{t+1}}$; $t > 0$, an integer. Shrinking of the noisy wavelet coefficients is done as follows [33–37]:

$$\bar{X} = F\lambda \tag{7.31}$$

Here, λ is defined in terms of S^2 as follows:

$$\lambda = \left(1 - \frac{T_{AW}^2}{S^2}\right)_+ \tag{7.32}$$

We describe another denoising method [41] that provides a shrinkage factor based on thresholding and neighboring window of each wavelet coefficient. In this method, the wavelet coefficients in every subband of the noisy image are thresholded in an adaptive manner. This method performs better than the NeighShrink, ModiNeighShrink, and IIDMWT methods for various noise levels and different neighboring window sizes. This method uses the threshold, denoted by T_{GI}, as defined below:

$$T_{GI} = \sigma\sqrt{2\log \hat{M}} - k \tag{7.33}$$

where $\hat{M} = \dfrac{M}{2^k}$ is the image dimension at the kth decomposition level, and σ^2 is the noise variance defined in Equation 7.9.

Shrinking of the noisy wavelet coefficients is done as follows [41]:

$$\bar{X} = F\lambda \tag{7.34}$$

It has been found that using the shrinkage factor λ of the ModiNeighShrink from Equation 7.24, there are blurring and aberration problems for the high noise level. Therefore, this method does not provide some image details. In order to overcome the problems of blurring and aberration, we define the following shrinkage factor, denoted by λ, for any value of n, as follows:

$$\lambda = \left(1 - \frac{n}{(n+1)^2}\frac{T_{GI}^2}{S^2}\right)_+ \tag{7.35}$$

where S^2 is given in Equation 7.22. The threshold T_{GI} is defined in Equation 7.33, and n is a positive integer, that is, $0 < n < \infty$. Here, the choice of n is independent of the image, noise, subband, and scale. It has been observed that taking a higher value of n gives good quality of the image, that is, a high PSNR for a high noise value.

The fuzzy-based wavelet shrinkage methods are used for neighbor dependency and uncorrelated nature of noise [47–49]. Hence, the fuzzy MFs based on fuzzy features are used to enhance the wavelet noisy coefficients in subbands during the shrinkage. This feature space distinguishes between important coefficients belonging to image discontinuity and noisy coefficients. Therefore, we describe the fuzzy MF, the fuzzy-based rule, and the fuzzy-based wavelet shrinkage.

7.3.1 Membership Function

The MF such as Gaussian is used for fuzzy-based wavelet shrinkage method to reduce Gaussian noise from a corrupted image [49]. Therefore, the fuzzy theorem is used to select the best value with respect to the threshold, which means that most of the coefficients under the threshold are noisy and most of the coefficients above the threshold are signal. The image data are converted from the input level into the membership level, and the membership values can be modified with fuzzy rule–based methods, thus giving noise-free image data. In fuzzy-based methods, a window $W(m,n)$ of odd size is considered, which is centered at the main (central) wavelet coefficient. The average value $X(m,n)$ of its neighboring coefficients in $W(m,n)$ at location (m,n) is calculated by [49]

$$X(m,n) = \frac{\displaystyle\sum_{i=1}^{L}\sum_{j=1}^{L}\left|W(m+i,n+j)\right| - \left|W(m,n)\right|}{(2L+1)^2 - 1} \;;\quad 1 \le i,j \le L, \tag{7.36}$$

where L is a positive odd integer.

If the average value of neighboring coefficients is more than the central coefficient, it is the signal component. If both the central coefficient and the average value of neighboring coefficients are small, the central coefficient is the noisy coefficient. The MF is used to determine whether the variable is small, large, or a degree of being large. For both the wavelet coefficient $W(m,n)$ and the average value of neighborhood $X(m,n)$, two MFs for $W(m,n)$ and $X(m,n)$ denoted by μ_W and μ_X, respectively, are defined as [49]

$$\mu_W = \begin{cases} 0, & W > T_1 \\ \dfrac{-(W(m,n)-T_1)^2}{2T_2^2}, & T_1 \le W(m,n) \le T_2 \\ 1, & W > T_2 \end{cases} \tag{7.37}$$

$$\mu_X = \begin{cases} 0, & X = t \\ e^{\frac{-(T_3)^2}{2t^2}}, & t \le X(m,n) \le T_3 \\ 1, & X > T_3 \end{cases} \tag{7.38}$$

In order to construct all the above MFs, three thresholds are needed: two for μ_W and one for μ_X. In this study, the values of thresholds are chosen from ref. [48], which are $T_1 = \sigma$, $T_2 = 2\sigma$, and $T_3 = 2.9\sigma - 2.625$. In simulation, we consider different values of σ: 10, 20, 30, 50, 75, and 100, and the parameter t for Gaussian is set as a negligible value, that is, near zero (here, the value of t is set to 0.01) [47].

7.3.2 Fuzzy Shrinkage Rules

Rule base is the main part of a fuzzy system, and the quality of results of a system depends on the fuzzy rules. The fuzzy rules can be expressed with the natural language in the following manner:

if a is small and b is middle, then c is great.

The variables a, b, and c are linguistic type. The fuzzy rules in the domain of wavelet shrinkage can be defined as follows [47–49]:

Fuzzy Rule 1:
IF $(|X(m,n)|)$ is a large variable *OR*
        $(|W(m,n)|)$ is a large coefficient *AND* $(|X(m,n)|)$ is a large variable
THEN $W(m,n)$ is a signal of interest signal

In this rule, there are one T-norm and one S-norm that means the first antecedent contains an *AND* (intersection), and between the first and second antecedent, an *OR* (union) is used. The fuzzy rule 1 is used to produce an equation for T-norm, which is $(a \cdot b)$, and the potential sum equation for S-norm is $(a + b - a \cdot b)$. Based on these assumptions, according to the criterion in the antecedent part of the fuzzy rule 1, it can be translated into a "truth" value: $\mu_X(|X(m,n)|) \cdot \mu_W(|W(m,n)|)$, where μ_W and μ_X are the MFs for the fuzzy set large variables and large coefficient, respectively [48–50].

7.3.3 Fuzzy-Based Wavelet Shrinkage

The shrinkage factor based on fuzzy logic is calculated to shrink the noisy coefficients in order to give noise-free coefficients as follows [47,48]:

$$\bar{X}(m,n) = \gamma(W(m,n), X(m,n)) \cdot W(m,n) \tag{7.39}$$

where $\gamma(W(m,n), X(m,n))$ denotes the degree of activation of fuzzy rule 1 for the wavelet coefficient $W(m,n)$. This value indicates the membership degree in the fuzzy set signal of interest for the wavelet coefficient $W(m,n)$ that is calculated as [47]

$$\gamma(W(m,n), X(m,n)) = \alpha + (1 - \alpha) \cdot \mu_X(|X(m,n)|) \tag{7.40}$$

If the membership degree has a value 1, the coefficient is certainly a proper signal and should not be changed (should not be shrunk), whereas a degree zero indicates that the coefficient is certainly noise and should be set equal to zero. The parameter α is calculated by [47]

$$\alpha = \mu_X(X(m,n)) \cdot \mu_W(X(m,n)) \tag{7.41}$$

So far, we have discussed various denoising methods whose performance needs to be evaluated. Before discussing the performance evaluation of the above discussed methods, we describe the performance parameters.

7.4 Performance Parameters

The image quality measures play an important role in image processing applications. The image quality evaluation parameters can be described in terms of objective and subjective aspects. The subjective aspect is based on human judgment and operates without reference to explicit criteria. The objective aspect is based on comparisons by using explicit numerical criteria. There are two types of quality or distortion assessment approaches. The first is mathematically defined measures, such as MSE and PSNR. The second one considers human visual system (HVS) characteristics to incorporate the perceptual quality measures. To evaluate performance of the denoising methods discussed in this chapter, we consider two assessment measures, namely, PSNR and SSIM, that are applied to obtain the fair and complete performance evaluation. The PSNR value approaches infinity as the MSE approaches zero. This implies that a higher PSNR value provides higher image quality. At the other end of the scale, a small value of the PSNR implies high numerical difference between images. The SSIM is a well-known quality metric used to measure the similarity between two images. The SSIM is designed by modeling any image distortion as a combination of three factors: loss of correlation, luminance, and contrast distortions. The PSNR is defined as follows:

$$\text{PSNR} = 10 \log_{10} \frac{2^L - 1}{\text{MSE}} \tag{7.42a}$$

L is the index of an image, that is, the number of bits used to represent a pixel and the MSE is given by

$$\text{MSE} = \frac{1}{M^2} \sum_{m,n=1}^{M} (x(m,n) - \hat{X}(m,n))^2 \tag{7.42b}$$

where $x(m,n)$ and $\hat{X}(m,n)$ are the original image without noise and the estimation of the noise-free image pixels at location (m,n), respectively; $M \times M$ is the original image size.

The SSIM is defined as follows:

$$\text{SSIM}(x,X) = l(x,X)c(x,X)s(x,X) \tag{7.43}$$

where x and X represent two discrete nonnegative signals that have been aligned with each other. The luminance, contrast, and structure comparison measures, denoted by l, c, and s, respectively, are given by

$$l(x,X) = \frac{2\mu_x \mu_X + a_1}{\mu_x^2 + \mu_X^2 + a_1} \tag{7.44a}$$

$$c(x, X) = \frac{2\sigma_x \sigma_X + a_2}{\sigma_x^2 + \sigma_X^2 + a_2} \qquad (7.44b)$$

$$s(x, X) = \frac{\sigma_{xX} + a_3}{\sigma_x \sigma_X + a_3} \qquad (7.44c)$$

where μ_x, μ_X, σ_x^2, σ_X^2, and σ_{xX} denote the mean, variance, and covariance of x and X, respectively; a_1, a_2, and a_3 are small constants that are given by

$$a_1 = (b_1 L)^2, \quad a_2 = (b_2 L)^2, \quad a_3 = \frac{a_2}{2} \qquad (7.45)$$

L is the dynamic range of a pixel value ($L = 255$ for 8 bits/pixel gray scale images), and $b_1 \ll 1$ and $b_2 \ll 1$ are two scalar constants.

In Section 7.5, we discuss experimental results of the above discussed denoising methods.

7.5 Experimental Results and Discussions

The experimental study has been performed on the following test images, each of size 512×512 (see Figure 7.6): Lena, Barbara, Cameraman, Goldhill, and Mandrill, using wavelet- and

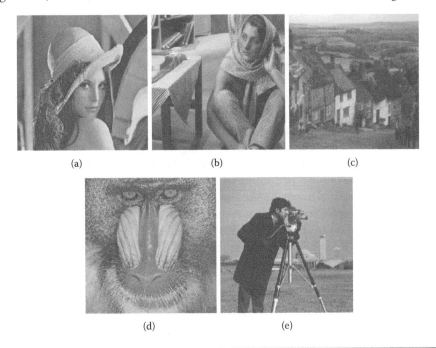

(a)   (b)   (c)

(d)   (e)

Figure 7.6   Original test gray images, each of 512×512 pixels: (a) Lena, (b) Barbara, (c) Goldhill, (d) Mandrill, and (e) Cameraman.

nonwavelet-based methods without and with fuzzy logic. These images are corrupted by the additive zero-mean Gaussian noise with the following noise levels: 10, 20, 30, 50, 75, and 100. In these experiments, we use Symlet wavelet of length eight up to four decomposition levels and the 3×3 square window for block-by-block approach. The experimental results in terms of PSNRs, SSIMs [50], and visual quality of the restored images have been considered for objective and subjective qualities.

Tables 7.1 and 7.2 contain PSNR values for the wavelet-based methods (using term-by-term and block-by-block approaches, respectively) for test images: Lena, Barbara, Goldhill, Mandrill, and Cameraman, corrupted with different noise levels. Table 7.3 contains PSNR values for fuzzy-based nonwavelet methods for the test images corrupted with different noise levels. Tables 7.4 and 7.5 contain SSIM values for the same scenarios as those for Tables 7.1 and 7.2. Table 7.6 contains SSIM values for the same scenario as those for Table 7.3 using fuzzy logic. The original test images are shown in Figure 7.6a–e. The Lena, Barbara, Goldhill, Mandrill, and Cameraman images have been corrupted with noise levels 20, 30, 50, 75, and 100, respectively, which are shown in Figure 7.7a–e.

Figure 7.8a–f shows denoised Lena image using (a) NeighShrink, (b) ModiNeighShrink, (c) IAWDMNC, (d) ref. [39], (e) ref. [40], and (f) ref. [41]. Figures 7.9a–h and 7.10a–h show denoised Barbara and Goldhill images, respectively, using (a) VisuShrink, (b) SureShrink, (c) BayesShrink, (d) ref. [28], (e) ref. [29], (f) ref. [30], (g) ref. [31], and (h) ref. [32]. Figure 7.11a–f shows denoised Mandrill image using (a) NeighShrink, (b) ModineighShrink, (c) IAWDMNC, (d) ref. [39], (e) ref. [40], and (f) ref. [41].

Figures 7.12a–f and 7.13a–f show denoised Cameraman and Barbara images, respectively, using (a) Median, (b) Weiner, (c) ATMAV, (d) ATMED, (e) FTS, and (f) ref. [49].

It is evident from Figures 7.8a–f, 7.9a–h, 7.10a–h, 7.11a–f, 7.12a–f, and 7.13a–f that the wavelet-based recent developments [28–32,39–41] on the image denoising methods provide the denoised images with better visual quality. Similar results were obtained for other noise levels and images; however, because of the repetitive nature, those results have not been shown. We observe that the recently developed fuzzy-based wavelet methods [28–32,39–41,49] outperform the state-of-the-art denoising methods in terms of PSNRs and SSIMs. The results of these methods are either better or comparable for all the noise levels: 10, 20, 30, 50, 75, and 100 for all test images under consideration (see Tables 7.1 through 7.6 and Figures 7.8a–f, 7.9a–h, 7.10a–h, 7.11a–f, 7.12a–f, and 7.13a–f). We have also shown the experimental results graphically for their quick analysis. We observe that the new denoising methods having term-by-term approach [28–32] perform better than the VisuShrink, SureShrink, and BayesShrink methods. The new methods having block-by-block approach [39–41] perform better than the NeighShrink, ModiNeighShrink, and IAWDMNC in terms of PSNR for all noise levels.

The fuzzy-based nonwavelet denoising methods (ATMAV, ATMED, and FTS) perform better than (or comparative with) the median and Weiner methods. The fuzzy-based wavelet methods [46–49] perform better than the nonwavelet-based denoising methods: median, Weiner, ATMAV, ATMED, and FTS, for higher noise levels. We have shown PSNR graphs for various methods: (a) VisuShrink, SureShrink, BayesShrink, and refs. [28–32]; (b) NeighShrink, ModiNeighShrink, IAWDMNC, and refs. [39–41]; and (c) Median, Weiner, ATMAV, ATMED, FTS, and ref. [49], respectively, in Figure 7.14a–c for Lena image only. Indeed, we got similar results for other images, and because of their repetitive nature, they are not shown graphically. Here denoising methods are implemented in MATLAB® 7.5.0, running on a 3.20-GHz Pentium IV personal computer with 504 MB RAM.

Table 7.1 PSNRs (in db) with Various Noise Levels 10, 20, 30, 50, 75, and 100 for Test Images Lena, Barbara, Cameraman, Goldhill, and Mandrill Using Term-by-Term Approach for Wavelet Methods

Image Names	Noise Levels	VisuShrink	SureShrink	BayesShrink	Ref. [28]	Ref. [29]	Ref. [30]	Ref. [31]	Ref. [32] n = 1
Lena	10	29.34	30.96	31.34	29.95	30.24	30.77	33.57	32.78
	20	26.40	26.43	29.09	26.80	27.83	28.42	30.49	29.92
	30	24.83	25.21	27.73	25.62	26.34	26.48	28.84	28.39
	50	23.00	23.84	25.91	24.17	24.42	23.79	26.59	26.48
	75	21.66	22.95	24.57	23.23	22.79	22.81	24.43	24.88
	100	20.76	22.38	23.67	22.61	21.58	22.01	23.82	23.73
Barbara	10	26.40	29.33	29.22	26.72	26.70	24.80	32.28	32.15
	20	23.39	24.13	26.36	23.54	24.59	23.67	28.19	28.37
	30	22.07	22.28	24.66	22.51	23.35	22.18	26.08	26.23
	50	20.75	21.32	22.84	21.57	21.94	21.64	23.47	23.83
	75	19.80	20.72	21.84	20.91	20.01	20.19	22.41	22.37
	100	19.11	20.33	21.22	20.48	20.07	18.73	21.52	21.48

(continued)

Table 7.1 (Continued) PSNRs (in db) with Various Noise Levels 10, 20, 30, 50, 75, and 100 for Test Images Lena, Barbara, Cameraman, Goldhill, and Mandrill Using Term-by-Term Approach for Wavelet Methods

Image Names	Noise Levels	VisuShrink	SureShrink	BayesShrink	Ref. [28]	Ref. [29]	Ref. [30]	Ref. [31]	Ref. [32] $n = 1$
Cameraman	10	27.96	31.13	30.78	28.00	29.69	28.63	32.83	32.33
	20	24.93	27.71	27.87	25.36	26.80	26.48	29.29	29.13
	30	23.39	24.10	26.04	24.03	25.16	24.95	27.56	27.35
	50	21.62	22.20	24.04	22.58	23.20	23.12	25.35	25.27
	75	20.32	21.18	22.78	21.56	21.69	21.95	23.53	23.56
	100	19.44	20.55	21.93	20.82	20.56	21.08	22.09	22.28
Goldhill	10	27.67	31.20	31.17	27.78	29.42	30.24	32.22	31.83
	20	25.25	27.86	28.33	25.85	27.12	26.39	29.09	28.75
	30	23.99	25.12	26.85	24.82	24.74	25.52	27.54	27.28
	50	22.51	23.32	25.21	23.64	23.92	23.68	25.69	25.55
	75	21.41	22.58	24.01	22.87	22.59	21.15	24.25	24.21
	100	19.24	22.10	23.18	22.24	21.87	21.62	23.46	23.32
Mandrill	10	23.74	27.76	27.75	24.26	24.31	27.49	29.80	30.03
	20	21.21	24.43	24.54	20.95	22.48	22.39	25.67	25.90
	30	20.20	21.57	22.79	20.28	21.44	21.94	23.27	23.81
	50	19.34	19.62	21.02	19.64	20.23	20.03	21.55	21.70
	75	18.84	19.29	20.07	19.04	19.47	19.32	20.34	20.50
	100	18.51	19.09	19.54	18.70	18.99	18.90	19.80	19.85

Table 7.2 Experimental Results (PSNRs in db) with Various Noise Levels 10, 20, 30, 50, 75, and 100 for Images Lena, Mandrill, Barbara, Cameraman, and Goldhill Using Block-by-Block Approach for Wavelet Denoising Methods

Images	Noise Levels	Denoising Methods				Ref. [40]	Ref. [41]	Ref. [49]
		NeighShrink	ModiNeighShrink	IAWDMNC	Ref. [39]	$t = 2$	$n = 2$	
Lena	10	33.22	33.50	33.83	33.65	34.25	34.04	25.97
	20	28.58	28.89	29.64	29.22	30.08	30.69	25.57
	30	26.09	26.38	27.07	26.74	27.56	28.21	25.38
	50	23.47	23.66	24.47	24.01	24.80	25.45	24.83
	75	22.52	22.64	22.96	22.77	23.12	23.51	23.91
	100	22.06	22.11	22.40	22.17	22.43	22.61	22.89
Mandrill	10	27.26	27.68	28.52	27.91	29.43	29.42	22.38
	20	21.90	22.21	22.80	22.48	23.66	24.25	22.32
	30	20.12	20.26	20.66	20.47	21.22	21.70	22.23
	50	19.37	19.40	19.60	19.46	19.70	19.89	21.95
	75	19.14	19.14	19.24	19.14	19.25	19.30	21.46
	100	19.04	19.04	19.02	19.04	19.04	19.02	20.85
Barbara	10	31.05	31.39	31.83	31.60	32.41	32.45	22.29
	20	25.24	25.65	26.32	25.96	26.93	27.73	22.19

(continued)

Table 7.2 (Continued) Experimental Results (PSNRs in db) with Various Noise Levels 10, 20, 30, 50, 75, and 100 for Images Lena, Mandrill, Barbara, Cameraman, and Goldhill Using Block-by-Block Approach for Wavelet Denoising Methods

| Images | Noise Levels | Denoising Methods | | | | Ref. [40] | Ref. [41] | Ref. [49] |
		NeighShrink	ModiNeighShrink	IAWDMNC	Ref. [39]	t = 2	n = 2	
Barbara	30	22.57	22.78	23.59	23.01	23.90	24.65	22.10
	50	21.07	21.19	21.60	21.36	21.80	22.16	21.83
	75	20.39	20.43	20.76	20.48	20.83	21.07	21.35
	100	20.18	20.18	20.37	20.20	20.31	20.42	20.76
Cameraman	10	32.70	33.04	33.29	33.30	33.89	33.81	25.35
	20	26.96	27.29	27.76	27.42	28.38	29.16	25.24
	30	24.60	24.85	25.46	25.04	25.82	26.47	25.07
	50	21.90	22.18	23.01	22.37	23.21	23.85	24.55
	75	20.37	20.49	21.11	20.50	21.23	21.79	23.69
	100	19.87	19.91	20.32	19.88	20.31	20.60	22.71
Goldhill	10	30.68	30.99	31.27	31.20	32.04	32.06	25.97
	20	26.72	26.97	27.33	27.24	27.92	28.41	25.57
	30	24.79	24.97	25.49	25.26	26.02	26.55	25.38
	50	23.43	23.53	23.78	23.67	24.11	24.46	24.83
	75	22.67	22.77	23.06	22.91	23.15	23.35	23.91
	100	22.20	22.20	22.59	22.23	22.55	22.76	22.89

Table 7.3 Experimental Results (PSNRs in db) with Various Noise Levels: 10, 20, 30, 50, 75, and 100 for Images: Lena, Mandrill, Barbara, Cameraman, and Goldhill for Fuzzy-Based Non-Wavelet Methods

Image Names	Noise Levels	Denoising Methods				
		Median	*Weiner*	*ATMAV*	*ATMED*	*FTS*
Lena	10	32.11	33.55	32.28	32.47	32.31
	20	28.38	28.99	29.38	29.16	29.19
	30	25.54	25.70	26.80	26.46	26.52
	50	21.55	21.40	22.96	22.56	22.62
	75	18.20	17.95	19.64	19.23	19.29
	100	15.79	15.49	17.22	16.80	16.86
Barbara	10	24.90	29.87	25.02	25.03	25.05
	20	23.84	26.82	24.31	24.20	24.30
	30	22.61	24.29	23.34	23.15	23.25
	50	20.14	20.66	21.18	20.89	20.98
	75	17.50	17.55	18.72	18.37	18.45
	100	15.37	15.25	16.66	16.28	16.35
Cameraman	10	29.26	32.77	28.44	29.25	28.74
	20	26.89	28.73	26.84	27.19	27.02
	30	24.62	25.52	25.11	25.16	25.11
	50	21.07	21.23	22.09	21.85	21.89
	75	17.94	17.82	19.19	18.84	18.90
	100	15.61	15.39	16.95	16.55	16.62
Goldhill	10	29.92	31.78	30.19	30.26	30.24
	20	27.30	28.26	28.13	27.94	28.01
	30	24.96	25.35	26.06	25.76	25.84
	50	21.33	21.27	22.63	22.26	22.33
	75	18.11	17.89	19.48	19.08	19.15
	100	15.74	15.45	17.12	16.71	16.78
Mandrill	10	23.39	26.50	23.33	23.49	23.11
	20	22.58	24.79	22.81	22.84	22.88
	30	21.57	23.08	22.07	21.98	22.05
	50	19.47	20.13	20.34	20.10	20.19
	75	17.10	17.30	18.21	17.89	17.97
	100	15.11	15.10	16.33	15.97	16.04

Table 7.4 **SSIMs with Various Noise Levels 10, 20, 30, 50, 75, and 100 for Test Images Lena, Barbara, Cameraman, Goldhill, and Mandrill Using Term-by-Term Approach for Wavelet Methods**

Image Names	Noise Levels	VisuShrink	SureShrink	BayesShrink	Ref. [28]	Ref. [29]	Ref. [30]	Ref. [31]	Ref. [32] n = 1
Lena	10	0.81	0.84	0.82	0.80	0.83	0.81	0.75	0.87
	20	0.75	0.73	0.76	0.75	0.77	0.72	0.70	0.80
	30	0.71	0.70	0.72	0.71	0.71	0.68	0.64	0.75
	50	0.66	0.66	0.68	0.67	0.62	0.62	0.64	0.69
	75	0.63	0.63	0.64	0.64	0.53	0.54	0.58	0.63
	100	0.61	0.61	0.62	0.62	0.46	0.50	0.54	0.59
Barbara	10	0.77	0.83	0.81	0.77	0.81	0.72	0.87	0.90
	20	0.64	0.66	0.70	0.64	0.72	0.51	0.78	0.81
	30	0.57	0.57	0.63	0.58	0.62	0.60	0.71	0.72
	50	0.51	0.51	0.56	0.53	0.54	0.47	0.60	0.61
	75	0.47	0.48	0.52	0.50	0.46	0.37	0.52	0.53
	100	0.45	0.47	0.49	0.48	0.40	0.29	0.48	0.49

Image	Noise								
Cameraman	10	0.82	0.84	0.77	0.82	0.85	0.83	0.78	0.79
	20	0.75	0.74	0.69	0.75	0.77	0.72	0.73	0.79
	30	0.71	0.71	0.66	0.72	0.71	0.65	0.68	0.73
	50	0.67	0.66	0.62	0.68	0.61	0.52	0.56	0.66
	75	0.64	0.62	0.58	0.64	0.51	0.39	0.53	0.61
	100	0.61	0.60	0.56	0.62	0.44	0.29	0.50	0.56
Goldhill	10	0.69	0.82	0.82	0.70	0.77	0.78	0.81	0.86
	20	0.59	0.71	0.72	0.61	0.69	0.54	0.74	0.75
	30	0.55	0.57	0.65	0.57	0.60	0.60	0.67	0.68
	50	0.50	0.51	0.58	0.53	0.52	0.48	0.57	0.59
	75	0.47	0.49	0.54	0.50	0.44	0.34	0.51	0.52
	100	0.46	0.47	0.51	0.48	0.39	0.30	0.47	0.49
Mandrill	10	0.63	0.84	0.84	065	0.70	0.83	0.84	0.87
	20	0.44	0.70	0.71	0.43	0.58	0.62	0.73	0.74
	30	0.35	0.53	0.61	0.36	0.50	0.46	0.65	0.61
	50	0.29	0.29	0.46	0.31	0.38	0.40	0.48	0.46
	75	0.26	0.27	0.36	0.28	0.32	0.28	0.38	0.37
	100	0.25	0.26	0.31	0.27	0.27	0.20	0.33	0.32

Table 7.5 Experimental Results (SSIMs) with Various Noise Levels 10, 20, 30, 50, 75, and 100 for Images Lena, Mandrill, Barbara, Cameraman, and Goldhill Using Block-by-Block Approach for Wavelet Methods

Images	Noise Levels	Denoising Methods				Ref. [40]	Ref. [41]	Ref. [49]
		NeighShrink	ModiNeighShrink	IAWDMNC	Ref. [39]	t = 2	n = 2	
Lena	10	0.87	0.88	0.88	0.88	0.89	0.88	0.71
	20	0.78	0.79	0.80	0.80	0.82	0.83	0.70
	30	0.71	0.72	0.74	0.73	0.76	0.77	0.69
	50	0.64	0.65	0.67	0.66	0.68	0.70	0.66
	75	0.62	0.62	0.63	0.63	0.64	0.64	0.61
	100	0.61	0.61	0.62	0.61	0.62	0.62	0.56
Mandrill	10	0.79	0.81	0.84	0.82	0.87	0.87	0.56
	20	0.48	0.51	0.56	0.53	0.62	0.67	0.55
	30	0.32	0.33	0.37	0.35	0.42	0.47	0.55
	50	0.27	0.27	0.29	0.27	0.29	0.31	0.53
	75	0.26	0.26	0.26	0.26	0.27	0.27	0.50
	100	0.26	0.26	0.26	0.26	0.26	0.26	0.46

Barbara	10	0.88	0.89	0.90	0.89	0.91	0.90	0.69
	20	0.70	0.72	0.74	0.73	0.78	0.80	0.68
	30	0.57	0.58	0.63	0.60	0.64	0.68	0.66
	50	0.49	0.50	0.52	0.51	0.53	0.55	0.62
	75	0.47	0.47	0.48	0.47	0.49	0.50	0.58
	100	0.46	0.46	0.47	0.46	0.47	0.47	0.49
Cameraman	10	0.90	0.90	0.91	0.91	0.92	0.90	0.57
	20	0.78	0.79	0.80	0.80	0.82	0.84	0.57
	30	0.72	0.73	0.74	0.74	0.76	0.77	0.56
	50	0.66	0.66	0.67	0.67	0.69	0.70	0.54
	75	0.61	0.61	0.62	0.62	0.64	0.64	0.51
	100	0.59	0.59	0.60	0.59	0.60	0.60	0.47
Goldhill	10	0.79	0.80	0.81	0.81	0.84	0.85	0.32
	20	0.63	0.64	0.66	0.65	0.69	0.71	0.32
	30	0.55	0.55	0.58	0.57	0.60	0.63	0.32
	50	0.50	0.50	0.51	0.51	0.52	0.54	0.31
	75	0.49	0.49	0.49	0.49	0.50	0.50	0.30
	100	0.48	0.48	0.48	0.48	0.48	0.49	0.28

Table 7.6 Experimental Results (SSIMs) with Various Noise Levels: 10, 20, 30, 50, 75, and 100 for Images: Lena, Mandrill, Barbara, Cameraman, and Goldhill for Fuzzy-Based Non-Wavelet Methods

Image Names	Noise Levels	Denoising Methods				
		Median	Weiner	ATMAV	ATMED	FTS
Lena	10	0.82	0.86	0.85	0.84	0.84
	20	0.65	0.69	0.70	0.69	0.70
	30	0.51	0.53	0.57	0.55	0.56
	50	0.33	0.33	0.38	0.37	0.37
	75	0.21	0.21	0.25	0.24	0.24
	100	0.14	0.15	0.17	0.17	0.17
Barbara	10	0.74	0.85	0.74	0.74	0.75
	20	0.61	0.73	0.64	0.63	0.64
	30	0.49	0.60	0.54	0.53	0.53
	50	0.34	0.40	0.39	0.37	0.38
	75	0.23	0.26	0.27	0.26	0.26
	100	0.16	0.18	0.20	0.18	0.19
Cameraman	10	0.82	0.87	0.84	0.84	0.84
	20	0.63	0.70	0.67	0.66	0.67
	30	0.47	0.52	0.53	0.51	0.52
	50	0.29	0.31	0.34	0.33	0.33
	75	0.19	0.20	0.22	0.21	0.22
	100	0.13	0.14	0.16	0.15	0.15
Goldhill	10	0.78	0.83	0.80	0.80	0.80
	20	0.64	0.70	0.69	0.68	0.68
	30	0.52	0.56	0.58	0.56	0.57
	50	0.34	0.36	0.40	0.38	0.39
	75	0.21	0.22	0.16	0.25	0.25
	100	0.14	0.15	0.18	0.17	0.17
Mandrill	10	0.67	0.78	0.67	0.67	0.67
	20	0.59	0.71	0.61	0.61	0.62
	30	0.51	0.62	0.55	0.54	0.55
	50	0.38	0.46	0.43	0.41	0.42
	75	0.27	0.32	0.32	0.30	0.31
	100	0.20	0.24	0.24	0.23	0.23

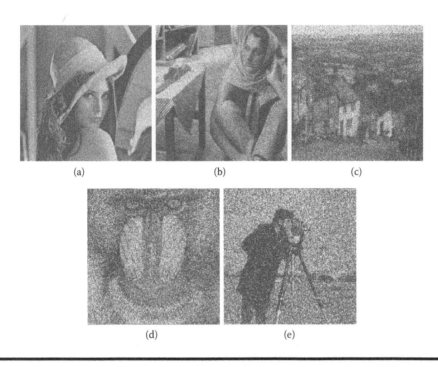

Figure 7.7 Noisy images with noise level (a) 20 for Lena, (b) 30 for Barbara, (c) 50 for Goldhill, (d) 75 for Mandrill, and (e) 100 for Cameraman.

Figure 7.8 Comparative performance of various methods on Lena image for noise level 20 with denoised image using (a) NeighShrink; (b) ModiNeighShrink; (c) IAWDMNC; (d) ref. [39]; (e) ref. [40]; and (f) ref. [41].

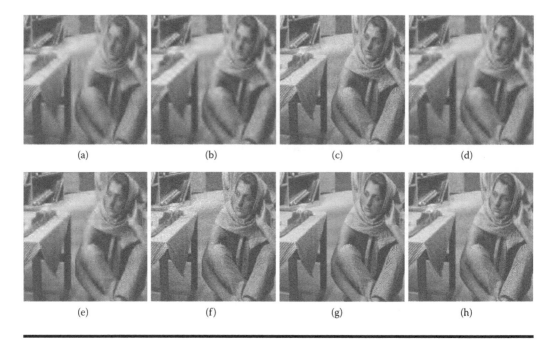

Figure 7.9 Comparative performance of various methods on Barbara image for noise level 30 with denoised image using (a) VisuShrink; (b) SureShrink; (c) BayesShrink; (d) ref. [28]; (e) ref. [29]; (f) ref. [30]; (g) ref. [31]; and (h) ref. [32].

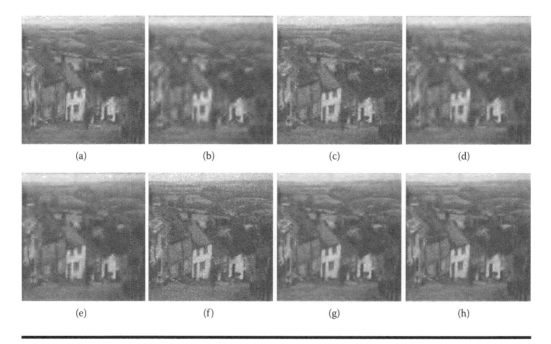

Figure 7.10 Comparative performance of various methods on Goldhill image for noise level 50 with denoised image using (a) VisuShrink; (b) SureShrink; (c) BayesShrink; (d) ref. [28]; (e) ref. [29]; (f) ref. [30]; (g) ref. [31]; and (h) ref. [32].

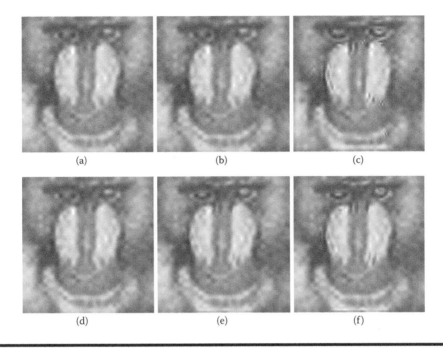

(a)   (b)   (c)

(d)   (e)   (f)

Figure 7.11 Comparative performance of various methods on Mandrill image for noise level 75 with denoised image using (a) NeighShrink; (b) ModineighShrink; (c) IAWDMNC; (d) ref. [39]; (e) ref. [40]; and (f) ref. [41].

(a)   (b)   (c)

(d)   (e)   (f)

Figure 7.12 Comparative performance of various methods on Cameraman image for noise level 100 with denoised image using (a) median; (b) Weiner; (c) ATMAV; (d) ATMED; (e) FTS; and (f) ref. [49].

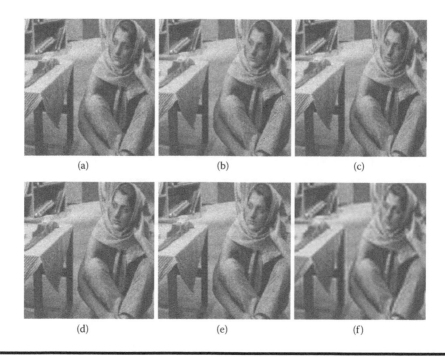

Figure 7.13 Comparative performance of various methods on Barbara image for noise level 30 with denoised image using (a) median; (b) Weiner; (c) ATMAV; (d) ATMED; (e) FTS; and (f) ref. [49].

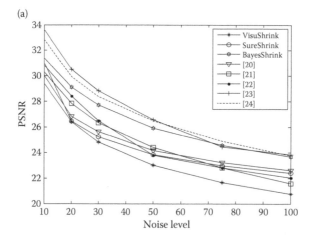

Figure 7.14 PSNR versus noise level of various methods: (a) VisuShrink, SureShrink, BayesShrink, and refs. [28–32].

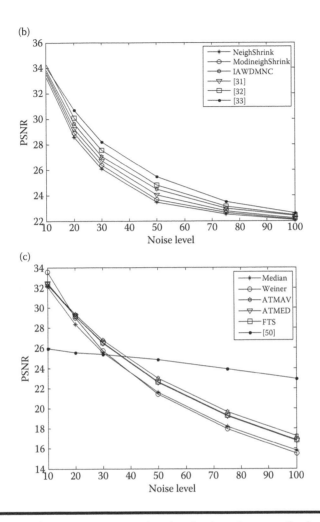

Figure 7.14 (Continued) PSNR versus noise level of various methods: (b) NeighShrink, ModiNeighShrink, IAWDMNC, and refs. [39–41]; and (c) median, Weiner, ATMAV, ATMED, FTS, and ref. [49].

7.6 Conclusion and Future Scope

Generally, image denoising imposes a compromise between noise reduction and preservation of significant image details. To achieve good performance in this respect, a denoising algorithm has to be adaptive to image discontinuities. In this chapter, we have done case study of several image denoising methods based on intelligence and non-intelligence approaches that follow term-by-term and block-by-block approaches in nonwavelet and wavelet domain on the standard natural test images corrupted with white Gaussian noise. Based on our experimental results, we conclude that the recently developed denoising methods have better performance for all test images and for all noise levels. They remove the noise and retrieve the significant image features of the noisy image. Apart from that, there is much room/sufficient scope for further development of the algorithms using other transforms such as discrete Hartley transform, Curvelet, Slantlet, and Contourlet. Furthermore, we can train denoising methods using various AI techniques like fuzzy logic, artificial neural network (ANN), and genetic algorithm (GA) in order to attain the best output without performing calculations for each and every combination. Using AI techniques will lead to the optimal solution with less tedious work.

References

1. Jain, A. K. 1989. *Fundamentals of Digital Image Processing*. Prentice Hall Information and System Sciences Series, Englewood Cliffs: Prentice Hall.
2. Gonzalez, R. C., and R. E. Woods. 2008. *Digital Image Processing*. Pearson Education, 3rd Edition, Upper Saddle River, NJ: Prentice-Hall.
3. Pratt, W. K. 2001. *Digital Image Processing*. New York: John Wiley & Sons.
4. Pitas, I., and A. N. Venetsanopoulos. 1990. *Nonlinear Digital Filters*. New York: Springer-Verlag.
5. Astola, J., and P. Kuosmanen. 1997. *Fundamentals of Nonlinear Digital Filtering*. Boca Raton, FL: CRC Press.
6. Hartley, R. V. L. 1942. A more symmetrical Fourier analysis applied to transmission problems. *Proceedings of the IRE* 30:144–150.
7. McVeigh, E. R., R. M. Henkelman, and M. J. Bronskill. 1985. Noise and filtration in magnetic resonance imaging. *Medical Physics* 12:586–591.
8. Hamza, A. B., and H. Krim. 2001. Image denoising: A nonlinear robust statistical approach. *IEEE Transactions on Signal Processing* 49:3045–3054.
9. Kosko, B. 1992. *Neural Networks and Fuzzy Systems*. Englewood Cliffs, NJ: Prentice-Hall.
10. Lin, C. T., and C. S. George Lee. 1996. *Neural Fuzzy Systems*. Englewood Cliffs, NJ: Prentice-Hall.
11. Durairaj, D. C., M. C. Krishna, and R. Murugesan. 2007. A neural network approach for image reconstruction in electron magnetic resonance tomography. *Computers in Biology and Medicine* 37:1492–1501.
12. Russo, M. 2000. Genetic fuzzy learning. *IEEE Transactions on Evolutionary Computation* 4:259–273.
13. Ali, S. A., S. Vathsal, and K. Lal kishore. 2010. A GA-based window selection methodology to enhance window-based Multi-wavelet transformation and thresholding aided CT image denoising technique. *International Journal of Computer Science and Information Security* 7:280–288.
14. Thavavel, V., and R. Murugesan. 2007. GA-based adaptive wavelet denoising of low-dose medical images application to EMR tomograms. *International Conference on Conference on Computational Intelligence and Multimedia Applications* 1:487–492.
15. Thanh, N. M., and M. S. Chen. 2007. Image denoising using adaptive neuro-fuzzy system. *IAENG International Journal of Applied Mathematics* 36:1–7.
16. Rafiee, A., M. H. Moradi, and M. R. Farzaneh. 2004. Novel genetic-neuro-fuzzy filter for speckle reduction. *Journal of Digit Imaging* 17:292–300.
17. Weaver, J. B., X. Yansun, D. M. J. Healy, and L. D. Cromwell. 1991. Filtering noise from images with wavelet transforms. *Magnetic Resonance in Medicine* 24:288–295.
18. Xu, Y., and J. B. Weaver. 1994. Wavelet transform domain filters: A spatially selective noise filtration technique. *IEEE Transactions on Image Processing* 3:747–757.
19. Johnstone, I. M., and B. W. Silverman. 1997. Wavelet threshold estimators for data with correlated noise. *Journal of Royal Statistical Society: Series B* 59:319–351.
20. Donoho, D. L., and I. M. Johnstone. 1995. Wavelet shrinkage: Asymptotic. *Journal of American Statistical Association, Series B* 57:301–369.
21. Daubechies, I. 1992. *Ten Lectures on Wavelets*. Philadelphia, PA: Society for Industrial and Applied Mathematics.
22. Mallat, S. 1999. *A Wavelet Tour of Signal Processing*. New York: Academic.
23. Goswami, J. C., and A. K. Chan. 1999. *Fundamentals of Wavelets*. New York: John Wiley & Sons, Inc.
24. Donoho, D. L. 1995. De-noising by soft thresholding. *IEEE Transactions on Information Theory* 41:613–627.
25. Donoho, D. L., and I. M. Johnstone. 1995. Adapting to unknown smoothness via wavelet shrinkage. *Journal of American Statistical Association* 90:1200–1224.

26. Donoho, D. L., and I. M. Johnstone. 1994. Ideal spatial adaptation via wavelet shrinkage. *Biometrika* 81:425–455.
27. Chang, S. G., B. Yu, and M. Vetterli. 2000. Adaptive wavelet thresholding for image denoising and compression. *IEEE Transactions on Image Processing* 9:1532–1546.
28. Om, H., and M. Biswas. 2013. An enhanced image denoising scheme. *International Journal on Information and Communication Technologies* 6:6–10.
29. Om, H., and M. Biswas. 2012. A new image denoising scheme using soft-thresholding. *Journal of Signal and Information Processing* 3:360–363.
30. Biswas, M., and H. Om. 2012. A new soft-thresholding image denoising method. *Procedia Technology* 6:10–15.
31. Biswas, M., and H. Om. 2012. Selective parameters based image denoising method. *Advances in Intelligent Systems and Computing* 182:325–332.
32. Biswas, M., and H. Om. 2013. An image denoising threshold estimation method. *Advances in Computer Science and its Applications* 2:377–381.
33. Cai, T. T., and B. W. Silverman. 2001. Incorporating information on neighboring coefficients into wavelet estimation. *Sankhya: The Indian Journal of Statistics, Series B* 63:127–148.
34. Chen, G. Y., and T. D. Bui. 2003. Multiwavelets denoising using neighboring coefficients. *IEEE Signal Processing Letters* 10:211–214.
35. Chen, G. Y., T. D. Bui, and A. Krzyzak. 2004. Image denoising using neighbouring wavelet coefficients. *IEEE International Conference on Acoustics, Speech and Signal Processing (ICASSP)* 917–920.
36. Rao, B. C., and M. M. Latha. 2011. Selective neighbouring wavelet coefficients approach for image denoising. *International Journal of Computer Science and Communication* 2:73–77.
37. Mohideen, S. K., S. A. Perumal, and M. M. Sathik. 2008. Image de-noising using discrete wavelet transform. *International Journal of Computer Science and Network Security* 8:213–216.
38. Jiang, J., J. Guo, W. Fan, and Q. Chen. 2010. An improved adaptive wavelet denoising method based on neighboring coefficients (IAWDMBNC). *World Congress on Intelligent Control and Automation*, China, 2894–2898.
39. Om, H., and M. Biswas. 2012. An improved image denoising method based on wavelet thresholding (IIDMWT). *Journal of Signal and Information Processing* 3:109–116.
40. Biswas, M., and H. Om. 2013. An adaptive wavelet thresholding image denoising method. *IEEE Xplore* 1–5.
41. Om, H., and M. Biswas. 2013. A generalized image denoising method using neighbouring wavelet coefficients (GIDMNWC). *Signal Image and Video Processing* 1–5, doi:10.1007/s11760-013-0434-5.
42. Farbiz, F., and M. B. Menhaj. 2000. A fuzzy logic control based approach for image filtering. *Fuzzy Techniques in Image Processing* 52:194–221.
43. Van De Ville, D., M. Nachtegael, D. Van Der Weken, E. E. Kerre, and W. Philips. 2003. Noise reduction by fuzzy image filtering. *IEEE Transactions on Fuzzy Systems* 11:429–436.
44. Kwan, H. K., and Y. Cai. 2002. Fuzzy filters for image filtering. *Symposium on Circuits and Systems* 3:672–675.
45. Arunkumar, S., R. Akula, R. Gupta, and M. R. Vimala Devi. 2009. Fuzzy filters to the reduction of impulse and Gaussian noise in gray and color images. *International Journal of Recent Trends in Engineering* 1:398–402.
46. Saeedi, J., M. H. Moradi, and A. Abedi. 2010. Image denoising based on fuzzy and intra-scale dependency in wavelet transform domain. *International Conference on Pattern Recognition* 2672–2675.
47. Schulte, S., B. Huysmans, A. Pižurica, E. E. Kerre, and W. Philips. 2006. A new fuzzy-based wavelet shrinkage image denoising technique. *Lecture Notes in Computer Science* 4179:12–23.
48. Tavassoli, S., A. Rezvanian and M. M. Ebadzadeh. 2010. A new method for impulse noise reduction from digital images based on adaptive neuro-fuzzy system and fuzzy wavelet shrinkage. *International Conference on Computer Engineering and Technology* 4:297–301.
49. Adeli, A., F. Tajeripoor, M. J. Zomordian, and M. Neshat. 2012. Comparison of the fuzzy-based wavelet shrinkage image denoising techniques. *International Journal of Computer Science* 9:211–215.
50. Wang, Z., A. C. Bovik, H. R. Sheikh, and E. P. Simoncelli. 2004. Image quality assessment: From error visibility to structural similarity. *IEEE Transactions on Image Processing* 13:600–612.

Chapter 8

Fuzzy Relevance Vector Machines with Application to Surface Electromyographic Signal Classification

Hong-Bo Xie, Hu Huang, and Socrates Dokos

Contents

This chapter presents a multiclass fuzzy relevance vector machine (FRVM) learning mechanism and evaluates its performance to classify multiple hand motions using surface electromyographic (SEMG) signals. The relevance vector machine (RVM) is a sparse Bayesian kernel method, which avoids some limitations of the support vector machine (SVM). However, the RVM still suffers from the difficulty of possible unclassifiable regions in multiclass problems. We propose two fuzzy membership function–based FRVM algorithms to solve such problems, based on experiments conducted on seven subjects with six hand motions. Two feature sets, namely, time domain (TD) and wavelet transform (WT) features, are extracted from the recorded electromyographic (EMG) signals. Fuzzy support vector machine (FSVM) analysis was also conducted for comparison. For both TD and WT features, FRVM demonstrates less sensitivity to membership functions, while FSVM provides quite-different classification accuracies when using various membership functions. FRVM yielded comparable classification accuracy with dramatically fewer support vectors in comparison with FSVM. Furthermore, the processing delay of FRVM was much less than that of FSVM. The results indicate that an FRVM classifier can achieve comparable generalization capability as FSVM with significant sparsity in multichannel EMG classification, which is more suitable for EMG-based real-time control applications.

8.1 Introduction

Biomedical signal processing is a rapidly expanding field with applications ranging from the designing of artificial limbs and aids for disabled persons to the development of sophisticated image diagnosis systems. During a voluntary contraction of skeletal muscles, for example, the electrical activity of activated motor units can be detected with surface electrodes [1]. The resulting electromyographic (EMG) signal is the summation of motor unit action potentials discharged by muscle fibers near the recording electrodes and contains rich information on motor unit recruitment, firing, motion intention, and the general physiological state of the neuromuscular system. EMG pattern classification has been widely used in prosthetic hand and exoskeletal control, functional electrical stimulation devices, and other human–machine interface (HMI) control for the elderly, amputees, and those with various neuromuscular disorders [2–5].

Artificial intelligence and machine learning play important roles in EMG pattern recognition, with many techniques based on these having been explored for the control of EMG-based HMI. In the first pattern recognition–based prosthetic hand control schemes developed in the 1970s, simple statistical classifiers were used to recognize hand motions from amplitude-based features, achieving about 75% accuracy in a four-class EMG classification problem [6]. This accuracy was then improved by using two artificial neural network (NN) classifiers, namely, a discrete Hopfield NN and a multilayer perceptron (MLP), as described by Kelly et al. [7]. Hudgins et al. [8] successfully applied the MLP NN, trained by a standard backpropagation (BP) algorithm, to develop a real-time EMG pattern control system with approximately 10% error rate in classifying four types of upper limb motion. Since EMG signals are nonstationary and noisy, varying during limb motions even when they are similar, BP-based NNs are not able to achieve high learning and discrimination performance [1,9]. Several other NN-based machine learning methods, such as radial basis function networks [10], time-delayed artificial NNs [11], and self-organizing feature maps [12,13], have also been evaluated for their applicability to EMG classification.

EMG signals are not always strictly repeatable and may sometimes even be contradictory due to the shift of electrodes, sweat, and muscle fatigue [14]. Since one of the most useful properties of fuzzy logic systems is that contradictions in the data can be tolerated, fuzzy logic systems are advantageous in EMG signal classification. Compared with an MLP network, several fuzzy logic approaches have shown improved accuracy and robustness to noise in EMG classification [14–16].

NNs exhibit some problems inherent to their architecture, such as overtraining, overfitting, and the large number of controlling parameters. Other problems relate to the reproducibility of results, due mainly to random initialization of the networks and variability in stopping criteria [17]. Support vector machine (SVM) classification, which is based on the idea of structural risk minimization, is a new technique that has drawn much attention in the field of biomedical engineering in recent years.

The good generalization ability of SVM is achieved by finding a large margin between two classes [18–20]. Performance of binary SVMs can match or exceed MLP and linear discriminant analysis when combined in an efficient manner to classify EMG signals of hand/wrist motions [18–20].

Despite the fact that SVM classifiers provide improved performance over traditional learning machines, a number of significant and practical disadvantages exist [21]. Although relatively sparse, the number of support vectors (SVs) typically grows linearly with the size of the training set, and hence, SVM makes unnecessarily liberal use of basis functions. SVM does not directly provide probability estimates and therefore is not suitable for classification tasks in which posterior probabilities of class membership are necessary. In addition, estimation of the regularizing parameter in SVM construction, which generally entails a cross-validation procedure, is wasteful of computational time and data. Finally, the SVM kernel function must satisfy Mercer's condition, namely, it must be a continuous symmetric kernel of a positive integral operator [21].

To overcome these problems of SVM efficiently, Tipping [21] developed a new kernel-based machine learning technique, termed *relevance vector machine* (RVM). The RVM shares many of the characteristics of the SVM while avoiding its principal limitations. It uses the sparse Bayesian learning framework, in which an *a priori* parameter structure is placed based on automatic relevance determination theory for removing irrelevant data points [22]. Hence, it produces sparse models as well as a comparable generalization performance to that of the SVM. Most importantly, RVM classification requires dramatically fewer relevance vectors (RVs) compared with the number of SVs for SVM classification. This can significantly reduce the computational cost, making the RVM more suitable for real-time applications [23–26]. Many EMG-based controls, including prosthetic hand and exoskeletal control, as well as wheelchair and robotic control, need to be performed in real time [2,3,5,6,9,13]. The RVM is thus a potentially promising tool to classify EMG patterns. Similar to the SVM, the original RVM is a binary classifier. As for multiclass recognition, several coding schemes have been proposed using binary classifiers [18,21]. However, indecisive regions often exist when a binary RVM classifier ensemble is used to accommodate a multiclass problem (explained in Section 8.2). In order to solve for unclassifiable regions in the RVM, we define two membership functions in a direction perpendicular to the optimal hyperplane that separates the pair of classes. We evaluate the performance of the proposed fuzzy relevance vector machines (FRVMs) in classification of six hand motions using four-channel EMG signals. Fuzzy support vector machines (FSVMs) based on a least-squares algorithm are compared in terms of classification accuracy, sparsity, and processing delay.

8.2 Fuzzy Relevance Vector Machine

As a sparse kernel technique, the central idea of the RVM is to map a set of inputs to a high-dimensional feature space through kernel functions, providing posterior probabilistic outputs of the class membership for constructing decision boundaries. The compelling feature of the RVM is that it utilizes dramatically fewer kernel functions, while its generalization performance is comparable to the equivalent SVM [21].

8.2.1 Binary RVM

Given a data set $\{\mathbf{x}_n, t_n\}_{n=1}^{N}$ where $\mathbf{x}_n$ denotes the input to be classified and t_n represents its class label, we write the targets as a vector $\mathbf{t} = (t_1, \ldots, t_N)^T$ and express it as the sum of an approximation vector $\mathbf{y} = (y(\mathbf{x}_1), \ldots, y(\mathbf{x}_N))^T$ and an "error" vector $\boldsymbol{\varepsilon} = (\varepsilon_1, \ldots, \varepsilon_N)^T$:

$$\mathbf{t} = \mathbf{y} + \boldsymbol{\varepsilon} = \boldsymbol{\Phi}\mathbf{w} + \boldsymbol{\varepsilon}. \tag{8.1}$$

where $\mathbf{w} = (w_1, \ldots, w_M)^T$ is a "weight" parameter vector and $\mathbf{\Phi} = [\mathbf{\Phi}_1 \ldots \mathbf{\Phi}_M]$ is an $N \times M$ design matrix whose columns comprise the complete set of M "basis vectors." Applying the logistic sigmoid link function $\sigma(y) = (1 + e^{-y})^{-1}$ to $y(\mathbf{x})$ and adopting the Bernoulli distribution, the likelihood of the complete data set can be represented as

$$P(t \mid \mathbf{w}) = \prod_{n=1}^{N} \sigma\{y(\mathbf{x}_n; \mathbf{w})\}^{t_n} [1 - \sigma\{y(\mathbf{x}_n; \mathbf{w})\}]^{1-t_n}, \tag{8.2}$$

where the targets $t_n \in \{0, 1\}$. To control the complexity of the model and avoid overfitting, a zero-mean Gaussian prior distribution is defined over $\mathbf{w}$:

$$p(\mathbf{w} \mid \boldsymbol{\alpha}) = \prod_{i=0}^{N} \mathcal{N}\left(w_i \mid 0, \alpha_i^{-1}\right) = \prod_{i=0}^{N} \sqrt{\frac{\alpha_i}{2\pi}} \exp\left(-\frac{\alpha_i w_i^2}{2}\right), \tag{8.3}$$

with $\boldsymbol{\alpha} = [\alpha_0, \alpha_1, \ldots, \alpha_N]^T$ a vector of $N + 1$ hyperparameters. An individual hyperparameter is associated independently with every weight, moderating the strength of the prior, with the hyperparameter itself having a gamma prior. The parameter α for each w is intuitively called the "relevance" of that feature, in the sense that the bigger the α becomes, the more likely the feature weight w is driven to zero. However, the weights w cannot be integrated out analytically, precluding closed-form expressions for either the weight posterior $p(\mathbf{w} \mid \mathbf{t}, \boldsymbol{\alpha})$ or the marginal likelihood $P(\mathbf{t} \mid \boldsymbol{\alpha})$. Thus, the Laplace approximation procedure is utilized as described in the following [21].

Since $p(\mathbf{w} \mid \mathbf{t}, \boldsymbol{\alpha}) \propto P(\mathbf{t} \mid \mathbf{w}) p(\mathbf{w} \mid \boldsymbol{\alpha})$, finding the optimal weights is equivalent to finding the maximum of

$$\log\{P(\mathbf{t} \mid \mathbf{w}) p(\mathbf{w} \mid \boldsymbol{\alpha})\} = \sum_{n=1}^{N} [t_n \log y_n + (1 - t_n) \log(1 - y_n)] - \frac{1}{2} \mathbf{w}^T \mathbf{A} \mathbf{w}, \tag{8.4}$$

for the most probable weight $\mathbf{w}_{\text{MP}}$, with $y_n = \sigma\{y(\mathbf{x}_n; \mathbf{w})\}$ and $\mathbf{A} = diag(\alpha_i)$ for the current values of α. This represents a penalized logistic log-likelihood function, and it requires iterative maximization, using an iterative reweighted least-squares algorithm to find $\mathbf{w}_{\text{MP}}$.

To carry out the iterative procedure, we require the gradient vector and Hessian matrix of the log posterior distribution, which can be found by differentiating twice:

$$\nabla_{\mathbf{w}} \log p(\mathbf{w} \mid \mathbf{t}, \boldsymbol{\alpha})\big|_{\mathbf{w}_{\text{MP}}} = \mathbf{\Phi}^T (\mathbf{t} - \mathbf{y}) - \mathbf{A} \mathbf{w} \tag{8.5}$$

$$\nabla_{\mathbf{w}} \nabla_{\mathbf{w}} \log p(\mathbf{w} \mid \mathbf{t}, \boldsymbol{\alpha})\big|_{\mathbf{w}_{\text{MP}}} = -(\mathbf{\Phi}^T \mathbf{B} \mathbf{\Phi} + \mathbf{A}), \tag{8.6}$$

where $\mathbf{B}$ is an $N \times N$ diagonal matrix with elements $b_n = y_n(1 - y_n)$, with vector $\mathbf{y} = (y_1, \ldots, y_N)^T$, and $\mathbf{\Phi}$ the design matrix with elements $\mathbf{\Phi}_{ni} = \phi_i(\mathbf{x}_n)$. The approximation to the posterior distribution corresponding to the mean of the Gaussian approximation is obtained by inverting Equation 8.6. The mean and the covariance of the Laplace approximation can be now given as

$$\Sigma = (\boldsymbol{\Phi}^T \mathbf{B} \boldsymbol{\Phi} + \mathbf{A})^{-1} \tag{8.7}$$

$$\mathbf{w}_{MP} = \mathbf{A}^{-1} \boldsymbol{\Phi}^T (\mathbf{t} - \mathbf{y}). \tag{8.8}$$

Using the statistics Σ and $\mathbf{w}_{MP}$ of the Gaussian approximation, we can follow Tipping's approach [21] to update the hyperparameters α_i by

$$\alpha_i^{new} = \frac{1 - \alpha_i \Sigma_{ii}}{\mathbf{w}_{MP}^2}, \tag{8.9}$$

where Σ_{ii} is the ith diagonal element of the covariance matrix. During the optimization process, many α_i will have large values, and thus, the corresponding model weights will be pruned out, leading to sparse representation. Those samples remaining with $\mathbf{w}_i \neq 0$ are termed RVs, corresponding to SVs in the SVM.

The aforementioned training procedure is typically slow. In order to speed up the training process, Tipping and Faul [27] proposed a highly accelerated learning algorithm in which a single hyperparameter α_i is fully optimized at each step. If we define

$$\hat{\mathbf{t}} = \boldsymbol{\Phi} \mathbf{w}_{MP} + \mathbf{B}^{-1}(\mathbf{t} - y), \tag{8.10}$$

the approximate log marginal likelihood can be written in the form

$$L(\boldsymbol{\alpha}) = \log p(\mathbf{t} \mid \boldsymbol{\alpha}, \beta) = -\frac{1}{2} \left\{ N \log(2\pi) + \log|\mathbf{C}| + (\hat{\mathbf{t}})^T \mathbf{C}^{-1} \hat{\mathbf{t}} \right\}, \tag{8.11}$$

where

$$\mathbf{C} = \mathbf{B} + \boldsymbol{\Phi} \mathbf{A} \boldsymbol{\Phi}^T. \tag{8.12}$$

Considering the dependence of $L(\boldsymbol{\alpha})$ on a single hyperparameter α_i, $i \in \{1, 2, \ldots, M\}$, the contribution from α_i in the matrix $\mathbf{C}$ is then factored out to give

$$\mathbf{C} = \mathbf{C}_{-i} + \alpha_i^{-1} \phi_i \phi_i^T, \tag{8.13}$$

where $\mathbf{C}_{-i}$ is $\mathbf{C}$ with the contribution of basis vector i removed. Established matrix determinant and inverse identities may be used to write the relevant terms in $L(\boldsymbol{\alpha})$ as

$$|\mathbf{C}| = |\mathbf{C}_{-i}| \left| 1 + \alpha_i^{-1} \phi_i^T \mathbf{C}_{-i}^{-1} \phi_i \right|, \tag{8.14}$$

$$\mathbf{C}^{-1} = \mathbf{C}_{-i}^{-1} - \frac{\mathbf{C}_{-i}^{-1} \phi_i \phi_i^T \mathbf{C}_{-i}^T}{\alpha_i + \phi_i^T \mathbf{C}_{-i}^T \phi_i}. \tag{8.15}$$

Using these results, the log marginal likelihood function (Equation 8.10) can be written in the form

$$L(\mathbf{\alpha}) = L(\mathbf{\alpha}_{-i}) + \frac{1}{2}\left[\log\alpha_i - \log(\alpha_i + s_i) + \frac{q_i^2}{a_i + s_i} \right] = L(\mathbf{\alpha}_{-i}) + \lambda(\alpha_i). \tag{8.16}$$

Here, two quantities are introduced:

$$s_i = \phi_i^T \mathbf{C}_{-i}^{-1} \phi_i, \tag{8.17}$$

$$q_i = \phi_i^T \mathbf{C}_{-i}^{-1} \mathbf{t}, \tag{8.18}$$

where s_i is the *sparsity* and q_i is the *quality* of ϕ_i. A large value of s_i relative to q_i means that the basis vector ϕ_i is more likely to be pruned from the model. The *sparsity* measures the extent to which basis vector ϕ_i overlaps with the other basis vectors in the model. The *quality* represents a measure of alignment of basis vector ϕ_n with the error between the training set values $\mathbf{t} = (t_1, t_2, ..., t_N)^T$ and the vector $\mathbf{y}_{-i}$ of predictions that would result from the model with the vector ϕ_i excluded [27].

8.2.2 Multiclass RVM

The RVM was originally developed for solving regression and binary classification problems. However, most practical applications need to handle multiclass discrimination problems. Several techniques have been proposed to extend a binary classifier to multiclass problems, including one-against-all (OAA), one-against-one (OAO, also known as pairwise), and error-correcting output code (ECOC) [27,28]. In the OAA scheme, a k-class problem is converted into k two-class problems, and for the ith two-class problem, class i is discriminated from the remaining classes. As for a multiclass RVM, Tipping and Faul [27] adopted this scheme and extended the original RVM to a multiclass model using a generalized multinomial form of likelihood for Equation 8.2. However, raising the number of classes would lead to a significant increase in the OAA computational load. More importantly, OAA generally produces a poor result [28,29] since it does not consider the pairwise correlation and hence creates several indecisive regions, shown in Figure 8.1.

In the OAO scheme, the k-class problem is converted into $k(k-1)/2$ two-class problems, which cover all pairs of classes. For an unknown sample x, the inferred discriminant function for i,j class pair is given by

$$D_{ij}(\mathbf{x}) = \mathbf{\Phi}\mathbf{w}_{\mathrm{MP}}. \tag{8.19}$$

The logistic sigmoid function can be applied here to transfer $D_{ij}(\mathbf{x})$ into the probability of $P(x, C_i)$ and $P(x, C_j)$. In practice, a "max wins" strategy is used in the OAO decision process, which first calculates the score function

$$D_i = \sum_{j \neq i, j=1}^{k} \mathrm{sgn}(D_{ij}(\mathbf{x})), \tag{8.20}$$

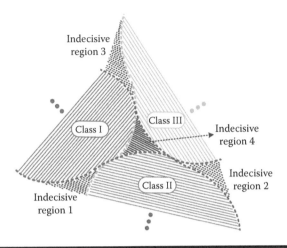

Figure 8.1   Indecisive regions in one-against-all classification strategy.

and classifies x into the class

$$\arg\max_{i=1,\cdots,k} (D_i(\mathbf{x})). \tag{8.21}$$

Although this method is more computationally efficient, an unclassifiable region may also exist for OAO if Equation 8.21 is satisfied by multiple i's. For example, if the discriminant functions satisfy $D_{12}(x) < 0$, $D_{23}(x) < 0$, and $D_{13}(x) > 0$, the test sample x in the central region of Figure 8.2a is obviously unclassifiable.

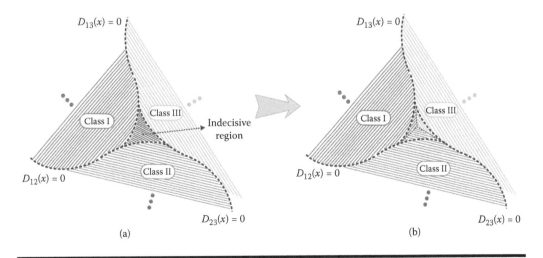

Figure 8.2   An indecisive region in a one-against-one (OAO) classification strategy (a) solved by using fuzzy membership functions to separate each pair of classes (b).

8.2.3 Fuzzy RVM

In order to solve the unclassifiable regions in OAO, we can define a choice of two fuzzy membership functions to indicate the probability of **x** belonging to each class.

Let $m_{i,ij}(\mathbf{x})$ and $m_{j,ij}(\mathbf{x})$ represent membership values of sample x belonging to classes i and j from the binary classifier RVM_{ij}. We define the first fuzzy membership function (MF I) as

$$m_{i,ij}(\mathbf{x}) = \begin{cases} 1 & D_{ij}(\mathbf{x}) \geq 1 \\ D_{ij}(\mathbf{x}) & -1 \leq D_{ij}(\mathbf{x}) < 1 \\ -1 & otherwise \end{cases} \tag{8.22}$$

$$m_{j,ij}(\mathbf{x}) = \begin{cases} -1 & D_{ij}(\mathbf{x}) \geq 1 \\ -D_{ij}(\mathbf{x}) & -1 \leq D_{ij}(\mathbf{x}) < 1. \\ 1 & otherwise \end{cases} \tag{8.23}$$

A second alternative membership function (MF II) is defined as

$$m_{i,ij}(\mathbf{x}) = \begin{cases} 1 & D_{ij}(\mathbf{x}) \geq 0 \\ \dfrac{1 + D_{ij}(\mathbf{x})}{2} & -1 < D_{ij}(\mathbf{x}) < 0, \\ 0 & otherwise \end{cases} \tag{8.24}$$

$$m_{j,ij}(\mathbf{x}) = \begin{cases} 0 & D_{ij}(\mathbf{x}) \geq 1 \\ \dfrac{1 - D_{ij}(\mathbf{x})}{2} & 0 < D_{ij}(\mathbf{x}) < 1. \\ 1 & otherwise \end{cases} \tag{8.25}$$

Using either of these membership functions, we then implement a minimum operator to determine $m_i(\mathbf{x})$, the membership function of **x** belonging to class i from all possible RVMs:

$$m_i(\mathbf{x}) = \min_{j=1,\cdots,k} m_{ij}(\mathbf{x}). \tag{8.26}$$

The input sample **x** is then classified into the class

$$\arg \max_{i=1,\cdots,k} (m_i(\mathbf{x})). \tag{8.27}$$

Using fuzzy functions, the unclassifiable region problem in the OAO strategy of RVM is now solved as indicated in Figure 8.2b.

8.3 Data Acquisition and Feature Extraction

We evaluate the FRVM technique by classifying experimental EMG signals, aiming at real-time control of various HMIs. Four channels of EMG were collected from seven subjects (three males and four females aged between 22 and 38 years). Six classes of hand/wrist motions to be classified were grasp (GR), hand open (OP), wrist flexion (WF), wrist extension (WE), ulnar deviation (UD), and radial deviation (RD), as shown in Figure 8.3. All participants were right-hand dominant without any known neuromuscular disorders. Human subject ethics approval was obtained from the relevant committee in Jiangsu University, Zhenjiang, Jiangsu Province, China and informed consent was obtained from all subjects prior to the experiment. EMG signals were acquired from the forearm using bipolar Ag–AgCl electrodes (dual electrode #272, Noraxon USA Inc., Scottsdale, AZ). Electrodes were placed on the extensor digitorum, the extensor carpi radialis, the palmaris longus, and the flexor carpi ulnaris around the forearm. The distance between two adjacent surface electrodes was 2 cm. Relevant skin areas were abraded beforehand with alcohol. An additional Ag–AgCl electrode was placed on the elbow to provide a common ground reference. EMG signals were amplified by a custom-made amplifier with a gain of 2000, filtered using an 8–500 Hz band-pass analog filter within the amplifier, then digitized by a 12-bit data acquisition card (NI PCI-6024E, National Instruments, Austin, TX), with a sample frequency of 1 kHz.

During the experiment, subjects were required to perform three repeated 60 s continuous contractions. Within each session, each limb motion was held in a random order for about 10 s. The participants were allowed to relax between each session to avoid fatigue. The first session was used as a training set, while the second and third were the validation and test sets, respectively. All the data were segmented into consecutive 256 ms epochs.

Two sets of features were extracted from the recorded EMG signals in the time and time-frequency (TF) domains. The first set was composed of fourth-order autoregressive model coefficients and the root mean square, referred to as TD [8,30]. For time-frequency features, a set of wavelet transform energy values at each scale using a Coiflet wavelet family (Coif 4) with four levels was extracted. A majority-vote strategy was then conducted to improve the accuracy [6].

Figure 8.3 Six hand/wrist motions used in the experiments. From left to right: grasp (GP), hand open (OP), wrist extension (WE), wrist flexion (WF), ulnar deviation (UD), and radial deviation (RD).

8.4 Results

8.4.1 Effect of Membership Functions

Typical raw EMG signals collected from subject 2 are shown in Figure 8.4. Two membership functions (Equations 8.22–8.25) were used to train $6(6-1)/2 = 15$ binary classifiers of both RVMs and SVMs. Their outputs were then processed by the proposed fuzzy strategies to recognize six patterns. Figure 8.5 shows the averaged classification accuracy and standard deviation of two membership functions across all subjects. When using TD features, FRVMs exhibited similar performance over all subjects for both membership functions. The averaged accuracy using MF I was slightly higher than that of MF II. In the case of WT features, averaged accuracy of the two membership functions was similar, while MF II demonstrated higher standard deviation. From the practical perspective, the performance of MF I was superior, and thus, it was employed in the

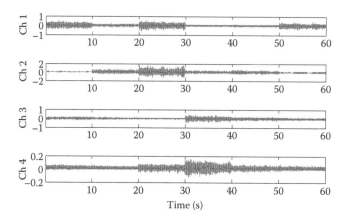

Figure 8.4 Typical four-channel raw EMG signals recorded from subject 2.

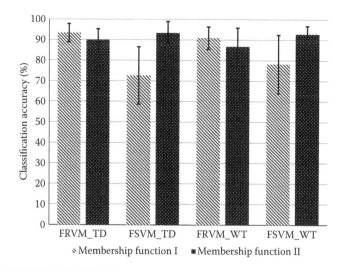

Figure 8.5 Averaged classification accuracy and standard deviation across all subjects obtained by FRVMs and FSVMs using two membership functions.

subsequent FRVMs evaluations. On the other hand, the results were quite different in the FSVM case. When using MF I, classification accuracy was much worse than MF II for both feature sets, indicating that MF II was more matched to FSVMs. In other words, the performance of FSVM was more sensitive to the membership functions than that of FRVM.

8.4.2 Classification Performance

Since averaged accuracies of RVMs with MF I and FSVMs with MF II were higher than other combinations, we further compared their performance in terms of each motion pattern, sparsity, and testing time. Figure 8.6 shows the classification accuracy and the percentage of vectors used in training these two classifiers for subject 2. In terms of classification accuracy, results were slightly worse for FRVMs but were still acceptable for both TD and WT features. For FRVMs, only 3.65% and 3.93% of the vectors were used in training for TD and WT features, respectively. However, a least-squares SVM was used as a base binary classifier for FSVMs [19,20], which utilized 100% of vectors as SVs without any sparseness.

The mean classification accuracy and standard deviation of each motion across all subjects after a majority vote are indicated in Figure 8.7. When using TD features, the total classification accuracy and standard deviation were similar for both classifiers, that is, 93.22 ± 4% for FRVMs and 93.28 ± 7% for FSVMs. In the case of WT features, although the discrimination capability of FRVMs was worse than FSVMs for the last two motions (UD and RD), the average classification accuracy of the former (90.86 ± 6%) was comparative to that of the latter (92.81 ± 4%). However, similar to subject 2, the RVs used in the training of other subjects varied from 3% to 5%, much lower than the 100% SV proportion for FSVMs.

FRVMs utilize multiple binary classifiers to achieve their final decision. The processing delay for EMG classification is another important issue, since the *response time* should not introduce a delay perceivable by the user for many EMG-based real-time control systems [31]. For example, the time threshold for acquiring EMG data plus the processing time for generating classified control commands for prosthetic hand control is typically regarded to be roughly 300 ms [31]. Testing times for FRVMs and FSVMs were empirically evaluated using a 2.2 GHz Intel-based computer, with computations performed in MATLAB® (version 8.0, The Mathworks, Natick, MA) and matrix multiplication built-in functions. Table 8.1 illustrates testing times for both TD and WT

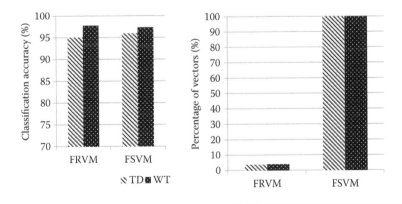

Figure 8.6 Classification accuracy (left) and percentage of vectors used in training (right) for subject 2 using FRVMs and FSVMs with both TD and WT features.

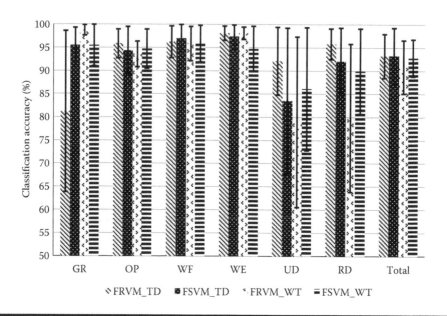

Figure 8.7 Mean classification accuracy and standard deviation of each motion across all subjects using FRVMs with MF I and FSVMs with MF II.

features across all subjects. The mean processing time of FSVMs for a motion was about 120 ms for both TD and WT features. In some extreme cases, the response time was larger than 200 ms. Normally, the minimal epoch length for EMG data is at least 128 ms for a 1000 Hz sampling rate [32]. In such cases, FSVMs are potentially unable to satisfy the real-time demand since the total time of signal acquisition, feature extraction, and FSVM recognition would exceed 300 ms. However, FRVMs could discriminate these motions in much less time than FSVMs due to fewer RVs used in the discriminant function. These results demonstrated that FRVMs could achieve comparable EMG classification accuracy in a more computationally efficient manner, more suitable for real-time applications.

Table 8.1 The Processing Delay (ms) of FRVMs and FSVMs with Both TD and WT Features for All Subjects

Subject	FRVM-TD	FSVM-TD	FRVM-WT	FSVM-WT
1	15.6	84.9	5.2	89.1
2	105.2	234.9	20.3	229.7
3	49.5	84.9	12.5	88.5
4	15.1	90.1	12.5	90.6
5	18.2	88.5	6.3	88.5
6	20.3	182.8	22.9	186.5
7	15.1	91.1	4.7	85.9
Mean ± Std	34.1 ± 33.6	122.4 ± 60.9	12.1 ± 7.3	122.6 ± 59.6

8.5 Discussion and Conclusion

This chapter presented an FRVM learning mechanism and evaluated its application in classifying hand motions using EMG signals. Its performance was compared with FSVMs in terms of accuracy, sparsity, and response time. The SVM is a binary classifier with a good generalization capability derived from structural risk minimization. Previous studies have extended the SVM to the FSVM and demonstrated that FSVMs are superior to artificial NN classifiers in several respects [19,20]. However, both the SVM and the FSVM still suffer from a number of limitations. The RVM is a Bayesian extension of the SVM. Key attractions of the RVM relative to the SVM are the removal of the need to define a regularizing parameter, a reduced sensitivity to hyperparameter settings, an ability to use non-Mercer kernels, the provision of a probabilistic output, and a typical requirement for considerably fewer basis functions (RVs) for a given analysis.

Focusing on the problem of unclassifiable regions in the RVM, we proposed an improved FRVM sparse kernel method. Two types of membership functions were presented as fuzzy logic functions to divide the indecisive regions. In an EMG classification experiment, FRVMs showed similar accuracy over both membership functions, while FSVMs were more dependent on one over the other. The combination of the RVM with membership function I was comparable to the SVM with MF II.

FRVM training resulted in much fewer RVs compared with the number of SVs obtained for FSVMs. Hence, classification could be carried out faster with FRVMs. Though various high-speed microprocessors have been developed, the proposed computationally efficient algorithm is beneficial for saving hardware resources. It is particularly useful for many biosignal-based practical applications with real-time requirements including EMG prosthetic control. However, it should be noted that FRVMs require longer training time to converge to fewer RVs in comparison with FSVMs. Another disadvantage of FRVMs related to fewer RVs is that it remains less robust to reduced training samples.

Nowadays, incremental learning is an open issue in artificial intelligence, which means taking new information and classes in evolving the classifier without fully retraining [33–35]. It is particularly useful for improving the flexibility of EMG classification–based prosthetic hands or exoskeletons by gradually increasing new classes in training the amputees without heavy burdens. The FRVM proposed in this chapter allows incremental learning. If a new sample of class $\mathbf{x}_{n+1}$ is used to retrain the FRVM classifiers, this sample will become a positive sample in training N pairs of binary FRVMs corresponding to the original data set $\{\mathbf{x}_n, t_n\}_{n=1}^{N}$. Compared with those traditional NN architectures, FRVMs can integrate the training samples of this new class into the previously trained model without retraining the entire system again. The performance of such an FRVM incremental learning scheme in EMG classification will be evaluated in our future study.

References

1. Xie, H. B., and Wang, Z. Z. 2006. Mean frequency derived via Hilbert-Huang transform with application to fatigue EMG signal analysis. *Computer Methods & Programs in Biomedicine* 82: 114–20.
2. Hung, H., Xie, H. B., Guo, J. Y., and Chen, H. J. 2012. Ant colony optimization-based feature selection method for surface electromyography signals classification. *Computers in Biology & Medicine* 42: 30–8.
3. Khokhar, Z. O., Xiao, Z. G., and Menon, C. 2010. Surface EMG pattern recognition for real-time control of a wrist exoskeleton. *Biomedical Engineering Online* 9: 41. http://www.biomedical-engineering -online.com/content/pdf/1475-925X-9-41.pdf.

4. Yu, W. W., Yamaguchi, H., Yokoi, H., Maruishi, M., Mano, Y., and Kakazu, K. 2002. EMG automatic switch for FES control for hemiplegics using artificial neural network. *Robotics and Autonomous Systems* 40: 213–24.

5. Ahsan, M. R., Ibrahimy, M. I., and Khalifa, O. O. 2009. EMG signal classification for human computer interaction: A review. *European Journal of Scientific Research* 33: 480–501.

6. Englehart, K., and Hudgins, B. 2003. A robust, real-time control scheme for multifunction myoelectric contrl. *IEEE Transactions on Biomedical Engineering* 50: 848–54.

7. Kelly, M. F., Parker, P. A., and Scott, R. N. 1990. The application of neural networks to myoelectric signal analysis: A preliminary study. *IEEE Transactions on Biomedical Engineering* 37: 221–30.

8. Hudgins, B., Parker, P., and Scott, R. N. 1993. A new strategy for multifunction myoelectric control. *IEEE Transactions on Biomedical Engineering* 40: 82–94.

9. Fukuda, O., Tsuji, T., Kaneko, M., and Otsuka, A. 2003. A human-assisting manipulator teleoperated by EMG signals and arm motions. *IEEE Transactions on Robotics and Automation* 19: 210–22.

10. Chaiyaratana, N., Zalzala, A. M. S., and Datta, D. 1996. Myoelectric signals pattern recognition for intelligent functional operation of upper-limb prosthesis. In *Proceedings of 1st International Conference on Disability, Virtual Reality & Associate Technologies*, Maidenhead, UK, pp. 151–60.

11. Au, A. T. C., and Kirsch, R. F. 2000. EMG-Based prediction of shoulder and elbow kinematics in able-bodied and spinal cord injured individuals. *IEEE Transactions on Rehabilitation Engineering* 8: 471–80.

12. Eom, K. H., Choi, Y. J., and Sirisena, H. 2002. EMG pattern classification using SOFMs for hand signal recognition. *Soft Computing* 6: 436–40.

13. Chu, J. U., Moon, I., and Mun, M. S. 2006. A real-time EMG pattern recognition system based on linear-nonlinear feature projection for a multifunction myoelectric hand. *IEEE Transactions on Biomedical Engineering* 53: 2232–9.

14. Chan, F. H. Y., Yang, Y. S., Lam, F. K., Zhang, Y. T., and Parker, P. A. 2000. Fuzzy EMG classification for prosthesis control. *IEEE Transactions on Rehabilitation Engineering* 8: 305–11.

15. Kiguchi, K., Tanaka, T., and Fukuda, T. 2004. Neuro-fuzzy control of a robotic exoskeleton with EMG signals. *IEEE Transactions on Fuzzy Systems* 12: 481–90.

16. Ajiboye, A. B., and Weir, R. F. 2005. A heuristic fuzzy logic approach to EMG pattern recognition for multifunctional prosthesis control. *IEEE Transactions on Neural System and Rehabilitation Engineering* 13: 280–91.

17. Xie, H. B., Zheng, Y. P., Guo, J. Y., and Chen, X. 2009. Estimation of wrist angle from sonomyography using support vector machine and artificial neural network models. *Medical Engineering and Physics* 31: 384–91.

18. Oskoei, M. A., and Hu, H. S. 2008. Support vector machine-based classification scheme for myoelectric control applied to upper limb. *IEEE Transactions on Biomedical Engineering* 55: 1956–65.

19. Yan, Z. G., Wang, Z. Z., and Xie, H. B. 2008. The application of mutual information-based feature selection and fuzzy LS-SVM-based classifier in motion classification. *Computer Methods and Programs in Biomedicine* 90: 275–84.

20. Yan, Z. G., Wang, Z. Z., and Xie, H. B. 2008. Joint application of rough set-based feature reduction and fuzzy LS-SVM classifier in motion classification. *Medical and Biological Engineering and Computing* 46: 519–27.

21. Tipping, M. E. 2001. Sparse Bayesian learning and the relevance vector machine. *Journal of Machine Learning Research* 1: 211–44.

22. MacKay, D. J. C. 1992. The evidence framework applied to classification networks. *Neural Computation* 4: 720–36.

23. Demir, B., and Ertürk, S. 2007. Hyperspectral image classification using relevance vector machines. *IEEE Geoscience and Remote Sensing Letters* 4: 586–90.

24. Majumder, S. K., Ghosh, N., and Gupta, P. K. 2005. Relevance vector machine for optical diagnosis of cancer. *Laser in Surgery and Medicine* 36: 323–33.

25. Wang, X., Ye, M., and Duanmu, C. J. 2009. Classification of data from electronic nose using relevance vector machines. *Sensors and Actuators B: Chemical* 140: 143–8.

26. Williams, O., Blake, A., and Cipolla, R. 2005. Sparse Bayesian learning for efficient visual tracking. *IEEE Transactions on Pattern Analysis and Machine Intelligence* 27: 1292–304.

27. Tipping, M. E., and Faul, A. 2003. Fast marginal likelihood maximization for sparse Bayesian models. In *Proceedings of Ninth International Workshop on Artificial Intelligence and Statistics*, Key West, FL.
28. Mianji, F. A., and Zhang, Y. 2011. Robust hyperspectral classification using relevance vector machine. *IEEE Transactions on Geoscience and Remote Sensing* 49: 2100–12.
29. Vong, C. M., Wong, P. K., Ip, W. F., and Chiu, C. C. 2013. Simultaneous-fault diagnosis of automotive engine ignition systems using prior domain knowledge and relevance vector machine. *Mathematical Problems in Engineering* 2013: 974862. http://www.hindawi.com/journals/mpe/2013/974862/.
30. Englehart, K. B., Hudgins, B. S., Parker, P. A., and Stevenson, M. 1999. Classification of the myoelectric signal using time-frequency based representations *Medical Engineering and Physics* 21: 431–8.
31. Xie, H. B., Zheng, Y. P., and Guo, J. Y. 2009. Classification of the mechanomyogram signal using a wavelet packet transform and singular value decomposition for multifunction prosthesis control. *Physiological Measurement* 30: 441–57.
32. Parker, P., Englehart, K., and Hudgins, B. 2006. Myoelectric signal processing for control of powered limb prostheses. *Journal of Electromyography and Kinesiology* 16: 541–8.
33. Joshi, P., and Kulkarni, P. 2012. Incremental learning: Areas and methods—A survey. *International Journal of Data Mining & Knowledge Management Process* 2: 43–51.
34. Tangruamsub, S., Takada, K., and Hasegawa O. 2012. A fast online incremental learning method for object detection and pose classification using voting and combined appearance modelling. *Signal Processing: Image Communication* 27: 75–82.
35. Ade, R. R., Pune, G., Deshmukh, P. R., and Amravati, S. T. 2013. Methods for incremental learning: A survey. *International Journal of Data Mining & Knowledge Management Process* 3: 119–25.

Chapter 9

Intelligent Remote Operating System Detection

João P. Souza Medeiros, João B. Borges Neto,
Gutto S. Dantas Queiroz, and Paulo S. Motta Pires

Contents

This chapter addresses the identification of a remote operating system, across a computer network, with the aid of computational intelligence. Based on an introductory presentation of fundamental concepts of remote operating system detection, we present a survey on the use of computational intelligence in this area. This study points to new research directions that are developed in this work. Specifically, this work presents advances in (1) the algorithm used to extract distinguishable characteristics from reliable data and (2) the procedure used to minimize the amount of data necessary to classification. Considering a set of 16 operating systems, the results indicate that it is possible to perform identification using only 25 network messages with high levels of accuracy, reaching a correct classification rate above 98%.

9.1 Introduction

Remote operating system detection (ROSD) is a process that aims to discover the operating system (OS) running on a remote machine. This process is based on the concept that any OS has distinguishable characteristics that can be used to differentiate it from others. These characteristics are used to compose the OS fingerprint [1], analogous to the human fingerprint. Generally, these characteristics are derived from the implementation details of the OS functioning, which impacts on its behavior and responses. Once it is possible to observe a specific behavior of an OS and to characterize it in computational terms, it can be used to compose the OS fingerprint. However, it is convenient to consider some characteristics that will provide a more accurate identification, preferably the ones that cannot be forged in the OS.

A common approach to performing ROSD is to use control data from network messages sent from the remote machine. For example, hereafter, we describe how the values of Internet Protocol version 4 (IPv4) [2] headers can be used to distinguish different OS implementations of this protocol. The reachability responses from a web search host, that is, Internet Control Message Protocol (ICMP) echo replies [3], are shown in Figure 9.1.

The messages are presented in the output format of tcpdump [4], a standard and classical tool for network traffic analysis [5]. The output was handled to hide the real hosts and message time stamps. To perform a comparison with the responses of the web search host in Figure 9.1, the responses from a free e-mail service are presented in Figure 9.2.

```
IP (tos 0x0, ttl 52, id 2506, offset 0, flags [none], proto ICMP (1), length 84)
    searchengine.example.com > local: ICMP echo reply, id 21213, seq 1, length 64
IP (tos 0x0, ttl 52, id 2506, offset 0, flags [none], proto ICMP (1), length 84)
    searchengine.example.com > local: ICMP echo reply, id 21213, seq 2, length 64
IP (tos 0x0, ttl 52, id 2506, offset 0, flags [none], proto ICMP (1), length 84)
    searchengine.example.com > local: ICMP echo reply, id 21213, seq 3, length 64
```

Figure 9.1   ICMP echo reply messages of a remote web search host.

```
IP (tos 0x0, ttl 241, id 62891, offset 0, flags [DF], proto ICMP (1), length 84)
    emailservice.example.com > local: ICMP echo reply, id 21224, seq 1, length 64
IP (tos 0x0, ttl 241, id 7584, offset 0, flags [DF], proto ICMP (1), length 84)
    emailservice.example.com > local: ICMP echo reply, id 21224, seq 2, length 64
IP (tos 0x0, ttl 241, id 16983, offset 0, flags [DF], proto ICMP (1), length 84)
    emailservice.example.com > local: ICMP echo reply, id 21224, seq 3, length 64
```

Figure 9.2   ICMP echo reply messages from a remote e-mail service.

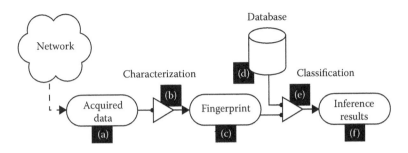

Figure 9.3   Remote operating system detection process illustrated. (a) Data acquired from the network; (b) the process of extraction of relevant information; (c) representation of the information extracted from acquired data; (d) database of representations of labeled operating systems; (e) the classifications process of the representation; and (f) the method used to present the classification results.

For simplicity, the OS of the search engine host in Figure 9.1 will be denoted by G and the OS of the free e-mail service host in Figure 9.2 by H. Based on the behavior of both replies, three differences can be highlighted: (1) the identification field in G's messages is always 2506, whereas in H's messages, it seems random; (2) the "don't fragment" bit is set in H's messages and unset in G's messages; and (3) the initial time to live (TTL) of G's messages seems to be 64, while for H's, it seems to be 256 [1]. These distinctions from IP header fields also exist in other protocols (cf. [6,7]). Therefore, ROSD can be accomplished by using network data originated from the remote machine according to the process illustrated in Figure 9.3.

The process consists of the following procedure: the network data (Figure 9.3a) are captured and used to characterize the computer system (Figure 9.3b), producing the system description, or fingerprint (Figure 9.3c), which is then compared to other descriptions cataloged in the database (Figure 9.3d) through a matching algorithm (Figure 9.3e). Finally, the result of the identification is presented (Figure 9.3f).

9.1.1 Applications

The process of remote characterization and identification of computers has many applications in network security and forensics. The process of discovering the OS of a networked machine is an initial requirement for a large range of network security tasks. Among these tasks, we can highlight the following: (1) identifying vulnerable hosts, (2) guiding the process of exploitation, and (3) performing network inventory [1]. On network forensics, this process can be used together with intrusion detection systems to characterize suspicious machines of remote attackers. In this case, the identification system could create a fingerprint of a remote networked machine used by the suspect, and when equipment is seized, the computer expert will be able to check the previous fingerprint with the one generated by the seized equipment. This application was exemplified by Novotny et al. [8,9], where this approach was used to capture digital evidence of criminal activity in chat rooms and websites.

9.1.2 Fundamentals

As illustrated by Figure 9.3, the ROSD process can be divided in two subsequent tasks: characterization and classification. In the characterization task, a fingerprint is created for an OS, while in the classification, some procedure is applied to a database of fingerprints to match the remote

OS fingerprint. The techniques used for this purpose differ according to the data they use and how these data are acquired. According to how data are created and captured, the methods can be grouped into the following.

- *Active*: The machine that performs the identification sends messages to the remote machine. The responses to these messages (or the lack of responses) are used in the identification process.
- *Passive*: The machine that performs the identification does not send messages through the network to perform identification. The remote machine data are captured when it communicates with a third machine. This implies that the identification machine must have access to the communication channel between the remote and the third machine.

To categorize and evaluate different techniques, it is convenient to define some criteria. The following definitions create a basis to evaluate the performance of the different types of ROSD techniques and tools.

1. *Availability*: considers the existence of the necessary data to perform ROSD
2. *Effectiveness*: concerned with the accuracy of the characterization and classification techniques used to distinguish OSs in the ROSD process
3. *Efficiency*: takes into account the amount of data and time needed to perform ROSD, where performance is often inverse to the amount of data and processing time needed
4. *Detectability*: qualifies the risks of the ROSD processes being detected while performed
5. *Reliability*: concerned with the veracity of data and the quality of characterization and classification when performing ROSD
6. *Tractability*: considers the qualitative aspect of not interfering in the expected function of the remote OS while performing ROS

These definitions can be used as a qualitative performance measure associated with the use of different ROSD techniques. From now on, we describe the goal of this chapter according to the aforementioned qualitative metrics.

9.1.3 Goal

In this chapter, we aim to develop a new classification mechanism to perform ROSD, which has the following requirements: (1) high availability of the data used to perform characterization; (2) high effectiveness, both in characterization and classification; (3) high efficiency; (4) low detectability; (5) high reliability; and (6) high tractability. To achieve this, it is insightful to use computational intelligence, a claim that will be enforced later, for the purposes of characterization and classification.

9.1.4 Document Outline

The state of the art in the use of computational intelligence in ROSD is an initial step to build up a method to achieve this goal. This survey in presented in Section 9.2. In Section 9.3, we present the theory and method used to achieve the goal previously defined. The characterization process and its results are described in Section 9.4 and the classification process and its results in Section 9.5. Finally, in Section 9.6, the goal requirements are revisited, and we discuss our achievements and possible future work.

9.2 Survey

Given the process presented in Figure 9.3, it is possible to highlight the application of computational intelligence in the following moments: (1) data preparation and feature selection and extraction from raw network data; (2) methods for classification of fingerprints; and (3) inference result projection, representation, and visualization. In this section, we present the state of the art in the use of computational intelligence in ROSD processes. The main referenced works are classified into three categories, according to the aforementioned possible applications of intelligence.

9.2.1 Feature Selection and Extraction

The feature selection and extraction consist of the first moment of an ROSD process. The goal at this moment is to obtain a proper fingerprint of the remote OS, which permits the ROSD process to perform an acceptable identification, according to the performance criteria presented in Section 9.1.2.

Although the Nmap OS detection tool [1] can provide an effective ROSD, it is unable to provide tractability or low detectability. The use of common ROSD tools like that may harm sensitive TCP/IP (Transmission Control Protocol [10]/Internet Protocol [2]) stack implementations, such as those of some industrial automation devices, and may cause communication interruption in these systems. Motivated by this, Medeiros et al. [11] propose a method that uses only TCP SYN (synchronization) messages to collect the contents of their TCP ISN (initial sequence number), a field of the TCP message header. Extracting features from these samples, the authors created representations of the pseudorandom number generator (PRNG) of the initial sequence of numbers. These representations are illustrated in Figure 9.4.

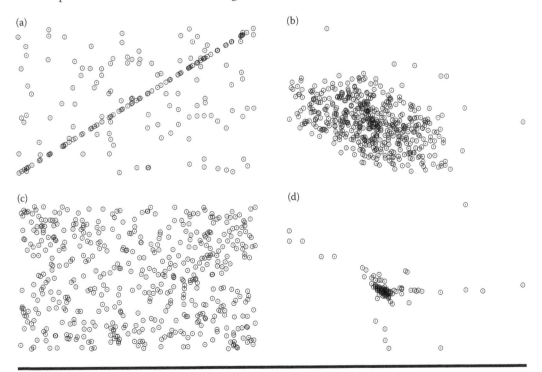

Figure 9.4 Attractors of some OS PRNG. (a) FreeBSD attractor; (b) NetBSD attractor; (c) OpenBSD attractor; and (d) Linux attractor.

These PRNG representations are discussed in Section 9.3. For now, it is convenient to highlight that the achievements in the work of Medeiros et al. [11] are quite important to availability and effectiveness, since these packets are valid TCP synchronization packets for open ports, and attractors are distinguishable.

Another application of computational intelligence in ROSD is associated with the use of information theory [12]. Greenwald and Thomas [13,14] demonstrated successful fingerprinting with 1 to 3 packets, while Nmap [1] uses 16. This result is quite important to perform ROSD efficiently and effectively. Furthermore, these packets are valid TCP synchronization packets for open ports, which are tractable and less likely to be detected.

9.2.2 Representation and Visualization

The representation and visualization of ROSD inference results can improve the capability of identifying unknown OSs and evaluating fingerprint entries in the classification database. These characteristics are vital to achieve the criteria of effectiveness and reliability, respectively.

As an application to industrial informatics, Medeiros et al. [15,16] propose a new method to improve the classification effectiveness of automation devices. The proposal makes use of self-organizing maps (SOMs) to build a contextual feature map [17] that organizes OS labels according to the similarities of their TCP/IP fingerprints. This map is used to identify the OS of a device under test and may help to select security tests according to the class to which it belongs. Figure 9.5 illustrates this contextual feature map.

Medeiros et al. [18,19] propose three new representations of the Nmap [1] ROSD database that can express how OSs are similar to each other with regard to their TCP/IP stack implementations. Specifically, beyond the use of SOM [20], growing neural gas (GNG) [21] and the *k*-means algorithm [22] are also used to assess the abilities of these algorithms on fingerprint database processing. In addition, they highlight applications in (1) improvement of the identification of unknown OSs; (2) compression of fingerprint databases; and (3) fingerprint corruption evaluation.

IOS	IOS	IOS	SonicOS	AIX	FreeBSD	Mac OS	Mac OS	FreeBSD	FreeBSD
IOS	IOS	QNX	SonicOS	FreeBSD	FreeBSD	FreeBSD	FreeBSD	FreeBSD	FreeBSD
IOS	IOS	QNX	SCO OS	BSD/OS	IRIX	IRIX	FreeBSD	FreeBSD	HP-UX
Windows	Windows	NetBSD	NetBSD	NetBSD	OpenBSD	OpenBSD	OpenBSD	Solaris	Solaris
Windows	Windows	IBM OS	IBM OS	Minix	OpenBSD	Linux	OpenBSD	Solaris	Solaris
Windows	Windows	IBM OS	IBM OS	NetWare	Linux	Linux	Linux	Linux	Solaris
Windows	Windows	Windows	Windows	Linux	Linux	Linux	Linux	Linux	Linux
Windows	Windows	Windows	Linux	Linux	Linux	Linux	Linux	Linux	Linux
Windows	Windows	Windows	Linux	Linux	Linux	Linux	Linux	Linux	Linux
Windows	Windows	Symbian	Linux	Linux	Linux	Linux	Linux	Linux	Linux

Figure 9.5 Illustration of self-organizing map of fingerprints.

9.2.3 Methods for Classification

The final step in the ROSD process consists of classifying the OS under observation by comparing the detected fingerprint with the entries of labeled fingerprints in a database. The first widespread scientific reference on the use of computational intelligence for ROSD is the work by Beverly [23], which used probabilistic learning to build up a Bayesian classifier (BC) [24] that can identify remote OSs in a passive manner. Consequently, improvements in OS classification when compared to rule-based systems, for example, early versions of p0f [25], are verified. Apparently not aware of this previous work, Li et al. [26] provide similar results using data from the passive remote OS fingerprinting tool p0f [25]. However, instead of probabilistic learning, the authors use a back-propagation algorithm [27] combined with the Levenberg–Marquardt algorithm (LMA) [28,29] to train a multilayer perceptron (MLP) [27] network, which produces better classification results.

The first work to deal with computational intelligence applied to active ROSD is that of Burroni and Sarraute [30], refined in the work of Sarraute and Burroni [31]. The authors deal with ROSD as an inference problem and classify the OS of remote hosts as the most likely to generate the captured traffic. To achieve this, they use an MLP neural network to classify the fingerprints according to known patterns. The proposed neural network provided a more reliable classification mechanism.

In papers by Gagnon and Esfandiari [32] and Gagnon et al. [33], the use of answer set programming (ASP) [34] is presented as a solution to address the problem of ROSD by logically specifying the problem and providing solutions through automated reasoning. This is the first computational intelligence method applied to ROSD that does not use a neural network. The results support the fact that using a knowledge base to keep previously deduced information enhances classification accuracy.

Another work proposes a method to perform ROSD with a support vector machine (SVM) [35], in which the authors present experimental results on identification of signatures in the fingerprint database of different Nmap [1] versions. Using the fingerprint database of the older version to perform classification, they show that their method is effective in the discovery of the signatures in the database of the newer version not included in the older one. It is convenient to say that since the SVM has the ability to simultaneously minimize the empirical classification error and maximize the geometric margin classification space [36], it usually produces optimal classification results.

Finally, Medeiros et al. [37] propose a method that uses only TCP SYN messages to collect TCP ISN samples. Using signal processing tools for classification, they show that it is possible to recognize OSs using only one open TCP port on the target machine without affecting device operation. The results also show that their technique cannot be fooled by Honeyd [38].

9.2.4 New Directions

In general, the current state of the art in intelligent ROSD consists of the use of classifiers that outperform the rule-based matching algorithms of passive and active fingerprinting tools, that is, p0f [25] and Nmap [1], respectively. The exceptions are the works of Medeiros et al. [11,37], which do not use any previous database to perform characterization and classification of remote machines. Moreover, the technique presented by these papers seems to be the most reliable nowadays. Motivated by these new findings, we summarized the results of the tests for tools that perform ROSD. These tools were evaluated under network scenarios built in order to decrease the classification performance of ROSD, which are (1) network address and port translation (NAPT) [39], (2) packet normalization or protocol scrubbing [40,41], (3) TCP synchronization mechanisms [42,43], and (4) Honeyd [38,44]. The evaluated tools were Nmap [1], p0f [25], SinFP [45], Xprobe [6,46], and Zion [37,47]. The results are presented in Table 9.1.

Table 9.1 Qualitative Performance Analysis of Some ROSD Tools

Network Setup	Nmap	p0f	SinFP	Xprobe	Zion
NAPT	Imprecise	Correct	Correct	Wrong	Correct
Protocol scrubbing	Imprecise	Imprecise	Correct	Wrong	Correct
TCP SYN cache	Wrong	Wrong	Wrong	Wrong	Correct[1]
Honeyd	Wrong	Wrong	Wrong	Wrong	Correct[2]

Source: Medeiros, J.P.S. et al., A qualitative survey of active TCP/IP fingerprinting tools and techniques for operating systems identification, *Proceedings of the International Workshop on Computational Intelligence in Security for Information Systems (CISIS)*, Lecture Notes in Computer Science, 2011.

The notes in each part of Table 9.1 are associated with these facts and events: (1) The tool was able to recognize the use of the SYN proxy, and (2) the tool was able to recognize the use of Honeyd. It is important to note that the performance of these tools is justified in terms of the data used to characterize OSs, not the classification algorithm. Therefore, the use of TCP ISN samples seems to be the most promising data to be explored in the field of ROSD research. However, the collection of TCP ISN may be characterized as a TCP SYN flooding attack. To minimize this side effect, it is important to reduce the amount of samples needed to perform characterization, which is in the order of 10^4 in the work of Medeiros et al. [37]. Hereafter, we explore the characterization process proposed in that work since it is already shown to be of high availability, effectivity, reliability, and tractability. After that, we have to reduce the amount of data required to perform ROSD and achieve our initial goal, defined in Section 9.1.3, in the sense of high efficiency and low detectability.

9.3 Method

In this section, the steps taken to achieve the goal defined in Section 9.1.3 are described. First, the theory of TCP ISN generators is explained, followed by a discussion about how to classify OSs using only this kind of data. Furthermore, we present an architecture that will be used to characterize and classify OSs using only TCP ISN samples.

9.3.1 Initial Sequence Numbers

Security specialist Michal Zalewski [25] presented an original way of characterization of TCP ISN PRNGs. Although this was originally used to exploit PRNG weakness and shows the possibility of spoof TCP sessions, it can be also used to detect OSs remotely. From the work of Bellovin [48] and Gont and Bellovin [49], we can extract the following recommendation for the generation of TCP initial sequence numbers:

$$s(c_{id}, t) = m(t) + f(c_{id}, t), \tag{9.1}$$

where $s(c_{id}, t)$ is the initial sequence number for a connection identity c_{id} (source address and port, and destination address and port) at instant t, and $m(t)$ is an incremental function, generally represented by

$$m(t) = m(t - 1) + r(t), \tag{9.2}$$

where $r(t)$ is a random number generator. The function $f(c_{id},t)$ is a connection-dependent term that is constant most of the time, represented by

$$f(c_{id},t) = h(c_{id},\ k(t)), \tag{9.3}$$

where $h(\cdot)$ is a hash function in which the second argument $k(t)$ is an optional secret key input that may change over time. Medeiros et al. [37] used the PRNG $r(t)$ function to classify OSs. Using Equations 9.1, 9.2, and 9.3, it is possible to recover samples of $r(t)$ using the relation

$$\hat{r}(t) = s(c_{id},t) - s(c_{id},t-1), \tag{9.4}$$

which, using Equations 9.1 and 9.2, may be rewritten as

$$\hat{r}(t) = r(t) + [f(c_{id},t) - f(c_{id},t-1)]. \tag{9.5}$$

Because $f(c_{id},t)$ will only change eventually, it will be constant for most of the time, and for the majority of cases, $\hat{r}(t)$ will be equal to $r(t)$; however, when $k(t)$ changes in $f(c_{id},t)$, the estimated value $\hat{r}(t)$ differs from $r(t)$.

Not surprisingly, there exist OSs that do not follow the initial recommendation of Bellovin [48] or the standard [49]. There are two common other alternative approaches to generate ISN: (1) use constant increments instead of random increments and (2) use pseudorandom sequences directly instead of the incremental approach. In the second case, we use the proper function $s(c_{id},t)$ as the true estimator for $r(t)$.

The approach adopted by the OS to implement $s(c_{id},t)$ is the first distinguishable characteristic we can highlight, more precisely, whether or not the TCP ISN follows the recommendation of Gont and Bellovin [49]. Another consideration is that the function $m(t)$ could be implemented as a timer whose increments are fixed. On these implementations, two consecutive TCP ISN samples could have the same value. Therefore, the existence of consecutive equal TCP ISN samples is another distinguishable characteristic of $s(c_{id},t)$.

Beyond consecutive equal samples, there is the possibility of different usage of the bits in the TCP sequence field. As shown in Section 9.4, some systems do not use some bits of this field. This is the third distinguishable characteristic used. Finally, we consider the shape of the function $\hat{r}(t)$. Figure 9.6 shows the shape of the PRNG in most common cases: purely random (left) and random increments (right).

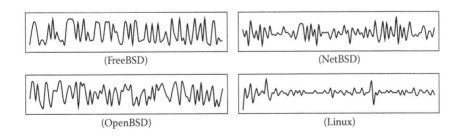

(FreeBSD) (NetBSD)

(OpenBSD) (Linux)

Figure 9.6 Comparison between operating systems TCP ISN PRNG.

Although the shapes presented in Figure 9.6 can be used to distinguish the PRNG with some effort, they are not the best way to characterize $\hat{r}(t)$. In fact, the representations in Figure 9.4 are much more distinguishable and do not change as frequently as the representations in Figure 9.6. Hereafter, we describe how to build up these representations called attractors.

9.3.2 Representation of Random Sequences

As discussed in Section 9.2.2, the representation of the raw data is a mode to extract some distinguishable characteristics that were not easily noted. To be able to perform an effective and reliable ROSD, another feature that can be extracted from the PRNG samples is their attractors. In order to obtain this feature, we may visualize the PRNG sequences in a graphical plot, which can highlight the $\hat{r}(t)$ dynamics.

A possible way to create effective representations is by the use of delayed coordinates, in which each point in the graphical plot is given by the relation

$$[x, y] = [\hat{r}(t), \hat{r}(t-1)], \tag{9.6}$$

where t, in this case, is interpreted as an integer iterated from the unity to the size of the sequence. The visualization of the sequences of four general-purpose OSs was already presented in Figure 9.4. A visual analysis of those portraits makes it possible to conclude that the PRNGs of the TCP implementations of each OS are viable solutions for the characterization step. However, an automated procedure to perform ROSD should be considered.

9.3.3 System Development and Architecture

Before delving into the details of the proposed intelligent ROSD architecture, it is necessary to consider the requirements to develop a classifier in accordance with the performance criteria discussed in Section 9.1.2:

- *Availability*: The proposed system must require only one open TCP port in order to acquire TCP ISN samples.
- *Tractability*: Since the classifier will only use normal TCP SYN messages, there is no chance of system damage on the target side.
- *Reliability*: Because TCP ISN does not suffer influence from protocol scrubbing, NAPT can detect SYN proxies and tools like Honeyd.
- *Efficiency* and *detectability*: The system should use a minimal number of TCP ISN samples to perform classification and avoid its detection.
- *Effectiveness*: The classification rates should be close to 100% accurate for each OS considered.

The proposed system architecture to achieve this is presented in Figure 9.7.

To achieve the requirements of efficiency, detectability, and effectiveness, it is necessary to build up a strategy to minimize the amount of samples needed for classification, without compromising the system effectiveness. This proposed system is able to intelligently perform an ROSD by the use of a neural network that can classify the remote OS according to the fingerprint presented to it. The necessary procedures and components for the training of the system are described as follows:

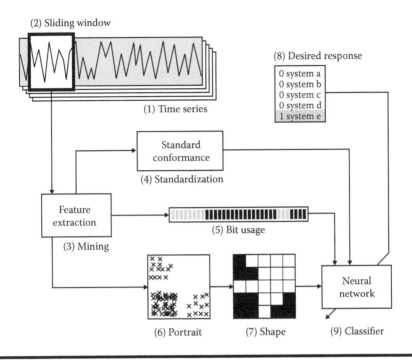

Figure 9.7   Neural network classifier training procedure.

1. The first procedure to be performed is to obtain TCP ISN samples. These samples are treated as a time series.
2. However, as discussed earlier, one of the main requirements of the system is its capability to achieve a high level of efficiency without losing detectability. Thus, we propose a sliding window strategy as a way of minimizing the number of TCP ISN samples to be considered for the feature extraction component of the system.
3. The feature extraction component is responsible for creating the fingerprint of the remote OS. Its main objective is to mine the TCP ISN samples in order to extract the distinguishable characteristics that will be used to compound the fingerprint submitted to the neural network.
4. The first feature extracted from the TCP ISN samples is related to the standard conformance of the remote OS. This feature consists of an assertion on the implementation of the OS, whether or not it follows the standard recommendations [48,49].
5. The second extracted distinguishable feature is the analysis of the bit usage of the TCP ISN field. This feature consists of the observation of the phenomenon presented by the PRNG of the remote OS.
6. Another important feature that is used as a distinguishable characteristic of the remote OS is its attractor. An OS attractor consists of a graphical representation of the estimated PRNG of the remote OS, which will be seen as a portrait of the OS for system analyses.
7. In order to make attractors an available feature to be presented to the neural network, an additional preprocessing step is necessary. To accomplish this requirement, we propose a graphical presentation of the portrait shape by a discretization process.

8. Once the fingerprint of the remote OS is created by combining these three extracted features during the training phase, it is submitted to the neural network together with the desired response.

9. After the training period, an SVM neural network will be able to classify the submitted fingerprint. The SVM was used due to its optimality characteristic [36], which is appropriate to estimate the minimum amount of samples necessary to perform classification accurately.

This architecture is used to build up a performance analysis of the classification rate using two free parameters: (1) the amount of TCP ISN samples and (2) the resolution of the shape of the attractor portrait. In Section 9.4, the characteristics that should compose the OS fingerprint are explored, while in Section 9.5, the performance of the classification system is addressed.

9.4 Characterization

To accomplish the proposed requirements of the ROSD system architecture, the intelligent system must consider previous knowledge about the target OSs. In our case, we consider the OSs presented in Table 9.2. The criteria for choosing these systems were (1) that the OS is well known and popular, (2) that it is easily accessible and available to the experiment, and (3) the diversity of

Table 9.2   List of Analysis Systems and Their Details

Number	System	Version	Purpose
1	3com OS	3.10	Network
2	FreeBSD	9.2	General
3	HP Printer	2600	Embedded
4	Cisco IOS	12.3.11	Network
5	Linux	2.6.32	General
6	Linux	3.2.29	General
7	Mac OS X	10.8.4	General
8	NetBSD	5.1.2	Network/embedded
9	OpenBSD	4.3	Network/security
10	Plan9	4	Embedded/network/grid
11	QNX	6.5	Real time
12	Solaris	11.1	General/cloud
13	SonicOS	5.8	Network/security
14	Windows	8	General
15	Windows	XP	General
16	Xerox Printer	3220	Embedded

the OS purposes. Although items 3 and 16 of Table 9.2 are not proper OSs, but printer devices, we call them by this term for convenience, since the OS is unknown.

Probably, the only missing OS purposes are those for mobile applications. This is justified by the fact that these OSs usually do not have open TCP ports, and therefore, TCP ISN samples are not available information. For each OS, we determined the characterization of its fingerprint, to be presented to the neural network, according to the features previously discussed. After this, we explored the usual behavior of these features and presented it to highlight which features can be used to distinguish the OSs. These characterizations are summarized and illustrated in Figure 9.8. This figure exemplifies the common behavior of these OSs, detected during observations with 400 TCP ISN samples for each of them.

To represent the standard conformance feature of an OS, we consider observations on the behavior of the ISN samples, looking for the presence of an incremental pattern. To argue that the OS follows the standards is a hard problem; however, it is possible to know, with tolerable accuracy, when an OS does not follow the standards. Thus, we consider the assumption that if the observed TCP ISN values are not incremental in most cases, this is an indication that the OS does not follow the standard recommendation [49]. This feature is represented as a Boolean value, assuming the value 1 if the TCP ISN is incremental or 0 otherwise.

The second feature expresses the existence of equal consecutive TCP ISN values. To represent this behavior, we consider two characteristics: (1) if repetitions were detected on the ISN samples and (2) what the frequency of this repetition was. The first characteristic is represented with 1 if there are repeated samples and 0 if the consecutive samples always differ. If there are repeated samples, the amount of times they repeat is represented as a 10-bit discretization of the percentage rate regarding the overall samples. The rate is rounded off to the nearest decimal percentage and should be read from the leftmost bit.

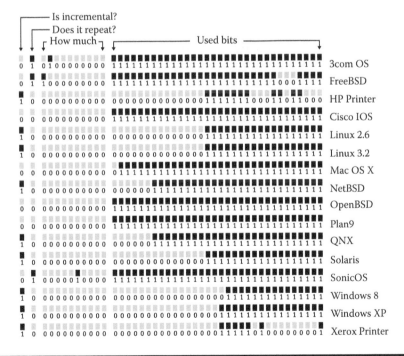

Figure 9.8 Conformance and bit usage for each OS.

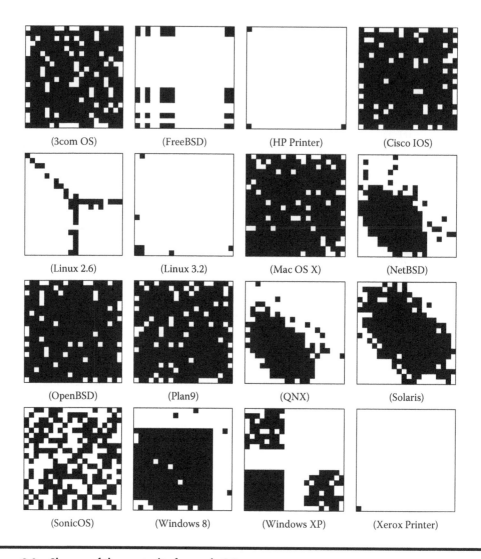

Figure 9.9 Shapes of the portraits for each OS.

As presented in Figure 9.7, the attractors of each OS must be preprocessed before being presented to the neural network. The chosen way for preprocessing this feature was the discretization of the attractors as a shape for each portrait. The shapes of the portraits for each OS are presented in Figure 9.9.

The shape of an attractor portrait can be taken as a matrix of pixels, where each pixel is set if its coordinates contain an attractor point. For this illustration, we consider a 20 × 20 matrix, where a black pixel represents the existence of at least one of the points in the original attractor.

9.5 Classification

To achieve the requirements of high efficiency and low detectability, it is necessary to find out the sufficient number of TCP ISN samples, denominated $|S_o|$, and the most suitable size of the portrait shape, denominated d_o. These values were obtained by using the following estimation procedure: (1) Compute the classification performance using a fixed high number of TCP ISN samples $|S|$ while increasing the value of d; and (2) compute the classification performance increasing the number of samples $|S|$ proportional to the increase in d. Figure 9.10 describes the performance for each strategy.

In the fixed case, $|S| = 400$ was used, while in the incremental approach, the relation was $|S| = d^2$. Moreover, from Figures 9.8 and 9.9, it is possible to conclude that there is not enough information to distinguish Cisco IOS, OpenBSD, and Plan9. Therefore, it is necessary to treat them as being one grouping class, with alias (a). The same occurs with NetBSD and QNX, which will compose group (b). The classification performance considering these groups is presented in Figure 9.11.

This result clearly shows that there is no need to use more than 25 samples for a high correct classification rate. More specifically, the classification performance using data from 25 ($d_o = 5$) TCP ISN samples using an SVM is presented in Table 9.3.

Summing the rates of classes (a) and (b), all systems have correct classification rates above 93%, and the mean classification performance is above 98%. The feature extraction step reached the correct classification of most of the OSs using only the data presented in Figure 9.8. In fact, the incremental approach for $d = 2$ in Figure 9.11 achieves a performance of appropriately 86% using only four samples. However, it was not possible to distinguish between Linux versions without the use of attractors. Hence, the proposed architecture results also meet the requirements of efficiency, detectability, and effectiveness.

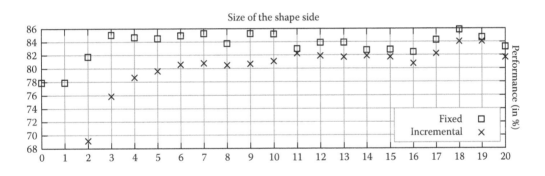

Figure 9.10   Classification performance for each OS.

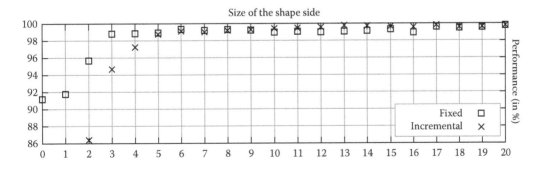

Figure 9.11   Classification performance grouping similar PRNGs.

Table 9.3 Classification Performance using 25 Packets

	3com OS	FreeBSD	HP Printer	(a) Cisco IOS	(a) OpenBSD	(a) Plan9	Linux 2.6	Linux 3.2	Mac OS X	(b) NetBSD	(b) QNX	Solaris	SonicOS	Windows 8	Windows XP	Xerox Printer
3com OS	.99	–	–	–	–	–	–	–	–	–	–	–	.01	–	–	–
FreeBSD	–	1.0	–	–	–	–	–	–	–	–	–	–	–	–	–	–
HP Printer	–	–	1.0	–	–	–	–	–	–	–	–	–	–	–	–	–
Cisco IOS (a)	–	–	–	.27	.54	.19	–	–	–	–	–	–	–	–	–	–
OpenBSD (a)	–	–	–	.32	.52	.16	–	–	–	–	–	–	–	–	–	–
Plan9 (a)	.03	–	–	.23	.48	.25	–	–	–	–	–	–	.01	–	–	–
Linux 2.6	–	–	–	–	–	–	.95	.04	–	–	–	.01	–	–	–	–
Linux 3.2	–	–	–	–	–	–	.07	.93	–	–	–	–	–	–	–	–
Mac OS X	–	–	–	–	–	–	–	–	1.0	–	–	–	–	–	–	–
NetBSD (b)	–	–	–	–	–	–	–	–	–	.74	.26	–	–	–	–	–
QNX (b)	.01	–	–	–	–	–	–	–	–	.67	.32	–	–	–	–	–
Solaris	–	–	–	–	–	–	.01	–	–	–	–	.99	–	–	–	–
SonicOS	.01	–	–	–	–	–	–	–	–	–	–	–	.99	–	–	–
Windows 8	–	–	–	–	–	–	–	–	–	–	–	–	–	1.0	–	–
Windows XP	–	–	–	–	–	–	–	–	–	–	–	–	–	–	1.0	–
Xerox Printer	–	–	–	–	–	–	–	–	–	–	–	–	–	–	–	1.0

9.6 Conclusion

In this chapter, we propose a system architecture to perform an intelligent ROSD, based on fingerprinting techniques and neural networks, to identify the OSs. This architecture is defined in order to achieve reasonable levels of availability, effectiveness, efficiency, detectability, reliability, and tractability when identifying a remote OS. To meet these requirements, we consider performing TCP/IP stack fingerprinting using only TCP ISN samples. We present results that show that the proposed architecture is able to perform effective, efficient, and reliable OS detection, having correct classification rates above 98%. The use of only 25 TCP ISN samples also makes it possible to achieve low detectability and detection with tractability. Future works include the analysis of other OSs with the discovery of other interesting features in these TCP messages.

Acknowledgments

The authors thank Aguinaldo Bezerra Batista Júnior for the insightful comments and review and Professor Agostinho de Medeiros Brito Júnior for the rich involvement in the early development of this work.

References

1. G. F. Lyon. *Nmap Network Scanning: The Official Nmap Project Guide to Network Discovery and Security Scanning*. Insecure.Com LLC, Synnyvale, CA, 2009.
2. J. Postel. *RFC 791 (Internet Standard), Internet Protocol—DARPA Internet Program, Protocol Specification*. Internet Engineering Task Force (IETF), Sept. 1981.
3. J. Postel. *RFC 792 (Internet Standard), Internet Control Message Protocol—DARPA Internet Program, Protocol Specification*. Internet Engineering Task Force (IETF), Sept. 1981.
4. V. Jacobson, C. Leres, and S. McCanne. TCPDUMP/LIBPCAP public repository, June 2012. Version 4.3.0, released on June 2012.
5. S. McCanne, and V. Jacobson. The BSD packet filter: A new architecture for user-level packet capture. In *Proceedings of the USENIX Winter 1993 Conference*, pages 259–269, 1993.
6. O. Arkin, and F. Yarochkin. ICMP based remote OS TCP/IP stack fingerprinting techniques. *Phrack Magazine*, 11(57), Aug. 2001.
7. G. F. Lyon. Remote OS detection via TCP/IP fingerprinting. *Phrack Magazine*, 8(54), Dec. 1998.
8. J. Novotny, D. Schulte, G. Manes, and S. Shenoi. Remote computer fingerprinting for cyber crime investigations. In *Proceedings of the Seventeenth Annual Working Conference on Data and Applications Security*, Data and Applications Security XVII, pages 3–15, 2004.
9. J. M. Novotny, A. Meehan, D. Schulte, G. W. Manes, and S. Shenoi. Evidence acquisition tools for cyber sex crimes investigations. In *Proceedings of the SPIE, Sensors, and Command, Control, Communications, and Intelligence (C3I) Technologies for Homeland Defense and Law Enforcement*, volume 4708, pages 53–60, 2002.
10. J. Postel. *RFC 793 (Internet Standard), Transmission Control Protocol—DARPA Internet Program, Protocol Specification*. Internet Engineering Task Force (IETF), Sept. 1981.
11. J. P. S. Medeiros, A. M. Brito, and P. S. M. Pires. A new method for recognizing operating systems of automation devices. In *Proceedings of the 14th IEEE International Conference on Emerging Technologies and Factory Automation (ETFA)*, pages 1–4, 2009.
12. C. E. Shanon. A mathematical theory of communication. *Bell System Technical Journal*, 27(3):379–423, 1948.
13. L. G. Greenwald, and T. J. Thomas. Toward undetected operating system fingerprinting. In *Proceedings of the First USENIX Workshop on Offensive Technologies (WOOT)*, 2007.

14. L. G. Greenwald, and T. J. Thomas. Understanding and preventing network device fingerprinting. *Bell Labs Technical Journal*, 12(3):149–166, 2007.

15. J. P. S. Medeiros, A. C. Cunha, A. M. Brito, and P. S. M. Pires. Application of Kohonen maps to improve security tests on automation devices. In *Proceedings of the 2nd International Workshop on Critical Information Infrastructure Security (CRITIS)*, pages 235–240, 2007.

16. J. P. S. Medeiros, A. C. Cunha, A. M. Brito, and P. S. M. Pires. Automating security tests for industrial automation devices using neural networks. In *Proceedings of the 12th IEEE International Conference on Emerging Technologies and Factory Automation (ETFA)*, pages 772–775, 2007.

17. T. Kohonen. Self-organized formation of topologically correct feature maps. *Biological Cybernetics*, 43(1):59–69, 1982.

18. J. P. S. Medeiros, A. M. Brito, and P. S. M. Pires. A data mining based analysis of Nmap operating system fingerprint database. In *Proceedings of the 2nd International Workshop on Computational Intelligence in Security for Information Systems (CISIS)*, pages 1–8, 2009.

19. J. P. S. Medeiros, A. M. Brito, and P. S. M. Pires. Using intelligent techniques to extend the applicability of operating system fingerprint databases. *Journal of Information Assurance and Security*, 5(4):554–560, 2010.

20. T. Kohonen. *Self-Organizing Maps*, 3rd edition, Springer, Berlin, 2001.

21. B. Fritzke. A growing neural gas network learns topologies. In G. Tesauro, D. Touretzky, and T. Leen, editors, *Advances in Neural Information Processing Systems*, volume 7, pages 625–632. MIT Press, Cambridge, MA, 1995.

22. J. B. MacQueen. Some methods for classification and analysis of multivariate observations. In *Proceedings of 5th Berkeley Symposium on Mathematical Statistics and Probability*, volume 1, pages 281–297, 1967.

23. R. Beverly. A robust classifier for passive TCP/IP fingerprinting. In *Proceedings of the 5th International Workshop in Passive and Active Measurements (PAM)*, pages 158–167, 2004.

24. G. F. Cooper, and E. Herskovits. A bayesian method for the induction of probabilistic networks from data. *Machine Learning*, 9(4):309–347, 1992.

25. M. Zalewski. *Silence on the Wire: A Field Guide to Passive Reconnaissance and Indirect Attacks*, 1st edition. No Starch Press, San Francisco, 2005.

26. W. Li, D. Zhang, and J. Yang. Remote OS fingerprinting using BP neural network. In *Proceedings of the Second international conference on Advances in Neural Networks*, pages 367–372, 2005.

27. D. E. Rumelhart, G. E. Hinton, and R. J. Williams. Learning representations by back-propagating errors. *Nature*, 323(6088):533–536, 1986.

28. K. Levenberg. A method for the solution of certain non-linear problems in least squares. *Quarterly of Applied Mathematics*, 2:164–168, 1944.

29. D. W. Marquardt. An algorithm for least-squares estimation of nonlinear parameters. *Journal of the Society for Industrial and Applied Mathematics*, 11(2):431–441, 1963.

30. J. Burroni, and C. Sarraute. Using neural networks for remote OS identification. In *Proceedings of the 3rd Pacific Security Conference (PacSec)*, 2005.

31. C. Sarraute, and J. Burroni. Using neural networks to improve classical operating system fingerprinting techniques. *Electronic Journal of SADIO*, 8(1):35–47, 2008.

32. F. Gagnon, and B. Esfandiari. Using answer set programming to enhance operating system discovery. In *Proceedings of the 10th International Conference on Logic Programming and Nonmonotonic Reasoning*, pages 579–584, 2009.

33. F. Gagnon, B. Esfandiari, and L. Bertossi. A hybrid approach to operating system discovery using answer set programming. In *Proceedings of the 10th IFIP/IEEE International Symposium on Integrated Network Management (IM)*, pages 391–400, 2007.

34. V. W. Marek, and M. Truszczyński. Stable models and an alternative logic programming paradigm. In K. R. Apt, V. W. Marek, M. Truszczyński, and D. S. Warren, editors, *The Logic Programming Paradigm: A 25-Year Perspective*, pages 375–398. Springer, Berlin, 1999.

35. B. Zhang, T. Zou, Y. Wang, and B. Zhang. Remote operating system detection based on machine learning. In *Proceedings of the International Conference on Frontier of Computer Science and Technology*, pages 539–542, 2005.

36. C. Cortes, and V. Vapnik. Support-vector networks. *Machine Learning*, 20(3):273–297, 1995.

37. J. P. S. Medeiros, A. M. Brito, and P. S. M. Pires. An effective TCP/IP fingerprinting technique based on strange attractors classification. In *Proceedings of the 2nd International Workshop on Autonomous and Spontaneous Security (SETOP)*, pages 208–221, 2010.

38. N. Provos. A virtual honeypot framework. In *Proceedings of the 13th USENIX Security Symposium*, 2004.

39. P. Srisuresh, and M. Holdrege. *RFC 2663 (Informational), IP Network Address Translator (NAT) Terminology and Considerations*. Internet Engineering Task Force (IETF), Aug. 1999.

40. D. Watson, M. Smart, G. Malan, and F. Jahanian. Protocol scrubbing: network security through transparent flow modification. In *Proceedings of the DARPA Information Survivability Conference and Exposition II (DISCEX)*, pages 108–118, 2001.

41. D. Watson, M. Smart, G. Malan, and F. Jahanian. Protocol scrubbing: network security through transparent flow modification. *IEEE/ACM Transactions on Networking*, 12(2):261–273, 2004.

42. W. M. Eddy. Defenses against TCP SYN flooding attacks. *The Internet Protocol Journal*, 9(4):2–16, 2006.

43. W. M. Eddy. *RFC 4987 (Informational), TCP SYN Flooding Attacks and Common Mitigations*. Internet Engineering Task Force (IETF), Aug. 2007.

44. N. Provos, and T. Holz. *Virtual Honeypots: From Botnet Tracking to Intrusion Detection*. Addison-Wesley, Boston, 2008.

45. P. Auffret. SinFP, unification of active and passive operating system fingerprinting. *Journal in Computer Virology*, 6:197–205, 2010.

46. O. Arkin. A remote active OS fingerprinting tool using ICMP. *;login:*, 27(2), Apr. 2002.

47. J. P. S. Medeiros, A. M. Brito, and P. S. M. Pires. A qualitative survey of active TCP/IP fingerprinting tools and techniques for operating systems identification. In *Proceedings of the International Workshop on Computational Intelligence in Security for Information Systems (CISIS)*, Lecture Notes in Computer Science, pages 68–75, 2011.

48. S. Bellovin. *RFC 1948 (Informational), Defending Against Sequence Number Attacks*. Internet Engineering Task Force (IETF), May 1996.

49. F. Gont, and S. Bellovin. *RFC 6528 (Standards Track), Defending Against Sequence Number Attacks*. Internet Engineering Task Force (IETF), Feb. 2012.

Chapter 10

An Automated Surveillance System for Public Places

Kumar S. Ray, Debayan Ganguly, and Kingshuk Chatterjee

Contents

We consider an automated surveillance system for public places. In this chapter, by the term *public place*, we mean a shopping mall, an airport, and so forth. However, with some modification, the present concept of automated surveillance can be applied to any public place like a daily market, railway station, public meeting hall, and so forth. The reason for choosing a shopping mall and an airport as two public places of interest is to handle the surveillance problem at two different levels of surveillance, namely, a bottleneck point (i.e., the entry point of the shopping mall or the airport) and the general area of the shopping mall and airport after the entry point. Based on this particular model of a public place, we design our algorithm for an automated surveillance system. The exits of the shopping mall and the airport are normally kept open and we do not consider any direction of motion at the exit points. At the bottleneck points, the problem of surveillance reduces to an event recognition problem, whereas the problem of surveillance of the areas of a shopping mall and an airport after the entry point reduces to tracking multiple objects. The method of handling event recognition is based on vertical and horizontal histogram analyses of the blob identified by which we can determine the number of objects present in the blob. Subsequently, the detection of a monotonic sequence of centroids of the detected blob is performed. Multiple-object tracking inside the shopping mall and the airport is based on the method of linear assignment and Kalman filter. Using a Kalman filter, we can handle a tracking problem under occlusion.

10.1 Introduction

We consider an automated surveillance system in public places like airports and shopping malls. The concept of this chapter can be applied with some modifications to the surveillance of any other public places like a daily marketplace, railway station, meeting hall, and so forth. We restrict ourselves to public places like shopping malls and airports simply because such places have two features, namely, a bottleneck feature or a bottleneck point and a general area accessible to the public after the entry point. Based on this particular model of a public place, we design our algorithm for an automated surveillance system. The problem of surveillance at the bottleneck point is treated as an event recognition problem. By the term *event recognition*, we mean to say that if any object is identified or detected that is represented by a blob, then a basic event occurs. Next, our task is to determine whether the event is caused by the presence of a single person or multiple persons.

This task is performed through vertical and horizontal histogram analyses of the blobs that are obtained from the detected objects. Once we detect the presence of multiple persons, we immediately raise an alarm; otherwise, we go for verifying the monotonicity of the sequence of the x-coordinate of the centroid of the blob. The purpose of verifying the monotonicity of the sequence of the x-coordinate of the centroid of the blob is to check the direction of the individual person, that is, whether he/she is moving in the right direction. Once this is done, the person entering the mall or airport is free to move at his/her freedom. The problem of surveillance of the area after the entry point is treated as a multiple-object tracking problem, which is essentially considered as a linear assignment problem (LAP). Now, if the objects are partially or completely occluded by each other, under these circumstances, the tracking of the object continues using a Kalman filter.

Note that in the present approach, detection of a moving object is essentially required for both the bottleneck point and the broader area after the bottleneck point of the shopping mall or the airport. For object detection, the primary task is to estimate the background of the video sequence and then subtract the background from the image. Subsequently we use a modified version of frame differencing to identify the moving objects. At the bottleneck point, the moment object/ objects is/are detected, we immediately obtain an event to be considered for further use. Next, we count the number of moving objects using a vertical and horizontal histogram. If the count assures the presence of a single object at the bottleneck point, we consider the problem of event recognition by considering the direction of motion of an object based on an idea of a monotonically increasing sequence formed by the x-coordinate of the centroid of the blob detected. The advantage of the present approach is that we do not have to perform any task of counting the number of objects present and checking the direction of movements at every instant. We initiate the process of surveillance when the event occurs (i.e., when the object is detected). When the first phase of the bottleneck problem is over, we go for multiple-object tracking in the broader areas of the shopping mall and the airport. In this case also, the detection of objects is the primary task, and for such detection, we adopt the process as we have stated prior.

Object tracking is very important in vision-based systems such as (1) surveillance systems, (2) human–computer interaction, (3) traffic monitoring, (4) vehicle navigation, (5) action recognition, and (6) navigation of autonomous robots. Several approaches have been presented in the past [1]. But they differ from each other with respect to the object representation method, features used for tracking, tracking methods employed, and so forth. For instance, objects can be represented as a point, that is, the centroid [2] or set of points [3]; primitive geometric shapes such as rectangles and ellipses [4]; the object contour, which is used to represent nonrigid objects [5]; and others. The important features used for tracking the objects are color in different color spaces such as RGB, YcbCr, and HSV. But none of these color spaces are unanimously accepted as all of them are affected by noise [6]. Features like edges, which can be easily detected because of their distinct changes in intensity, can also be used for tracking. Edges have the advantage that they are not susceptible to illumination changes, like color. Tracking algorithms that track on the basis of object boundaries use edge-finding algorithms. The most popular algorithm among the existing edge-finding algorithms is Canny's [7] edge detection algorithm. Similarly, some approaches use the optical flow of the objects as the feature, which is a dense field of displacement vectors computed assuming a constant brightness of corresponding pixels in consecutive frames [8,9]. The algorithms for object detection are numerous in nature; for instance, the popular techniques for object detection are interest point detectors, which are usually unique to an object and are not susceptible to illumination or camera viewpoint changes. The Harris interest point detector [10] and Scale Invariant Feature Transform (SIFT) detector [11] belong in this category. Background subtraction can also be used for object detection. In this technique, a background model is formed, and each incoming frame is compared with the background to identify changes, which represent the foreground objects. The most popular approach for background models is the mixture of Gaussians method [12,13]. Segmentation is another technique for object detection. The aim of a segmentation algorithm is to partition the image into similar regions. The most popular segmentation technique is mean shift clustering [14]. Next to object detection, the most important task is the tracking of objects on the basis of the features extracted from one frame to the next. The tools employed to track objects depend on the features used to represent the objects. For instance, objects represented by points are tracked based on their location and motion information. For this, a Kalman filter is a very popular tool, which has been in use since 1986 [15]. A Kalman filter is used for estimating object location when object states are assumed to have a Gaussian distribution. For non-Gaussian objects, state particle filters are used [16]. Modification of the Kalman filter to an extended form has also been successfully employed in object tracking [17]. An object represented by a kernel (i.e., basic geometrical shapes) uses template matching, which is the simplest and most popular technique to track an object [18]. Another very efficient method for tracking is a kernel-tracking algorithm. It uses the concepts of mean shift clustering, which was developed by Comaniciu [4]. In this approach, the kernel histogram information is used. Comaniciu combined the mean shift algorithm with a Kalman filter to give a faster solution to the tracking problem. Another tracking technique, very similar in operation to the kernel-tracking technique, uses the object boundary along with the object histogram information to track objects [19], which is known as silhouette tracking.

Using the previously stated techniques and some new techniques, many multiobject tracking algorithms have come into existence. Each of these techniques has its own set of advantages and disadvantages. In the work of Li et al. [20], a Kalman filter is used to track multiple objects where distance and dimension are considered as features. The algorithm is fast but does not deal with static occlusion, and, moreover, it considers dynamically merged objects as new objects. Some multiobject tracking employs modified versions of existing tracking techniques, such as in the work of Mishra et al. [21], which employs a modified version of mean shift tracking, but the objects to be tracked need to be indentified manually. Moreover, it does not deal with partial occlusion. There is an algorithm that does multiobject tracking using a *k*-means algorithm [22]. The tracking algorithm does not pose any restriction on the location, color, or dimension of the objects but imposes other restrictions, for instance, objects neither appear nor disappear but, at certain locations, do not move quickly and cannot share a place with any other objects. The work of Khan [23] is one of the few papers that deal with long-time occlusion. It uses anisotropic mean shift and particle filters but does not deal with multiobject tracking. Particle swarm optimization has also been employed successfully in multiobject tracking in recent years [24,25]. Multiobject tracking in nonstationary video has also been done in the work of Nguyen and Bir [26]. The work of Pushpa and Sheshadri [27] deals with multiple-object tracking using a greedy algorithm, but the occlusion handling is not very robust.

From the previously discussed tracking algorithms, we experience that the assumptions used by these tracking algorithms such as prior object dimension information, minimal amount of occlusion, constant illumination, high contrast between foreground objects and background, arbitrary initialization of model parameters, and so forth, do not always work in an efficient manner in the real world. In this chapter, we aim to eliminate some of the aforementioned problems in multiobject tracking. We try to detect objects under partial and/or complete occlusion. We aim to build a real-time object tracking system that is capable of tracking objects in any given video sequence provided that the video is an unedited continuous video from a static camera. Here, the background model of the given video sequence is developed using an approximated median filter (AMF) algorithm. Then, frame differencing is used to detect objects. The features used to represent objects are its location, color histogram, and dimension of its bounding box. The location of the detected objects in the next frame is estimated using a Kalman filter. The Kalman filter is initialized properly so that it converges to the correct estimation quickly. Truth verification of the Kalman estimate is done to update the parameters of the Kalman filter. A different Kalman filter is introduced for each new track identified. Objects indentified in the next frame are assigned to a previously existing track using a linear assignment approach. Partial and/or complete occlusions are handled using Kalman estimates.

This chapter is divided into two parts; the first part deals with the bottleneck problem, which essentially deals with event recognition, and the second part deals with tracking multiple objects in the broader area of the shopping mall and the airport after the entry point.

10.2 Methodology

10.2.1 Bottleneck Problem

The bottleneck problem consists of four steps; (1) background estimation, (2) object detection, (3) counting the number of objects, and (4) determination of the direction of motion of moving objects. Experimental results of the bottleneck point are reported in Section 10.2.1.4.

10.2.1.1 Background Estimation

As the method of background estimation is an essential task to solve in the bottleneck problem for event recognition as well as to solve in the tracking problem in the boarder area of the shopping mall and the airport after the bottleneck point, we discuss this agenda in detail so that the methodology of this background estimation can be unifiedly used when it is necessary. Moving-object identification from a video sequence is a fundamental and critical task in many computer-vision applications. A common approach to this problem is to perform background subtraction, which identifies moving objects from the portion of a video frame that differs significantly from a background model. There are many challenges in developing a good background subtraction algorithm. First, it must be robust against changes in illumination. Second, it should avoid detecting nonstationary background objects such as swinging leaves, rain, snow, and shadows cast by moving objects. Finally, the background model that is stored internally should react quickly to changes in the background, such as starting and stopping of vehicles. One popular technique is to model each pixel feature in a video frame with the mixture of Gaussians (MOG) method [28]. The MOG method can deal with periodic motions from a cluttered background, slow lighting changes, and so forth. However, it is not adaptive to the quick variations in dynamic environments [29]. Other pixel-wise modeling techniques include kernel density estimation [30,31], codebook approach [32], and so forth. Due to the large memory requirements of nonrecursive filtering, McFarlane and Schofield [33] propose a simple recursive filter to estimate the background using the concept of a median, which requires less memory. This technique has been used in background modeling for urban traffic monitoring [34]. In this scheme, the running estimate of the median is incremented by 1 if the input pixel is larger than the estimate and is decreased by 1 if smaller. This estimate eventually converges to a value for which half of the input pixels are larger and half are smaller; that is the median. For estimation of background, we consider AMF. As far as accuracy is concerned, AMF is not as good as MOG and a median filter (MF). But it produces good performance with extremely simple implementation. Since the amount of background update (+1 or –1) is independent of the foreground pixels, it is very robust against moving traffic. It requires less memory, and also it works faster than MOG and MF. The only drawback of this approximated scheme is that it adapts slowly to a large change in the background. That is why to compensate for a large change in the background, in the object detection phase in Section 10.2.1.2, we use frame differencing. The results obtained in a video sequence as shown in Figure 10.1 are found using the aforementioned AMF approach.

10.2.1.2 Object Detection

The methodology of object detection is equally important and applicable for solving the bottleneck problem and object-tracking problem after the bottleneck point. Hence, this methodology is also discussed in a generalized fashion, so that it can be utilized when it is required.

In this section, object detection is done by means of a modified version of frame differencing. The block diagram of this phase is shown in Figure 10.2.

Frame differencing has been in use since the late 1970s [35]. The basic idea of the frame-differencing technique is to subtract a temporally adjacent frame from the current frame to identify the objects that are moving in the current frame. The advantage of frame differencing is that certain changes in a background, especially in an external scene such as illumination, weather becoming cloudy, or a car being parked, can be incorporated as the background very easily. But it is very difficult for the background estimation model to incorporate such phenomena immediately. However, there are some disadvantages of the frame-differencing model; for example, it evidently works only in particular conditions of objects' speed and frame rate and is very sensitive to the chosen thresholds that are ad hoc in nature. Hence, we modify the frame-differencing method to remove the aforementioned disadvantages. The major disadvantage of the frame-differencing technique is that if the movements of the objects are very slow, then there is no significant change

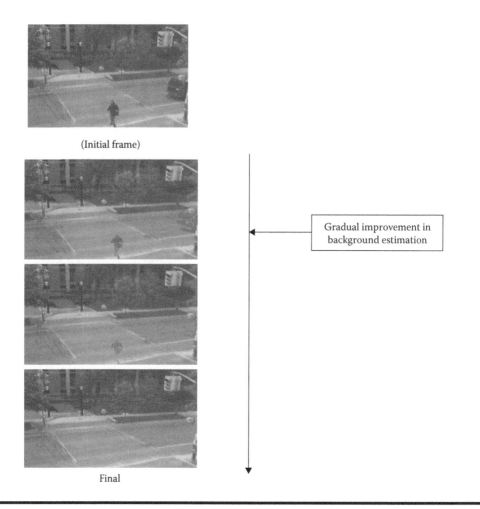

(Initial frame)

Gradual improvement in background estimation

Final

Figure 10.1   The results obtained in a video sequence using the AMF.

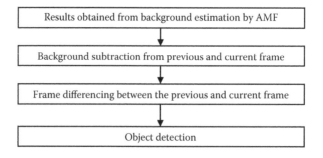

Results obtained from background estimation by AMF

Background subtraction from previous and current frame

Frame differencing between the previous and current frame

Object detection

Figure 10.2   Object detection by frame differencing.

in the temporarily adjacent frames. A very easy solution to this problem is to increase the distance between the adjacent frames, that is, instead of using the adjacent frames, we can use the frames that are a number of frames before the current frame so that we can also detect the motion of the slow objects. But it further introduces a problem, which is shown in Figure 10.3a. In Figure 10.3a, the resulting image contains two objects that are primarily the same object: one is the object located in the previous frame and one in the current frame. So a further modification is required, that is, we have to devise a way by which only the object in the current frame is detected and not the previous one. This is achieved by the following method.

The estimated background obtained from the background estimation algorithm is subtracted from the previous frame, and the process of this subtraction is as follows:

If $P(x,y) >$ th, where x,y are the coordinate of the pixel P and 'th' is the threshold,
then $P(x,y) = 1$,
else $P(x,y) = 0$.

Thus, we obtained two images, as shown in Figure 10.3b and c. We are able to identify the two target objects in the two images, but they are still corrupted with some noise, which is due to the estimation error of the background. If it is noise due to wrong estimation of the background, then it will be present in both the previous and current images. Here, the concept of frame differencing is used to eliminate this noise. The process of frame differencing is stated as follows.

We subtract the binarized image of the current frame from the binarized image of the previous frame. Then for each pixel $P(x,y)$,

if $P(x,y) > 0$, where x,y are the coordinates of the pixel P,
then $P(x,y) = 1$,
else $P(x,y) = 0$.

Now, we obtain an image as shown in Figure 10.3d, which contains only the moving object of the current frame and devoid of any noise due to error in background estimation. Thus, the moving objects are detected. In case any fragmentation of objects occurs, we use a distance-based criterion, which connects blobs very close to one another if they are within a certain threshold. We further illustrate the prior computation for object detection in another example. Figure 10.4 shows successful object detection in a video frame. Figure 10.4a is the actual background; Figure 10.4b is the estimated background that contains error as a car has parked in the scene and has

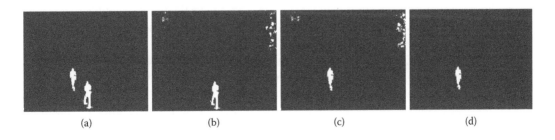

(a)　　　　　　(b)　　　　　　(c)　　　　　　(d)

Figure 10.3 (a) **The problem of frame differencing. (b) Previous frame—estimated background. (c) Current frame—estimated background. (d) Object is detected successfully.**

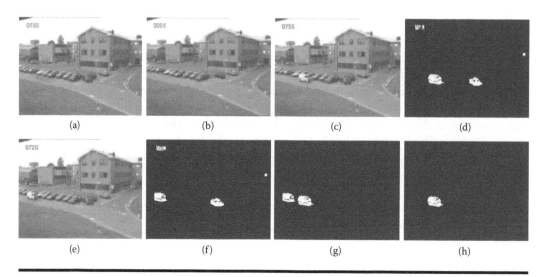

Figure 10.4 **(a) Actual background. (b) Estimated background. (c) Current frame. (d) Image after subtraction of estimated background from current frame. (e) Previous frame. (f) Image after subtraction of estimated background from previous frame. (g) Frame differencing. (h) Modified frame differencing for successful object detection.**

become part of background; but as AMF takes time to accommodate this change in the background, wrong background estimation occurs. Now, when this estimated background is subtracted from the current image, Figure 10.4c, two objects are detected: one is the actual moving object, and another is due to wrong estimation of the background. Moreover, there is some noise too, as shown in Figure 10.4d. When the estimated background is subtracted from a previous frame (see Figure 10.4e), the same noise and wrong objects are found, as shown in Figure 10.4f. Now the frame differencing between the current and previous frames is done. As a result, we obtain Figure 10.4g, where the problem, as stated with respect to Figure 10.3b, remains the same. Finally, when we apply the modified frame differencing, we detect the object successfully, as shown in Figure 10.4h.

10.2.1.3 Counting Number of Objects

This methodology is exclusively required to solve the event recognition problem at the entry point in the shopping mall and the airport. In case, at the object detection stage, multiple persons are detected, the surveillance system generates an alarm for safety; otherwise, the algorithm for the surveillance system will proceed further.

Detection of a single person is simple when persons are apart from each other. For instance, if in a frame, there are two persons who are apart from each other, then there are two separate blobs, as shown in Figure 10.5. Thus, there are two moving objects in a frame, and an alarm is raised. But a problem arises when persons are holding hands or are very close to each other. For instance, in Figure 10.6a,b, two persons are very close to each other in a frame, and they form a single blob. This problem can be solved by using the vertical and horizontal histograms.

A vertical histogram is the sum of all the 1 pixels in a particular column, and this is done for all the columns of the bounding box of the blob. Similarly, a horizontal histogram is the sum of all the 1 pixels in a particular row, and this is done for all the rows of the bounding box of the blob.

Figure 10.5 Showing two different blobs for two different persons.

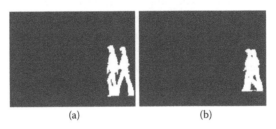

(a)   (b)

Figure 10.6 (a and b) A single blob comprising two different persons.

Here, we consider that if the bounding box of the blob comprises a group of people and if all of them are standing, then their heads will be visible in all the cases except when a person completely occludes another. Under such occlusion, we will not be able to identify two different heads. But chances of two persons walking exactly in tandem such that one's head is occluded by another throughout the entry path are very small. So counting of heads is a good method for identifying the number of persons in a group.

The idea that is employed in identifying the heads is based on a vertical histogram, which was used in the work of Haritaoglu [36] along with convex hull points to identify heads in a group. Instead of computing the convex hull, which is computationally heavy, we suggest a simpler alternative approach. We employ a horizontal histogram along with a vertical histogram to identify the heads. The number of peaks in the vertical histogram is equal to the number of heads in the binary bounding box of the blob. But this results in a problem, as shown in Figure 10.7b, which is the vertical histogram of Figure 10.7a. We see that it has two peaks, although the number of persons

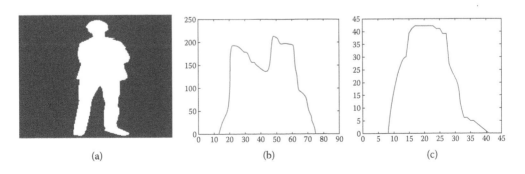

(a)   (b)   (c)

Figure 10.7 (a) An image frame containing a single blob. (b) A vertical histogram for the image frame. (c) A vertical histogram of the same image when taken from torso level; it contains only one peak.

in the bounding box is one. This is due to the fact that the two legs separated from one another along with the body and heads give two peaks. To overcome this problem, we compute the vertical histogram of the group of objects above the torso because the head is always above the torso. Then, only one peak will be obtained for each head in the group. The torso level is identified first by removing columns from the object matrix from the first column until we find a column whose sum of pixels is greater than the vertical histogram mean. A similar thing is done starting from the other end too. The new object matrix is obtained. Then, the horizontal histogram is computed. The torso level will have a value greater than the mean value in the horizontal histogram. So we scan downward from the top of the bounding box until we come across a row whose horizontal histogram value is greater than the mean horizontal histogram value of the bounding box. Thus, the corresponding row is the torso level in the object matrix. Now, if we consider the vertical histogram for the object matrix only up to that level, we will get only one peak for each head. Thus, counting the number of peaks above the mean value of the vertical histogram enables us to find the number of people in the bounding box. If the number of people is more than one, an alarm is raised. Figures 10.8, 10.9, and 10.10 show successful counting for different blobs.

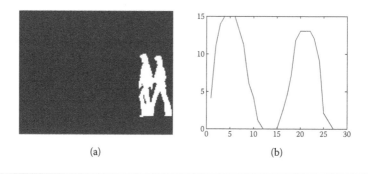

(a)   (b)

Figure 10.8   (a) An image frame with two persons in a single blob. (b) Vertical histogram with two peaks.

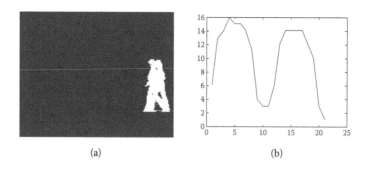

(a)   (b)

Figure 10.9   (a) Another image frame with two persons in a single blob. (b) Vertical histogram of 10.9(a) has two peaks.

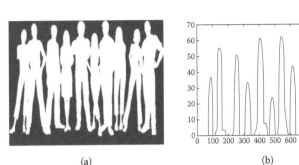

(a)   (b)

Figure 10.10 **(a) An image frame with 10 persons in a single blob. (b) Vertical histogram with 10 peaks.**

10.2.1.4 *Determination of Direction of Motion of Moving Objects*

We consider the concept of event recognition [37,38] for detection of the direction of motion of a moving object in a video sequence.

10.2.1.4.1 Centroid Representation

The previous steps ensure that if an image reaches this point, then it contains only one blob having one object. We can get the x-coordinate of the centroid. So we replace each image frame that we come across by the x-coordinate of the centroid of the blob in that frame. Thus, we obtain a one-dimensional array of x-coordinates of blobs for a video sequence as shown in Figure 10.11.

10.2.1.4.2 Recognition of Monotonically Increasing Sequence

To illustrate this method, let us consider a codebook of, say, 10 images as shown in Figure 10.12, which correctly represent the exact direction of motion. In this case, a video sequence depicting

```
Z =
    Columns 1 through 13
    1   2   2   2   2   2   2   2   2   3   3   3   3
    Columns 14 through 16
    3   3   3   3   4   4   4   4   4   4   4   4   4
    Columns 27 through 39
    5   5   5   5   5   5   5   5   6   6   6   6   6
    Columns 40 through 52
    6   6   6   6   7   7   7   7   7   7   7   7   8
    Columns 53 through 65
    8   8   8   8   8   8   8   9   9   9   9   9   9
    Columns 66 through 68
    9   9   10
```

Figure 10.11 **60-8-frame image sequence represented by the symbols of the codebook.**

the motion from right to left is used as the codewords. For each image chosen, the centroid of the blob is found out for that image. The *x*-coordinate of the centroids is stored as a codeword. Each codeword is assigned a number, which is its position in the codeword array.

Each image is represented by a centroid of the blob present, and each such centroid is given a symbol; also, the codeword is shown. The codeword array =

```
Columns 1 through 4
165.9813 150.6519 134.8950 118.0149
Columns 5 through 8
100.2220 82.7927 65.0165 47.0062
Columns 9 through 129.2550 13.0577
```

Now, a time sequential image sequence that has been represented as an array of the *x*-coordinate of centroids is compared to the codewords. Each image in the sequence is assigned a symbol, as shown in Figure 10.11, depending on which codeword it most closely matches. The image gets the same symbol as that of the matched codeword. This matching is done using minimum Euclidian distance. Thus, a time sequential image is converted to a series of symbols.

Now, this symbol sequence is checked. If the same symbol occurs in the sequence continuously more than twice the number of frames per second of the video sequence, then it is a still object, and an alarm is raised; otherwise, checking for increasing monotonicity of the sequence is done. If it is monotonically increasing, then the motion is in the right direction. The process flow is shown in Figure 10.13.

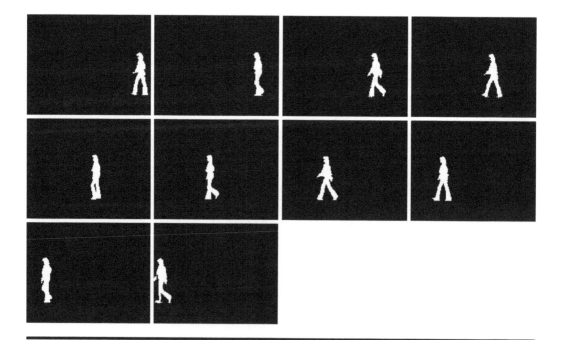

Figure 10.12   The images chosen for event recognition.

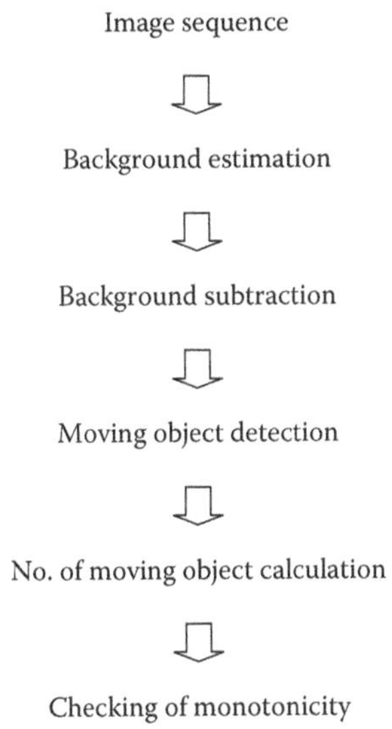

Image sequence

Background estimation

Background subtraction

Moving object detection

No. of moving object calculation

Checking of monotonicity

Figure 10.13   The process flow.

10.2.1.5 Experimental Results at the Bottleneck Point

10.2.1.5.1 Experimental Conditions

This algorithm is tested on time sequential images. The monotonicity of the centroid position is used to recognize the correct direction of motion, which is taken from right to left. In our experiment, there were eight different persons, some walking from left to right (L TO R) and the others walking from right to left (R TO L). One person A is used to form the codebook. The system, when tested with different persons, is able to determine the correct direction of motion for 10 out of 10 motions.

10.2.1.5.2 Experimental Results

Table 10.1 represents the experimental details for multiple-object counting, Table 10.2 represents the percentage of multiple objects successfully counted, Table 10.3 represents the experimental details for event recognition, and Table 10.4 represents the percentage of event recognition.

10.2.2 Multiple-Object Tracking

The proposed methodology consists of five basic steps. In the first step, background estimation is done using an AMF algorithm. In the second step, object detection is done using frame differencing. In the third step, feature extraction of the detected objects is performed. In the fourth step, multiple-object tracking is treated as an LAP. In the fifth step, tracking of objects, under occlusion, is dealt with using a Kalman filter. Finally, in the sixth step, solving the merging problem is done. The steps involved in the proposed methodology are shown in Figure 10.14.

Table 10.1 Experimental Details for Multiple-Object Counting

Number of Persons in Sequence	Direction of Motion	Number of Persons Detected by the System
2 (coming from opposite side)	One person moving from L to R and another person moving from R to L	2
2 (coming from same side a certain distance apart from each other)	Both the persons moving from L to R	2
2 (coming from same side nearly beside one another)	Both the persons moving from L to R	2
2 (coming from same side, one occluded by the other)	Both the persons moving from L to R	2
2 (coming from the same side a certain distance apart from each other)	Both the persons moving from R to L	2
2 (coming from same side nearly beside one another)	Both the persons moving from R to L	2
2 (coming from same side, one occluded by the other)	Both the persons moving from R to L	2
1	Moving from L to R	1
1	Moving from R to L	1

Table 10.2 Multiple-Object Count Score

No. of Image Sequences with Multiple Persons	No. of Correct Identification of Multiple Persons	% Correctness
7	7	100%

The first two steps are already described in Sections 10.2.1.1 and 10.2.1.2. Here, we start from feature extraction of detected objects. The experimental results after the bottleneck point are reported in Section 10.2.1.4.

10.2.2.1 Feature Extraction

After object detection, the next stage is feature extraction so that the detected objects can be represented and tracked in the next frame. Objects are represented as points [2], kernels (having geometrical shape) [3], contours [5], and others. In addition to these, many features such as the color histogram of the object, its SIFT detectors, and so forth are used to represent objects. Here, we primarily use three features to represent an object: (1) the centroid of the object detected, (2) the height and width of the smallest bounding box of the object, and (3) the 16-bin RGB normalized

Table 10.3   Experimental Details for Event Recognition

Person ID	Direction of Motion	Direction Estimated
A	R TO L	R TO L
B	R TO L	R TO L
C	R TO L	R TO L
D	L TO R	NOT (R TO L)
E	R TO L	R TO L
F	R TO L	R TO L
F	L TO R	NOT (R TO L)
E	L TO R	NOT (R TO L)
G	L TO R	NOT (R TO L)
H	L TO R	NOT (R TO L)
A	STILL	NOT (R TO L)
D	STILL	NOT (R TO L)
E	STILL	NOT (R TO L)

Table 10.4   Event Recognition Score

No. of People	No. of Walks from R to L or L to R or Still	No. of Correct Motion Identification	% Correctness
8	13	13	100%

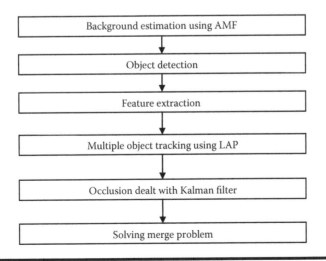

Figure 10.14   The basic steps of the tracking algorithm.

color histogram of the region within the bounding box, that is, the object. The features previously stated are shown in Figure 10.15. The two features, the centroid and the bounding box, as shown in Figure 10.15a are directly obtained from the object detection phase, whereas the normalized color histogram as shown in Figure 10.15b is obtained at the stage of feature extraction. The object details, that is, the stated features, are stored in the form of an array of dimension $n \times 52$, where n is the number of objects detected in a particular frame. The object array for Figure 10.15 is shown in Figure 10.16. For the present example of Figure 10.15, the value of n is 1. The other details are as follows: x-coordinate of centroid, y-coordinate of centroid, width of bounding box, height of bounding, 16-bin histogram values of red, 16-bin histogram values of green, and 16-bin histogram values of blue.

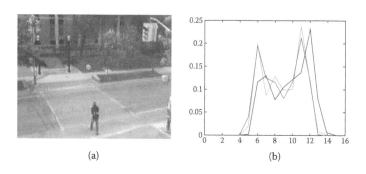

(a)   (b)

Figure 10.15   **(a) Object representation in the frame. (b) The object's color histogram.**

Columns 1 through 11

178.5000 238.0000 23.0000 72.0000   0   0   0   0 0.0381 0.1936 0.1239

Columns 12 through 22

0.1144 0.0804 0.1126 0.2126 0.1233 0.0012   0   0   0   0   0

Columns 23 through 33

0   0 0.0191 0.2001 0.0852 0.1292 0.0983 0.0995 0.2388 0.1221 0.0077

Columns 34 through 44

0   0   0   0   0   0   0 0.0018 0.1161 0.1304 0.0768

Columns 45 through 52

0.1048 0.1203 0.1358 0.2323 0.0762 0.0054   0   0

Figure 10.16   **The array of features for Figure 10.15.**

10.2.2.2 Multiple-Object Tracking

The problem of multiple-object tracking is considered as an LAP, as stated here.

Let there be a set of existing tracks and a set of new objects be identified in the next frame. The problem is to assign the said new objects either to the existing tracks or to the new tracks such that the cost of assigning the object is minimum. The block diagram of this phase is shown in Figure 10.17.

The cost that we calculate is as follows.

In the video sequence when, for the first time, there is a frame that contains an (some) object (objects), there is no existing track. We introduce tracks where the features of the said object/objects are stored along with the track number. The features are the centroid of the objects, the width and height of the bounding box of the objects, and the normalized 16-bin RGB histogram of the objects. Now, in the next frame, a set of objects are detected, among which some of the objects belong to the earlier frame and some are appearing for the first time. Here, the question of linear assignment arises. Depending on the number of newly detected objects, we generate a set of tracks that are empty at present. Now, the cost of assigning each object from the newly detected set of objects to the existing track is calculated. Figure 10.18 shows the existing tracks for the previous frame. We compute the Euclidian distance between the centroid value, which is stored in track 1 of the previous frame (see Figure 10.18), and the centroid value of each object of the newly detected set. If this measure is less than or equal to either the width or the height of the bounding box stored in track 1 (see Figure 10.19), then we assign

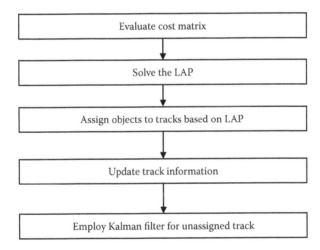

Figure 10.17 Steps involved in multiple-object tracking.

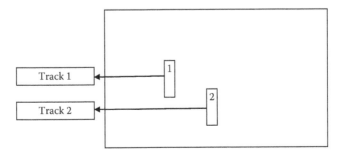

Figure 10.18 The existing tracks of the previous frame.

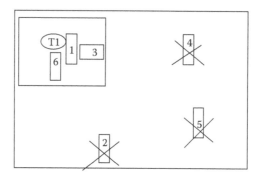

Figure 10.19 **The distance cost being evaluated for track 1.**

0 values, which indicate that they are the promising candidate objects to be assigned to track 1 of the previous frame; otherwise, a high value (say 10,000) will be assigned (see, for example, Figure 10.20). Now, for the objects that are promising candidates (for example, objects 1, 3, and 6 of Figure 10.19) to be assigned to track 1, we calculate the cost of matching the dimension of the bounding box. If both the width and the height of the bounding boxes of the promising candidate objects are within 25% of the stored value of those in track 1, then their cost will be assigned as 0; otherwise, a high value (say 10,000) will be assigned. For example, consider Figure 10.21, where the dimensions of the bounding box of object 3 do not satisfy the aforementioned conditions. Thus, the array of Figure 10.20 is revised, as shown in Figure 10.22. The next step is to check the normalized 16-bin RGB histogram cost. Here, the threshold value is chosen as 0.5 (see Section 10.2.2.2.3). Thus, we obtain Figures 10.23 and 10.24,

T1	0	10,000	0	10,000	10,000	0

Figure 10.20 **The cost values for track 1 after distance cost evaluation.**

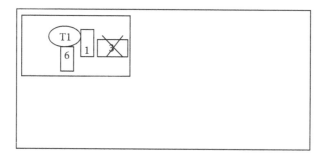

Figure 10.21 **The dimension cost being evaluated for track 1.**

T1	0	10,000	10,000	10,000	10,000	0

Figure 10.22 **The cost values for track 1 after dimension cost evaluation.**

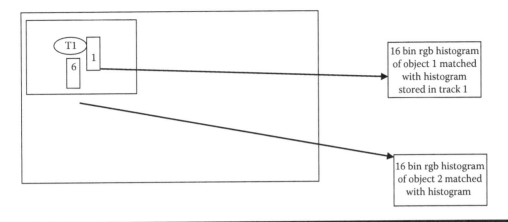

Figure 10.23 The normalized histogram cost being evaluated.

Figure 10.24 The cost values for track 1 after histogram cost evaluation.

which clearly indicate that object 1 is the most promising candidate to be assigned to track 1. We repeat the same process for all the existing tracks. Figure 10.25 shows the complete cost matrix. In the cost matrix of Figure 10.25, the entries having values of 5000 indicate the new tracks. Section 10.2.2.2.4 gives some further clarification on assigning cost values to the new tracks.

In the following paragraphs, detailed computations of different costs for linear assignment are stated one after another.

Tracks	1	2	3	4	5	6
T1	0.2040	10,000	10,000	10,000	10,000	0.4855
T2	10,000	0.1844	10,000	10,000	10,000	10,000
T3	5000	5000	5000	5000	5000	5000
T4	5000	5000	5000	5000	5000	5000
T5	5000	5000	5000	5000	5000	5000
T6	5000	5000	5000	5000	5000	5000
T7	5000	5000	5000	5000	5000	5000
T8	5000	5000	5000	5000	5000	5000

Figure 10.25 The cost matrix.

10.2.2.2.1 Distance Cost (*D*)

Remark: (x_i, y_i) is the centroid of track i, and (x_j, y_j) is the centroid of the *j*th object in the current frame. Width$_i$ and height$_i$ are the dimensions of the bounding box of track i, and cost$_{ij}$ is the cost of assigning object j to track i.

$$D = ((x_i - x_j)^2 + (y_i - y_j)^2)^{0.5}.$$

```
If(D>width_i and D>height_i)
cost_ij=10,000
else
cost_ij=0
and calculate the next cost.
```

Figure 10.19 shows the distance cost being evaluated for track 1. Here, the square box whose side is equal to width$_i$ or height$_i$, whichever is greater, shows the region beyond which the distance cost is set to the arbitrary large value 10,000. Thus, objects 2, 5, and 4 of the current frame are assigned an arbitrary large cost. Objects 1, 3, and 6 are within the box dimensions and are assigned a distance cost 0. For these three objects, dimension cost is evaluated. Figure 10.20 shows the cost values for track 1 after distance cost evaluation.

10.2.2.2.2 Dimension Cost (DM)

Remark: Width$_i$ and height$_i$ are the dimensions of the bounding box of track I, and width$_j$ and height$_j$ are the dimensions of the bounding box of object j.

```
If((|width_j-width_i|/width_i*100)>25 OR (|height_j-height_i|/height_i*100)>25)
cost_ij=10,000
else
cost_ij=0
and calculate the next cost.
```

Figure 10.23 shows the dimension cost being evaluated for track 1. Here, the dimension of object 3 is not within the 25% limit; thus, the cost is set to an arbitrary large value: 10,000. Objects 1 and 6 are assigned a dimension cost 0. Figure 10.24 shows the cost values for track 1 after dimension cost evaluation.

10.2.2.2.3 Normalized Histogram Cost

The normalized histogram of the bounding box region of the object j and the histogram information stored in the tracker i are matched as follows.

```
For k=1 to 16
r1=abs(red bin(k) value of object j-red bin(k) value of track i)
g1=abs(green bin(k) value of object j-green bin(k) value of track i)
b1=abs(blue bin(k) value of object j-blue bin(k) value of track i)
r=r+r1
g=g+g1
b=b+b1
```

```
end for
NH=(r+g+b)/3
if (NH>0.5)
cost_ij=10,000
else
cost_ij=NH.
```

Figure 10.23 shows the normalized histogram cost being evaluated. Here, both the objects have a low histogram value, but object 1 has a lesser value than the object 6. Figure 10.24 shows the cost values for track 1 after normalized histogram cost evaluation.

10.2.2.2.4 Introduction of New Tracks at Each Current Frame

As the problem of linear assignment (i.e., LAP) is to assign objects to tracks, it may so happen that for a current frame, all the objects detected do not belong to any previously existing tracks. They are new objects that have been detected for the first time, and the old tracked objects have moved out of the scene or are occluded. Hence, they are not detected. To solve this problem, we introduce n number of new tracks every time an assignment is to be done, where n is the number of objects detected in the current frame. The cost of assigning objects to each such new track is 5000. After the assignment procedure, if no object is assigned to a new track, it is removed. Thus, the LAP is primarily a cost matrix where the number of tracks is always greater than the number of objects detected. Hence, all the objects are always assigned. Figure 10.25 shows the cost matrix for Figure 10.19. As there are six objects in the frame, the cost matrix contains six new rows along with the existing two previous tracks. Figure 10.26 shows actual histogram matching in a video frame. The assignment algorithm considered here is from Jonker and Volgenant [39]. Now, the aforementioned methodology for multiple-object tracking is applied to a video scene, and we obtain successful tracking results, as shown in Figures 10.27 and 10.28.

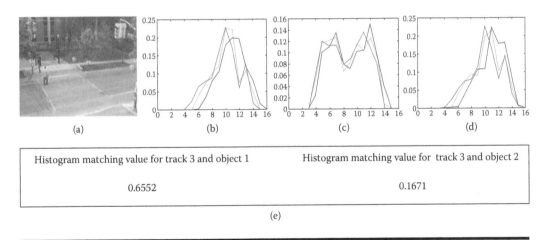

(a)　　(b)　　(c)　　(d)

Histogram matching value for track 3 and object 1	Histogram matching value for track 3 and object 2
0.6552	0.1671

(e)

Figure 10.26 **Actual histogram matching in a video sequence. (a) Objects present in the frame. (b) Histogram information stored in track 3 (which was tracking object 3 of the current frame). (c and d) Normalized color histogram for objects 1 and 3, respectively. (e) Result of color histogram matching: We find that object 1 gives a value higher than 0.5, whereas object 3, which track 3 was tracking, gives a very low value.**

Figure 10.27   Successful tracking in indoor scene.

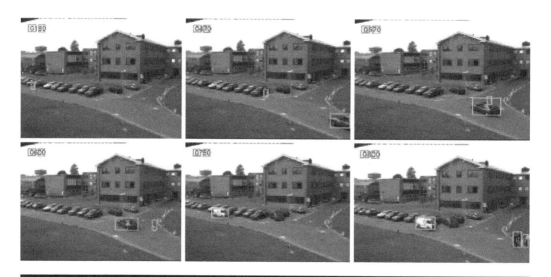

Figure 10.28   Successful tracking in outdoor scene.

10.2.2.3 Occlusion Problem

A Kalman filter is used to solve the tracking problem under occlusion of an object. For a detailed discussion on Kalman filters, interested readers are referred to the appendix. When an object is detected for the first time and assigned a new track, its corresponding Kalman filter is initialized with the centroid values of the object assigned to the track. When that track is reassigned an object in the next frame, then its corresponding Kalman filter is again reinitialized with the centroid and velocity information. Finally, when the track is assigned an object for the third time, it is again initialized for the last time so that the centroid, velocity, and acceleration values are

(a)   (b)

Figure 10.29   (a and b) Successful tracking under partial occlusion.

properly initialized. The first two initializations are done so that if a track is not assigned an object for three frames, even then, the Kalman filter will be able to predict a location, though the prediction may not be very accurate. This process of initialization is done because a proper initialization of the Kalman filter enables it to predict the next location in the coming frames more accurately. A Kalman filter deals with the system model represented by Q (see Equations 1 through 5 of the appendix). The greater the knowledge about the system, the lesser the value of Q. But as we are tracking all kinds of objects such as humans, cars, and so forth, the system knowledge is very little because we do not know the type of objects that are going to be tracked. Therefore, we set the value of Q high as object motion in general is not predictable. If the same is used for, say, a highway to track cars, we may set the value of Q low as chances of a car changing speed suddenly on highways are less. Whenever a track is assigned an object, the corrections are made to the Kalman filter parameters according to the previously stated rules, and the next predicted location is determined. If an existing track is not assigned an object from the current frame, we can assume that the object got occluded partially or completely by some other object; hence, it is not detected. Here, we use the Kalman filter prediction for that track if the Kalman prediction for the location of the object is within the image dimension. We assume that the occluded object is located in that particular location, and the centroid information of the corresponding track is updated. All other information remains the same. The Kalman prediction for occluded objects is shown in Figure 10.29a and b.

10.2.2.4 Solving Merge Problem

The occlusion-handling technique as mentioned in Section 10.2.2.3 performs well only when the occlusion is complete or when partial occlusion occurs where one object occludes the other by more than 50%. This is so because when the occlusion is less than 50%, a completely new set of features are associated with the merged blob, which is obtained due to the dynamic occlusion of the merging objects, as shown in Figure 10.30a. The false new object is identified along with the merged object. To deal with this problem, a modification is done to the previously stated method of occlusion handling. After the linear assignment stage, if a new object is identified and is associated with a new track, the new track is not stored. But before assigning the object to the new track, it is checked whether there are previously existing tracks that have not been assigned an object. For each such track, the distance between the Kalman-predicted location of the track and the merged blob is calculated, and if it is within the distance threshold value, it is recognized as a candidate track for the merged blob. If there are no such tracks, then the new object is assigned the new track. If there is only one such track, the previously stated algorithm will be able to handle the merging problem. If there is more than one track of this type, then the new object obtained is

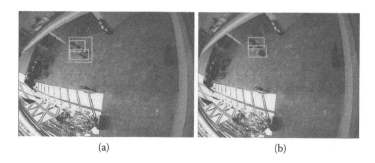

(a)   (b)

Figure 10.30   (a) Result of tracking without using the merging solution when the occlusion between objects 2 and 3 is less than 50%. The occlusion handling and tracking module considers the dynamic occlusion between 2 and 3 as a new object. (b) Successful merge implementation.

not assigned to the new track as it is concluded that the new object is a merged object composed of the existing tracks. The location of the existing tracks is updated along with their Kalman filter. The dimension and color are not updated. The merged object is stored in another array, which is composed of the location of the blob, the color information of the blob, the tracks that make up the blob, and its dimensions. In the next frame, it is this merged object that is assigned an object first using the location, dimension, and color information, and the location of the corresponding tracks associated with it is updated. Then the previously stated LAP is used to assign tracks to the other objects that are not merged. If the merged tracks split, then the merged object will not exist. So the merged track will not be assigned an object. In that case, we check the tracks that were involved in the merged object, and using the Kalman filter–predicted location and the dimension and color information stored in those tracks, we assign the split objects to those tracks. If no such object exists, we use the Kalman filter to identify its location. The shortcoming of this method is that if the dynamic occlusion occurs for a long time such that the color and dimension of the occluded object change drastically, then it will not be able to identify the split objects.

10.2.2.5 Experimental Results

The system is tested on four types of image sequences (see Table 10.5), all of which are continuous and unedited and from a static camera. The system is highly successful in all these types shown in Table 10.6. The result shows that the system is not that efficient only when it's an outdoor scene

Table 10.5   Details of the Different Video of Types Used for Tracking (PETS Data and Other Available Video Data of Shopping Mall and Airport)

Scene	Number of Videos	Number of Objects
Outdoor	1	Many
Outdoor	3	Few
Indoor (shopping mall)	1	Many
Indoor (airport)	2	Few

Table 10.6   Results of Tracking

Scene	Number of Objects	Number of Objects Present	Number of Objects Tracked Successfully	Percentage of Success
Outdoor	Many	26	18	69%
Outdoor	Few	12	10	83.3%
Indoor (shopping mall)	Few	11	11	100%
Indoor (airport)	Many	9	7	77%

with many objects present, which is primarily due to the failure of the object detection part rather than the tracking part.

10.3 Complexity Analysis

The previously stated algorithm comprises two parts: one is the background estimation part, which is independent of the tracking part and does not affect the complexity of the tracking algorithm. The tracking part is composed of three subparts.

First is the object detection part using the estimated background and the frame-differencing technique. The complexity of the object detection phase is dependent on the size of the input video. If the input video frames comprise $m \times n$ pixels, then the complexity of the frame-differencing phase is $O(mn)$.

The second subpart of tracking is the linear assignment phase. If there are x existing tracks in frame k and the number of objects detected in frame k is y, then the distance cost, dimension cost, and histogram cost will all take $O(xy)$, that is, for each track, its cost with all objects is evaluated. But in the average case, most of the time, the distance cost will be evaluated for all the objects. Only for those objects that satisfy the distance criteria the other costs will be evaluated. So in the average case, the time of cost evaluation is reduced drastically. The next is the assignment phase. The worst-case time for Jonker's assignment algorithm is $O(x^3)$ as the number of tracks is, most of the time, greater than the number of objects. So the complexity of the tracking phase is $O(x^3)$.

Finally, the third part is dealing with occlusion, primarily when the merging occurs. All other occlusions are handled in the assignment stage. If all tracks are occluded, which is the worst case, then the occlusion-finding algorithm will take $O(x)$. Thus, the tracking algorithm's time complexity for the worst case is $O(x^3)$. Though the tracking complexity of the algorithm shows $O(x^3)$ due to solving of LAP, it is merely mathematical manipulation. The main time-consuming operation is the cost estimation stage, that is, $O(x * y)$ phase.

10.4 Conclusion

We have successfully presented an automated surveillance system for public places, namely, shopping malls and airports. As stated earlier, the present concept can be extended, with some modifications, to any other public place like a daily market, railway station, public meeting hall, and so forth. At the first stage of our surveillance, we handle the event recognition problem at the bottleneck point of an airport and a shopping mall. We have successfully determined the presence of person/persons in an identified blob at the bottleneck point. If a single person is identified at the bottleneck point, then his/her correct direction of motion is also successfully determined. At the second stage of surveillance, we consider tracking of multiple objects at the broader area of an airport or shopping mall after the bottleneck point. Successful tracking of multiple objects is done using an LAP. Tracking of multiple objects under occlusion is performed using a Kalman filter. In the case of an outdoor scene, we have experienced that if the scene is overcrowded and if the objects are overlapped by each other (partial occlusion/complete occlusion), then detection of an individual object in real time becomes computationally heavy and sometimes impossible. We have further experienced that under overlapped conditions as stated previously, when the overlapped object moves in the next frame and becomes separated in that frame, then we cannot track them individually due to a lack of detailed information obtained from the previous frame.

Both the problems as stated previously reduce the recognition score in real time, but if we incorporate a more improved background subtraction and segmentation method, which is the scope of our future experiment, we may have more improved performance in terms of recognition score. Note that there are already several sophisticated methods existing for background subtraction and segmentation, but we have to modify them further to make them perform in real time, keeping in mind that computation of such real-time algorithms is not time consuming. However, the said problems are the challenge of real life, and we have to tackle them depending upon the situation at hand. As a whole, the overall performance of multiple-object tracking is quite satisfactory, which is verified through experimental results.

References

1. Yilmaz, A., Javed, O., and Shah, M. Object tracking: A survey. *ACM Comput. Surv.* 38, 4, Article 13(Dec. 2006), 45 pp. DOI:10.1145/1177352.1177355, 2006.
2. Veenman, C., Reinders, M., and Backer, E. Resolving motion correspondence for densely moving points. *IEEE Trans. Patt. Analy. Mach. Intell.* 23, 1, 54–72, 2001.
3. Serby, D., Koller-Meier, S., and Gool, L. V. Probabilistic object tracking using multiple features. In IEEE International Conference of Pattern Recognition (ICPR), 184–187, 2004.
4. Comaniciu, D., Ramesh, V., and Meer, P. Kernel-based object tracking. *IEEE Trans. Patt. Analy. Mach. Intell.* 25, 564–575, 2003.
5. Yilmaz, A., Li, X., and Shah, M. Contour based object tracking with occlusion handling in video acquired using mobile cameras. *IEEE Trans. Patt. Analy. Mach. Intell.* 26, 11, 1531–1536, 2004.
6. Song, K. Y., Kittler, J., and Petrou, M. Defect detection in random color textures. *Israel Verj. Cap. J.* 14, 9, 667–683, 1996.
7. Canny, J. A computational approach to edge detection. *IEEE Trans. Patt. Analy. Mach. Intell.* 8, 6, 679–698, 1986.
8. Horn, B., and Schunk, B. Determining optical flow. *Artific. Intell.* 17, 185–203, 1981.
9. Lucas, B. D., and Kanade, T. An iterative image registration technique with an application to stereo vision. In International Joint Conference on Artificial Intelligence, 1981.
10. Harris, C., and Stephens, M. A combined corner and edge detector. In 4th Alvey Vision Conference, 147–151, 1988.
11. Lowe, D. Distinctive image features from scale-invariant keypoints. *Int. J. Comput. Vision* 60, 2, 91–110, 2004.

12. Wren, C., Azarbayejani, A., and Pentland, A. Pfinder: Real-time tracking of the human body. *IEEE Trans. Patt. Analy. Mach. Intell.* 19, 7, 780–785, 1997.
13. Stauffer, C., and Grimson, W. Learning patterns of activity using real time tracking. *IEEE Trans. Patt. Analy. Mach. Intell.* 22, 8, 747–767, 2000.
14. Comaniciu, D., and Meer, P. Mean shift: A robust approach toward feature space analysis. *IEEE Trans. Patt. Analy. Mach. Intell.* 24, 5, 603–619, 2002.
15. Broida, T., and Chellappa, R. Estimation of object motion parameters from noisy images. *IEEE Trans. Patt. Analy. Mach. Intell.* 8, 1, 90–99, 986.
16. Tanizaki, H. Non-gaussian state-space modeling of nonstationary time series. *J. Am. Statist. Assoc.* 82, 1032–1063, 1987.
17. Bar-shalom, Y., and Foreman, T. *Tracking and Data Association.* Academic Press Inc., USA, 1988.
18. Schweitzer, H., Bell, J. W., and Wu, F. Very fast template matching. In European Conference on Computer Vision (ECCV), 358–372, 2002.
19. Kang, J., Cohen, I., and Medioni, G. Object reacquisition using geometric invariant appearance, model. In International Conference on Pattern Recognition (ICPR), 759–762, 2004.
20. Xin, L., Wang, K., Wang, W., and Li, Y. A multiple object tracking method using Kalman filter. In Proceedings of the 2010 IEEE, International Conference on Information and Automation, Harbin, China, 1862–1866, June 20–23, 2010.
21. Rahul, M., Chouhan, M. K., and Nitnawwre, D. Multiple object tracking by kernel based centroid method for improve localization. *Int J Adv Res Comput Sci Soft Eng* 2, 7, 2012.
22. Berclaz, J., Francois, F., Turetken, E., and Fua, P., Senior Member, IEEE. Multiple object tracking using K-shortest paths optimization. *IEEE Trans. Patt. Analy. Mach. Intell.* 33, 9, 2011.
23. Khan, Z. H., Student Member, IEEE, Gu, I. Y.-H., Senior Member, IEEE, and Backhouse, A. G. Robust visual object tracking using multi-mode anisotropic mean shift and particle filters. *IEEE Trans. Circuits Syst. Video Technol.* 21, 1, 2011.
24. Hsu, C.-C., and Dai, G.-T. Multiple object tracking using particle swarm optimization. *World Acad Sci Eng Technol* 68, 2012.
25. Xiaoqin, Z., Hu, W., Qu, W., and Maybank, S. Multiple object tracking via species-based particle swarm optimization. *IEEE Trans Circuits Syst. Video Technol.* 20, 11, 2010.
26. Nguyen, H., and Bhanu, B. Multi-object tracking in non-stationary video using bacterial foraging swarms. In Proceeding ICIP'09 Proceedings of the 16th IEEE International Conference on Image Processing, 873–876, 2009.
27. Pushpa, D., and Sheshadri, H. S. Multiple object detection and tracking in cluttered region with rational mobile area. *Int J Comput Appl (0975–8887)* 39, 10, 2012.
28. Stauffer, C., and Grimson, W. E. L. Learning patterns of activity using real-time tracking. *TPAMI* 22, 8, 747–757, 2000.
29. Javed, O., Shafique, K., and Shah, M. A hierarchical approach to robust background subtraction using color and gradient information. In IEEE Workshop on Motion and Video Computing, 22–27, 2002.
30. Elgammal, A., Harwood, D., and Davis, L. Non-parametric model for background subtraction. *ECCV* 2, 751–767, 2000.
31. Sheikh, Y., and Shah, M. Bayesian modeling of dynamic scenes for object detection. *TPAMI* 27, 11, 1778–1792, 2005.
32. Kim, K., Chalidabhongse, T. H., Harwood, D., and Davis, L. Real-time foreground-background segmentation using codebook model. *Real-Time Imaging* 11, 3, 167–256, 2005.
33. McFarlane, N., and Schofield, C. Segmentation and tracking of piglets in images. *Mach Vis Appl* 8, 3, 187–193, 1995.
34. Remagnino, P. An integrated traffic and pedestrian model-based vision system. In Proceedings of the Eighth British Machine Vision Conference, 380–389, 1997.
35. Jain, R., and Nagel, H. On the analysis of accumulative difference pictures from image sequences of real world scenes. *IEEE Trans. Patt. Analy. Mach. Intell.* 1, 2, 206–214, 1979.
36. Ismail, H., Harwood, D., and Davis, L. S. W4 real time surveillance of people and their activities. *IEEE Trans. Patt. Analy. Mach. Intell.* 22, 8, 2000.

37. Yamato, J., Ohya, J., and Ishii, K. Recognizing human action in time sequential images using hidden Markov model. In Proceedings of IEEE Conference on Computer Vision and Pattern Recognition, 379–385, 1992.
38. Starner, T. E. Visual recognition of American sign language using hidden Markov model. Submitted to the program in Media Arts and Sciences School of Architecture and Planning at the Massachusetts Institute of Technology, February 1995.
39. Jonker, R., and Volgenant, A. A shortest augmenting path algorithm for dense and sparse linear assignment problems. *Computing* 38, 4, 325–340, 1987.

Appendix: Kalman Filter

The Kalman filter (KF) is a set of mathematical equations that provides an efficient computational (recursive) means to estimate the state of a process, in a way that minimizes the mean of the squared error. The filter is very powerful in several aspects: it supports estimations of past, present, and even future states, and it can do so even when the precise nature of the modeled system is unknown. This section formulates the general filtering problem and explains the conditions under which the general filter simplifies to a KF.

Figure 10.A1 illustrates the application context in which the KF is used. A physical system (e.g., a mobile robot, a chemical process, a satellite) is driven by a set of external inputs or controls, and its outputs are evaluated by measuring devices or sensors, such that the knowledge on the system's behavior is solely given by the inputs and the observed outputs. The observations convey errors and uncertainties in the process, namely, sensor noise and system errors. Based on the available information (control inputs and observations), it is required to obtain an estimate of the system's state that optimizes given criteria. This is the role played by a filter. In particular situations, explained in the following, this filter is a KF.

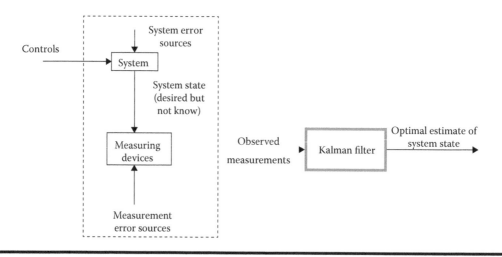

Figure 10.A1   Typical application of the KF.

State Space Models

The state variable vector is denoted by $X = (x \; y \; v_x \; v_y \; a_x \; a_y)^T$. This vector summarizes the relevant information from the system at any time and describes how the system changes as a function of time and input. The k and $k - 1$ subscripts represent the time of the vector.

The equation for generation of a next state variable is $X_k = \mathbf{A}X_{k-1}$, where

$$
\mathbf{A} = \begin{bmatrix}
1 & 0 & 1 & 0 & 0 & 0 \\
0 & 1 & 0 & 1 & 0 & 0 \\
0 & 0 & 1 & 0 & 1 & 0 \\
0 & 0 & 0 & 1 & 0 & 1 \\
0 & 0 & 0 & 0 & 1 & 0 \\
0 & 0 & 0 & 0 & 0 & 1
\end{bmatrix}
$$

The KF equations are represented by Equations A.1–A.5. In general, **A** is a matrix relating the state variables at a previous time step to the state variables at a current time step, which, in our case, has been derived from the equations of motion, and **B** is a matrix relating the input to the state variables, which is a null matrix in our case. Y is the output (or measurement) variable vector, and **C** is a matrix relating the state variables to the measurement variables. In this case, **C** is the identity matrix. To generalize, any system that is finite dimensional, causal (the output does not depend on future input values), and time-invariant can be described by a set of variables that constitute the important aspects of the system's internal behavior. These variables can be combined into a vector that, at any time, contains the information required to characterize the system. This type of model is known as a state space model and is commonly used in control system modeling and signal processing. The equations represent a linear, discrete-time state-space model. This is called the measurement model, and it describes how the sensor data vary as a function of the state variables. The time update projects the state variable vector estimate ahead in time taking into account the input into the system. Thus, it makes a prediction of the new state. The measurement update adjusts the time update state estimate to take into account measurements made during the time interval.

$$
\widehat{X}_{k|k-1} = A\widehat{X}_{k-1|k-1} + Bu_k \tag{A.1}
$$

$$
\mathbf{P}_{k|k-1} = A\mathbf{P}_{k-1|k-1}A^T + Q \tag{A.2}
$$

$$
J_k = \mathbf{P}_{k|k-1}\mathbf{C}^T (C\mathbf{P}_{k|k-1}C^T + R)^{-1} \tag{A.3}
$$

$$
\widehat{X}_{k|k} = \widehat{X}_{k|k-1} + J_k(Y_k - \mathbf{C}\widehat{X}_{k|k-1}) \tag{A.4}
$$

$$
\mathbf{P}_{k|k} = (I - J_k\mathbf{C})\mathbf{P}_{k|k-1} \tag{A.5}
$$

Before we start using the KF, we need to make an estimate of the initial value of the state variable vector and error covariance matrix.

Step 1: The Time Update

Equations A.1 and A.2 are the time update equations. Equation A.1 calculates the a priori estimate of the state variable vector—an estimate of X at time k given measurements up to time $k - 1$. This updates the state estimate based on the knowledge of the previous time state and the input to the system since the last time update. Equation A.2 updates the a priori error covariance matrix **P**. This update represents the fact that knowledge of the system gradually decays over time due to errors in the assumed input or in the model, which contribute to the uncertainty in the estimate.

Step 2: Measurement Update

Equations A.3–A.5 are the measurement update equations. The time update state estimate in the previous step is corrected based on the feedback from the sensor measurements that have been taken during the time interval. Equation A.3 calculates the Kalman gain J to minimize the a posteriori error covariance matrix **P**. Equation A.4 calculates the a posteriori estimate of the state variable vector—an estimate of X at time k given measurement data up to time k. This updates the state variable estimate for the new measurement. It compares the actual sensor measurement (Y) with the sensor measurement predicted from the state estimate (**C**X) and uses the difference between these values (called the "innovation" or "residual") and the Kalman gain to determine the amount by which to adjust the time update state estimate. Equation A.5 calculates the a posteriori error covariance matrix **P**. We further notice that Equations A.1 and A.4 combined are the same as the Observer equation above. These equations are repeated at every time interval. If the KF does not receive any measurement information, it performs time update (Equations A.1 and A.2) and no measurement update.

Chapter 11

Nature-Inspired Intelligence: A Modern Tool for Warfare Strategic Decision Making

Lavika Goel

Contents

The chapter discusses a methodology inspired from nature using remote sensing inputs based on swarm intelligence for strategic decision making in modern warfare. The chapter presents a hybrid ant colony–biogeography-based optimization technique (ACO-BBO) for predicting the deployment strategies of enemy troops in the war theatre and finding the shortest and the best feasible path for attack on the enemy base station. The hybrid algorithm begins by predicting the most suitable destination for the enemy troops to position their forces, for which it uses BBO and, after finding the shortest and the best feasible path for attacking the enemy base station, uses the ACO technique, thus combining the strengths of both the techniques. Hence, the algorithm can be used to improve the ACO approach, which is currently used to predict enemy troop mobility since it lacks the ability to predict the destination and can only find a suitable path to the given destination, leading to coordination problems and target misidentification, which can lead to severe casualties. The algorithm can be of major use for the commanders in the battlefield who have been using traditional decision-making techniques of limited accuracy for predicting destination. Using the hybrid ACO-BBO technique can help in enabling commanders for intelligent preparation in the battlefield by automating the process of assessing the likely base stations of the enemy and the ways in which these can be attacked, given the environment and the terrain considerations.

11.1 Introduction

In modern warfare, it has become imperative to have the ability to anticipate the likely actions of the enemy's maneuver and the troop mobilization strategies. The ability to accurately predict the deployment strategy of the enemy troops—identifying the most likely location for the enemy to position their forces and finding a feasible route to it—is of critical importance to the commanders in the battlefield. There are a few works available in this field of anticipatory computing for situation awareness, which we modify to suit our purpose of intelligent battlefield planning, some of which are on disaster situation awareness (Jaiswal et al. 2002), terrorist camp detection (Sahin and Ercan 2008), and electronic situation awareness (Hew 2006). But as such, no computing method is available for the prediction of enemy base stations directly. The known available methods for the prediction of the enemy base camps are still the conventional methods employed by the military, which involve manual study of the geography of the area and various other factors (Sun Tzu, 6th century BC). To understand and simulate the best available routes for attacking the enemy forces and to predict the ability of the enemy to position forces and mount attack, this chapter puts forward a hybrid algorithm of ant colony and biogeography-based optimization (ACO-BBO), both of which are included in the of population-based optimization techniques (Goel et al. 2010, 2012a,b).

ACO is a swarm intelligence technique that studies the collective behavior of decentralized, self-organized systems. It is in the nature of ant colonies to discover and travel upon the shortest and the safest path from their nest to the food source. This search for the shortest path is based on a heuristic function and update of pheromone values upon each iteration (Dorigo and Stutzle 2004). BBO, first introduced by Dan Simon in December 2008, is an optimization technique based on the geographical distribution of the biological species (Simon 2008). Geographical areas that are well suited for biological species are said to have a high habitat suitability index (HSI), which is determined by factors called the suitability index variables (SIVs). Habitats with a high

HSI are characterized by a large number of species, a low species immigration rate, a static species distribution, and a high species emigration rate, whereas low-HSI habitats are characterized by a small number of species, a high species immigration rate, a dynamic species distribution, and a low species emigration rate (Ergezer et al. 2009; Simon 2008).

In our presented work, we consider a collection of ideal SIVs as the feature habitat against which we compare our candidate base stations, which are put in the universal habitat. We use HSI for comparison between the two solutions. HSI is the measure of the similarity threshold between the habitats. We also consider an isolated habitat that consists of zero species, that is, this habitat has no solution class (Ergezer et al. 2009; Goel et al. 2012c). SIVs are the set of features possessed by the habitat that is an indication of the suitability of the terrain for the enemy troops to deploy their forces. After each iteration, the candidate base station's HSI is determined. After the completion of all the iterations, we are left with the base station with the maximum HSI, which corresponds to the maximum collection of SIVs from the feature habitat. Having found the destination, now we proceed to find the shortest and the safest path to this base station using the ACO technique. The mechanism at work in the ACO algorithm that is responsible for the discovery of good routes is the positive feedback given by the pheromone update by the ants. The safer and the more feasible the route, the higher the amount of pheromones deposited by the ants on the cities of its route (Kaur et al. 2010). This implies the fact that these cities have a higher probability of being selected in the subsequent iteration of the algorithm. This process is followed by pheromone evaporation on areas that have already or never received additional pheromone deposits. This, in turn, leads us to the shortest path.

The motivation of this research is to merge the migration strategy of the BBO approach with the shortest-path–finding nature of ants in order to see how the techniques can be of mutual benefit to each other. Deciding on efficient routes has so far been an intuitive and a cognitive process for the troop commanders. Automated simulation of the terrain (of the war area) and of the available routes will allow the commanders to understand the implications of the terrain for effective maneuver, and when simulated on the enemy's terrain coupled with the provision for the automated prediction of the enemy's base station, it will help them to predict the intents of the enemy's troop deployment. Though geographic features are not the only source for determining the same, here, we are only considering the remote sensing inputs, that is, the satellite images of the area. The decisions over the suitability of a geographic feature for the probability of finding the enemy base station and path finding thereafter were taken on the basis of expert knowledge in the military domain. The methodology developed is tested on two case studies, those of the regions of Alwar and Mussourie.

Section 11.2 gives a brief review of the BBO and the ACO techniques. Section 11.3 gives the terminology used in this chapter with their respective meanings for both phases of the presented nature-inspired framework. Section 11.4 elucidates on the functional architecture that was used for the presented work. Section 11.5 provides the results of the experimental study conducted over the two regions. Finally, Section 11.6 concludes the chapter.

11.2 A Brief Review of BBO and ACO Techniques

The soft computing technique to tackle the problem of predicting the enemy base station selected in this work is BBO from the swarm intelligence techniques (Goel et al. 2010, 2011). So going by the technique, we consider the probable base stations as "islands" (Goel et al. 2010). These islands have an HSI determined on the basis of certain factors, here referred to as SIVs (Simon 2008). The following is the BBO algorithm proposed by Dan Simon (2008):

1. Initialize the BBO parameters.
2. Initialize a random set of habitats, each habitat corresponding to a potential solution to the given problem.
3. For each habitat, map the HSI to the number of species, the immigration rate, and the emigration rate.
4. Probabilistically use immigration and emigration to modify each nonelite habitat, and then recompute each HSI.
5. For each habitat, update the probability of its species count using step 2. Then, mutate each nonelite habitat based on its probability, and recompute each HSI.
6. Go to step 3 for the next iteration. This loop can be terminated after a predefined number of generations or after an acceptable problem solution has been found.

The algorithm proposed by Dan Simon is used in its variant form to suit to the problem statement of this work (Goel et al. 2012b).

The technique for finding the shortest and the safest path that we use in our application is the ACO technique. The mechanism at work in the ACO algorithm that is responsible for the discovery of good routes is the positive feedback given by pheromone updates by ants. The safer and the more feasible the route, the higher the amount of pheromones deposited by the ants on the cities of its route (Dorigo and Stutzle 2004). This implies the fact that these cities have a higher probability of being selected in the subsequent iteration of the algorithm. This process is followed by pheromone evaporation on areas that have already or never received additional pheromone deposits. This, in turn, leads us to the shortest path. The algorithm for ACO shortest-path finding is as follows:

```
For each ant in ant colony
        Initialize the position
        Choose the next nearest node to the target
        If node is obstacle
        Then choose the other nearest node
        Else move and deposit pheromone
        End
    Calculate the distance and update pheromone
    End-for
Find shortest path.
```

11.3 Terminology Used

11.3.1 Fixing Parameters for the First Phase of the Nature-Inspired Framework for Battlefield Planning

11.3.1.1 SIVs

In accordance with the problem statement and expert knowledge of military domain, the following are the SIVs taken into consideration for deciding the HSI for the base stations (Goel et al. 2012c):

1. *Elevation of the area (elev_area)*: The greater the elevation of that area is, the more the base stations on that area are visible. Hence, the enemy would like to have its base station located on such an area that is out of the line of sight of others.
2. *Evenness of the area (even_area)*: The evenness of the area is important as a base station would not be possible on an uneven surface that has pits and peaks. There has to be certain evenness of surface in that area for the construction of a base station.
3. *Area covered under slope (slope_area)*: The more the vertical area is covered, the higher the probability is of locating a base station there.
4. *Aspect (direction/angle) of area (asp_area)*: The more the aspect is vertically aligned toward the enemy, the higher the probability is of having their base station there as it acts as a natural shield for them.
5. *Degree of urbanity (urb_deg)*: The more the area under consideration is urban, the lower the probability is of having a base station there, as civilians are kept as far away from military operations as possible.
6. *Degree of water (wat_deg)*: For a base station, the degree of water of that area should be from low to medium, as little water could be of help for their daily household work. But if it is in excess, the probability of hiding their base station decreases.
7. *Degree of forest (for_deg)*: The greater the degree of forest in that area, the greater the ease for them to situate their base station, as that is the best location to maintain the anonymity of the base station.
8. *Degree of barren land (bar_deg)*: The more barren the land in the area, the less the chances of constructing a base station there, as it would easily be detectable in satellite images.
9. *Degree of rocky land (roc_deg)*: A medium level of rocky land is the best for the construction of a base station, but both the extremities are not suited for the construction of a base station.

11.3.1.2 Scales for SIVs

These SIVs were then determined for each area on a scale of one to five.

1. *Elevation of the area (elev_area)*: The ranges were determined after calculating the minimum, maximum, average, mode, median, and mid of all digital elevation model (DEM) values for the stretch of the area taken under consideration.
2. *Evenness of the area (even_area)*: This was determined by considering a small area into consideration at a particular time. If the neighboring area was of similar height, then the area was considered even. The levels were decided by considering the percentage of the area (around the area under consideration) that is even.
3. *Area covered under slope (slope_area)*: This was determined by scaling the area on a scale of four, depending on the percentage of the area coming under the slope.
4. *Aspect (direction/angle) of area (asp_area)*: This was determined by calculating the angle for each area and was then categorized into eight categories, that is, 0° to 45° first, 45° to 90° second, 90° to 135° third, 135° to 180° fourth, 180° to 225° fifth, 225° to 270° sixth, 270° to 315° seventh, and 315° to 360° eighth. Then, using these categories, we scale the aspect of an area on a scale of five.
5. *Degree of urbanity (urb_deg)*: The area was scaled on a scale of one to five by determining if the area itself is urban or what percentage of the area around is urban.
6. *Degree of water (wat_deg)*: The area was scaled on a scale of one to five by determining if the area itself is water or what percentage of the area around is water.

7. *Degree of forest (for_deg)*: The area was scaled on a scale of one to five by determining if the area itself is water or what percentage of the area around is forest.

8. *Degree of barren land (bar_deg)*: The area was scaled on a scale of one to five by determining if the area itself is water or what percentage of the area around is barren land.

9. *Degree of rocky land (roc_deg)*: The area was scaled on a scale of one to five by determining if the area itself is water or what percentage of the area around is rocky land.

11.3.1.3 Weights Assigned to SIV

These SIVs are given weights from a scale of 1 to 10 according to their importance in deciding the location of the base station. These weights are then utilized in determining the effort for migration from this base station to the ideal base station. This effort further helps in determining the selectivity factor of the base station.

11.3.1.4 Ideal Enemy Base Station

For ideal base station, the value of each SIV was taken, as per expert knowledge in the military domain, on a scale of one to five.

11.3.1.5 Habitat Suitability Index

First, the HSI of the ideal base station is calculated, and then the HSIs of all the other base stations are calculated using the following formula (the formula was generated by the interpretation of military data and the meaning of the ideal base station in terms of its SIVs) (Goel et al. 2012c; Arora 2010):

$$
\begin{aligned}
&\text{if asp\_area} > 3 \\
&\quad HSI = \text{for\_deg} + \left(\frac{\text{elev\_area}}{\text{even\_area}} \right) + \text{mod}((6 - \text{roc\_deg}), 4) \\
&\qquad + \left(\frac{\text{asp\_area} * \text{slope\_area}}{10} \right) - \text{urb\_deg} - \text{bar\_deg} - \text{wat\_deg} - 2) \\
&\text{else} \\
&\quad HSI = \text{for\_deg} + \left(\frac{\text{elev\_area}}{\text{even\_area}} \right) + \text{mod}((6 - \text{roc\_deg}), 4) \\
&\qquad - \left(\frac{\text{asp\_area} * \text{slope\_area}}{10} \right) - \text{urb\_deg} - \text{bar\_deg} - (\text{wat\_deg} - 2)
\end{aligned}
$$

where for_deg, elev_area, even_area, roc_deg, asp_area, slope_area, urb_deg, bar_deg, and wat_deg are SIVs of the island whose HSI is being calculated.

11.3.1.6 Probable Enemy Base Station

The initial base station selection is based on the drainage pattern of the area under consideration. The drainage pattern helps in deciding the areas that would have higher denser canals (canal means a line in a drainage map, and density of canal means the number of the subcanals that join to form this canal), which actually implies the probability of the groundwater at that place.

11.3.2 Fixing Parameters for the Second Phase of the Nature-Inspired Framework for Battlefield Planning

A. T_{ij} = Pheromone value
B. $N_{ij} = 1/d_{ij}$, where d_{ij} represents the heuristic information
C. D_{ij} = Distance between city i and city j
D. F_{ki} = Feasible neighborhood of the ant k when being at city i
E. P_{ij} = Probability of choosing j as the next city when at city i
F. a and b are the parameters that determine the relative influence of the pheromone trail and the heuristic information
  1. If $a = 0$, the closest nodes are more likely to be selected
  2. If $b = 0$, then only pheromones are used to select the next node without using the heuristics

Hence, P_{ij} is given by the following equation:

$$P_{ij}^k = \frac{[T_{ij}]^a [N_{ij}]^b}{\sum l \in N_{ij} [T_{il}]^a [N_{il}]^b}$$

if $j \in n$.
where n is the feasible neighborhood of ant k when at city i.

11.4 Nature-Inspired Intelligent Framework for Battlefield Planning

This section presents the algorithm for the nature-inspired intelligent framework for intelligent preparation of the battlefield. The presented architecture combines the process of finding the destination enemy base station and also the best feasible path of attack on it. The aforementioned framework is hence divided into two phases. In the first phase, we present the biogeography-based anticipatory computing framework, and in the second phase, we present the modified ACO technique for finding the shortest path of attack.

11.4.1 First Phase

In the first phase, we present the biogeography-based anticipatory computing framework. To solve the problem of finding the highly probable enemy base station through BBO, the following functional architecture was modeled and used.

Input: Set of candidate base stations suitable for the enemy to position its forces and mount attack (derived based on the drainage pattern of the area under consideration).

Output: Best feasible base station for the enemy troops as anticipated by the presented algorithm.

11.4.1.1 Assumptions

1. Initially, it is considered that there exists a universal habitat consisting of all the candidate base stations.
2. It has been assumed that the SIVs migrate between the universal habitat, feature habitat, and isolated habitat.

3. All the candidate base stations are considered exactly once.

4. At the completion of the algorithm, we get a base station that is best suited as the destination base station.

11.4.1.2 Algorithm for Predicting the Location of Enemy Base Station

1. Get the set of suitable base stations for the enemy to position its forces.

   No. of habitats = no. of candidate solutions to the problem.

2. Put the set of the determined base stations in the universal habitat.

3. Consider an isolated habitat with zero SIVs. This habitat represents the state of no solution in the initial stage of the algorithm.

4. Define HSI, S_{max}, immigration rate (λ), and emigration rate (μ) for each of the base stations in the universal habitat.

5. Construct a standard habitat that is analogous to the base station with ideal characteristics that are best suited for the enemy troops. This habitat is called the feature habitat and consists of the collection of standard SIVs (or ideal SIVs) on the basis of historic and intelligence data obtained through a statistical survey of the area, the parameters (SIVs) of which were defined before. The feature habitat is used for comparison with the candidate base stations in the universal habitat.

6. Calculate the HSI of the feature habitat based on its SIVs, and hence calculate the ideal HSI value (SIV_{ideal}).

7. Calculate the threshold HSI value by taking one-third of the ideal HSI value (based on military inputs).

8.
   a. Now, calculate the HSI for the candidate base station based on its SIVs as given by the HSI formula derived in Section 11.2, applying the corresponding HSI formula depending upon the value of "asp_area," where asp_area is the aspect (direction/angle) of the area under consideration. If asp_area > 3, then the first formula is applicable, or else the second one.

   b. Compare the HSI of the habitat (candidate base station) with the threshold HSI. The threshold HSI denotes that the candidate base stations of the universal habitat can only be made a feature habitat after migration if their HSI falls within this range, that is, it is greater than the threshold HSI.

      • If the HSI is greater than the threshold HSI value, then find out the SIVs to be migrated and probabilistically use immigration and emigration to modify the non-elite base station by immigrating the ideal SIVs of the feature habitat that match with the SIVs of the input base station of the universal habitat to the universal habitat and emigrating the SIVs of the input base station that do not match with the ideal SIVs of the feature habitat from the universal habitat to the isolated habitat.

      • If the HSI is less than the threshold, transfer the SIVs of this base station to an isolated habitat. This base station will not be considered further and is removed from the universal habitat.

9. Repeat step 8 for each of the candidate base stations in the universal habitat.

10. Next, compare the HSI values of all the remaining base stations in the universal habitat. The base station with the highest HSI value is the most suitable base station for the enemy troops for their deployment, and this will be the destination base station for the friendly troops to mount attack on.

The described algorithm can be summarized as in Figure 11.1.

1. Input all the candidate base stations to be considered in the universal habitat. Also input the isolated habitat and the feature habitat.
2. **For** each candidate base station in the universal habitat
   Calculate the HSI using the corresponding HSI formula
   /* depending upon whether the value of asp_area (Aspect/ Direction) > 3 or not. */
   Calculate the HSI of the feature habitat and the threshold HSI by taking 1/3 of the ideal HSI value, i.e., 1/3 × HSI ideal
   Compare the HSI of the input base station with the ideal HSI.
   If the HSIinput < HSI Threshold,
   Then
   Transfer the SIVs of this base station to the isolated habitat, i.e., remove this base station from the universal habitat.
   End
   End For

3. Compare the HSI of all the base stations. The base station with the highest HSI value is the destination enemy base station.

Figure 11.1   First phase: algorithm for biogeography-based anticipatory computation.

11.4.2 Second Phase

Input: Friendly base station and the best suited enemy base station obtained as the output of the first phase.

Output: The shortest and the safest path for attacking the enemy base station.

A modified ACO algorithm for finding the shortest as well as an obstacle-free path (i.e., best feasible path of attack) from the friendly to the destination enemy base station used in the second phase of the presented system (hybrid approach for cross-country path planning [Kaur et al. 2010]) is summarized in Figure 11.2. The image is classified into accessible and inaccessible regions, and morphological operations are applied to smoothen the image. After these operations, many

1. Take satellite image as input image
2. **For** each candidate position
   Calculate the fitness value at that position
   Find global best position
   Update position and velocity
   End-For
3. Calculate the threshold value (path extracted and obstacles detected)
4. Refine paths using morphological operations
5. **For** each ant in ant colony
   Initialize the position
   Choose the next nearest node to the target
   If node is obstacle
   Then choose the other nearest node
   Else move and deposit pheromone
   End
   Calculate the distance and update pheromone
   End-For
6. Find shortest path

Figure 11.2   Second phase: algorithm for finding shortest and safest path using ACO technique.

possible paths are extracted amidst the cross-country path. Now, ants are created and randomly initialized from the starting point. They randomly chose different ways of getting to the target. While moving to the target, they deposit pheromones; after reaching the target, they retrace their respective paths. The path of the ant that reaches the starting point earliest is considered the shortest. Now the shortest path is obtained. While finding the way to the next node, they check for obstacles; if an obstacle occurs, they choose the next node. Hence, the ants avoid obstacles in their way, where a black area would depict the inaccessible area and white would depict the accessible path. On the whole, we have the safest and shortest path.

Algorithm (shortest_path_attack_enemy_base_station)

{
1. Represent the paths on the enemy terrain as a connected graph G (N, A) where N is the set of cities and A is the set of possible paths to them. Each path on the graph is weighted according to the distance between the two cities.
2. Define the friendly and the enemy base station, that is, the source and the destination.
3. Place the ants at the source station and initialize all the paths with a constant pheromone value; this value should be slightly higher than the expected amount of pheromone deposited by the ants in one iteration. This is done so that the search is not biased by the initial tours constructed by the ants.
4. The iteration ends when all the ants have reached the destination city.

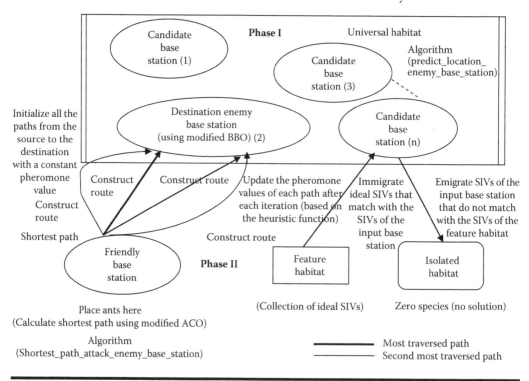

Figure 11.3 An integrated nature-inspired intelligent framework using the hybrid ACO-BBO approach for battlefield planning.

5. After the first iteration, when all the ants have constructed their routes, update the pheromone values (which serves as a heuristic function to decide the shortest path to the destination base station). This means increasing the amount of pheromone values on the paths that have been used by the ants and decreasing the pheromone values on the paths that have not been used.

6. After successive iterations, we get the shortest route that is best suited for the friendly base station to attack the enemy base station.

}

The algorithm is summarized in Figure 11.2. The complete framework for the discussed hybrid ACO-BBO algorithm is represented in Figure 11.3.

11.5 Experimental Study

For the purpose of experiment, the Alwar region (India) and Mussoorie region (India) were selected as these have all the geographic features (Kiefer and Lillesand 2006; Zhou and Wei 2008). The results obtained after applying the work described in this chapter are as follows.

11.5.1 Alwar Region in Rajasthan

From military inputs, the ideal values of the SIVs {even_area, elev_area, slope_area, asp_area, urb_deg, wat_deg, roc_deg, bar_deg, for_deg} are taken as 1, 5, 2, 5, 1, 1, 1, 1, and 5, from which the ideal HSI value is calculated. Hence, the HSI for the ideal base station is taken as 9. We have considered five base stations for demonstration purposes and fed their SIV values, which were given by an expert, to our algorithm. However, the number of base stations may change depending upon the terrain characteristics, but the procedure followed for detection of the best feasible base station will be the same. For our given terrain data set, five feasible base stations could be identified, and hence, we take $n = 5$. Figure 11.4a shows the candidate base stations marked in dotted circles. From Table 11.1, it can

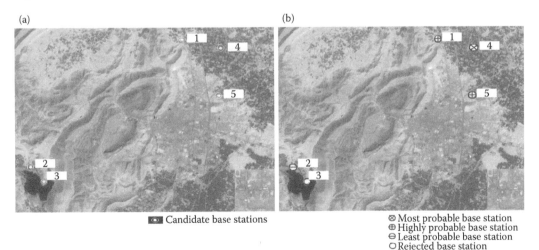

(a)   (b)

▣ Candidate base stations

⊗ Most probable base station
⊕ Highly probable base station
⊖ Least probable base station
○ Rejected base station

Figure 11.4 (a) Alwar image with the candidate base stations marked in dotted circles. (b) Alwar image with the base stations categorized into respective classes. The symbol codes are as follows: most probable, cross; probable, plus; least probable, minus; rejected base stations, blank.

Table 11.1 HSI Calculations for Alwar

Base Station No.	even_area	elev_area	slope_area	asp_area	urb_deg	wat_deg	roc_deg	bar_deg	for_deg	HSI
1	3	5	1	2	1	1	1	2	5	5.47
2	3	5	1	4	1	1	1	5	5	3.07
3	4	5	2	3	1	1	5	1	1	1.65
4	2	5	1	4	1	1	1	1	5	7.10
5	3	5	1	4	1	1	1	3	5	5.07

Table 11.2   Final Categorization of the Probable Enemy Base Stations

Base Station	Category
4	Most probable base station
1, 5	Probable base stations
2	Least probable base station
3	Rejected base station

be seen that the HSI values of base station 3 is 1.65, which is less than the threshold HSI of 3.0; hence, this base station is rejected, and no further calculations are made for this base station. The HSIs for the remaining base stations are 5.47, 3.07, 7.10, and 5.07 for base stations 1, 2, 4, and 5, respectively. From these values, the base stations are classified as in Table 11.2. Figure 11.4b presents the base stations categorized into most probable, probable, least probable, and rejected base stations, marked in symbols as cross, plus, minus, and blank, respectively. The next phase of the algorithm is to find the shortest and the best feasible path of attack on the enemy base station, for which we use the hybrid cross-country path-planning algorithm as described in Section 11.4 (Kaur et al. 2010).

The algorithm serves a dual purpose of finding the shortest path that is also obstacle free, using the ACO technique, given the source and the destination locations. In our case, the source is the friendly base station, and the destination is the destination enemy base station provided as the output of the first phase of our two-phase intelligent framework. Figure 11.5a represents a portion of the Alwar image with the source (friendly) base station and the destination enemy base station identified. The destination enemy base station is obtained as the output of the first phase of the two-phase system where we obtained the base station numbered 4 ($n = 4$) as the destination enemy base station.

The source base station is chosen to demonstrate the second phase of the intelligent system. The algorithm extracts the possible paths by categorizing the image into accessible and inaccessible regions, where a black area depicts an inaccessible area and white depicts the accessible path, after which these paths are refined by applying morphological operations. The aforementioned

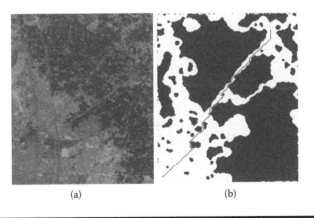

(a)   (b)

Figure 11.5   (a) Portion of the Alwar image with the source and the destination base stations identified. (b) Alwar image with the line representing the safest and the shortest path from the source (friendly) base station to the target destination enemy base station.

categorization of regions is achieved by creating histograms of accessible and inaccessible ranges of digital number values implemented in MATLAB. After these operations, many possible paths are extracted amidst the cross-country path of the Alwar region. Now the shortest path is obtained using path planning by ACO, wherein the Euclidean distance is calculated from the friendly base station to the destination enemy base station, and the shortest path is thus identified. While finding the way to the next node/image pixel, the algorithm checks for the obstacle; if an obstacle occurs, the next node is chosen. On the whole, we have the safest and shortest path, as depicted by Figure 11.5b.

11.5.2 Mussourie Region in Himachal Pradesh

From military inputs, the ideal values of the SIVs {even_area, elev_area, slope_area, asp_area, urb_deg, wat_deg, roc_deg, bar_deg, for_deg} are taken as 1, 5, 2, 5, 1, 1, 1, 1, and 5, from which the HSI value for the ideal base station is calculated as 9. We consider four base stations whose SIV values generated by the expert knowledge are taken as input to our algorithm. The number of base stations in a plain and a hilly region are in the ratio of 4:5 based on military inputs. Hence, the number of base stations for the Mussourie region is taken as 4 for demonstration purposes. Figure 11.6a presents the Mussourie image with the candidate base stations marked in dotted circles. From Table 11.3, it can be seen that the HSI values of base station 1 is 1.55, which is less than the threshold HSI of 3.0; hence, this base station is rejected, and no further calculations are made for this base station. The HSI values are calculated for the remaining base stations. The HSI values for base stations 2, 3, and 4 are 7.4, 5.9, and 6.6, respectively. Hence, the base stations are classified as in Table 11.4. Figure 11.6b presents the base stations categorized into most probable, probable, least probable, and rejected base stations, marked in symbols as a cross, plus, minus, and blank, respectively.

Figure 11.7a represents a portion of the Mussourie image with the source (friendly) base station and the destination enemy base station identified in the image. The destination enemy base

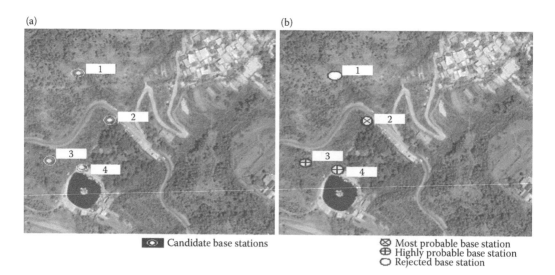

(a) (b)

■ Candidate base stations

⊗ Most probable base station
⊕ Highly probable base station
◯ Rejected base station

Figure 11.6 (a) Mussourie image with the candidate base stations marked in dotted circles. (b) Mussourie image with the base stations categorized into respective classes. The symbol codes are as follows: most probable, cross; probable, plus; rejected base station, blank.

Table 11.3 HSI Calculations for Mussoorie

Base Station No.	even_area	elev_area	slope_area	asp_area	urb_deg	wat_deg	roc_deg	bar_deg	for_deg	HSI
1	4	3	2	4	1	1	3	5	2	1.55
2	1	3	3	2	1	1	1	1	5	7.4
3	2	3	2	3	1	1	1	1	5	5.9
4	5	2	3	4	1	1	1	1	5	6.6

Table 11.4   Final Categorization of the Probable Enemy Base Stations

Base Station	Category
2	Most probable base station
3, 4	Highly probable base stations
1	Rejected base station

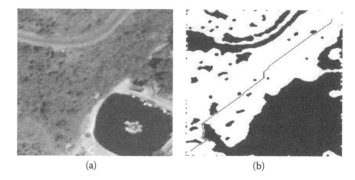

(a)   (b)

Figure 11.7   (a) Portion of the Mussourie image with the source and the destination base stations identified. (b) Mussourie image with the line representing the safest and the shortest path from the source (friendly) base station to the target destination enemy base station.

station is obtained as the output of the first phase of the two-phase intelligent framework where we obtained the base station numbered 2 ($n = 2$) as the destination enemy base station. The algorithm extracts the possible paths by categorizing the image into accessible and inaccessible regions, where a black area depicts an inaccessible area and white depicts the accessible path, after which these paths are refined by applying morphological operations through histogram creation in MATLAB. After these operations, many possible paths are extracted amidst the cross-country path of the Alwar region. Now the shortest path is obtained using Euclidean distance as the measure. While finding the way to the next node, the algorithm checks for the obstacle; if an obstacle occurs, the next node is chosen. On the whole, we have the safest and shortest path, as depicted by Figure 11.7b.

11.5.3 Performance Analysis

Next, we compare the performance of the first phase of the anticipatory system with the traditional decision-making techniques that have been used to date for anticipating the probable enemy base stations but have shown limited accuracy. Tables 11.2 and 11.4 present the results of anticipation on the data sets of the Alwar and Mussourie regions. From the results in Tables 11.2 and 11.4, we know that the proposed model for predicting the enemy base station resulted in the fourth and second base stations as the destination enemy base stations for the Alwar and the Mussourie images, respectively. However, if traditional decision making would have been applied,

Table 11.5 Comparison of Results of Path Planning on the Given Data Sets by Various Techniques

	Evolutionary Strategy	*Fuzzy Inference*	*Proposed Model*
Alwar	358	361	357
Mussourie	316	319	315

the SIV values should have been added up linearly for each of the candidate base stations, and the value that is nearest to the ideal value will be chosen as the output base station. Using traditional decision making, base stations 1, 3, and 4 are taken as the output base stations since these are the nearest to the ideal HSI value of 22. However, it can be seen that traditional decision making does not produce a unique output and is therefore imprecise. Also, base stations 1 and 3 have been categorized as "highly probable base station" and "rejected base station" by our algorithm, which further adds on to the impreciseness in the results. For the Mussourie region, base station 4 is taken as the output base station; however, this base station is indicated as only "highly probable" by our algorithm and not as the most suited base station for the Mussourie data set. Thus, we can see the improvement in the results anticipated by the proposed model when compared with the traditional decision-making techniques.

For the second phase of the anticipatory system, we compare the performance of the proposed model with the results obtained by the use of the recent techniques of fuzzy inference mechanism (Afaq and Saini 2011; Kim et al. 1999) and evolutionary strategy (Back 1996; Yao et al. 1999) that have been used extensively for path-planning applications. Table 11.5 presents the results of path-planning implementation for the Alwar as well as the Mussourie images using the aforementioned optimization techniques when compared with the proposed model. The figures in the table are the pixel count of the path planned from the source to the destination base station. From the table, it can be seen that the proposed technique employed in the second phase produces the lowest pixel count of 357 for the Alwar and 315 for the Mussourie region when compared to the other techniques.

11.6 Conclusion and Future Scope

From the previous discussion, we conclude that nature-inspired intelligence can be used as a modern tool in warfare planning and strategic decision making (Sun Tzu, 6th century BC). In the described system, the military application of the most suitable enemy base station prediction, and thereafter, finding the path of attack on this predicted destination, has been solved using two nature-inspired intelligent techniques, biogeography-based optimization and ACO, respectively. Based on the results of the presented algorithm, the commanders in the war theatre will have an increased battlefield awareness since they can now anticipate the destined enemy base station. This will be of prime importance since in the modern warfare strategies, the ability of an army to position its troops at an effective geographical location (having predicted the location of the enemy base station), in the shortest possible time, will significantly give a tactical advantage over the enemy and prove to be the deciding factor for winning (Hew 2006; Zhou and Wei 2008). Thus, the demonstrated system is very well suited for anticipating the next action of the enemy—to anticipate the enemy's deployment strategies—and can replace the currently employed traditional decision-making techniques.

There is a lot of scope in the future for the development of the proposed technique to be a more practical anticipatory system since the proposed system has the limitation that it can only capture a small set of SIVs of the input base station and hence presents an incomplete and imprecise assessment of the base station's feasibility. Also, the SIVs that require human interpretation cannot be captured by the proposed algorithm. In the future, the proposed system can be improved by adding those SIVs that need human interpretation, and hence, we can aid in better anticipation while designing the war/battlefield strategies. Also, we can sample the aforementioned SIVs round the year to generate very precise and accurate results. This would also enable us to detect any changes if there are any, hence giving us the capability of any kind of movement detection, thereby enhancing anticipatory capabilities. Also, one of the limitations of the proposed system is that the SIV values of each of the input candidate base stations are fed manually into the anticipatory system, and the values are decided based on military inputs. However, in the future, the system can be made more autonomous by directly retrieving the SIV values of the candidate base stations from the multispectral satellite images or Google Earth images itself by using image analysis tools for measuring the slope, evenness, elevation, aspect, and other terrain characteristics and hence sophisticating the process of assessing the likely base stations of the enemy on the given terrain.

References

Afaq, H., Saini, S., 2011. On the solutions to the travelling salesman problem using nature inspired computing techniques. *IJCSI International Journal of Computer Science Issues*, 8(4): 326–334.

Arora, S., 2010. Biogeography based battlefield situation awareness. Master of Engineering (M.E.) Thesis. Submitted to Delhi College of Engineering (now Delhi Technological University), Delhi, India.

Back, T., 1996. *Evolutionary Algorithms in Theory and Practice*. Oxford, UK: Oxford Univ. Press.

Dorigo, M., Stutzle, T., 2004. *Chapter 3, Ant Colony Optimization*, MIT Press, Cambridge, UK.

Ergezer, M., Simon, D., Du, D., 2009. Population distributions in biogeography-based optimization algorithms with elitism. In: *IEEE International Conference on Systems, Man and Cybernetics*, San Antonio, TX, 991–996.

Goel, L., Gupta, D., Panchal, V.K., 2011. Information sharing in swarm intelligence techniques: A perspective application for natural terrain feature elicitation in remote sensing images. *International Journal of Computer Applications (IJCA)*, 32(2): 34–40.

Goel, L., Gupta, D., Panchal, V.K., 2012a. Hybrid bio-inspired techniques for land cover feature extraction: A remote sensing perspective. *Applied Soft Computing*, Elsevier Publications, 12(2): 832–849.

Goel, L., Gupta, D., Panchal, V.K., Abraham, A., 2012b. Taxonomy of computational intelligence: A remote sensing perspective. In: *World Congress on Nature and Biologically Inspired Computing (NaBIC)*, IEEE Publications, Mexico City, Mexico, 200–206.

Goel, L., Gupta, D., Panchal, V.K., 2012c. Biogeography based anticipatory computing framework for intelligent battlefield planning. In: *International Conference on Hybrid Intelligent Systems (HIS)*, Pune, 41–46.

Goel, L., Panchal, V.K., Gupta, D., Bhola, R., 2010. Hybrid ACO-BBO Approach for predicting the deployment strategies of enemy troops in a military terrain application. In: *4th International Multi Conference on Intelligent Systems & Nanotechnology (IISN)*.

Hew, P.C., 2006. *The Generation of Situational Awareness within Autonomous Systems—A Near to Mid Term Study*. Issues by Defence Systems Analysis Division Information Sciences Laboratory DSTO-GD-0467, DSTO Information Sciences Laboratory, Edinburgh, South Australia: DSTO.

Jaiswal, R.K., Mukherjee, S., Raju, K.D., Saxena, R., 2002. Forest fire risk zone mapping from satellite imagery and GIS. *International Journal of Applied Earth Observation and Geoinformation*, Elsevier Publications, 4: 1–10.

Kaur, P., Kaur, S., Aulakh G.S. Panchal, V.K., Gill, I.S., 2010. Hybrid approach using PSO and ACO for cross-country path planning. In: *International Conference on Artificial Intelligence and Pattern Recognition (AIPR-10)*, Florida, 1–6.

Kiefer, R.W., Lillesand, T.M., 2006. *Principles of Remote Sensing*, John Wiley & Sons, New York.

Kim, B.N., Kwon, O.S., Kim, K.H., Lee, E.H., Hong, S.H., 1999. A study on path planning for mobile robot based on fuzzy logic controller. *IEEE TENCON*, Cheju Island, 2: 1002–1005.

Sahin, Y.G., Ercan, T., 2008. Detection of hidden hostile/terrorist groups in harsh territories by using animals as mobile biological sensors. *Sensors*, 8: 4365–4383. doi: 10.3390/s8074365.

Simon, D., 2008. Biogeography-based optimization. *IEEE Transactions on Evolutionary Computation*, IEEE Computer Society Press, 12(6): 702–713.

Tzu, S., 6th Century BC. *The Art of War, A Chinese Military Treatise*, China, Chapter 3.

Yao, X., Liu, Y., Lin, G., 1999. Evolutionary programming made faster. *IEEE Transactions on Evolutionary Computing*, 3: 82–102.

Zhou, G., Wei, D., 2008. Survey and analysis of land satellite remote sensing applied in highway transportations infrastructure and system engineering. *IGARSS*, Boston: IEEE, 4: 479–482.

Chapter 12

High-Utility Patterns Discovery in Data Mining: A Case Study

Chiranjeevi Manike and Hari Om

Contents

Over the last decade, high-utility pattern mining has become an emerging research topic in the field of data mining. There is a strong need for scalable and efficient mining techniques in this area as the size of data increases gigantically. For example, on YouTube, 48 h of video is uploaded every minute; there are currently 1.97 billion Internet users worldwide, and the unstructured data are growing at a rate of 80% per year. The high-utility pattern mining may be considered as an extension of frequent-pattern mining in which the frequency of the itemsets' occurrence is considered. In some cases, the frequent itemsets may only contribute a small portion of the overall profit, whereas the nonfrequent itemsets may contribute a large portion of profit. High-utility pattern mining discovers more valuable knowledge from the transaction databases by considering different values of individual items as utilities. Utility mining is more complex than frequent-pattern mining. It has many applications in retail-chain data analysis, online analytical processing, network traffic analysis, web-server log and click-stream mining, telecommunication data analysis, e-business and stock data analysis, sensor network data analysis, and so forth.

In this chapter, we select four significant algorithms in this area, namely, generation of temporal maximal utility itemsets from data streams using landmark window (GUIDE [LM]), high-utility itemset miner (HUI-Miner), high-utility mining using maximal itemset property (UMMI), and Two-Phase algorithm, based on the following concepts: number of database scans, pruning strategies, and summary structures. A case study on the retail data set with real application is also presented. The main purpose of this chapter is to show the performance and usefulness of the chosen algorithms based on analysis of the retail data set in order to design more efficient algorithms. Moreover, it will be useful to researchers interested in the area to learn why all past attempts have failed to discover high-utility patterns.

12.1 Introduction

The first question that arises in utility mining is *why is high-utility pattern mining challenging and more important than frequent-pattern mining?*

We first address this point and then define the problem in a structured way. Generally, data mining is the process of data analysis from different contexts and summarizing it into qualitative information—information that can be used by business analysts for making decisions to increase total revenue, decrease total costs, or both. Data-mining software is one among a number of analytical tools for data analysis that allows users to analyze data from many different aspects or angles, categorize them, and summarize the relationships found in them. Technically, data mining can be defined as the process of finding correlations or patterns among a huge number of attributes in large data sets/databases. Retail markets have been using powerful computers to shift through volumes of supermarket scanner data and analyze market research reports for years. However, uninterrupted innovations in computer processing power, storage, and mining software are rapidly increasing the accuracy of analysis while driving down the cost.

In data mining, association rule learning is one of the popular and well-researched methods for discovering interesting correlations between variables in large data sets/databases. Association rule mining from a database is a two-step process (Agrawal and Srikant 1994):

■ Finding frequent patterns from the transaction database with minimum support threshold, specified by the user
■ Generating rules among the frequent patterns identified in the first step

Thee second step is a straight forward process, whereas the first step is more costly than the second (Li et al. 2008a). So, the problem of mining frequent patterns from a transaction database becomes most important. Frequent itemsets are the patterns/itemsets that appear together in a database frequently. For example, a set of items, such as toothpaste and toothbrush, that appear frequently together in a transaction database is a frequent itemset. Finding these frequent patterns has been playing an essential role in mining associations, correlations, and many other significant relationships among the data. Moreover, it is useful in classification, clustering, and other data-mining tasks. Thus, frequent-pattern mining has become an important data-mining task and a focused topic of research in data mining. The goal of mining frequent itemsets is to generate all the frequent itemsets whose frequency is more than the user-defined minimum support threshold, which is given by the ratio of the number of transactions containing the itemset.

Agrawal and Srikant (1994) report a novel idea (called Apriori property) that the frequent itemsets at level L_i are generated from the frequent itemsets at level L_{i-1}. That is, candidate itemsets at level L_i are generated from the frequent itemsets at level L_{i-1}, and after generating candidate itemsets, their support values can be calculated by scanning the database, which may help in pruning the low-support itemsets. This is an iterative process, also called level-wise candidate generation and test, in which at each level, candidates are generated and tested to identify the frequent itemsets. Based on the Apriori property, lots of redundant itemsets are pruned to reduce the extra computation cost. However, there are some drawbacks to this Apriori approach.

The Apriori approach has two main drawbacks: one is the cost associated with the candidate generation process, and the other is the cost of rescanning the database multiple times. To overcome the drawbacks in the Apriori approach, a novel approach, called frequent-pattern growth (FP-Growth) (Han et al. 2000), has been discussed, which finds frequent patterns without generating a huge number of candidates, thus completely removing the cost associated with the candidate generation process. Next, the FP-Growth builds a compact data structure, called FP-Tree, to store itemset information by scanning a database twice, which effectively reduces the cost associated with multiple database scans. However, all frequent-pattern mining algorithms consider only the frequency of an itemset in a transaction database. In association rule mining, support is defined over the binary domain 0, 1, where 1 indicates the presence of an item in a transaction, and 0 its absence, which is shown in Figure 12.1a.

The frequency of an itemset may not be a sufficient measure of interestingness (Silberschatz and Tuzhilin 1996; Liu et al. 2000), because it only reflects the number of transactions in the database that contain the itemset. It does not reveal the actual utility of an itemset, which can be measured in terms of cost, profit, or other expressions of user preference. For example, consider the transaction database shown in Figure 12.1b, which contains information of actual sold quantity of each item in a transaction. In this database, items A, B, and C have total sales quantities of 3, 11, and 40, respectively, but their frequencies are the same (i.e., 3). Frequent-itemset mining gives equal importance to all these items even though all of them have different quantities. In the worst case, if all these three items are associated with the same profit value (i.e., unit profit is the same), the total profit on item C is obviously more than the others. In some cases, low-frequency patterns may contribute more to the total profit. Therefore, to know information like which patterns are contributing more to the total profit, we need to consider the sold quantity of each itemset.

Item	A	B	C	D	E		Item	A	B	C	D	E
T1	0	0	1	0	1		T1	0	0	12	0	2
T2	0	1	0	1	1		T2	0	6	0	1	1
T3	1	1	0	0	1		T3	1	4	0	0	1
T4	1	0	1	1	1		T4	1	0	1	15	1
T5	1	1	1	0	0		T5	1	1	27	0	0
(a)							(b)					

Figure 12.1 Transaction database for (a) frequent and (b) high utility pattern mining.

In view of this, high-utility pattern mining was introduced in 2003 to mine patterns by considering actual utilities of items in the transaction database. High-utility patterns are the pattern having utility more than the specified minimum utility threshold. To understand the necessity of high-utility patterns in today's market, we have considered a small example in the real-world market basket database, wherein different items have different profit values and different items in a transaction have different selling quantities.

Another important and more challenging topic is to find high-utility patterns from the data streams. Pattern mining from a data stream is more challenging than that from a static database. Due to the characteristics of high speed, rapid rate, and continuous arrival of a data stream, it needs a one-pass algorithm (Shie et al. 2012), with efficient processing time and limited memory.

In data stream mining, three different models have been considered based on the end-user requirements, which are the sliding window (SW) model, landmark window (LW) model, and time-fading window (TW) model (Shie et al. 2012). The SW model is used to keep recent information, and it is useful for those who are interested to know the recent information. This model holds information like sales in the last 3 h, last 1 week, last 15 days, and so forth. The main problem with the SW model is that when the window is sliding, we need to load new information, and at the same time, we have to delete outdated information. In LW, data are maintained from the specified time point to present time, for example, since June 2012 to the present time, whereas TW captures the data from LW, but it uses a time decay function to decrease the importance of the outdated data.

The remaining part of this chapter is organized as follows: Section 12.2 provides the high-utility pattern mining problem definition. In Section 12.3, we discuss relevant research works. In Section 12.4, we give a brief description about each algorithm that we have selected, and each algorithm is illustrated with a common example. Section 12.5 provides a case study. In Section 12.6, we present performance analysis of the considered algorithms. Finally, the conclusion is given in Section 12.7.

12.2 Problem Definition

Let $I = \{i_1, i_2, i_3, \ldots, i_m\}$ be a set of items and DB a transaction database $\{T_1, T_2, T_3, \ldots, T_n\}$, where each transaction contains a set of items, which is a subset of I. Utility table U contains the utility of each item in I. Transaction identifier can be denoted as either T_1 or T1 and itemset can also be denoted as either {AB} or AB.

The problem of high-utility pattern mining is to find all patterns in the transaction database DB with utility values higher than the minimum utility threshold, for the given utility table. We adopt definitions similar to those presented in the literature (Liu et al. 2005a, b; Liu and Qu 2012; Shie et al. 2012).

Definition 12.1

The internal utility of item i_p in transaction T_q, denoted as $iu(i_p, T_q)$, is the purchased quantity value associated with i_p in T_q in the transaction database, for example, $iu(B, T_2) = 6$ in Figure 12.1b. ■

Definition 12.2

The external utility of item i_p, denoted as $eu(i_p)$, is the utility value of i_p in the utility table, for example, $eu(C) = 1$, in Figure 12.2a. ■

Item	Profit ($)
A	3
B	10
C	1
D	6
E	5

(a)

Tid	TU
T1	22
T2	71
T3	48
T4	99
T5	40

(b)

Item	TWU
A	187
B	159
C	161
D	170
E	240

(c)

Figure 12.2 Profits, transaction utility (TU), and transaction weighted utility (TWU) of items. (a) Utility (U), (b) TU, and (c) TWU tables.

Definition 12.3

The utility of item i_p in transaction T_q, denoted as $u(i_p, T_q)$, is the product of $u(i_p, T_q)$, and $eu(i_p)$, where $u(i_p, T_q) = iu(i_p, T_q) \times eu(i_p)$, for example, $u(D, T_4) = 15 \times 6 = 90$ in Figure 12.1b and Figure 12.2a. ■

Definition 12.4

The utility of itemset X in transaction T_q, denoted as $u(X, T_q)$, is the sum of the utilities of all items in X in T_q in which X is contained, where $u(X, T_q) = \Sigma_{i_p \in X \in T_q} u(i_p, T_q)$, for example, $u(AB, T_3) = 43$ in Figures 12.1b and 12.2a. ■

Definition 12.5

The utility of transaction T_q, denoted as $tu(T_q)$, is the sum of utilities of all items in T, where $tu(T) = \Sigma_{i \in T} u(i, T)$, for example, the transaction utility of T_1 is $u(C, T_1) + u(E, T_1) = 22$ in Figure 12.2b. ■

Definition 12.6

The transaction-weighted utility (TWU) of itemset X in transaction database, denoted as $twu(X)$, is the sum of utilities of all transactions containing X in transaction database, where $twu(X) = \Sigma_{T \in DB X \in T} tu(T)$, for example, $twu(A) = tu(T_3) + tu(T_4) + tu(T_5) = 187$ in Figure 12.2b and c. ■

Definition 12.7

The minimum utility threshold minUtility () is given by a percentage of the total transaction utility values of the database, where minUtility $= \delta \times \Sigma_{T_q \in DB} tu(T_q)$. ■

Definition 12.8

The total utility of database DB is the sum of utilities of all transactions in DB, where total DB utility $= \Sigma_{T_q \in DB} u(T_q)$. ■

Definition 12.9

A pattern X is a high-utility pattern, if $u(X) \geq$ minUtility. Finding high-utility patterns means determining all patterns X that satisfy the criterion $u(X) \geq$ minUtility.   ■

12.3 Literature Review

In this section, we briefly review high-utility pattern mining algorithms in static and dynamic environments.

12.3.1 Mining from Static Databases

The practical usefulness of frequent-itemset mining is limited by the significance of the discovered itemsets. There are two limitations. First, a huge number of frequent itemsets that are not interesting to the user are often generated when the minimum support is set to low. For example, there may be thousands of combinations of products that occur in 1% of the transactions. If too many uninteresting frequent itemsets are found, the user is forced to do additional work to select the itemsets that are indeed interesting. Second, support, defined based on the frequency of itemsets, is not an adequate measure of a typical user interest. Suppose that a sales manager is more interested to find the itemsets that can generate a profit higher than a threshold.

Frequent-itemset mining considers the measure called support (i.e., percentage of transactions in the transaction database containing the particular itemset) to estimate the usefulness of an association rule. It does not consider the other utility values of an itemset like purchased quantity, cost, profit, and so forth. Hence, the share measure (Barber and Hamilton 2003) has been discussed to overcome the shortcomings of support. This is an alternative measure to the importance of itemsets that may be defined as the percentage of the total that is contributed by the items in an itemset. Like frequent itemsets, the share-frequent itemsets do not hold Apriori property. Lu et al. (2001) discuss the vertical and mixed weighted association rules in which the database is divided into several time intervals and is assigned weights for each interval to identify the important items. Wang et al. (2002) discuss an approach, called profit mining, with the objective of promoting the sales of target items based on the nonprofit items. Chan et al. (2003) discuss an alternative approach for mining high-utility patterns.

Yao et al. (2004) generalize the concept of itemset share and give a theoretical model for utility mining. In their approach, two types of utilities are defined for items: transaction utility and external utility. Later on, they designed two efficient pruning strategies and also developed two algorithms (UMining, UMining_H) by incorporating these pruning strategies (Yao and Hamilton 2006). These algorithms are based on the problem of a level-wise search approach. Liu et al. (2005a, b) discuss an algorithm, called Two-Phase, and identified the Apriori property among TWU values of the itemsets. In phase I, this algorithm generates high transaction-weighted utility itemsets (HTWUI), where the TWU value of an itemset ≥ minimum utility threshold, and in phase II, it calculates actual utilities of itemsets. This algorithm may also be said to be based on the level-wise search approach, in which a huge number of candidate itemsets are generated.

An algorithm based on the pattern growth approach, compressed transaction utility (CTU)-Mine, is discussed by Erwin et al. (2007b). They also discuss the CTU-PROL algorithm (Erwin et al. 2008), which efficiently mines both the dense and sparse data sets that fit into the main memory. The CTU-PROL algorithm mines the complete set of high-utility itemsets (HUIs) from both the sparse and dense data sets that have short or long high-utility patterns (Erwin et al. 2008). Yu et al. (2008) discuss a hybrid method by composing intertransaction and Two-Phase algorithms to mine the HUIs with high dimensions or long patterns. This method does not work well under long transaction environments without using an optimization technique.

In view of the level-wise candidate generation-and-test problem, Li et al. (2008b) discuss an efficient strategy, isolated itemset discarding strategy (IIDS), that reduces the number of candidates by pruning isolated items during the level-wise pattern generation processes. It applies two share mining methods, Share-counted Fast Share Measure (ShFSM) and direct candidates generation (DCG) to the utility mining model to increase the speed of finding high-utility patterns. Le et al. (2009) discuss an algorithm, called TWU-Mining, based on the Weighted Itemset-Tedset (WIT) tree, an extension of the IT-tree (Erwin et al. 2007b), which performs better than the Apriori-based algorithms (Wang et al. 2002) and requires a single database scan. Xian-shan et al. (2010) discuss the high-motivation (HM) two-phase miner by introducing a new measure, called motivation, and a transaction-weighted motivation downward-closure property. Though the aforementioned algorithms prune the search space of utility mining increasingly, they utilize the Apriori-based level-wise candidate generation-and-test process that requires scanning a database multiple times. Ahmed et al. (2009) discuss a novel tree-based candidate pruning technique, called high-utility candidate (HUC)-Prune, which efficiently mines the high-utility patterns without the level-wise candidate generation-and-test problem.

To effectively generate HTWUIs in phase I of the study by Liu et al. (2005a, b) and to reduce the database scans, the incremental HUP lexicographic tree (IHUP-Tree)-based algorithm has been discussed for maintaining the HUIs (Ahmed et al. 2009). In this algorithm, three tree structures are designed: $IHUP_L$-Tree (IHUP lexicographic tree), $IHUP_{TF}$-Tree (IHUP transaction frequency tree), and $IHUP_{TWU}$-Tree (IHUP TWU tree), based on the items' lexicographic order, transaction frequency (descending order), and TWU. Wu et al. (2011) discuss an efficient algorithm for finding compact high-utility patterns from the transactional databases, called closed + high utility itemset discovery (CHUD).

Chu et al. (2009) discuss a novel method, HUI mining with negative item values (HUINIV)-Mine, for efficiently and effectively mining the HUIs from the large databases with consideration of negative item values. Tseng et al. (2010) discuss the utility pattern growth (UP-Growth) that reduces the estimated utilities effectively in the UP-Trees during the mining processes and the number of HTWUIs. Lin et al. (2010b) discuss the IHUP for incremental mining by modifying the high-utility pattern (HUP) (Lin et al. 2009) in which all the transactions are processed in batch-by-batch fashion.

Silberschatz and Tuzhilin (1996) design a HUP tree (HUP-Tree) and HUP-Growth mining algorithm to derive the HUPs effectively and efficiently. This algorithm integrates a Two-Phase procedure for utility mining (Liu et al. 2005a, b) and an FP-Tree (Han et al. 2000) concept to utilize the downward-closure property to generate a compressed tree structure. In the traditional mining of HUIs, an increase in the length of the itemset leads to an increase in the utility of the itemset. Hence, making decisions among the itemsets of different lengths with the same threshold is not fair. To eliminate the effect of this length, the average utility of an itemset has been discussed in the work of Hong et al. (2011), Lin et al. (2010a), and Bashir et al. (2009). Silberschatz and Tuzhilin (1996) discuss an algorithm, high on-self utility itemsets (HOUI), by designing periodical transaction total utility (PTTU), which increases the execution efficiency.

Liu and Qu (2012) discuss an algorithm, HUI-Miner, using a novel structure, called utility list, to store the itemset utility information and heuristic information of the itemsets for pruning the search space of HUI-Miner. It avoids multiple calculations and effectively reduces the candidate itemsets. To filter the HUPs from the huge number of patterns, Lan et al. (2011) design an efficient algorithm, projection-based (PB) utility mining algorithm with pruning strategies (PPS), that is more efficient than the two-phase (Liu et al. 2005a) and PB (Lan et al. 2010) algorithms. Recently, an algorithm, high-utility mining using maximal itemset property (UMMI) (Lin et al. 2012), based on two steps has been discussed. In the first step, it reduces the number of potential itemsets significantly, and in the second step, it uses an effective lexicographic tree structure to determine all of the HUIs.

12.3.2 Mining from Dynamic Databases

Tseng et al. (2006) design the first algorithm, called temporal HUIs (THUI-Mine), to mine the HUIs from the data streams by extending the framework of two-phase (Liu et al. 2005a) and SW filtering (SWF) (Lee et al. 2001) algorithms. It addresses the problem of discovering the THUIs over the data streams, that is, finding the itemsets larger than the threshold in the current time window of the data stream by partitioning the transaction database into several partitions. The THUI-Mine operates based on the filtering threshold in each partition to deal with the TWU itemsets (TWUIs) generated. Yeh et al. (2008) discuss two efficient algorithms, namely, incremental utility mining (IUM), based on a Two-Phase algorithm (Liu et al. 2005a, b) and fast incremental utility mining (FIUM), based on the ShFSM algorithm (Li and Yeh 2005). Another two efficient one-pass algorithms, mining HUIs based on BITvector (MHUI-BIT) and mining HUIs based on TIDlist (MHUI-TID), are discussed by Li et al. (2008a).

Ahmed et al. (2011) discuss a novel framework by introducing a useful measure, called frequency affinity/correlation, to discover the HUPs in the data streams in a single database scan. A new tree structure called high-utility stream tree (HUS-Tree) and a novel algorithm, HUP mining over stream data (HUPMS), are discussed for SW-based HUP mining (Erwin et al. 2007a). Shie et al. (2012) discuss generation of temporal maximal utility itemsets from data streams (GUIDE) by extending their previous work (2010) to find the temporal maximal HUIs from the data streams for LW. The GUIDE framework can indeed find maximal HUIs from the data streams with different models, that is, LW, SW, and TW models.

12.4 HUP Mining Algorithms

In this section, we give a brief introduction about each of the selected algorithms and illustrate them using a common and simple example for better understanding of the HUP mining process.

12.4.1 GUIDE (LM) Algorithm

An efficient framework, called GUIDE, was proposed by Shie et al. (2012), to find maximal HUIs from the data streams with different models, that is, LW, SW, and TW models. The main aim of this framework is to find a compact form of HUPs (i.e., maximal HUIs) from the data streams. A novel tree structure, Maximal high Utility Itemset Tree (MUI-Tree), was proposed to maintain the essential information captured from the data streams. A bottom-up tracing strategy has been used to find all target patterns from the MUI-Tree.

In this GUIDE framework, the algorithm implemented for LW, called GUIDE (LM), is selected for our performance analysis, which first generates projections of each loaded transaction, and then all these projections are updated in the MUI-Tree. Finally, by using a bottom-up tracing strategy, it generates all HUPs. In our analysis, we change the bottom-up tracing process and use a top-down tracing strategy in which every node of the tree is visited to find all HUPs. For a better understanding of GUIDE (LM), Example 12.1.

Pruning strategy: GUIDE (LM) uses an efficient pruning strategy, called bottom-up tracing, to find maximal HUPs (MHUI). The process of tracing an MUI-Tree starts from the leftist node and checks the node's utility; if it is more than the user-specified minimum utility, the itemset corresponding to this node is generated as MHUI, and then the node pointer is moved to its parent node. In this way, the algorithm outputs all MHUIs. But, in our implementation of this algorithm, we have changed the tracing process in such a way that it can find all HUIs.

Example 12.1

Consider a transaction database and utility table, as shown in Figures 12.1b and 12.2a, respectively. First, transaction T_1 is loaded, and at the same time its utility (Figure 12.2b) is added to total database utility; accordingly, the projections are generated. The transaction projections are given in Figure 12.3. The projections of T_1 are {C}, {E}, {CE}, and the utility value of each (i.e., 12, 10, and 22) projection is also calculated at the same time. Updating the process of each projection into an MUI-Tree is shown in Figure 12.4. While adding the first projection of T_1, that is, {C}, we check whether that node exists in the tree or not. If the node does not exist, a new node is created; otherwise, the utility value is updated. In this manner, all transaction projections are added to the tree.

After constructing the MUI-Tree, the algorithm GUIDE (LM) finds all HUIs, and from them, it generates maximal HUIs. Let us assume that the user-specified minimum utility is 25% (i.e., 280 × 25 = 70); the algorithm generates the following HUIs: ACDE: 99, BDE: 71, CDE: 96, DE: 106. According to the definition of maximal itemset, the ACDE: 99 and BDE: 71 itemsets are filtered as the maximal HUIs among the generated HUIs. Our implementation of GUIDE (LM) with another tracing method generates the following HUIs: ACD: 94, ACDE: 99, B: 110, BDE: 71, CD: 91, CDE: 96, D: 96, and DE: 106, with a minimum utility threshold of 25%, as shown in Figure 12.5.

T1	{E}, {C}, {CE} = {10, 12, 22}
T2	{E}, {D}, {DE}, {B}, {BD}, {BDE} = {5, 6, 11, 60, 66, 71}
T3	{E}, {B}, {BE}, {A}, {AB}, {ABE} = {5, 40, 45, 3, 43, 48}
T4	{E}, {D}, {DE}, {C}, {CD}, {CDE}, {A}, {AC}, {ACD}, {ACDE} = {5, 90, 95, 1, 91, 96, 3, 4, 94, 99}
T5	{C}, {B}, {BC}, {A}, {AB}, {ABC} = {27, 10, 37, 3, 13, 40}

Figure 12.3   Transaction projections.

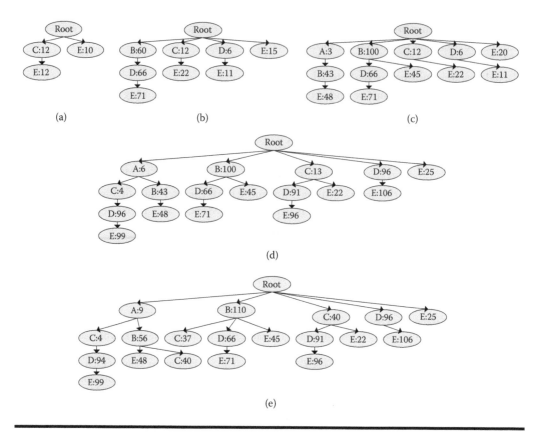

(a) (b) (c)

(d)

(e)

Figure 12.4 Updating of MUI-Tree. After inserting projection of (a) T_1, (b) T_2, (c) T_3, (d) T_4, (e) T_5.

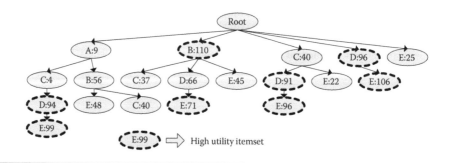

Figure 12.5 Tracing MUI-tree.

12.4.2 HUI-Miner Algorithm

To identify HUIs, most of the existing algorithms first generate candidate itemsets by over-estimating their utilities and subsequently compute the exact utilities of these candidates. These algorithms suffer from the problem of level-wise candidate generation and test. Most of the candidates are found as not having high utility after their exact utilities have been computed. In view of this, Liu and Qu (2012) have recently discussed an algorithm, HUI-Miner, for mining HUIs. HUI-Miner uses a novel structure, called utility list, in which each entry contains three fields: transaction id (Tid), iutility (i.e., item utility), and rutility (i.e., remaining utility), to store both the utility information about an itemset and the information for pruning the search space.

HUI-Miner first finds the TWU of each item in the transaction database and then discards the item/s having a TWU less than the minimum utility threshold. The discarded items are no longer considered in future calculations. All remaining items are sorted in an ascending order according to the TWU, and all items from each transaction are processed in the same order. Based on this order, the initial utility lists, 2-itemset utility lists, and so on are constructed. After constructing the initial utility lists, the algorithm efficiently mines all HUIs.

Example 12.2

This algorithm calculates TWUs of all items in the first scan of the transaction database (i.e., A: 187, B: 159, C: 161, D: 170, E: 240). When scanning the database again, the algorithm revises each transaction for constructing initial utility-lists. The database view in Figure 12.6 lists all revised transactions derived from the transaction database in Figure 12.1b. The item/s with TWU less than the minimum utility threshold (i.e., 70) are discarded. Here, all items have a TWU more than the minimum utility, so no item is discarded. The remaining items are sorted in an ascending order based on the TWU (i.e., $B < C < D < A < E$). While scanning the database again, the algorithm revises each transaction for constructing the initial utility lists. After constructing the initial utility list for each item, the 2-itemset utility lists are constructed by intersecting the initial utility lists. For example, consider the construction of 2-itemset {BC} by intersecting the initial utility lists {B} and {C} in Figure 12.7. There is one common Tid, so the itemset {BC} is constructed with one entry; the three fields in the first entry are filled with common Tid, the sum of utility values in the corresponding entry. The remaining utility of {C} (i.e., {C} is before {B}) is the corresponding entry. We follow the same process to construct all 2-itemsets. For constructing k-itemset ($k \geq 3$), we have to use the formula $u(i_1 \ldots i_{(k-2)} i_{(k-1)} i_k, T) = u(i_1 \ldots i_{(k-2)} i_{(k-1)}, T) + u(i_1 \ldots i_{(k-2)} i_k, T) - u(i_1 \ldots i_{(k-2)}, T)$.

Let us take a look at the construction of 3-itemset BCA, which is constructed from the two 2-itemsets BC and BA. There is one common Tid in both the itemsets, that is, 5, so the Tid field of the first entry of the BCA is filled with 5, and the item utility field is filled with the value 40, which is the summation of the corresponding item utility values in BC and BA (i.e., 37 + 13 = 50, where Tid is 5) minus the item utility value of B in the corresponding entry (i.e., 10). HUI-Miner first checks all initial utility lists according to the TWU, and it recursively constructs extensions for every initial utility list. If the initial utility list with the total item utility (i.e., sum of all item utilities) exceeds the minUtility, it is considered as HUI. If an initial utility list having the sum of all iutilities and rutilities ≥ minUtility, it is considered for constructing its extensions. Let us consider the initial utility list E in Figure 12.7. Its sum of iutilities is 25 < minUtility, and the sum of all iutilities and rutilities is 25 < minUtility. Due to the first reason, it is not an HUI, and for the second reason, it is considered for constructing its extensions.

Tid	Item	Utility	Item	Utility	Item	Utility	Item	Utility	TU
T1	C	12	E	10					22
T2	B	60	D	6	E	5			71
T3	A	3	B	40	E	5			48
T4	A	3	C	1	D	90	E	5	99
T5	A	3	B	10	C	27			40

Figure 12.6   Database view.

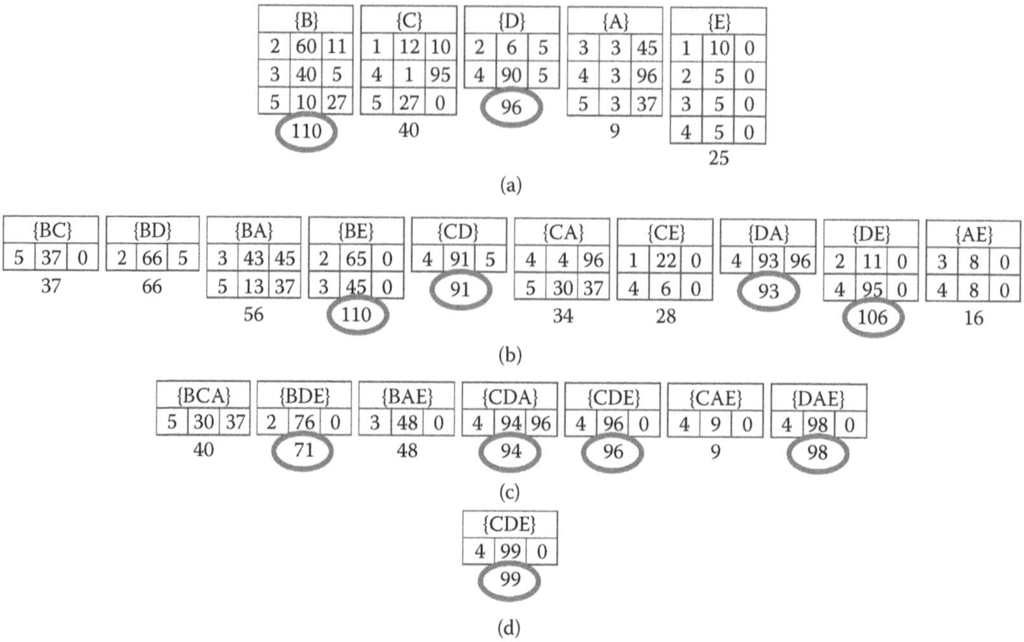

{B}			{C}			{D}			{A}			{E}		
2	60	11	1	12	10	2	6	5	3	3	45	1	10	0
3	40	5	4	1	95	4	90	5	4	3	96	2	5	0
5	10	27	5	27	0	*(96)*			5	3	37	3	5	0
(110)			40						9			4	5	0
												25		

(a)

{BC}			{BD}			{BA}			{BE}			{CD}			{CA}			{CE}			{DA}			{DE}			{AE}		
5	37	0	2	66	5	3	43	45	2	65	0	4	91	5	4	4	96	1	22	0	4	93	96	2	11	0	3	8	0
37			66			5	13	37	3	45	0	*(91)*			5	30	37	4	6	0	*(93)*			4	95	0	4	8	0
						56			*(110)*						34			28						*(106)*			16		

(b)

{BCA}			{BDE}			{BAE}			{CDA}			{CDE}			{CAE}			{DAE}		
5	30	37	2	76	0	3	48	0	4	94	96	4	96	0	4	9	0	4	98	0
40			*(71)*			48			*(94)*			*(96)*			9			*(98)*		

(c)

{CDE}		
4	99	0
(99)		

(d)

Figure 12.7 Utility lists construction. (a) Initial, (b) 2-itemsets, (c) 3-itemsets, and (d) 4-itemsets utility lists.

12.4.3 UMMI Algorithm

The algorithm UMMI (Lin et al. 2012) improves the performance of HUP mining. It uses an efficient tree structure called a lexicographic tree to store the captured information. This algorithm first finds all HTWUIs (1-itemsets) by scanning the database. The itemsets with a TWU less than the minimum utility threshold are discarded; they are no longer used in further computations. All 1-itemsets are sorted in an ascending order based on TWU values, and the items of each transaction in the transaction database are processed in the same order. The high-TWU (HTWU) pattern (HTP) tree is constructed by reading each transaction in the transaction database and by updating the TWU of the corresponding nodes representing the transaction itemset. After building the HTP tree, a conditional database of each item is constructed, and the MTWU itemsets are mined. Each MTWU itemset is inserted into the MLexTree, next, actual utilities of MTWU itemsets is stored in MLexTree by scanning database. All HUIs are generated by traversing MLexTree.

Example 12.3

How does the UMMI algorithm find high-utility itemsets?

Like HUI-Miner, the UMMI algorithm calculates the TWU value of each item in the first scan of the database. The items with low TWU (i.e., less than 70) are discarded; the remaining items are sorted in an ascending order based on TWU (i.e., $B < C < D < A < E$). Every transaction item in the transaction database is processed in the same order. Figure 12.8 shows the transaction database after the items are reordered. After constructing the HTP tree (i.e., Figure 12.9), the conditional database (Han et al. 2000) of each item is constructed to mine the HTWUIs instead of finding

Item	Items (reordered)	TU
T1	C, E	22
T2	B, D, E	71
T3	B, A, E	48
T4	C, D, A, E	99
T5	B, C, A	40

Figure 12.8 Database transactions (items reordered).

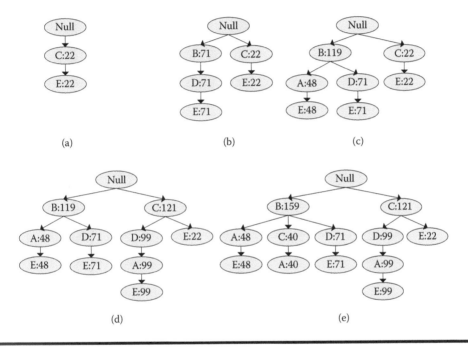

(a) (b) (c)

(d) (e)

Figure 12.9 HTP tree construction. After adding (a) T_1, (b) T_2, (c) T_3, (d) T_4, and (e) T_5.

the maximal HTWUIs. The following are the HTWUIs mined from each item's conditional database: {A}, {B}, {C}, {D}, {E}, {AB}, {AC}, {AD}, {AE}, {BD}, {BE}, {CD}, {CE}, {DE}, {ABE}, {ACD}, {ACE}, {ACDE}. We then have constructed a tree like MUI-Tree (Bashir et al. 2009) and inserted all these itemsets. By scanning the transaction database again, the actual utilities of itemsets are stored in the corresponding nodes of the tree. Finally, by tracing the tree, all HUIs are identified.

12.4.4 Two-Phase Algorithm

To address the drawbacks in mining using expected utility (MEU) (Yao et al. 2004), Liu et al. (2005b) discuss a novel algorithm—Two-Phase. In phase I, it follows the concept of level-wise candidate generation-and-test process that uses a transaction-weighted downward-closure property. By using this, in each level, the candidate itemsets are identified with the TWU more than the user-specified minimum utility threshold. In phase II, the algorithm generates actual HUIs and also filters the overestimated itemsets in phase I by scanning the database again.

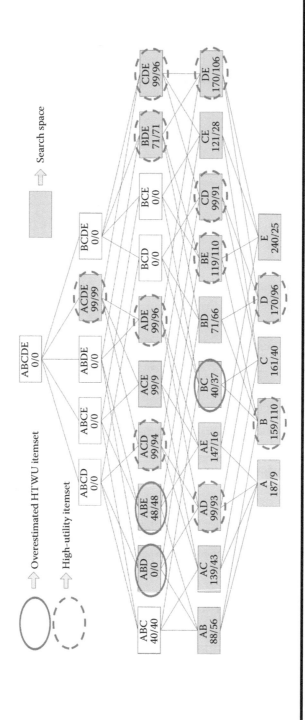

Figure 12.10 Itemset lattice related to example. Minimum utility = 70. Numbers in each box are transaction-weighted utility/itemset utility.

Example 12.4

Like HUI-Miner and UMMI, the two-phase algorithm also depends on TWU. Phase I of this algorithm generates HTWU candidate itemsets by following the Apriori approach. That is, in each level, it first generates candidates and tests their HTWU values (i.e., HTWU ≥ minUtility). The candidates qualified in this test are considered for generating the candidates in the next level. Let us consider 1-itemsets in the first level (Figure 12.10), all having TWU ≥ minUtility. All items are considered for generating candidate itemsets at this level because TWU ≥ minUtility. After generating candidate itemsets, the two-phase algorithm tests their HTWU values (i.e., HTWU ≥ minUtility). The candidate itemset BC is not an HTWUI that is shown in Figure 12.10; it is indeed an overestimated itemset. In phase II, the algorithm checks the actual utilities of all the generated candidate itemsets and produces all HUIs by doing one more scan. Overestimated itemsets in phase I are also filtered out in phase II; the total number of candidates generated for minUtility 70 is 23. Out of 23 HTWUIs, 3 are overestimated, shown as shaded squares and ellipses, respectively, in Figure 12.10.

12.5 Case Study: Real Retail Data Set

The retail data set has been obtained from the FIMI repository (http://fimi.ua.ac.be/data/retail. dat), in which the transaction records have been taken from an anonymous Belgian retail supermarket store. It contains a total of 88,163 transactions; the number of distinct items is 16,470, and the average number of distinct items per transaction is 13.

From this data set, we have filtered 29,475 transactions with a maximum number of distinct items per transaction of 5 and a total number of distinct items of 10,310. In this data set, 10.23% of the transactions contain a single item, 18.71% of the transactions contain two items, 23.47% of the transactions contain three items, 24.46% of the transactions contain four items, and 23.11% of the transactions contain five items. This data set does not provide the item utility (i.e., profit) and internal utility of items in the transactions. Based on the performance evaluation of the algorithms (Liu et al. 2005a, b; Ahmed et al. 2009; Tseng et al. 2006), the internal utilities are generated randomly, ranging from 1 to 5, and the utilities (i.e., profits) for items are generated between 1 and 20, using the lognormal distribution as shown in Figure 12.11. This case study focuses on the use of four significant HUP algorithms, that is, GUIDE (LM), HUI-Miner, UMMI, and two-phase, on a real

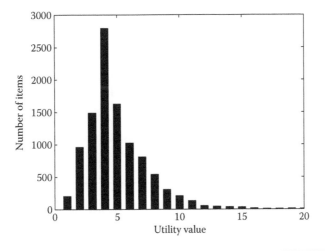

Figure 12.11 Utility value distribution.

Total number of transactions: 29,475
Maximum number of items per transaction: 5
Total number of items: 10,310
Purchased quantity range: 1 to 5
Profit range: 1 to 20
Total DB utility: 1,554,082

Minimum utility (%)	Runtime (s)				Memory (MB)				HUI count			
	GUIDE (LM)	HUI-Miner	UMMI	Two-phase	GUIDE (LM)	HUI-Miner	UMMI	Two-phase	GUIDE (LM)	HUI-Miner	UMMI	Two-phase
0.001	3.135	59.044	56.391	1119.148	20.1	9.95	85.16	87.49	106,681	213,386	213,552	213,552
0.002	3.088	55.081	53.824	1078.484	20.1	10.76	86.15	91.93	80,253	161,166	163,018	163,018
0.003	3.08	51.883	51.403	959.9	20.1	12.26	84.4	104.06	53,382	103,639	107,249	107,251
0.004	3.083	46.756	41.133	700.612	20.1	9.2	78.91	68.14	31,205	56,548	60,092	60,107
0.005	3.085	42.513	33.761	452.602	20.1	6.36	46.3	49.2	17,830	30,929	33,283	33,305
0.006	3.097	39.951	27.758	265.33	20.1	8.34	45.47	37.72	10,055	17,451	18,632	18,659
0.007	3.079	38.156	23.704	163.188	20.1	11.07	22	36.36	6519	11,640	12,156	12,172
0.008	3.077	36.498	21.15	110.596	20.1	11.51	16.63	28.44	4523	8333	8531	8547
0.009	3.082	35.883	19.452	85.054	20.1	8.66	17.8	26.73	3547	6641	6716	6723
0.01	3.079	34.556	17.799	69.513	20.1	8.19	21.28	23.92	2909	5547	5560	5566
0.02	3.088	26.924	10.255	28.553	20.1	7.84	10.06	22.43	1138	2059	2057	2059
0.03	3.093	22.618	6.935	16.867	20.1	7.51	8.14	19.4	692	1206	1205	1206
0.04	3.085	20.015	5.255	11.911	20.1	5.82	5.63	22.72	466	816	816	816
0.05	3.095	17.722	4.574	8.789	20.1	4.4	5.56	21.45	354	607	607	607
0.06	3.087	16.117	3.405	6.731	20.1	4.56	7.11	17.27	290	477	477	477
0.07	3.077	14.675	2.906	5.483	20.1	5.19	5.3	15.24	230	384	384	384
0.08	3.095	13.585	2.442	4.601	20.1	4.17	7.15	21.56	194	326	326	326
0.09	3.098	12.776	2.158	3.899	20.1	3.29	5.9	19.54	175	282	282	282
0.1	3.095	12.087	1.902	3.399	20.1	3.75	4.51	20.63	155	248	247	248
0.2	3.084	8.651	0.944	1.355	20.1	6.27	2.98	18.01	68	99	99	99
0.3	3.095	7.086	0.692	0.826	20.1	5.93	5.41	15.81	45	61	61	61
0.4	3.113	6.14	0.541	0.585	20.1	5.84	4.29	14.96	34	45	45	45
0.5	3.109	5.445	0.462	0.446	20.1	5.54	3.72	14.62	28	37	37	37
0.6	3.081	5.056	0.428	0.369	20.1	6.08	3.37	14.45	24	32	32	32
0.7	3.081	4.829	0.404	0.336	20.1	5.52	2.72	14.46	21	24	24	24
0.8	3.077	4.683	0.387	0.296	20.1	5.3	3.03	14.28	18	21	21	21
0.9	3.077	4.42	0.379	0.27	20.1	5.28	2.93	14.28	14	18	18	18
1	3.078	4.16	0.365	0.261	20.1	5.27	2.81	14.28	11	17	17	17

Figure 12.12 Experimental results of case study.

retail data set. The goal of this case study is to find the HUPs from the retail data set and analyze the performance of these algorithms. Therefore, the performance analysis provided may be useful to the researchers for their future research in this area to design more efficient HUP mining algorithms.

Business analysts are interested to know the information on all itemsets, particularly those contributing more than the specified profit limit. Here, profit limit is specified as minUtility in the utility mining. The itemsets with utility more than the specified minUtility are called the HUIs. HUP mining aims to find these patterns from a given input data set with a specified minimum utility threshold. In this case study, HUP mining is done using four algorithms, namely, GUIDE (LM), HUI-Miner, UMMI, and Two-Phase. All these algorithms are run on the same data set with minUtility ranges from 0.001 to 0.009, 0.01 to 0.09, and 0.1 to 1. In these experiments, the runtime, memory consumption and total HUIs generated by each algorithm are observed. There is another important measure we may consider, the number of candidates reduced with their pruning strategy, but this will be reflected in the aforementioned measures. These observations are shown in Figure 12.12. Results give the information of how many patterns there are in the specified profit range, that is, how many patterns are contributing to the specified percentage of profit and to the total profit of the transaction database. This information is useful to business analysts to make quality decisions in order to increase profit and other required parameters. From Figure 12.12, we can observe that the runtime and memory consumption of the GUIDE (LM) algorithm are approximately the same for all minimum utility threshold values. The main reason behind this is that it maintains all pattern information in its MUI-Tree irrespective of utility values. We can also observe the number of HUPs generated by four algorithms. The GUIDE (LM) algorithm HUI count is different from all others for all minimum utility threshold values because of limited potential patterns generated by transaction projection, which was already discussed in Section 12.4.1. We can also observe that the HUI count of UMMI and HUI-Miner is different from Two-Phase at low utility threshold values.

12.6 Performance Analysis

In this chapter, we have selected four important algorithms and the two algorithms, GUIDE (LM) and UMMI, with the objective of finding the HUPs. The primary contribution of this chapter is to show how the HUP mining tasks can be applied on the transaction databases in order to obtain useful information and to give a clear idea of how much memory and time are consumed in the process. It also gives an idea of how the performance of algorithms varies based on the data set characteristics. In this chapter, we have performed a case study by showing the application of HUP mining on retail transaction data by generating the number of HUPs for different minimum utility ranges. In this case study, we have made a performance comparison of the algorithms in terms of memory, runtime, and HUP count. From Figure 12.13a, b, and c, we observe that the GUIDE (LM) algorithm requires constant memory consumption (i.e., 20 MB) in all three ranges of minUtility. For any value of minUtility, the memory consumption is the same for this data set. The main reason for the constant memory consumption of this algorithm is that it builds the tree without considering minUtility value. Tree construction takes a maximum number of nodes $2^n - 1$, where n is the maximum number of distinct items in a transaction database. For example, consider the transaction database shown in Figure 12.1b in which the number of distinct items is 5, so the maximum number of nodes that it can create to store a transaction database is $2^5 - 1 = 31$, as shown in Figure 12.14. We observe that the two-phase algorithm consumes more memory than HUI-Miner and UMMI for the minUtility ranging from 0.001 to 0.01. UMMI consumes approximately the same memory as the two-phase algorithm. HUI-Miner consumes less memory for the minUtility

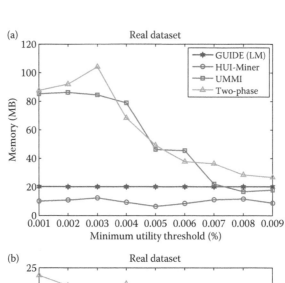

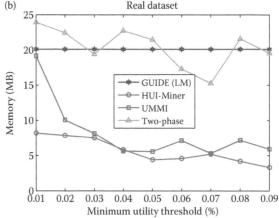

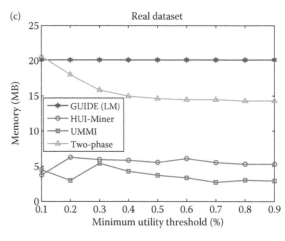

Figure 12.13   Memory consumption with various ranges of δ: (a) from 0.001% to 0.009%; (b) from 0.01% to 0.09%; (c) from 0.1% to 0.9%.

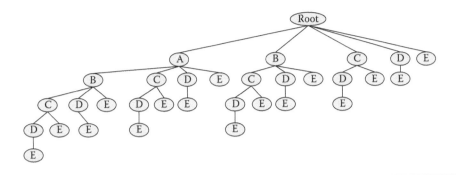

Figure 12.14   Complete MUI-tree.

ranging from 0.001 to 0.1. For the range from 0.2 to 1, its requirement is higher than UMMI. Figure 12.15a, b, and c shows that the runtime of the two-phase algorithm increases exponentially with decreasing mining utility value, and it becomes much less as compared to the other algorithms in the range from 0.1 to 1. The runtime of HUI-Miner is lower than the two-phase algorithm in low minUtility ranges, as shown in Figure 12.15a, but it is higher than all algorithms, as shown in Figure 12.15b and c. The UMMI has an overall runtime performance better than all other algorithms.

Figure 12.16a shows that HUI-Miner, UMMI, and two-phase algorithms do not generate the exact number of HUPs within the minUtility ranges. Figure 12.16b and c shows that for the minUtility from 0.04 to 1, these three algorithms generate the same number of HUPs. As far as the counts of HUPs of GUIDE (LM) are concerned, they are much less compared to that of others, and the difference decreases by increasing the minUtility value.

Why does the GUIDE (LM) algorithm generate a different and smaller number of patterns compared to the other three algorithms? From an n number of items in a transaction, HUI-Miner, UMMI, and two-phase algorithms generate a maximum of $2^n - 1$ number of patterns, but in GUIDE (LM), the procedure transaction projection (Shie et al. 2012) generates only $n(n + 1)/2$ number of patterns. So there is a huge number of pattern losses in GUIDE (LM). For example, a

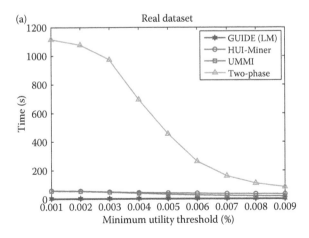

Figure 12.15   Runtime with various ranges of δ: (a) from 0.001% to 0.009%.

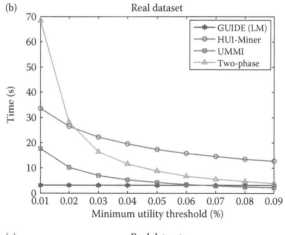

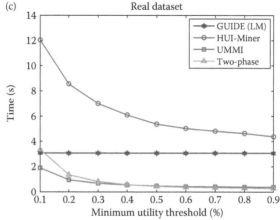

Figure 12.15 **(Continued) Runtime with various ranges of δ: (b) from 0.01% to 0.09%; (c) from 0.1% to 0.9%.**

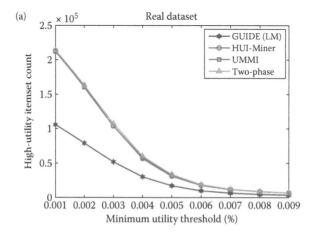

Figure 12.16 **High-utility itemset count with various ranges of δ: (a) from 0.001% to 0.009%.**

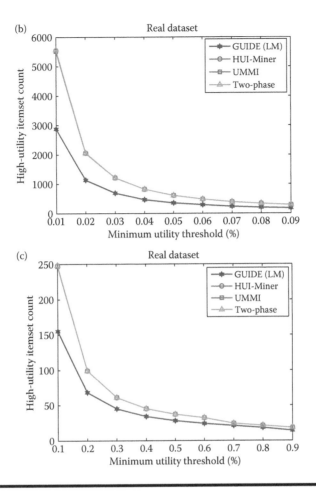

Figure 12.16   (Continued) High-utility itemset count with various ranges of δ: (b) from 0.01% to 0.09%; (c) from 0.1% to 0.9%.

transaction contains 5 distinct items; GUIDE (LM) generates 15 patterns, whereas others generate 31 patterns. If we consider all patterns, GUIDE (LM) definitely takes much memory and time to process.

12.7 Conclusions

In this chapter, we mainly focused on four important algorithms, namely, two-phase, HUI-Miner, GUIDE (LM), and UMMI, with the objective of finding the HUPs from real retail data sets. The primary contribution of this is to show how the HUP mining tasks can be applied on the transaction databases in order to obtain the useful information and to give a clear idea of how much memory and time are consumed to process. It also gives an idea of how the performance of algorithms varies based on the data set characteristics. We also performed a case study by showing the application of high-utility pattern mining on retail transaction data by generating the number of HUPs for different minimum utility ranges. We have made a performance comparison of the algorithms in terms of memory, runtime, and HUP count.

Here, the performance of the algorithms mainly depends on the pruning strategy, the number of database scans, and the summary structure used for maintaining HUPs. Hence, there is a huge scope in developing efficient algorithms with effective pruning strategy and fewer database scans to reduce the potential patterns. Therefore, the required memory and time will be minimized, and the quality of generated patterns will be improved.

References

Agrawal, R., and Srikant, R., 1994. Fast algorithms for mining association rules, in: *Proc. 20th Int. Conf. Very Large Data Bases, VLDB*, vol. 1215, 487–499.

Ahmed, C.F., Tanbeer, S.K., Jeong, B.S., and Choi, H.J., 2011. A framework for mining interesting high utility patterns with a strong frequency affinity, *Information Sciences*, 181 (21), 4878–4894.

Ahmed, C.F., Tanbeer, S.K., Jeong, B.S., and Lee, Y.K., 2009. An efficient candidate pruning technique for high utility pattern mining, in: *Advances in Knowledge Discovery and Data Mining*, Springer, 749–756.

Barber, B., and Hamilton, H.J., 2003. Extracting share frequent itemsets with infrequent subsets, *Data Mining and Knowledge Discovery*, 7 (2), 153–185.

Bashir, S., Jan, Z., and Baig, A.R., 2009. Fast algorithms for mining interesting frequent itemsets without minimum support, *arXiv preprint arXiv:0904.3319*.

Chan, R., Yang, Q., and Shen, Y.D., 2003. Mining high utility itemsets, in: *Data Mining, 2003. ICDM 2003. Third IEEE International Conference on*, IEEE, 19–26.

Chu, C.J., Tseng, V.S., and Liang, T., 2009. An efficient algorithm for mining high utility itemsets with negative item values in large databases, *Applied Mathematics and Computation*, 215 (2), 767–778.

Erwin, A., Gopalan, R.P., and Achuthan, N., 2007a. A bottom-up projection based algorithm for mining high utility itemsets, in: *Proceedings of the 2nd International Workshop on Integrating Artificial Intelligence and Data Mining*, vol. 84, Australian Computer Society, Inc., 3–11.

Erwin, A., Gopalan, R.P., and Achuthan, N., 2007b. Ctu-mine: An efficient high utility itemset mining algorithm using the pattern growth approach, in: *Computer and Information Technology, 2007. CIT 2007. 7th IEEE International Conference on*, IEEE, 71–76.

Erwin, A., Gopalan, R.P., and Achuthan, N., 2008. Efficient mining of high utility itemsets from large datasets, in: *Advances in Knowledge Discovery and Data Mining*, Springer, 554–561.

Han, J., Pei, J., and Yin, Y., 2000. Mining frequent patterns without candidate generation, *in: ACM SIGMOD Record*, vol. 29, 1–12.

Hong, T.P., Lee, C.H., and Wang, S.L., 2011. Effective utility mining with the measure of average utility, *Expert Systems with Applications*, 38 (7), 8259–8265.

Lan, G.C., Hong, T.P., and Tseng, V.S., 2010. Projection-based utility mining with an efficient indexing mechanism, in: *Technologies and Applications of Artificial Intelligence (TAAI), 2010 International Conference on*, IEEE, 137–141.

Lan, G.C., Hong, T.P., Tseng, V., and Chen, C.H., 2011. Using pruning and filtering strategies to speed-up projection-based utility mining, in: *System Science and Engineering (ICSSE), 2011 International Conference on*, IEEE, 400–404.

Le, B., Nguyen, H., Cao, T.A., and Vo, B., 2009. A novel algorithm for mining high utility itemsets, in: *Intelligent Information and Database Systems, 2009. ACIIDS 2009. First Asian Conference on*, IEEE, 13–17.

Lee, C.H., Lin, C.R., and Chen, M.S., 2001. Sliding-window filtering: An efficient algorithm for incremental mining, in: *Proceedings of the Tenth International Conference on Information and Knowledge Management*, ACM, 263–270.

Li, H.F., Huang, H.Y., Chen, Y.C., Liu, Y.J., and Lee, S.Y., 2008a. Fast and memory efficient mining of high utility itemsets in data streams, in: *Data Mining, 2008. ICDM'08. Eighth IEEE International Conference on*, IEEE, 881–886.

Li, Y.C., and Yeh, J.S., 2005. C.: Efficient algorithms for mining share-frequent itemsets, in: *In Proceedings of the 11th World Congress of Intl. Fuzzy Systems Association*, Citeseer.

Li, Y.C., Yeh, J.S., and Chang, C.C., 2008b. Isolated items discarding strategy for discovering high utility itemsets, *Data & Knowledge Engineering*, 64 (1), 198–217.

Lin, C., Hong, T., and Lu, W., 2009. High utility pattern trees, in: *The 20th Workshop on Object-Oriented Technology and Applications*.

Lin, C.W., Hong, T.P., and Lu, W.H., 2010a. Efficiently mining high average utility itemsets with a tree structure, in: *Intelligent Information and Database Systems*, Springer, 131–139.

Lin, C.W., Hong, T.P., and Lu, W.H., 2010b. Maintaining high utility pattern trees in dynamic databases, in: *Computer Engineering and Applications (ICCEA), 2010 Second International Conference on*, vol. 1, 304–308.

Lin, M.Y., Tu, T.F., and Hsueh, S.C., 2012. High utility pattern mining using the maximal itemset property and lexicographic tree structures, *Information Sciences*, 215, 1–14.

Liu, B., Hsu, W., Chen, S., and Ma, Y., 2000. Analyzing the subjective interestingness of association rules, *Intelligent Systems and Their Applications, IEEE*, 15 (5), 47–55.

Liu, M., and Qu, J., 2012. Mining high utility itemsets without candidate generation, in: *Proceedings of the 21st ACM International Conference on Information and Knowledge Management*, ACM, 55–64.

Liu, Y., Liao, W.K., and Choudhary, A., 2005a. A fast high utility itemsets mining algorithm, in: *Proceedings of the 1st International Workshop on Utility-Based Data Mining*, ACM, 90–99.

Liu, Y., Liao, W.K., and Choudhary, A., 2005b. A two-phase algorithm for fast discovery of high utility itemsets, in: *Advances in Knowledge Discovery and Data Mining*, Springer, 689–695.

Lu, S., Hu, H., and Li, F., 2001. Mining weighted association rules, *Intelligent Data Analysis*, 5 (3), 211–225.

Shie, B.E., Tseng, V.S., and Yu, P.S., 2010. Online mining of temporal maximal utility itemsets from data streams, in: *Proceedings of the 2010 ACM Symposium on Applied Computing*, ACM, 1622–1626.

Shie, B.E., Yu, P.S., and Tseng, V.S., 2012. Efficient algorithms for mining maximal high utility itemsets from data streams with different models, *Expert Systems with Applications*, 39 (17), 12947–12960.

Silberschatz, A., and Tuzhilin, A., 1996. What makes patterns interesting in knowledge discovery systems, *Knowledge and Data Engineering, IEEE Transactions on*, 8 (6), 970–974.

Tseng, V.S., Chu, C.J., and Liang, T., 2006. Efficient mining of temporal high utility itemsets from data streams, in: *Second International Workshop on Utility-Based Data Mining*, Citeseer, 18.

Tseng, V.S., Wu, C.W., Shie, B.E., and Yu, P.S., 2010. Up-growth: An efficient algorithm for high utility itemset mining, in: *Proceedings of the 16th ACM SIGKDD International Conference on Knowledge Discovery and Data Mining*, ACM, 253–262.

Wang, K., Zhou, S., and Han, J., 2002. Profit mining: From patterns to actions, in: *Advances in Database Technology EDBT 2002*, Springer, 70–87.

Wu, C.W., Fournier-Viger, P., Yu, P.S., and Tseng, V.S., 2011. Efficient mining of a concise and lossless representation of high utility itemsets, in: *Data Mining (ICDM), 2011 IEEE 11th International Conference on*, IEEE, 824–833.

Xian-Shan, Z., Liang, W., and Guang-Zhu, Y., 2010. Study of high motivation itemsets mining, in: *Computer Science and Information Technology (ICCSIT), 2010 3rd IEEE International Conference on*, vol. 5, 634–637.

Yao, H., and Hamilton, H.J., 2006. Mining itemset utilities from transaction databases, *Data & Knowledge Engineering*, 59 (3), 603–626.

Yao, H., Hamilton, H.J., and Butz, C.J., 2004. A foundational approach to mining itemset utilities from databases, in: *The 4th SIAM International Conference on Data Mining*, 482–486.

Yeh, J.S., Chang, C.Y., and Wang, Y.T., 2008. Efficient algorithms for incremental utility mining, in: *Proceedings of the 2nd International Conference on Ubiquitous Information Management and Communication*, ACM, 212–217.

Yu, G., Li, K., and Shao, S., 2008. Mining high utility itemsets in large high dimensional data, in: *Proceedings of the 1st International Conference on Forensic Applications and Techniques in Telecommunications, Information, and Multimedia and Workshop*, ICST (Institute for Computer Sciences, Social-Informatics and Telecommunications Engineering), 47.

Chapter 13

Bag of Riemannian Words for Virus Classification

Masoud Faraki and Mehrtash Harandi

Contents

The efficiency of covariance descriptors (CovDs) has been explored in several image/video categorization tasks. CovDs lie on Riemannian manifolds known as tensor manifolds. Therefore, the non-Euclidean geometry should be taken into account in devising inference methods that exploit them. In this chapter, we extend the conventional bag-of-words model from Euclidean space to non-Euclidean Riemannian manifolds. To this end, we elaborate on an intrinsic bag-of-Riemannian-words (BoRW) model, which takes into account the true geometry of tensors in obtaining its codebook and histogram. Experiments on challenging a virus texture data set show that the proposed BoRW on CovDs obtains notable improvements in discrimination accuracy, in comparison to popular bag-of-words models.

13.1 Introduction

In computer vision, texture classification has received significant attention with applications including, but not limited to, medical image analysis (Wu et al. 1992), object categorization (Zhang et al. 2007), industrial inspection, (Mäenpää et al. 2003), and content-based image retrieval (Belongie et al. 1998). Its challenge lies in the presence of intraclass variations as well as a wide variety of possible 3-D variations due to changes in camera pose and illumination directions.

Many effective texture recognition approaches rely on bag-of-words (BoW) image representation. In the BoW framework, texture is defined as a visual pattern characterized by the repetition of a few basic primitives, or *textons*, obtained by clustering local image features. The texture image is then represented as a histogram of the resulting textons. The BoW representation can be obtained from filter responses (Schmid 2001; Leung and Malik 2001), intensity-based features (Varma and Zisserman 2009; Lowe 2004; Lazebnik et al. 2005), or difference-based features (Ojala et al. 2002; Liu et al. 2012). In both cases, texture appearance features are captured under varying rotation and scale conditions in a complicated design.

In this work, we propose a natural method of combining multiple features in a unified framework for the task of virus classification. To this end, we utilize a region covariance descriptor (CovD) in a BoW framework. Tuzel et al. (2006) first introduced the CovD image descriptor. Then, it has been employed successfully for object tracking (Porikli et al. 2006), face recognition (Pang et al. 2008), analyzing diffusion tensor images (Pennec 2006), and action/gesture recognition (Sanin et al. 2013).

Utilizing CovDs as a region descriptor has several advantages: (1) It is a natural way of fusing different (correlated) features. (2) It is a low-dimensional descriptor and is independent of the size of the image. (3) Through the averaging process in its computation, the impact of the noisy samples is reduced. (4) Efficient methods for its fast computation exist.

Despite the aforementioned appealing properties, CovDs are symmetric positive-definite (SPD) matrices that form a connected Riemannian manifold. This makes developing inference methods on CovDs quite challenging. On the other hand, recent studies show that considering Riemannian geometry of SPD matrices leads to improved performances, as in Pennec (2006). In this work, we generalize the conventional BoW model to its Riemannian version and name it the bag-of-Riemannian-words (BoRW) model. The BoRW model takes into account the true Riemannian geometry of SPD matrices in obtaining its codebook and histogram. This is consistent with the recent trends in extending machineries from vector spaces to their Riemannian counterparts (Faraki et al. 2013; Harandi et al. 2012a, b; Sanin et al. 2013; Tuzel et al. 2008).

Contributions. In a nutshell, there are three main novelties in this work.

1. We propose the use of CovDs for texture classification.
2. We elaborate on an intrinsic BoRW model.
3. We compare and contrast our proposed algorithm against popular BoW methods, namely, local binary pattern (LBP)-BoW (Ojala et al. 2002) and scale-invariant feature transform (SIFT)-BoW (Lowe 2004), on a virus texture data set (Kylberg et al. 2011).

The rest of the chapter is organized as follows. Section 13.2 provides a brief review of some texture classification methods. Section 13.3 is dedicated to Riemannian geometry and serves as a grounding for follow-up sections. Section 13.4 discusses the intrinsic BORW model. In Section 13.5, we compare the performance of the proposed method with baseline approaches on virus texture data sets (Kylberg et al. 2011). The main findings and possible future directions are summarized in Section 13.6.

13.2 Related Work

The texton codebook–based approach has received a great deal of attention for texture classification. The underlying idea is to utilize local image structures with rich statistical properties to encode texture images. In the classification stage, the frequency histogram of the textons is taken as the image representation. A key issue of texton codebook–based approaches is how to describe local patches with the highest discriminative ability.

Several studies propose filter banks for analyzing texture images. Basically, special filters are devised in order to capture the texture properties under different conditions (e.g., rotation, pose, illumination). Notable examples are Leung and Malik (LM) and maximum response (MR) filter sets (Leung and Malik 2001; Varma and Zisserman 2005). The LM set consists of 48 filters at multiple scales and orientations. However, this leads to high-dimensional and rotation-sensitive descriptors. The MR filter bank consists of 38 isotropic and anisotropic filters at various orientations and scales. Only a few filters (eight or four) are selected for texture modeling by measuring their responses across orientations.

Nevertheless, directly using the intensities or differences in a local small patch can produce superior classification performance to filter banks with large support. A recent study by Varma and Zisserman (2009) demonstrates that joint distribution of intensity values over compact neighborhoods can outperform filter banks significantly.

The emergence of LBPs (Ojala et al. 2002) inspired several studies to explore difference-based descriptors for texture classification. An LBP operator converts a local image patch to a binary code by thresholding neighboring intensity values of a center pixel and reading the resulting values sequentially. In order to achieve rotation invariance, Ojala et al. (2002) propose to record the minimum code by considering all possible codes from circularly shifting the original code. Local ternary patterns (LTPs) and dominant local binary patterns (DLBP) are other successful variants of LBP (Tan and Triggs 2007; Liao et al. 2009). Very recently, a computationally efficient method has been proposed by Liu et al. (2012) for rotationally invariant texture classification. In the work of Liu et al. (2012), a set of random measurements from sorted pixel differences is used in a BoW model for classification.

In this work, we propose to create BoW models using CovDs, which encode the second-order statistics of textural information. We will show that BoW models on CovDs are astonishingly rich and can outperform complex machineries even with simple classifiers. Nevertheless, since CovDs are lying on a Riemannian manifold, generating BoW models is not trivial.

13.3 Differential Geometry Background

In this section, we introduce some basic notions of Riemannian geometry and manifold of real SPD matrices. Throughout this chapter, $\mathcal{S}_{++}^{d}$ denotes the space of $d \times d$ SPD matrices.

Before delving more into differential geometry, we formally define CovDs and, without loss of generality, we confine ourselves here to grayscale images. Let $I(x,y)$ be a $W \times H$ image and

$\mathbb{O} = \{\boldsymbol{o}_i\}_{i=1}^n, \boldsymbol{o}_i \in \mathbb{R}^d$ be a set of d-dimensional observations (feature vectors) extracted from $I(x,y)$. Then, the region $R \subset I$ can be represented by a $d \times d$ covariance matrix of the observations as

$$C_R = \frac{1}{n-1}\sum_{i=1}^n (\boldsymbol{o}_i - \mu)(\boldsymbol{o}_i - \mu)^T ,$$

$$\mu = \frac{1}{n}\sum_{i=1}^n \boldsymbol{o}_i .$$

(13.1)

The entries on the diagonal of matrix C_R are the variances of each feature and the nondiagonal entries are their pairwise correlations.

13.3.1 Riemannian Geometry

We start the discussion here by first introducing an analytic manifold. An *analytic manifold* $\mathcal{M}$ is a Hausdorff, topological space equipped with a complete atlas (Subbarao and Meer 2009). A set X and a family of its subsets T (including the empty set and X) form a *topological space* if the union and intersection of any finite number of sets in T also lie in T. As a simple example, one can consider the intervals on a real line. Let $X = \{(1,3)\}$ be the set of real numbers lying in the open interval (1,3) and $T = \{(1,3),(1,2),[2,3),\{2\},\{\}\}$. Then, T is called a *topology* of X. A *Hausdorff* (separated) space is a topological space such that any two points belonging to it can be separated by disjoint neighborhoods. So, in our example, the set X is a Hausdorff space. A complete *atlas* is a set of all smoothly overlapping neighborhood-mapping (U, ϕ) pairs, such that U is an open interval on the m-dimensional manifold $\mathcal{M}$ and ϕ is a one-to-one and onto mapping (also called homeomorphic) from U to some Euclidean space $\mathbb{R}^m$. Therefore, a manifold can be understood as a (topological) space that resembles Euclidean space at a small neighborhood of each point. An intuitive example of manifold is the surface of a sphere that is not a vector space but can be perceived flat (Euclidean) in a small neighborhood of each point of the surface.

The *tangent space* of the manifold is a generalization of the directional derivatives in Euclidean space. Let $\mathcal{M}$ denote a manifold and $\boldsymbol{P} \in \mathcal{M}$; then, the tangent space at point $\boldsymbol{P}$ is denoted by $T_P(\mathcal{M})$ and defined as the vector space of the tangent vectors to all the possible curves passing by the point $\boldsymbol{P}$. More formally, assume that the set $\{\boldsymbol{\rho}^i\}_{i=1}^n$ denotes a local coordinate system in $\mathbb{R}^n$. The tangent space at point $\boldsymbol{P}$ is then the vector space spanned by the differential operators $\frac{\partial}{\partial\rho^1}, \frac{\partial}{\partial\rho^2}, \cdots, \frac{\partial}{\partial\rho^n}$ and can be seen geometrically as the tangent vector to the ith $(1 \leqslant i \leqslant n)$ coordinate curve (see Figure 13.1 for an illustration). For analytic manifolds, the tangent space is a vector space of the same dimension and, hence, is an important notion in the study of the analytic manifolds.

On the manifold, a *Riemannian metric* is defined as a continuous collection of dot products on the tangent space $T_P(\mathcal{M})$ at each $\boldsymbol{P} \in \mathcal{M}$. Given the basis set $\{\boldsymbol{\rho}^i\}_{i=1}^n$ and an inner product $\langle,\rangle_P$ on the tangent space $T_P(\mathcal{M})$, the Riemannian metric is defined by positive-definite matrices $\boldsymbol{G}(\boldsymbol{P}) = [g_{ij}(\boldsymbol{P})]$ where each element is given by $g_{ij}(\boldsymbol{P}) = \langle \frac{\partial}{\partial\rho^i}, \frac{\partial}{\partial\rho^j} \rangle_P$ (i.e., the dot product of the tangent vector to the coordinate curves).

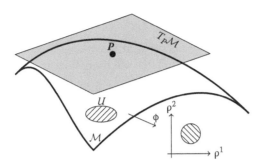

Figure 13.1   Illustration of the tangent space at point *P* and a neighborhood-mapping (*U*,φ) pair on a Riemannian manifold $\mathcal{M}$.

The Riemannian metric of the manifold enables us to define geometric notions on the manifold such as lengths and angles. The *geodesic distance* between two points on the manifold is defined as the length of the shortest curve connecting the two points. The shortest curves are known as geodesics (also called Riemannian distance) and are analogous to straight lines in Euclidean space.

A *Riemannian manifold* ($\mathcal{M}$,g) consists of the analytic manifold $\mathcal{M}$ and its associated metric $g_X(.,.): \mathcal{M} \times \mathcal{M} \to \mathcal{R}$ that varies smoothly on $T_X(\mathcal{M})$. The function g has a symmetric, positive definite bilinear form on each $P \in T_X(\mathcal{M})$. Also, it is chosen to provide robustness to some geometrical transformations.

13.3.2 *Geometry of SPD Matrices*

The space of real $d \times d$ SPD matrices $\mathcal{S}^d_{++}$, forms a Lie group. A Lie group is an algebraic group with a manifold structure (i.e., more algebraic structure than a manifold). It is natural to use the language of Riemannian manifolds and all the related concepts of differential geometry when discussing $\mathcal{S}^d_{++}$.

The *affine-invariant Riemannian metric* (AIRM) (Pennec 2006) is the most popular choice to handle the non-Euclidean structure of SPD matrices and is shown to be advantageous for several applications (Tuzel et al. 2008). For $P \in \mathcal{S}^d_{++}$ and two tangent vectors $\Delta, \Gamma \in T_P\mathcal{M}$, the AIRM is defined as

$$\langle \Delta, \Gamma \rangle_P \triangleq \langle P^{-1/2}\Delta P^{-1/2}, P^{-1/2}\Gamma P^{-1/2} \rangle$$
$$= \text{Tr}(P^{-1}\Delta P^{-1}\Gamma). \tag{13.2}$$

For two $X, Y \in \mathcal{S}^d_{++}$, the geodesic distance induced by AIRM is

$$\delta_R(X,Y) = \left\| \log(X^{-1/2}YX^{-1/2}) \right\|_F, \tag{13.3}$$

where $\|.\|_F$ denotes the Frobenius norm and $\log(\cdot)$ is the matrix principal logarithm. The invariance to affine transformations for Equation 13.3 is defined as $\delta^2_R(X,Y) = \delta^2_R(AXA^T, AYA^T)$ for an arbitrary $d \times d$ real invertible matrix A.

13.4 Bag of Riemannian Words

In computer vision, the BoW approach has been the widely used way of image representation in different applications including texture classification (Leung and Malik 2001; Varma and Zisserman 2009), video retrieval (Sivic and Zisserman 2003), and scene categorization (Fei-Fei and Perona 2005). In this section, we discuss how a conventional BoW model can be extended to incorporate the Riemannian structure of CovD descriptors.

In the standard BoW representation, a feature detector first abstracts image information by applying various tests at every image point in order to extract salient image patches. Two popular detectors are *Harris–Laplace* (Mikolajczyk and Schmid 2004) and *maximally stable extremal regions* (MSERs) (Matas et al. 2004). After feature detection, a feature descriptor converts the extracted patches to numerical vectors. A descriptor is usually selected to have the desired insensitivity to intensity, scale, rotation, and affine variations for the application on hand. For example, SIFT (Lowe 2004) has shown to be superior to many descriptors (Mikolajczyk and Schmid 2005), and rotation-invariant feature transform (RIFT) and SPIN (Lazebnik et al. 2005) have obtained good performances in the context of texture classification. Descriptors are then grouped into a codebook, with those that are similar assigned into the same code word. The final descriptor is a sparse vector (known as a *histogram*) of occurrence counts of a codebook of local descriptors.

To devise a BoRW model, we should address two subproblems:

1. Given a set of points on an SPD manifold (each point on the manifold corresponds to a CovD), how can a Riemannian codebook be trained?
2. Given a Riemannian codebook, how can a histogram be obtained for a query image?

13.4.1 Learning the Riemannian Codebook

Learning a codebook is crucial to our proposed BoRW method. Formally, given a set of training samples $\mathbb{X} = \{X_i\}_{i=1}^m, X_i \in \mathcal{S}_{++}^d$, we seek to estimate k clusters $C_1, C_2, \ldots, C_k$ with centers $\{S_i\}_{i=1}^k$ such that the sum of squared distances over all clusters is minimized, that is,

$$\min_{C_1, C_2, \ldots, C_k} \sum_{i=1}^k \sum_{X_j \in C_i} \delta^2(X_j, S_i), \tag{13.4}$$

where δ is a metric on $\mathcal{S}_{++}^d$.

A straightforward way of learning a codebook over SPD matrices is to vectorize them and apply a k-means algorithm on the resulting vectors. In this case, clusters are determined by computing the arithmetic mean of the nearest training vectors to that cluster. Nevertheless, several studies argue against exploiting Euclidean geometry and the vector form of SPD matrices for inference (Pennec 2006; Tuzel et al. 2008). For example, as shown by Pennec (2006), the determinant of the weighted mean could become greater than samples' determinants, an undesirable outcome known as swelling effect (Arsigny et al. 2007). Therefore, we seek possibilities to consider the geometry of SPD matrices in creating the codebook.

A codebook can be obtained by an intrinsic k-means algorithm that does not rely on the embedding Euclidean space and depends only on the manifold. The core ingredient of an intrinsic k-means algorithm is the Karcher mean (Pennec 2006). Given an abstract manifold $\mathcal{M}$, the classical general-ization of the Euclidean mean for a set of points $\{X_i\}_{i=1}^m, X_i \in \mathcal{M}$ is given by the Karcher mean (also referred as Fréchet mean) as the point minimizing the following metric dispersion:

$$\arg\min_X \sum_{i=1}^m \delta_g^2(X_i, X), \tag{13.5}$$

where $\delta_g : \mathcal{M} \times \mathcal{M} \to \mathbb{R}^+$ is the associated geodesic distance function.

The discussion of the existence and uniqueness value of the Karcher mean is given in Pennec (2006). Since, at the optimum point, the gradient is zero, a gradient descent algorithm can be uti-lized to obtain the mean value. The details of computing the Karcher mean over SPD manifolds are given in Algorithm 13.1.

Algorithm 13.1: Karcher Mean Algorithm over $\mathcal{S}_{++}^d$

Input:

- A set of points $\left\{X_i\right\}_{i=1}^m$ on the underlying $\mathcal{S}_{++}^d$ manifold
- *maxIter*, maximum number of iterations

Output:

- The sample Karcher mean μ
  1. Let $\mu^{(0)}$ be an initial estimate of the Karcher mean, for example, by selecting a sample from $\{X_i\}_{i=1}^m$ randomly.
  2. **while** $t < maxIter$ **do**
  3.   For each point X_i, compute the tangent vector v_i on the current estimate of the Karcher mean, that is, $v_i = \log_{\mu^{(t)}}(X_i)$.
  4.   Compute the average tangent vector $\bar{v} = \dfrac{1}{k} \sum_{i=1}^m v_i$.
  5.   If $\|\bar{v}\|_2$ is small, then $\mu = \exp_{\mu^{(t)}}(\bar{v})$ and break the while. Else, compute the new estimate of Karcher mean $\mu^{(t+1)}$ by moving along the average tangent direction, that is, $\mu^{(t+1)} = \exp_{\mu^{(t)}}(\varepsilon\bar{v})$, where $\varepsilon > 0$ is small step size.
  6. $t \leftarrow t + 1$.
  7. **end while**

Algorithm 13.2: Intrinsic k-Means Algorithm over $\mathcal{S}_{++}^d$ for Learning the Codebook

Input:

- Training set $\mathbb{X} = \left\{X_i\right\}_{i=1}^N$ from the underlying $\mathcal{S}_{++}^d$ manifold
- *nIter*, the number of iterations

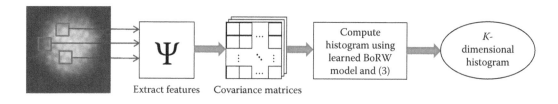

Extract features   Covariance matrices

Figure 13.2   Block diagram showing computations of BoRW histogram.

Output:

- Codebook $\mathbb{S} = \{S_i\}_{i=1}^k, S_i \in \mathcal{S}_{++}^d$
  1. Initialize the dictionary $\mathbb{S} = \{S_i\}_{i=1}^k$ by selecting N samples from X randomly.
  2. **for** $t = 1 \rightarrow nIter$ **do**
  3. Assign each point X_i to its nearest cluster in $\mathbb{S}$ by computing $\delta_R(X_i, S_j) = \left\| \log(X_i^{-1/2} S_j X_i^{-1/2}) \right\|_F$, $1 \le i \le N$, $1 \le j \le k$.
  4. Recompute cluster centers $\{S_i\}_{i=1}^k$ by Karcher mean algorithm.
  5. **end for**

Similar to its Euclidean counterpart, intrinsic k-means solves Equation 13.4 by using an expectation maximisation (EM)-based approach. The algorithm starts by selecting k points from $\mathbb{X}$ randomly as the cluster centers. In the E-step, we assign each of the points of the data set to the nearest cluster center. Then in the M-step, the cluster centers are recomputed using the Karcher mean. The procedure is summarized in Algorithm 13.2.

13.4.2 Encoding Local Image Descriptors

Having a codebook, $\mathbb{S} = \{S_i\}_{i=1}^k$, at our disposal, we seek to group a set of CovDs, $\mathbb{Q} = \{Q_i\}_{i=1}^p$, extracted from a query image, in order to find a discriminative representation. We follow the simplest form of BoW representation and hard-assign local descriptors to their closest code words. This obviously requires $p \times k$ comparisons. Comparisons are done using the AIRM, (i.e., Equation 13.2) as it is invariant to affine transforms. The resulting histogram is ℓ_2 normalized in the end. The conceptual diagram of a BoRW histogram computation is illustrated in Figure 13.2.

13.5 Empirical Evaluations

In this section, we compare and contrast the performance of the proposed BoRW against two baseline methods, namely, bag of SIFT words (SIFT-BoW) and bag of LBP words (LBP-BoW), for the task of texture categorization.

In our experiments, a set of small overlapping blocks is extracted from images, and the CovD for each block is obtained. The amount of overlap for consecutive blocks is 75%. Before delving into experiments, we elaborate how a descriptive representation of textures can be attained by CovDs. To this end, from each texture image, a set of CovDs is extracted and then passed to BoRW to generate an image histogram. To generate CovDs from an image, a feature vector is assigned to each pixel in the image through using a Gabor filter bank. More specifically, each pixel is described by

$$F_{(x,y)} = \left[I(x,y), x, y, \left|\frac{\partial I}{\partial x}\right|, \left|\frac{\partial I}{\partial y}\right|, \left|\frac{\partial^2 I}{\partial x^2}\right|, \left|\frac{\partial^2 I}{\partial y^2}\right|, \left|G_{(0,0)}(x,y)\right|, \left|G_{(0,1)}(x,y)\right|, \ldots, \left|G_{(u,v)}(x,y)\right| \right]$$

where $I(x,y)$ is the intensity value at position x,y; $\left|\frac{\partial I}{\partial x}\right|$, $\left|\frac{\partial I}{\partial y}\right|$ are the magnitude of gradients along the x and y directions; $\left|\frac{\partial^2 I}{\partial x^2}\right|$, $\left|\frac{\partial I^2}{\partial y^2}\right|$ are the magnitude of Laplacians along the x and y directions; and $G_{(u,v)}$ (x,y) is the response of a 2-D Gabor wavelet (Lee 1996) centered at x,y with orientation u and scale v:

$$G_{(u,v)}(x,y) = \frac{k_v^2}{4\pi^2} \sum_{t,s} e^{-\frac{k_v^2}{8\pi^2}\left((x-s)^2+(y-t)^2\right)}$$

(13.6)

$$\left(e^{ik_v\left((x-t)\cos(\theta_u)+(y-s)\sin(\theta_u)\right)} - e^{-2\pi^2} \right),$$

with $k_v = \frac{1}{\sqrt{2^{v-1}}}$ and $\theta_u = \frac{\pi u}{8}$.

We extracted Gabor wavelets at four orientations and three scales. Therefore, each region is described by a 19 × 19 covariance matrix formed from these features (intensity, 2 positions, 4 image gradients, and 12 Gabor features). To classify histograms, support vector machines (SVMs) (Bishop 2006) were employed.

13.5.1 Evaluation on Virus Texture Data Set

For our evaluations, we have used a virus texture data set (Kylberg et al. 2011). The virus images are presented in 15 different classes with 100 samples per class. The images are formed from a transmission electron microscopy (TEM) technique and resampled to 41 × 41 pixel grayscale images. This data set is challenging due to variations of viruses in size and shape. A binary mask is provided for the whole data set. Tenfold validation is considered as the test protocol here. We emphasize that only foreground pixels will be considered in computing the CovD of each block. Examples of this data set are shown in Figure 13.3.

We compare the proposed BoRW approach against baseline texture categorization systems, SIFT-BoW (Lowe 2004) and LBP-BoW (Ojala et al. 2002), on the virus texture data set (Kylberg et al. 2011).

SIFT is fundamental to many of the core computer vision problems. The SIFT feature descriptor approach transforms an input image into a large collection of local feature vectors. Each of the extracted feature vectors is robust to any scaling, rotation, or translation of the input image and moderately robust to perspective transformations and illumination variations. In the original formulation, the SIFT descriptor consists of four stages. In the first stage, a set of stable key points is extracted from an image in scale space using the difference of Gaussians (DoG) technique at multiple scales. The key points are local extrema pixels of the DoG within the neighboring points

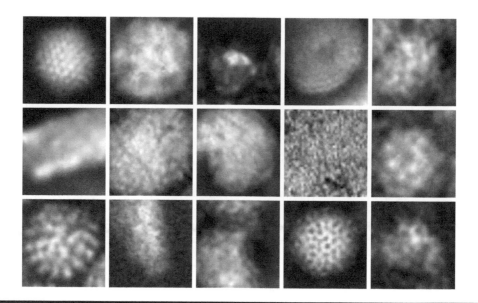

Figure 13.3 Sample images drawn randomly from virus texture data set. Each image is taken from one category. (With kind permission from Springer Science+Business Media: *Progress in Pattern Recognition, Image Analysis, Computer Vision*, Virus texture analysis using local binary patterns and radial density profiles, 2011, Kylberg, G. et al.)

at the same, up, and down one scales. Next, key points are added with an offset coming from interpolating a quadratic Taylor expansion of the DoG (at the key point location) to obtain more accurate location. Also, low-contrast or poorly localized points along the edges (which might be unstable) are rejected from the key points' list. To this end, Lowe (2004) formulated a criterion in terms of the ratio between the eigenvalues of the Hessian matrix of the input image's scale-space representation. In the third stage, a histogram of local gradients in eight directions around the interest point is computed. Then, a dominant orientation is determined from the orientations of the gradient vectors in the neighborhood. It is used for orienting the grid over which the histogram is computed to achieve rotational invariance. Finally, for each of the eight orientation planes, the image gradients are sampled over a 4 × 4 grid and weighted by a Gaussian window function. This results in a 128-dimensional feature vector.

LBPs have proved to be effective mostly for texture classification (Ojala et al. 2002). An LBP operator probes image pixels locally and compares the intensity value at the central pixel with the neighboring pixels in a circle. An eight-digit binary number is generated by assigning 1 where the center pixel's value is greater than the neighbor's value and 0 otherwise. The codes with more than two transitions from 0 to 1 (or equivalently, 1 to 0) are considered nonuniform and rejected. To obtain rotation invariance, codes are shifted circularly, and the minimum number is preserved as the final descriptor. Finally, a histogram of the LBP numbers is constructed in the local patch. The resulting histograms are concatenated in the end.

In Table 13.1, we compare our proposed BoRW against SIFT-BoW and LBP-BoW methods for a specific codebook size. As shown in the table, our BoRW significantly outperforms the baseline methods. We have used the functions from Vedaldi and Fulkerson (2008) for LBP-BoW and SIFT-BoW. We note that the same BoW configurations and classifiers were used in the experiments.

Table 13.1 Comparisons Between the Proposed BoRW Method and Baseline BoW Methods on Virus Texture Data Set

Method	Accuracy
SIFT-BoW, Lowe (2004)	40.1
LBP-BoW, Ojala et al. (2002)	56.0
Proposed BoRW	67.5

Source: With kind permission from Springer Science+Business Media: *Progress in Pattern Recognition, Image Analysis, Computer Vision*, Virus texture analysis using local binary patterns and radial density profiles, 2011, Kylberg, G. et al. $K = 512$.

Note: Mean accuracy is reported.

13.5.2 Efficiency of CovD and Effect of Codebook Size

We justify our choice of the CovD descriptor and analyze the performance of BoRW for texture categorization in the following. To this end, we compare the performance of BoRW against two aforementioned BoW methods for various codebook sizes in Figure 13.4. For all codebook sizes, BoRW outperforms the SIFT-BoW and LBP-BoW significantly. The difference between BoRW and SIFT-BoW exceeds 10 percentage points for a codebook size of 1024.

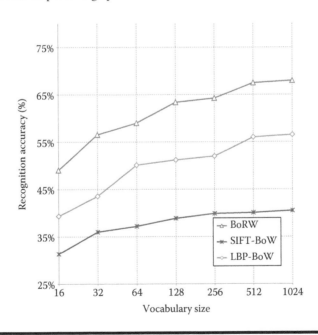

Figure 13.4 Performance versus size of codebook for BoRW and baseline BoW methods on virus texture data set. (With kind permission from Springer Science+Business Media: *Progress in Pattern Recognition, Image Analysis, Computer Vision*, Virus texture analysis using local binary patterns and radial density profiles, 2011, Kylberg, G. et al.)

13.6 Conclusions

In this chapter, we proposed an approach to extend the popular BoW models to a special class of non-Euclidean spaces, the space of SPD matrices formed by CovDs (Tuzel et al. 2006). To this end, we elaborated on how a Riemannian codebook could be obtained from CovDs and devised an intrinsic extension of conventional BoW using Riemannian geometry of SPD matrices. The main motivation comes from previous studies that demonstrate benefits of utilizing true geometry of the space and the need for intrinsic tools for inference (Arsigny et al. 2007; Pennec 2006). Texture classification experiments on challenging a virus texture data set (Kylberg et al. 2011) indicate that the proposed BoRW approach obtains notable improvements in discrimination accuracy compared to two popular BoW methods, namely, SIFT-BoW (Lowe 2004) and LBP-BoW (Ojala et al. 2002). We believe that our work motivates future research on extending well-known machine learning inference tools to their non-Euclidean versions. Moreover, we are keen to explore the efficiency of our proposal on different categorization tasks and assess its performance against Euclidean counterparts.

References

Arsigny, V., P. Fillard, X. Pennec, and N. Ayache. Geometric means in a novel vector space structure on symmetric positive-definite matrices. *SIAM Journal on Matrix Analysis and Applications*, 29(1):328–347, 2007.

Belongie, S., C. Carson, H. Greenspan, and J. Malik. Color- and texture-based image segmentation using em and its application to content-based image retrieval. In *Computer Vision, 1998. Sixth International Conference on*, pp. 675–682. IEEE, 1998.

Bishop, C. M. *Pattern Recognition and Machine Learning*. Springer, New York, 2006.

Faraki, M., M. T. Harandi, A. Wiliem, and B. C. Lovell. Fisher tensors for classifying human epithelial cells. *Pattern Recognition*, 47:2348–2359, 2013.

Fei-Fei, L., and P. Perona. A bayesian hierarchical model for learning natural scene categories. In *Computer Vision and Pattern Recognition, 2005. CVPR 2005. IEEE Computer Society Conference on*, volume 2, pp. 524–531. IEEE, 2005.

Harandi, M. T., C. Sanderson, R. Hartley, and B. C. Lovell. Sparse coding and dictionary learning for symmetric positive definite matrices: A kernel approach. In *Proc. European Conference on Computer Vision (ECCV)*, pp. 216–229. Springer, 2012a.

Harandi, M. T., C. Sanderson, A. Wiliem, and B. C. Lovell. Kernel analysis over Riemannian manifolds for visual recognition of actions, pedestrians and textures. In *IEEE Workshop on the Applications of Computer Vision (WACV)*, pp. 433–439, 2012b.

Kylberg, G., M. Uppström, and I.-M. Sintorn. Virus texture analysis using local binary patterns and radial density profiles. In *Progress in Pattern Recognition, Image Analysis, Computer Vision, and Applications*, pp. 573–580. Springer, Berlin Heidelberg, 2011.

Lazebnik, S., C. Schmid, and J. Ponce. A sparse texture representation using local affine regions. *Pattern Analysis and Machine Intelligence, IEEE Transactions on*, 27(8):1265–1278, 2005.

Lee, T. S. Image representation using 2d Gabor wavelets. *IEEE Transactions on Pattern Analysis and Machine Intelligence*, 18(10):959–971, 1996.

Leung, T., and J. Malik. Representing and recognizing the visual appearance of materials using three-dimensional textons. *International Journal of Computer Vision (IJCV)*, 43(1):29–44, 2001.

Liao, S., M. W. K. Law, and A. C. S. Chung. Dominant local binary patterns for texture classification. *Image Processing, IEEE Transactions on*, 18(5):1107–1118, 2009.

Liu, L., P. Fieguth, D. Clausi, and G. Kuang. Sorted random projections for robust rotation-invariant texture classification. *Pattern Recognition*, 45(6):2405–2418, 2012.

Lowe, D. G. Distinctive image features from scale-invariant keypoints. *International Journal of Computer Vision (IJCV)*, 60(2):91–110, 2004.

Mäenpää, T., M. Turtinen, and M. Pietikäinen. Real-time surface inspection by texture. *Real-Time Imaging*, 9(5):289–296, 2003.

Matas, J., O. Chum, M. Urban, and T. Pajdla. Robust wide-baseline stereo from maximally stable extremal regions. *Image and Vision Computing*, 22(10):761–767, 2004.

Mikolajczyk, K., and C. Schmid. Scale and affine invariant interest point detectors. *International Journal of Computer Vision*, 60(1):63–86, 2004.

Mikolajczyk, K., and C. Schmid. A performance evaluation of local descriptors. *Pattern Analysis and Machine Intelligence, IEEE Transactions on*, 27(10):1615–1630, 2005.

Ojala, T., M. Pietikainen, and T. Maenpaa. Multiresolution gray-scale and rotation invariant texture classification with local binary patterns. *IEEE Transactions on Pattern Analysis and Machine Intelligence*, 24(7):971–987, 2002.

Pang, Y., Y. Yuan, and X. Li. Gabor-based region covariance matrices for face recognition. *IEEE Transactions on Circuits and Systems for Video Technology*, 18(7):989–993, 2008.

Pennec, X. Intrinsic statistics on Riemannian manifolds: Basic tools for geometric measurements. *Journal of Mathematical Imaging and Vision*, 25(1):127–154, 2006.

Porikli, F., O. Tuzel, and P. Meer. Covariance tracking using model update based on Lie algebra. In *Proc. IEEE Conference on Computer Vision and Pattern Recognition (CVPR)*, pp. 728–735, 2006.

Sanin, A., C. Sanderson, M. T. Harandi, and B. C. Lovell. Spatio-temporal covariance descriptors for action and gesture recognition. In *IEEE Workshop on the Applications of Computer Vision (WACV)*, pp. 103–110, 2013.

Schmid, C. Constructing models for content-based image retrieval. In *Computer Vision and Pattern Recognition, 2001. CVPR 2001. Proceedings of the 2001 IEEE Computer Society Conference on*, volume 2, pp. II–39. IEEE, 2001.

Sivic, J., and A. Zisserman. Video google: A text retrieval approach to object matching in videos. In *Computer Vision, 2003. Proceedings. Ninth IEEE International Conference on*, pages 1470–1477. IEEE, 2003.

Subbarao, R., and P. Meer. Nonlinear mean shift over riemannian manifolds. *International Journal of Computer Vision*, 84(1):1–20, 2009.

Tan, X., and B. Triggs. Enhanced local texture feature sets for face recognition under difficult lighting conditions. In *Analysis and Modeling of Faces and Gestures*, pp. 168–182. Springer, Berlin Heidelberg, 2007.

Tuzel, O., F. Porikli, and P. Meer. Region covariance: A fast descriptor for detection and classification. In *Proc. European Conference on Computer Vision (ECCV)*, volume 3952, pp. 589–600, 2006.

Tuzel, O., F. Porikli, and P. Meer. Pedestrian detection via classification on Riemannian manifolds. *IEEE Transactions on Pattern Analysis and Machine Intelligence*, 30(10):1713–1727, 2008.

Varma, M., and A. Zisserman. A statistical approach to texture classification from single images. *International Journal of Computer Vision (IJCV)*, 62(1–2):61–81, 2005.

Varma, M., and A. Zisserman. A statistical approach to material classification using image patch exemplars. *IEEE Transactions on Pattern Analysis and Machine Intelligence*, 31(11):2032–2047, 2009.

Vedaldi, A., and B. Fulkerson. VLFeat: An open and portable library of computer vision algorithms. Available at http://www.vlfeat.org/, 2008.

Wu, C.-M., Y.-C. Chen, and K.-S. Hsieh. Texture features for classification of ultrasonic liver images. *Medical Imaging, IEEE Transactions on*, 11(2):141–152, 1992.

Zhang, J., M. Marszałek, S. Lazebnik, and C. Schmid. Local features and kernels for classification of texture and object categories: A comprehensive study. *International Journal of Computer Vision*, 73(2):213–238, 2007.

Chapter 14

Normalized Ordinal Distance: A Performance Metric for Ordinal, Probabilistic-Ordinal, or Partial-Ordinal Classification Problems

Mohammad Hasan Bahari and Hugo Van Hamme

Contents

In this chapter, a novel application-independent performance metric for ordinal, probabilistic-ordinal, and partial-ordinal classification problems is introduced. Conventional performance metrics for ordinal classification problems, such as mean absolute error of consecutive integer labels and ranked probability score, are difficult to interpret and may lead to fraudulent results about the true performance of the classifier. In this chapter, first, the ordinal distance between two arbitrary vectors in Euclidean space is introduced. Then, a new performance metric, namely, normalized ordinal distance, is proposed based on the introduced ordinal distance. This performance metric is conceptually simple, computationally inexpensive, and application-independent. The advantages of the proposed method over the conventional approaches and its different characteristics are shown using several numerical examples.

14.1 Introduction

A large number of real-world classification problems are ordinal, where there is intrinsic ordering between the categories. For example, in quality prediction systems, the task is to categorize the quality of a product into bad, good, or excellent (Erdural 2006). In human age group recognition from speech or images, the categories can be child, young, middle-aged, and senior (Bahari and Van hamme 2011b; Li et al. 2013). In the classification of therapeutic success, the classes are good recovery, moderate disability, severe disability, and fatal outcome (Cardoso and da Costa 2007). In all ordinal classification problems (C_O), the class labels are ordinal numbers, that is, there is intrinsic ordering between the categories.

Probabilistic-ordinal and partial-ordinal classification problems, labeled C_O^{Pr} and C_O^{Pa}, respectively, are well-known generalizations of the C_O. In C_O^{Pr}, for a test data point, the classifier calculates the probability of belonging to each category. In C_O^{Pa}, instead of the crisp class labels, each data point has a degree of membership to every class (Verwaeren et al. 2012). These types of problems, explained in Sections 14.2.2 and 14.2.3 in detail, can be found in many domains, such as natural language processing, social network analysis, bioinformatics, and agriculture (Verwaeren et al. 2012).

Scientists have proposed different methods to solve C_O, C_O^{Pr}, and C_O^{Pa} (Verwaeren et al. 2012; McCullagh 1980; Chu and Keerthi 2007; Cheng et al. 2008; Chu and Ghahramani 2004; Shevade and Chu 2006). For example, McCullagh (1980) introduce an ordinal classifier, namely, the proportional odds model (POM), based on logistic regression. In the work of Chu and Keerthi (2007), C_O is addressed using a generalization of support vector machines (SVMs), namely, support vector ordinal regression (SVOR). A neural network approach for the C_O is suggested in the work of Cheng et al. (2008). Chu and Ghahramani (2004) suggest Gaussian processes for C_O.

In the work of Verwaeren et al. (2012), kernel-based proportional odds models is introduced to solve the C_O^{Pa}.

To measure the performance of these classifiers, different approaches have been suggested. For example, mean zero–one error (E_{mzo}) and mean absolute error of consecutive integer labels $\left(E_{ma}^{cil}\right)$ are widely applied to measure the performance of the classifiers in C_O (Chu and Keerthi 2007; Cheng et al. 2008; Chu and Ghahramani 2004; Shevade and Chu 2006). However, none of these methods are applicable to C_O^{Pr} and C_O^{Pa}. The percentage of correctly fuzzy classified instances (P_{cfci}) and average deviation (E_{ad}) have been suggested to measure the classifier performance in C_O^{Pr} and C_O^{Pa} (Verwaeren et al. 2012; Manel et al. 2002; Van Broekhoven et al. 2007; Mouton et al. 2009). The main drawback of P_{cfci} is that it does not consider the order of categories (Manel et al. 2002; Van Broekhoven et al. 2007). E_{ad} suggests a simple idea to solve this problem (Van Broekhoven et al. 2007; Mouton et al. 2009). Although E_{ad} is attractive from several aspects, the interpretation of its results is difficult, because the range of its output depends on the application. The same difficulty is observed in E_{ma}^{cil}. Application dependency makes the interpretation of E_{ma}^{cil} and E_{ad} very challenging. The average of ranked probability scores (E_{rps}) are also applied as a performance metric in C_O^{Pr} and C_O^{Pa} (Bougeault 2003; Murphy 1969). In this method, the order of categories is important, and the range of the output is fixed between 0 and 1. This method can be applied to C_O, C_O^{Pr}, and C_O^{Pa}. However, analysis reveals that E_{rps} overestimates the performance of classifiers in many situations. This issue, which leads to an erroneous interpretation of classifier performance, is illustrated by some numerical examples in Section 14.5.

In this chapter, we investigate different characteristics of these performance metrics, and finally, a novel application-independent performance metric, namely, normalized ordinal distance (OD), $\left(E_{nod}^{p}\right)$, is introduced. The MATLAB code of the suggested approach, which can be applied to all three types of considered problems C_O, C_O^{Pr}, and C_O^{Pa}, can be downloaded from our website.*

This chapter is organized as follows. In Section 14.2, the mathematical formulations of C_O, C_O^{Pr}, and C_O^{Pa} are presented. In Section 14.3, five different conventional performance metrics are explained. The proposed performance metric is elaborated in Section 14.4. In Section 14.5, the effectiveness of the proposed approach is illustrated using some numerical examples. The chapter ends with a conclusion in Section 14.6.

14.2 Problem Formulation

In this section, the ordinal, probabilistic-ordinal, and partial-ordinal problems are formulated.

14.2.1 Ordinal Classification

Assume that we are given a training data set $S^{tr} = \{(X_1, Y_1),...,(X_n, Y_n),...,(X_N, Y_N)\}$, where $X_n = [x_{n,1},...,x_{n,i},...,x_{n,I}]$ denotes a vector of observed characteristics of the data item and $Y_n = [y_{n,1},..., y_{n,d},...,y_{n,D}]$ denotes a label vector. The label vector is defined as follows if X_n belongs to class C_d:

$$y_{n,j} = \begin{cases} 1 & j = d \\ 0 & j \neq d \end{cases} \tag{14.1}$$

---

* http://www.esat.kuleuven.be/psi/spraak/downloads/.

In ordinal problems, there is an intrinsic ordering between the classes, which is denoted as $C_1 \prec \cdots \prec C_d \prec \cdots \prec C_D$, like low, medium, and high (Verwaeren et al. 2012). The goal is to approximate a classifier function (G), such that for the mth unseen observation X_m^{tst}, $\hat{Y}_m = G\left(X_m^{tst}\right)$ is as close as possible to the true label. For a crisp classifier, $\hat{Y}_m$ is defined as follows if the dth class is chosen for X_m^{tst}:

$$\hat{y}_{m,j} = \begin{cases} 1 & j = d \\ 0 & j \neq d \end{cases}$$

(14.2)

14.2.2 Probabilistic-Ordinal Classification

The probabilistic-ordinal classification problem $\left(C_O^{Pr}\right)$ is a generalization of the C_O, where each element of the classifier output vector ($\hat{Y}$) represents the probability of belonging to the corresponding category. In this type of classification, Y_n is defined by Equation 14.1. However, $\hat{Y}_m$ is defined as follows:

$$\hat{Y}_m = \left\{ \left[\hat{y}_{m,1}, \ldots, \hat{y}_{m,d}, \ldots, \hat{y}_{m,D}\right] \in \mathbb{R}^D \,\middle|\, \hat{y}_{m,d} \geq 0; \sum_{d=1}^{D} \hat{y}_{m,d} = 1 \right\}$$

(14.3)

where $\mathbb{R}$ denotes the set of real numbers.

14.2.3 Partial-Ordinal Classification

The partial-ordinal classification problem $\left(C_O^{Pa}\right)$ is another generalization of C_O (Verwaeren et al. 2012). In ordinal problems, each data object is limited to belong to a single category, that is, out of all D elements of Y_n, only one is nonzero. However, this is too conservative in the case of noncrisp or fuzzy classes. This limitation is relaxed in C_O^{Pa} by rephrasing Y_n as follows:

$$Y_n = \left\{ \left[y_{n,1}, \ldots, y_{n,d}, \ldots, y_{n,D}\right] \in \mathbb{R}^D \,\middle|\, y_{n,d} \geq 0; \sum_{d=1}^{D} y_{n,d} = 1 \right\}$$

(14.4)

Therefore, each data point has a degree of membership to all classes. Like in ordinal problems, the final goal is to approximate a classifier function (G), such that for an unseen observation X^{tst}, $\hat{Y}_m = G\left(X_m^{tst}\right)$ is as close as possible to the true label. In this type of classification, $\hat{Y}_m$ is also defined by Equation 14.3.

14.3 Conventional Performance Metrics

In this section, five widely used conventional metrics, namely, E_{mzo}, E_{ma}^{cil}, P_{cfci}, E_{ad}, and E_{rps}, are introduced (Verwaeren et al. 2012; McCullagh 1980; Chu and Keerthi 2007; Cheng et al. 2008; Chu and Ghahramani 2004; Shevade and Chu 2006; Manel et al. 2002; Van Broekhoven et al. 2007; Mouton et al. 2009; Murphy 1969; Kohonen and Suomela 2005; Toda 1963).

14.3.1 Mean Zero–One Error (E$_{mzo}$)

Performance metric E_{mzo} is the fraction of incorrect predictions, which is calculated as follows (Chu and Keerthi 2007; Cheng et al. 2008; Chu and Ghahramani 2004; Shevade and Chu 2006):

$$E_{mzo} = \frac{1}{M} \sum_{m=1}^{M} 1_{\hat{y}_m \neq y_m} \tag{14.5}$$

where M is the total number of test set data points, $\hat{y}_m$ is the predicted label of the mth test set data point, and y_m is the true label of the mth test set data point. The main advantage of E_{mzo} is its simplicity. However, it does not consider the order of the categories. Furthermore, it is not applicable to measure the performance in C_O^{Pr} or C_O^{Pa}.

14.3.2 Mean Absolute Error of Consecutive Integer Labels $\left(E_{ma}^{cil}\right)$

To calculate E_{ma}^{cil}, first, both true labels and predicted labels of the test set data points are transformed into consecutive integers so that if the dth column of the label vector is 1, then the transformed label is equal to d (Chu and Keerthi 2007; Cheng et al. 2008; Chu and Ghahramani 2004; Shevade and Chu 2006). After label transformation, E_{ma}^{cil} is calculated as follows:

$$E_{ma}^{cil} = \frac{1}{M} \sum_{m=1}^{M} \left| \hat{U}_m - U_m \right| \tag{14.6}$$

where $\hat{U}_m$ is the transformed predicted label of the mth test set data point, and U_m is the transformed true label of the mth test set data point. E_{ma}^{cil} enjoys the advantage of taking the order of categories into account. However, it cannot be applied to evaluate the classifiers in C_O^{Pr} or C_O^{Pa}. Moreover, the range of its output is application-dependent. Therefore, the interpretation of this metric is challenging. This is shown in Section 14.5 using some numerical examples.

14.3.3 Percentage of Correctly Fuzzy Classified Instances (P$_{cfci}$)

Performance metric P_{cfci} has been applied to measure the performance of probabilistic or fuzzy classifiers (Manel et al. 2002; Van Broekhoven et al. 2007). It is calculated as follows:

$$P_{cfci} = \frac{100}{M} \sum_{m=1}^{M} \left(1 - \frac{1}{2} \sum_{d=1}^{D} \left| \hat{y}_{m,d} - y_{m,d} \right| \right) \tag{14.7}$$

As can be inferred from this relation, the order of the categories is not considered in P_{cfci}.

14.3.4 Average Deviation (E_ad)

Performance metric E_{ad} was originally introduced by Van Broekhoven (2007) to evaluate the classifiers in fuzzy ordered classification problems. It was also applied in different applications with other names (Verwaeren et al. 2012; Mouton et al. 2009). E_{ad} is calculated as follows:

$$E_{ad} = \frac{1}{M} \sum_{m=1}^{M} \left\{ \sum_{d=1}^{D-1} \left| \sum_{i=1}^{d} \hat{y}_{m,i} - \sum_{i=1}^{d} y_{m,i} \right| \right\} \tag{14.8}$$

It can be interpreted from this relation that the order of categories is important in E_{ad}. E_{ad} is also useful for classifier evaluation in C_O^{Pr} or C_O^{Pa}. However, similar to E_{ma}^{cil}, the range of E_{ad} is application-dependent and hence difficult to interpret.

14.3.5 Average Ranked Probability Scores (E_rps)

The ranked probability score was originally introduced to score the output of probabilistic classifiers (Bougeault 2003; Murphy 1969). It is defined as follows:

$$RPS_Y(\hat{Y}) = \frac{1}{D-1} \left\{ \sum_{d=1}^{D-1} \left(\sum_{i=1}^{d} \hat{y}_i - \sum_{i=1}^{d} y_i \right)^2 \right\} \tag{14.9}$$

This scoring rule can be easily extended to measure the performance of classifiers in C_O, C_O^{Pr} and C_O^{Pa} using the following relation:

$$E_{rps} = \frac{1}{M(D-1)} \sum_{m=1}^{M} \sum_{d=1}^{D-1} \left(\sum_{i=1}^{d} \hat{y}_{m,i} - \sum_{i=1}^{d} y_{m,i} \right)^2 \tag{14.10}$$

As can be interpreted from this relation, the order and the number of categories are important in E_{rps}. It is assumed that the maximum of the nominator of E_{rps} is $M(D-1)$. Therefore, to fix the range of E_{rps} between 0 and 1, the nominator is divided by its maximum possible value $M(D-1)$. However, this assumption is very conservative so that in many practical cases, the maximum of the nominator of E_{rps} is less than $M(D-1)$. Consequently, this assumption may lead to an erroneous interpretation of the classifier performance. Numerical examples in Section 14.5 reveal this issue clearly.

14.4 Proposed Performance Metric

In this section, first, OD of two vectors in Euclidean space is introduced. Then, a new performance metric, namely, normalized ordinal distance $\left(E_{nod}^p\right)$, is developed based on the ordinal distance.

14.4.1 Ordinal Distance

In this section, the definition of a distance function is recaptured. Then, the Minkowski distance is described, and finally, the OD is introduced as an extension of the Minkowski distance.

14.4.1.1 Distance

By definition, a distance function of two points $A = [a_1, \ldots, a_d, \ldots, a_D]$ and $B = [b_1, \ldots, b_d, \ldots, b_D]$ is a function $D : \mathbb{R}^D \times \mathbb{R}^D \to \mathbb{R}$, which satisfies the following three conditions (Deza and Deza 2009):

1. $D(A, B) \geq 0$ and $D(A, B) = 0 \Leftrightarrow A = B$
2. $D(A, B) = D(B, A)$
3. $D(A, C) \leq D(A, B) + D(B, C)$

A variety of distance functions have been introduced by scientists for different applications such as Minkowski distance, Mahalanobis distance, Chebyshev distance, and Hamming distance (Deza and Deza 2009).

14.4.1.2 Minkowski Distance of Order p

The Minkowski distance of order p or p-norm is a distance function, which satisfies all conditions of a distance function:

$$\|A - B\|_p = \left(\sum_{d=1}^{D} |a_d - b_d|^p \right)^{1/p} \tag{14.11}$$

where p is a real number not less than 1. As can be interpreted from Equation 14.11, in p-norm, the order of the elements of two points A and B is not important.

14.4.1.3 OD of Order p

The notion of OD is previously used to measure the differences of two strings (Morovic et al. 2002) or two histograms (Luxenburger 2008). In this chapter, an OD of two vectors in Euclidean space is introduced. The OD of order p between two points A and B is defined in Equation 14.12.

$$\|A - B\|_p^{\text{OD}} = \left(\sum_{d=1}^{D} |\bar{a}_d - \bar{b}_d|^p \right)^{1/p} \tag{14.12}$$

$$\bar{a}_d = \sum_{i=1}^{d} a_i$$

$$\bar{b}_d = \sum_{i=1}^{d} b_i$$

where p is a real number not less than 1. Since Equation 14.12 is a Minkowski distance between $\bar{A} = [\bar{a}_1, \ldots, \bar{a}_d, \ldots, \bar{a}_D]$ and $\bar{B} = [\bar{b}_1, \ldots, \bar{b}_d, \ldots, \bar{b}_D]$, it follows that the OD of order p satisfies the conditions of Section 14.4.1.1.

Figure 14.1 shows the diagram of a unit circle using Minkowski and ODs of orders 1, 2, and infinity.

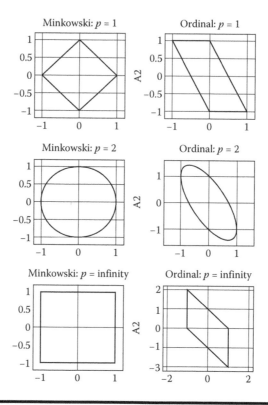

Figure 14.1 Diagram of unit circle using Minkowski and ordinal distances of orders 1, 2, and infinity.

14.4.2 *Normalized OD* $\left(E_{nod}^p\right)$

In this section, a new performance metric, namely, normalized OD $\left(E_{nod}^p\right)$, is introduced to measure the performance classifiers in C_O, C_O^{Pr}, and C_O^{Pa}.

$$E_{nod}^p = \frac{\sum_{m=1}^{M}\left\|Y_m - \hat{Y}_m\right\|_p^{OD}}{\sum_{m=1}^{M}\psi_{Y_m}^p} \tag{14.13}$$

where $\psi_{Y_m}^p$ is the upper bound of $\left\|Y - \hat{Y}\right\|_p^{OD}$ for any possible $\hat{Y}$ in its defined range. ψ_Y is defined as follows:

$$\psi_Y^p \triangleq \max_T \left\|Y - T\right\|_p^{OD} \tag{14.14}$$

where $T = \{t_1,\ldots,t_{d},\ldots,t_D\}$ is an arbitrary vector with the same specifications of $\hat{Y}$ mentioned in Equation 14.2. ψ_Y^p can be calculated using Theorem 14.1.

In E_{nod}^p, OD is used to take the order of categories into account, and it is normalized by the largest possible OD because not all test cases (Y_m) are equally difficult and the possible OD for some test cases is larger than others. Without this normalization, the OD is difficult to interpret. In this chapter, we are performing a macroaveraging, while a microaveraging variant could also be studied.

Theorem 14.1

The upper bound of $\left\|Y - \hat{Y}\right\|_p^{OD}$ for any possible $\hat{Y}$ can be obtained as follows:

$$\psi_Y^p = max\left(\left\|Y - L_1\right\|_p^{OD}, \ldots, \left\|Y - L_d\right\|_p^{OD}, \ldots, \left\|Y - L_D\right\|_p^{OD}\right) \qquad (14.15)$$

or equivalently

$$\psi_Y^p = max\left(\left\|Y - L_1\right\|_p^{OD}, \left\|Y - L_D\right\|_p^{OD}\right) \qquad (14.16)$$

where L_d is a vector of size Y. The dth element of L_d is equal to 1, and the rest of the elements are 0. As can be interpreted from Equations 14.15 and 14.16, although the latter one is more restrictive, it provides an easier way to calculate ψ_Y^p. ■

Proof

We first prove Equation 14.15, which helps us to show the correctness of Equation 14.16.
Proof of Equation 14.15:
By definition

$$\left\|Y - T\right\|_p^{OD} = \left\|\Lambda(Y - T)\right\|_p \qquad (14.17)$$

where Λ is a lower triangular matrix of size $D \times D$ with all diagonal and lower diagonal elements equal to 1. Since $\left\|(Y - T)\right\|_p$ is a convex function of T and a convex function remains convex under an affine transformation, $\left\|\Lambda(Y - T)\right\|_p$ is also convex.

On the other hand, a convex function on a compact convex set attains its maximum at an extreme point of the set (Kincaid and Cheney 2002). In this problem, $T \in \left\{\left[t_1, \ldots, t_d, \ldots, t_D\right] \in \mathbb{R}^D \middle| t_d \geq 0; \sum_{d=1}^{D} t_d = 1\right\}$. The extreme points of this compact convex set are L_d with $d \in \{1, \ldots, D\}$.

Therefore,

$$\underset{T}{max}\left\|\Lambda(Y - T)\right\|_p = max\left(\left\|\Lambda(Y - L_1)\right\|_p, \ldots, \left\|\Lambda(Y - L_d)\right\|_p, \ldots, \left\|\Lambda(Y - L_D)\right\|_p\right) \qquad (14.18)$$

Consequently,

$$\max_{T} \left\| Y - T \right\|_p^{\text{OD}} = \max \left(\left\| Y - L_1 \right\|_p^{\text{OD}}, \ldots, \left\| Y - L_d \right\|_p^{\text{OD}}, \ldots, \left\| Y - L_D \right\|_p^{\text{OD}} \right) \tag{14.19}$$

Proof of Equation 14.16:

Equation 14.16 is now shown by contradiction. Suppose Equation 14.15 is not equivalent with Equation 14.16. Then there must be a $k \in \{2, \ldots, D - 1\}$ such that

$$\left\| Y - L_k \right\|_p^{\text{OD}} > \left\| Y - L_1 \right\|_p^{\text{OD}} \tag{14.20}$$

$$\left\| Y - L_k \right\|_p^{\text{OD}} > \left\| Y - L_D \right\|_p^{\text{OD}} \tag{14.21}$$

Expansions of Equations 14.20 and 14.21 are

$$\sum_{d=1}^{k-1} \left(\sum_{i=1}^{d} y_i \right)^p + \sum_{d=k}^{D-1} \left(1 - \sum_{i=1}^{d} y_i \right)^p > \sum_{d=1}^{D-1} \left(1 - \sum_{i=1}^{d} y_i \right)^p \tag{14.22}$$

$$\sum_{d=1}^{k-1} \left(\sum_{i=1}^{d} y_i \right)^p + \sum_{d=k}^{D-1} \left(1 - \sum_{i=1}^{d} y_i \right)^p > \sum_{d=1}^{D-1} \left(\sum_{i=1}^{d} y_i \right)^p \tag{14.23}$$

After some manipulations, Equations 14.22 and 14.23 lead to

$$\sum_{d=1}^{k-1} \left[\left(\sum_{i=1}^{d} y_i \right)^p - \left(1 - \sum_{i=1}^{d} y_i \right)^p \right] > 0 \tag{14.24}$$

$$\sum_{d=k}^{D-1} \left[\left(1 - \sum_{i=1}^{d} y_i \right)^p - \left(\sum_{i=1}^{d} y_i \right)^p \right] > 0 \tag{14.25}$$

If Equation 14.24 holds, $\left(\sum_{i=1}^{d} y_i \right) > \left(1 - \sum_{i=1}^{d} y_i \right)$; hence, $\left(\sum_{i=1}^{d} y_i \right) > 0.5$ for at least one d between 1 and $k - 1$. Likewise, from Equation 14.25, $\left(\sum_{i=1}^{d} y_i \right) < 0.5$ for at least one d between k and $D - 1$. This is impossible, since $\sum_{i=1}^{d} y_i$ is an increasing function of d, and hence, Equation 14.16 holds.

14.5 Results and Discussion

In this section, different characteristics of E_{nod}^p are discussed, and its advantages to conventional performance metrics, namely, E_{mzo}, P_{cfci}, E_{ad}, E_{rps}, and E_{ma}^{cil}, are demonstrated.

14.5.1 Cumulative Probability Mass Distribution

As can be interpreted from Equation 14.13, E_{nod}^p calculates the OD between $\hat{Y}$ and Y, which is equivalent to the Minkowski distance between cumulative probability mass distributions (CMDs) of $\hat{Y}$ and Y; hence, the order of categories is important. The effect of using CMD is shown in Figure 14.2 by comparing two cases. Figure 14.2a and b shows the probability mass distributions (MDs) and the CMD of $\hat{Y}$ and Y, respectively, for case 1. Figure 14.2c and d illustrates the MD and the CMD of $\hat{Y}$ and Y, respectively, for case 2. As shown in these figures, $\hat{Y}$ and Y are closer to each other in the second case compared to the first case. While the Minkowski distance between the MD of $\hat{Y}$ and Y does not reflect this fact, the Minkowski distance between CMD of $\hat{Y}$ and Y (their OD) shows this closeness effectively.

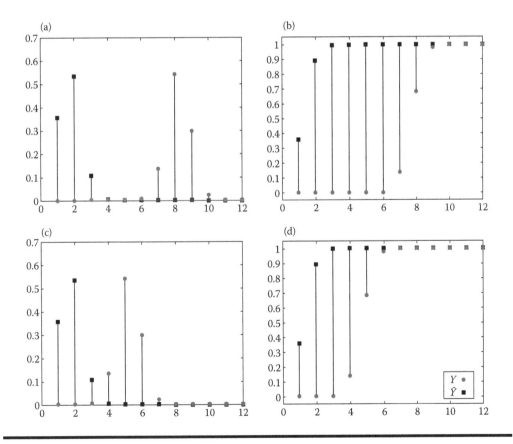

Figure 14.2 **Effect of using cumulative mass distribution.**

14.5.2 Order of Categories

In Example 1, it is shown that P_{cfci} and E_{mzo} are not suitable for measuring the performance of ordinal classifiers, because these methods do not consider the order of categories.

Example 1: For an ordinal three-class classification problem, classifier 1 and classifier 2 result in confusion matrix 1, labeled as CM_1 and CM_2, respectively. In these matrices, each column represents the instances in a predicted class, and each row shows the instances in an actual class.

$$CM_1 = \begin{bmatrix} 4 & 1 & 0 \\ 0 & 5 & 0 \\ 0 & 0 & 10 \end{bmatrix} CM_2 = \begin{bmatrix} 4 & 0 & 1 \\ 0 & 5 & 0 \\ 0 & 0 & 10 \end{bmatrix} \quad (14.26)$$

Table 14.1 shows the performance of two classifiers measured by E_{mzo}, E_{ad}, E_{ma}^{cil}, P_{cfci}, E_{rps}, E_{nod}^1, E_{nod}^2, and E_{nod}^∞. As can be interpreted from this table, E_{mzo}, P_{cfci}, and E_{nod}^∞ fail to reflect the degradation of performance from classifier 1 to classifier 2. However, E_{nod}^1, E_{nod}^2, E_{ad}, E_{rps}, and E_{ma}^{cil} perfectly show that classifier 1 outperforms classifier 2.

14.5.3 Number of Categories

In Example 2, it is shown that the number of categories in the classification problem influences the interpretation of E_{ad} and E_{ma}^{cil}.

Example 2: Consider the following three ordinal and partial-ordinal classification problems.

Problem 1: For a test data point, the true label and the estimated label are $Y_1 = [1\ 0]$ and $\hat{Y}_1 = [0\ 1]$, respectively.

Problem 2: For a test data point, the true label and the estimated label are $Y_1 = [0\ 0\ 0\ 0\ 0.5\ 0.5\ 0\ 0\ 0\ 0]$ and $\hat{Y}_1 = [0\ 0\ 0.5\ 0.5\ 0\ 0\ 0\ 0\ 0\ 0]$, respectively.

Table 14.1 Performance of Two Classifiers Measured by E_{mzo}, E_{ad}, E_{ma}^{cil}, P_{cfci}, E_{rps}, E_{nod}^1, E_{nod}^2, and E_{nod}^∞ in Example 1

Performance Metric	Problem 1	Problem 2
E_{mzo}	0.05	0.05
E_{ad}	0.05	0.1
E_{ma}^{cil}	0.05	0.1
P_{cfci}	97.5	97.5
E_{rps}	0.025	0.05
E_{nod}^1	0.0286	0.0571
E_{nod}^2	0.0381	0.0540
E_{nod}^∞	0.05	0.05

Table 14.2 Performance of Two Classifiers Measured by E_{mzo}, E_{ad}, E_{ma}^{cil}, P_{cfci}, E_{rps}, E_{nod}^1, E_{nod}^2, and E_{nod}^∞ in Example 2

Performance Metric	Problem 1	Problem 2	Problem 3
E_{ad}	1	2	1
E_{ma}^{cil}	1	–	1
E_{rps}	1	0.17	0.25
E_{nod}^1	1	0.444	0.50
E_{nod}^2	1	0.594	0.71
E_{nod}^∞	1	1	1

Problem 3: In this problem, each of the two neighboring categories of Y_1 in Problem 2 are merged such that the new true and estimated labels are $Y_1 = [0\ 0\ 1\ 0\ 0]$ and $\hat{Y}_1 = [0\ 1\ 0\ 0\ 0]$, respectively.

Table 14.2 shows the performance of classifiers in these problems obtained using E_{ad}, E_{ma}^{cil}, E_{rps}, E_{nod}^1, E_{nod}^2, and E_{nod}^∞ in Example 2. As can be interpreted from Table 14.2, E_{ad}, E_{ma}^{cil}, and E_{nod}^∞ treated the classifiers of the first and third problems in the same manner. However, the estimated label of the first problem is completely incorrect, while the estimated label in the third problem is close to the true label. Performance metrics E_{rps}, E_{nod}^1, and E_{nod}^2 reflect the higher performance of the third classifier compared to the first one.

The second and third problems are naturally similar to each other because the categories in the third problem are obtained by merging the neighboring categories in the second problem. An appealing characteristic of a performance metric is remaining invariant to the number of classes. It can be interpreted from Table 14.2 that the calculated performances using E_{ad}, E_{rps}, E_{nod}^1, and E_{nod}^2 are changed by 200%, 32%, 11%, and 16%, respectively, from Problem 3 to Problem 2. Therefore, E_{nod}^1 and E_{nod}^2 are robust against variability in the number of classes.

14.5.4 Relation to Ranked Probability Score

There is a close relationship between E_{rps} and E_{nod}^p, especially for $p = 2$. In both E_{rps} and E_{nod}^p, denominators are assumed to be the upper bound of the numerator and are used to keep the range of the performance metric between 0 and 1. In E_{rps}, it is assumed that the upper bound of the numerator is $M(D-1)$ (Murphy 1969; Déqué et al. 1994). However, this is a conservative bound in many situations. In E_{nod}^p, this upper bound is explicitly defined by Equation 14.14 and calculated by Equation 14.16. The following examples show that the conservative assumption of E_{rps} results in a misleading or erroneous interpretation of the classifiers' performance.

Example 3: Consider the following two cases.

Case 1:
For an ordinal three-class classification problem, a completely useless classifier is applied, which results in CM_3.

$$CM_3 = \begin{bmatrix} 0 & 0 & 0 \\ 5 & 0 & 5 \\ 0 & 0 & 0 \end{bmatrix} \tag{14.27}$$

Case 2:
For another ordinal three-class classification problem, consider a classifier with CM_4.

$$CM_4 = \begin{bmatrix} 5 & 0 & 0 \\ 0 & 5 & 0 \\ 10 & 0 & 0 \end{bmatrix} \tag{14.28}$$

The performance of classifiers in cases 1 and 2 calculated by E_{mzo}, P_{cfci}, E_{ad}, E_{rps}, E_{nod}^p, and E_{ma}^{cil} are listed in Table 14.3.

As can be seen from Table 14.3, the performance of the applied classifier in case 1 measured by E_{rps} is 0.50, while all estimated labels are incorrect and the classifier is totally useless. The outputs of E_{nod}^p and P_{cfci} are 1 and 0, respectively, which appropriately reflect that the applied classifier is useless in this case. The table also indicates that E_{rps}, E_{ad}, and E_{ma}^{cil} result in the same values for both cases, while we know that the applied classifier in the second case is much more effective than the first one. This is appropriately reflected by E_{nod}^1, E_{nod}^2, and E_{nod}^∞.

Example 4: This example shows the disadvantage of E_{rps} in measuring the performance of classifiers in C_O^{Pa}. Consider that in an ordinal three-class classification problem, a probabilistic classifier is applied. The test set data points along with their corresponding classifier outputs are shown in Table 14.4. The result for performance metric E_{rps} suggests that the classifier error is 0.2667, while it can be concluded from Table 14.4 that the applied classifier is not useful. In this example, the results for E_{nod}^1, E_{nod}^2, and E_{nod}^∞ are 1, 0.73, and 0.60, respectively. Obviously, E_{nod}^p better reflects the performance of the applied probabilistic classifier especially for $p = 1$ compared to E_{rps}.

Table 14.3 Performance of Two Classifiers Measured by E_{mzo}, E_{ad}, E_{ma}^{cil}, P_{cfci}, E_{rps}, E_{nod}^1, E_{nod}^2, and E_{nod}^∞ in Example 3

Performance Metric	Case 1	Case 2
E_{mzo}	1	0.5
E_{ad}	1	1
E_{ma}^{cil}	1	1
P_{cfci}	0	50
E_{rps}	0.50	0.50
E_{nod}^1	1	0.5714
E_{nod}^2	1	0.5395
E_{nod}^∞	1	0.5

Table 14.4   Test Set Data Points and Their Corresponding Classifier Outputs in Example 4

	Actual Label (Y)			Classifier Output (Ŷ)		
Data point 1	0	1	0	0.3	0	0.7
Data point 2	0	1	0	0.6	0	0.4
Data point 3	0	1	0	0.5	0	0.5

Example 5: In this example, E_{rps} and E_{nod}^p are evaluated in measuring the performance of two classifiers in a real-world C_O problem, namely, age group classification from speech recordings (Bahari and Van hamme 2011a). In this experiment, speech signals of 555 speakers from the *n*-best evaluation corpus (Van Leeuwen et al. 2009) were used. The corpus contains live and broadcast commentaries, news, interviews, and reports broadcast in Belgium. The speakers in this dataset are categorized into three age categories, namely, young (18–35), middle (36–45), and senior (46–81). The number of young, middle, and senior speakers in this database is 138, 201, and 216, respectively. Among all speakers in the database, 400 are selected for model training, and the rest are used for testing. Two approaches are applied for age group recognition. The first method is a random classifier, where $P(\hat{Y} = [1\ 0\ 0]) = P(\hat{Y} = [0\ 1\ 0]) = P(\hat{Y} = [0\ 0\ 1]) = \dfrac{1}{3}$. The second approach, which is introduced by Bahari and Van hamme (2011a), applies well-known speech processing tools and supervised nonnegative matrix factorization (SNMF) (Bahari and Van hamme 2012) to recognize the age of speakers. The resulting confusion matrices of both methods can be

$$\text{CM}_{\text{SNMF}} = \begin{bmatrix} 15 & 15 & 9 \\ 18 & 22 & 16 \\ 9 & 11 & 40 \end{bmatrix} \text{CM}_{\text{random}} = \begin{bmatrix} 13 & 13 & 13 \\ 18 & 18 & 19 \\ 20 & 20 & 20 \end{bmatrix} \tag{14.29}$$

The results of using performance metrics E_{rps} and E_{nod}^p are listed in Table 14.5.

A subjective study on the obtained results shows that the SNMF-based age group recognizer is more effective than a random classifier. As can be interpreted from Table 14.5, this performance drop is better revealed in E_{nod}^p compared to E_{rps}. In this experiment, the error of the random

Table 14.5   Performance of Two Classifiers Measured by E_{rps}, E_{nod}^1, E_{nod}^2, and E_{nod}^∞ in Example 5

Performance Metric	SNMF	Random
E_{rps}	0.30	0.44
E_{nod}^1	0.37	0.54
E_{nod}^∞	0.41	0.60
E_{nod}^∞	0.46	0.67

classifier measured by E_{rps} is only 0.44, which is not rational. By contrast, the results of E_{nod}^1, E_{nod}^2, and E_{nod}^∞ effectively reflect the nature of the applied random classifier.

14.5.5 Partial-Ordinal Problems

Examples 6 and 7 show the advantages of E_{nod}^p over P_{cfci}, E_{rps}, and E_{ad} in measuring the performance of the classifiers in C_O^{Pa}, where other conventional approaches are not applicable.

Example 6: In this example, P_{cfci}, E_{ad}, E_{rps}, and E_{nod}^p are evaluated in measuring the performance of classifiers in C_O^{Pa}. Consider an eight-class C_O^{Pa}. In this problem, the test data point label is $Y = [0.1\ 0.1\ 0.1\ 0.1\ 0.1\ 0.1\ 0.2\ 0.2]$. Two classifiers are applied in this problem. Table 14.6 shows the output of the applied classifiers. The measured performance of these classifiers using P_{cfci}, E_{ad}, E_{rps}, E_{nod}^1, E_{nod}^2, and E_{nod}^∞ is presented in Table 14.7. As can be understood from Table 14.6, the estimated label of the second classifier is more similar to the true label compared to that of the first classifier. However, the output of the P_{cfci} is the same for both of them. This is due to the fact that the order of categories has no effect on the output of P_{cfci}. In this example, E_{ad}, E_{rps}, E_{nod}^1, E_{nod}^2, and E_{nod}^∞ reflect the performance improvement from the first classifier to the second one.

Example 7: In this example, the behavior of E_{nod}^p and E_{rps} in a C_O^{Pa} is analyzed. Consider a five-class C_O^{Pa}. In this problem, a special classifier is applied to recognize the labels of an infinite number of data points. The actual label of all data points is the same, $Y = [0.2\ 0.2\ 0.2\ 0.2\ 0.2]$.

The applied classifier is random and crisp, in which $P(\hat{Y}=[1\ 0\ 0\ 0\ 0]) = P(\hat{Y} = [0\ 1\ 0\ 0\ 0]) = P(\hat{Y} = [0\ 0\ 1\ 0\ 0]) = P(\hat{Y} = [0\ 0\ 0\ 1\ 0]) = P(\hat{Y} = [0\ 0\ 0\ 0\ 1]) = 0.2$. The error of the applied classifier expressed by E_{rps} is 0.20. However, since the classifier is absolutely random, this result is not rational. The measured error using E_{nod}^1, E_{nod}^2, and E_{nod}^∞ is 0.80, 0.7983, and 0.80, respectively, which perfectly matches the characteristics of this classifier.

Table 14.6 Output of Applied Classifiers in Example 6

	Classifier Output ($\hat{Y}$)							
Classifier 1	0.2	0.2	0.1	0.1	0.1	0.1	0.1	0.1
Classifier 2	0.1	0.1	0.1	0.1	0.1	0.2	0.2	0.1

Table 14.7 Performance of Two Classifiers Measured by P_{cfci}, E_{ad}, E_{rps}, E_{nod}^1, E_{nod}^2, and E_{nod}^∞ in Example 6

Performance Metric	Classifier 1	Classifier 2
E_{ad}	1.2	0.2
P_{cfci}	80	80
E_{rps}	0.0314	0.0029
E_{nod}^1	0.2927	0.0488
E_{nod}^2	0.2828	0.0853
E_{nod}^∞	0.2222	0.1111

14.6 Conclusion

In this chapter, the OD between two arbitrary vectors in Euclidean space has been introduced. Then, normalized OD $\left(E_{\text{nod}}^p\right)$ as an application-independent performance metric for ordinal, probabilistic-ordinal, or partial-ordinal classification problems has been presented. Different advantages of E_{nod}^p over conventional performance metrics such as mean absolute error of consecutive integer labels $E_{\text{ma}}^{\text{cil}}$, mean zero–one error ($E_{\text{mzo}}$), correctly fuzzy classified instances (P_{cfci}), average deviation (E_{ad}), or ranked probability score (E_{rps}) have been shown using a number of numerical examples.

Acknowledgments

This work is supported by the European Commission as a Marie-Curie Initial Training Networks (ITN) project (FP7-PEOPLE-ITN-2008), namely, Bayesian Biometrics for Forensics (BBfor2), under Grant Agreement number 238803.

The authors also thank Jort F. Gemmeke for his help to accomplish this work.

References

Bahari, M., Van hamme, H., 2011a. Age and gender recognition from speech patterns based on supervised non-negative matrix factorization, in: *20th Annual Conference of the International Association of Forensic Phonetics and Acoustics*, pp. 3–5.

Bahari, M., Van hamme, H., 2012. Speaker age estimation using hidden markov model weight supervectors, in: *Proc. 11th International Conference on Information Science, Signal Processing and Their Applications (ISSPA)*, pp. 517–521.

Bahari, M.H., Van hamme, H., 2011b. Speaker age estimation and gender detection based on supervised non-negative matrix factorization, in: *Proc. IEEE Workshop on Biometric Measurements and Systems for Security and Medical Applications (BIOMS)*, pp. 1–6.

Bougeault, P., 2003. *The WGNE Survey of Verification Methods for Numerical Prediction of Weather Elements and Severe Weather Events*. Toulouse: Météo-France.

Cardoso, J., da Costa, J., 2007. Learning to classify ordinal data: The data replication method. *Journal of Machine Learning Research* 8, 6.

Cheng, J., Wang, Z., Pollastri, G., 2008. A neural network approach to ordinal regression, in: *Neural Networks, 2008. IJCNN 2008. (IEEE World Congress on Computational Intelligence). IEEE International Joint Conference on*, pp. 1279–1284.

Chu, W., Ghahramani, Z., 2004. Gaussian processes for ordinal regression. *Journal of Machine Learning Research* 6, 1019–1041.

Chu, W., Keerthi, S., 2007. Support vector ordinal regression. *Neural Computation* 19, 792–815.

Déqué, M., Royer, J., Stroe, R., France, M., 1994. Formulation of Gaussian probability forecasts based on model extended-range integrations. *Tellus A* 46, 52–65.

Deza, M., Deza, E., 2009. *Encyclopedia of Distances*. Springer, Berlin Heidelberg, Germany.

Erdural, S., 2006. *A Method for Robust Design of Products or Processes with Categorical Response*. METU: Ankara.

Kincaid, D., Cheney, E., 2002. *Numerical Analysis: Mathematics of Scientific Computing*, volume 2. Amer Mathematical Society, Pacific Grove, California, United States.

Kohonen, J., Suomela, J., 2005. Lessons learned in the challenge: Making predictions and scoring them. *Lecture Notes in Artificial Intelligence* 3944, 95–116.

Li, M., Han, K.J., Narayanan, S., 2013. Automatic speaker age and gender recognition using acoustic and prosodic level information fusion. *Computer Speech and Language* 27, 151–167.

Luxenburger, J., 2008. Modeling and exploiting user search behavior for information retrieval. PhD thesis, Universität des Saarlandes, Saarlandes, Germany.

Manel, S., Williams, H., Ormerod, S., 2002. Evaluating presence–absence models in ecology: The need to account for prevalence. *Journal of Applied Ecology* 38, 921–931.

McCullagh, P., 1980. Regression models for ordinal data. *Journal of the Royal Statistical Society. Series B (Methodological)*, Issue 2, 42, 109–142.

Morovic, J., Shaw, J., Sun, P., 2002. A fast, non-iterative and exact histogram matching algorithm. *Pattern Recognition Letters* 23, 127–135.

Mouton, A., De Baets, B., Van Broekhoven, E., Goethals, P., 2009. Prevalence-adjusted optimisation of fuzzy models for species distribution. *Ecological Modelling* 220, 1776–1786.

Murphy, A., 1969. On the ranked probability score. *Journal of Applied Meteorology* 8, 988–989.

Shevade, S., Chu, W., 2006. Minimum enclosing spheres formulations for support vector ordinal regression, in: *Data Mining, 2006*. ICDM'06. Sixth International Conference on, IEEE. pp. 1054–1058.

Toda, M., 1963. Measurement of subjective probability distributions. Technical Report. DTIC Document.

Van Broekhoven, E., Adriaenssens, V., De Baets, B., 2007. Interpretability-preserving genetic optimization of linguistic terms in fuzzy models for fuzzy ordered classification: An ecological case study. *International Journal of Approximate Reasoning* 44, 65–90.

Van Leeuwen, D.A., Kessens, J., Sanders, E., Van Den Heuvel, H., 2009. Results of the n-best 2008 Dutch speech recognition evaluation. *NOVA* 6, 11–15.

Verwaeren, J., Waegeman, W., De Baets, B., 2012. Learning partial ordinal class memberships with kernel-based proportional odds models. *Computational Statistics and Data Analysis* 56, 928–942.

Chapter 15

Predictive Data Mining for Oral Cancer Treatment

Neha Sharma and Hari Om

Contents

This chapter presents a case study wherein five data mining models are designed to predict the survival rate of oral cancer patients who visit the Ear, Nose and Throat-Out Patients Department (ENT-OPD). The predictive models are single tree, TreeBoost, decision tree forest, multilayer perceptron, and support vector machine that address the classification problem. This study helps identify the most effective model for predicting the survivability of oral cancer by examining 1025 patients who visited a tertiary care center from January 2004 to December 2009. For all these models, there is no misclassified row in any category, and all cases have correctly been classified. The performance of the models are estimated on the basis of validation method, misclassification table, confusion matrix, sensitivity and specificity report, lift and gain chart and area under ROC curve. The diagnostic biopsy has been identified as the most important attribute by all these models. All the models present similar results in terms of misclassification statistics, confusion matrix, sensitivity, and specificity as well as lift and gain. The single tree model takes the minimum time for analysis. The experimental results in terms of probability calibration and threshold analysis are better in the support vector machine model, thus making it the most favorable model for predicting the survival rate of oral cancer patients.

15.1 Introduction

There are approximately 2,000,000 deaths worldwide and 46,000 deaths particularly in India that are caused by oral cancer [1]. Studies show that developing countries like Melanesia, South-Central Asia, and Central and Eastern Europe have the highest rate of oral cavity cancer, whereas developed countries like Africa, Central America, and Eastern Asia have the lowest rate, for both males and females [2]. Oral cancer, with its widely variable rate of occurrence, has one of the highest incidences in the Indian subcontinent, ranking among the top three types of cancer in the country [3]. Age-adjusted rate of oral cancer in India is 20 per 100,000 population, which accounts for over 30% of all cancerous persons in the country [4]. It is very important as far as public health is concerned because it has been estimated that 83,000 new oral cancer cases occur each year in India [5,6]. The difficulty level is high because it is usually diagnosed at later stages, which results in low treatment outcomes and considerably high cost to the patients, who typically cannot afford this type of treatment [7]. The prognosis for patients with oral cancer also remains poor in spite of advances in therapy of many other malignancies. Early diagnosis and treatment remain the key to improve patient survival. To achieve success in treatment, it is essential to determine the hidden patterns and trends in the oral disease data to help health care practitioners in effective decision making.

Manual extraction of patterns from the data has occurred for centuries. The Bayes theorem and regression analysis were considered to be early methods of identifying patterns in the data. In fact, they are still being used in their different variants. The proliferation, ubiquity, and increasing power of computer technology have dramatically increased data collection, storage, and manipulation ability [8]. Since the data sets have grown in size and complexity, manual extraction is extremely impossible, and hence, the direct "hands-on" data analysis has increasingly been augmented with indirect, automated data processing, aided by other discoveries in computer science, such as neural networks (NNs), cluster analysis, genetic algorithms, decision trees, and support vector machines (SVMs). Data mining is basically a process of applying some suitable methods for identifying or uncovering the hidden patterns in large data sets [9].

The objective of this case study is to develop various predictive data mining models and analyze their performance in terms of survivability of oral cancer patients. The tool used for developing the data mining models is DTREG. The DTREG (pronounced D-T-reg) is a predictive modeling software tool that builds classification and regression decision trees, NNs, SVMs, group method of data handling (GMDH) polynomial networks, gene expression programs, *k*-means clustering, discriminant analysis, and logistic regression models that can describe data relationships. It indeed can help predict values for future observations and has full support for time series analysis. It accepts a data set in the form of a table containing a number of rows, and each column represents an attribute/variable. One of the variables is "target variable," whose value is to be modeled and predicted as a function of the "predictor variables." The DTREG analyzes the data and generates a model showing how it best predicts the values of the target variable based on the values of predictor variables [10].

15.2 Related Work

Milovic and Milovic [11] discuss data mining in health care by providing ways for physicians to determine diagnoses and prognoses and apply for patients. A detailed survey on various methods for identification and classification of oral cancer detection at an earlier stage is discussed by Anuradha and Sankaranarayanan [12]. Various significant prevention factors for a particular type of cancer are discussed in the work of Nahar et al. [13] by using Apriori, predictive Apriori, and tertius algorithms against a specific type of cancer. It is reported that the Apriori is the most useful association rule-mining algorithm for discovery of the prevention factors. Chuang et al. [14] and Gadewal and Zingde [15] report that the performance of the holdout cross-validation is much better than cross-validation, and the best classification accuracy is 64.2%. Kent [16] provides a diagnosis method for oral cancer using genetic programming to solve many complex problems, which provides programs to diagnose oral cancer and precancer. Kaladhar et al. [17] classify cancer survival using tenfold cross-validation and a training data set and report that the random forest technique is more accurate as compared to other methods. Kaladhar et al. [18] discuss cancer identification and classification based on genes and accordingly suggest proper treatment selection and drug development.

In the work of Swami et al. [19], preventive measures have been discussed by modeling smoking habits. Sung Ho Ha and Seong Hyeon Joo [20] and RuthRamya et al. [21] discuss the methods of association rule and classification trees to help physicians to make fast and accurate classification of chest pain disease. Gupta et al. [22] provide a method for recognizable proof and forecast of micro ribo nucleic acid (miRNA) in infections through artificial neural networks (ANNs). In the work of

Abual-Rub [23], a hybrid harmony search algorithm (HHSA) is discussed for an initio protein tertiary structure prediction problem. HariKumar et al. [24] compares the classification accuracy of the tumor, lymph node, and metastatis (TNM) staging system along with that of the chi-square test and NNs. An important study is presented by Exarchos et al. [25] to monitor oral cancer evolvement and progression during the whole follow-up period (i.e., 24 months). It evaluates the posttreatment condition of a patient to infer about the probability as well as approximate timing of a potential reoccurrence. In the work of Sankaranarayanan [26], the epidemiologic and clinical aspects of the oral cancer in India are discussed. Causal association between oral cancer and the chewing of betel quids containing tobacco leaves or stems and other tobacco habits has extensively been studied. In Section 15.3, we briefly discuss data mining.

15.3 Data Mining

Data mining is a process of extracting nontrivial and potentially useful information, or knowledge, from the enormous data sets available in experimental sciences (historical records, reanalysis, global climate modeling [GCM] simulations, etc.), providing explicit information that has a readable form and can be used to solve diagnosis, classification, or forecasting problems [27–30]. Traditionally, these problems were solved by direct hands-on data analysis using standard statistical methods, but the increasing volume of data has motivated the study of automatic data analysis using more complex and sophisticated tools that can operate directly on the data. Thus, data mining identifies trends within data that go beyond simple analysis. It bridges the gap from applied statistics and artificial intelligence (which usually provide the mathematical background) to database management by exploiting the way the data are stored and indexed in databases to execute the algorithms more efficiently, thus allowing such methods to be applied to ever-larger data sets. The overall goal of the data mining process is to extract information from a data set and transform it into an understandable structure for further use [28]. Apart from the raw analysis, it involves database and data management aspects, data preprocessing, model and inference considerations, interestingness metrics, complexity considerations, postprocessing of discovered structures, visualization, and online updating [28]. There are various data mining tools available that can be used to predict behaviors and future trends, allowing businesses to make proactive and knowledge-driven decisions. They can answer business questions that traditionally are too time consuming to resolve. They scour databases for hidden patterns for finding predictive information that the experts may miss because it lies outside their expectations. The information gained can be used to develop a model for prediction and classification of new data [31].

15.4 Oral Cancer

Oral cancer is a subtype of head and neck cancer in which cancerous tissue growth is located in the oral cavity [32]. It may arise as a primary lesion originating in any of the oral tissues, by metastasis from a distant site of origin, or by extension from a neighboring anatomic structure, such as the nasal cavity. The oral cancers may also originate in any of the tissues of the mouth. They may be of varied histologic types: teratoma, adenocarcinoma derived from a major or minor salivary gland, lymphoma from tonsillar or other lymphoid tissue, or melanoma from the pigment-producing cells of the oral mucosa. Among the various types of oral cancers, around 90% are squamous cell carcinomas (SCCs) [33] that originate in the tissues lining the mouth and lips. Oral or mouth cancer may also occur on the floor of the mouth, cheek lining, gingiva (gums), lips, or palate (roof of the mouth), but it most commonly involves the tongue. Most oral cancers look very similar under the microscope, and they are called SCC.

There is not a single factor causing oral cancer but, rather, multiple factors. Oral malignancy is most likely caused by a combination of extrinsic and intrinsic factors acting in concert over a period of time. Its symptoms demonstrate that there is at least a contributing component related to a genetic susceptibility of the individual exposed to carcinogens and a potential for malignant transformation of the oral tissue. The epidemiologic data indicate that a strong correlation exists between the exposure to many potential carcinogens and the increased risk of oral cancer following long exposure or early exposure to these carcinogens. Many reports indicate that the age, gender, race, tobacco use, alcohol use (especially tobacco and alcohol in combination), presence of a synchronous cancer of the upper aerodigestive tract, poor nutritional status, infection with certain viruses, oral lichen planus, and immune deficiencies all increase the relative risk for developing an oral cancer.

Public health authorities, private treatment centers, and scholastic medicinal centers in India have distinguished oral disease as a grave issue [34], and great emphasis is being laid by the government and nongovernment organizations toward effective tobacco control. Over the last several decades, billions of rupees have been spent to educate the public, implement laws effectively, rehabilitate tobacco growers, build cessation facilities, create health infrastructures, and so forth to reduce the usage of smokeless tobacco. However, oral cancer, which is an uncommon disease in the west, continues to be a major cause of cancer death in India; about 2000 deaths per day are tobacco related [35]. Therefore, oral cancer, which is of noteworthy public health importance in the country, has been undertaken as a study.

The symptoms of oral cancer at an earlier stage [36] include the following: (1) patches inside the mouth or on lips that are white, red, or a mixture of white and red; (2) any sore or area in the mouth whose discoloration does not heal after more than 14 days; (3) bleeding in the mouth; (4) difficulty or pain when swallowing; and (5) a lump in the neck. These symptoms identify possible candidates for cancer. Treatments for oral cancer include surgery, radiation therapy, and chemotherapy [37]. But all these are not always successful as 70% of the cases after treatment lead to relapse, resulting in death. The treatment is successful only if the lesion is diagnosed early, but sadly, many times, it is ignored. The patient reports when the lesion has spread so much that treatment is impossible or, even if done, the long-term prognosis is poor. Prognosis of oropharyngeal SCC (oral cavity and pharynx) depends on early diagnosis. Despite advanced surgical techniques and adjuvant treatment, the 5-year survival rate remains ~40%–50% [38,39], and the treatment cost is about 3.5 lakh. In spite of this cost, there is no guarantee that it will surely be cured. The surgery requires cutting half the face and tongue and extending to the neck, resulting in the patient looking horrible after surgery.

15.5 Predictive Models

Data mining, an analytic process, has been designed to explore data in search of consistent patterns and/or systematic relationships between variables and then to validate the findings by applying the detected patterns to new subsets of data. Its ultimate goal is prediction, and predictive data mining is the most common type of data mining and the one that has the most direct business applications. Predictive modeling is a process by which a model is created or chosen to try to best predict the probability of an outcome. The process of data mining consists of three stages: (1) initial exploration, (2) model building or pattern identification with validation/verification, and (3) deployment (i.e., the application of the model to new data in order to generate predictions). The following predictive models have been designed for oral cancer treatment.

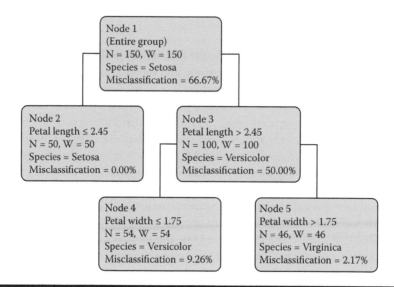

Figure 15.1 Decision tree. (Courtesy of the DTREG Manual.)

15.5.1 Decision Tree Model (DT)

A decision tree is a logical model represented as a binary (two-way split) tree to show how the value of a target variable can be predicted by using the values of a set of predictor variables. The rectangular boxes in the tree are called nodes; each represents a set of records (rows) from the original data set (refer to Figure 15.1). Nodes having child nodes are called interior nodes, and those not having child nodes are called terminal or leaf nodes. The topmost node is called the root node. The root node represents all the rows in the data set. A decision tree is constructed by a binary split that divides the rows in a node into two groups (child nodes), as shown in Figure 15.1. The same procedure is then used to split the child groups. This process is called recursive partitioning. The split is selected to construct a tree that can be used to predict the value of the target variable [10].

15.5.2 TreeBoost Model (TB)

Boosting is a technique for improving the accuracy of a predictive function by applying the function repeatedly in a series and combining the output of each function with weight so that the total error of the prediction is minimized (Figure 15.2). In many cases, the predictive accuracy of such a series greatly exceeds the accuracy of the base function used alone. Mathematically, a TreeBoost (TB) model can be described as

$$\text{Predicted target} = F0 + B1*T1(X) + B2*T2(X) + \dots + BM*TM(X)$$

where F0 is the starting value for the series (the median target value for a regression model); X is a vector of pseudo-residual values remaining at this point in the series; T1(X) and T2(X) are trees

Figure 15.2 TreeBoost.

fitted to the pseudo-residuals; and B1, B2, and so forth are coefficients of the tree node predicted values that are computed by the TB algorithm [10].

The first tree is fitted to the data. The residuals (error values) from the first tree are then fed into the second tree, which attempts to reduce the error. This process is repeated through a series of successive trees. The final predicted value is formed by adding the weighted contribution of each tree.

15.5.3 Decision Tree Forest Model (DTF)

A decision tree forest consists of an ensemble (collection) of decision trees whose predictions are combined to make the overall prediction for the forest. It is similar to a TB model in the sense that a large number of trees are grown. However, the TB generates a series of trees, with the output of one tree going into the next tree in the series. In contrast, a DTF grows a number of independent trees in parallel, and they do not interact until all of them have been built [10]. Both the TB and DTFs produce high-accuracy models. Experiments show that the TB works better with some applications and the DTFs with others. Thus, it is best to try both methods and compare the results.

15.5.4 Multilayer Perceptron Model (MLP)

The ANN is one of the most commonly used models based on human cognitive structure. Some different types of ANN like multilayer perception, radial basis function (RBF) NN, and Kohonen's self-organizing map have been discussed to solve nonlinear problems by learning. The terms NN and ANN usually refer to a multilayer perceptron network (MLP), when used without qualification. The diagram shown in Figure 15.3 illustrates a perceptron network with three layers. It has an input layer (on the left) with three neurons, one hidden layer (in the middle) with three neurons, and an output layer (on the right) with three neurons. There is one neuron in the input layer for each predictor variable $(x_1...x_p)$. In the case of categorical variables, $N - 1$ neurons are used to represent the N categories of the variable.

The network diagram in Figure 15.3 is a fully connected, three-layered, feed-forward, perceptron NN. Fully connected means that the output from each input and hidden neuron is distributed to all neurons in the following layer. Feed-forward means that the values move only from input to hidden to output layers; no values are fed back to earlier layers. When there is more than one hidden layer, the output from one hidden layer is fed into the next hidden layer, and the separate weights are applied to the sum going into each layer [40,41].

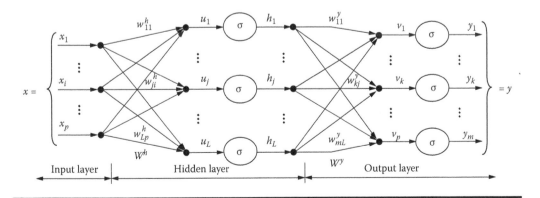

Figure 15.3   Multilayer perceptron neural network.

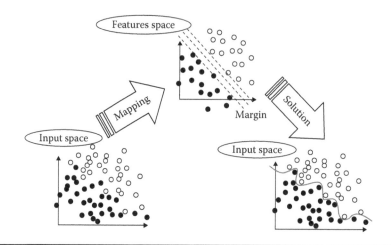

Figure 15.4   Support vector machine. (Courtesy of the DTREG Manual.)

15.5.5 Support Vector Machine (SVM)

An SVM performs classification by constructing an N-dimensional hyperplane that optimally separates the data into two categories. SVM models are closely related to NNs. In fact, an SVM model using a sigmoid kernel function is equivalent to a two-layer, feed-forward NN and is an alternative training method for polynomial, RBF, and multilayer perceptron classifiers in which the weights of the network are found by solving a quadratic programming problem with linear constraints, rather than by solving a nonconvex, unconstrained minimization problem as in standard NN training [42–44]. In the parlance of SVM literature, a predictor variable is called an attribute, and a transformed attribute that is used to define the hyperplane is called a feature. The task of choosing the most suitable representation is known as feature selection. A set of features that describes one case (i.e., a row of predictor values) is called a vector. So the goal of SVM modeling is to find the optimal hyperplane that separates clusters of a vector in such a way that cases with one category of the target variable are on one side of the plane and cases with the other category are on the other side of the plane. The vectors near the hyperplane are the support vectors, and the same is shown in Figure 15.4.

15.6 Experimental Results

The database for this case study has been created by collecting data related to oral cancer through a retrospective chart review from ENT and head and neck departments; the records of the cancer registries of tertiary care hospitals; and OPD data sheets and archives of departments of histopathology, surgery, and radiology. The clinical details, personal history, and habits were collected manually from the records to complete the data sheet of the patients. The data collection was done using a nonrandomized or nonprobabilistic method as all the data in the registries for the period of 5 years were considered. The data set is based on the records of all the patients who reported with a lesion and were treated at the center from January 2004 to June 2009. The complete process of data preparation, data integration, and data cleaning (i.e., removing missing values, noisy data, and inconsistent data) was strictly followed to create the database of oral cancer patients [45].

A database of 1024 oral cancer patients has been created that has 33 data columns (variable), as shown in Table 15.1. The database is stored in a comma-separated values (csv) file format, which is the acceptable file format for the DTREG tool. All data rows are used for data subsetting. The total weights for all rows are equal, and there are no rows with missing target or weight values. However, there is only one row with a missing predictor value.

Table 15.1   Variables and Their Domains

No.	Variable	Domain
1	Sex	Male, female
2	Socioeconomic status	Good, average, poor, above average, below average
3	Clinical symptoms	Burning sensation, ulcer, loosening of tooth, none
4	History of addiction	Tobacco chewing, tobacco smoking, gutka, alcohol, smoking and alcohol, none
5	History of addiction1	Tobacco chewing, tobacco smoking, gutka, alcohol, smoking and alcohol, none
6	Comorbid condition	Hypertension, diabetes, immunocompromised, none
7	Comorbid condition1	Hypertension, diabetes, immunocompromised, none
8	Gross examination	Ulceroproliferative, infiltrative, verrucous, plaque-like, polypoidal
9	Site	BM, LA, RMT, LIP, tongue, UA, palate
10	Predisposing factor	Leukoplakia, erythoplakia, submucous fibrosis, linchen planus, none
11	Tumor size	<2 cm, 2 to 4 cm, >4 cm
12	Neck node	Present, absent
13	LFT	Normal, deranged
14	FNAC of neck node	Yes, no
15	Diagnostic biopsy	Squamous cell carcinoma, variant of SCC, benign
16	USG	Yes, no
17	CT scan/MRI	Bony involvement, normal
18	Diagnosis	SCC, verrucous, benign, plaque-like, sarcomatoid, acantholytic, adenoca, lymphoepithelioma-like
19	Staging	I, II, III, IV
20	Surgery	Yes, no
21	Radiotherapy	Yes, no

(continued)

Table 15.1 (Continued) Variables and Their Domains

No.	Variable	Domain
22	Chemotherapy	Yes, no
23	Histopathology	Variant of SSC—verrucous, adenoca, basaloid, plaque-like, sarcomatoid, acantholytic, lymphoepithelioma-like
24	1st follow-up symptoms	Difficulty in swallowing, swelling
25	1st follow-up examination	Ulceroproliferative, infiltrative, verrucous, plaque-like, polypoidal
26	2nd follow-up symptoms	Difficulty in swallowing, swelling
27	2nd follow-up examination	Ulceroproliferative, infiltrative, verrucous, plaque-like, polypoidal
28	3rd follow-up symptoms	Difficulty in swallowing, swelling
29	3rd follow-up examination	Ulceroproliferative, infiltrative, verrucous, plaque-like, polypoidal
30	4th follow-up symptoms	Difficulty in swallowing, swelling
31	4th follow-up examination	Ulceroproliferative, infiltrative, verrucous, plaque-like, polypoidal
32	5th follow-up symptoms	Difficulty in swallowing, swelling
33	5th follow-up examination	Ulceroproliferative, infiltrative, verrucous, plaque-like, polypoidal
34	Survival	Yes, no

Note: BM, buccal mucosa; LA, lower alveolus; RMT, revto molar trigone; UA, upper alveolus.

15.6.1 Building a Model

There are five prediction models that have been developed as a case study. The attribute "survival" is considered as a target variable for all the models. Classification technique is used for analysis, category weights are distributed over the entire data file, misclassification costs are equal (unitary), and variable weights are also equal.

15.6.1.1 DT Model

The maximum number of splitting levels of the model is 10, and the splitting algorithm used is Gini. The minimum size node to split is 10, whereas the minimum number of rows allowed in a node is 5. The maximum number of categories for continuous predictors is 1000. A cross-validation method with 10 folds is used for tree pruning and validation. Minimum cost complexity (0.00 S.E.) is used as a tree pruning criterion. The maximum depth of the tree is 2. The total number of group splits is 1. The full tree has two terminal nodes. The minimum validation relative error occurs with two nodes. The relative error value is 0.0000 with a standard error of 0.0000.

15.6.1.2 TB Model

The maximum number of trees in a TB series is 400. The maximum number of splitting levels is 5. The minimum size node to split is 10. The maximum number of categories for continuous predictors is 1000. A random sampling (20%) validation method is used in this model. Tree pruning criterion is minimum absolute error. All 18 predictors were considered for each split. The full series has 400 trees. The minimum error with the training data occurs with 30 trees. The minimum error with the test data also occurs with 30 trees. The minimum point is smoothed by 5 trees. The specified minimum number of trees is 10. The tree series will be pruned to 30 trees. The maximum depth of any tree in the series is 2. The average number of group splits in each tree is 1.0.

15.6.1.3 DTF Model

The maximum number of trees in DTF is 200. The maximum number of splitting levels is 50. The minimum size node to split is 2. The maximum number of categories for continuous predictors is 1000. Surrogate splitters are used for missing values. An out of bag (OOB) tree validation method is used for this model. The full forest has 200 trees. Four predictors (out of 18) were used for each split. The maximum depth of any tree in the forest is 4. The average number of group splits in each tree is 1.5.

15.6.1.4 MLP Model

The number of layers is 3 (input, hidden, and output). Hidden layer 1 neurons search from 2 to 20. The hidden layer and output layer activation function used in this model is logistic. A cross-validation method with 10 folds is used for validation, whereas network size evaluation is performed using fourfold cross-validation. The network is built using two neurons for hidden layer 1. The architecture of MLP is presented in Table 15.2. The category weights (prior probabilities) and training statistics of the network are given in Tables 15.3 and 15.4, respectively.

Table 15.2   Architecture of Multilayer Perceptron Network

Layer	Neurons	Activation	Min. Weight	Max. Weight
Input	34	Passthru	–	–
Hidden 1	2	Logistic	−1.678e+000	3.371e+000
Output	2	Logistic	−3.760e+000	3.463e+000

Table 15.3   Category Weight of Multilayer Perceptron Network

Category	Probability
Survival = D	0.6748047
Survival = A	0.3251953

Table 15.4   Training Statistics of Multilayer Perceptron Network

Process	Time	Evaluations	Error
Conjugate gradient	00:00:00.3	91,372	3.7266e−007

15.6.1.5 SVM Model

The Type of SVM model built is C-SVC. RBF is the SVM kernel function. A cross-validation method with 10 folds is used for validation. The search criterion used by the model is minimize total error. A total of 148 points are evaluated during search. No error is found by search. SVM grid and pattern searches found optimal values for parameters: epsilon = 0.001, C = 0.1, and gamma = 0.001.

Number of support vectors used by the model = 666.

15.6.2 Misclassification Table

If the target variable is categorical and a classification tree is built, then a misclassification summary table presents the number of rows with a particular category that were misclassified by the tree, for both a training as well as a validation data set. Misclassification statistics are the same for decision tree (DT), decision tree forest (DTF), multilayer perceptron (MLP), and support vector machine (SVM) for both training and validation data, as shown in Table 15.5, whereas the misclassification statistics of the TreeBoost (TB) model for both training and validation data are shown in Tables 15.6 and 15.7, respectively. However, overall accuracy for the entire aforementioned model is 100.00%.

Table 15.5   Misclassification for DT, DTF, MLP, and SVM (Training and Validation Data)

Category	Actual		Misclassified			
	Count	Weight	Count	Weight	%	Cost
A	333	333	0	0	0.000	0.000
D	691	691	0	0	0.000	0.000
Total	1024	1024	0	0	0.000	0.000

Table 15.6   Misclassification for TB (Training Data)

Category	Actual		Misclassified			
	Count	Weight	Count	Weight	%	Cost
A	266	266	0	0	0.000	0.000
D	553	553	0	0	0.000	0.000
Total	819	819	0	0	0.000	0.000

Table 15.7   Misclassification for TB (Validation Data)

Category	Actual		Misclassified			
	Count	Weight	Count	Weight	%	Cost
A	67	67	0	0	0.000	0.000
D	138	138	0	0	0.000	0.000
Total	205	205	0	0	0.000	0.000

Table 15.8   Confusion Matrix (DT, DTF, MLP, and SVM)

	Training Data		Validation Data	
	Predicted Category		Predicted Category	
Actual Category	A	D	A	D
A	333	0	333	0
D	0	691	0	691

Table 15.9   Confusion Matrix (TB)

	Training Data		Validation Data	
	Predicted Category		Predicted Category	
Actual Category	A	D	A	D
A	266	0	67	0
D	0	533	0	138

15.6.3 Confusion Matrix

A confusion matrix provides detailed information about how data rows are classified by the model. The matrix has a row and column for each category of the target variable. The categories shown in the first column are the actual categories of the target variable. The categories shown across the top of the table are the predicted categories. The numbers in the cells are the weights of the data rows with the actual category of the row and the predicted category of the column. The numbers in the diagonal cells are the weights for the correctly classified cases where the actual category matches the predicted category. The off-diagonal cells have misclassified row weights. The confusion matrix for both training and validation data for DT, DTF, MLP, and SVM is the same and is shown in Table 15.8. The confusion matrix of the TB model for both training and validation data is shown in Table 15.9.

15.6.4 Sensitivity and Specificity

The sensitivity and specificity report is generated only for classification problems (categorical target variable). One category of the target variable is called the positive category, and the other is called the negative category. True positive (TP) means patients who are predicted as malignant among malignant patients. True negative (TN) means patients who are predicted as nonmalignant among nonmalignant patients. False positive (FP) means patients who are predicted as nonmalignant among malignant patients. False negative (FN) means patients who are predicted as malignant among nonmalignant patients. The sensitivity and specificity were calculated by TP, TN, FP, and FN as shown in Table 15.10. Sensitivity means the probability that the algorithms can correctly predict nonmalignancy. Specificity means the probability that the algorithms can correctly predict malignancy.

Table 15.10 Sensitivity and Specificity

Actual Class	Predicted Class	
	True	*False*
True	TP	FP
False	FN	TN
	TP + FN	FP + TN

Note: Sensitivity = TP/(TP + FN); Specificity = TN/(FP + TN).

Survival = D is considered as a positive and survival = A is considered as negative for all the models developed. The positive/negative ratio, accuracy, TP, TN, FP, FN, sensitivity, specificity, geometric mean of sensitivity and specificity, positive predictive value (PPV), negative predictive value (NPV), and geometric mean of PPV and NPV for training and validation data for all the models developed are shown in Table 15.11.

Table 15.11 Sensitivity and Specificity

Details	(DT, DTF, MLP, and SVM Model) (Training, Validation)	TreeBoost Model	
		Training Data	*Validation Data*
Total records	1024	819	205
Positive/negative ratio	2.08	2.08	2.08
Accuracy	100%	100%	100%
TP	691 (67.5%)	553 (67.5%)	138 (67.5%)
TN	333 (32.5%)	266 (32.5%)	67 (32.5%)
FP	0 (0.0%)	0 (0.0%)	0 (0.0%)
FN	0 (0.0%)	0 (0.0%)	0 (0.0%)
Sensitivity	100%	100%	100%
Specificity	100%	100%	100%
Geometric mean of sensitivity and specificity	100%	100%	100%
PPV	100%	100%	100%
NPV	100%	100%	100%
Geometric mean of PPV and NPV	100%	100%	100%
Precision	100%	100%	100%

15.6.5 Probability Calibration

The probability calibration report shows how the predicted probability of a target category is distributed and provides a means for gauging the accuracy of predicted probabilities. The probability calibration report is generated only when a classification analysis is performed and there are two target categories (e.g., survival = dead [D] or alive [A]). If the model is accurate, the predicted probability of an event occurring should match the actual proportion of times that the event occurs. For problems where probability estimates are important, the following values are excellent overall indicators of the quality of the model:

1. *Average weighted probability error*: This is the average error between the predicted probability and the actual occurrence rate weighted by the number of rows.
2. *Average weighted squared probability error*: This is computed in the same way as the average error, except that the error is squared before being multiplied by the weight and added into the sum. After the total squared error is added up, the square root is computed, and that is the result reported for this statistic.

The probability calibration report for survival = dead (D) as well as survival = alive (A) is generated for all the models, which provides a breakdown for making a comparison.

15.6.5.1 DT

Probability calibration for survival = D or A is the same.
Average weighted probability error for training and validation data = 0.000000.
Average weighted squared probability error for training and validation data = 0.000000.

15.6.5.2 TB

Probability calibration for survival = D or A is the same for this model as well and is shown in Figure 15.5. Average weighted probability error for training data = 0.324473.

Average weighted squared probability error for training data = 0.346345.
Average weighted probability error for validation data = 0.008016.
Average weighted squared probability error for validation data = 0.008553.

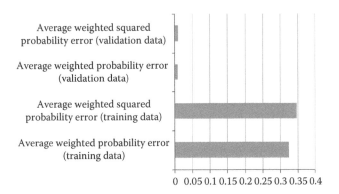

Figure 15.5 Probability calibration for TB model (survival = D or A).

15.6.5.3 DTF

In this model also, probability calibration for survival = D or A is the same and is shown in Figure 15.6.

Average weighted probability error for training data = 0.000042.
Average weighted squared probability error for training data = 0.000073.

15.6.5.4 MLP

In this model, the probability calibration for survival = D and A is different and is shown in Figure 15.7.
Probability calibration for survival = D:

Average weighted probability error for training data = 0.100202.
Average weighted squared probability error for training data = 0.100202.
Average weighted probability error for validation data = 0.133785.
Average weighted squared probability error for validation data = 0.11579.

Probability calibration for survival = A:

Average weighted probability error for training data = 0.100202.
Average weighted squared probability error for training data = 0.100202.
Average weighted probability error for validation data = 0.108394.
Average weighted squared probability error for validation data = 0.104252.

15.6.5.5 SVM

In this model also, probability calibration for survival = D and A is the same and is shown in Figure 15.8.

Average weighted probability error for training data = 0.002174.
Average weighted squared probability error for training data = 0.002646.
Average weighted probability error for validation data = 0.002415.
Average weighted squared probability error for validation data = 0.002939.

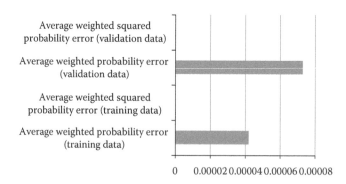

Figure 15.6   Probability calibration for DTF model (survival = D or A).

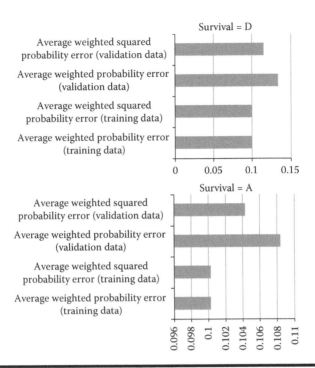

Figure 15.7   Probability calibration for MLP model.

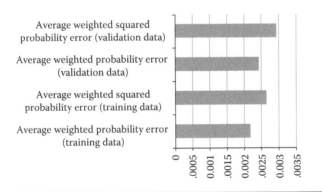

Figure 15.8   Probability calibration for SVM model (survival = D or A).

15.6.6 *Probability Threshold*

The probability threshold report provides information about how different probability thresholds would affect target category assignments. The threshold report provides a convenient way to see the trade-off between impurity and loss as the probability threshold is varied. The probability threshold report is generated only when a classification analysis is performed and there are two target categories. Probability threshold analysis is carried out for survival = D for all the models.

15.6.6.1 DT

Area under the receiver operation characteristic (ROC) curve (AUC) for training and test data = 1.000000.
Threshold to minimize misclassification for training and test data = 0.000000.
Threshold to minimize weighted misclassification for training and test data = 0.000000.
Threshold to balance misclassifications for test data = 0.000000.

15.6.6.2 TB

AUC for training data = 1.000000.
Threshold to minimize misclassification for training data = 0.499121.
Threshold to minimize weighted misclassification for training data = 0.499121.
Threshold to balance misclassifications for training data = 0.249561.
AUC for test data = 1.000000.
Threshold to minimize misclassification for test data = 0.012298.
Threshold to minimize weighted misclassification for test data = 0.012298.
Threshold to balance misclassifications for test data = 0.006149.

15.6.6.3 DTF

AUC = 1.000000.
Threshold to minimize misclassification = 0.028571.
Threshold to minimize weighted misclassification = 0.028571.
Threshold to balance misclassifications = 0.021429.

15.6.6.4 MLP

AUC for training data = 1.000000.
Threshold to minimize misclassification for training data = 0.100113.
Threshold to minimize weighted misclassification for training data = 0.100113.
Threshold to balance misclassifications for training data = 0.100107.
AUC for test data = 1.000000.
Threshold to minimize misclassification for test data = 0.103332.
Threshold to minimize weighted misclassification for test data = 0.103332.
Threshold to balance misclassifications for test data = 0.102676.

15.6.6.5 SVM

AUC for training data = 1.000000.
Threshold to minimize misclassification for training data = 0.000003.
Threshold to minimize weighted misclassification for training data = 0.000003.
Threshold to balance misclassifications for training data = 0.484782.
AUC for test data = 1.000000.
Threshold to minimize misclassification for test data = 0.000007.
Threshold to minimize weighted misclassification for test data = 0.000007.
Threshold to balance misclassifications for test data = 0.481395.

15.6.7 Lift and Gain

The lift and gain table is a useful tool for measuring the value of a predictive model. Lift and gain values are especially useful when a model is being used to target (prioritize) marketing efforts. The basic idea of lift and gain is to sort the predicted target values in a decreasing order of purity on some target category and then compare the proportion of cases with the category in each bin with the overall proportion. In the case of a model with a continuous target variable, the predicted target values are sorted in a decreasing target value order and then compared with the mean target value. The lift and gain values show how much improvement the model provides in picking out the best 10%, 20%, and so forth of the cases.

15.6.7.1 DT, DTF, MLP, and SVM

Lift and gain for training data as well as validation data for the models are the same, which are mentioned in the following:

Lift/gain for survival = A
Average gain = 2.012
Percentage of cases with survival = A: 32.52%

Lift/gain for survival = D
Average gain = 1.366
Percentage of cases with survival = D: 67.48%

15.6.7.2 TB

Lift and gain for training data are shown in the following:

Lift/gain for survival = A
Average gain = 2.018
Percentage of cases with survival = A: 32.48%

Lift/gain for survival = D
Average gain = 1.367
Percentage of cases with survival = D: 67.52%

Lift and gain for validation data are shown in the following:

Lift/gain for survival = A
Average gain = 1.990
Percentage of cases with survival = A: 32.68%

Lift/gain for survival = D
Average gain = 1.361
Percentage of cases with survival = D: 67.32%

15.6.8 Overall Importance of Variables

The most important attribute according to most of the models is "diagnostic biopsy." However, the overall importance of attributes as per the DTF model is presented in Table 15.12.

15.6.9 Analysis Run Time

The minimum analysis time is taken using the single tree model, whereas multilayer perceptron was used for the maximum time for analysis. The analysis time of all the models is presented in Table 15.13.

Table 15.12 Importance of Variables

Variable	Importance
Diagnostic biopsy	100.000
Diagnosis	65.210
Radiotherapy	50.881
Gross examination	41.033
Histopathology	38.369
Clinical symptom	25.738
Staging	25.238
Neck nodes	13.800
Chemotherapy	11.243
Predisposing factor	6.072
Tumor size	4.863
USG	4.062
LFT	2.510
Comorbid condition	2.142
Site	1.393
History of addiction	0.985

Table 15.13 Analysis Run Time

Model	Analysis Run Time
Single tree	00:00.40
Decision tree forest	00:00.56
TreeBoost	00:01.24
Multilayer perceptron	00:05.37
Support vector machine	02:02.94

15.6.10 Comparison of Models

We provide a comparison of all five models on the basis of performance, given as follows. The DT, MLP, and SVM use the cross-validation method with 10 folds. The DTF uses the OOB validation method, and the TB model uses a random sampling (20%) validation method. The MLP uses logistic as an activation function at the hidden and output layer. The RBF is the SVM kernel function.

1. *Misclassification*: There is no row in any category that is misclassified, and misclassification costs are equal for all the models.
2. *Confusion matrix*: All the cases have been correctly classified, and the actual category matches the predicted category in all the models. The off-diagonal cells have "0," which indicates there is no misclassified row in any of the models.
3. *Sensitivity and specificity*: It is 100% for all the models.
4. *Probability calibration*: Comparison of probability calibration for survival = D and A for all the models on training data as well as validation data shows that the multilayer perceptron model and SVM are better, and the same is presented in Tables 15.14 and 15.15, respectively.

Table 15.14 Probability Calibration of DT, TB, DTF, MLP, and SVM for Survival = A

	Survival = A				
Probability Calibration	*DT*	*TB*	*DTF*	*MLP*	*SVM*
Average weighted probability error (training data)	0.0	0.324473	0.000042	0.100202	0.002174
Average weighted squared probability error (training data)	0.0	0.346345	–	0.100202	0.002646
Average weighted probability error (validation data)	0.0	0.008016	0.000073	0.108394	0.002415
Average weighted squared probability error (validation data)	0.0	0.008553	–	0.104252	0.002939

Table 15.15 Probability Calibration of DT, TB, DTF, MLP, and SVM for Survival = D

	Survival = D				
Probability Calibration	*DT*	*TB*	*DTF*	*MLP*	*SVM*
Average weighted probability error (training data)	0.0	0.324473	0.000042	0.100202	0.002174
Average weighted squared probability error (training data)	0.0	0.346345	–	0.100202	0.002646
Average weighted probability error (validation data)	0.0	0.008016	0.000073	0.133785	0.002415
Average weighted squared probability error (validation data)	0.0	0.008553	–	0.115790	0.002939

5. *Threshold analysis*: Comparison of probability threshold analysis for survival = D on training data as well as validation data shows that the AUC is 1.000000 for all the models. Threshold analysis to "minimize the misclassification," "minimize the weighted misclassification," and "balance misclassification" shows better results in the SVM model, and the comparison is presented in Tables 15.16 and 15.17 and Figures 15.9 and 15.10.

Table 15.16   Threshold Analysis for Training Data of DT, TB, DFT, MLP, and SVM

Threshold Analysis	Training Data			MLP	SVM
	DT	TB	DTF		
Area under ROC curve	1.000000	1.000000	1.000000	1.000000	1.000000
Threshold to minimize misclassification	0.000000	0.499121	0.028571	0.100113	0.000003
Threshold to minimize weighted misclassification	0.000000	0.499121	0.028571	0.100113	0.000003
Threshold to balance misclassifications	0.000000	0.249561	0.021429	0.100107	0.484782

Table 15.17   Threshold Analysis for Test Data of DT, TB, DFT, MLP, and SVM

Threshold Analysis	Test Data			MLP	SVM
	DT	TB	DTF		
Area under ROC curve	1.000000	1.000000	1.000000	1.000000	1.000000
Threshold to minimize misclassification	0.000000	0.012298	0.028571	0.103332	0.000007
Threshold to minimize weighted misclassification	0.000000	0.012298	0.028571	0.103332	0.000007
Threshold to balance misclassifications	0.000000	0.006149	0.021429	0.102676	0.481395

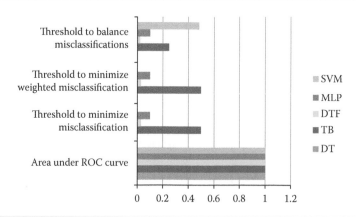

Figure 15.9   Comparison: threshold analysis for training data of DT, TB, DFT, MLP, and SVM.

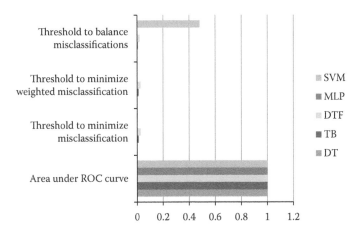

Figure 15.10   Comparison: threshold analysis for test data of DT, TB, DFT, MLP, and SVM.

6. *Lift and gain*: All the models show similar results.
7. *Importance of the variable*: The variable "diagnostic biopsy" is the most important variable according to all the models. However, the variable "diagnosis" is the next most important variable as per the DTF model, whereas the variable "Radiotherapy" is the next most important variable as per the TB model.
8. *Analysis run time*: The single tree model took minimum analysis time, whereas multilayer perceptron took the maximum analysis time.

15.7 Conclusion

In this chapter, we have built five models for oral cancer prediction. All the models have similar results and performance as far as oral cancer prediction is concerned. The cases have been correctly classified by all the models. The sensitivity and specificity of these models is 100%. The lift and gain for all the models have similar results. "Diagnostic biopsy" has been identified as the most important attribute by all the models. The single tree model takes minimum time for analysis. All the models have given similar results in terms of misclassification statistics, confusion matrix, sensitivity and specificity, as well as lift and gain. However, the experimental results in terms of probability calibration and threshold analysis show better results in the SVM model, making it the most favorable model for predicting the survival rate of oral cancer patients.

References

1. Jemal, A., Siegel, R., Xu, J. and Ward, E. Cancer statistics. *CA: A Cancer Journal for Clinicians*. Vol. 60, pp. 277–300, 2010.
2. Ferlay, J., Shin, H. R. and Bray, F. Estimates of worldwide burden of cancer in 2008: GLOBOCAN 2008. *International Journal of Cancer*. Vol. 12, pp. 2893–2917, 2010.
3. Elango, J. K., Gangadharan, P., Sumithra, S. and Kuriakose, M. A. Trends of head and neck cancers in urban and rural India. *Asian Pacific Journal of Cancer Prevention*. Vol. 7, no. 1, pp. 108–112, 2006.
4. Sankaranarayanan, R., Ramadas, K. and Thomas, G. Effect of screening on oral cancer mortality in Kerala, India: A cluster-randomised controlled trial. *The Lancet*. Vol. 365, no. 9475, pp. 1927–1933, 2005.

5. Manoharan, N., Tyagi, B. B. and Raina, V. Cancer incidences in rural Delhi—2004–05. *Asian Pacific Journal of Cancer Prevention*. Vol. 11, no. 1, pp. 73–78, 2010.

6. Agrawal, M., Pandey, S., Jain, S. and Maitin, S. Oral cancer awareness of the general public in Gorakhpur City, India. *Asian Pacific Journal of Cancer Prevention*. Vol. 13, pp. 5195–5199, 2012.

7. Khandekar, P. S., Bagdey, P. S. and Tiwari, R. R. Oral cancer and some epidemiological factors: A hospital based study. *Indian Journal of Community Medicine*. Vol. 31, no. 3, pp. 157–159, 2006.

8. Han, J., Kamber, M. and Pei, J. *Data Mining: Concepts and Techniques*, Third Edition. Morgan Kaufmann Publishers Inc., San Francisco, 2012.

9. Kantardzic and Mehmed. *Data Mining: Concepts, Models, Methods, and Algorithms*. John Wiley & Sons, Inc., Hoboken, NJ, 2013.

10. Available at http://www.dtreg.com.

11. Milovic, B. and Milovic, M. Prediction and decision making in health care using data mining. *International Journal of Public Health Science*. Vol. 1, no. 2, pp. 69–78, 2012.

12. Anuradha, K. and Sankaranarayanan, K. Identification of suspicious regions to detect oral cancers at an earlier stage—A literature survey. *International Journal of Advances in Engineering & Technology*. Vol. 3, no. 1, pp. 84–91, 2012.

13. Nahar, J., Kevin, S. T., Ali, A. B. M. S. and Chen, Y. P. Significant cancer prevention factor extraction: An association rule discovery approach. *Journal of Medical Systems*, Springer, Vol. 35, no. 3, pp. 353–367, June 2011.

14. Chuang, L. Y., Wu, K. C., Chang, H. W. and Yang, C. H. Support vector machine-based prediction for oral cancer using four SNPS in DNA repair genes. Proceedings of the International Multi Conference of Engineers and Computer Scientists, March 16–18, 2011.

15. Gadewal, N. S. and Zingde, S. M. Database and interaction network of genes involved in oral cancer: Version II. *Bioinformation*. Vol. 6, no. 4, pp. 169–170, 2011.

16. Kent, S. Diagnosis of oral cancer using genetic programming—A technical report. CSTR -96-14, 1996.

17. Kaladhar, D. S. V. G. K., Chandana, B. and Kumar, P. B. Predicting cancer survivability using Classification algorithms. *International Journal of Research and Reviews in Computer Science (IJRRCS)*. Vol. 2, no. 2, pp. 340–343, 2011.

18. Shah, S. and Kusiak, A. Cancer gene search with data-mining and genetic algorithms. *Computers in Biology and Medicine*, Vol. 37, pp. 251–261, 2007. Available at http://www.intl.elsevierhealth.com/journals/cobm.

19. Swami, S., Thakur, R. S. and Chande, L. R. S. Multi-dimensional association rules extraction in smoking habits database. *International Journal of Advanced Networking and Applications*. Vol. 3, no. 3, pp. 1176–1179, 2011.

20. Ha, S. H. and Joo, S. H. A hybrid data mining method for medical classification of chest pain. *World Academy of Science, Engineering and Technology*. Vol. 37, pp. 608–613, 2010.

21. RuthRamya, K., Anusha, K., Chanti, K., Srividya, V. and Praveen, P. A class based approach for medical classification of chest pain. *International Journal of Engineering Trends and Technology*. Vol. 3, no. 2, pp. 89–93, 2012.

22. Gupta, M. K., Agarwal, K., Prakash, N., Singh, D. B. and Mishra, K. Prediction of miRNA in HIV-1 genome and its targets through artificial neural network: A bioinformatics approach. *Network Modeling Analysis in Health Informatics and Bioinformatics*. Vol. 1, no. 4, pp. 141–151, 2012.

23. Abual-Rub, M. S., Ai-Betal, M. A., Abdullah, R. and Khader, A. T. A hybrid harmony search algorithm for ab initio protein tertiary structure prediction. *Network Modeling Analysis in Health Informatics and Bioinformatics*. Vol. 1, no. 3, pp. 69–85, 2012.

24. HariKumar, R., Vasanthi, N. S. and Balasubramani, M. Performance analysis of artificial neural networks and statistical methods in classification of oral and breast cancer stages. *International Journal of Soft Computing and Engineering (IJSCE)*. Vol 2, no. 3, pp. 263–269, 2012.

25. Exarchos, K. P., Rigas, G., Goletsis, Y. and Fotiadis, D. I. Modelling of oral cancer progression using dynamic Bayesian networks. *Data Mining for Biomarker Discovery, Springer Optimization and its Applications*. pp. 199–212, 2012.

26. Sankaranarayanan, R. Oral cancer in India: An epidemiologic and clinical review. *Oral Surgery, Oral Medicine, Oral Pathology*. Vol. 69, no. 3, pp. 325–330, 1990.

27. Fayyad, U. M., Piatetsky-Shapiro, G. and Smyth, P. *From Data Mining to Knowledge Discovery: An Overview. Advances in Knowledge Discovery and Data Mining.* AAAI Press/MIT Press, Menlo Park, Cambridge, MA, pp. 1–36, 1996.
28. Chakrabarti, S., Ester, M., Fayyad, U., Gehrke, J., Han, J., Morishita, S., Piatetsky-Shapiro, G., and Wang, W. Data Mining Curriculum—A Proposal (Version 0.91), ACM SIGKDD. April 30, 2006.
29. Clifton, C. *Encyclopædia Britannica: Definition of Data Mining,* 2010, http://www.britannica.com /EBchecked/topic/1056150.data-mining.
30. Hastie, T., Tibshirani, R. and Friedman, J. *The Elements of Statistical Learning: Data Mining, Inference, and Prediction,* 2nd edition, Springer, LLC, 2009.
31. Cunningham, S. J. and Holmes, S. Developing innovative applications in agriculture using data mining. Proceedings of the Southeast Asia Regional Computer Confederation Conference, 1999.
32. Werning, J. W. *Oral Cancer: Diagnosis, Management, and Rehabilitation.* Thieme Medical Publishers, New York, 2007.
33. Available at http://www.oralcancerfoundation.org/facts/index.htm.
34. Coelho, K. R. Challenges in oral cancer burden in India. *Journal of Cancer Epidemiology.* Hindawi Publishing Corporation. Vol. 2012, 2012.
35. Available at http://www.oralcancerawareness.org.
36. Scully, C., Bagan, J. V., Hopper, C. and Epstein, J. B. Oral cancer: Current and future diagnostics techniques—A review article. *American Journal of Dentistry.* Vol. 21, no. 4, pp. 199–209, 2008.
37. Available at www.yourtotalhealth.ivillage.com.
38. Jemal, A., Thimas, A., Murray, T. and Thun, M. Cancer statistics. *CA: A Cancer Journal for Clinicians.* Vol. 52, pp. 181–182, 2002.
39. Woolgar, J. A., Scott, J., Vaughan, E. D., Brown, J. S., West, C. R. and Rogers, S. Survival, metastasis and recurrence of oral cancer in relation to pathological features. *Annals of the Royal College of Surgeons of England.* Vol. 77, pp. 325–331, 1995.
40. LeCun, Y. Modeles connexionnistes de l'apprentissage (connectionist learning models). Doctoral dissertation, Université P. et M. Curie (Paris 6), 1987.
41. Rumelhart, D., Hinton, G. and Williams, R. Learning internal representations by backpropagating errors. In D. Rumelhart and J. Mc-Clelland (Eds.), *Parallel Distributed Processing: Explorations in the Microstructure of Cognition,* Vol. 1, pp. 318–362. MIT Press, Cambridge, 1986.
42. Vapnik, V. *The Nature of Statistical Learning Theory,* Second Edition. Springer, New York, 1995.
43. Lippmann, R. P. An introduction to computing with neural nets. *IEEE ASSP Magazine,* Vol. 4, pp. 4–22, 1987.
44. Cristianini, N. and Shawe-Taylor, J. *An Introduction to Support Vector Machines.* Cambridge University Press, Cambridge, 2000.
45. Sharma, N. and Om, H. Framework for early detection and prevention of oral cancer using data mining. *International Journal of Advances in Engineering and Technology,* Vol. 4, no. 2, pp. 302–310, 2012.

Chapter 16

Human Identification Using Individual Dental Radiograph Records

Omaima Nomir and Mohamed Abdel-Mottaleb

Contents

The goal of forensic dentistry is to identify individuals based on their dental characteristics. In this chapter, we present a system for automating that process by identifying people from dental x-ray images. Given a dental record of a postmortem (PM), the proposed system retrieves the best matches from an antemortem (AM) database. The system automatically segments dental x-ray images into individual teeth and extracts representative feature vectors for each tooth, which are later used for retrieval. We developed a new method for teeth segmentation and three different methods for representing and matching teeth. The system relies on the three different types of dental radiographs for identification. The identification procedure is carried out by integrating the results of using an individual's three available types of dental radiographs. In this chapter, we address the problem of identifying individuals based on more than one type of dental radiographs for the first time, where three available types of dental radiographs are used. The experimental results show that using the three types of dental radiographs enhances the overall human identification procedure. Also, the experimental results of the different modules and the results of fusing the matching techniques are presented. To increase the accuracy of the identification process, the three matching techniques are fused together to improve the overall performance. We introduce some scenarios for fusing the three matchers at the score level as well as at the decision level.

16.1 Introduction

Human identification is a fundamental activity at the heart of our society and culture. For many applications, ensuring the identity and authenticity of people is a prerequisite. Biometrics identification refers to identifying an individual based on his or her distinguishing characteristics. It is being accepted by government and industry alike that automated biometric identification will become a necessary fact of life.

Forensic identification is typically defined as the use of science or technology in identifying human beings in the court of law. It may take place prior to death and is referred to as antemortem (AM) identification. Identification may as well be carried out after death and is called postmortem (PM) identification. While behavioral characteristics (e.g., speech) are not suitable for PM identification, most of the physiological characteristics are not appropriate for PM identification as well, especially under severe circumstances encountered in mass disasters (e.g., airplane crashes) or when identification is being attempted more than a couple of weeks PM, because of the decay of soft tissues of the body. Therefore, a PM biometric identifier has to survive such severe conditions and resist early decay that affects body tissues. Because of their survivability, the best candidates for PM biometric identification are the dental features, and now the importance of using dental records for human identification is well recognized (Jain and Ross 2002).

Forensic odontology (Brogdon 1998) is the branch of forensics concerned with identifying humans based on their dental features. Dental identification is a comparative technique, where the PM dental records are analyzed and compared against AM records to confirm identity and establish the degree of certainty that the dental records obtained from the remains of a decedent and the AM dental records of a missing person are from the same individual. Currently the identification is carried out manually by comparing extracted features from a PM dental record to extracted fractures from a database of AM records. According to forensic experts (Brogdon 1998), dental characteristics preserve their shape after death for a long period of time. Several individual teeth may get missed or filled after its AM record is taken; hence, dental features need to be recorded based on the contour/shape of individual teeth rather than the contour of the whole jaw.

The objective of our research is to automate the process of forensic odontology using image processing and pattern recognition techniques. There are several advantages for automating this procedure. An automatic system can perform identification on a large-scale database, whereas a manual or semiautomatic system is useful for verification on a small data set. Also, automating this process will come up with an ordered list of closest matches that we may refer to in order to decide the best match. Accordingly, this will facilitate for forensic odontologists to only manually verify through this best match short list instead of manually searching a large number of AM records. In order to achieve this goal, we need to automate the process of segmenting the dental radiographs and to separate each individual tooth. For the automated identification, the dental records are usually available as radiographs. An automated dental identification system (ADIS) consists of two main stages: feature extraction and feature matching. During feature extraction, certain salient information of the teeth such as contours, artificial prosthesis, and the number of cuspids is extracted from the radiographs.

In this chapter, we present a fully automated dental biometrics system. A block diagram of the proposed dental identification system is shown in Figure 16.1. This dental identification system can be used by both law enforcement and security agencies in both forensic and biometric

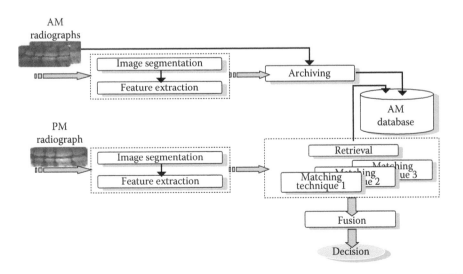

Figure 16.1 Dental identification system logical diagram.

identification. The system archives AM dental images in a database and searches the database for the best matches to a given PM image. The AM images are archived by segmenting and separating the individual teeth in the three different types (bitewing, panoramic, and periapical) of x-ray radiographs, and then extracting a set of features for each individual tooth.

Because of the poor quality of some radiographs, which is the main challenge in the identification procedure, in this chapter, we integrate the results when using the individual's dental records of the three available different types of dental radiographs (Nomir and Abdel-Mottaleb 2010). In order to achieve this, we enlarge the dental radiograph database, where different types of radiographs for a single person are available. This is the first research that integrates the results of using the three different types of dental radiographs for human identification.

The goal of the segmentation is to separate the teeth from the rest of the radiograph. Then, the individual teeth are separated by first separating the upper jaw from the lower jaw and then separating each tooth; this step is achieved using integral projection. After separating each tooth, we use and compare between three different methods to search the database for a given PM subject. In the first method, a set of salient points on the contour of each tooth is identified, and signatures for these points are extracted. These signatures are vectors that are extracted for each salient point. During searching, matching scores are generated based on the distances between the signature vectors of AM and PM teeth. In the second method, we use a hierarchical edge matching algorithm at different resolution levels. The technique is based on matching teeth contours using hierarchical chamfer distance. Using this hierarchical structure, the search space, as well as the computational load, is reduced significantly. In the third method, instead of using only the contour points as features, we combine region and boundary information to overcome the inherent limitations of using either representation alone. The process of matching is carried out based on two sets of features, where the first set is extracted using a force field transformation to represent the appearance of the tooth, and the second set consists of the Fourier descriptors of the contour of the tooth to represent the shape.

Finally, to increase the accuracy of the overall identification process, we fuse the three matching techniques. The fusion of information is an integral part of any identification systems. We analyze some scenarios for fusing the introduced matchers. Some scenarios are Boolean whereas others are statistical, and accordingly, the results are recorded using the different fusion scenarios.

There are only a few published works for dental image matching. Jain et al. (2003, 2004, 2005) propose a method for dental x-ray image segmentation and contour matching. They measure the distance between the PM and AM radiographs by combining the distance between the contours of the teeth and the distance between the shapes of the dental work.

Said et al. (2006) propose a method for dental radiograph registration based on genetic algorithms. This method is a preprocessing step of the image comparison component of ADIS. They used two multiresolution techniques—image subsampling and wavelet decomposition—to reduce the search space. A genetic algorithm was adopted to search for the best transformation parameters that give the maximum similarity score.

Zhou and Abed-Mottaleb (2005) present a system for archiving and retrieval of dental images to be used in identification based on dental images. The system includes steps for dental image classification, automatic segmentation of bitewing dental x-ray images, and teeth shape matching. They separated the tooth into crowns and roots. They extracted a set of features that are later used for identification.

We introduced an ADIS (Fahmy et al. 2004a,b,c, 2005; Nomir and Abdel-Mottaleb 2005, 2006) for identifying individuals using their dental x-ray records. ADIS is a process automation tool, for PM identification, designed to achieve accurate and timely identification results with minimum amount of human intervention. To this end, ADIS automates and facilitates some of the steps taken by forensic experts to examine missing and unidentified person (MUP) cases.

The rest of this chapter is organized as follows: Section 16.2 presents the automatic dental image segmentation technique, Section 16.3 presents the matching techniques, Section 16.4 presents the fusion of the three matching techniques using different scenarios to increase the accuracy of the overall identification process, and Section 16.5 concludes the chapter.

16.2 Radiograph Segmentation

Dental x-ray images are classified according to the view from which they are captured and their coverage (Brogdon 1998). The most commonly used dental x-ray radiographs are panoramic, periapical, and bitewing. Figure 16.2 shows an example of dental image types. The bitewing images hold more information about the curvature and the roots, and these images are the most common views made by dentists; therefore, we previously used them in our system. In this chapter, we extend our system to use the three different types of dental x-ray radiographs for the identification procedure (Nomir et al. 2010).

This section introduces our automatic dental segmentation technique (Nomir et al. 2005; Abdel-Mottaleb et al. 2003).

During the segmentation step, we use a checking criterion to classify the dental radiograph type into one of the three dental types (Nomir et al. 2010). The classification step is guided by the description of the three dental radiograph types: panoramic, periapical, and bitewing.

Our segmentation method consists of two stages. The first stage separates the teeth from the background using a two-step thresholding technique; this stage is detailed in Section 16.2.1. The second stage separates each individual tooth using integral projection; this stage is detailed in Section 16.2.2. Figure 16.3 shows a block diagram of the main steps of the segmentation algorithm. In Section 16.2.3, the experimental results for the segmentation algorithm are presented.

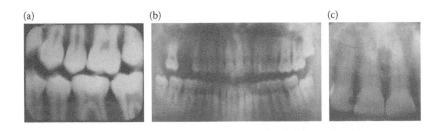

Figure 16.2   Example of x-ray dental images. (a) Bitewing; (b) panoramic; and (c) periapical.

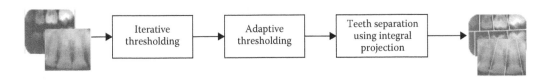

Figure 16.3   Segmentation algorithm.

16.2.1 Radiograph Segmentation

Dental x-ray images have three different regions: (1) the background or air, which has the lowest intensity and corresponds to soft tissues; (2) the bone areas, which have average intensity; and (3) the teeth, which have the highest intensity. In some cases, the intensity of the bone areas is close to the intensity of the teeth, which makes it difficult to use a single threshold for segmenting the whole image.

One important challenge that badly affects the accuracy of any identification system is the poor quality of some x-ray radiographs, which badly affects the final segmentation results.

Dental radiographs often suffer from uneven exposure and low contrast, which accordingly badly affects the performance of the dental x-ray segmentation technique; therefore, applying an enhancement step before the segmentation takes place usually helps the segmentation. Our enhancement procedure introduced in Zhou and Abdel Mottaleb (2005) is applied before the segmentation step in order to improve the dental x-ray radiograph segmentation results.

In Zhou and Abdel Mottaleb (2005), two morphological filters are used: the top-hat filter and the bottom-hat filter. Both filters are used to extract dark objects (or, conversely, light ones) on a light (or dark) slowly changing background. Both top-hat and bottom-hat filters are applied on the original dental x-ray radiograph. The enhanced dental x-ray radiograph is achieved by adding to the original dental x-ray radiograph the top-hat filter's result and subtracting the bottom-hat filter's result.

The first stage of the radiograph segmentation is to separate the teeth from the background using a two-step thresholding technique. It starts by iterative thresholding followed by adaptive thresholding (Gonzalez and Wood 2003) to segment the teeth from both the background and the bone areas. Figure 16.4 shows an example after applying the two-step thresholding technique.

16.2.2 Radiograph Classification and Teeth Separation

After segmenting the teeth from the background, each tooth is separated from its surroundings in order to prepare for feature extraction. This step is achieved by applying the horizontal integral projection followed by vertical integral projection Jain et al. (1995).

In this step, we classify the radiographs into three different types, the horizontal integral projection is applied to a given x-ray dental radiograph, and then we look for the line that produces the minimum horizontal projection. By checking the position of this line, we can classify radiographs as periapical in one class and panoramic and bitewing in the other class. In the periapical, the line

(a)   (b)

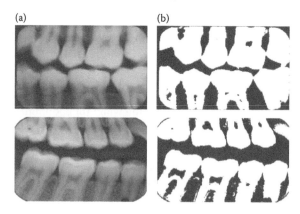

Figure 16.4 Result of applying the two-step thresholding technique. (a) Original image and (b) image after applying the technique.

will lie close to the upper or lower radiograph's edge, whereas in the panoramic and bitewing, it will lie close to the radiograph's center. The place for the line in the periapical will classify the radiographs into lower or upper periapical. If the line is close to the upper edge, the periapical radiograph is lower periapical; otherwise, it is upper periapical.

16.2.2.1 Horizontal Projection

As we mentioned before, the horizontal projection is used to discriminate between the different types of dental x-ray radiographs; after applying the horizontal projection and from the line that produces the minimum horizontal projection, we can discriminate them into two sets. One set has the periapical radiographs, and the second set has the panoramic and the bitewing radiographs.

As an example for the second set, if we consider the first bitewing image in Figure 16.4, it is clear that a horizontal or a near horizontal line can separate the upper jaw from the lower jaw.

This can be achieved by using horizontal projection as follows. Let $f(i,j)$ be an $m \times n$ (m columns × n rows) binary image obtained from the segmentation stage. The horizontal integral projection $H(i)$ is obtained by

$$H(i) = \sum_{j=1}^{n} f(i,j) \tag{16.1}$$

Assuming that it is possible to separate the upper jaw from the lower jaw by a straight line, the integral projection along that line will be minimal.

Since it is not always the case that this line is horizontal, we need to rotate the image in a small range of angles. To estimate that range of angles, we randomly selected 40 images from the database as a training set and found that the range [–20:20] is a suitable range of angles. We iteratively rotate the image in that range and find the angle at which a line that produces the minimum horizontal projection, θ, is obtained. This is achieved as follows:

$$\theta, i = \arg\min_{\theta, i} H_{\theta, i}(i) \tag{16.2}$$

where $H_{\theta}(i)$ is the horizontal integral projection obtained by rotating $f(i,j)$ with an angle θ. In Figure 16.5a, the minimum horizontal projection point is marked with a circle, and Figure 16.5b shows the corresponding horizontal line in the image. It is clear that this is the best horizontal line that can separate the two jaws without cutting through the teeth.

(a)　　　　　　　　　　　(b)

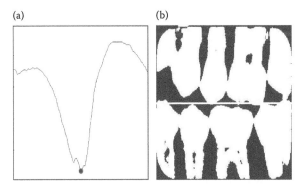

Figure 16.5 (a) Horizontal integral projection and (b) initial line segmenting the two jaws.

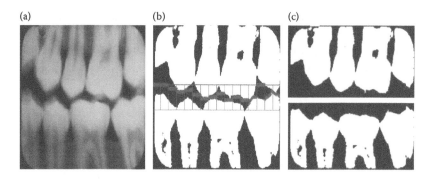

Figure 16.6 (a) Original image; (b) binary image with the exact locations for separating the two jaws; and (c) upper and lower jaws after separation.

In many cases, there is no single straight line that can separate the upper and lower jaws. Therefore, the initial straight line obtained from the horizontal projection is incrementally modified by reapplying the projection process in adjacent vertical strips in order to find the piecewise linear separation of the two jaws. The stripes are $h \times w$ pixels around the line, where h is the height of the strip and w is the width of the strip; in our experiments, we used $h = 40$ and $w = 20$. Figure 16.6 shows an example of separating the two jaws using this method. Figure 16.6a shows a case where there is no single line that can separate the two jaws. Figure 16.6b and c shows the result of using the piecewise separation method and the upper and lower jaws after the separation, respectively.

16.2.2.2 Separating Each Individual Tooth (Vertical Projection)

To separate each individual tooth, we use a technique similar to the one used in the horizontal projection. The goal is to find the lines that separate the adjacent teeth. This can be achieved by using the integral projection method in the vertical direction. If $f(i,j)$ is the $m \times n$ binary image obtained from the segmentation stage, the vertical projection $V(j)$ is calculated by

$$V(j) = \sum_{i=1}^{m} f(i,j) \tag{16.3}$$

The separating lines are located by finding valleys in the result of the vertical projection. Due to different teeth alignment, the lines are always neither vertical nor parallel. Therefore, we rotate the image in a small range of angles, for example, [–20:20] (we used a set of training data to estimate this range), and calculate the vertical projection for each angle in this range. For each projection, we use a threshold value to obtain the valleys that identify locations of vertical lines between adjacent teeth. In the experiments, we used a threshold value equal to 0.35 of the maximum number of the ones in the result of the projection. We then select the separating lines and the corresponding angles, which produce the minimum vertical projection among all the rotation angles. Figure 16.7 shows the detected separating lines overlaid over the original image.

Also, by applying the vertical integral projection and checking the number of separated teeth, we can classify the radiograph into panoramic or bitewing. If the number of teeth in the upper or lower jaws exceeds six, it is classified as panoramic; otherwise, the radiograph is classified as bitewing.

In case the radiograph is classified as periapical, we only need to apply the vertical integral projection.

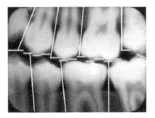

Figure 16.7 Result of teeth separation.

16.2.3 Experiments and Results

Our database was provided by the FBI's Criminal Justice Information Service (CJIS) division, which includes records of different dental radiograph types of AM as well as PM records. The database includes 50 subjects, 279 bitewing, 59 periapical, and 48 panoramic dental x-ray images.

First, all dental images in the database are enhanced. Then, the segmentation technique is applied to the enhanced dental images in the database. In case of the panoramic and bitewing dental images, the segmentation technique always correctly segments the upper jaw from the lower jaw for all the dental x-ray radiographs.

The results of the segmentation technique are shown in Table 16.1. The segmentation results of some teeth are shown in Figure 16.8. The cases where teeth were not correctly segmented are due to the poor quality of the dental radiographs. We also notice that the segmentation results

Table 16.1 Dental Radiograph Segmentation Results

	% of Correctly Segmented Teeth	
Radiograph Type	*Upper Jaw*	*Lower Jaw*
Bitewing	89%	85%
Periapical	88%	85%
Panoramic	84%	81%

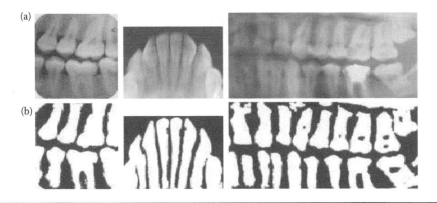

Figure 16.8 Teeth segmentation results for different radiographs types. (a) Original dental radiographs and (b) segmented teeth.

of the bitewing and periapical dental radiographs are much better than those for the panoramic radiographs. The reason is that the panoramic radiographs do not show details as fine as those in bitewing and periapical dental radiographs.

16.3 Dental X-Ray Teeth Matching

This section introduces our dental radiograph matching techniques. Each technique extracts a set of features from the previously segmented x-ray images.

Section 16.3.1 introduces a dental x-ray teeth matching technique that uses signature vectors. Section 16.3.2 introduces the hierarchal contour matching technique. Section 16.3.3 introduces the matching technique based on teeth shapes and appearances. Finally, Section 16.3.4 discusses the experimental results.

16.3.1 Dental X-Ray Teeth Matching Using Signature Vectors

This method relies on selecting a set of salient points from the object's contour and generating a signature vector for each salient point (Nomir et al. 2005; Abdel-Mottaleb et al. 2003). The signature vectors capture the curvature information for each salient point (Yamany and Farag 2003). Each element in the vector is the distance between the salient point and a point on the contour. Teeth matching is then performed by minimizing the Euclidean distance between the signature vectors of the PM and the AM teeth. Salient points are identified as the points of high curvature on the contour.

16.3.1.1 Contour Extraction and Teeth Numbering

To extract the contour points from the binary image that results from the segmentation, a connected component analysis using 8-connectivity (Gonzalez and Wood 2003) is applied.

For all the teeth in the database as well as for the PM query teeth, each tooth contour is represented by an equal number of points by applying an equal point sampling technique on the extracted tooth contour pixels. To increase the accuracy of our matching and to reduce the search space when matching, we only consider the corresponding teeth (i.e., teeth that have the same number). Each tooth is automatically numbered according to the universal teeth numbering system (Figure 16.9) using our algorithm described in Mahoor and Abdel-Mottaleb (2005). The algorithm used Bayesian classification to classify the teeth in a given bitewing image into molars and premolars and assign an absolute number to each tooth based on the common numbering system used in dentistry. This method is used to automatically number the panoramic and bitewing images. We modify the algorithm to automatically number the periapical images.

16.3.1.2 Generating Signature Vectors and Matching

We developed a method for shape description and matching. The method relies on selecting a set of salient points from the object's contour and generating a signature vector for each salient point (Yamany and Farag 2003). The algorithm calculates the curvature for every point on the contour and then selects the N points with the highest curvature as the salient points. A test is performed to eliminate spike points that have considerable higher curvature than their neighbors. These points are considered as noise. Figure 16.10 shows an example where the contour of the tooth is

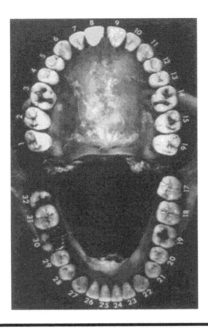

Figure 16.9   Upper and lower jaws with teeth numbered according to the universal system.

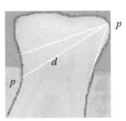

Figure 16.10   Generating the signature vector V_p for point p.

marked with black. For each salient point, p, defined by its *2D* coordinates, each point p_i on the contour can be related to p by the distance

$$d_i = \|p - p_i\| \tag{16.4}$$

and the signature vector V_p of the point p is defined as

$$V_p = [d_1, d_2, \ldots\ldots, d_M] \tag{16.5}$$

where M is the number of points on the tooth contour. This is done for all the N salient points; in the experiments, we chose $N = 20$.

Before matching, the contour of each tooth in a PM image has to be aligned with the contour of a corresponding tooth (i.e., have the same universal tooth number) in an AM image. There may be variations between the AM and PM teeth, regarding scale, rotation, and translation. To solve this problem, we apply a transformation T for aligning both teeth, which results in the minimum matching distance between both teeth. The alignment step assumes that the image of the PM tooth, P, is transformed with respect to the image of the AM tooth, P', by an affine transformation as follows:

$$T(p) = A \times P + \tau \tag{16.6}$$

where $P = (x, y)^T$ represents a point in the query contour, and $T(P)$ is the result of applying the affine transformation to the query tooth P. A is a transformation matrix that includes both rotation and scaling. τ is a translation vector. The parameters A and τ can be represented as

$$A = \begin{bmatrix} \cos\theta & \sin\theta \\ -\sin\theta & \cos\theta \end{bmatrix} X \begin{bmatrix} S_x & 0 \\ 0 & S_y \end{bmatrix} \tag{16.7}$$

$$\tau = \begin{bmatrix} \tau_x \\ \tau_y \end{bmatrix} \tag{16.8}$$

where θ is the rotation angle, S_x and S_y are the vertical and horizontal scale factors, respectively, and τ_x and τ_y are the vertical and horizontal translations, respectively. The five parameters (i.e., θ, S_x, S_y, τ_x, τ_y) are optimized to obtain the minimum matching distance between the transformed contour of the query AM tooth and the contour of the AM database tooth. Suppose we have a query tooth contour, q, and a database tooth contour, k. Their signature vectors Q_i and K_i are defined as follows:

$$Q_{i,j} = \lfloor \lVert qc_i - q_j \rVert \rfloor, i = 1...N, j = 1....M \tag{16.9}$$

where qc_i is a high curvature point, q_j is a point on the contour of the PM tooth, N is the number of high curvature points, and M is the number of points on the contour, and

$$K_{i,j} = \lfloor \lVert kc_i - k_j \rVert \rfloor, i = 1...N, j = 1....M \tag{16.10}$$

where kc_i is a high curvature point, and k_j is a point on the contour of the AM database tooth. After aligning the contour of a PM tooth with the contour of a corresponding tooth in an AM image, the matching distance is calculated by

$$D(T(q), K) = \sqrt{\sum_{i=1}^{N} \frac{1}{k_i'} \sum_{j=1}^{M} (Q_{i,j}' - K_{i,j})^2} \tag{16.11}$$

where $Q_{i,j}'$ is the feature j in the signature vector Q_i after applying the transformation T to the query PM tooth, q. By ranking the values of D in an ascending order, the best matching AM tooth corresponds to the minimum D. In order to obtain the best matching image, majority voting is used so that the best matching AM image is the image with the maximum number of teeth ranked first. For a given PM image, we order the matched AM images according to the maximum number

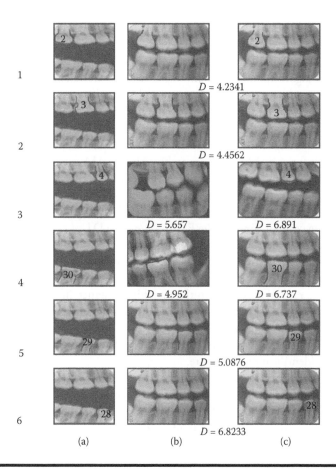

Figure 16.11 **Example of the retrieval results using the signature vectors matching (a) query tooth marked with black; (b) best-matched tooth in the database (1, 2, 5, and 6 are correct matches); and (c) best-matched tooth in the database when using classification and numbering technique (1, 2, 4, 5, and 6 are correct matches).**

of teeth that ranked first, then to the maximum number of teeth that ranked second, and so on. The best AM match is the first image in the list. If there is a tie, the one that has the minimum average matching distance for the whole AM image is chosen.

Figure 16.11 shows the retrieval results for one of the query PM images; the left column shows the PM query tooth, the middle column shows the retrieved AM tooth without applying the classification and numbering techniques, and the right column shows the retrieved AM tooth when applying the classification and numbering techniques before matching. The matching distance D is listed under each retrieved tooth. The PM image in Figure 16.11a contains six teeth; Figure 16.11b shows that four out of the six teeth are correctly matched to an AM image of the same person. Figure 16.11c shows that five out of the six teeth are correctly matched to the same person.

16.3.2 Hierarchal Contour Matching of Dental X-Ray Radiographs

In this section, we introduce the second technique for dental x-ray matching (Nomir and Abdel-Mottaleb 2006, 2008a). This technique is based upon edge matching using the hierarchical chamfer matching algorithm (Borgefors 1998). The algorithm finds the best match for a given image by minimizing a predefined matching criterion in terms of the distance between the contour points of the two dental radiographs. The matching is performed in a hierarchical fashion using multiresolution levels. The algorithm has two main stages: feature extraction and teeth matching. At the feature extraction stage, the contour pixels are extracted, and a distance transformation (DT) image (Borgefors 1998) is built for all the AM teeth in the AM database. Then, a hierarchical structure that contains the DT images at different resolution levels is constructed for each tooth from the AM tooth information at the higher resolution level, as will be explained in Section 16.3.2.1. The DTs at all resolution levels for each AM tooth are archived in the AM database. At the teeth matching stage, given a PM query image, the teeth are first segmented and then numbered.

At any resolution level, the matching scores are generated based on the distance between the contours of the PM tooth and each AM tooth that have the same tooth number. This is achieved by superimposing the contour pixels of the PM tooth on the DT of each AM tooth and then calculating the distance between the PM and the AM contours. The contour of the PM tooth at any resolution level is constructed from the contour of the PM tooth at the higher resolution level, as will be explained in Section 16.3.2.1.

The AM teeth are ranked according to the matching distance in an ascending order, that is, the first ranked AM tooth is the one with the minimum matching distance and so on. Then, majority voting is used, as explained in Section 16.3.1.

The DT can be computed by two methods as will be detailed later. Our goal is to reduce the retrieval time of the identification procedure.

Using the multiresolution hierarchy, the search space is significantly reduced and consequently the computational load. Accordingly, the retrieval time is improved. The details of the feature extraction step are presented in Section 16.3.2.1, and the details of the matching step are presented in Section 16.3.2.2. Also the experimental results are presented in Section 16.3.2.3.

16.3.2.1 Feature Extraction

The technique starts by extracting the contour pixels for all the AM teeth in the database. A DT (Barrow et al. 1977) is created and archived for each AM tooth. For each AM tooth contour, the DT is computed iteratively by setting each contour point to zero and noncontour points to infinity; each pixel obtains a new value $v_{i,j}^k$ equal to

$$v_{i,j}^k = \min \begin{cases} v_{i,j}^{k-1} \\ v_{i,p}^{k-1} + 3 & p = j-1, j+1 \\ v_{m,j}^{k-1} + 3 & m = i-1, i+1 \\ v_{m,p}^{k-1} + 4 & m = i-1, i+1; p = j-1, j+1 \end{cases} \tag{16.12}$$

where $v_{i,j}^k$ is the value of the pixel in position i,j at iteration k. Equation 16.12 is iteratively updating the DT for each pixel depending on its neighboring pixels at a previous iteration. This equation calculates all the possible assigned values for a pixel at a given iteration and selects the minimum among them, which is the idea behind using the DT. This iterative procedure continues until no changes occur in the values. We can notice that the global distances in the DT image are approximated by propagating local distances, that is, distances between neighboring pixels over

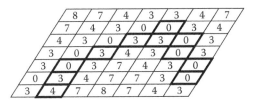

Figure 16.12 Example of the DT: the zero entries represent the pixels' positions of an AM tooth contour. The dark-edge entries represent the pixels' positions of a given PM tooth contour.

the image, which is the main idea of building the DT. This computation is only applied for an area around the contour points rather than the whole image, which further reduces the number of computations. From our experimental results, 10 to 15 iterations were sufficient for convergence. Figure 16.12 shows an example of a DT.

The DT can be computed by two methods. In the first method, given the contour of the AM tooth, at a certain resolution level, the contour of the AM tooth is constructed from its contour information at the higher resolution level. Then the DT (Barrow et al. 1977) is computed from the AM tooth contour information at that resolution level (Nomir et al. 2006). In the second method, given the contour of the AM tooth, the DT is computed first for the highest resolution level (Nomir et al. 2008a). For the following, lower resolution, levels, the DT is computed using the DT information from the higher resolution level without creating the pyramid of the AM contours. This method requires less computation than the first method.

Using the first method, the tooth contour image at a given resolution level in the hierarchical pyramid is constructed from the contour image at the higher resolution level by replacing each block of four pixels by one pixel. This new pixel is the result of the "OR" of the four parent pixels. In Borgefors (1998), this process is repeated until only one pixel is left. But from our experimental results, we found that it is sufficient to use six levels. This is due to the fact that there is no much detail in the lower resolution levels. This previous procedure is applied to the contour of all the AM teeth in the database. Using the second method, the DT at a given resolution level in the hierarchical pyramid is constructed from the DT at the higher resolution level by replacing each block of four pixel values by one pixel. This new pixel value is the result of averaging the four parent pixel values.

For the PM tooth, we need to construct the contour images at the different resolutions to perform matching. The contour image at a given resolution level in the hierarchical pyramid is constructed from the contour image at the higher resolution level by replacing each block of four pixels by one pixel. This new pixel is the result of the "OR" of the four parent pixels.

For a given resolution level, *l*, if the coordinates of a point at the original image are *x* and *y*, then the corresponding pixel coordinates at resolution level *l* will be

$$x_l = 2^{-l}(x + 2^l - 1) \tag{16.13}$$

$$y_l = 2^{-l}(y + 2^l - 1) \tag{16.14}$$

16.3.2.2 Teeth Matching

The idea of our matching technique is to perform matching using different resolution levels. Starting at a low-resolution level, the search space is large, that is, contains all the images, while the matching between two teeth is fast. At each resolution level, the distance between the AM and the PM teeth contours is calculated. Then, the AM teeth are arranged in an ascending order based upon the calculated distance. Half of the AM teeth with the largest distances are removed from the search space, and the remaining AM teeth are marked as the possible candidates for further match. As a result, the search space is decreased while moving to higher resolution levels. Before calculating the matching distance between a PM image and an AM image, the contour of each tooth in the PM image has to be aligned with the contour of the corresponding tooth (i.e., tooth that has the same number) in the AM image using the same transformation previously mentioned in Section 16.3.1. The matching distance is

$$D(T(q),k) = \sqrt{\frac{1}{M}\sum_{i=1}^{M} v_i^2} \tag{16.15}$$

where q is the query tooth, $T(q)$ is the query tooth after applying the transformation T, k is the AM database tooth, v_i is the value of the DT at position i after superimposing the transformed contour of the PM tooth, where position i lies on the transformed contour of the PM tooth, and M is the number of contour points. D will be zero if we have a perfect match between the contours of the AM and the PM teeth.

Our goal is to search for the best match between a given PM and the AM teeth in the database. This is one of the important advantages of using hierarchal algorithm, that is, to speed up the search. In order to obtain the best matched image, majority voting is used, as explained in Section 16.3.1, so that the best matched AM image is the image with the maximum number of teeth ranked first.

Figure 16.13 shows the retrieval results for one query PM image. Each row contains the query PM tooth and the best matched AM tooth from the database, in columns *a* and *b*, respectively. Column *c* shows the corresponding AM tooth for the same person when it is not ranked first. The matching distance D is shown under each retrieved tooth. The PM image in Figure 16.13 contains six teeth; four out of the six teeth were correctly matched to an AM image of the same person, whereas for the other two incorrectly matched teeth, their correct matches were ranked fourth and third.

16.3.3 Matching X-Ray Dental Radiographs Using Teeth Shapes and Appearances

The contour is one of the important features that can discriminate between teeth. However, because of the poor quality of some images, the resulting contours can have poor quality and this strongly affects the final matching results (Nomir et al. 2005, 2006, 2008a; Abdel-Mottaleb et al. 2003). In this section, we introduce a teeth-matching technique that uses two sets of features (Nomir and Abdel-Mottaleb 2007a), which overcomes the drawback of using only the contour of the tooth in matching. It uses features that represent the contour as well as features that describe the appearance of the tooth.

The contour is represented using Fourier descriptors, and the appearance is described using force field energy function. Fourier descriptors are calculated for the contour of the tooth; hence, they represent the shape of the contour. On the other hand, the calculation of the force field function uses the pixels within the tooth area; hence, it emphasizes the texture. The overall feature vector is the concatenation of the features extracted by the two methods.

The extracted features for the AM images are archived in a database. During searching, matching scores are generated based on the Euclidean distance between the features extracted from the AM and the PM teeth. The result of this search will be a set of AM candidates that best match the PM query image.

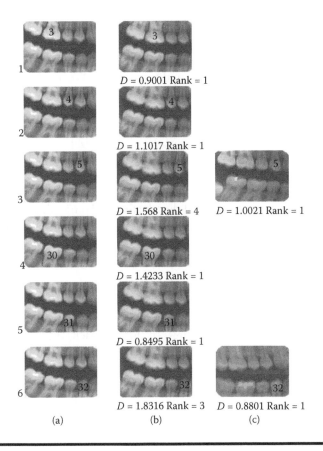

D = 0.9001 Rank = 1

D = 1.1017 Rank = 1

D = 1.568 Rank = 4   D = 1.0021 Rank = 1

D = 1.4233 Rank = 1

D = 0.8495 Rank = 1

D = 1.8316 Rank = 3   D = 0.8801 Rank = 1

(a)   (b)   (c)

Figure 16.13   Retrieval results using the hierarchical matching algorithm. (a) Query PM tooth marked with black; (b) AM tooth for the correct person marked with black; and (c) ranked first tooth, when matched with a wrong person, marked with black (rows 3 and 6).

The details of the feature extraction step are presented in Section 16.3.3.1, and the details of the matching step are presented in Section 16.3.3.2.

16.3.3.1 Feature Extraction

In feature extraction using Fourier descriptors, considering the *2D N* points of the tooth's contour as a discrete function $u(n) = (x(n), y(n))$ (Arbter et al. 2002), we can define a discrete complex function, $f(n)$, to represent the contour of the tooth as

$$f(n) = x(n) + jy(n) \qquad (16.16)$$

By assuming that $f(n)$ is a periodic signal with period N (Arbter et al. 2002), and applying discrete Fourier transformation (DFT) to the complex function, we obtain

$$F(s) = \frac{1}{N} \sum_{i=0}^{N-1} f(i) e^{\frac{-2\pi si}{N}}, s = 0, 1, \dots N - 1 \qquad (16.17)$$

The coefficients $F(s)$ are called Fourier descriptors. By setting the first Fourier descriptor $F(0)$ to 0, which moves the centroid of the contour to 0, dividing the remaining coefficients by $F(1)$, and taking only the absolute values of the F's, we can achieve translation invariance, scale invariance, and rotation invariance, respectively (Costa and Cesar 2000). We use the feature vector that corresponds to the low-frequency components as follows:

$$V = \left[\frac{|F(2)|}{|F(1)|}, \frac{|F(3)|}{|F(1)|}, \ldots\ldots\ldots, \frac{|F(21)|}{|F(1)|} \right] \tag{16.18}$$

Using a set of training images, we found that the first 20 Fourier descriptors were sufficient to characterize each individual tooth.

Teeth Analysis and Feature Extraction Using Force Field Transformation

A set of features are extracted to represent each individual tooth. First, the tooth is preprocessed by applying an energy transformation method called force field transformation. This transformation was used in Hurley et al. (2000, 2002) for ear recognition. It smoothes the original gray-scale image while preserving the important features. In this approach, the *2D* intensity image $f(x, y)$ is treated as a surface. The surface is defined as $w = f(x, y)$, where w is the image intensity at pixel (x, y). Under this representation, the most distinctive features are surface feature points. The algorithm starts by converting a tooth image into a force field by pretending that each pixel exerts an isotropic force on all the other pixels. Following the gradient direction of the potential energy associated with that force field forms energy channels along the way. Eventually, these channels become trapped in a small number of energy wells. These wells are the peaks of the potential energy surface, and they are used to describe the appearance of each individual tooth. Assume that each tooth image has N pixels. A pixel at position r_i with intensity $p(r_i)$ is considered to exert a spherically symmetrical force field $F_i(r_j)$ on a pixel of unit intensity at the pixel location r_j defined as follows:

$$F_i(r_j) = p(r_j) * d_{ji} \tag{16.19}$$

$$d_{ji} = \frac{(r_i - r_j)}{|r_i - r_j|^3} = \frac{1}{((x_i - x_j)^2 + (y_i - y_j)^2} \angle \theta \tag{16.20}$$

where $r_i = [x_i, y_i]$ and $r_j = [x_j, y_j]$, d_{ji} is represented by an absolute, and an angle value $\theta = \tan^{-1} \frac{(y_i - y_j)}{(x_i - x_j)}$ is the angle that gives the direction of the force field. This force field is associated with potential energy field $E_i(r_j)$, which is given by

$$E_i(r_j) = \frac{p(r_i)}{|r_i - r_j|} \tag{16.21}$$

To calculate the total potential energy at a given pixel j, the sum of the potential energy functions from all pixels within the region is taken into account and is given by

$$E(r_j) = \sum_{i=0, i \neq j}^{N-1} E_i(r_j) \tag{16.22}$$

Figure 16.14b is the energy potential surface for the tooth image in Figure 16.14a.

To extract the potential wells, an initialization procedure takes place. The initialization procedure starts by arranging a set of 100 test pixels (see Figure 16.15a) in an ellipse around each tooth and is allowed to iteratively follow the gradient of the potential energy, which captures the general flow of the force field.

By following the field lines, each field line will continue moving until it reaches a maximum in the potential energy surface. The field lines flow into a small number of channels. The channel is modulating the natural flow of the field lines toward a single well at the center of the field. The field lines flow eventually and terminate in wells, the maximum in the potential energy surface

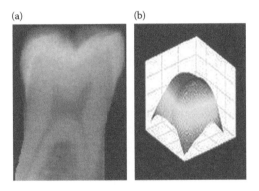

Figure 16.14 The potential energy surface. (a) Original tooth and (b) potential energy surface for the tooth in (a).

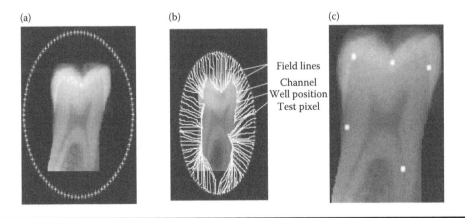

Figure 16.15 Extraction of potential wells and channels (a) 100 pixels for initialization; (b) field lines are terminating into five wells; and (c) well positions.

where no force is exerted and no further movement is possible, joining up with other channels on the way. The locations for the image in Figure 16.15a are shown in Figure 16.15c. Using a set of training data, we found that initializing the procedure with 100 pixels is enough for extracting all the wells. We apply this procedure to all the images of the AM teeth in the database. Also, the same procedure is applied for the teeth of a given PM image to obtain the corresponding feature vector. Suppose that a tooth has W wells. We define the feature vector as

$$V^t = [d_{1,2}, d_{1,3}, \ldots\ldots, d_{w-1,w}], \tag{16.23}$$

$$d_{j,k} = \frac{1}{d'}\left\|w_j - w_k\right\| \tag{16.24}$$

where $d_{j,k}$ is the normalized distance between well j, w_j and well k, w_k; W is the total number of wells; $j = 1,\ldots,W - 1$; $k = j + 1,\ldots, W$; $j \neq k$, and d' is the mean value of the components of the tooth's feature vector V. d' is used to normalize the distance between each pair of wells, for example, j and k, to be independent of the scale.

We found from the experimental results, using a set of training images, that each tooth has around four to seven wells on average. We store the positions of all the extracted wells for each tooth in our database. During matching, when we match two teeth with a different number of wells, the matching is based on the smallest number of wells as will be explained later in Section 16.3.3.2.

The computational cost for extracting the wells is high since the force field calculation uses all the pixels within the tooth area. Converting the tooth image into force field requires that each pixel exerts an isotropic force on all other pixels, which is time consuming.

In order to reduce the computations, we examined the locations of the extracted wells for a set of training images. We found that the wells are usually located in an area around the contour of the tooth. Based on this observation, we only apply the force field energy function for a subset of pixels around the tooth's contour, which tremendously reduces the number of computations compared with the number of computations when we use all the pixels. After locating the well positions, the feature vector is calculated by computing the normalized distances between all extracted wells.

16.3.3.2 Teeth Matching

Matching is performed by minimizing the matching distance between the feature vector of the PM tooth and the feature vector of the AM tooth. There may be variations in scale, rotation, and translation between the AM and the PM teeth. During matching, the image of a PM tooth is aligned with that of a corresponding AM tooth (they should also have the same universal tooth number). We use the same transformation mentioned in the matching technique introduced in Section 16.3.1. Suppose we have a query tooth with feature vector Q and a database tooth with feature vector K, which are defined as

$$Q = [q_i], i = 1, \ldots, ((W-1)*W/2) + 20 \tag{16.25}$$

$$K = [k_j], j = 1, \ldots, ((W-1)*W/2) + 20 \tag{16.26}$$

where q_i is the ith feature in the Q vector, k_j is the jth feature in the K vector, W is the number of wells, $(W-1)*W/2$ is the number of features corresponding to the well positions, and the remaining 20 features are the Fourier descriptors.

As the number of extracted wells in both the query and the database teeth may be different, if the number of wells in the query and the database teeth are W_i and W_j, respectively, we only need to compare the corresponding W wells in the AM and the PM teeth, where

$$W = \min(W_i, W_j) \tag{16.27}$$

This is achieved by choosing the W wells from the AM and the PM teeth, which result in the minimum distance between AM and PM teeth. This technique has the advantage of representing each tooth by a small set of features that represent both shape and appearance in order to avoid the drawbacks of using only incorrect contours obtained in case of poor quality images. The best matches are obtained by minimizing the distance, $D_{q,k}$, between the PM tooth, q, and the AM tooth, k, considering the transformation T as follows:

$$D_{T(q),k} = \sqrt{\sum_{i=1}^{((W-1)*W/w)+20} (q'_i - k_i)^2} \tag{16.28}$$

where $T(q)$ is the transformed query tooth, and q'_i is the ith feature of the query tooth after applying the transformation T. The best matched AM tooth, with distance D, corresponds to the minimum $D_{T(q),k}$:

$$D = \arg \min_k D_{T(q),k} \tag{16.29}$$

In order to obtain the best matched image, majority voting is used as explained in Section 16.3.1, so that the best matching AM image is the image with the maximum number of teeth ranked first.

Figure 16.16 shows the retrieval results for one of the query PM images. The left column shows the well positions superimposed on each PM query tooth. The second column shows the corresponding AM teeth for the same subject with the well positions marked. The third and fourth columns show the AM teeth that best match the query teeth along with the complete AM image if the correct AM tooth was not ranked first. The matching distance D is listed under each retrieved tooth. The PM image in Figure 16.16 contains seven teeth, where five out of the seven teeth were correctly matched to an AM image of the same person, while the correct match for the two mismatched teeth was ranked second. Majority voting is then used to find the best matched AM image. In our example, since five out of seven teeth were ranked first and retrieved from the same person, it is considered the best match.

16.3.4 Experiments and Results

We tested the matching techniques on a set of AM dental radiographs. The AM database contains 231 bitewing, 37 periapical, and 27 panoramic AM dental images. Figure 16.17 shows a sample of the x-ray images in the AM database. The AM images are enhanced, segmented, and numbered. During matching, given a subject PM record (the record contains some different type of

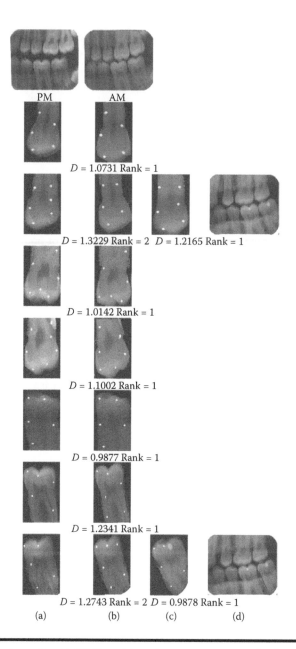

Figure 16.16   Retrieval results. (a) Well positions in a query PM tooth; (b) well positions in the matching tooth in the corresponding AM image and its rank; (c) ranked first AM tooth if the correct AM tooth was not ranked first; and (d) complete AM image for the tooth in (c), marked with black if the correct AM tooth was not ranked first.

radiographs for the same subject), the subject's x-ray dental radiographs are enhanced, segmented, and numbered. Then, the best matched AM tooth in the database is searched for each segmented PM tooth (both teeth should have the same universal tooth number) by calculating the matching distance. The best matched AM tooth is the one with the minimum matching distance. The results from different dental types for the same subject are combined. In this case, we rely on

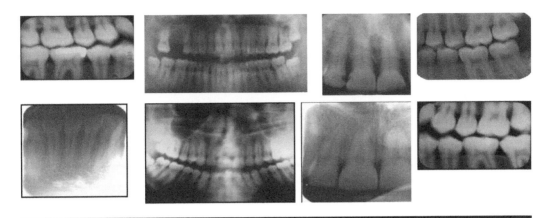

Figure 16.17   Sample of x-ray AM images from the database.

matching more than dental radiograph for the same subject, if available. The matching techniques were evaluated using 50 PM query subjects. The 50 PM subjects are represented by 58 bitewing, 22 periapical, and 21 panoramic query images. The correct matches were always retrieved for the PM query images using the three matching techniques. Table 16.2 shows the results.

The matching performance curves for the three matching techniques are shown in Figures 16.18, 16.19, and 16.20, respectively, when using the three types of the x-ray dental radiographs.

Studying the experimental results of the matching techniques and combining the results of the three types of the dental radiographs improve the performance of the three matchers as shown in Table 16.2. Also, one other reason for improving the performance is using the enhancement step, which improves the segmentation results.

By studying the results of the matching techniques, we found that there are different reasons for the misclassified subjects. One reason is that, if the PM images are captured long time after

Table 16.2   Results of Three Matching Techniques Using 50 Subjects

Radiograph Types	Signature Vectors Technique		Hierarchical Technique		Force Field Technique	
	Correct Matches	*%*	*Correct Matches*	*%*	*Correct Matches*	*%*
Bitewing only	40	80	42	84	43	86
Three types	41	82	44	88	45	90

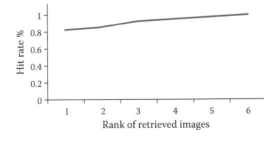

Figure 16.18   Performance curve for the signature vector matching technique.

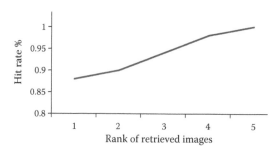

Figure 16.19   Performance curve for the hierarchical matching technique.

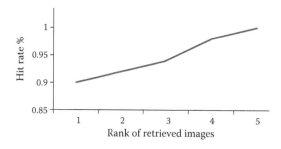

Figure 16.20   Performance curve for the force field matching technique.

the AM images, this can result in change in the teeth's shapes because of artificial prosthesis, teeth growth, and teeth extraction. In other cases, because the x-ray image is a 2D projection of a 3D object, the 2D shapes of the contours were similar, which leads to wrong matches. Also, it is important to note that, in some cases, the problem arises from the segmentation step because of the dental radiograph's poor quality where the tooth contour is not correctly extracted.

16.4 Fusion of Matching Techniques

In this section, we fuse the matching techniques introduced in Section 16.3 using two approaches, fusion at the matching level, which is detailed in Section 16.4.1, and fusion at the decision level, which is detailed in Section 16.4.2. The goal is to improve the performance of the fused matchers, that is, the three matchers that were introduced in Section 16.3 (Nomir and Abdel-Mottaleb 2007b,c, 2008b).

16.4.1 Fusion at the Matching Level

In this approach, the scores or decisions of an individual matcher are available for fusion, whereas the features used by one matcher are not accessible to others. As mentioned in Section 16.3, our final result from the matching step is an ordered list. This representation may not be appropriate for fusion at the matching level because fusion at this level requires fusing the scores of these matchers. Therefore, for a given PM image, we have to assign a score to each AM image proportional to the distance between the given PM image and that AM image.

In the following sections, we discuss some scenarios for fusing the three matchers at the matching level. Section 16.4.1.1 introduces the scenario for fusing the three matchers using the average sum of the normalized scores for the three matchers. Section 16.4.1.2 introduces the scenarios for fusing the three matchers by estimating a weight for each matcher that results in the minimum total error.

16.4.1.1 Score Summation

The easiest way for fusion at the matching level is by score summation. The idea is to calculate the average of the matching scores produced by the three different matchers. According to the average scores, a decision of rejection or acceptance takes place. Before applying this method, the generated scores are first normalized. The normalization typically involves mapping the scores from multiple domains into a common domain. We use tanh to normalize the matching scores (Snelick et al. 2005). The tanh technique maps the raw scores to the (0, 1) range and computes the new normalized score value as

$$S = \frac{1}{2}\left[\tanh\left(0.01\frac{(S_b - \mathrm{mean}_{S_b})}{\mathrm{std}_{S_b}}\right) + 1\right] \tag{16.30}$$

where S_b and S are the score values before and after the normalization, respectively, whereas mean_{S_b} and std_{S_b} represent the mean and the standard deviation of all possible values of S_b that will be observed, respectively.

16.4.1.2 Weight Estimation

Weights are used to indicate the importance of each individual matcher for the fusion. In this section, we introduce three scenarios to estimate a weight for each individual matcher. These calculated weights are used to fuse the three matchers together. The fusion of the three matchers' scores will be the weighted sum of the individual matchers' normalized scores. The first scenario uses exhaustive search to estimate the weights, which results in the minimum total error using a set of training data (Jain et al. 2002). The second scenario uses a defined function of the normalized scores of each individual matcher for a set of training data to estimate the weight for that matcher (Cheung et al. 2005). The third scenario uses each matchers' performance on a set of training data to obtain the weights.

16.4.1.2.1 Calculating Weights Using Exhaustive Search

A different weight is initially assigned for each individual matcher. The method exhaustively searches the space of weights (w_1, w_2, and w_3) for the three matchers such that the total error rate for a training set is minimized. The weights are considered to be multiples of 0.01 over the range [0, 1]. The fused score is computed under the constraints

$$w_1 + w_2 + w_3 = 1, \tag{16.31}$$

$$w_i \geq 0, \; i = 1,2,3 \tag{16.32}$$

and it is equal to

$$S_j = \sum_{i=1}^{3} w_i S_{i,j} \tag{16.33}$$

where $S_{i,j}$ is the normalized score of matcher i for subject j, and S_j is the fused score for subject j.

The search for the optimum weights is achieved by iteratively changing the value of each weight by 0.01 while applying the constraints in Equations 16.31 and 16.32, and then calculating the total error in each iteration. Applying all possible weight combinations and then choosing the set of weights that minimizes the total error, which is in the form of costs associated with the two types of errors, over the training data set

$$E = C_{FA} F_{AR} + C_{FR} F_{RR} \tag{16.34}$$

where C_{FA} is the cost of accepting a false match, F_{AR} is the false acceptance rate, C_{FR} is the cost of falsely rejecting a true match, and F_{RR} is the false rejection rate. For simplicity, we assign equal costs ($C_{FA} = C_{FR} = 1$), that is, the risk is equivalent to the total error.

This scenario needs many iterations to choose the final weights, since all possible combinations of the weight values need to be considered.

16.4.1.2.2 Deriving the Weights from the Scores

Each matcher is assigned a weight that is a function of the matcher's normalized scores derived using a set of training data. In this case, each matcher weight is inversely proportional to the error rate, and it is in the form

$$w_{i,j} = \frac{\exp\left(\left(s_{i,j} - \mu_i/2\sigma_i^2\right)\right)}{\sum_{j=1}^{m} \exp\left((s_{i,j} - \mu_i)^2/2\sigma_i^2\right)} \tag{16.35}$$

where $w_{i,j}$ is the weight of matcher i for subject j, $s_{i,j}$ is the normalized score of matcher i for subject j, μ_i is the mean score for matcher i, σ_i is the standard deviation for matcher i's scores, and m is the number of the training subjects.

$$\mu_i = \frac{\sum_{j=1}^{m} s_{i,j}}{m} \tag{16.36}$$

$$\sigma_i^2 = \frac{1}{m} \sum_{j=1}^{m} (s_{i,j} - \mu_i)^2 \tag{16.37}$$

After calculating the weights for the three matchers, the weights are normalized so that $w_{1,j} + w_{2,j} + w_{3,j} = 1$. Then, the set of weights that results in the minimum total error is selected.

16.4.1.2.3 Assigning Weights Based on the Performance

Different weights may be assigned to each matcher based on their individual performance (Ross et al. 2006). In this scenario, we assign for each matcher a weight that is a function of the matcher's performance derived using a set of training data. The weights are calculated as follows

$$w_i = \frac{1 - (F_{AR_i} + F_{RR_i})}{3 - \sum_{j=1}^{3} (F_{AR_j} + F_{RR_j})} \tag{16.38}$$

where w_i is the weight for matcher i, F_{ARi} and F_{RRi} are the false acceptance rate and the false rejection rate for matcher i, respectively, and $i = 1, 2, 3$.

The values for F_{ARi} and F_{RRi} are threshold dependent, that is, when the value of the operation point (F_{ARi} and F_{RRi}) for each matcher is changed, the weights assigned to the individual matcher will be suitably modified.

16.4.2 Fusion at the Decision Level

In this approach, a separate decision is made for each matcher. These decisions are then combined into a final vote. This approach has become increasingly popular in multibiometric systems. Many different strategies are available to combine the distinct decisions into a final decision. They range from majority votes to sophisticated statistical methods (Ross and Jain 2003). In practice, however, developers seem to prefer the easiest method: Boolean conjunctions. In the following sections, we discuss some scenarios for fusing our introduced matchers at the decision level; some are Boolean, whereas others are statistical.

16.4.2.1 Boolean Scenarios

The most prevalent rules for fusing multiple matchers are the AND and OR rules. Given the decisions from the three matching techniques, D_{M1}, D_{M2}, and D_{M3}, we fuse the three matchers using the Boolean functions.

- AND rule (D_{M1}.AND. D_{M2}.AND. D_{M3}): this requires a positive decision from the three matchers; otherwise, it fails to identify.

    F_{ARi} is the false acceptance rate, and F_{RRi} is the false rejection rate for matcher i, where $i = 1, 2, 3$. Using the AND rule, a false accept can only occur for the fused matchers if the three matcher outcomes are falsely accepted because Boolean AND requires all its variables to be true. However, that also means a false reject occurs if at least one matcher outcome is falsely rejected.
- OR rule (D_{M1}.OR. D_{M2}.OR. D_{M3}): this scenario requires positive decision from at least one matcher in order to accept. For the OR rule, a false accept can occur if at least one matcher outcome is falsely accepted. On the other hand, a false reject can only occur if the three matcher outcomes are falsely rejected.
- AND–OR rule ((D_{M1}.AND. D_{M2}).OR. (D_{M1}.AND. D_{M3}).OR. (D_{M2}.AND. D_{M3})): this scenario is more reliable than the AND rule because it requires positive decision from only two matchers at a time.

16.4.2.2 Statistical Scenario

Let X_i, for $i = 1,..., N$, be a set of independent random variables that represent the decisions of N matchers. $p(X_i/w_j)$ is the conditional probability function for X_i, where $j = T/F$ (True/False), w_T represents a true match, and w_F represents a false match.

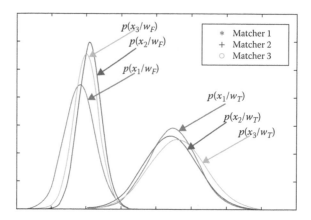

Figure 16.21 Probability density functions for the three matchers.

For a given matcher, the class-conditional probability density functions ($p(X_i/w_T)$ and $p(X_i/w_F)$) are usually unknown. A critical issue in this decision fusion scheme is to estimate the class conditional probability density functions from a set of training data. Assuming that X_i, $i = 1, 2, 3$, are independent decisions from the three matchers, and using a set of training data, the probability density functions for the three matchers are shown in Figure 16.21, and the joint probability density function has the following form:

$$p(X_1, \ldots \ldots X_N \mid w_j) = \prod_{i=1}^{3} p(X_i/w_j) \qquad (16.39)$$

A given observation $X^0 = \left(X_1^0, X_2^0, X_3^0 \right)$ is classified as

$$\left(X_1^0, X_2^0, X_3^0 \right) \varepsilon \begin{cases} w_T & \text{if } \dfrac{p\left(X_1^0, X_2^0, X_3^0/w_T \right)}{p\left(X_1^0, X_2^0, X_3^0/w_F \right)} > \lambda \\ \\ w_F & \text{otherwise} \end{cases} \qquad (16.40)$$

where λ depends on the performance requirements of the fusion result. It is usually specified in terms of C_{FA} (cost of accepting a false match) and C_{FR} (cost of rejecting a true match) for the result of fusion. By assigning a value for λ, the decision for any given observation can be obtained using Equation 16.40.

16.4.3 Experimental Results

The matching techniques were fused using the scenarios previously introduced. Sections 16.4.3.1 and 16.4.3.2 show the results of the fusion of the three matchers at the matching level and at the decision level.

16.4.3.1 Fusion at the Matching Level

Using the score summation scenario, Figure 16.22 shows the performance of the sum rule compared to the performance of the three individual matchers, where each matcher is assigned an equal weight (1/3). From the receive operating characteristic (ROC) curves in Figure 16.22, we can notice that the overall performance of the sum is better than the performance of each individual matcher.

Using the weight estimation scenario, based on the exhaustive search, we found that the weights for the matchers that result in the minimum error are $w_1 = 0.31$, $w_2 = 0.33$, and $w_3 = 0.37$, respectively. Figure 16.23 shows the performance of the exhaustive search scenario. Using the scenario for deriving the weights from the scores, we found that the weights for the matchers that result in the minimum error are $W_1 = 0.24$, $W_2 = 0.26$, and $W_3 = 0.53$, respectively. Figure 16.24 shows the performance curve for this fusion scenario.

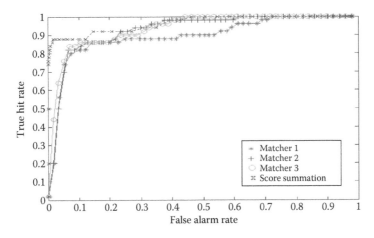

Figure 16.22 ROC curves showing an improvement in performance when scores are combined using the sum rule with equal weights.

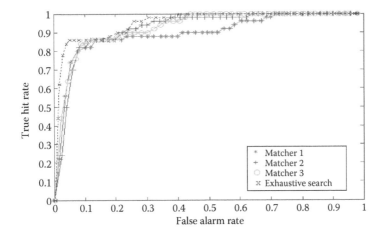

Figure 16.23 ROC curves showing the performance when matchers' weights are derived using exhaustive search.

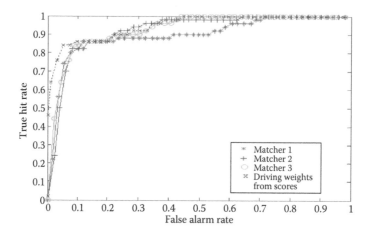

Figure 16.24 ROC curve showing the performance when matchers' weights are derived from the scores.

Table 16.3 Calculated Weights Based on Matchers' Performance

	F_{RR}	F_{AR}	*Weight*
Matcher 1	17%	6.3%	0.30
Matcher 2	14%	6.0%	0.35
Matcher 3	13%	4.3%	0.37

Using the scenario that assigns weights based on the performance, Table 16.3 shows the calculated weights corresponding to given operating points (F_{AR} and F_{RR}) for each matcher, and Figure 16.25 shows the performance of this fusion scenario.

From the ROC curves, we can notice that the overall performance of the fused matchers when calculating the weights based on the matcher's performance (using a certain operating point) is

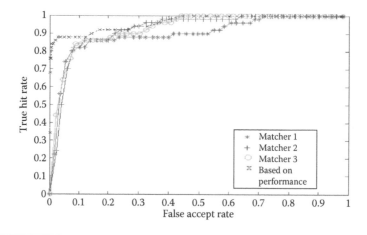

Figure 16.25 ROC curve showing the performance when weights are derived from the individual matcher performance.

better than the overall performance of the fused matchers when calculating the weights using exhaustive search or deriving the weights from the normalized scores.

16.4.3.2 Fusion at the Decision Level

Figures 16.26, 16.27, and 16.28 show the performance of fusing the three matchers using the AND, OR, and AND–OR rules, respectively.

Comparing the ROC curves of the three scenarios for fusing the matchers using Boolean functions, we can notice that, when we use the AND rule, the F_{RR} (false rejection rate) for the fused matchers is higher than the F_{RR} for any individual matcher. Also, we can notice that, when we use the OR rule, the F_{AR} (false acceptance rate) for the fused matchers is higher than the F_{AR} for any

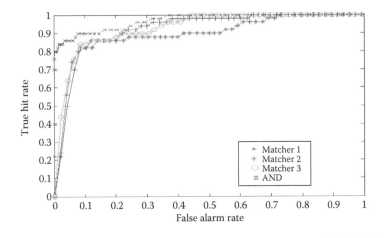

Figure 16.26   ROC curve showing the performance of the three matchers fused using AND rule.

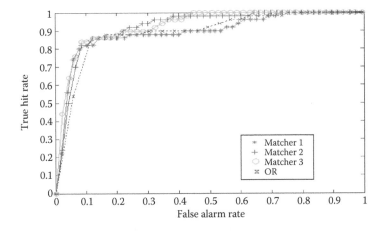

Figure 16.27   ROC curve showing the performance of fusing the three matchers using OR rule.

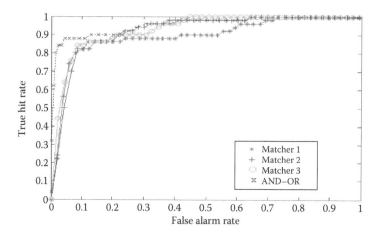

Figure 16.28   ROC curve showing the performance of fusing the matchers using AND–OR rule.

individual matcher. AND function is preferred when designing fused matchers with a high rejection rate, whereas OR function is preferred when designing fusion matchers with a high acceptance rate.

16.5 Conclusion

With the advancements in information technology and the huge volume of cases that need to be investigated by forensic specialists, automation of forensic identification became inevitable. In this chapter, we have introduced an ADIS. The system archives AM dental images in a database and searches the database for the best matches to a given PM image. The system can be used by both law enforcement and security agencies in both forensic and biometric identification. The goal of our research is to automate the process of extracting a representation from the dental radiographs and to automate the process of matching PM and AM records. An automatic system can perform identification on a large-scale database, whereas a manual or semiautomatic system is useful for verification on a small data set. Also, automating this process will come up with an ordered list of closest matches that we may refer to in order to decide the best match. Accordingly, this will facilitate for forensic odontologists to only manually verify a short list instead of manually searching a large number of AM records.

Because of the poor quality of some radiographs, which is the main challenge in any human identification procedure, in this chapter, we propose to combine the results when using the individual's dental records of the three available different types of dental radiographs. We address the problem of identifying individuals based on more than one type of dental radiographs for the first time. To achieve that, we enlarge the database; different types of radiographs for a single person are available. Our previously introduced system was relying only on the bitewing x-ray dental radiograph in the identification process. In this chapter, the identification procedure was extended to handle panoramic and periapical radiographs. The identification procedure is carried out by integrating the results of using the individual's three available types of dental radiographs.

We presented a new technique for dental x-ray image segmentation as well as three techniques for teeth matching. These techniques address the issues of representing each individual tooth by a set of features and calculating the similarity between a query tooth and archived teeth based on these features. The query PM subject's teeth are segmented, and the representative features are extracted. Then, a similarity measure is used to search for the best matching teeth in the AM database for each PM tooth; accordingly, finding the best matched subject is by combining the results of each individual matched tooth using the majority voting.

The experimental results show that using the three types of dental radiographs enhances the overall human identification procedure. To improve the overall system performance, we fuse the three matchers. We introduced some scenarios to fuse the matchers at the matching level as well as at the decision level.

References

Abdel-Mottaleb, M., Nomir, O., Nassar, D., Fahmy, G., and Ammar, H. (2003). Challenges of Developing an Automated Dental Identification System. *IEEE Mid- West Symposium for Circuits and Systems*, 411–414, Cairo, Egypt.

Arbter, K., Snyder, W. E., Burhardt, H., and Hirzinge, G. (2002). Content-Based Image Retrieval Using Fourier Descriptors on a Logo Database. *Journal of Pattern Recognition*, 3:521–524.

Barrow, H. G., Tenenbuam, J. M., Bolles, R. C., and Wolf, H. C. (1977). Parametric Correspondence and Chamfer Matching: Two New Techniques for Image Matching. *Proc. 5th Int. Joint Conf. Artificial Intelligence*, 659–663, Cambridge, MA.

Borgefors, G. (1998). Hierarchical Chamfer Matching: A Parametric Edge Matching Algorithm. *IEEE Transactions on Pattern Analysis and Machine Intelligence*, 10(6):849–865.

Brogdon, B. G. (1998). *Forensic Radiology*. CRC Press, Boca Raton, FL.

Cheung, M., Mak, M., and Kung, S. (2005). A Two-Level Fusion Approach to Multimodal Biometric Verification. *International Conference on Acoustics, Speech, and Signal Processing*, 5:485–488, Philadelphia, PA.

Costa, L. F., and Cesar, R. M. (2000). *Shape Analysis and Classification: Theory and Practice*. CRC Press, Boca Raton, FL.

Fahmy, G., Nassar, D., Said, E., Chen, H., Nomir, O., Zhou, J., Howell, R., Ammar, H., Abdel-Mottaleb, M., and Jain, A. K. (2004a). Towards an Automated Dental Identification System. *IEEE International Conference of Biometric Authenticity*, 789–796, Hong Kong.

Fahmy, G., Nassar, D., Said, E., Chen, H., Nomir, O., Zhou, J., Howell, R., Ammar, H., Abdel-Mottaleb, M., and Jain, A. K. (2004b). A Web Based Tool for an Automated Dental Identification System (ADIS). *Proc. of National Conference on Digital Government Research*, 1–2, Seattle, WA.

Fahmy, G., Nassar, D., Said, E., Chen, H., Nomir, O., Zhou, J., Howell, R., Ammar, H., Abdel-Mottaleb, M., and Jain, A. K. (2004c). Automated Dental Identification System (ADIS). *Proc. of National Conference on Digital Government Research*, 1–2, Seattle, WA.

Fahmy, G., Nassar, D., Said, E. H., Chen, H., Nomir, O., Zhou, J., Howell, R., Ammar, H., Abdel-Mottaleb, M., and Jain, A. K. (2005). Towards an Automated Dental Identification System (ADIS). *Journal of Electronic Imaging*, 14(4):1–13.

Gonzalez, R., and Wood, R. (2003). *Digital Image Processing*. Addison Wesley, Boston.

Hurley, D., Nixon, M., and Carter, J. (2000). Automatic Ear Recognition by Force Field Transformation. *IEEE Colloquium on Visual Biometrics*, 789–796, London.

Hurley, D., Nixon, M., and Carter, J. (2002). Force Field Energy Function for Image Feature Extraction. *Image Vision Computing*, 20:311–317.

Jain, A. K., and Chen, H. (2004). Matching of Dental X-ray Images for Human Identification. *Pattern Recognition*, 37(7):1519–1532.

Jain, A. K., and Chen, H. (2005). Alignment and Matching of Dental Radiographs. *IEEE Transactions on Pattern Analysis and Machine Intelligence*, 27(8):319–1326.

Jain, A. K., and Ross, A. (2002). Learning User-Specific Parameters in a Multibiometric System. *Proc. International Conference on Image Processing*, 1:57–60, Rochester, NY.

Jain, A. K., Chen, H., and Minut, S. (2003). Dental Biometrics: Human Identification using Dental Radiographs. *4th International Conference of Audio and Video-Based Biometric Person Authentication, AVBPA2003*, 429–437, Guildford, UK.

Jain, R., Kasturi, R., and Schnck, B. G. (1995). *Machine Vision*. McGraw-Hill Inc., New York.

Mahoor, M., and Abdel-Mottaleb, M. (2005). Classification and Numbering of Teeth in Bitewing Dental Images. *Journal of Pattern Recognition*, 38:577–586.

Nomir, O., and Abdel-Mottaleb, M. (2005). A System for Human Identification from X-Ray Dental Radiographs. *Journal of Pattern Recognition*, 38(8):1295–1305.

Nomir, O., and Abdel-Mottaleb, M. (2006). Hierarchical Dental X-Ray Radiographs Matching. *International Conference on Image Processing ICIP*, 2677–2680, Atlanta, GA.

Nomir, O., and Abdel-Mottaleb, M. (2007a). Dental Biometrics: Matching X-Ray Dental Images Using Teeth Shapes and Appearances. *IEEE Transactions on Information Forensics and Security*, 2(2):188–197.

Nomir, O., and Abdel-Mottaleb, M. (2007b). Combining Matching Algorithms for Human Identification Using Dental X-Ray Radiographs. *International Conference on Image Processing ICIP*, 409–412, San Antonio, TX.

Nomir, O., and Abdel-Mottaleb, M. (2007c). Human Identification Based on Fusing Matching Algorithms Using Dental X-Ray Radiographs. *International Conference on Computer Theory and Applications*, 85–88, Alexandria, Egypt.

Nomir, O., and Abdel-Mottaleb, M. (2008a). Hierarchical Contour Matching for Dental X-Ray Radiographs. *Journal of Pattern Recognition*, 41(1):130–138.

Nomir, O., and Abdel-Mottaleb, M. (2008b). Fusion of Matching Algorithms for Human Identification Using Dental X-Ray Radiographs. *IEEE Transactions on Information Forensics and Security*, 3(2):223–233.

Nomir, O., and Abdel-Mottaleb, M. (2010). Human Identification Using the Individual's Dental Radiographs. *Sixth IASTED International Conference on Advances in Computer Science and Applications*, 148–154.

Ross, A., and Jain, A. K. (2003). Information Fusion in Biometrics. *Pattern Recognition Letters*, 24:2115–2125.

Ross, A., Nandakumar, K., and Jain, A. K. (2006). *Handbook of Biometrics*. Springer-Verlag, New York, Inc. Secaucus, NJ.

Said, E. H,. Nassar, D., Fahmy, G., and Ammar, H. (2006). Teeth Segmentation in Digitized Dental X-Rays Films using Mathematical. *IEEE Transactions on Information Forensics and Security*, 1(2):178–189.

Snelick, R., Uludag, U., Mink, A., Indovina, M., and Jain, A. K. (2005). Large-Scale Evaluation of Multimodal Biometric Authentication Using State-of-the-Art Systems. *IEEE Transactions on Pattern Analysis and Machine Intelligence*, 27(3):450–455.

Yamany, S., and Farag, A. (2003). Adaptive Object Identification and Recognition Using Neural Networks and Surface Signatures. *IEEE Conference on Advanced Video and Signal Based Surveillance*, 137–142, Miami, FL.

Zhou, J. D., and Abdel-Mottaleb, M. (2005). A Content-Based System for Human Identification Based on Bitewing Dental X-Ray Images. *Pattern Recognition*, 38:2132–2142.

Chapter 17

A Novel Hybrid Bayesian-Based Reasoning: Multinomial Logistic Regression Classification and Regression Tree for Medical Knowledge-Based Systems and Knowledge-Based Systems

Patcharaporn Paokanta

Contents

Over the past decades, Bayesian-based reasoning, a data and knowledge engineering technology (DKET) approach and reasoning method, has played an important role in knowledge-based systems (KBSs). The well-known concept of this theory is that a parameter source is generated by a random process and experience or prior probability of events of interest; the posterior probability depends not only on the likelihood but also on the history of data. In this chapter, a novel hybrid ontology called multinomial logistic regression (Markov chain Monte Carlo)–C5.0–classification and regression tree (MLR (MCMC)–C5.0–CART) for thalassemia KBS is revealed in terms of theory and comparing the performances of the proposed algorithms. The obtained results show that MLR (MCMC)–C5.0–CART provides satisfactory results with Markov chain error in the range 0.0112–0.2473 for 500,000 iterations. In the future, hybrid intelligent computing such as Bayesian-based reasoning (BBR), artificial neural networks–based reasoning (ANNBR), fuzzy-based reasoning (FBR), evolutionary-based reasoning (EBR), and MLR (MCMC)–C5.0–CART will be constructed for thalassemia KBS.

17.1 Introduction

Among data and knowledge engineering technologies (DKETs), the technology for discovering knowledge (problems and solutions) and solving problems by using the discovered solutions, a well-known DKET for solving complex problems based on experience or historical data called prior probability is Bayesian-based reasoning (BBR). Various BBR systems have been developed for medical diagnosis, production and operation research, quality control, etc. [1–6]. In these developed systems, knowledge-based systems (KBSs) play an important role in handling complex problems through its inference engine. It is well known that KBSs have three components: inference engine, rules, and facts. Part of the inference engine needs knowledge discovery (KD) methodologies to discover solutions for solving a specific problem. BBR is a KD method that constructs the inference engine with prior experience, learning, or knowledge. Generally, BBR is always used in medical KBSs since diagnosis processes are complex problems that need the experience of experts to identify the causes of diseases and their appropriate treatments. One common genetic disorder is thalassemia, which requires experts to specify several types of Thlassemia to give patients suitable treatments.

BBR has a wide variety of applications. For example, the study of Lunn et al. proposed the excellent BBR software called WinBUGS. This tool is a well-known Bayesian modeling framework. They presented the concepts, structure, extensibility, statistics, and computation of this application. In the BUGS project, they presented the evolution, critique, and future directions of statistics in medicine through a user interface of the software. The model can be analyzed using Markov chain Monte Carlo (MCMC) techniques based on dialogue boxes and menu commands of this tool. As a useful MCMC method, it has lead to dramatic growth of MCMC and BBR publications, which can be proved with a number of related Bayesian books such as *Markov Chain Monte Carlo in Practice* by Gilks et al. Moreover, the well-known book of Thomas et al. for the BBR approach revealed a program that performs Bayesian inference using Gibbs sampling called BUGS. In addition, Hastings presented applications of the Monte Carlo sampling method using Markov chains through a sampling method called the Metropolis algorithm [7–11].

There are several BBR applications, but for hybrid BBR methods, a few studies are applied to medical systems such as neural BBRs in the study of Lamirel; this project proposed the combination of neural clustering and unsupervised BBR in a multiview context for efficient diachronic analysis, similar to the study of Ishwaran, which revealed applications of hybrid Monte Carlo to Bayesian generalized linear models (quasi-complete separation and neural networks). Furthermore, the study of Niu presented short-term load forecasting using Bayesian neural networks based on the hybrid Monte Carlo algorithm. Another study on hybrid BBRs was conducted by Zhou et al.; they proposed the hybrid Monte Carlo sampling implementation of BBR and support vector machines (SVMs) [12–15].

In this chapter, a novel hybrid ontology called multinomial logistic regression (Markov chain Monte Carlo)–C5.0–classification and regression tree (CART) for thalassemia KBS is presented as a concept, and the methodology performance of different methods on thalassemia data sets is compared. The chapter is organized as follows: a literature review of knowledge discovery in databases is discussed in Section 17.2, experimental results are discussed in Section 17.3, and conclusions are provided in Section 17.4.

17.2 Knowledge Discovery in Database or Data Mining

Knowledge discovery in databases (KDDs) or data mining (DM) is one of the selected DKET techniques for constructing the inference engines of KBSs. This technique can be categorized into three main types of algorithms: machine learning, statistics, and soft computing. Machine learning is the algorithm that works on training and testing data sets. Some machine learning algorithms related to this study, such as MLR, C5.0, and CART, are described as theoretical reviews below.

17.2.1 MCMC and Maximum Likelihood

Multinomial logistic regression (MLR) is a statistical analysis method relying on unknown parameter estimation methods such as least squares method, maximum likelihood (ML), Bayesian approach (MCMC), etc. [16–18]. Among these parameter estimation methods, the two popular methods selected are ML and the Bayesian approach (MCMC). The proposed main difference between Bayesian and classical statistics is the source of unknown parameters (θ). In Bayesian theory, the source of θ is described to be generated by a random process. On the other hand, in ML, θ is generated from the likelihood of data by a fixed process. Moreover, in classical statistical theory, when n is large, θ is unbiased because this theory was developed by the laws of large numbers (LLN) theory. However in real-world situations, it is difficult to collect a large amount of data, especially medical data sets. For these reasons, the LLN, central limit theorem, and Bayes' theorem, which are the bases of Bayesian and classical statistics, are illustrated as theoretical reviews below.

17.2.1.1 Laws of Large Number

Over the past decades, the LLN has played an important role in several areas. The concept of this theory involves the ratio of the number of repeated measurements of an event of interest (n). This ratio is almost consistent when the measurement is repeated. The value of the parameter is near the expected ratio when n is large ($n \rightarrow \infty$). The LLN can be separated into two main types: the weak and strong law of large numbers. The definitions and proofs of each type are discussed below.

The concept of a weak law of large numbers (WLLN) is based on the defined large n; $\bar{X}_n$ is presumably close to μ. This implies that the WLLN allows the probability that $|x - \mu| \geq \varepsilon$. This theory can be proven by Chebychev's inequalities and Taylor's theorem, which is called the convergence of characteristic functions. In this chapter, the proof of the WLLN is described by Chebychev's inequalities.

Theorem 17.1: Chebychev's Inequalities

If the random variable X has μ and σ^2 for every $k \geq 1$, then $P\left(\left|X - \mu\right| \geq k\sigma\right) \leq \dfrac{1}{k^2}$. This means that if the variance of X is small, then the value of X is close to the mean with high probability. ■

Proof 17.1

Let $f(x)$ be the probability mass function (PMF) of the random variable X; thus

$$\sigma^2 = E[(X - \mu)^2]$$

$$= \sum_{x \in R} (X - \mu)^2 f(x) \qquad (17.1)$$

$$= \sum_{x \in A} (X - \mu)^2 f(x) + \sum_{x \in A'} (X - \mu)^2 f(x)$$

When $A = \{x : |x - \mu| \geq k\sigma\}$, the second term of Equation 17.1 is the summation of positive numbers and is greater than or equal to 0. If this term is 0,

$$\sigma^2 \geq \sum_{x \in A} (X - \mu)^2 f(x)$$

However, when the set of A is $|x - \mu| \geq k\sigma$,

$$\sigma^2 \geq \sum_{x \in A} (k\sigma)^2 f(x) = (k\sigma)^2 \sum_{x \in A} f(x)$$

as

$$\sum_{x \in A} f(x) = P(X \in A)$$

Thus,

$$\sigma^2 \geq (k\sigma)^2 P(X \in A) = k^2 \sigma^2 P(|X - \mu| \geq k\sigma)$$

Therefore,

$$P\left(\left|X - \mu\right| \geq k\sigma\right) \leq \frac{1}{k^2}$$

Let $\varepsilon = k\sigma$; hence

$$P\left(\left|X - \mu\right| \geq \varepsilon\right) \leq \frac{\sigma^2}{\varepsilon^2} \tag{17.2}$$

Equation 17.2 refers to the probability that the value of X differs from μ minimally to $k\sigma$ and is less than or equal to $\frac{1}{k^2}$. Moreover, the probability that the value of X differs from μ is less than $k\sigma$ and is not less than or equal to $\frac{1}{k^2}$. Hence,

$$P\left(\left|X - \mu\right| < k\sigma\right) \geq 1 - \frac{1}{k^2}$$

or $P\left(\left|X - \mu\right| < \varepsilon\right) \geq 1 - \frac{\sigma^2}{\varepsilon^2}$ in the case that $\varepsilon = k\sigma$.

Chebychev's inequalities relate to the WLLN. Its definition is given as follows. ■

Theorem 17.2: Weak Law of Large Numbers

Let $S = X_1, X_2, \ldots, X_n$ be a set of independent random variables that have the same probability distribution. These random variables have $E(X_i) = \mu$, where $E(|X|) < \infty$ and $\mathrm{Var}(X_i) = \sigma^2$ when $i = 1, 2, 3, \ldots, n$ for every $\varepsilon > 0$. This leads to $\lim_{n \to \infty} P\left(\left|\bar{X}_n - \mu\right| \geq \varepsilon\right) = 0$ or $\lim_{n \to \infty} P\left(\left|\bar{X}_n - \mu\right| < \varepsilon\right) = 1$. Then $\bar{X}_n$ is the convergence of $\bar{X}_n \xrightarrow{P} \mu$. ■

Proof 17.2

According to Chebychev's inequalities (Equation 17.2)

$$P\left(\left|X - \mu\right| \geq \varepsilon\right) \leq \frac{\sigma^2}{\varepsilon^2}$$

Thus

$$P\left(\left|\bar{X}_n - \mu_{\bar{X}_n}\right| \geq \varepsilon\right) \leq \frac{\sigma^2}{n\varepsilon^2}$$

so

$$\lim_{n \to \infty} P\left(\left|\bar{X}_n - \mu_{\bar{X}_n}\right| \geq \varepsilon\right) \leq \lim_{n \to \infty} \frac{\sigma^2}{n\varepsilon^2} = 0$$

and therefore

$$\bar{X}_n \xrightarrow{\ p\ } \mu$$

■

Theorem 17.3: Strong Law of Large Numbers (SLLN)

Let $P\left(\lim_{n \to \infty} Y_n = c\right) = 1$ where Y_n is the convergence of c with a probability of 1 when $n = 1, 2, 3,\dots$.

■

17.2.1.2 Central Limit Theorem

According to the LLN, which relates to the classical statistics approach, the other well-known theory concerned with the classical approach is the central limit theorem. In this section, the theory of this approach is demonstrated.

Theorem 17.4: Central Limit Theorem

Let $S = X_1, X_2,\dots, X_n$ be the set of independent random variables that have the same distribution. This set has the mean $E(X_i) = \mu$ and variance $\mathrm{Var}(X_i) = \sigma^2$. When n is large, the parameter is given by

$$Y_n = \frac{\sum_{i=1}^{n} X_i - n\mu}{\sqrt{n}\sigma}$$

or

$$Y_n = \frac{\bar{X} - \mu}{\sigma/\sqrt{n}}$$

which is the convergence of random variables (Y). It follows a normal distribution with mean $\mu = 0$ and variance $\sigma^2 = 1$. Y_n is the asymptotically standard normal.

In conclusion, in CLT theory, if the size of the data is large, the parameters are given by

$$\sum_{i=1}^{n} X_i \sim N(n\mu, n\sigma^2)$$

and

$$\bar{X} \sim N\left(\mu, \frac{\sigma^2}{n}\right)$$

no matter what their distribution is.

■

17.2.1.3 Maximum Likelihood

As a review of the related theory of classical statistics, Bayesian statistics is discussed in this section. Generally, the generated models for the specific problems can be constructed by two main approaches, fixed and random effects, which have unknown parameters especially linear programming. Among parameter estimation methods, which include ordinary least squares (OLS), generalized least squares (GLS), and the best linear unbiased estimator (BLUE), ML is one of the more popular estimation methods. In this paper, the definition and proof of ML are presented and discussed.

OLS estimators are built based on $y = X\beta + \varepsilon$ where $E(\varepsilon) = 0$ and $V(\varepsilon) = I\sigma_\varepsilon^2$. On the other hand, the estimators of GLS, ML, and BLUE are generated on the basis of $y = X\beta + \varepsilon$ where $E(\varepsilon) = 0$ and $V(\varepsilon) = V$.

Theorem 17.5: Maximum Likelihood

Let $S = x_1, x_2,...,x_n$, be a set of random variables of a population with a distribution $f(x;\theta)$, where θ is a parameter. Then the likelihood function is

$$L(\theta) = \sum_i^n f(x_i;\theta)$$

This equation can be rewritten as $L(\theta; x_1, x_2,......,x_n)$ or $L(\theta)$. ▪

Theorem 17.6: ML Estimator

The ML estimator (MLE) of θ is $\hat{\theta} = \hat{\theta}(X_1, X_2,.....,X_n)$, which maximizes the likelihood function $L(\theta)$. ▪

17.2.1.4 Bayes' Theorem

Bayes' theorem was developed by Thomas Bayes, an English mathematician. In his view, the probability of an event of interest relies not only on the likelihood of data but also on the experience or prior probability or history of data. His derived mathematical equation is as follows:

$$P(\theta \mid x) = \frac{P(x \mid \theta) * P(\theta)}{P(x)} \tag{17.3}$$

This equation describes $P(\theta|x)$ as

posterior probability $\propto$ prior probability and likelihood

As the perspective of this approach, the source of probability is a random process and not a fixed process. Moreover, it is efficiently used for a small sample size (less than 30 records), which a classical statistics approach like ML cannot handle. Generally, Bayesian normally uses Markov chain Monte Carlo such as the Metropolis–Hastings algorithm or Gibbs sampling to generate a sample for estimating the unknown parameter of the posterior distribution.

17.2.2 Multinomial Logistic Regression

MLR is the extension of binomial logistic regression (BLR). This algorithm is also known as softmax regression or multinomial logit. The purpose of this model is to forecast categorical data. The assumptions of MLR are as follows:

■ The independent variables are not necessary to be statistically independent from each other.
■ Colinearity is relatively low.

In the case where Y has two possible outcomes, the BLR model can be derived as follows:

$$\log\left[\frac{P(C_i)}{1 - P(C_i)}\right] = \beta_0 + \beta_1 X_1 + \ldots + \beta_n X_n \tag{17.4}$$

where $\log\left[\dfrac{P(C_i)}{1 - P(C_i)}\right]$ is called log(odds) or logit.

On the other hand, in the case where Y has more than two possible outcomes, Y is called MLR. For example, if $J > 2$, then the number of logit is $J - 1$. Each value is compared to a baseline category logit; for example, if the baseline category is a constant J, then the logit of category i can be derived as

$$\log\left[\frac{P(C_i)}{P(C_J)}\right] = \beta_{i0} + \beta_{i1} X_1 + \ldots + \beta_{in} X_n \tag{17.5}$$

$\beta_{i0}, \beta_{i1}, \ldots, \beta_{in}$ are the coefficients of the ith category, and the coefficient of baseline category should be $\beta_{i0} = \beta_{i1} = \ldots = \beta_{in} = 0$.

17.2.3 Markov Chain Monte Carlo

In Bayes' theorem, in the case that the posterior distribution is not the general distribution, computation of a parameter's expectation from a posterior distribution is an important issue in Bayesian modeling. MCMC is the proposed technique to solve this problem. It is a sampling technique in which the random variables are taken from a posterior density function. The concept of MCMC is sequence generation of random variables $\{K_0, K_1, \ldots \ldots, K_{j+1}\}$ where K_{j+1} is randomized from the distribution $p(K_{j+1}|K_j)$ when $j \geq 0$. This means that K_{j+1} is only randomized based on K_j, and it does not depend on $\{K_0, K_1, \ldots \ldots, K_{j+1}\}$; thus, $p(K_{j+1}|K_j)$ is a transitional kernel. Transitional kernel is the probability of changing state j to state $j + 1$ when j increases. $\{K_0, K_1, \ldots, K_{j+1}\}$ is called the stationary distribution, and it can be used to estimate the expectation of X_c for that forecasting model. For generating the MCMC technique, there are several algorithms to construct an MCMC approach such as Metropolis–Hastings and Gibbs sampling [19].

17.2.4 C5.0 and CART

Among the decision methods, decision trees have been widely selected to be implemented in KBS over the past decades in the academic community. C5.0 and CART are two popular association rule techniques, which association rule is a task of knowledge discovery techniques or Data Mining techniques. C5.0 and CART obtain the If–Then rules generated by an induction process from related data sets. C5.0 is the commercial version of C4.5, which is an improvement from ID3. On the other hand, CART was developed by Breiman, Freidman, Olshen, and Stone in the 1980s. This methodology involves a set of questions that receive a binary answer such as yes or no. The first question is separated to the lower branches by using the learning data sample. Moreover, the concept of this approach consists of two main methodologies: classification and regression parts. In the classification part, the splitting rules are generated based on maximum homogeneity of child nodes, which can be defined as the impurity function $i(t)$. The popular methods to generate the impurity function are the Gini splitting rule and the Towing splitting rule. For the regression part, this methodology involves splitting nodes through a squared residual minimization algorithm.

There are well-known differences between C5.0 and CART. C5.0 has multibranches, whereas CART gives a binary output. Moreover, the test selection criterion of C5.0 is an information-based criterion, whereas CART's is based on a diversity index. For the pruning process, C5.0 is a single pass based on binomial confidence limits; CART uses a cross-validated method called the cost-complexity model. Finally, another difference between the two techniques is in dealing with missing values: C5.0 apportions values probabilistically among outcomes, whereas CART surrogates tests to approximate outcomes.

This is the review of KD methodology, which included the classical and Bayesian approaches through different methodologies such as ML, MCMC, and related theorems. Moreover, decision tree algorithms called C5.0 and CART were also demonstrated.

17.3 Methodology and Results

Before describing the materials and methodology of this study, the author will illustrate related studies of medical systems in the case study of a thalassemia screening system, including the differences between those studies and this one.

The study of Amendolia et al. shows thalassemia screening indicators by using principle component analysis (PCA), in which the selected features are RBC, Hb, Ht, and MCV. They compared the result of K-nearest neighbor (KNN), SVM, and multilayer perceptron (MLP) for thalassemia screening. The obtained result of MLP (95%) is better than that of SVM, even though the sensitivity values of MLP and SVM are 92% and 83%, respectively [20].

The study of Wongseree et al. presents thalassemia classification using neural networks and genetic programming (GP), where the data set includes a mature red blood cell, a reticulocyte, and a platelet. Twenty indicators were collected to be classified using MLP and GP, with 90% classification accuracy for 13 input features and 82% for 15 input features [21].

In another related study, Piroonratana et al. propose the classification of hemoglobin typing chromatograms using neural networks and decision trees for thalassemia screening, and the best result is 97.24% by using C4.5 for classifying 13 classes based on discrete attributes of high-performance liquid chromatography results. On the other hand, the results of random forests and MLP obtained 96.00% and 93.44%, respectively [22].

Moreover, the study of Setsirichok et al. presents the classification of complete blood count and hemoglobin typing data by a C4.5 decision tree, a naive Bayes classifier, and a multilayer perceptron for thalassemia screening. The obtained results of using naive Bayes classifier and a multilayer perceptron to classify 18 classes with 8 input features are 93.23% and 92.60%, respectively [23].

According to previous studies, different conclusions between them and this study can be derived, which include the following:

1. *The data sets*: This study uses 11 input features including F-Cell and HbA_2 of children, fathers, and mothers with β-thalassemia, and 1 output feature including phenotypes of children collected from a laboratory, which differs from the data sets of the previous studies. Moreover, the results of C5.0 and CART are used to improve the performance of the methodology also. One hundred twenty-seven records of β-thalassemia patients are collected from the hospital in northern Thailand.
2. *The purpose of the study*: The purpose of this study is to discover a suitable model for thalassemia KBS by using the Bayesian estimation framework.
3. *Methodologies*: In this study, statistical-based reasoning, fuzzy-based reasoning (FBR), evolutionary-based reasoning, and artificial neural networks–based reasoning are used to discover appropriate results and methodology. Moreover, the ensemble method is also used.

For the review of related studies and materials, in Section 17.3.1, the methodology used in this study will be described.

The first step in the implementation of BBR-MLR (MCMC)–C5.0–CART involves the knowledge elicitation process such that an expert interviews and related documents are reviewed using the diagnostic template of CommonKADs suit [24]. Then related factors are defined to collect and clean before the filtering process. Afterward, the filtered variables are clustered by a fuzzy approach or other clustering techniques such as fuzzy C-means, fuzzy-GAs, and K-mean clustering to confirm the quality of the data. In the next step, these clustered variables are provided and transformed using classification techniques such as machine learning techniques (naive Bayes, BNs, etc.). Moreover, there are not only machine learning techniques but also statistical techniques such as BLR (ML), BLR (MCMC), and MLR that are also used to discover essential knowledge. Furthermore, soft computing techniques such as GAs-KNN classified the types of thalassemia, and the best result among the several algorithms used is selected to construct the thalassemia KBS. Finally, the results of the thalassemia KBS are compared by using DKET called BBR-MLR (MCMC)–C5.0–CART (see the results of the previous studies of the author in Section 17.4). The obtained experimental results of this methodology will be presented in the Section 17.3.1.

17.3.1 MLR (MCMC)–C5.0–CART Results

After the filtering process, the obtained results of using Pearson's chi square and Fisher's extract were used to generate MLR (MCMC), C5.0, and CART to classify types of β-thalassemia for thalassemia KBS. The results are shown in Table 17.1.

Table 17.1 reveals the parameter estimation for MLR using MCMC at several numbers of iterations. The MC errors decrease in every parameter from 100,000 to 500,000 iterations. Beta [*i*, *j*] is the proportion between the *i* and *j* class. Figures 17.1 through 17.3 reveal the trace plot of 1–500,000 iterations, which represents the history of samples for each parameter. These results are the generated sample sets for monitoring the consistency of parameters and completing the update.

Table 17.1   Parameter Estimation of C5.0 and CART using MLR (MCMC)

Iterations	Parameters	Means	SD	MC Error
100,000	Beta[1,2]	−21.66	6.8	0.3497
	Beta[1,3]	−24.02	7.048	0.3554
	Beta[2,2]	13.97	6.462	0.3397
	Beta[2,3]	12.48	6.465	0.3404
	Beta[3,2]	2.363	1.086	0.0224
	Beta[3,3]	4.682	1.02	0.0227
200,000	Beta[1,2]	−22.46	7.443	0.3145
	Beta[1,3]	−24.8	7.661	0.3181
	Beta[2,2]	14.81	7.135	0.3075
	Beta[2,3]	13.3	7.12	0.3077
	Beta[3,2]	2.333	1.114	0.0167
	Beta[3,3]	4.661	1.028	0.0169
300,000	Beta[1,2]	−22.82	7.729	0.293
	Beta[1,3]	−25.16	7.933	0.295
	Beta[2,2]	15.14	7.422	0.2867
	Beta[2,3]	13.64	7.411	0.2871
	Beta[3,2]	2.346	1.119	0.0136
	Beta[3,3]	4.668	1.036	0.0136
400,000	Beta[1,2]	−22.68	7.759	0.2702
	Beta[1,3]	−25	7.973	0.2721
	Beta[2,2]	15	7.448	0.2643
	Beta[2,3]	13.5	7.444	0.2647
	Beta[3,2]	2.342	1.119	0.0116
	Beta[3,3]	4.663	1.039	0.0119
500,000	Beta[1,2]	−22.44	7.654	0.2473
	Beta[1,3]	−24.77	7.896	0.2504
	Beta[2,2]	14.76	7.315	0.2412
	Beta[2,3]	13.25	7.319	0.2421
	Beta[3,2]	2.346	1.13	0.0111
	Beta[3,3]	4.671	1.047	0.0112

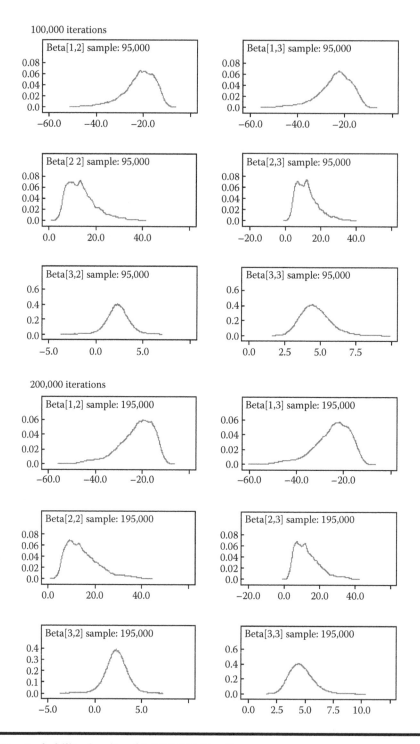

Figure 17.1   Probability density of 1–200,000 iterations.

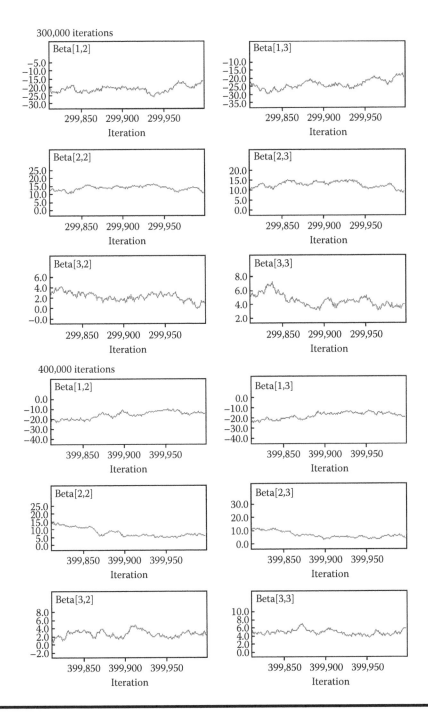

Figure 17.2   Trace of 300,000–400,000 iterations.

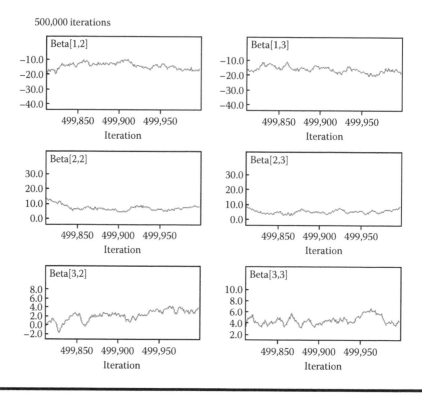

Figure 17.3   Trace of 500,000 iterations.

17.4 Conclusion

In conclusion, the obtained results of MLR (MCMC)–C5.0–CART are satisfactory with the MC error in the range 0.0112–0.2473 for 500,000 iterations. In the future, hybrid intelligent computing, which includes the BBR, artificial neural networks–based reasoning and fuzzy-based reasoning, and MLR (MCMC)–C5.0–CART, will be constructed for thalassemia KBS. The results will be used to construct thalassemia KBS and to compare to previous results through the following:

■ Pearson's chi square test and machine learning such as BNs, KNN, MLP, MLR, and naive Bayes with 85.83, 88.98, 87.40, 84.25, and 84.25 accuracy percentages, respectively [24]

■ Pearson's chi square test, PCA, and machine learning such as BNs, KNN, MLP, MLP, MLR, and naive Bayes with 85.04, 85.83, 86.61, 83.46, and 85.04 accuracy percentages, respectively for PCA [25]

■ C5.0 and CART with 84.25 and 77.17 accuracy percentages, respectively [16]

■ Polychromatic set theory and reasoning matrices [17]

■ DBNs [18]

■ BLR (MCMC) and BLR (ML) [26]

■ DBNs–BLR (MCMC)–GAs–KNN with 89.76 accuracy percentage [27]

■ K-means clustering, fuzzy C-means, and fuzzy-GAs with 86.99, 86.48, and 85.65 accuracy percentages, respectively [28]

■ FBR–GAs–CBR–C5.0–CART with 94.90 accuracy percentage [29]

In conclusion, the discovered knowledge obtained from this study is 94.90 accuracy percentage using FBR–GAs–C5.0–CART to classify three classes in the case that has 23 variables (11 laboratory variables, 10 symptom variables, and the results of using C5.0 and CART).

References

1. Chang, R., Stetter, M., and Brauer, W. 2008. Quantitative inference by qualitative semantic knowledge mining with Bayesian model averaging. *IEEE Transactions on Knowledge and Data Engineering* 20, 12: 1587–1600.
2. Metropolis, N., and Ulam, S. 1949. The Monte Carlo method. *Journal of the American Statistical Association* 44, 247: 335–341.
3. Green, P.J. 1995. Reversible jump Markov chain Monte Carlo computation and Bayesian model determination. *Biometrika* 82, 4: 711–732.
4. Gasparini, M., Pellerey, F., and Proietti, M. 2012. Bayesian hierarchical models to analyze customer satisfaction data for quality improvement: A case study. *Applied Stochastic Models in Business and Industry* 28, 6: 571–584.
5. Geman, S., and Geman, D. 1984. Stochastic relaxation, Gibbs distributions, and the Bayesian restoration of images. *IEEE Transactions on Pattern Analysis and Machine Intelligence PAMI* 6, 6: 721–741.
6. Lee, J.J., and Chu, C.T. 2012. Bayesian clinical trials in action. *Statistics in Medicine* 31, 25: 2955–2972.
7. Lunn, D.J., Thomas, A., Best, N., and Spiegelhalter, D. 2000. WinBUGS—A Bayesian modelling framework: Concepts, structure, and extensibility. *Statistics and Computing* 10, 4: 325–337.
8. Lunn, D., Spiegelhalter, D., Thomas, A., and Best, N. 2009. The BUGS project: Evolution, critique and future directions. *Statistics in Medicine* 28, 25: 3049–3067.
9. Gilks, W.R., Richardson, S., and Spiegelhalter, D.J. 1996. *Markov Chain Monte Carlo in Practice*. London: Chapman & Hall.
10. Thomas, A., Spiegelhalter, D.J., and Gilks, W.R. 1992. *BUGS: A Program to Perform Bayesian Inference Using Gibbs Sampling Bayesian Statistics*. Oxford: Oxford University Press.
11. Hastings, W.K. 1970. Monte Carlo sampling methods using Markov chains and their applications. *Biometrika* 57, 1: 97–109.
12. Lamirel, J.-C. 2013. Combining neural clustering with intelligent labeling and unsupervised Bayesian reasoning in a multiview context for efficient diachronic analysis. *Advances in Intelligent Systems and Computing* 198: 245–254.
13. Ishwaran, H. 1999. Applications of hybrid Monte Carlo to Bayesian generalized linear models: Quasi-complete separation and neural networks. *Journal of Computational and Graphical Statistics* 8, 4: 779–799.
14. Niu, D.-X., Shi, H.-F., and Wu, D.D. 2012. Short-term load forecasting using Bayesian neural networks learned by Hybrid Monte Carlo algorithm. *Applied Soft Computing Journal* 12, 6: 1822–1827.
15. Zhou, Y., Li, J., and Liu, L. 2013. Hybrid Monte Carlo sampling implementation of Bayesian support vector machine. *Advances in Information Sciences and Service Sciences* 5, 1: 284–290.
16. Paokanta, P., Ceccarelli, M., Harnpornchai, N., Chakpitak, N., and Srichairatanakool, S. 2012. Rule induction for screening thalassemia using machine learning techniques: C5.0 and CART. *ICIC Express Letters* 6, 2: 301–306.
17. Paokanta, P. 2012. Reasoning matrices and polychromatic set for screening thalassemia. *Journal of Medical Research and Science* 1, 1: 144–152.
18. Paokanta, P., and Harnpornchai, N. 2012. Risk analysis of thalassemia using knowledge representation model: Diagnostic Bayesian networks. Proceedings of International Conference on Biomedical and Health Informatics, Hong Kong, China.
19. Harnpornchai, N., and Paokanta, P. 2009. Introduction to Bayesian Modeling, Research Report of College of Arts, Media and Technology, Chiang Mai University, Thailand.
20. Amendolia, S.R., Cossu, G., Ganadu, M.L., Golosio, B., Masala, G.L., and Mura, G.M. 2003. A comparative study of k-nearest neighbour, support vector machine and multi-layer perceptron for thalassemia screening. *Chemometrics and Intelligent Laboratory Systems* 69, 1: 13–20.

21. Wongseree, W., Chaiyaratana, N., Vichittumaros, K., Winichagoon, P., and Fucharoen, S. 2007. Thalassaemia classification by neural networks and genetic programming. *Information Sciences* 177: 771–786.

22. Piroonratana, T., Wongseree, W., Assawamakin, A., Paulkhaolarn, N., Kanjanakorn, C., Sirikong, M., Thongnoppakhun, W., Limwongse, C., and Chaiyaratana, N. 2009. Classification of haemoglobin typing chromatograms by neural networks and decision trees for Thalassaemia screening. *Chemometrics and Intelligent Laboratory Systems* 99: 101–110.

23. Setsirichok, D., Piroonratana, T., Wongsereea, W., Usavanarong, T., Paulkhaolarn, N., Kanjanakorn, C., Sirikong, M., Limwongse, C., and Chaiyaratana, N. 2012. Classification of complete blood count and haemoglobin typing data by a C4.5 decision tree, a naive Bayes classifier and a multilayer perceptron for Thalassaemia screening. *Biomedical Signal Processing and Control* 7: 202–212.

24. Paokanta, P., Ceccarelli, M., and Srichairatanakool, S. 2010. Proceedings of the 3rd International Symposium on Applied Sciences in Biomedical and Communication Technologies ISABEL, Rome, Italy.

25. Patcharaporn, P. 2012. β-thalassemia knowledge elicitation using knowledge and data engineering: PCA, Pearson's chi square and machine learning. *International Journal of Computer Theory and Engineering* 4, 5: 702–706.

26. Paokanta, P., Harnpornchai, N., Chakpitak, N., Ceccarelli, M., and Srichairatanakool, S. 2012. Parameter estimation of binomial logistic regression based on classical (ML) and Bayesian (MCMC) approach for screening β-thalassemia. *International Journal of Intelligent Information Processing* 3, 1: 90–100.

27. Paokanta, P. 2012. DBNs-BLR (MCMC)-GAs-KNN: A novel framework of hybrid system for thalassemia expert system. *Lecture Notes in Computer Science* 7666, 4: 264–271.

28. Paokanta, P., Harnpornchai, N., Chakpitak, N., Srichairatanakool, S., and Ceccarelli, M. 2013. Knowledge and data engineering: Fuzzy approach and genetic algorithms for clustering β-2013. Thalassemia of knowledge based diagnosis decision support system. *ICIC Express Letters* 7, 2: 479–484.

29. Paokanta, P. 2013. A new methodology for web-knowledge-based system using systematic thinking, KM process and data and knowledge engineering technology: FBR-GAs-CBR-C5.0-CART. *International Journal of Engineering and Technology* 5, 5: 3420–4325.

Chapter 18

Application of Backpropagation Neural Networks in Calculation of Robot Kinematics

R. R. Srikant and Ch.Srinivasa Rao

Contents

In the present-day scenario of automated industries, the use of robots has increased exponentially. However, the use of robots is limited by the difficulty of positioning the end effectors as per requirements. Previously, robots were physically positioned by an operator, but with automation, robot control has gone into the hands of computers. Robot kinematics is an essential concept in the positioning of robotic manipulators. Generally, for serial manipulators, direct kinematics is easy, and for parallel manipulators, inverse kinematics is simple. The present work tries to take advantage of this, and inverse kinematics is calculated for a serial manipulator and direct kinematics for a parallel manipulator (i.e., the more difficult ones) using backpropagation neural networks. A simple interface has been developed using Visual Basic for easier interaction.

18.1 Introduction

With the growth of a competitive market, automation has gained momentum due to lesser idle time and greater precision. In flexible automation, robotics occupies a place of prominence. Robots are characterized by their high precision and accuracy. They are widely used in several applications like spray painting, welding, assembly, and so forth. With the growth in their usage, their complexity has increased manyfold. For precise location of the robotic arm or the end effector, knowledge of their kinematics is essential. There are basically two different categories of kinematics: direct and reverse. In direct kinematics, the link and joint parameters are known, and we end up calculating the position of the end effector. In reverse kinematics, we know the end effector position, and we calculate the joint angles/link orientations (Figure 18.1). Usually, for a serial robotic manipulator, direct kinematics is simpler as compared to reverse kinematics, whereas for a parallel manipulator, the reverse is true (Tsai 1996).

The calculation of kinematics is done using Denavit–Hartenberg (D–H) parameters. D–H parameters provide the arm equation and transformation matrix (T) from a previous joint to the current joint (Craig 2008).

The transformation matrix from joint $k - 1$ to k is given by

$$
{}^{k-1}_{k}T = \begin{bmatrix}
c\theta_k & -s\theta_k & 0 & a_{k-1} \\
s\theta_k c\alpha_{k-1} & c\theta_k c\alpha_{k-1} & -s\alpha_{k-1} & -s\alpha_{k-1}d_k \\
s\theta_k s\alpha_{k-1} & c\theta_k s\alpha_{k-1} & c\alpha_{k-1} & c\alpha_{k-1}d_k \\
0 & 0 & 0 & 1
\end{bmatrix}
$$

The rules for obtaining the different parameters are as follows [2,3]:

1. Rotate $\{k - 1\}$ about the x_{k-1} axis by α_{k-1} (z_{k-1} coincides with z_R).
2. Translate $\{R\}$ along the x_R axis by a_{k-1} (z_R coincides with z_P).
3. Rotate $\{Q\}$ about the z_Q axis by θ_k (x_Q coincides with x_P).
4. Translate $\{P\}$ along the z_P axis by d_k (x_P coincides with x_k).

The overall transformation matrix is obtained by premultiplying/postmultiplying the individual transformation matrices. In Figure 18.2, x_{k-1}, y_{k-1}, and z_{k-1} are the axes corresponding to joint $k - 1$, and x_k, y_k, and z_k are the axes corresponding to joint k. α_{k-1} is the angle through which the axis has to be rotated to coincide z_{k-1} with z_k, θ_k is the angle of rotation to make x_{k-1} coincide with x_k, and a_k and d_k are the translations to make z_{k-1} coincide with z_k, and x_{k-1} coincide with x_k, respectively. C and S are the abbreviations to represent cosine and sine of an angle.

The obtained overall transformation matrix provides a basis for the inverse kinematics. Based on the matrix, the joint angles are estimated (Klafter et al. 1989). Several researchers

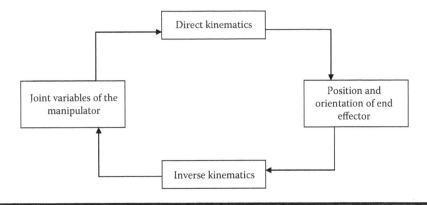

Figure 18.1   Representation of direct and reverse kinematics.

have tried different techniques to solve these problems. In the initial stages, conventional kinematics were the only solution; however, at later stages, different artificial intelligence techniques were used.

Chen et al. (2002) applied fuzzy logic to solve in conjunction with fuzzy logic to solve the inverse kinematics problem. However, direct kinematics was not dealt with. Jamwal et al. (2010) applied a similar technique to find the forward kinematics. However, the major problem with fuzzy logic is that the implementation requires framing of inference rules. Sardana et al. (2013) applied a geometric method to find out the inverse kinematics of a robot used in biopsy. Morell et al. (2013) applied a support vector regression method for forward kinematics. In all works, either forward or inverse kinematics is studied, not both. Also, the methods applied cannot be used without prior knowledge about the method or the system. This chapter concentrates on demonstrating how direct kinematics and inverse kinematics can be easily estimated using neural networks for parallel and serial manipulators, respectively.

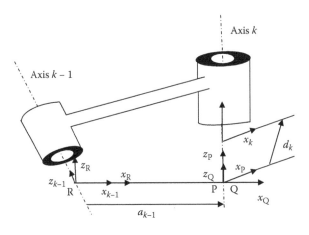

Figure 18.2   Joint parameters in D–H method.

18.2 Backpropagation Neural Network

An artificial neural network (ANN) is an information-processing paradigm that is inspired by the way biological nervous systems, such as the brain, process information. An ANN consists of multiple layers of simple processing elements called neurons. An ANN executes in cycles; a whole network of neurons is executed in series in response to some input. Several types of ANNs, based on particular computing abilities of the human brain, are proposed. The choice of a particular neural network depends on the application.

Of the available ANNs, the backpropagation network has gained importance due to the shortcomings of other available networks. The network is a multilayer network (multilayer perceptron) that contains at least one hidden layer in addition to input and output layers (Figure 18.3). The number of hidden layers and the number of neurons in each hidden layer are to be fixed based on the application, complexity of the problem, and the number of inputs and outputs. Use of a nonlinear, log-sigmoid transfer function enables the network to simulate nonlinearity in practical systems. Due to its numerous advantages, a backpropagation network is chosen for the present work (Hagan 2008).

Implementation of the backpropagation model consists of two phases. Each neuron receives input and produces output. Neurons are connected within a layer and among different layers. The strength of connection within the network, otherwise known as weight structure, is initially assumed to be random-valued and is fixed by learning or training. Once network parameters are fixed, output is obtained by presenting the input patterns to the network. This process is termed testing of the network.

Training is based on a gradient descent rule that tends to adjust weights and reduce system error in the network. The input layer has neurons equal in number to that of the inputs. Similarly, the output-layer neurons are the same in number as the outputs. The number of hidden-layer neurons is decided by a trial-and-error method using the experimental data.

18.2.1 Weight Structure

Every input-layer neuron is connected to all hidden-layer neurons by interlayer connections (Figure 18.3). Every connection carries a weight factor, initially assigned by a random generator algorithm. Weights are scaled in the range of –0.5 to +0.5 and are represented by *Wij* (where i = 1, 2, 3, …, 7 and j = 1 to 3). Output- and hidden-layer neurons are connected similarly, and the interconnection

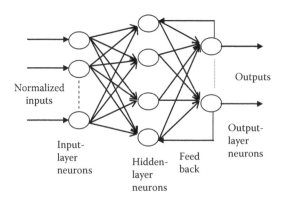

Figure 18.3   Training in backpropagation neural network.

weights are represented by *Wij*2 (where i = 1 to 3 and j = 1). The same random generator initially generates weights on these connections.

18.2.2 Normalization

The backpropagation network is based on the *delta rule*, according to which a change in weights in successive iterations varies proportionally with inputs. Hence, it is evident that in successive iterations, a change in weight depends on the magnitude of inputs. To avoid an abnormal increase in weight structures, inputs are scaled to a range of 0 to 1. Values of each pattern are normalized for efficient processing by the network. Normalization is carried out by dividing each input by the length of the corresponding vector, considering data to be used for both training and testing.

18.2.3 Training

Success of the implementation of neural networks is influenced by the choice of parameters of the network. The choice of parameters of the network greatly influences the accuracy of implementation of neural networks. A heuristic method of optimization is used to overcome the threat of local minima with the help of momentum. The momentum rate in the present network was fixed as 0.75, as a large value creates inconsistencies in the network, and smaller ones are futile. For the network to adapt to new input patterns, the learning rate should be high; however, too-high learning rates tend to destabilize the network. As a trade-off, the value was fixed as 0.45 for the present network. The D–H parameters of the manipulator are taken as inputs for the network to predict the position of the end effector in direct kinematics. In inverse kinematics, the position of the end effector is taken as input to the network to predict the joint angles. Normalized input patterns were presented to the network for training, and the size of the network was optimized by trial and error. Initially, the number of hidden layers was determined. After optimizing the number of hidden layers, the number of neurons in the hidden layer was determined. To assess the number of neurons in the hidden layer, experimental data were presented to the network to examine the variation in error with a change in the number of hidden-layer neurons. The final parameter to be determined is the number of iterations of the network. The network was trained with the data, and the variation in error was observed for a change in the number of iterations.

Each of the inputs, Ii, is multiplied by weights on interlayer connections of a hidden-layer neuron, Wij_1, and added to bias to produce activation, a_1.

$$a_1 = Wij_1{}^*IT + \phi$$

where

Ii is the output of the input layer
Wij_1 is the weight structure between the input and hidden layers
ϕ is the bias

A log-sigmoid activation function that transforms activation of hidden-layer neurons to a scaled output O_1 can be written as

$$O_1 = 1/(1 + \exp(-a_1))$$

Outputs from hidden-layer neurons are treated as inputs to output-layer neurons. Summation of the product of all hidden-layer outputs and weights between hidden and output layers added to bias constitutes the activation a_2 of output-layer neurons. A log-sigmoid transfer function or pure linear function can be applied, and output O_2 is computed. In the present work, a pure linear function is used so as to reduce the nonlinearity in the system and help in the faster convergence of the network. Error is estimated as the difference between actual and computed outputs. This procedure constitutes the forward flow of the backpropagation phase, and error computed is backpropagated through the same network to update weights. Weights are updated using the generalized delta rule:

$$Wnew = Wold + \beta eI$$

where

    $Wnew$ is the weight after modification
    $Wold$ is the weight structure before modification
    β is the learning rate, usually taken between 0 and 1
    e is the error obtained

Weight change is calculated for all connections. Errors for all patterns are summed, and the algorithm is run until the error falls below a specified value (Figure 18.3).

Backpropagation algorithms attempt to minimize the error of the mathematical system represented by a neural network's weights and thus walk downhill to the optimum values for weights. Unfortunately, due to the mathematical complexity of even the simplest neural network, there are many minima, some deeper than others. The deepest minimum is the ideal one and is called the *global minimum*, whereas inferior minima are termed *local minima*. Local minima present a problem to the gradient descent algorithms as the algorithm is invariably attracted to the nearest minimum, which may not be the global one. The problem is revealed by the fact that two identical neural networks trained on the same set of data for same processing time will almost certainly produce different results, because one network reaches one minimum while the other reaches a different one due to different random starting weights representing different starting locations on the mathematical landscape. Hence, to reach the global minimum, the aid of heuristic optimization techniques is sought in the present work. The present work uses the concept of *momentum* to overcome local minima and speed up the process of attaining a stable weight structure. Momentum acts as a disturbance and makes the network escape minimum error.

The technique lies in adding a portion of the previous weight changes in the weight modification relation, as shown in the folowing:

$$W_2 (k + 1) = W_2(k) + \beta eI + \Omega W_2(k)$$

where

    Ω is the momentum rate, usually taken to be around 0.5 to 0.8
    k denotes the number of the present iteration

Momentum plays a role similar to a low-pass filter that smoothens out high-frequency variations in error surface, which tend to cause divergent oscillations. Thus, momentum helps in reaching a stable weight structure at a faster rate.

Obtained weights corresponding to the minimum error are stored. These trained weights are used in testing to predict the output for new data (that have not been used in training).

18.2.4 Testing

After stable weights are obtained by the training network, interconnections are assigned corresponding weights. Normalized input patterns other than those used for training are fed to the network, where only a forward pass takes place.

Each of the inputs, Ii, is multiplied by weights on interlayer connections of a hidden-layer neuron, Wij_1, and added to bias to produce activation, a_1.

A log-sigmoid activation function is used to transform activation of the hidden-layer neurons to a scaled output O_1.

Outputs from the hidden-layer neurons are treated as inputs to the output-layer neurons. Summation of the product of all the hidden-layer outputs and weights between hidden and output layers added to bias constitutes activation a_2 of the output-layer neurons. A log-sigmoid transfer function is applied, and output O_2 is computed. Outputs are in a normalized form. To obtain true values, denormalization is carried out.

18.2.5 Denormalization

Output values range from 0 to 1. The obtained outputs are multiplied with the length of the corresponding vector to obtain results in true magnitudes. This process is termed denormalization.

18.3 Application of Backpropagation Neural Network to Robot Kinematics

In the present case study, a 3-degree-of-freedom (dof) serial manipulator (Figure 18.4) is considered. In the initial step, the position of the end effector is calculated using the D–H parameter, and then, using inverse kinematics, starting from the end effector position, the joint parameters are estimated. This is illustrated in more detail in the following.

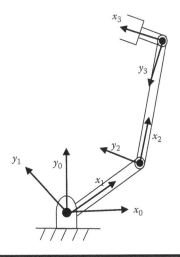

Figure 18.4   3-dof manipulator.

Table 18.1   D-H Parameters

i	α_{i-1}	d_i	a_{i-1}	θ_i
1	0	0	0	θ_1
2	0	0	l_1	θ_2
3	0	0	l_2	θ_3

18.3.1 Direct Kinematics

The axes of the manipulator are fixed for convenience. Once the axes are fixed, the D–H parameters are tabulated (Table 18.1).

The algebraic solution for the different transformations can be obtained as

$$
{}_1^0T = \begin{bmatrix}
c\theta_1 & -s\theta_1 & 0 & a_0 \\
s\theta_1 c\alpha_0 & c\theta_1 c\alpha_0 & -s\alpha_0 & -s\alpha_0 d_1 \\
s\theta_1 s\alpha_0 & c\theta_1 s\alpha_0 & c\alpha_0 & c\alpha_0 d_1 \\
0 & 0 & 0 & 1
\end{bmatrix} = \begin{bmatrix}
c\theta_1 & -s\theta_1 & 0 & 0 \\
s\theta_1 & c\theta_1 & 0 & 0 \\
0 & 0 & 1 & 0 \\
0 & 0 & 0 & 1
\end{bmatrix}
$$

$$
{}_2^1T = \begin{bmatrix}
c\theta_2 & -s\theta_2 & 0 & l_1 \\
s\theta_2 & c\theta_2 & 0 & 0 \\
0 & 0 & 1 & 0 \\
0 & 0 & 0 & 1
\end{bmatrix} \quad
{}_3^2T = \begin{bmatrix}
c\theta_3 & -s\theta_3 & 0 & l_2 \\
s\theta_3 & c\theta_3 & 0 & 0 \\
0 & 0 & 1 & 0 \\
0 & 0 & 0 & 1
\end{bmatrix}
$$

The overall transformation can be shown as

$$
{}_3^0T = \begin{bmatrix}
c_{123} & -s_{123} & 0 & l_1 c_1 + l_2 c_{12} \\
s_{123} & c_{123} & 0 & l_1 s_1 + l_2 s_{12} \\
0 & 0 & 1 & 0 \\
0 & 0 & 0 & 1
\end{bmatrix}
$$

18.3.2 Inverse Kinematics

The inverse kinematics starts with the end solution of the direct kinematics. The final position of the end effector is assumed as

$$
{}_W^B T = \begin{bmatrix}
c_\phi & -s_\phi & 0 & x \\
s_\phi & c_\phi & 0 & y \\
0 & 0 & 1 & 0 \\
0 & 0 & 0 & 1
\end{bmatrix}
$$

By comparison,

$$c_\phi = c_{123} \qquad s_\phi = s_{123}$$

$$x = l_1 c_1 + l_2 c_{12}$$

$$y = l_1 s_1 + l_2 s_{12}$$

Hence,

$$x^2 + y^2 = l_1^2 + l_2^2 + 2l_1 l_2 c_2$$

$$c_2 = \frac{x^2 + y^2 - l_1^2 - l_2^2}{2l_1 l_2}$$

$$s_2 = \pm\sqrt{1 - c_2^2} \quad \Rightarrow \theta_2 = A\tan 2(s_2, c_2).$$

The cosine function has the problem that the value of cosine of an angle and that of its negative are the same, that is, $\cos(\theta) = \cos(-\theta)$. So, we do not know exactly whether the angle is positive or negative. The problem with sine is that as the angle approaches zero, sine may give inaccurate answers. To prevent these problems, tangent is generally considered (Figure 18.5).

Using $c_{12} = c_1 c_2 - s_1 s_2$ and $s_{12} = c_1 s_2 - c_2 s_1$:

$$x = k_1 c_1 - k_2 s_1$$

$$y = k_1 s_1 + k_2 c_1$$

where $k_1 = l_1 + l_2 c_2$ and $k_2 = l_2 s_2$.
To solve these equations, take

$$r = +\sqrt{k_1^2 + k_2^2} \text{ and } \gamma = A\tan 2(k_2, k_1).$$

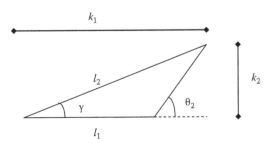

Figure 18.5 Depiction of angles.

Then, $k_1 = r \cos \gamma$, $k_2 = r \sin \gamma$, and we can write

$$x/r = \cos \gamma \cos \theta_1 - \sin \gamma \sin \theta_1$$

$$y/r = \cos \gamma \sin \theta_1 + \sin \gamma \cos \theta_1$$

$$\text{or } \cos(\gamma + \theta_1) = x/r, \sin(\gamma + \theta_1) = y/r$$

Hence, $\gamma + \theta_1 = a\tan2(y/r, x/r) = a\tan2(y, x)$
Therefore, $\theta_1 = a\tan2(y, x) - a\tan2(k_2, k_1)$
Finally, θ_3 can be solved from $\theta_1 + \theta_2 + \theta_3 = \phi$

It can be seen from the previous discussion how cumbersome the process is. In order to avoid the complex mathematical solving of the parameters, an ANN-based technique has been used. A backpropagation neural network (BPNN) is chosen. The formulated values of D–H parameters (Table 18.1) are given as inputs. It must be noted that one trained neural network can be used only for a similar type of a manipulator. For instance, if a 3-dof manipulator's D–H parameters are used for training, then the network can be used to be tested on 3-dof manipulators of different orientations but not on a manipulator of more or fewer degrees of freedom. In order to control this limitation, several networks are trained.

18.4 Developed User Interface

To aid in simpler application of the network, a user-friendly front end is created. Visual Basic 6.0 has been used in the front end (Schneider 2003). Several C++ programs have been employed in the back end (Kanetkar 2002). Upon choosing an option, a particular program activates. The input has to be provided in .dat file format. Outputs are saved as .txt files. The number of input-layer neurons, the number of hidden layers, the number of iterations, the value of learning rate, and the value of momentum can be chosen by the user. There is an option for the user to take the default values. These default values are set using the training data, aiming at minimum error (Freeman 1999). The values are fixed by trial and error. After these parameters are given to the system, the network trains itself with data already pertaining to the same number of degrees of freedom as chosen by the user. After testing, the new inputs are taken, and the results are calculated. Screenshots of the developed user interface are shown in Figure 18.6.

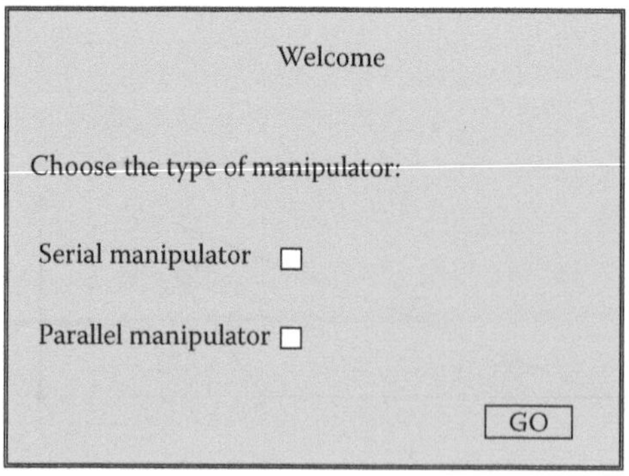

Figure 18.6   Choice of manipulator.

Only a few screenshots are shown in the present chapter for brevity. Figure 18.6 shows the initial screen of the developed user interface. Here, the user is prompted to choose the type of manipulator. In the next screen, the user is prompted to choose the number of degrees of freedom. After the number of degrees of freedom is chosen, the user chooses the type of kinematic calculation required. At this stage, the required program for use is pinpointed by the interface. For all future calculations and inputs, this particular program will be used. In the next stage, the user will be prompted to give the parameters for BPNN as discussed previously or to choose to use the default values. After inputting the values for BPNN, the program directs the user to different screens, depending on his/her choice of direct or inverse kinematics. In the case of direct kinematics, the D–H parameters are to be stored in a .dat file and given to the system (Figure 18.7).

For inverse kinematics (Figure 18.8), the position of the end effector is given by the user. Then the program corresponding to the inverse kinematics is triggered, and the output is generated. The main advantage of this developed interface is facilitating the easy calculation of robot kinematics; however, this suffers from certain limitations like constraints on the number of degrees of freedom. This has been prepared only for academic purposes and can be improved for greater flexibility.

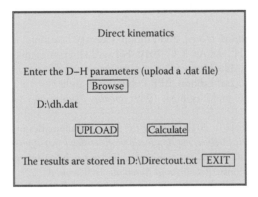

Figure 18.7 Calculation of direct kinematics.

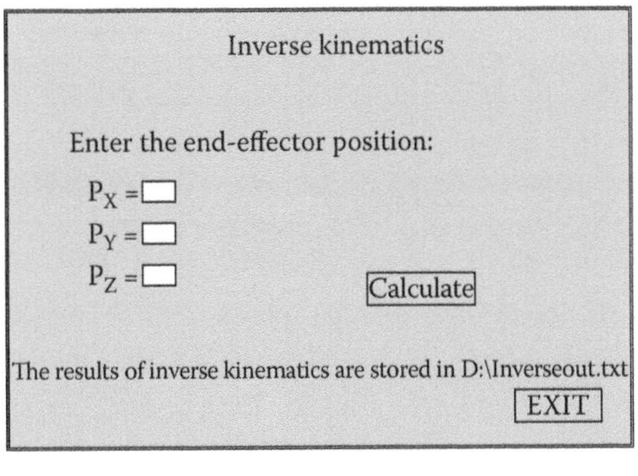

Figure 18.8 Calculation of inverse kinematics.

18.5 Conclusion

Robot kinematics is essential in robotic control and application. However, the calculation of robot kinematics is difficult and requires a lot of mathematical background. To make this process simpler, the use of ANNs is helpful. A user interface has been developed using Visual Basic 6.0 and C++ for easier implementation of the neural networks to solve the robot kinematics.

The work can be extended by using different types of networks like Radial Basis Function (RBF), General Probabilistic Regression Neural Networks (GPRNN) and so forth, and the efficiency of these networks can be compared. However, this would depend, to a large extent, on the data taken and the scenario. Further, other parameters like trajectory generation can be included in the program, and the suggested output graphs can be obtained.

References

Chen C.-Y., M.-G. Her, Y.-C. Hung and M. Karkoub. 2002. Approximating a robot inverse kinematics solution using fuzzy logic tuned by genetic algorithms. *The International Journal of Advanced Manufacturing Technology*. 20(5): 375–380.

Craig J.J. 2008. *Introduction to Robotics: Mechanics and Control*, 3rd Edition. Pearson, India.

Freeman J.A. and Skapura D.M. 1999. *Neural Networks Algorithms, and Programming Techniques*. Addison-Wesley, USA.

Hagan M.T. 2008. *Neural Network Design*, 2nd Edition. Cengage Learning, Michigan.

Jamwal P.K., Xie S.Q., Tsoi Y.H. and Aw K.C. 2010. Forward kinematics modelling of a parallel ankle rehabilitation robot using modified fuzzy inference. *Mechanism and Machine Theory*. 45(11): 1537–1554.

Kanetkar Y. 2002. *Let Us C++*, 2nd Edition. BPB Publications, India.

Klafter R.D., Chmielewski T.A. and Negin M. 1989. *Robotics Engineering: An Integrated Approach*. Prentice Hall, India.

Morell A., Tarokh M. and Acosta L. 2013. Solving the forward kinematics problem in parallel robots using support vector regression. *Engineering Applications of Artificial Intelligence*. 26(7): 1698–1706.

Sardana L., Sutar M.K. and Pathak P.M. 2013. A geometric approach for inverse kinematics of a 4-link redundant *In-Vivo* robot for biopsy. *Robotics and Autonomous Systems*. 61(12): 1306–1313.

Schneider D.I. 2003. *An Introduction to Programming with Visual Basic 6.0*, Update Edition. Prentice Hall, USA.

Tsai L.-W. 1996. *Robot Analysis: The Mechanics of Serial and Parallel Manipulators*. Wiley-Interscience, John Wiley & Sons Inc., New York.

Chapter 19

Conceptual Modeling of Networked Organizations: The Case of Aum Shinrikyo

Saad Alqithami, Jennifer Haegele, and Henry Hexmoor

Contents

In an open dynamic environment, autonomous agents form a network organization (NO) by engaging in active connections with other autonomous agents in order to achieve common goals. In some situations, due to an agent's scale of dynamism, these connections may include agents that have had no previous experience (i.e., no prior associations); thus, agents are required to coordinate their actions and cooperate toward a common goal. As a result, agent members of NOs are more likely to cohesively collaborate as a means to build and maintain their network. Moreover, an NO behaves as a complicated system interwoven with commonplace social relationships, not as a closed system. Thus, the magnitude of these networks' interactions and the pace of social change that they produce are context specific. To this end, this chapter will describe the general construction (i.e., formation and internal structure) of an NO as they can affect the internal and external ties and interactions of agents within the NO. This chapter will also present the methods of agent-based modeling as a means to define specific tools (e.g., norms, roles, capabilities, utilities) that inherently affect agent behaviors and help them to socially connect with other agents through the formation, modification, and expansion of the organization. A case study of a terrorist organization known as Aum Shinrikyo (Aum) will be analyzed using a classic bottom-up perspective of influence on autonomous agents through the social structure. As this study theorizes that average global utility will decrease when there is a strong fluctuation in agent contributions, the bottoms-up perspective will be able to address these fluctuations. Furthermore, a dynamic explanation is considered for any prospective fluctuations prevalent in small groups, as large groups are more likely to be involved in a collective action. Consequently, using NetLogo as a prototyping platform, a simulation is implemented to illustrate that such fluctuations may have a dramatic impact on the average utility of the group.

19.1 Introduction

Within the past decade, there has been an increasing amount of research on what is characterized as a network organization (NO). Unlike living organizations (i.e., traditional organizations), NOs exhibit how participants are linked to one another through various social structures. Inactive agents, who have not been linked with any of the others, are simply omitted from the organization, and the structure is evaluated without them. Agents in NOs are typically active collaborators producing particularistic-seeming ties among them with the aim of maintaining a sense of continuity toward their organizational goals. This has narrowed our perspectives when perceiving organizations. In light of this, this chapter elucidates on evaluating and modeling NO using a real-world case study.

Agency theory frequently applies organizational models in order to model coordination in open multiagent system (MAS) environments (Easley and Kleinberg 2010; Eisenhardt 1989). This will allow them to adapt dynamically to environmental changes. Two perspectives should be considered when modeling NOs: (1) structural perspectives, including nodes (e.g., agents, resources, objects), ties (e.g., norms, role, resource access, etc.), as well as ontology; and (2) functional perspectives that classify the various types of activities and ties within an NO. To this end, it becomes clear that organizational modeling plays an important role in evaluating open dynamic MAS.

There exists a systematic overlap in NOs between the type of structure and quotidian social networks, which results in mobilization pathways and organizational subdivisions. This is elicited from tracing an agent's sustained set of interactions favoring the nuanced relationship between the set and the social structure. Dynamic social interactions can help NO resilience, while fragment confrontation does not, since the magnitude and pace of an NO are situation specific (Easley and Kleinberg 2010; Hartmann et al. 2008). For instance, in terrorist organizations, agents are dynamically changing their actions based on the direction from the leader of the group in retaliation to actions by the society.

More broadly, emergent properties of agents' actions based on their attributes and norms about organizational behavior help in forming an NO. For this, different forms of NO should be theorized explicitly to assist with introducing agent-based modeling (ABM) into the case study of the terrorist network Aum. The network organizational structure may be characterized into different types including hierarchies, holarchies, coalitions, teams, congregations, societies, federations, markets, and matrix organizations (Easley and Kleinberg 2010; Horling and Lesser 2005). A hierarchical organization, such as the case with Aum, is the traditional structure used in many organizations.

In hierarchical structures, those with higher rankings possess wider, more global organizational scopes and greater authority than those individuals who rank below them. The resources travel up the hierarchical structure in order to provide a broader view for NOs, whereas control has the opposite tendency (i.e., travel down). If the problem space is divided into layers and task partitioning can parallel the problem structure, hierarchy is a good paradigm (Easley and Kleinberg 2010; Horling and Lesser 2005). A hierarchical organization begins with at least three agents and two levels to form a network; this includes the upper-level (e.g., leader), which is in control of the data streaming since it produces a global view, and the lower level (e.g., subordinate), which responds to the commands of the leader. This type of hierarchy can affect the characteristics of global and local behavior (Easley and Kleinberg 2010; Horling and Lesser 2005).

There are several models proposed for analyzing, designing, and building NOs. Nevertheless, most of them are grounded on real object-oriented or knowledge-based models. Matson and DeLoach (2005) showed the procedure of building an adaptive and fault tolerance organizational model through their study of the Gulf War in 1990. This study has mimicked the command and control procedure developed by Krackhardt and Carley (1998) in order to evaluate the battlefield information system. Previous works that have also been developed in the area of using MAS for modeling NOs vary depending on the organization type studied. Alqithami and Hexmoor (2012b) modeled their organization in terms of how rapidly it adapts to new interiors and what is the fastest way possible. Their model was based on four major components: (1) the role of the agents inside the organization, (2) utility of each actor, (3) their capability, and (4) de facto norms. Similarly, Hexmoor (2011) used a model to describe his organization depending on the team capabilities, roles, departments, and norms. These models, however, are abstract and nonspecific in evaluating NOs even though they have been useful. This chapter proposes that earlier models can be enhanced with formalisms incorporating network complexities while building upon their ABM.

Presented in Section 19.2 is a case study analyzing terrorist organizations using the classic top-down direction of influence from autonomous agents to social groups. It addresses the fluctuations of individual contributions to global NO utility. Such fluctuations may have a dramatic impact on the average utility of a group (i.e., this utility decreases when there is a strong fluctuation in the individuals' contributions to the global utility). We consider this a dynamic explanation for the fact that large groups are more likely than small groups to get involved in collective action, pointing to fluctuations as stronger in small groups.

19.2 Aum Shinrikyo

19.2.1 The NO of Aum Shinrikyo: From Finances to Recruitment

In 1984, a charismatic and partially blind guru named Chizuo "Shoko Asahara" Matsumoto founded a yoga school and publishing house he then called Aum, Inc. (Bellamy 2013; Danzig et al. 2011; Reader 1996; Staff 1995; START 2013; Walsh 2001). Establishing only a few clients when the shop first opened, Asahara soon decided to try and increase his client populace by utilizing the popular Japanese magazine *Twilight Zone* to release a public announcement that depicted him as a deity having the capability to levitate (Bellamy 2013; Danzig et al. 2011; Walsh 2001). Although the group was not yet religious, it was not long before his newfound messianic reputation throughout Japan attracted a number of people wanting to obtain the same power to levitate (Bellamy 2013; Danzig et al. 2011). It was not until 1985, after a trip to North Japan in search of self-discovery, that Asahara began advocating esoteric mysticism to his members despite the fact that he possessed all six terrorist leader characteristics* identified by Parachini and Tucker (1999). Preaching meditation, introspection, and nonviolence to his members enabled him to formalize his group of approximately 24 members into an organization, and they changed their name to Aum Shinsen-no Kai (translated as "Group of Gods/Supreme Beings") by 1986 (Bellamy 2013; Danzig et al. 2011; Reader 1996; Walsh 2001).

It was also during this time that Asahara began claiming he could prevent a catastrophe, which he foresaw developing from a "materialist and spiritually void society" (Danzig et al. 2011). However, in order for him to prevent the cataclysm, he asserted that he would need to open centers around the world and acquire thousands of spiritually enlightened practitioners; thus, Asahara urged laypeople to renounce their society and contribute donations for their initiation as a practitioner. Although money came from their various front companies (i.e., businesses) selling services, literature, tests, and advanced courses, it was through its members (i.e., membership fees and donations) that Aum procured the majority of their funding (Parachini and Tucker 1999; Staff 1995; START 2013). By the fall of 1986, his scam to collect money from unsuspecting followers had worked, and he was able to begin opening monastic communities throughout Japan (Bellamy 2013; Danzig et al. 2011).

Then, in 1987, the organization changed their name again, this time to Aum "Aum" Shinrikyo (translated as the "Supreme Truth"), as well as began shifting their spiritual beliefs to one requiring blood rituals (Danzig et al. 2011; Reader 1996; Staff 1995; START 2013; Walsh 2001). According to Danzig et al. (2011), Aum had generated so much popularity over a 2-year period, through recruitment efforts and word of mouth, that by 1987, the organization had grown to include nearly 1300 members with 30 monks and nuns, around 2300 members by 1988 with 117 monks and nuns, and almost 4000 members by 1989 with 390 monks and nuns. It was also in 1989 that the Tokyo Metropolitan Government finally granted Aum official religious corporation status (Danzig et al. 2011; Staff 1995; START 2013). Upon registration as a legally recognized religion, Aum gained many privileges from the Japanese government, such as de facto immunity from official oversight and prosecution, as well as massive tax breaks (Danzig et al. 2011; Staff 1995; START 2013).

After Aum's religious legalization, membership again rose dramatically from 4,000 members in 1989 to nearly 10,000 members by 1992 and approximately 50,000 worldwide by 1995 (Parachini and Tucker 1999; Reader 1996; Staff 1995; START 2013). Moreover, Aum's 1989 net worth of less than 430 million yen (approximately 4.3 million USD) more than doubled, growing to well over 100 billion yen (1 billion USD) by 1995 (Staff 1995; START 2013). As a result, Aum began utilizing their government immunities and extensive capital to expand their operations to include bases in six other countries, including Australia, Germany, Indonesia, Russia, Taiwan, and the United States, with more than 130 front companies worldwide (Parachini and Tucker 1999; Staff 1995; START 2013). Operating out of a number of these newly established front companies, similar to that of the yoga school in Japan, members began purchasing chemicals and biological agents; developing software and data mining; procuring weapon materials from Russia, Australia, Sri Lanka, Zaire, and North Korea; as well as acquiring helicopters from Russia and training pilots in the United States (Parachini and Tucker 1999; Staff 1995; START 2013; Vogel 1999). At the same time, Aum began reorganizing and expanding their leadership in order to assemble their own militia (Parachini and Tucker 1999; Reader 1996; Staff 1995; START 2013).

Aum had a strategy to recruit from the military, officers of the Japanese Self-Defense Force (JDF), placing high priority on the First Airborne Brigade, and the police as a means to further their militarization and intelligence functions. Furthermore, they targeted Japan's top universities

---

* The six terrorist leader characteristics include (1) charismatic leadership, (2) no external constituency, (3) apocalyptic ideology, (4) loner or splinter group, (5) a sense of paranoia and grandiosity, and (6) defense aggression.

in order to actively recruit students and professionals. Having acquired a considerable amount of brilliant members—who have obtained degrees in such fields as medicine, biochemistry, architecture, biology, and genetic engineering—each department or ministry was run by those whom many considered the "best and brightest" of their fields (Staff 1995). Subsequently, Aum shadowed the structure of the Japanese government and organized into a hierarchical organization with 21 identifiable ministries and departments, with each one headed by 21 of the 23 members closest to Asahara (Table 19.1) (Danzig et al. 2011; Hudson 1999; Reader 1996; START 2013). With the title of supreme leader reserved for Asahara, his wife Tomoko Ishii/Matsumoto and his mistress Hisako Ishii were second and third in command, respectively; six individuals were considered

Table 19.1 Aum's System of Ministries

Affiliation	Name
Founder	Shoko Asahara
Household Agency	Tomomasa Nakagawa
Secretariat	Reika Matsumoto
Ministry of Commerce	Yofune Shirakawa
Ministry of Construction	Kiyohide Hayakawa
Ministry of Defense	Tetsuya Kibe
Ministry of Education	Shigeru Sugiura
Ministry of Finance	Hisako Ishii
Ministry of Foreign Affairs (Public Relations)	Fumihiro Joyu
Ministry of Healing	Ikuo Hayashi
Ministry of Health and Welfare	Seiichi Endo
Ministry of Home Affairs	Tomomitsu Niimi
Ministry of Intelligence	Yoshihiro Inoue
Ministry of Justice	Yoshinobu Aoyama
Ministry of Labor	Mayumi Yamamoto
Ministry of Post and Telecommunications	Tomoko Ishii
Ministry of Science and Technology	Hideo Murai
Ministry of Vehicles	Naruhito Noda
Eastern Followers Agency	Eriko Iida
New Followers Agency	Sanae Ouchi
Western Followers Agency	Kazuko Miyakozawa

Sources: Hudson, R., *Federal Research Division,* Library of Congress, Washington, DC, 1999. Brackett, D., *Holy Terror: Armageddon in Tokyo.* Weatherhill, New York, 1996.

"senior advisors," and six individuals not only were involved in the group's biological and chemical program but also were considered by Asahara as his "inner-circle members." Despite Aum's structure being developed in a hierarchical fashion, with the exception of the 3 Followers Agencies (Western, Eastern, and New) and the Ministry of Science and Technology, the remaining 17 agencies did not oversee anyone, as they were only responsible for the coordination of any event that utilized their skills and services. Ultimately, due to the secrecy of Asahara's master plans, only one or more of the 23 individuals under Asahara coordinated and implemented all major attacks, and the approximately 50,000 followers were generally not even involved in minor attacks since they were mainly recruited to generate revenue.

19.2.2 Mass Violence in the Name of Religion

Having an idea that Aum should become a government entity rather than one of religion, Asahara and 25 members of his inner circle attempted to run for office in the 1990 Japanese parliamentary elections. However, despite Aum's many efforts in campaigning under the Shinrito ("Supreme Truth") Party, no members were elected (Danzig et al. 2011; Pate and Ackerman 2001; Staff 1995; START 2013). As a result, Asahara became infuriated with the Japanese government and accused them of rigging the elections; thus, Asahara evolved his worldview into one of apocalyptic nihilism (Pate and Ackerman 2001; Reader 1996; START 2013). It was under this new worldview that Asahara started justifying murder on spiritual grounds and transforming his teachings around cultic behaviors—predominately involving Buddhism but including an amalgam of New Age thought, Hinduism, Christianity, elements of Nostradamus' prophecies, and science fiction—which encouraged followers to confront the Japanese establishment through various acts of terrorism (Pate and Ackerman 2001; Reader 1996; START 2013; Walsh 2001).

Over a span of 5 years, Aum had initiated 17 chemical and biological warfare (CBW) attacks—10 chemical and 7 biological—with goals ranging from assassination to mass murder; fortunately, 10 of those attempts failed (Ballard et al. 2001; Tucker 2000). According to Ballard et al. (2001), of the seven biological agent attacks, four attacks used anthrax, and three used botulinum; all seven of these attacks were unsuccessful as they were nonvirulent microbial strains. For instance, in order to test the dissemination device, six key Aum members (Fomihiro Joyu, Seiichi Endo, Hideo Murai, Kiyohide Hayakawa, Kazumi Watabe, and Masaya Takahashi) and several other unknown members sprayed *Bacillus anthracis*, "anthrax," from the roof of their Tokyo midrise office building in 1993. However, the attack attempt failed as the cult had acquired a nonlethal vaccine strain (Ballard et al. 2001; START 2013). Conversely, of the 10 chemical attacks, 4 attacks used sarin, four attacks used VX, one attack used phosgene, and one attack used hydrogen cyanide (Ballard et al. 2001; Tucker 2000). For instance, in an attempt to kill three judges who were presiding on a fraud case against Aum in 1994, seven key Aum members (Seiichi Endo, Hideo Murai, Tomoitsu Niimi, Tomomasa Nakagawa, Yasuo Hayashi, Masami Tsuchiya, and Satoru Hashimoto) disseminated sarin gas into a residential neighborhood in the city of Matsumoto. Although they did not kill the targeted judges, they killed 7 people and injured 144 others, who indicated symptoms of headache, vision impairment, nausea, and so forth (Ballard et al. 2001; START 2013). However, it was not until 1995 that Aum committed their first and last large-scale attack on Japan.

By March of 1995, Aum had accumulated enough chemicals to make sarin gas to kill millions of people, and after approving the next attack, Asahara assigned the task of field supervisor to Yoshihiro Inoue and the task of carrying out the attack to Hideo Murai (Associated Press 1996; Eate 2008). Upon assignment, Murai met with Ikuo Hayashi (treatment minister), Tomomasa Nakagawa (Asahara's personal doctor), and Seiichi Endo (health and welfare minister) to develop the plan, which resulted in the decision to use sarin gas. It was also decided that Ikuo Hayashi, Toru Toyoda, Yasuo Hayashi, Masato Yokoyama, and Kenichi Hirose were to place the sarin bags on their designated train lines. At the same time, Tomomitsu Niimi, Shigeo Sugimoto, Kouichi Kitamura, Katsuya Takahashi, and Kyotaka Sotozaki were designated as lookouts and drivers for the attack (Staff 1995). And on March 20, 1995, five containers of sarin were released in Tokyo's subway in an attempt to impede an investigation into Aum's activities. Utilizing these 10 key members of Aum, they carried out the attack at the central crossing of the subway, right near the main police station (Ballard et al. 2001; Murakami 2001; Parachini and Tucker 1999; Pate and Ackerman 2001; START 2013; Tucker 2000; Vogel 1999). Sitting outside in the getaway vehicle nearby, Tomomitsu Niimi waited for Ikuo Hayashi while he released one of the five containers carrying sarin gas onto the Chiyoda Line. Similarly, Koichi Kitamura and Katsuya Takahashi waited outside in their own getaway vehicles while Kenichi Hirose and Toru Toyoda each released their containers of sarin gas onto two different trains of the Marunouchi Line. At the same time, Kiyotaka Tonozaki and Shigeo Sugimoto also waited outside in their own getaway vehicles while Masato Yokoyama and Yasuo Hayashi each released their containers of sarin gas onto two different trains of the Hibiya Line. The attack, conducted during peak Monday morning rush hour, killed a total of 12 people and injured over 5000 others (Ballard et al. 2001; Murakami 2001; Parachini and Tucker 1999; Pate and Ackerman 2001; START 2013; Tucker 2000; Vogel 1999).

Within the first 24 hours of the attack, the Japanese Metropolitan Police had designated four members of Aum as National Police Agency (NPA) most wanted suspects and arrested at least 41 others who were suspected of either murder or being a murder accomplice (NPA 1996). In the months following, police tracked down and arrested Asahara, many of the main leaders of the sect, as well as nearly 200 other members of Aum for their involvement in the subway attack and other terrorist activities. However, it was not until June 2012 that Tokyo police finally arrested the last fugitive, Katsuya Takahashi, wanted for the attack. Currently, 13 members including Asahara are on death row, while hundreds more have been released or received prison sentences, which they are still serving (Associated Press 1996; Ballard et al. 2001; Murakami 2001; Reuters Staff 2012; Staff 1995; START 2013; Vogel 1999).

19.2.3 Where Are They Now?

Despite their terrorist activities, the Japanese government did not outlaw Aum. In 1999, Fumihiro Joyu, former Aum minister of foreign affairs (i.e., public relations), became the new head of the organization after the arrest and subsequent trial verdict of Asahara (Ballard et al. 2001; Staff 1995; START 2013). Under new leadership, Aum has not only apologized for its past acts of terrorism and paid reparation to the victims of the Tokyo underground sarin attack but has also undergone many revisions. Such revisions have included changing their name to Aleph in 2000, redefining Asahara as "founder" rather than "supreme leader," as well as forbidding members from killing anyone who was against the group, among many others (Ballard et al. 2001; Staff 1995; START 2013). However, not all followers of Aum have appreciated the new direction of Aleph, and some have decided to branch off into a new group. While Joyu continues to lead Aleph, Tatsuko Muraoka and Asahara's biological children lead the splinter group. Muraoka continues to follow Asahara's original teachings, and it has been discovered that their group has committed various illegal activities since the 1995 Tokyo subway attack (see also Ballard et al. 2001; Staff 1995; START 2013). For instance, the cult hacked into several computer networks belonging to nuclear power plants located in Russia, Ukraine, China, South Korea, Taiwan, and Japan. Joyu has claimed that Aleph has no connection with these plans (Ballard et al. 2001; Staff 1995;

START 2013). However, according to START (2013), authorities have reported that although there has been considerable depletion in membership, "approximately 1,650 people in Japan and 300 in Russia still believe in Asahara's teachings. The cult holds 50 seminars a month for current and potential members. Aleph has offices all over Japan, including Tokyo, and reportedly maintains approximately 100 safe houses throughout the country. It has been reported that at least 700 members are monk-like devotees and that mind control techniques are still part of Aleph's activities (Kyodo News International 1999; Mukai 2012)." Moreover, because enough suspicion has remained around the group, Japan has passed a law allowing authorities to monitor Aum or Aleph activities for 3 years, with the ability to extend monitoring capabilities at the end of each 3-year period. The last extension of this monitoring law occurred in January 2006 (START 2013).

19.3 NO Modeling

19.3.1 ABM of NOs

Modeling the hierarchical structure of an NO requires a basic understanding of agent characteristics such as behaviors, norms, and roles. The interactional types and patterns of agents inside and outside the NO largely influence the aforementioned characteristics and often result in increased homophily. Homophily, a type of collaboration, is an agent's objective to associate and bond with other agents that have similar objectives to their own, and it can be divided into one of two types: status-homophily and value-homophily (Lazarsfeld and Merton 1954). Status-homophily argues that agents are more likely to collaborate with others intentionally rather than merely by chance when they have similar social statuses. Value-homophily claims that agents are more likely to collaborate with others despite their social status, as long as they think similarly (Currarini and Vega-Redondo 2013; Easley and Kleinberg 2010). For instance, Asahara had a tendency to allow only a very small fraction of members (i.e., the 23 leaders and select followers) to know the "master plan" of the group. Although all members were technically considered an internal tie, the members who did not know the master plan operated as an external tie since they were only there to provide funding. Furthermore, nonmembers also operated as an external tie. Thus, external ties affected the distribution of in-group ties from the baseline form of homophily. As such, ignoring other agents' attitudes and assembly mechanisms, only a small concentration of individuals committed their major attacks. Thus, it must also be noted that collaboration is a more demanding process than cooperation* because it allows agents to share information, share resources, and evaluate a program of activities in order to accomplish a certain goal and then generate common value together (Alqithami and Hexmoor 2013; Currarini and Vega-Redondo 2013; Easley and Kleinberg 2010).

More broadly, the type and pattern of interaction may not always result in congruent homophily, since different types of ties can affect structure and behavior positively. The development of ties transpires when an agent generates utilities with another agent while also relying on the organization to decide whether it will be a tie of inbreeding (i.e., connections restricted to one agent) or outbreeding (i.e., connections extended to a whole group) (Alqithami and Hexmoor 2013; Currarini and Vega-Redondo 2013; Easley and Kleinberg 2010). Moreover, ties can be explicit or implicit, where implicit affinities can be seen inside the organization when the member has more than one interest to share. However, if any of those members has a connection with any other

---

* Cooperation includes communication, information exchange, activity adjustment, and resource sharing to accomplish compatible goals (Tuomela 2000).

members of another organization, this connection will immediately be considered an explicit affinity. Therefore, implicit connections produce bonding, which in result helps build homogenous networks, while explicit ties result in bridging several organizations to shape a heterogeneous society. The bonding matrix has a positive relationship with the role of social capital among agents and is represented through the fraction of six times the length of total vectors by the length of two paths (Alqithami and Hexmoor 2012a, 2013; Easley and Kleinberg 2010). Relatedly, the bridging matrix measures outside connections (i.e., ties) to represent the betweenness among all participant members.* As a result, the repeated interaction of bonding or bridging among agents inside and/or outside the organization produces a cohesive network. In other words, cohesion is made of a combination of bonding and bridging matrices and can play the same role as a clustering coefficient to measure the triadic closure in a sociogram (i.e., a graph) (Alqithami and Hexmoor 2012a, 2013; Easley and Kleinberg 2010).

Since an NO has periodic patterns of connections, ties have an effect on organizational performance as well as the agents' intraorganizational network, which are dependent on their type: state ties and event ties. State ties are measured concerning intensity, strength, and duration over continuous time, while event ties are measured on the subject of frequency over a discrete time slot. Ties have a positive correlation with the social capital of an NO (e.g., when the organization has a strong social capital, ties are also strengthened) (Alqithami and Hexmoor 2012a, 2013; Borgatti and Halgin 2011; Easley and Kleinberg 2010). In the case of Aum, these kinds of ties evaluate (i.e., enable, limit, or constrain) the flow of information as members engage in various types of interactions. For instance, in 1995, the leader (i.e., Asahara) engaged in interactions (state type ties) with his members (i.e., the individuals who were justified with committing acts of terror) in order to commit to releasing sarin gas (i.e., an event-type tie) on five trains in the Tokyo subway system, killing 13 commuters and seriously injuring 5000 others. However, this event would not have been accomplished had Asahara not been able to seed (i.e., grow or strengthen) his network.

19.3.2 The Seeding of Aum Shinrikyo

In general, the seeding of Aum is similar to many other NOs in that Asahara was able to strengthen his ties in the yoga shop before he started overexaggerating his religious capabilities, thus bridging his ties. The seeding of his organization started when 23 members were seeking a foundation of faith in him as a means to fill a void in their scientific-based lives. Their beliefs were only a normative social influence through mirroring of his behavior and attitude. And looking for more resources to spread his ideas and gain money (i.e., utility), Asahara began to build a hierarchical structure through the 23 primary members in order to attract more followers to Aum (Figure 19.1). More broadly, Asahara's norms facilitated coordinating agents' diversity, heterogeneity, and autonomy inside an NO instead of direct control of their socialites. It allowed the leader to determine satisfactions, punishments, and rewards, as well as control over agents' behaviors and interactions for a consistent and efficient process. Furthermore, the leader used roles to determine and control the normative attitudes toward his followers' interactions, which, in result, differentiated their ties. Oftentimes, roles are applied endogenously or exogenously to an NO. In the present case study, it appears as though Aum's roles were exogenously applied since the leader was responsible for assigning roles during formation; however, it became self-organized over time (i.e., roles were endogenously applied).

---

* Betweenness is the number of shortest paths from all vertices to all others that pass through that agent.

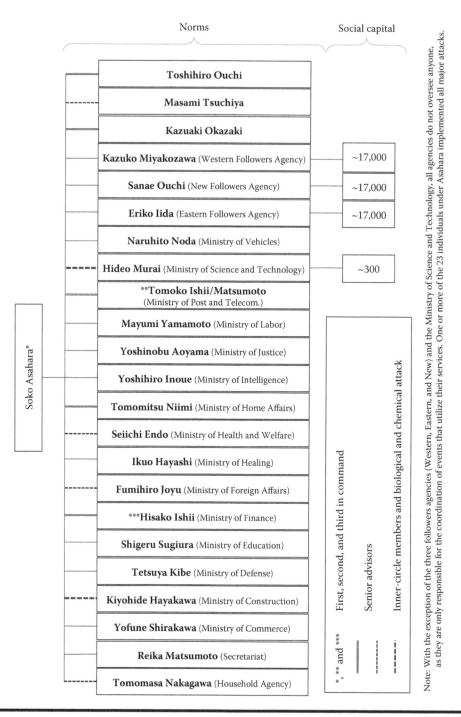

Figure 19.1 The hierarchical structure of AUM and its stages. (Adapted from Staff, *Global Proliferation of Weapons of Mass Destruction: A Case Study on the Aum Shinrikyo*, Senate Government Affairs Permanent Subcommittee, 1995. Danzig, R. et al., *Aum Shinrikyo Insights into How Terrorists Develop Biological and Chemical Weapons*, Center for a New America Security, 2011.)

As previously mentioned, the formation of Aum was based on strong ties, which allowed the NO to grow virally with the acceptance of every new member, eventually accumulating over 50,000 members. It is obvious that the formation of Aum was based on three main parameters of an NO: capabilities, preferences, and resources. (1) Capability is what the member-agent has in order to handle certain tasks. The agents were chosen based on their knowledge and achievements. (2) Preference is considered when some of the leaders were considered senior advisors and allowed to have more power than others. (3) Resources are the most important key in forming this organization. The resources provided by lower-level followers helped the leader in structuring these ties in order to build an NO, as well as allowed the extension of their views and opening of several more base locations in different countries. Therefore, the capabilities of members within Aum played an important role since the leader attracted followers with higher educational and financial achievements. As such, this study simulates the primary formation of Aum when Asahara's aim was to have more power and control, not commit harmful actions or acts of terror. Moreover, it will show how each of the 24 primary members gains utility, and the person with the most utility maintains the position of the supreme leader.

19.3.3 A Simulation of Aum Shinrikyo

In an organization, ties can differ depending on the aforementioned descriptions and may have varying values (i.e., from 0.0 [the minimum value] to +1.0 [the maximum value]) depending on the form of coevolution. The three main forms of coevolution that an organization uses in order to extend its connections are harmony, cohesion, and spontaneity, with the maximal or near-maximal values of their associated parameters (Figure 19.2).

In Figure 19.2, the three main forms of coevolution are presented in their simplest forms. Figure 19.2a presents a structure of network nodes in which harmony is the highest among agents. The positive or negative signs depict whether the social harmony was balanced or unbalanced. We assume that the harmony is equal to +1.0 when the whole network is balanced; otherwise, it will be graded based on the balancing ratio. Figure 19.2b shows two types of cohesion, where the dashes present the local bridging, while the solid line presents bonding (Easley and Kleinberg 2010). The cohesion is equal to +1.0 when the organization has a fair amount of interactions, which can be generated inside the organization through bonding or outside the organization through bridging (Alqithami and Hexmoor 2013). Spontaneity, seen in Figure 19.2c, links the different types of agents who may behave irrationally, where the different shapes in the graph depict

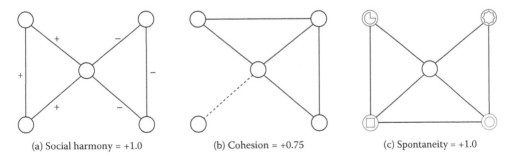

(a) Social harmony = +1.0   (b) Cohesion = +0.75   (c) Spontaneity = +1.0

Figure 19.2   Three forms of coevolution inside an organization. (Modified from Alqithami, S., and Hexmoor, H., *Qualities of Interest for Spontaneous Networked Organizations,* **Proceedings of the 2013 AASRI Conference on Intelligent Systems and Control, Canada, 2013.)**

the various kinds of agents, actions, and future interests. Spontaneity is satisfied and presented by +1.0 when any agent ties with another agent of a different type, while it becomes lower when the agent corresponds with others of similar capabilities, activities, and resources, until the value reaches a minimum of 0.0. Leadership and connections are related to many open social environments. Thus, leadership affects more than the social harmony among the agents to further impact the cohesion of the organization. Furthermore, spontaneity indicates that separate agents may have implicit communications with one another indirectly based on shared affinities or interest.

These forms of coevolution are used to classify cooperation among agents in order to arrive at the total average utility of an organization such as Aum. The cooperation (δ) between two agents, *i* and *j*, is denoted as $\delta(i,j)$. Moreover, the agents' assignments were based on capabilities, preference, and resources, as discussed in detail previously. Preference usually plays the same role as resources (i.e., preference $\propto$ resources) since access to resources will become higher, and the opposite is possible; therefore, we will consider both preference and resources, as they both can be applied similarly. The capability of agent *i*, denoted (Ψ_i), is the sum of a set of different capabilities {ψ_1, ψ_2,…,ψ_n} for different tasks (*n*). To measure the activeness (β) of agent *i*, we propose Equation 19.1 depending on the role assigned ξ.

$$\beta_i = \sum_i \xi_i (\text{preference}_i \times \Psi_i) \qquad (19.1)$$

The utility of individual agent x_i is measured through Equation 19.2.

$$\varphi(x_i, \xi_i) = \beta_i + \frac{1}{\lambda} \sum_i^j \delta(i, j)$$

$$\lambda = \sum_i (\Psi_i | \Psi_i \in \xi_i) \qquad (19.2)$$

The average global utility (U_G) of such an NO is measured through Equation 19.3.

$$U_G = \sum_i^j \frac{\varphi(x_i, \xi_i)}{\mu} \qquad (19.3)$$

where μ is the total number of agents (i.e., $\mu = \sum_i x_i$). This shows the average satisfaction with respect to the role assigned for the majority of an NO.

Using these equations, the formula for finding the relative utility has been implemented to depict the case of Aum in order to discover who has the highest utility among Aum's members. Specifically, Equation 19.2 was used in the NetLogo implementation of this study to find the expected utility for each agent. Developed by Uri Wilensky in 1999, NetLogo is a programmable modeling environment used to simulate natural and social phenomena (i.e., agents) and runs on the Java virtual machine. The NetLogo programming environment allows the programmer to give instructions to a limitless number of independently operating agents as a means to model complex systems over time. Moreover, NetLogo provides programmers with the capability to explore the connections and patterns between (1) individual-level behaviors (i.e., interactions between agents) and/or (2) individual agents and their environments (Stonedahl and Wilensky 2009).

The simulation in this study presents each leader's utility through random connections. This is based on the type of ties that link them in order to show the hierarchical structure of this organization and how Asahara has the highest utility in Aum. Furthermore, the simulation shows that the size of an agent changes based on the number of ties for each member within the organization, and upon it, he or she will be assigned a title. The supreme leader (SL) Asahara is the main character in forming this organization; thus, his rank was the highest as he was in control of this hierarchical structure. His leaders (L)—which include ministry heads, senior advisors, and inner-circle members—are in the second stage of this hierarchy since they helped in forming, evaluating, and changing this organization based on the SL's needs, while followers (F) had ties that were generally not noticeable in comparison with others.

The preceding simulation output represents the rate at which Aum leaders gained utility. Figure 19.3a and b shows the progression of member classifications based on the diffusion of one idea (i.e., only one plan to implement), while Figure 19.4a and b shows the progression of member classifications based on a continuous set of actions assigned randomly (i.e., more than one plan to implement). Throughout the simulation, Asahara maintained the highest utility, qualifying him as the supreme leader of Aum, while the 23 leaders in the hierarchy below him had less utility than Asahara but more than the remaining 50,000 plus followers. Additionally, the simulation shows which of the 23 leaders under Asahara had the most utility among them, qualifying the leader with the most utility to become the supreme leader should something become of Asahara (e.g., death or imprisonment). For simplicity, the assumption in the simulation was based on those agents having random capabilities, resources, and preferences, which allow them to have different volumes of excessive interaction and different ranking in the hierarchical structure.

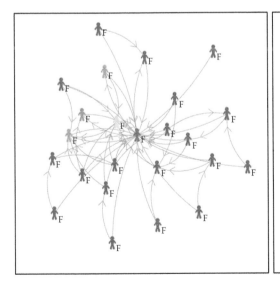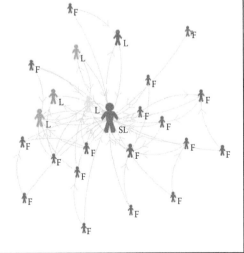

Figure 19.3   Simulation of member classifications based on the utility function with only one plan to implement.

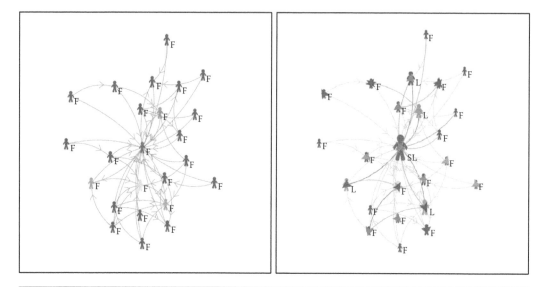

Figure 19.4   Simulation of member classifications based on the utility function with multiple plans to implement.

19.4 Conclusion and Future Work

In summary, this chapter presented the case study of a terrorist organization known as Aum. This organization has caused a lot of damage inside Japan with many of their activities, which resulted in many deaths and injuries. An evaluation of such an NO using MASs was presented. This chapter showed the impact of norms on the society with other important factors (i.e., roles, capabilities, preferences, and resources) and how Aum has benefited from it. The chapter progressed to cover the role of social capital in this organization and how it helped in maintaining the organization over time. The method of finding the global utility was proposed and implemented for validation using the Aum network. Additionally, this study shows not only how dependence on hierarchical structure can affect organizational performance but also how the types of ties, norms, roles, capabilities, resources, and preferences play an important role in forming the NO.

As our study only looked at the creation of NO ties within Aum, future research will include analysis of various tie disseminations and forms of negative social capital. These disseminations can be seen through the change of Aum's organizational goals (a reaction to outside forces that were not acceptable in Asahara's view), while negative social capital was the use of Aum's social capital for harmful purposes against other organizations (i.e., Japanese government). For instance, Asahara began triggering negative social capital from the sociality that existed in order to protect his organization, resulting in several terrorist attacks. Subsequently, the attacks led to the dissemination of their NO and the arrest of Asahara as well as several of the 23 leaders. Additionally, Aum leaders did not allow ties between followers to diminish due to the negative effect on the other members (i.e., followers who attempted to leave were viewed as a threat since they knew too much) (Eate 2008). As a result, when any member tried to leave Aum's NO, the individual was tracked down and brought back to be tortured, humiliated, or even killed. This has reflected on the dynamic organizational roles (i.e., the role is updated dynamically for every member over time), pointing to the awareness that leaving the group is impossible. By analyzing these aspects of

Aum's NO dissemination, we will be able to see how broken ties affected the utility of Aum and led to its fragmentation into small splinter groups, with Asahara no longer the supreme leader.

References

Alqithami, S. and H. Hexmoor. 2012a. Spontaneous organizations: Collaborative computing model of a networked organization. In *8th IEEE International Conference on Collaborative Computing: Networking, Applications and Work-sharing (Collaborative Communities for Social Computing)*, Pittsburgh, PA.

Alqithami, S. and H. Hexmoor. 2012b. Rapid adaptation in computational organizations. In *2012 International Conference on Artificial Intelligence*, Las Vegas, NV.

Alqithami, S. and H. Hexmoor. 2013. Qualities of interest for spontaneous networked organizations. In *Proceeding of the 2013 AASRI Conference on Intelligent Systems and Control*, Canada.

Associated Press. 1996. Ex-cultist said to lead police to cyanide cache. *Los Angeles Times*. Available at http://articles.latimes.com/1996-12-16/news/mn-9688_1_sodium-cyanide (accessed September 19, 2013).

Ballard, T., J. Pate, G. Ackerman, D. McCauley and S. Lawson. 2001. Chronology of Aum Shinrikyo's CBW activities. Available at http://cns.miis.edu/reports/pdfs/aum_chrn.pdf (accessed September 12, 2013).

Bellamy, P. 2013. False prophet: the Aum cult of terror. Crime library: Criminal minds and methods. Available at http://www.trutv.com/library/crime/terrorists_spies/terrorists/prophet/1.html (accessed September 18, 2013).

Borgatti, S. and D. Halgin. 2011. On network theory. *Organization Science* 22(5):1168–1181.

Brackett, D. 1996. *Holy Terror: Armageddon in Tokyo*. New York: Weatherhill.

Currarini, S. and F. Vega-Redondo. 2013. A simple model of homophily in social networks. Available at http://virgo.unive.it/seminari_economia/Currarini.pdf (accessed September 10, 2013).

Danzig, R., M. Sageman, T. Leighton, L. Hough, H. Yuki, R. Kotani and Z. Hosford. 2011. Aum Shinrikyo insights into how terrorists develop biological and chemical weapons. *Center for a New America Security*. Available at http://www.cnas.org/files/documents/publications/CNAS_AumShinrikyo_Danzig_1.pdf (accessed September 12, 2013).

Easley, D. and J. Kleinberg. 2010. *Networks, Crowds, and Markets, Reasoning about a Highly Connected World*. Cambridge: Cambridge University Press.

Eate, P. 2008. The replication and excess of disciplinary power in Sekigun and Aum Shinrikyo—A Foucaultian approach. *New Voices* 2:153–178. Available at http://newvoices.jpf-sydney.org/2/chapter8.pdf (accessed September 12, 2013).

Eisenhardt, K. 1989. Agency theory: An assessment and review. *The Academy of Management Review* 14(1):57–74.

Hartmann, W., P. Manchanda, H. Nair, M. Bothner, P. Dodds, D. Godes, K. Hosanagar and C. Tucker. 2008. Modeling social interactions: Identification, empirical methods and policy implications. *Marketing Letters: Springer* 19(3):287–304.

Hexmoor, H. 2011. Oversight of reorganization in massive multiagent systems. *Multiagent and Grid Systems* 7(6):269–289.

Horling, B. and V. Lesser. 2005. A survey of multi-agent organizational paradigms. *The Knowledge Engineering Review* 19(4):281–316.

Hudson, R. 1999. *The Sociology and Psychology of Terrorism: Who Becomes a Terrorist and Why? Federal Research Division*. Washington DC: Library of Congress.

Krackhardt, D. and K. Carley. 1998. A PCANS model of structure in organization. In *1998 International Symposium on Command and Control Research and Technology*, Vienna, VA: Evidence Based Research.

Kyodo News International. 1999. Ex-AUM member Tominaga appeals 18-year sentence. *The Free Library* (August, 9). Available at http://www.thefreelibrary.com/Ex-AUM member Tominaga appeals 18-year sentence.-a055433911 (accessed September 19, 2013).

Lazarsfeld, P. and R. Merton. 1954. Friendship as a social process: A substantive and methodological analysis. In *Freedom and Control in Modern Society*, eds. M. Berger and T. Abel, 18–66. New York: Van Nostrand.

Matson, E. and S. DeLoach. 2005. Formal transition in agent organizations. In *IEEE International Conference on Knowledge Intensive Multiagent Systems (KIMAS '05)*.

Mukai, A. 2012. Aum's Hirata, among Japan's most-wanted, surrenders in Tokyo. *Bloomberg News*. Available at http://www.bloomberg.com/news/2012-01-01/aum-s-hirata-among-three-most-wanted-surrenders-after-17-years.html (accessed September 19, 2013).

Murakami, H. 2001. *Underground: The Tokyo Gas Attack and the Japanese Psyche*. New York: Vintage International.

National Police Agency. 1996. Recollecting the series of Aum Shinrikyo (supreme truth) incidents. *Police White Paper*. Available at http://cns.miis.edu/pubs/eanp/wpap.pdf (accessed September 12, 2013).

Parachini, J. and J. Tucker. 1999. Combating terrorism: Assessing the threat. Statement before the House Subcommittee on National Security, Veterans Affairs, and International Relations. Available at http://www.gpo.gov/fdsys/pkg/CHRG-106hhrg63765/pdf/CHRG-106hhrg63765.pdf (accessed September 12, 2013).

Pate, J. and G. Ackerman. 2001. Assessing the threat of WMD terrorism. James Martin Center for Nonproliferation Studies. Available at http://cns.miis.edu/reports/wmdt.htm (accessed September 12, 2013).

Reader, I. 1996. *A Poisonous Cocktail?: Aum Shinrikyo's Path to Violence*. Copenhagen, Denmark: NIAS Books.

Reuters Staff. 2012. Last fugitive of Japan's Aum doomsday cult arrested for 1995 Tokyo gas attack. *Reuters FaithWorld*. Available at http://blogs.reuters.com/faithworld/2012/06/17/last-fugitive-of-japans-aum-doomsday-cult-arrested-for-1995-tokyo-gas-attack/ (accessed September 21, 2013).

Staff. 1995. Global proliferation of weapons of mass destruction: A case study on the Aum Shinrikyo. Senate Government Affairs Permanent Subcommittee. Available at http://www.fas.org/irp/congress/1995_rpt/aum/ (accessed September 12, 2013).

START. 2013. Terrorist organization profile: Aum Shinrikyo/Aleph. National Consortium for the Study of Terrorism and Responses to Terrorism. Available at http://www.start.umd.edu/start/data_collections/tops/terrorist_organization_profile.asp?id=3956 (accessed September 12, 2013).

Stonedahl, F. and U. Wilensky. 2009. NetLogo PageRank model. Center for Connected Learning and Computer-Based Modeling, Northwestern University, Evanston, IL. Available at http://ccl.northwestern.edu/netlogo/models/PageRank.

Tucker, J. 2000. *Toxic Terror Assessing Terrorist Use of Chemical and Biological Weapons*. Cambridge, MA: MIT Press.

Tuomela, R. 2000. *Cooperation*. 82:431. The Netherlands: Kluwer Academic Publishers.

Vogel, K. 1999. Ensuring the security of Russia's chemical weapons: A lab-to-lab partnering program. *The Nonproliferation Review*. Available at http://cns.miis.edu/npr/pdfs/vogel62.pdf (accessed September 12, 2013).

Walsh, J. 2001. Shoko Asahara: the making of a Messiah. *Time Magazine*. Available at http://content.time.com/time/magazine/article/0,9171,982749,00.html (accessed September 12, 2013).

Wilensky, U. 1999. NetLogo. Center for Connected Learning and Computer-Based Modeling. Available at http://ccl.northwestern.edu/netlogo/ (accessed September 10, 2013).

Chapter 20

Energy-Efficient Wireless Sensor Networks Using Learning Techniques

Sumit Tokle, Shamantha Rai Bellipady,
Rajeev Ranjan, and Shirshu Varma

Contents

Wireless sensor networks (WSNs) are self-configurable and infrastructure-less wireless networks that have nodes consisting of a wireless transceiver, a microcontroller, and an energy source assembled as one unit (Akyildiz et al. 2002). The sensor nodes in a WSN are resource constrained in terms of computational, storage, communication, and energy resources and capabilities. WSNs are energy constrained because they use battery power; therefore, minimizing energy consumption is of prime importance. Consequently, a better approach is to put the WSN node in sleep mode when it is not sensing any physical event. Artificial learning techniques are used to minimize the energy consumption of the WSN nodes, by putting them in sleep mode intelligently. This chapter combines features of many learning algorithms such as an offline critic function and real-time learning algorithms to enhance the lifetime of WSN nodes. The purpose of a machine learning algorithm is to guess the environmental behavior where it is deployed and to update the parameters of a WSN. We mainly focus on reinforcement learning (RL) (Sutton and Barto 1988) algorithms on each WSN node. The key involvement of this method is to validate theoretically and implement reward functions and offline critic functions that will achieve the desired energy savings.

20.1 Introduction

The thought of sensing physical events has been encouraged from biological living creatures (Marsland 2011). Sensor devices have been in use for a few decades now, and they are being used in everyday life. The conventional single-sensor system has been substituted by a huge array of small, automatic, self-powered sensors that can wirelessly link to the outer world via a base station (BS), which is aptly termed as a wireless sensor network (WSN). Several WSN nodes can be deployed collaboratively and cooperatively, which can be used in various applications like surveillance systems, military applications, health care, habitat monitoring, wildlife monitoring, natural hazards detection, and so forth (Arampatzis et al. 2005). Large numbers of sensors are added into the system for improving the performance and lifetime of the WSN. We could also use a single sensor to cover the whole area of our concern, but it is too costly and risky, and it gives a single point of failure. Thus, having multiple sensors clearly alleviates many problems in WSNs (Akyildiz et al. 2002). The WSN's expected lifetime is based upon many factors including, onboard battery capacity of the individual sensor nodes, layout of the WSN, total information that can be gathered, required number of sensor nodes, amount of processing that can take place, and finding the exact position of the gateway or BS or sink node. An onboard battery provides power for the sensor nodes in the network, which must be used minimally so as to achieve prolonged battery life (Chong and Kumar 2003; Culler et al. 2004). The impact of preserving power on every sensor node can have a more prominent effect on the total lifetime of the entire WSN, that is, the conserved power on each sensor node is directly proportional to the lifetime of the sensor network.

Two methods are employed to enlarge the lifetime of WSNs at different levels:

1. *Global level*: Redundant sensor nodes are increased in the WSN. These nodes are called backup nodes or redundant nodes. These nodes are used as alternative nodes for dying sensor nodes, and they carry out the tasks of sensing and signal communication.
2. *Local level*: In this level, changes are made to the sleep time, sensing time, and communication time, and each sensor node is operated in low power.

20.1.1 Need for a Learning Technique

A sensing node in a network can sense parameters like temperature, humidity, sound, vibration, and so forth in an environment and communicate these sensed data to other nodes such as a neighboring node, cluster head, and so forth, as long as its onboard power is available (Simic 2003). Nearly 60% of all of whole energy is underutilized because sensor nodes need to stay awake to communicate with neighboring nodes. Therefore, to maintain the lifetime of a WSN, power scheduling of individual sensor nodes has to be done, where the power source is alternately switched on and off. Figure 20.1 shows the on/off (sleep/awake mode) scheduling of sensor nodes. A WSN changes its behavior whenever the scheduling parameter is adjusted, which leads to analysis and observation of such changes.

The following procedure shows how a built-in power scheduling mechanism is inculcated by most sensor nodes:

1. Sleep: Power supply is off to all the sensor nodes except the clock.
2. Wake-up: Power supply is on to all circuits of sensor nodes.
3. Read the sensor sensing information from the analog to digital converter (ADC) port.
4. Communicate data with relevant node.
5. Go back to sleep.

The sensor nodes need to continuously sense the environment because events occur randomly in the environment. For saving energy, commercially existing sensor nodes such as crossbow and Micaz Motes have fixed sleep-and-wake cycles, due to which some critical events could be missed during the sleep time. However, when these sensor nodes are awake, there is no surety about the stochastic events that may or may not become noticeable at that instance. These situations drain battery power unnecessarily. Therefore, we have exploited a lot of learning algorithms with WSN and analyzed their advantages and disadvantages.

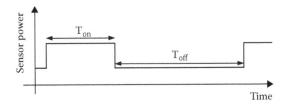

Figure 20.1   Sensor scheduling example.

20.2 Background: Machine Learning

Artificial intelligence (AI) gave birth to a significant concept called machine learning (Nilsson 1996). The core idea of machine learning is to make the system intelligent, in order to recognize composite patterns and control, predict, and make autonomous decisions based on data by using learning algorithms in a dynamically varying environment (Azarnoush et al. 2006). By using old data and experience, the system will give optimal performance, by applying these machine learning algorithms.

An AI system consists of four blocks, as shown in Figure 20.2; any change made to these blocks is called learning. Many learning mechanisms are used depending upon which block is going to be altered.

The main benefit of machine learning (Alpaydin 2004) is that if the system can learn the environment and automatically choose and follow such changes, then the system designer does not need to give a clarification to all possible situations.

20.2.1 Classification of Machine Learning

Machine learning algorithms can be organized into three different classifications based on the outcome of the algorithm.

20.2.1.1 Supervised Learning

In this learning model, parameters of the model are adjusted depending upon the training set of instances with the correct response (targets are provided). This learning technique needs to generalize to respond correctly to all possible inputs, that is, there are sets of information (training information) that contain a set of input information and a set of target information, which is the solution this algorithm must produce. This is commonly shown as a set of (X_i, T_i), where X_i stands for input information, T_i stands for target information, and i indicates the index number, which means it has a huge amount of data points, which range from 1 to N. Then, if our database contains an example for every possible piece of data it senses, we can put them closer together into a larger searching chart; also, there is no obligation of any machine learning. Conversely, new data

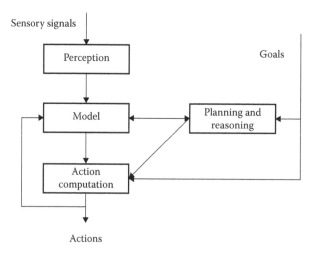

Figure 20.2   Architecture of AI system.

that are given to this learning technique that is obtained from the sensing device are not present in the training set; this makes the technique generalized from the instruction set to the entire unobserved state or a state that is not encountered during learning in a reasonable way. This method contains a set of rules for identifying the closest equivalent instruction of the instruction set; this set of laws is restricted in the sense that each cell learns without concerning other cell output. If there are M samples with the value F in the training set S, then we suppose that if we can search a hypothesis H that nearly corresponds with F for the members of S, then this hypothesis will be well estimated for F, particularly if S is huge. Curve fitting is the simplest example of supervised learning. Supervised learning problems are divided into classification and regression problems.

20.2.1.1.1 Classification

This problem accepts the input vectors and decides which of N categories they belong to, based on the training sets that are provided from good examples of each category. There are mainly two constraints present in classification problems:

- Each case is distinct and belongs to only one category.
- The set of categories covers the complete output space.

However, in the real world, sometimes, an example might fit into two different categories; in such cases, fuzzy classifiers are helpful to resolve this type of problem. Also, there are some unique places where fuzzy classifiers are not able to classify every possible input. For example, consider a machine where we are using a neural network to identify characteristics of all fruits. For that, we require that training be offered to the classifiers, to identify all different types of fruit, but what happens if we are given a ball (apple or orange shape) to classify? In that type of ambiguity, the classifier will recognize it as the orange or apple that is close to it in the visual aspects, but we do not want this result. Instead of this, the classifier must learn and identify that the given type of object is not a fruit that it was trained on. We call this type of problem novelty detection.

20.2.1.1.2 Regression

In this problem, the learning agent provides some data points as input. We can call these data points A and B and request to locate the value of output (we call it Y as it is not an agent's objective data point). If we say that when the value of $X = 0.24$, that is absent in the current input data point, and an agent would like to discover the approach to foretell its corresponding value. Then the agent assumes that this value is coming from some dynamic function, will try to find out what the function is, and then will come across the current value of Y matching X. This is called a well-known regression problem in statistics.

20.2.1.2 Unsupervised Learning

In this learning model, there is no supervisor provided. A learning agent only has the input data points, and the plan of this agent is to discover certain patterns. Here, an agent will attempt to find out what usually occurs and what does not. This statistical approach is called "density estimation." This kind of learning has conceptually different sources of problems. We cannot do regression here because to use regression, an agent must know output points for guessing the function. Then, can we use classification? The agent cannot perform direct classification too because none of the information is present on correct classes. However, when the algorithm works fine and finds out similarities among inputs that are similar, classification is done automatically. Therefore, to find the input agent, we first need to find a resemblance for it (Marsland 2009).

One way to locate the density is clustering (Dahnil et al. 2011), where the intention is to discover the clusters or group of inputs.

20.2.1.2.1 Clustering (*K*-Means Algorithm)

Suppose we need to split the input data into K different classes. The agent should decide the value of K depending upon which works best on certain conditions. Then depending on the plan, K cluster centers are allocated to the input space and will position that cluster center in the core of all clusters. However, the learning agent does not know where these clusters are. Therefore, an algorithm needs to find these clusters.

20.2.1.2.2 Distance Measure

The agent needs to determine the distance between the points; there are numerous techniques offered for measuring the distance, but the most commonly used is the Euclidean distance.

20.2.1.2.3 Mean Average

Once the learning agent knows the distance between points, it can calculate the central point from the existing data points. These central points are nothing but a mean average (the mean of two points is the halfway line between them).

Now the learning agent can imagine what could be the location of the cluster center; this is calculated by finding the main point of each cluster, $\mu_{c(i)}$; place the cluster center over there. Then to decide which points belong to which cluster, the point that is adjoining to the cluster center turns into an element of that cluster. This might change as the algorithm repeats until all points are converged. Some of the applications of unsupervised learning are bioinformatics, image compression, segmentation in customer relationship management, and so forth.

20.2.1.3 Reinforcement Learning

This learning method is somewhere in between unsupervised learning and supervised learning. Unlike supervised learning, in reinforcement learning (RL), the agent cannot provide training set data. Instead of this training set, they provide a different feedback signal, called a reward signal. This will tell the agent when it is performing well or when it is performing poorly. This learning algorithm will say something about a particular action or response, but it does not contribute any previous information such as how to determine the most optimal answer. RL is much tougher than supervised learning because the learning agents have to make a decision over time; hence, it is called sequential decision making. RL maps a current situation into action in order to enlarge the sum of expected rewards.

Mostly, a Markov decision process (MDP) is used to model RL problems in the real world. MDP contains five tuples:

- *State* (*S*) denotes the actual state of the environment or machine.
- *Action* (*A*) denotes the set of actions that the agent needs to select from available actions.

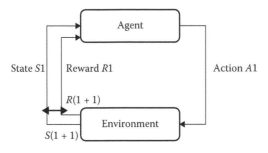

Figure 20.3   Architecture of RL.

- *Discount factor* (γ), also named learning factor, ranges from 0 to 1.
- *State transition probability* ($P(S,A)$) gives the subsequent condition of the mechanism, which is based on the probability of events of each state and each action.
- *Reward function* (R) function sets the goal of the learning problem. Generally, it represents each state action pair into a single number. The agent cannot alter this reward function; also, it indicates what is good in the immediate sense.

Figure 20.3 shows the architecture of RL using MDP tuples.

20.3 Learning Methods in Wireless Sensor Networks

Several learning methods have been proposed (Kulkarni et al. 2011) and used for a WSN to turn out to be an energy-efficient network. The following are a few important learning methods used in a WSN.

20.3.1 Energy-Efficient Technique Using Fuzzy Neural Network in Wireless Sensor Networks

Broadcast scheduling in WSNs using a fuzzy Hopfield neural network (Yu-Ju and Ming-Shi 2006) employs time division multiple access (TDMA) to share a channel between multiple users. In this method, the channel is divided into many time slots, and each sensor is given a unique slot to send data to another user. TDMA is used to solve the broadcast scheduling problem (BSP) in an ad hoc sensor network. Even et al. (1984) proved that this TDMA cycle solution is an NP-complete problem. Besides this, Funabiki and Takefuji (1992) invented the maximum neural network (MNN) framework. The MNN always gives a guaranteed solution, minimizing the searching space without the need for optimizing any parameter. It is applied to many NP-complete problems. Shi and Wang (2005) proposed two-stage hybrid methods, sequential vertex coloring (SVC) and noisy chaotic neural networks (NCNNs). SVC is used for to getting minimal frame length in the initial cycle and an NCNN is used for obtaining the maximum node transmission in the subsequent cycles. Unfortunately, the BSP methods take a long time in finding an optimal choice of parameters, which gave rise to several other methods to solve the BSP. Solutions are provided for finding the conflict-free time slot assignment in the TDMA cycle. For that, the fuzzy Hopfield neural Network (FHNN) algorithm for finding the smallest TDMA frame length with scheduling was proposed, which maps the discrete energy minimization problem into Hopfield neural networks.

There are two main constraints in node scheduling as presented by Chakraborty and Hirano (1998):

- No-conflicts: It contains primary conflicts and secondary conflicts. In primary conflicts, a node cannot transfer and receive at the same time, while in secondary conflicts, a node cannot receive more than one packet at the same time.
- No-transmission: Each sensor node is scheduled such that it can transfer at least once in each TDMA cycle.

In TDMA, on each time slot, only one transmitter can send packets in a synchronized way. The particular energy associated with this time is calculated by using

$$\sum_{x=1}^{n}\left(\sum_{i=1}^{c}\mu_{xi}-1\right)^{2} \tag{20.1}$$

where c is the number of nodes and n is the time slot. μ_{xi} indicates the time slot that is assigned to the ith node. If any sensor node has been assigned with time slot j, then other sensor nodes cannot be assigned j time slots. This type of constraint in energy is defined as

$$\sum_{y=1,y\neq i}^{n} d_{iy}\mu_{yj} \tag{20.2}$$

where d_{iy} is 1, if there is any connectivity among node i and node y. Also, a numerical formula is obtained to find the energy when node i has been assigned time slot j, and after what period of time its neighboring nodes can assign time slot j. An FHNN uses a scatter energy function, which is useful for converging rapidly into the smallest energy values. This algorithm will assign the weight by comparing the energy value of each sensor node using

$$W = \sum_{y=1}^{n} \frac{z_y}{\sum_{k=1}^{n}(\mu_{ki})m} \tag{20.3}$$

This synaptic weight value among the neuronal interconnections will force the network to converge into a well stable state, and at this moment, the network will be consuming minimal energy.

Where z indicates the data set, μ_{ki} indicates the timeslot k that is assigned to node i. An FHNN needs to classify the samples into classes by randomly generating the membership matrix states for all neuron function. To find the starting membership function, the following is used:

$$\mu_{xi} = \sum_{j=1}^{c}\left(\frac{\|z_x - v_i\|}{\|z_x - v_j\|}\right)^{\frac{-2}{m-1}} \tag{20.4}$$

where $x = 1, 2, \ldots n$; and $i = 1, 2, \ldots c$, c indicates the number of clusters, m is the fuzzification parameter, v indicates the cluster centroid, and z_x indicates the unclassified data sets. The FHNN will update the membership value, and then the new cluster centroid is calculated, after which the energy of the whole network is calculated.

20.3.2 Energy-Efficient Technique Using Evolutionary Algorithm in Wireless Sensor Networks

Dynamic alliance (DA) was proposed based on genetic algorithms (GAs) in WSNs (Zhang et al. 2006). DA refers to virtual corporations, which are like short-span unions created by some independent commercial corporations. The authors have given a new approach for a sleep scheduling technique for sensor nodes in a randomly located WSN using GAs. Such a network is static, that is, nodes, once deployed, will know their position and have the same sensing range as each other, and multiple redundant nodes are present to cover the whole area. With this assumption, the whole lifetime of a WSN has been divided into rounds. In every round, a set of nodes that are present in the DA is selected; also, the whole target area is covered, and at the same instant, other nodes remain in sleep mode. The scheduling process does not start until and unless all nodes are not able to form DA to completely cover the target area. In this method, the target area is divided into square sub-blocks. DA recommends that for each area, at most two nodes are selected from every group to form DA. After many rounds of DA, there might be a condition where there is no valid node in certain groups. At this point of time, they are again divided into small areas by changing the sub-block origin O by $(r\sqrt{2})/2$, where r is the sensing range of each node. The goal of the DA is to choose a subset of sensor nodes from a large group to cover the complete intended area, which is solved by employing a GA that works with chromosomes, which denotes solving optimization problems.

Figure 20.4 gives information related to coding used in a GA, where the set of node N can be shown as binary stream L as shown in Figure 20.4 in which $N_l^{(k)} = 1$ indicates that node in the jth subsquare is selected to form DA; else $N_l^{(k)} = 0$ it is not selected. A GA defines the fitness function that specifies the goal of the system. In order to construct the fitness function, positive points and negative points of the system need to be known:

$$f(t) = \frac{d^-}{d^+ + d^-} \tag{20.5}$$

$$d^-(t) = \|((C(t) - C^-), (N(t) - N^-))\| \tag{20.6}$$

$$d^+(t) = \|((C(t) - C^+), (N(t) - N^+))\| \tag{20.7}$$

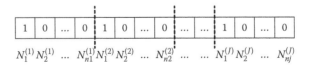

Figure 20.4 Coding used in GA.

where t of the generation *is* in the GA, $\|a\|$ means the norm of a, d^+ is the distance to the positive points, and d^- is the distance to negative points. A GA uses the roulette wheel selection procedure to select the population that is initially arranged from the largest to smallest values; also, two-point crossover operations use a probability from 0.6 to 1.0. Mutation is carried out by changing the random bit with the probabilities of $p_m = 0.34$. This model will choose 10 individuals along with their 10 optimum offspring; those who have more fitness values among the original population go into the next generation using mutation and crossover operators. When there is no change in two consecutive generations, that is, the change is not more than 0.01%, then this GA is stopped.

20.3.3 Energy-Efficient Technique Using Reinforcement Learning in Wireless Sensor Networks

20.3.3.1 RL-MAC: A Quality of Service (QoS)-Aware RL Based Media Access Control (MAC) Protocol for WSN (Liu 2006)

The RL MAC protocol employs a similar frame-based structure to that of Sensor-MAC (S-MAC) and Timeout-MAC (T-MAC). The difference between this method and other protocols is that both the frame active time and duty cycle are dynamically customized in accordance with a node's traffic load as well as its incoming traffic characteristics. At the start of each frame, an RL agent dynamically reserves slots as active times. In this slot, a node listens to the channel and tries to exchange packets with its neighbors. When a reserved active timer dies, the node pauses and resists from sending or receiving data transitions in the sleep state.

The main goals of an RL agent are the following:

1. RL will maximize an energy metric, which can be defined as the ratios of efficient transmit/receive time to the total reserves' active time.
2. RL is intended to improve the data throughput. RL-MAC refers to the term throughput as an actual payload's bits per second, excluding all protocol overheads. To achieve this goal, an RL agent chooses to employ queued transmission at the commencement of the frame, and this queue contains the number of packets that are organized to send. In addition, to find the efficient transmit/receive time ratio, the number of effectively transmitted packets and received packets during the reserved active period is recorded. It is further noted that by overhearing request to send/clear to send (RTS/CTS) messages or collisions, the sensor node transitions into sleep mode. Then the RL agent will find the reward value. This RL-MAC avoids the early sleeping scenarios where a node may go to sleep when its neighboring node still has packets designated for it by adding a 4-bit field in the data packet header called FAIL_ATTEMPTS; this field gives information to the receiving node regarding the number of failed transmission tries made by the transmitter, before the data correctly arrived. This kind of information is embedded by constructing a negative reward signal pertaining to previous actions. In the actor-critic learning (Mustapha and Lachiver 2000) algorithm, when there are many packets queued for the transition from a node, then the reserve time must be longer for that node. Therefore, the RL agent can specify the action space $A(S)$ for a given state S. Also, since the networking condition and the traffic load vary in this case, an agent will adopt the constant learning rate = 0.1. But once the traffic load is constant over a relatively longer period and the queued packet length is not varying by much, there will be a great increase in the learning procedure. To augment the QoS, an RL agent will maintain the three types of queue at each node; this will differentiate the traffic of each sensor node.

20.3.4 Adaptive Routing for Sensor Networks Using Reinforcement Learning (AdaR)

Wang and Wang (2006) suggested a routing scheme, AdaR, which adaptively learns the best route. AdaR is based on least-squares policy iteration (LSPI), which is more efficient in a model-free RL technique, and it need not be compulsorily trained with the whole model. To overcome the difficulties such as the large number of attempts to acquire the optimal solution, little modification can result in serious variation in routing performance. In this scheme, at the commencement of the training period, each source creates a packet. At each step, current node S selects one neighbor S' like the descendant based on the current Q values $Q(S, A) = \phi(S, A)T\dot{\omega}$. To accelerate exploration $\epsilon-$, a greedy way is used, that is, with probability ϵ, one can choose an action arbitrarily, and with probability $1 - \epsilon$, one can choose action with a maximum Q value. At each step record for a packet, $<S, A, S', \phi(S, A)>$ is generated. This packet is repeatedly sent from current node S to its successor node S' toward the BS. This cycle is completed once for each route until one of the following events is encountered, and this route gives a reward value R:

1. The packet is received at the BS. In this case, the affirmative reward is given as $R = R_{max}$.
2. When BS has not received the packet and the route length is exceeding a threshold value, L_{max} neutral reward is given.
3. When cycle appears in the route, then a negative reward is given by $R = -R_{max}/2$.

The present reward R is calculated as the reward of the entire path divided by path length, plus a combination of the features.

This proposed AdaR gets the samples from the surroundings as a set of tuples (S, A, S', R) and uses LSPI to update the weight $\dot{\omega}$ of the linear function $Q^{\Pi}(S, A)$ for the current policy Π. This restructured weight is used to develop the current policy Π. This method is recurring until an excellent policy is found, that is, the weights of policies between two nearby iterations do not differ significantly. Once this packet is reached at the BS, all the information about the complete routing path can be traced. The immediate reward r for each tuple (S, A, S') is then considered based on the superiority of the routing path. After a few samples are collected at the BS, one performs the LSPI method to approximate the new weight $\dot{\omega}'$ of the linear functions. Then new $\dot{\omega}'$ can be broadcasted inside the network, or it can be sent from the BS by using new weight $\dot{\omega}'$. The policy improvement is done easily at each sensor "S" by selecting action "A" with the topmost Q value.

20.3.5 Distributed Independent Reinforcement Learning Approach to Resource Management in Wireless Sensor Networks

Shah and Kumar (2007) introduced distributed independent reinforcement learning (DIRL) based on a Q-learning framework that does not require learning the model, such as environment, to enable independent adaptive application with built-in support for proficient resource management. In this method, WSNs can be prepared as a multiagent system (MAS) where each sensor node represents a goal-oriented agent, and they are called independent learners because a learning algorithm is functional on each sensor node by ignoring the existence of other sensor nodes; this will reduce the communication among the sensor node, and each node will selfishly try to improve its own rewards. DIRL maps the element of the RL system into wireless sensor areas, such as the following.

- *Agent*: Each sensor node is corresponding to the agent.
- *Environment*: The sensor node interacts with the surrounding environment.
- *Action*: The agent may take action such as alarm, actuate, aggregate, transmit, and receive.
- *State*: This RL element includes system-specific variables such as neighboring nodes, remaining energy, mobility, and communication ability and application of precise variables such as signal strength, sensor reading, and so forth. To classify this state into different classes, DIRL uses weighted hamming distance.
- *Policy*: It contains predicates and exploitation/exploration schemes.
- *Reward function*: DIRL implements a reward utility that gives the amount of reward obtained during each execution of that application.
- *Value function*: DIRL uses the Q-learning to find the value function. Q-learning is used with incremental step updates, as specified by $Q(s, t) = (1 - \alpha)Q(s, t) + \alpha(r + \gamma e(s'))$. At this time, α is a learning parameter, which is considered $\alpha = 0.5$ and γ is a discount factor, which is also considered as 0.5.

In DIRL, each node needs to execute the task from a set of tasks at each time cycle, for which it needs to execute one of the methods in between exploration and exploitation. To select one of the schemes, agents need to find "ϵ" using the Boltzmann equation. All the tasks are not executed all the time due to some constraints, so each task needs to be linked with an applicability predicate that needs to be evaluated accurately in order to execute a task. The DIRL algorithm initializes the utility function for the entire state s and task $t = 0$. Then the sensor will examine the present state s from the surroundings. Depending upon the policy, an agent will find the particular task t. Then it will implement that assignment and view the novel state s'. After that, with the assistance of hamming, a distance agent will find whether s' is similar to existing state s''; if they are analogous, it will assign $s' = s''$ along with working out the reward r for doing task t in state s. Then it will update the utility values for a particular task in state s with the aforementioned reward r value. They proved that DIRL is, on average, 90% more efficient than conventional resource management schemes.

Mihaylov et al. (2010) used the RL algorithm to enhance the lifetime and reduce the latency of WSNs in a decentralized manner. To achieve this, the authors developed energy-saving schemes that are deployed on each sensor node. Each sensor node tries to gain knowledge to reduce the pessimistic result of its actions on adjacent nodes in the scheme, depending on the reward function. This algorithm says that the power utilization of all nodes is based on their position. Those nodes that are closer to the sink need to forward more messages to the sink, and thus, in the majority of instances, they require to be awakened in the scheduling cycle, whereas the nodes that are far from the sink node can spend more time in sleep. For this reason, the performance of every sensor node of the network cannot be the same (Mihaylov et al. 2010; Predd et al. 2006). Each sensor agent uses an RL algorithm to learn best scheduling, which will increase the power efficiency in a distributed manner. Distributed learning maps the element of the RL system in the wireless sensor domain.

Action: The action set consists of a distinct number of sleep durations, and the value of this sleep duration is in incremental fashion within one frame length. A sensor agent can choose its action based on the probability distribution and can use the same action on a small number of frames, which is called a frame window. The reason to use the action on a few frames is that the agent will find additional time to identify the effect of that exploit on WSNs.

Reward: Reward function requires defining the energy efficiency (EE) of each sensor node, so EE for agent i in frame f is given by

$$EE = \alpha(1 - IL_{i,f}) + \beta(1 - OH_{i,f}) + \gamma(1 - UT_{i,f}) + \epsilon BLi + \delta(1 - DQ_{i,f}) \qquad (20.8)$$

where $IL_{i,f}$ is the idle listening duration for an agent i within frame f, $OH_{i,f}$ is the overhearing duration of agent i within frame f, $UT_{i,f}$ is the unsuccessful transmission amount of agent i within frame f, $DQ_{i,f}$ is the entire time interval that the packet sent in the queue of agent i within frame f, blue is the leftover battery life for every agent i, and α, β, γ, δ and ϵ are constant weights. This distributed learning considers that for progress to occur in the performance of the entire system, each sensor agent needs to care about other sensor agents. To achieve this, the concept of effect set (ES) of each node is used, which is a subset of the current node's neighborhood, with which it shares information within a frame window. Thus, EE of a sensor agent i directly depends on the action of all agents in set N_i and vice versa. These representations also consider that if each sensor agent tries to enhance not just its individual energy but also the efficiency of ES, this will help to improve the whole energy in the system. So the reward of each sensor node is equal to its average effect set energy efficiency (ESEE) over each frame window of size $|F|$. Thus, the agent always tries to enhance the significance of its ESEE by optimizing its own behaviors. ESEE of an agent i in the frame window F is given as

$$ESEE = \frac{1}{|F|} \cdot \sum_f^F \frac{EE_{i,f} + \sum_j EE_{j,f}}{|N_i| + 1} \qquad \forall_j \in N_i \qquad (20.9)$$

where $EE_{i,f}$ is the energy efficiency of an agent i in frame f, and $|N_i|$ is the number of agents in the ES of an agent i. A sensor node cannot find ESEE directly; to find the ESEE, the sensor node contains the value of its individual EE in a control packet such as RTS, CTS, and ACK, so the neighboring sensor agent also knows the value, and it can also communicate its ESEE. Now to update the rule, at the end of each frame window, an agent needs to find the average ESEE from past frames and use these values to learn the optimum sleep time that will minimize the latency and increase the efficiency. Action probabilities $p_i(x)$ are updated in the following way:

$$p_i(x) \leftarrow p_i(x) + \lambda * ESEE_{i,f} * (1.0 - p_i(x)) \qquad (20.10)$$

where λ is used to define the learning rate.

Thus, they develop an energy saving method without having any central mediator.

20.3.6 Optimal QoS and Adaptive Routing in Wireless Sensor Networks

Ouferhat and Mellouk (2006) have considered not only cost optimality for the improving routing path for each packet but also a QoS requirement to increase the overall sensor network performance based on RL techniques. They used a Q-routing method, which uses an RL algorithm to learn the best path to reach the destination node. Each node contains the RL module to randomly locate the most excellent path to the destination. Therefore, the principle idea behind this routing principle is as follows: let $Q, (y, d)$ be the time epoch that a node x estimates, to take a target packet P, bound for node d by means of x's neighboring sensor node y including whatever period that

P would contain to use in node *x*'s queue. On sending *P* to *y*, *x* directly gets back *y*'s approximation for the instance left in the journey. Therefore, every node holds information about *Q* values for every possible next hop. The node will send a packet by making a selection of the next hop that has a minimum accurate instant to arrive at the target, and it will send the current *Q* value to the previous node. When the network failure rate increases and the network becomes dubious, the agent is required to allocate the load of the circulation of node to node, in order to avoid dead nodes and to surmount the irregularity of the network, which uses RL based on Q-routing, because as soon as the system turns out to be doubtful, the RL will evade this component of the network by punishing it. This will reduce the number of packet losses due to the breakdown of nodes, which will also go up by increasing the rate of accomplishment per node. This algorithm shows that moving a packet from any starting point *s* to target point *d* can be done by considering some constraints of QoS.

20.3.6.1 Dynamic Power Management of an Embedded Sensor Network Based on Actor-Critic Reinforcement-Based Learning

Sridhar et al. (2007) discussed an actor-critic-dependent RL mechanism. The major role of this work is to develop a critic function (or value/reinforcement function) on every sensor node that can be valuable in dynamic power scheduling depending on dissimilar circumstances. There are three foremost elements in RL:

1. Policy: Observations that can be mapped to actions are called policy.
2. Reward function: It maps action into a unique scalar value; a learning agent is responsible for maximizing the reward value.
3. Critic or value function (*V*): It is used to locate what is superior in the long run and at instance *t*, which is specified by

$$V(t) = r(t) + \gamma r(t + 1) + \gamma 2r(t + 2)...$$

where *r* is an instant reward function that is differentiated and γ is a discounting factor. An important family of RL is the temporal difference (TD) learning strategy; this can immediately learn from knowledge, and it does not involve any fundamental model of the environment. The main task of the learning agent is to predict the expected rewards. One such TD method is actor-critic learning. Figure 20.5 shows the architecture of actor-critic learning.

The policy structure in RL is known as an actor, as it used to take action and calculate the value function to identify as a critic, as it criticizes the action that is completed by the actor. In this scheme, learning always depends on the policy. The actual critic function gives the total discounted sum of the next reward, which is given by

$$V(k) = \sum_{m=0}^{6} \gamma^{m} r(k+m), \quad \gamma = 0.6 \tag{20.11}$$

where γ is a discounting factor. If $\gamma = 0$, then the learning agent tries to maximize only the current reward; when $\gamma = 1$, then the agent assumes more subsequent rewards. So this discounting factor

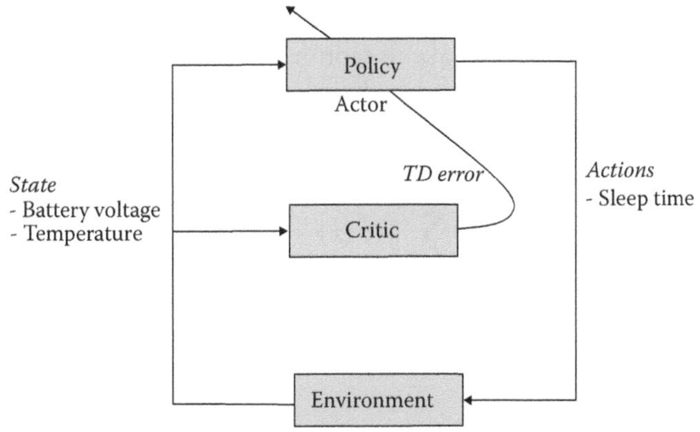

Figure 20.5 Architecture of actor-critic technique.

acts like a weighting factor to consider either future or current reinforcement. Equation 20.11 shows a set of $\gamma = 0.6$.

To implement power management in a WSN, an offline critic function was developed depending on the data set obtained by changing the temperature and sleep time. The estimated critic function is given by

$$\hat{V}(k) = \varnothing^T(k)\theta(k) \tag{20.12}$$

$$\in = V(k) - \hat{V}(k) \tag{20.13}$$

$$\theta(k) = \theta(k-1) + P(k)\varnothing(k-1)[V(k) - \varnothing(k-1)^T\theta(k-1)] \tag{20.14}$$

$$P(k) = P(k-1) - P(k-1)\varnothing(k-1)[1 + \varnothing(k-1)^T P(k-1)\varnothing(k-1)]^{-1}\varnothing(k-1)^T P(k-1) \tag{20.15}$$

where $\hat{V}(k)$ is the calculated discounted sum of future reward.

$\varnothing(k) = [r(k)\ r(k-1)...r(k-N+1)]^T$ is a value of earlier rewards. $\theta(k)$ is a value of scalar parameters that has equivalent size to that of $\varnothing(k)$. To find the estimated value of $\hat{V}(k)$, first the parameter vector $\varnothing(k)$ is discovered. To optimize this parameter vector, a recursive least-squares algorithm $P(k)$ is used. Here, a nonlinear static reward function is used to approximate the random behavior of the sensor network and the surroundings. The reward function r is given by

$$r(k) = \frac{bat(k)}{bat_{max}} * \frac{S(k)}{S_{avg}}^{\in|T(k)-T(k-1)|} \tag{20.16}$$

where $bat(k)$ and bat_{max} are the battery voltage at time instance k and at full charge, respectively; $S(k)$ is the sleep time at time k and S_{avg} is the mean sleep time; $\in$ is a scalar value; and $T(k)$ is the environment temperature. The design of this reward function is made by considering the details, such as the sensor node having to be awake to capture important events from the environment.

This approach shows the variation among the calculated critic value and the actual critic. The polynomial order 4 was to give less average calculated error given by

$$\in = \sum_{k=1}^{T} \| (V(k) - \hat{V}(k)) \| \tag{20.17}$$

where T is the entire time span.

20.3.6.2 Intelligent Sensing in Dynamic Environments Using Markov Decision Process

Thrishantha et al. (2011) have concentrated on a real-time machine learning scheme to exploit the lifetime of a sensor node to sense and pass on important environmental proceedings. To accomplish this objective, they must be able to put the sensor into sleep mode in a steady environment and keep it awake in a changing environment. They make use of stochastic methods such as MDP. Sometimes, problems are encountered such as the sensor node being expected to meet two possible contradictory objectives, that is, one is to hold on as long as possible with fixed battery energy, and another is to gather as much data from the surroundings as possible. Here, sensor nodes are used to sense ambient temperature changes. They can consider battery voltage at a given instance and that at complete charge, which is given by W_k/W_{max}, because this measures a likelihood of losing various important functionalities due to battery exhaust. Thus, smaller values of this measurement must minimize the reward level allotted for gathering new data. Also, whenever the temperature $\Delta T = |T_{i+1} - T_i|$ of the two successive walking up times $(i, I + 1)$ increases, then the reward that is allotted for capturing new data must be increased. Thereby with the demands of energy conservation and collecting new data, the reward function can be invented as shown in the following:

$$r(k) = \frac{W(k)}{W_{max}} * \frac{Sl(k)}{Sl_{avg}}^{\in|T(k) - T(k-1)|} \tag{20.18}$$

where $Sl(k)$ and Sl_{avg} are nodes sleep time and average sleep time. $\in$ is a variable parameter.

Based on this equation, if the sensor battery energy level $(W(k)/W_{max})$ drops, then simply one technique to get superior rewards is to go far beyond average sleeping plans so that temperature changes are still gathered from the environment among two successive wake-up instances. Still, this reward function cannot find a long-term best sleeping behavior of the sensor. So a critic utility was invented that can be used for discovering total future reward generated by the proposed reward function for an agent that is executing a particular strategy. The total expected future reward $\hat{V}(t)$ is specified by $\hat{V}(t) = \sum_{k=0}^{\infty} \gamma^k r(t + k)$. This can be extended to give

$$\hat{V}(t) = r(t) + \sum_{k=1}^{\infty} \gamma^k r(t + k) \tag{20.19}$$

$$\hat{V}(t) = r(t) + \gamma \sum_{k=0}^{\infty} \gamma^k r(t+k) \qquad (20.20)$$

$$\hat{V}(t) = r(t) + \gamma \hat{V}(t)(t+k) \qquad (20.21)$$

If prediction function $\hat{V}(t)$ is accurate, then only Equation 20.21 holds true. However, if $\hat{V}(t) \ne r(t) + \gamma \hat{V}(t+k)$, then the TD is given by $\Delta = r(t) + \gamma \hat{V}(t+k) - \hat{V}(t)$, as shown in Figure 20.6.

For learning the optimal value function, the inner parameter of the utility needs to be modified to reduce the fault Δ. As TD error Δ is a known quantity, learning a value function is purely a supervised learning scheme.

This system uses the critic function to guess the value function $\hat{V}(t)$, as well as to learn the optimal policy. Figure 20.7 shows how this critic can be used to discover the best possible policy. They consider the action space, which is a continuous one; each sensor situation can be treated as a Markov state. In this state, the critic function predicts the sum of the future reward, which is called $V(t)$. But then the policy can take an action from the available action. In this instance, no one can identify whether this chosen action $u(t)$ is the most excellent one to choose given the current state. Therefore, a normal distributed exploratory disturbance $N(0, \sigma)$ action is added. Since the disturbance is focused on an origin, it can be augmented or can reduce the significance of the action. Once this modified action is given to a sensor node, it will cooperate with the

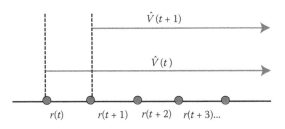

Figure 20.6   Relation between reward and critic function.

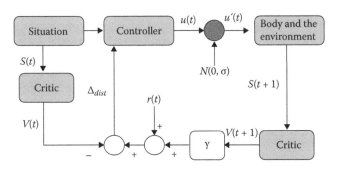

Figure 20.7   Actor-critic-based learning.

surroundings. It will result in a new situation that can be described by a new Markov state. Now the same critic will give expected total rewards from the next point of time. As a sensor knows the real reward value for this state, the TD of predictions made by the disturbance can be found.

When $\Delta_{dist} > 0$, this implies that the modified action is better than what the critic expected, $v(t)$. When $\Delta_{dist} < 0$, this implies that the modified action is giving a very low reward value. At this instance, the policy tries to move away from selecting an action on giving state $S(t)$.

20.4 Conclusion

In this chapter, we have dealt with a real-time learning procedure to enhance a lifetime of a sensor node. The objective of the new learning procedure is to link the sensor node's sleeping policy with the amount of data sensing, which is due to the occurrence of an event. Hence, the sensor nodes will periodically move into a sleep/wake state intelligently by monitoring the environment where it is deployed. We gave theoretical and experimental justification for different types of learning techniques such as the offline critic-based learning procedure, fuzzy neural networks, AI systems, and so forth that can be employed within clusters of sensors. We have shown that these proposed onboard programming algorithms are excellent ones to evaluate the scheduling procedures. For N number of nodes, the procedure will precisely reflect the scattered observation in the environment, where each cluster will provide information about local modifications such as temperature and relative humidity (RH).

References

Akyildiz, I. F., W. Su, Y. Sankarasubramaniam, and E. Cayirci. 2002. A survey on sensor networks. *Communications Magazine, IEEE*, Vol. 40, No. 8, pp. 102–114.

Alpaydin, E. 2004. Introduction to Machine Learning, Chapters 4, 5, 6. MIT Press, Cambridge, MA.

Arampatzis, T., J. Lygeros, and S. Manesis. 2005. A survey of applications of wireless sensors and wireless sensor networks. In *Intelligent Control, 2005. Proceedings of the 2005 IEEE International Symposium on, Mediterrean Conference on Control and Automation*, pp. 719–724.

Azarnoush, H., B. Horan, P. Sridhar, A. M. Madni, and M. Jamshidi. 2006. Towards optimization of a real-world robotic-sensor system of systems. In *World Automation Congress*, Budapest, Hungary.

Chakraborty, G., and Y. Hirano. 1998. Genetic algorithm for broadcast scheduling in packet radio networks. In *Evolutionary Computation Proceedings, 1998. IEEE World Congress on Computational Intelligence, The 1998 IEEE International Conference on*, pp. 183–188, IEEE.

Chong, C. Y., and S. P. Kumar. 2003 Sensor networks: Evolution, opportunities, and challenges. *Proceedings of the IEEE*, Vol. 91, No. 8, pp. 1247–1256.

Culler, D., D. Estrin, and M. Srivastava. 2004. Overview of sensor networks. *IEEE Magazine Computers*, Vol. 37, No. 8, pp. 41–49.

Dahnil, D. P., Y. P. Singh, and C. K. Ho. 2011. Energy-efficient cluster formation in heterogeneous wireless sensor networks: A comparative study. In *Advanced Communication Technology (ICACT), 13th International Conference on IEEE*, pp. 746–751.

Even, S., O. Goldreich, S. Moran, and P. Tong. 1984. On the np-completeness of certain network testing problems. *Networks*, Vol. 14, No. 1, pp. 1–24.

Funabiki, N., and Y. Takefuji. 1992. A neural network parallel algorithm for channel assignment problems in cellular radio networks. *Vehicular Technology, IEEE Transactions on*, Vol. 41, No. 4, pp. 430–437.

Kulkarni, R. V., A. Forster, and G. K. Venayagamoorthy. 2011. Computational intelligence in wireless sensor networks: A survey. *Communications Surveys & Tutorials, IEEE*, Vol. 13, No. 1, pp. 68–96.

Liu, Z., and I. Elhanany. 2006. RL-MAC: A QoS-aware reinforcement learning based MAC protocol for wireless sensor networks. In Networking, Sensing and Control, 2006. ICNSC'06. Proceedings of the 2006 IEEE International Conference on (pp. 768–773). IEEE.

Marsland, S. 2009. Using habituation in machine learning. *Neurobiology of Learning and Memory*, Vol. 92, No. 2, pp. 260–266.

Marsland, S. 2011. *Machine Learning: An Algorithmic Perspective*. CRC Press, Boca Raton.

Mihaylov, M., K. Tuyls, and A. Nowe. 2010. Decentralized learning in wireless sensor networks. In *Adaptive and Learning Agents,* pp. 60–73, Springer, Berlin, Heidelberg.

Mustapha, S., and G. Lachiver. 2000. A modified actor-critic reinforcement learning algorithm. In *Proc. of the Canadian Conference on Electrical and Computer Engineering*, Vol. 2, pp. 605–609.

Nilsson, N. J. 1996. *Introduction To Machine Learning*. Stanford University, Stanford.

Ouferhat, N., and A. Mellouk. 2006. Optimal QoS and adaptative routing in Wireless Sensor Networks. In *Information and Communication Technologies, 2006. ICTTA'06 2nd*, Vol. 2, pp. 2736–2741, IEEE.

Predd, J., S. Kulkarni, and V. Poor. 2006. Distributed learning in wireless sensor networks. *IEEE Signal Processing Magazine*, Vol. 23, No. 4, pp. 56–69.

Shah, K., and M. Kumar. 2007. Distributed independent reinforcement learning (DIRL) approach to resource management in wireless sensor networks. In *Mobile Adhoc and Sensor Systems. MASS 2007. IEEE Internatonal Conference on*, pp. 1–9, IEEE.

Shi, H., and L. Wang. 2005. Broadcast scheduling in wireless multihop networks using a neural-network-based hybrid algorithm. *Neural Networks*, Vol. 18, No. 5, pp. 765–771.

Simic, S. 2003. A learning-theory approach to sensor networks. *Proceedings of IEEE Pervasive Computing*, Vol. 2, pp. 44–49.

Sridhar, P., T. Nanayakkara, A. M. Madni, and M. Jamshidi. 2007. Dynamic power management of an embedded sensor network based on Actor-Critic reinforcement based learning. In *Proceedings of the 3rd International Conference on Information and Automation for Sustainability*, Vols. 4–6, pp. 76–81, IEEE, Melbourne, VIC, Australia.

Sutton, R., and A. Barto. 1988. *Reinforcement Learning: An Introduction*. MIT Press, Cambridge, MA.

Thrishantha, N., N. Malka, S. Prasann, and M. Asad. 2011. Intelligent sensing in dynamic environments using Markov decision process. *IEEE Sensors*, Vol. 11, No. 1, pp. 1229–1242.

Wang, P., and T. Wang. 2006. Adaptive routing for sensor networks using reinforcement learning. In *Computer and Information Technology. CIT'06. The Sixth IEEE International Conference on*, pp. 219–219, IEEE.

Yu-Ju, S., and W. Ming-Shi. 2006. Broadcast scheduling in wireless sensor networks using fuzzy Hopfield neural network. *Expert Systems with Applications*, Vol. 34, No. 2, pp. 900–907.

Zhang, S., Z. Zhang, Q. Lu, and J. Chen. 2006. Dynamic alliance based on genetic algorithms in wireless sensor networks. In *Wireless Communications, Networking and Mobile Computing. WiCOM. International Conference on*, pp. 1–4.

Chapter 21

Knowledge on Routing Nodes in MANET: A Soft Computing Approach

Senthilkumar K and Arunkumar Thangavelu

Contents

Mobile ad hoc networks (MANETs) is a technology that has been developed for real-world applications. The routing information of MANET can be said to be the backbone for the routing process, which also represents the characteristics or behaviors of routing nodes. The performance of MANET can be improved if the routing is done based on nodes' routing behaviors. Keeping this in view, we have proposed a knowledge model to analyze the routing node behaviors. Our proposed model uses routing attributes to classify the routing nodes based on a fuzzy proximity relation that induces the almost equivalence classes of routing nodes. On imposing an ordering relation on these equivalence classes, we have obtained ordered categorical classes of routing nodes. Further, we use association rules, Bayesian approach, and formal concept analysis (FCA) on ordered categorical classes to determine the behaviors, predict the hidden associations, and predict the implications and dependencies of routing attributes, respectively. Hence, this classification, prediction, and implication of routing nodes' behavior could lead to proper decision making through which an effective routing model can be developed for MANET.

21.1 Introduction

Mobile ad hoc networking is an essential technology for pervasive computing, and it has great potential for real-life applications such as commercial, emergency service, civilian, and military environments. Generally, a mobile ad hoc network (MANET) is based on self-creation, self-organization, and self-administration. The main characteristics and complexities of MANET are as follows (Chlamtac et al. 2003):

- Autonomous and infrastructure-less
- Multihop routing
- Dynamic network topology
- Device heterogeneity
- Energy-constrained operation
- Bandwidth-constrained variable capacity links
- Limited physical security
- Network scalability

In a MANET, each node can communicate directly with any other node that resides within its direct radio communication range. For communicating with nodes that reside beyond this range, the node needs to use intermediate nodes to relay the messages hop by hop. Routing protocols are needed to establish communication paths between nodes to exchange the messages with less overhead and computational burden in MANET. Routing protocols are classified into proactive, reactive, hybrid, and location-based protocols (Royer and Toh 1999; Abolhasan et al. 2004; Hu and Perrig 2004; Marina and Das 2005; Abusalah et al. 2008; Saeed et al. 2012). Proactive routing protocols maintain the route to all the nodes in the network by exchanging the routing control information periodically whenever the changes happen in the network topology, whereas reactive routing protocols initiate the route to the destination on demand, and these routes are kept alive as long as needed. Hybrid protocols have features of both proactive and reactive protocols. This type of protocol adopts a proactive mode when the destination node is very near (for example, less than two hops), whereas routes can be established through a reactive mode when the destination node is far away. The location-based routing protocol forwards the packets to other nodes through a location information service. Each type of protocol has its own advantages and disadvantages based on the different types of service and network environments, which have been discussed by various authors from different perspectives (Arora and Rama Krishna 2010; Cho et al. 2011). Numerous routing protocols and algorithms have been proposed, and their performance under various network environments and traffic conditions has been studied and compared (Yi et al. 2012; Kumar et al. 2012). Most routing protocols do not consider the routing attributes while selecting the routes. We observed that the elemental and essential part of any routing protocol is the routing information, which is dynamic in nature as there are frequent and unpredictable changes of topology and uncertainty in the network environment, which uplift the complex web for routing between the mobile nodes. Uncertainty and vagueness are pervasive characteristics of real-life applications. Since MANET has been developed to solve numerous real-life applications, the existence of uncertainty and vagueness in the routing information is the inevitable that may affect the overall performance of MANET. Hence, it is essential to study routing node behaviors through routing information. Keeping this in view, we study the behavior of routing nodes and their attributes through routing information using soft computing techniques such as association rules, naïve Bayesian, and formal concept analysis (FCA). Since these techniques have been discussed in the literatures of different domains of various applications, we have considered it for our proposed model. The rest of the chapter is organized as follows. Section 21.2 presents an overview of fuzzy proximity relations. We present ordered routing information in Section 21.3. Section 21.4 describes how soft computing techniques are useful in MANET. Our proposed model is discussed in Section 21.5, and its analysis is presented in Section 21.6. Finally, Section 21.7 provides the conclusion.

21.2 Overview of Fuzzy Proximity Relation

Let U be the universe of the routing nodes $(n_1, n_2, n_3, \ldots n_i)$ in MANET. An existence of crisp relations among the nodes is very rare in realistic environments. Therefore, a fuzzy proximity relation defined on the universe U is more appropriate for the nodes in MANET. We give the following definition and basic notions of fuzzy proximity relations (Senthilkumar et al. 2013a), which are highly essential for our proposed model.

Definition 21.1

Let U be a universe of routing nodes $(n_1, n_2, n_3, \ldots n_i)$. We define the fuzzy relation on U as a fuzzy subset of (UXU).

Definition 21.2

A fuzzy relation R on U is said to be a fuzzy proximity relation if

$$\mu_R(n_1, n_1) = 1; \quad \forall n_1 \in U$$

$$\mu_R(n_1, n_2) = \mu_R(n_2, n_1); \quad \forall n_1, n_2 \in U$$

Definition 21.3

Let R be a fuzzy proximity relation on U. Then, for the given membership value $\alpha \in [0,1]$, we say that the two nodes n_1 and n_2 are α-similar to R if $(n_1, n_2) \in R_\alpha$, that is, $\mu_R(n_1, n_2) \geq \alpha$, and we write $n_1 R_\alpha n_2$.

Definition 21.4

Let R be a fuzzy proximity relation on U. Then, for the given membership value $\alpha \in [0,1]$, we say that the two nodes n_1 and n_2 are α-identical to R if either n_1 is α-similar to n_2 or n_1 is transitively α-similar to n_2 with respect to R; that is, there exists a sequence of nodes $u_1, u_2, u_3 \ldots u_n$ such that $\mu_R(n_1, u_1) \geq \alpha$, $\mu_R(u_1, u_2) \geq \alpha$, $\mu_R(u_2, u_3) \geq \alpha$, $\ldots \mu_R(u_n, n_2) \geq \alpha$.

Definition 21.5

Let U be a universal set and R be a fuzzy proximity relation on U. The pair (U,R) is called a fuzzy approximation space. For any $\alpha \in [0,1]$, we denote by R_α^* the set of all equivalence classes of $R(\alpha)$. Also, we call $(U,R(\alpha))$ a generated approximation space associated with R and α.

21.3 Ordered Routing Information System

21.3.1 Information System

In this section, we discuss the basic notion of an information system (Pawlak 1991). The basic component of an information system is a finite nonempty set of objects U called the universe for a finite nonempty set A of attributes. With every attribute $a \in A$, there is associated a nonempty set V_a of values of an attribute a. V_a will be referred to as the domain of attribute a. The attributes are further classified into a set of condition attributes and decision attributes. The formal definition of the information system (IS) is $IS = (U,A,V,f)$, where U is a finite nonempty set of objects called the universe and A is a finite nonempty set of attributes, $V = \cup_{a \in A} V_a$. For every $a \in A$, V_a is a set of values that attribute a may have, whereas f is an information function, $f: U \times A \rightarrow V$. For every $a \in A$, $f_a: U \times A \rightarrow V_a$. For example, let us consider the simple patient information system defined as follows:

$$U = \{p_1, p_2, p_3, p_4, p_5\},$$

$$A = \{\text{headache, temperature, cough, body pain}\},$$

$$V = \{V_{\text{headache}} \cup V_{\text{temperature}} \cup V_{\text{cough}} \cup V_{\text{body-pain}}\}$$

where
$V_{\text{headache}} = \{\text{yes, no}\}$
$V_{\text{temperature}} = \{\text{normal, high, very high}\}$
$V_{\text{cough}} = \{\text{never, seldom, always}\}$ and
$V_{\text{body-pain}} = \{\text{yes, no}\}$

Table 21.1 Classical View of Patient Information System

Patients	Headache	Temperature	Cough	Body Pain
p_1	Yes	Normal	Seldom	No
p_2	Yes	High	Seldom	Yes
p_3	No	Very high	Always	No
p_4	No	Normal	Always	Yes
p_5	Yes	High	Never	Yes

A classical view of a patient information system is presented in Table 21.1. For example, the information about patient p_3 is characterized in Table 21.1 by the attribute value set (headache, no), (temperature, very high), (cough, always), and (body-pain, yes).

21.3.2 Routing Information System

Generally, nodes in MANET are recognized or quantified using a finite number of attributes. At the same time, it does not consider any semantic relationships between distinct values of a particular attribute. Different values of the same attribute are considered as different notions without any relation. However, in most real-life applications, it is observed that the attribute values are almost identical, so they would be considered as almost the same. This is because nodes are characterized by almost the same attribute values that are almost indiscernible. Hence, an effort has been made to generalize the Pawlak indiscernibility relation into an almost indiscernibility relation. The routing tables of each node represent the knowledge about the routing process in MANET. The routing data are often presented in a table in which columns are labeled by attributes and rows are labeled by nodes, and we denote it as a routing information system (*RIS*). Let $RIS = (U,A,V_a,f_a)$ be a routing information system, where U is a nonempty finite set of nodes that participate in the routing process known as universe and A is a nonempty finite set of routing attributes. For every $a \in A$, V_a is the set of values that attribute a may have and $f_a: U \rightarrow V_a$ is a routing information function. For example, consider the sample routing information system as presented in Table 21.2, where a_1, a_2, a_3, a_4, and a_5 represent route request (RREQ), route reply

Table 21.2 Tabular View of Routing Information System

Node	a_1	a_2	a_3	a_4	a_5
n_1	Very high	No	High	High	15
n_2	High	No	High	More	10
n_3	Low	Yes	Low	Less	5
n_4	Medium	Yes	Medium	More	10
n_5	Very high	No	Very high	High	15

(RREP), packet drop (PKT-DROP), control packet (CTRL-PKT), and speed of node (meter/second), respectively. Here,

$$U = \{n_1, n_2, n_3, n_4, n_5\}, A = \{a_1, a_2, a_3, a_4, a_5\}$$

$$V_{a_1} = \{\text{low, medium, high, very high}\}$$

$$V_{a_2} = \{\text{yes, no}\}$$

$$V_{a_3} = \{\text{low, medium, high, very high}\}$$

$$V_{a_4} = \{\text{less, more, high}\}$$

$$V_{a_5} = \{5, 10, 15\}$$

21.3.3 Ordered Routing Information System

We introduce a fuzzy proximity relation to find the attribute values that are α-identical prior to the ordering relations. This is because exact ordering is not possible when the attribute values are the same. For $\alpha = 1$, the almost indiscernibility reduces to Pawlak's indiscernibility relation. Therefore, we generalize at this point Pawlak's indiscernibility relation. The ordering rules give an idea on how the routing nodes could be ordered according to their attribute values. An ordered routing information system (*ORIS*) is a routing information system with an order relation. We define ordered routing information as $ORIS = (RIS, \{\prec_a : a \in A\})$, where RIS is a routing information system defined on U induced by the relation attribute a where $\prec_a$ represents an order relation on U. Node n_1 is more confident than node n_2 if and only if the node n_1 has higher priority order than n_2 based on the value of attribute a. However, the other ordered relations between n_1 and n_2 may also possible, and it may vary based on the network environment. For a subset of attributes $P \subseteq A$, we define

$$n_1\{\prec_a\}n_2 \Leftrightarrow f_a(n_1)\{\prec_a\}f_a(n_2)\forall a \in P$$

$$\Leftrightarrow \bigcap_{a \in P} f_a(n_1)\{\prec_a\}f_a(n_2)$$

$$\Leftrightarrow \bigcap_{a \in P}\{\prec_a\}$$

This formalization indicates that node n_1 is more confident than n_2 if and only if n_1 has higher priority order than n_2 according to all attributes in P. For example, the routing information system of Table 21.2 becomes an ordered routing information system by introducing the following ordering relations:

$$\prec_{a_1}: \text{low} \prec \text{medium} \prec \text{high} \prec \text{very high}$$

$$\prec_{a_2}: \text{yes} \prec \text{no}$$

$$\prec_{a_3}: \text{low} \prec \text{medium} \prec \text{high} \prec \text{very high}$$

$$\prec_{a_4}: \text{less} \prec \text{more} \prec \text{high}$$

$$\prec_{a_5}: 5 \prec 10 \prec 15$$

21.4 Soft Computing Techniques

21.4.1 Granular Computing

Many researchers have been attracted by granular computing (GrC) since it provides a structured approach, a natural way to understand, analyze, compute, and solve problems such as incompleteness, uncertainty, or vagueness occurring in real-world applications. The label "granular computing" was suggested by Professor T.Y. Lin, and it has been discussed in many established fields such as artificial intelligence, cluster analysis, machine learning, fuzzy set, rough set theory, binary relation models, and many others (Yao 2001; Liang and Shi 2004; Bargiela and Pedrycz 2006; Yao 2000; Senthilkumar and Thangavelu 2013c). The main component of GrC is granules. The granules can be any subset, class, object, or cluster of a universe based on similarity or proximity relations, and it may be crisp or fuzzy. Granules may have a different format and meaning based on the applications and uses. In MANETs, GrC can be used to study the behaviors or characteristics of routing nodes. We use a proximity relation to find the closeness of routing nodes. This result induces the almost-equivalence classes of routing nodes. Here, each class is considered as granule, and operation on granules is called granulation.

21.4.2 Association Rules

An association rule (Tripathy and Acharijya 2011; Senthilkumar and Thangavelu 2013c) is an expression $X \Rightarrow Y$, where X and Y are sets of attributes. If a set of attribute values is an association rule, all the attribute values in the set are said to be associated with one another. To check whether a set of attribute values is an association rule or not, we perform the AND operation among the bit representation of the attribute values of the set. If the number of 1s in the result of the AND operation is greater than or equal to minimum support, then it is an association rule; otherwise, it is not an association rule. Here, we use association rules to determine the behavior or identify the characteristics of the routing nodes and their attributes.

21.4.3 Naïve Bayesian Classifier

In general, Bayesian classification is derived from Bayes theorem and addresses the classification problem by learning the distribution of instances given different class values. The various classification algorithms and prediction of categorical and ordinal variables have been discussed in various domains

(Han and Kamber 2006; Lin and Haug 2008; Mitchell 1997; Acharjya et al. 2012; Senthilkumar and Arunkumar 2013b). The basic notion of Bayesian classification is as follows: Let E be the tuple and be considered as evidence in Bayesian theory, which possesses a set of n-attributes. Let H be some hypothesis such that the tuple E belongs to some specified class V. According to the Bayes theorem, we determine $P(H \mid E)$, the probability that the hypothesis H holds given the evidence E, as

$$P(H \mid E) = \frac{P(E \mid H)P(H)}{P(E)}$$

Let X be a training set of tuples from ORIS, which possesses n-dimensional attribute vector $E = (e_1, e_2, e_3, \ldots e_n)$, with $e_i = x(a_i)$, $i = 1, 2, 3 \ldots, n$, which represents that tuples are quantified with $a_1, a_2, a_3, \ldots, a_n$ attributes. Let us assume that the decision attribute da has m classes $V_1, V_2, V_3, \ldots, V_m$. That is, the value of da is denoted by $V_{da} = \{V_1, V_2, V_3, \ldots, V_m\}$. Given a tuple E, the classifier will predict that E belongs to the class having the highest posterior probability, conditioned on E. That is, the naïve Bayesian classifier predicts that tuple E belongs to class V_i if and only if $P(V_i \mid E) > P(V_j \mid E)$ for $j \neq i$; $1 \leq i, j \leq m$. The class V_i for which $P(V_i \mid E)$ is maximum is called maximum posteriori hypothesis and is represented by Bayes theorem as

$$P(V_i \mid E) = \frac{P(E \mid V_i)P(V_i)}{P(E)}$$

When $P(E)$ is constant for all classes, only $P(V_i \mid E)$ is maximized. If the class prior probabilities are not known, then it is assumed that $P(V_1) = P(V_2) = \ldots = P(V_m)$. Hence, we would maximize $P(E \mid V_i)$. Otherwise, the class prior probability $P(V_i) = |V_i|/|X|$ is to be estimated, where $|V_i|$ is the cardinality of the V_i and $P(E \mid V_i)P(V_i)$ is to be maximized. If the data set has many attributes, it is observed that computing $P(E \mid V_i)P(V_i)$ is computationally expensive. Thus, the "naïve" assumption of class conditional independence is made to reduce computations. By considering that the values of the attributes are conditionally independent of one another, given the class label of the tuple (i.e., that there are no dependence relationships among the attributes),

$$P(E \mid V_i) = \prod_{l=1}^{q} P(e_l \mid V_i)$$

where e_l refers to the value of attribute a_l of tuple E. We define $P(e_l \mid V_i) = n_v/n$, where n_v is the number of times that the attribute value t_l was seen with the label V_i and n represents the number of times V_i was seen in the decision attribute da. Sometimes, we may not see the value t_l with the label V_i and considered a zero probability, which is denoted as $n_v = 0$. This problem can be overcome by using m-estimate; we define $P(t_l \mid V_i)$ as

$$P(e_l \mid V_i) = \frac{n_v + mp}{n + m}$$

where p is the prior estimate of the probability and m is the equivalent sample size (constant). In the absence of other information, assume a uniform prior $p = \dfrac{1}{l}$, where $l = |V_{al}|$. Here, we use a naïve Bayesian approach to predict the hidden associations of routing attributes of routing nodes.

21.4.4 *Formal Concept Analysis*

The FCA has been applied in many domains, such as medicine, biology, and computer sciences, for conceptual analysis of data and knowledge discovery (Venter et al. 1997; Priss 2006; Kwon and Kim 2009; Aswanikumar and Sumangali 2012; Acharjya and Ezhilarasi 2011; Senthilkumar and Thangavelu 2013d). The FCA can be a righteous way of developing ontology from a set of objects using their attributes. Using the FCA, the concepts can be understood in the form of a philosophical approach; data can be conceptually organized by clustering and structuring. The structure of data can also be visualized in the form of implications and dependencies. A concept is divided into two mutually dependent parts: *extension* and *intension*. The *extension* refers to all objects that share all the attributes of the concept, whereas *intension* refers to the attributes that precisely describe the objects of the concept. We have used FCA to obtain more knowledge on routing nodes and their attributes.

Definition 21.6

A formal context $C = (U,A,R)$ consists of U, A, and R. The elements of U are called the objects, whereas A is called the attribute of the context, and R is a binary relation between U and A. That is, $R \subseteq U \times A$.

Definition 21.7

A formal concept of the context (U,A,R) can be defined as an ordered pair (X,Y) with $X \subseteq U$, $Y \subseteq A$, $X' = Y$, $Y' = X$. The set of all concepts of (U,A,R) is denoted as $L(U,A,R)$, where

$$X' = \{a \in A: uRa \ \forall \ u \in X\}$$

$Y' = \{u \in U: uRa \ \forall \ a \in A\}$. We call X the extent and Y the intent of the concept (X,Y). That is, objects in X share all properties Y, and only properties Y are possessed by all objects in X.

21.5 Proposed Knowledge Model

An abstract view of our proposed model is presented in Figure 21.1. We have considered different attributes of routing nodes such as RREQ, RREP, error packets (ERR-PKT), packets lost (PKT-LOST), CTRL-PKT, PKT-DROP, and the node speed (NS). These attributes are taken into consideration as they influence the routing process and make our analysis simple. However, other routing attributes can also be taken into consideration based on the network environment. We observed that the values in the routing information system are not exactly identical but, rather, almost identical, and most of the attribute values have vague or imprecise meanings. That is, nodes cannot be distinguished clearly by some of the attribute values. To decide on a ratio of similarity between attribute values of two nodes, we use a fuzzy proximity relation; here we generalize the Pawlak indiscernibility relation into almost-indiscernibility relation. If we consider the real-world data of any two objects in the same domain, the attribute values are almost identical, if not exactly identical. For example, if we consider all the apples in a basket, all are not exactly the same, but

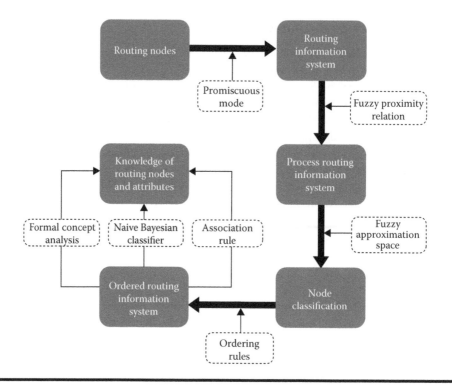

Figure 21.1 Abstract view of proposed granulation model.

they are almost the same. Since MANETs have been developed for real-world applications, it is more appropriate to characterize the behaviors of nodes in MANETs using a proximity relation. Hence, we have considered the almost-indiscernibility relation for our proposed model. We define the fuzzy proximity relation $r(n_i, n_j)$ based on the definitions in Section 21.2 to identify the almost indiscernibility among the nodes n_i and n_j, where

$$r(n_i, n_j) = 1 - \frac{|V_{n_i} - V_{n_j}|}{2(V_{n_i} + V_{n_j})}$$

The fuzzy proximity relation defined here uses routing attributes (RREQ, RREP, NS, etc.) to identify the almost indiscernibility among the nodes. By considering the almost indiscernibility on the result of a fuzzy proximity relation, we obtained almost-equivalence classes of routing nodes (i.e., node classification). It is vital that if we decreases the membership value of α, more and more, the number of attributes shall become indispensable. On imposing order relation on the almost-equivalence classes, we have obtained ordered categorical classes of routing nodes, which provides further knowledge on routing nodes. The different values of the same attribute could be ordered using ordering, and it can also be used to know which attributes play more important roles in determining the overall ordering, which attributes do not contribute at all to the overall ordering, and which subset of attributes would be sufficient to determine the overall ordering. After ordering, we obtained the confidence levels of each node by assigning weights to each categorical class and computed the confidence levels of each routing node involved in the routing process, which provided further knowledge of routing nodes. We first introduce the notion of ordered routing information tables as a generalization of routing information tables, and then we use an ordered routing information table to find the confidence levels of routing nodes on which any standard data mining and machine learning algorithms can be applied. We have used an association rule to determine the behavior or identify the characteristics of the routing nodes and their attributes. We have considered a naïve Bayesian approach to predict the hidden associations of routing attributes of routing nodes, and FCA was used to obtain a concept lattice that provides complete information in the form of a mathematical lattice structure and visualizes the sub/super concept hierarchy, relations between nodes and attributes, implications, and dependencies. All these processes are explained in Section 21.6.

21.6 Empirical Studies on Routing Nodes and Their Attributes

In our case studies, we have considered different network environments, and we assume that each node participating in the network should also be willing to forward packets to other nodes in the network and have features like promiscuous mode operation, omnidirectional transceivers, and comparable transmission and reception ranges of transceivers. We use a network simulator (NS2) tool to collect the data for our proposed model. Since the NS2 tool is widely used in the literature for MANET simulation, we have used it for the data collection. The data have been collected through a promiscuous mode based on a network that consists of different network sizes of mobile nodes; at a particular instance of time, we have randomly selected the few nodes that are involved in routing at various speed levels (5 to 20 m/s) in a random movement. We number the nodes sequentially because this would not affect our analysis and also to make our analysis simple and easy to understand. We chose a random way-point mobility model for our analysis because it has been used mostly in MANET literatures, and it has the possibility of configuring mobile nodes based on the network environment setup. The main key parameter in this model is *pause-time*. It determines how long a node can remain stationary at a point. In a simulation, each node in the network begins by remaining stationary at a randomly selected location in the simulation space for *pause-time* seconds. The node then moves to a randomly selected destination with a chosen speed. Once the location of the destination is reached, the node remains stationary for the *pause-time* period before the process is repeated. In general, the mobile NS and *pause-time* would have a major impact on any routing protocols that use a random way-point mobility model. The communication range of each node is set to 250 m for all our simulations, which is a commonly used frequency for a Cisco wireless interface running on 802.11 standard.

21.6.1 Using Granules and Association Rules

Data have been collected based on a network that consists of 40 mobile nodes; at a particular instance of time, we have randomly selected the 10 nodes that are involved in the routing process at various speed levels (5 to 15 m/s) in a random movement. The collected data have been presented in Table 21.3. The different attributes taken into consideration are RREQ, RREP, CTRL-PKT, PKT-DROP, and NS. The attribute NS is based on meters per second. The results of fuzzy proximity relations of attributes RREQ, RREP, CTRL-PKT, PKT-DROP, and NS are shown in Tables 21.4 through 21.8.

On considering the almost similarity of 95%, that is, $\alpha \geq 0.95$, it is observed from Table 21.4 that $r(n_0, n_0) = 1; r(n_0, n_5) = 0.96;$ and $r(n_0, n_7) = 0.97$. Therefore, the nodes $\{n_0, n_5, n_7\}$ belong to one

Table 21.3   Nodes Routing Information

Node	RREQ	RREP	CTRL-PKT	PKT-DROP	NS
n_0	31	17	180	9	5
n_1	53	35	313	24	10
n_2	46	39	282	27	10
n_3	112	62	621	50	15
n_4	86	57	512	39	15
n_5	36	20	213	13	5
n_6	82	48	492	42	15
n_7	28	14	163	11	5
n_8	79	49	503	45	15
n_9	49	31	344	29	10

class, and they are α-identical. Similarly, the other classes can also be obtained from Table 21.4. The equivalence class generated from Tables 21.4 through 21.8 is given as follows:

$$R^{\alpha}_{RREQ} = \{\{n_0, n_5, n_7\}, \{n_1, n_2, n_9,\}, \{n_4, n_6, n_8\}, \{n_3\}\}$$

$$R^{\alpha}_{RREP} = \{\{n_0, n_5, n_7\}, \{n_1, n_2, n_9,\}, \{n_3, n_4, n_6, n_8\}\}$$

$$R^{\alpha}_{CTRL-PKT} = \{\{n_0, n_5, n_7\}, \{n_1, n_2, n_9,\}, \{n_3, n_4, n_6, n_8\}\}$$

$$R^{\alpha}_{PKT-DROP} = \{\{n_0, n_5, n_7\}, \{n_1, n_2, n_9,\}, \{n_3, n_4, n_6, n_8\}\}$$

$$R^{\alpha}_{NS} = \{\{n_0, n_5, n_7\}, \{n_1, n_2, n_9,\}, \{n_3, n_4, n_6, n_8\}\}$$

Table 21.4   Fuzzy Proximity Relation for RREQ

	n_0	n_1	n_2	n_3	n_4	n_5	n_6	n_7	n_8	n_9
n_0	1.00	0.86	0.90	0.71	0.76	0.96	0.77	0.97	0.78	0.88
n_1	0.86	1.00	0.96	0.82	0.88	0.90	0.89	0.84	0.90	0.98
n_2	0.90	0.96	1.00	0.79	0.84	0.93	0.85	0.87	0.86	0.98
n_3	0.71	0.82	0.79	1.00	0.93	0.74	0.92	0.70	0.91	0.80
n_4	0.76	0.88	0.84	0.93	1.00	0.79	0.98	0.74	0.97	0.86
n_5	0.96	0.90	0.93	0.74	0.79	1.00	0.80	0.93	0.81	0.92
n_6	0.77	0.89	0.85	0.92	0.98	0.80	1.00	0.75	0.99	0.87
n_7	0.97	0.84	0.87	0.70	0.74	0.93	0.75	1.00	0.76	0.86
n_8	0.78	0.90	0.86	0.91	0.97	0.81	0.99	0.76	1.00	0.88
n_9	0.88	0.98	0.98	0.80	0.86	0.92	0.87	0.86	0.88	1.00

Table 21.5   Fuzzy Proximity Relation for RREP

	n_0	n_1	n_2	n_3	n_4	n_5	n_6	n_7	n_8	n_9
n_0	1.00	0.82	0.80	0.71	0.72	0.95	0.76	0.95	0.75	0.85
n_1	0.82	1.00	0.97	0.86	0.88	0.86	0.92	0.78	0.91	0.96
n_2	0.80	0.97	1.00	0.88	0.90	0.83	0.94	0.76	0.94	0.94
n_3	0.71	0.86	0.88	1.00	0.97	0.74	0.93	0.68	0.94	0.83
n_4	0.72	0.88	0.90	0.97	1.00	0.75	0.95	0.69	0.96	0.85
n_5	0.95	0.86	0.83	0.74	0.75	1.00	0.79	0.91	0.78	0.89
n_6	0.76	0.92	0.94	0.93	0.95	0.79	1.00	0.72	0.99	0.89
n_7	0.95	0.78	0.76	0.68	0.69	0.91	0.72	1.00	0.72	0.81
n_8	0.75	0.91	0.94	0.94	0.96	0.78	0.99	0.72	1.00	0.88
n_9	0.85	0.96	0.94	0.83	0.85	0.89	0.89	0.81	0.88	1.00

For example, from the equivalence class R^{α}_{RREQ}, it can be observed that the attribute RREQ has been classified into four categories such as $\{\{n_0, n_5, n_7\}, \{n_1, n_2, n_9\}, \{n_4, n_6, n_8\}, \text{and } \{n_3\}\}$. We categorize these classes into low, medium, high, and very high, respectively. Similarly, we categorized RREP (low, medium, high); CTRL-PKT (less, moderate, large); PKT-DROP (less, moderate, large); and NS (minimum, average, maximum) with proper notions. Now we impose an order relation on Table 21.3, and the obtained ordered routing information is presented in Table 21.9. We have assigned weights to each class, like very high; (high, large, maximum); (medium, moderate, average); and (low, less, minimum) as 1, 2, 3, and 4, respectively. We computed the total weights, and

Table 21.6   Fuzzy Proximity Relation for CTRL-PKT

	n_0	n_1	n_2	n_3	n_4	n_5	n_6	n_7	n_8	n_9
n_0	1.00	0.86	0.88	0.72	0.76	0.95	0.76	0.97	0.76	0.84
n_1	0.86	1.00	0.97	0.83	0.87	0.90	0.88	0.84	0.88	0.97
n_2	0.88	0.97	1.00	0.81	0.85	0.93	0.86	0.86	0.85	0.95
n_3	0.72	0.83	0.81	1.00	0.95	0.75	0.94	0.70	0.94	0.85
n_4	0.76	0.87	0.85	0.95	1.00	0.79	0.99	0.74	0.99	0.90
n_5	0.95	0.90	0.93	0.75	0.79	1.00	0.80	0.93	0.79	0.88
n_6	0.76	0.88	0.86	0.94	0.99	0.80	1.00	0.74	0.99	0.91
n_7	0.97	0.84	0.86	0.70	0.74	0.93	0.74	1.00	0.74	0.82
n_8	0.76	0.88	0.85	0.94	0.99	0.79	0.99	0.74	1.00	0.90
n_9	0.84	0.97	0.95	0.85	0.90	0.88	0.91	0.82	0.90	1.00

Table 21.7   Fuzzy Proximity Relation for PKT-DROP

	n_0	n_1	n_2	n_3	n_4	n_5	n_6	n_7	n_8	n_9
n_0	1.00	0.77	0.75	0.65	0.68	0.90	0.67	0.95	0.66	0.73
n_1	0.77	1.00	0.97	0.82	0.88	0.85	0.86	0.81	0.84	0.95
n_2	0.75	0.97	1.00	0.85	0.90	0.82	0.89	0.78	0.87	0.98
n_3	0.65	0.82	0.85	1.00	0.93	0.70	0.95	0.68	0.97	0.86
n_4	0.68	0.88	0.90	0.93	1.00	0.75	0.98	0.72	0.96	0.92
n_5	0.90	0.85	0.82	0.70	0.75	1.00	0.73	0.95	0.72	0.80
n_6	0.67	0.86	0.89	0.95	0.98	0.73	1.00	0.70	0.98	0.90
n_7	0.95	0.81	0.78	0.68	0.72	0.95	0.70	1.00	0.69	0.77
n_8	0.66	0.84	0.87	0.97	0.96	0.72	0.98	0.69	1.00	0.89
n_9	0.73	0.95	0.98	0.86	0.92	0.80	0.90	0.77	0.89	1.00

Table 21.8   Fuzzy Proximity Relation for NS

	n_0	n_1	n_2	n_3	n_4	n_5	n_6	n_7	n_8	n_9
n_0	1.00	0.83	0.83	0.75	0.75	1.00	0.75	1.00	0.75	0.83
n_1	0.83	1.00	1.00	0.90	0.90	0.83	0.90	0.83	0.90	1.00
n_2	0.83	1.00	1.00	0.90	0.90	0.83	0.90	0.83	0.90	1.00
n_3	0.75	0.90	0.90	1.00	1.00	0.75	1.00	0.75	1.00	0.90
n_4	0.75	0.90	0.90	1.00	1.00	0.75	1.00	0.75	1.00	0.90
n_5	1.00	0.83	0.83	0.75	0.75	1.00	0.75	1.00	0.75	0.83
n_6	0.75	0.90	0.90	1.00	1.00	0.75	1.00	0.75	1.00	0.90
n_7	1.00	0.83	0.83	0.75	0.75	1.00	0.75	1.00	0.75	0.83
n_8	0.75	0.90	0.90	1.00	1.00	0.75	1.00	0.75	1.00	0.90
n_9	0.83	1.00	1.00	0.90	0.90	0.83	0.90	0.83	0.90	1.00

the confidence level of each node is presented in Table 21.10. We may also consider that the last column (confidence level) of Table 21.10 represents the overall ordering of nodes. The granular computing view of routing information is presented in Table 21.11. To verify if a set of attribute values is an association rule or not, we performed an AND operation among the bit representation of the attribute values of this set. If the number of 1s in the result of an AND operation is greater than or equal to minimum support, then it is an association rule; otherwise, it is not an association rule. For example, we consider the attributes RREQ (low), PKT-DROP (less), and NS (minimum) to find the association rule. We compute an AND operation on bit representation of RREQ (low), PKT-DROP (less), and NS (minimum), displayed in Table 21.12. We assumed

Table 21.9   Ordered Routing Information

Node	RREQ	RREP	CTRL-PKT	PKT-DROP	NS
n_0	Low	Low	Less	Less	Minimum
n_1	Medium	Medium	Moderate	Moderate	Average
n_2	Medium	Medium	Moderate	Moderate	Average
n_3	Very high	High	Large	Large	Maximum
n_4	High	High	Large	Large	Maximum
n_5	Low	Low	Less	Less	Minimum
n_6	High	High	Large	Large	Maximum
n_7	Low	Low	Less	Less	Minimum
n_8	High	High	Large	Large	Maximum
n_9	Medium	Medium	Moderate	Moderate	Average

Notes: $\prec_{RREQ}$: low $\prec$ medium $\prec$ high $\prec$ very high;

$\prec_{RREP}$: low $\prec$ medium $\prec$ high;

$\prec_{CTRL-PKT}$: less $\prec$ moderate $\prec$ large;

$\prec_{PKT-DROP}$: less $\prec$ moderate $\prec$ large;

$\prec_{NS}$: minimum $\prec$ average $\prec$ maximum

Table 21.10   Nodes' Confidence Level

Node	RREQ	RREP	CTRL-PKT	PKT-DROP	NS	Total	Confidence
n_0	Low	Low	Less	Less	Minimum	20	Good
n_1	Medium	Medium	Moderate	Moderate	Average	15	Average
n_2	Medium	Medium	Moderate	Moderate	Average	15	Average
n_3	Very high	High	Large	Large	Maximum	9	Poor
n_4	High	High	Large	Large	Maximum	10	Poor
n_5	Low	Low	Less	Less	Minimum	20	Good
n_6	High	High	Large	Large	Maximum	10	Poor
n_7	Low	Low	Less	Less	Minimum	20	Good
n_8	High	High	Large	Large	Maximum	10	Poor
n_9	Medium	Medium	Moderate	Moderate	Average	15	Average

Table 21.11 Granular View of Ordered Routing Information

Attributes	Attribute Values	Granule as List	Granule as Bits
RREQ	Low	n_0,n_5,n_7	1 0 0 0 0 1 0 1 0 0
	Medium	n_1,n_2,n_9	0 1 1 0 0 0 0 0 0 1
	High	n_3	0 0 0 1 0 0 0 0 0 0
	Very high	n_4,n_6,n_8	0 0 0 0 1 0 1 0 1 0
RREP	Low	n_0,n_5,n_7	1 0 0 0 0 1 0 1 0 0
	Medium	n_1,n_2,n_9	0 1 1 0 0 0 0 0 0 1
	High	n_3,n_4,n_6,n_8	0 0 0 1 1 0 1 0 1 0
CTRL-PKT	Less	n_0,n_5,n_7	1 0 0 0 0 1 0 1 0 0
	More	n_1,n_2,n_9	0 1 1 0 0 0 0 0 0 1
	Large	n_3,n_4,n_6,n_8	0 0 0 1 1 0 1 0 1 0
PKT-DROP	Less	n_0,n_5,n_7	1 0 0 0 0 1 0 1 0 0
	More	n_1,n_2,n_9	0 1 1 0 0 0 0 0 0 1
	Large	n_3,n_4,n_6,n_8	0 0 0 1 1 0 1 0 1 0
NS	Minimum	n_0,n_5,n_7	1 0 0 0 0 1 0 1 0 0
	Average	n_1,n_2,n_9	0 1 1 0 0 0 0 0 0 1
	Maximum	n_3,n_4,n_6,n_8	0 0 0 1 1 0 1 0 1 0

Table 21.12 AND Operation on Granule Using Bit Representation

Attribute Values	Granule as Bits
RREQ	1 0 0 0 0 1 0 1 0 0
PKT-DROP	1 0 0 0 0 1 0 1 0 0
NS	1 0 0 0 0 1 0 1 0 0
AND	1 0 0 0 0 1 0 1 0 0

that the minimum support is 2. From Table 21.12, we can understand that attributes RREQ (low), PKT-DROP (less), and NS (minimum) are an association rule, and the nodes that are supporting the association rule are n_0, n_5, and n_7. That is, the nodes n_0, n_5, and n_7 possess the same characteristics or behaviors. Similarly, we can also find the association rules of the attributes like RREP (high), CTRL-PKT (large), and NS (maximum) by computing an AND operation on bit representation of these attributes, and we can understand that nodes n_3, n_4, n_6, and n_8 possess the same characteristics or behaviors. Using the same procedure, we can also find the association rules of length two, three, and so on.

21.6.2 Using Naïve Bayesian Classifier

Data have been collected based on a network that consists of 50 mobile nodes, at a particular instance of time, and we have randomly selected the 10 nodes that are involved in the routing process at various speed levels (5 to 15 m/s) in a random movement. The collected data are presented in Table 21.13. We have considered the routing attributes such as RREQ, RREP, CTRL-PKT, PKT-DROP, and NS for our analysis. The attribute NS is based on meters per second. The results of fuzzy proximity relations of attributes RREQ, RREP, CTRL-PKT, PKT-DROP, and NS are shown from Tables 21.14 through Table 21.18.

On considering the almost similarity of 95%, that is, $\alpha \geq 0.95$, it is observed from Table 21.14 that $r(n_0,n_0) = 1; r(n_0,n_6) = 0.96$; and $r(n_0,n_8) = 0.96$. Therefore, the nodes $\{n_0,n_6,n_8\}$ belong to one class, and they are α-identical. Similarly, the other classes can also be obtained from Table 21.14. The equivalence class generated from Tables 21.14 through 21.18 is given as follows:

$$R_{RREQ}^{\alpha} = \{\{n_2,n_4\},\{n_1,n_7\},\{n_0,n_6,n_8\},\{n_3,n_5,n_9\}\}$$

$$R_{RREP}^{\alpha} = \{\{n_1,n_4,n_7\},\{n_0,n_2\},\{n_3,n_5,n_6,n_8,n_9\}\}$$

$$R_{CTRL-PKT}^{\alpha} = \{\{n_1\},\{n_0,n_2,n_4,n_7\},\{n_3,n_5,n_6,n_8,n_9\}\}$$

$$R_{PKT-DROP}^{\alpha} = \{\{n_1,n_4,n_7\},\{n_0\},\{n_2,n_9\},\{n_3,n_5,n_6,n_8\}\}$$

$$R_{NS}^{\alpha} = \{\{n_0,,n_1,n_4,n_7\},\{n_2,n_6,n_8\},\{n_3,n_5,n_9\}\}$$

For example, from the equivalence class R_{RREQ}^{α}, it can be observed that the attribute RREQ has been classified into four categories such as $\{\{n_2,n_4\}, \{n_1,n_7\}, \{n_0,n_6,n_8\},$ and $\{n_3,n_5,n_9\}\}$, and we categorize these classes into low, medium, high, and very high, respectively. Similarly, we categorized RREP (low, medium, high);, CTRL-PKT (low, medium, high); PKT-DROP (low, medium, high,

Table 21.13 Nodes Routing Information

Node	RREQ	RREP	CTRL-PKT	PKT-DROP	NS
n_0	37	24	168	31	5
n_1	18	12	110	19	5
n_2	11	20	153	45	10
n_3	52	38	231	62	15
n_4	13	15	147	23	5
n_5	63	42	315	63	15
n_6	42	64	361	79	10
n_7	22	14	170	23	5
n_8	32	56	421	77	10
n_9	57	47	264	39	15

Table 21.14 Fuzzy Proximity Relation for RREQ

	n_0	n_1	n_2	n_3	n_4	n_5	n_6	n_7	n_8	n_9
n_0	1.00	0.82	0.72	0.91	0.76	0.87	0.96	0.87	0.96	0.89
n_1	0.82	1.00	0.87	0.75	0.91	0.72	0.80	0.95	0.86	0.74
n_2	0.72	0.87	1.00	0.67	0.95	0.64	0.70	0.83	0.75	0.66
n_3	0.91	0.75	0.67	1.00	0.70	0.95	0.94	0.79	0.88	0.97
n_4	0.76	0.91	0.95	0.70	1.00	0.67	0.73	0.87	0.78	0.68
n_5	0.87	0.72	0.64	0.95	0.67	1.00	0.90	0.75	0.83	0.97
n_6	0.96	0.80	0.70	0.94	0.73	0.90	1.00	0.84	0.93	0.92
n_7	0.87	0.95	0.83	0.79	0.87	0.75	0.84	1.00	0.90	0.77
n_8	0.96	0.86	0.75	0.88	0.78	0.83	0.93	0.90	1.00	0.85
n_9	0.89	0.74	0.66	0.97	0.68	0.97	0.92	0.77	0.85	1.00

very high); and NS (low, medium, high) with proper notions. Now, we impose an order relation on Table 21.13, and the obtained ordered routing information is presented in Table 21.19. We have assigned a priority order to each class, like very high, high, medium, and low as 1, 2, 3, and 4, respectively. We computed the total weights, and the link failures of each node are presented in Table 21.20. The analysis on data classifications can also be done using a Bayesian classifier. Since the classification of data has been done using fuzzy proximity relation with ordering, we now impose a naïve Bayesian classifier to predict the hidden association of routing attributes using Table 21.20 as training data. The outcome of this analysis provides further knowledge on

Table 21.15 Fuzzy Proximity Relation for RREP

	n_0	n_1	n_2	n_3	n_4	n_5	n_6	n_7	n_8	n_9
n_0	1.00	0.83	0.95	0.88	0.88	0.86	0.77	0.86	0.80	0.83
n_1	0.83	1.00	0.87	0.74	0.94	0.72	0.65	0.96	0.67	0.70
n_2	0.95	0.87	1.00	0.84	0.92	0.82	0.73	0.91	0.76	0.79
n_3	0.88	0.74	0.84	1.00	0.78	0.97	0.87	0.76	0.90	0.94
n_4	0.88	0.94	0.92	0.78	1.00	0.76	0.68	0.98	0.71	0.74
n_5	0.86	0.72	0.82	0.97	0.76	1.00	0.89	0.75	0.92	0.97
n_6	0.77	0.65	0.73	0.87	0.68	0.89	1.00	0.67	0.96	0.92
n_7	0.86	0.96	0.91	0.76	0.98	0.75	0.67	1.00	0.70	0.72
n_8	0.80	0.67	0.76	0.90	0.71	0.92	0.96	0.70	1.00	0.95
n_9	0.83	0.70	0.79	0.94	0.74	0.97	0.92	0.72	0.95	1.00

Table 21.16 Fuzzy Proximity Relation for CTRL-PKT

	n_0	n_1	n_2	n_3	n_4	n_5	n_6	n_7	n_8	n_9
n_0	1.00	0.89	0.97	0.92	0.96	0.84	0.81	0.99	0.78	0.88
n_1	0.89	1.00	0.91	0.82	0.92	0.75	0.73	0.89	0.70	0.79
n_2	0.97	0.91	1.00	0.89	0.99	0.82	0.79	0.97	0.76	0.86
n_3	0.92	0.82	0.89	1.00	0.88	0.92	0.89	0.92	0.85	0.96
n_4	0.96	0.92	0.99	0.88	1.00	0.81	0.78	0.96	0.75	0.85
n_5	0.84	0.75	0.82	0.92	0.81	1.00	0.96	0.85	0.92	0.95
n_6	0.81	0.73	0.79	0.89	0.78	0.96	1.00	0.82	0.96	0.92
n_7	0.99	0.89	0.97	0.92	0.96	0.85	0.82	1.00	0.78	0.89
n_8	0.78	0.70	0.76	0.85	0.75	0.92	0.96	0.78	1.00	0.88
n_9	0.88	0.79	0.86	0.96	0.85	0.95	0.92	0.89	0.88	1.00

routing nodes, and it may also help to make a proper decision during the routing process. For example, we consider the attribute values E = {RREQ = high, RREP = medium, CTRL-PKT = high, PKT-DROP = high, NS = high} to predict the possibilities of link failure (PLF). Let us consider E = {e_1,e_2,e_3,e_4,e_5}, where e_1 is RREQ = high; e_2 is RREP = medium; e_3 is CTRL-PKT = high; e_4 is PKT-DROP = high; and e_5 is NS = high. From Table 21.20, it is clear that the decision attribute PLF has three classes such as V_1 = low, V_2 = medium, and V_3 = high. But $P(e_i | V_1) = 0$ for i = 1,2,3,4,5 with $P(V_1)$ = 3/10; Hence, it dominates the classification of future instances as a Bayesian classifier multiplies $P(e_i | V_1)$ together. Therefore, by using m-estimate, we obtain $P(V_1)$ = 0.0002907, $P(V_2)$ = 0.0016410, and $P(V_3)$ = 0.011396. From the previous computation we can

Table 21.17 Fuzzy Proximity Relation for PKT-DROP

	n_0	n_1	n_2	n_3	n_4	n_5	n_6	n_7	n_8	n_9
n_0	1.00	0.88	0.90	0.83	0.90	0.82	0.78	0.92	0.78	0.94
n_1	0.88	1.00	0.79	0.73	0.97	0.73	0.69	0.95	0.69	0.82
n_2	0.90	0.79	1.00	0.92	0.81	0.91	0.86	0.83	0.86	0.96
n_3	0.83	0.73	0.92	1.00	0.75	0.99	0.93	0.77	0.94	0.88
n_4	0.90	0.97	0.81	0.75	1.00	0.75	0.71	0.97	0.71	0.85
n_5	0.82	0.73	0.91	0.99	0.75	1.00	0.94	0.76	0.95	0.88
n_6	0.78	0.69	0.86	0.93	0.71	0.94	1.00	0.72	0.99	0.83
n_7	0.92	0.95	0.83	0.77	0.97	0.76	0.72	1.00	0.73	0.87
n_8	0.78	0.69	0.86	0.94	0.71	0.95	0.99	0.73	1.00	0.83
n_9	0.94	0.82	0.96	0.88	0.85	0.88	0.83	0.87	0.83	1.00

Table 21.18   Fuzzy Proximity Relation for NS

	n_0	n_1	n_2	n_3	n_4	n_5	n_6	n_7	n_8	n_9
n_0	1.00	1.00	0.83	0.75	1.00	0.75	0.83	1.00	0.83	0.75
n_1	1.00	1.00	0.83	0.75	1.00	0.75	0.83	1.00	0.83	0.75
n_2	0.83	0.83	1.00	0.90	0.83	0.90	1.00	0.83	1.00	0.90
n_3	0.75	0.75	0.90	1.00	0.75	1.00	0.90	0.75	0.90	1.00
n_4	1.00	1.00	0.83	0.75	1.00	0.75	0.83	1.00	0.83	0.75
n_5	0.75	0.75	0.90	1.00	0.75	1.00	0.90	0.75	0.90	1.00
n_6	0.83	0.83	1.00	0.90	0.83	0.90	1.00	0.83	1.00	0.90
n_7	1.00	1.00	0.83	0.75	1.00	0.75	0.83	1.00	0.83	0.75
n_8	0.83	0.83	1.00	0.90	0.83	0.90	1.00	0.83	1.00	0.90
n_9	0.75	0.75	0.90	1.00	0.75	1.00	0.90	0.75	0.90	1.00

Table 21.19   Ordered Routing Information

Node	RREQ	RREP	CTRL-PKT	PKT-DROP	NS
n_0	High	Medium	Medium	Medium	Low
n_1	Medium	Low	Low	Low	Low
n_2	Low	Medium	Medium	High	Medium
n_3	Very high	High	High	Very high	High
n_4	Low	Low	Medium	Low	Low
n_5	Very high	High	High	Very high	High
n_6	High	High	High	Very high	Medium
n_7	Medium	Low	Medium	Low	Low
n_8	High	High	High	Very high	Medium
n_9	Very high	High	High	High	High

Notes: $\prec_{RREQ}$: low $\prec$ medium $\prec$ high $\prec$ very high;

$\prec_{RREP}$: low $\prec$ medium $\prec$ high;

$\prec_{CTRL-PKT}$: low $\prec$ medium $\prec$ high;

$\prec_{PKT-DROP}$: low $\prec$ medium $\prec$ high $\prec$ very high;

$\prec_{NS}$: low $\prec$ medium $\prec$ high.

Table 21.20 Possibilities of Link Failure on Routing Nodes

Node	RREQ	RREP	CTRL-PKT	PKT-DROP	NS	Total Weight	PLF
n_0	High	Medium	Medium	Medium	Low	15	Medium
n_1	Medium	Low	Low	Low	Low	19	Low
n_2	Low	Medium	Medium	High	Medium	15	Medium
n_3	Very high	High	High	Very high	High	9	High
n_4	Low	Low	Medium	Low	Low	19	Low
n_5	Very high	High	High	Very high	High	8	High
n_6	High	High	High	Very high	Medium	10	High
n_7	Medium	Low	Medium	Low	Low	18	Low
n_8	High	High	High	Very high	Medium	10	High
n_9	Very high	High	High	High	High	9	High

observe that $P(V_3)$ is maximum. Hence, it is an axiomatic fact that this hidden association of attribute values belongs to the decision class $V_3 = high$. That is, we can also interpret that *if RREQ is high, RREP is medium, CTRL-PKT is high, PKT-DROP is high, and NS is high, then PLF would be high*. We have computed some of the hidden associations, and their corresponding decision values are listed in Table 21.21.

Table 21.21 Prediction of Hidden Associations

HAS	RREQ	RREP	CTRL-PKT	PKT-DROP	NS	PLF
1	Very high	High	Medium	High	Medium	High
2	Low	Medium	Medium	Low	Low	Low
3	High	Medium	High	High	Medium	High
4	High	Low	Medium	High	Medium	Medium
5	Low	Low	Medium	Medium	Low	Low
6	Very high	Medium	Medium	High	High	High
7	Low	Medium	Medium	Medium	Medium	Medium
8	Low	Low	Medium	Low	Medium	Low
9	Low	Medium	High	Medium	Medium	Medium
10	Very high	Medium	Medium	Very high	High	High

21.6.3 Using Formal Concept Analysis

Data have been collected from a network that consists of 50 mobile nodes through a promiscuous mode, at a particular instance of time, and we have randomly selected the 10 nodes that are involved in a *dynamic source routing* process at various speed levels (5 to 20 m/s) in a random movement. The collected data are presented in Table 21.22.

On considering the almost similarity of 95%, that is, $\alpha \geq 0.95$, it is observed from Table 21.23 that $r(n_0,n_0) = 1$; $r(n_0,n_1) = 0.95$; $r(n_0,n_3) = 0.96$; $r(n_0,n_6) = 0.95$; and $r(n_0,n_9) = 0.97$. Therefore, the nodes $\{n_0,n_1,n_3,n_6,n_9\}$ belong to one class, and they are α-identical. Similarly, the other classes can

Table 21.22 Nodes Routing Information

Node	ERR-PKT	PKT-LOST	CTRL-PKT	PKT-DROP	NS
n_0	34	62	190	36	10
n_1	28	54	292	33	12
n_2	15	22	97	24	5
n_3	29	70	331	38	11
n_4	13	26	127	18	7
n_5	46	90	428	64	17
n_6	40	115	518	49	19
n_7	48	99	566	56	16
n_8	18	18	116	28	6
n_9	31	66	220	40	9

Table 21.23 Fuzzy Proximity Relation for ERR-PKT

	n_0	n_1	n_2	n_3	n_4	n_5	n_6	n_7	n_8	n_9
n_0	1.00	0.95	0.80	0.96	0.77	0.92	0.94	0.91	0.84	0.97
n_1	0.95	1.00	0.84	0.99	0.81	0.87	0.90	0.86	0.89	0.97
n_2	0.80	0.84	1.00	0.84	0.96	0.74	0.76	0.73	0.95	0.82
n_3	0.96	0.99	0.84	1.00	0.80	0.88	0.90	0.87	0.88	0.98
n_4	0.77	0.81	0.96	0.80	1.00	0.72	0.73	0.71	0.91	0.79
n_5	0.92	0.87	0.74	0.88	0.72	1.00	0.97	0.98	0.78	0.90
n_6	0.94	0.90	0.76	0.90	0.73	0.97	1.00	0.96	0.80	0.92
n_7	0.91	0.86	0.73	0.87	0.71	0.98	0.96	1.00	0.77	0.89
n_8	0.84	0.89	0.95	0.88	0.91	0.78	0.80	0.77	1.00	0.86
n_9	0.97	0.97	0.82	0.98	0.79	0.90	0.92	0.89	0.86	1.00

also be obtained from Table 21.23. The equivalence class generated from Tables 21.23 through Table 21.27 is given as follows:

$$R_{ERR-PKT}^{\alpha} = \{\{n_0, n_1, n_3, n_9\}, \{n_2, n_4, n_8,\}, \{n_5, n_6, n_7\}\}$$

$$R_{PKT-LOST}^{\alpha} = \{\{n_0, n_1, n_3, n_9\}, \{n_2, n_4, n_8,\}, \{n_5, n_6, n_7\}\}$$

$$R_{CTRL-PKT}^{\alpha} = \{\{n_0, n_9\}, \{n_1, n_3\}, \{n_2, n_4, n_8\}, \{n_5, n_6, n_7\}\}$$

$$R_{PKT-DROP}^{\alpha} = \{\{n_0, n_1, n_2, n_3, n_8, n_9\}, \{n_4\}, \{n_5, n_6, n_7\}\}$$

$$R_{NS}^{\alpha} = \{\{n_0, n_1, n_3, n_9\}, \{n_2, n_4, n_8,\}, \{n_5, n_6, n_7\}\}$$

Table 21.24 Fuzzy Proximity Relation for PKT-LOST

	n_0	n_1	n_2	n_3	n_4	n_5	n_6	n_7	n_8	n_9
n_0	1.00	0.96	0.76	0.96	0.79	0.90	0.85	0.88	0.72	0.98
n_1	0.96	1.00	0.78	0.93	0.82	0.87	0.81	0.85	0.75	0.95
n_2	0.76	0.78	1.00	0.73	0.95	0.69	0.66	0.68	0.95	0.75
n_3	0.96	0.93	0.73	1.00	0.77	0.93	0.87	0.91	0.70	0.98
n_4	0.79	0.82	0.95	0.77	1.00	0.72	0.68	0.70	0.90	0.78
n_5	0.90	0.87	0.69	0.93	0.72	1.00	0.93	0.97	0.66	0.92
n_6	0.85	0.81	0.66	0.87	0.68	0.93	1.00	0.96	0.63	0.86
n_7	0.88	0.89	0.68	0.91	0.70	0.97	0.96	1.00	0.65	0.90
n_8	0.72	0.75	0.95	0.70	0.90	0.66	0.63	0.65	1.00	0.71
n_9	0.98	0.95	0.75	0.98	0.78	0.92	0.86	0.90	0.71	1.00

Table 21.25 Fuzzy Proximity Relation for CTRL-PKT

	n_0	n_1	n_2	n_3	n_4	n_5	n_6	n_7	n_8	n_9
n_0	1.00	0.89	0.83	0.86	0.90	0.80	0.76	0.75	0.87	0.96
n_1	0.89	1.00	0.74	0.96	0.80	0.90	0.86	0.84	0.78	0.92
n_2	0.83	0.74	1.00	0.72	0.93	0.68	0.65	0.64	0.95	0.80
n_3	0.86	0.96	0.72	1.00	0.77	0.93	0.88	0.86	0.75	0.89
n_4	0.90	0.80	0.93	0.77	1.00	0.72	0.69	0.68	0.97	0.86
n_5	0.80	0.90	0.68	0.93	0.72	1.00	0.95	0.93	0.71	0.83
n_6	0.76	0.86	0.65	0.88	0.69	0.95	1.00	0.97	0.68	0.79
n_7	0.75	0.84	0.64	0.86	0.68	0.93	0.97	1.00	0.67	0.77
n_8	0.87	0.78	0.95	0.75	0.97	0.71	0.68	0.67	1.00	0.84
n_9	0.96	0.92	0.80	0.89	0.86	0.83	0.79	0.77	0.84	1.00

Table 21.26   Fuzzy Proximity Relation for PKT-DROP

	n_0	n_1	n_2	n_3	n_4	n_5	n_6	n_7	n_8	n_9
n_0	1.00	0.97	0.90	0.98	0.83	0.86	0.92	0.89	0.93	0.97
n_1	0.97	1.00	0.92	0.96	0.85	0.84	0.90	0.87	0.95	0.95
n_2	0.90	0.92	1.00	0.88	0.92	0.77	0.82	0.80	0.96	0.87
n_3	0.98	0.96	0.88	1.00	0.82	0.87	0.93	0.90	0.92	0.98
n_4	0.83	0.85	0.92	0.82	1.00	0.71	0.76	0.74	0.89	0.81
n_5	0.86	0.84	0.77	0.87	0.71	1.00	0.93	0.96	0.80	0.88
n_6	0.92	0.90	0.82	0.93	0.76	0.93	1.00	0.96	0.86	0.94
n_7	0.89	0.87	0.80	0.90	0.74	0.96	0.96	1.00	0.83	0.91
n_8	0.93	0.95	0.96	0.92	0.89	0.80	0.86	0.83	1.00	0.91
n_9	0.97	0.95	0.87	0.98	0.81	0.88	0.94	0.91	0.91	1.00

For example, from the equivalence class $R^\alpha_{CTRL-PKT}$, it is observed that the attribute CTRL-PKT has been classified into four categories such as $\{n_2,n_4,n_8\}$, $\{n_0,n_9\}$, $\{n_1,n_3\}$, and $\{n_5,n_6,n_7\}$. We categorize these classes into low, medium, high, and very high, respectively. Similarly, we categorized the other equivalence classes with proper notions. Now we impose an order relation on Table 21.22, and we have obtained ordered routing information, which is presented in Table 21.28. We have assigned weights to each class and computed the total weights, and the confidence level of each node is presented in Table 21.29. It is important to note that some of the nodes have the same weights, which indicates that these nodes cannot be distinguished with available attributes and their values. Thus, it requires further analysis on routing nodes and its attributes. To explore further knowledge on routing nodes, we have introduced FCA to obtain a concept lattice,

Table 21.27   Fuzzy Proximity Relation for NS

	n_0	n_1	n_2	n_3	n_4	n_5	n_6	n_7	n_8	n_9
n_0	1.00	0.95	0.83	0.97	0.91	0.87	0.84	0.88	0.87	0.97
n_1	0.95	1.00	0.79	0.97	0.86	0.91	0.88	0.92	0.83	0.92
n_2	0.83	0.79	1.00	0.81	0.91	0.72	0.70	0.73	0.95	0.85
n_3	0.97	0.97	0.81	1.00	0.88	0.89	0.86	0.90	0.85	0.95
n_4	0.91	0.86	0.91	0.88	1.00	0.79	0.76	0.80	0.96	0.93
n_5	0.87	0.91	0.72	0.89	0.79	1.00	0.97	0.98	0.76	0.84
n_6	0.84	0.88	0.70	0.86	0.76	0.97	1.00	0.95	0.74	0.82
n_7	0.88	0.92	0.73	0.90	0.80	0.98	0.95	1.00	0.77	0.86
n_8	0.87	0.83	0.95	0.85	0.96	0.76	0.74	0.77	1.00	0.90
n_9	0.97	0.92	0.85	0.95	0.93	0.84	0.82	0.86	0.90	1.00

Table 21.28 Ordered Routing Information

Node	ERR-PKT	PKT-LOST	CTRL-PKT	PKT-DROP	NS
n_0	Medium	Medium	Medium	Medium	Medium
n_1	Medium	Medium	High	Medium	Medium
n_2	Low	Low	Low	Medium	Low
n_3	Medium	Medium	High	Medium	Medium
n_4	Low	Low	Low	Low	Low
n_5	High	High	Very high	High	High
n_6	High	High	Very high	High	High
n_7	High	High	Very high	High	High
n_8	Low	Low	Low	Medium	Low
n_9	Medium	Medium	Medium	Medium	Medium

Notes: $\prec_{ERR-PKT}$: low $\prec$ medium $\prec$ high;

$\prec_{PKT-LOST}$: low $\prec$ medium $\prec$ high;

$\prec_{CTRL-PKT}$: low $\prec$ medium $\prec$ high $\prec$ very high;

$\prec_{PKT-DROP}$: low $\prec$ medium $\prec$ high;

$\prec_{NS}$: low $\prec$ medium $\prec$ high.

Table 21.29 Nodes' Confidence Level

Node	ERR-PKT	PKT-LOST	CTRL-PKT	PKT-DROP	NS	Total Weight	Confidence Level
n_0	Medium	Medium	Medium	Medium	Medium	15	Average
n_1	Medium	Medium	High	Medium	Medium	14	Average
n_2	Low	Low	Low	Medium	Low	19	Good
n_3	Medium	Medium	High	Medium	Medium	14	Average
n_4	Low	Low	Low	Low	Low	20	Good
n_5	High	High	Very high	High	High	9	Poor
n_6	High	High	Very high	High	High	9	Poor
n_7	High	High	Very high	High	High	9	Poor
n_8	Low	Low	Low	Medium	Low	19	Good
n_9	Medium	Medium	Medium	Medium	Medium	15	Average

Table 21.30   Context Table of Routing Information System

Node	a_1			a_2			a_3				a_4			a_5		
	a_{11}	a_{12}	a_{13}	a_{21}	a_{22}	a_{23}	a_{31}	a_{32}	a_{33}	a_{34}	a_{41}	a_{42}	a_{43}	a_{51}	a_{52}	a_{53}
n_0		×			×		×					×			×	
n_1		×			×				×			×			×	
n_2	×			×			×					×		×		
n_3		×			×				×			×			×	
n_4	×			×			×				×			×		
n_5			×			×				×			×			×
n_6			×			×				×			×			×
n_7			×			×				×			×			×
n_8	×			×			×					×		×		
n_9		×			×		×					×			×	

Notes: $V_{RREQ(a_1)} = \{\text{low}(a_{11}), \text{medium}(a_{12}), \text{high}(a_{13})\}$

$V_{RREP(a_2)} = \{\text{low}(a_{11}), \text{medium}(a_{12}), \text{high}(a_{13})\}$

$V_{CTRL-PKT(a_3)} = \{\text{low}(a_{31}), \text{medium}(a_{32}), \text{high}(a_{33}), \text{very high}(a_{34})\}$

$V_{PKT-DROP(a_4)} = \{\text{low}(a_{11}), \text{medium}(a_{12}), \text{high}(a_{13})\}$

$V_{NS(a_5)} = \{\text{low}(a_{11}), \text{medium}(a_{12}), \text{high}(a_{13})\}$

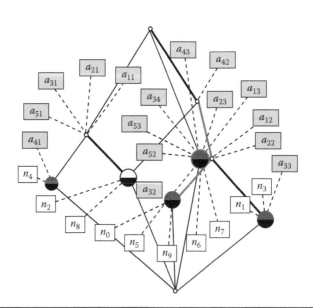

Figure 21.2   Lattice structure of routing information system.

Table 21.31   Attribute Implication Derived from Table 21.30

Sr. no.	Implication	Support	Sr. no.	Implication	Support
1	$a_{11} \Rightarrow a_{21}a_{31}a_{51}$	3	11	$a_{53} \Rightarrow a_{13}a_{23}a_{34}a_{43}$	3
2	$a_{12} \Rightarrow a_{22}a_{42}a_{52}$	4	12	$a_{13} \Rightarrow a_{23}a_{34}a_{43}a_{53}$	3
3	$a_{21} \Rightarrow a_{11}a_{31}a_{51}$	3	13	$a_{23} \Rightarrow a_{13}a_{34}a_{43}a_{53}$	3
4	$a_{22} \Rightarrow a_{12}a_{42}a_{52}$	4	14	$a_{34} \Rightarrow a_{13}a_{23}a_{43}a_{53}$	3
5	$a_{31} \Rightarrow a_{11}a_{21}a_{51}$	3	15	$a_{43} \Rightarrow a_{13}a_{23}a_{34}a_{53}$	3
6	$a_{32} \Rightarrow a_{12}a_{22}a_{42}a_{52}$	2			
7	$a_{33} \Rightarrow a_{12}a_{22}a_{42}a_{52}$	2			
8	$a_{41} \Rightarrow a_{11}a_{21}a_{31}a_{51}$	1			
9	$a_{51} \Rightarrow a_{11}a_{21}a_{31}$	3			
10	$a_{52} \Rightarrow a_{12}a_{22}a_{42}$	4			

attribute implication, and the importance of attributes that have been considered for the routing process. The context table of routing information is presented in Table 21.30. Figure 21.2 shows the concept lattice structure obtained by applying FCA on Table 21.30. From Figure 21.2, we can understand that the lattice structure is of height 4 and contains 10 concepts with 14 edges. Any two connected nodes in the concept lattice represent superconcept and subconcept. The upper one is superconcept, and the lower one is subconcept. The red color represents the nodes n_5, n_6, and n_7, which have common attributes and edges. There are 15 implications, derived from the context Table 21.30 using a Duquenne–Guigues (DG) base, which is presented in Table 21.31. The main advantage of DG is that it produces a minimal possible number of implications with 100% confidence. From attribute implication (Table 21.31), we observed that all the attributes we have considered for the routing process are significant.

21.7   Conclusion

The performance of the MANET depends on the behaviors of the routing nodes, and the behavior could be quantified with the help of routing information. Hence, it is essential to obtain knowledge on routing nodes for efficient communication. Classification of routing nodes and prediction of their routing behavior would help us to design and develop an effective routing model for MANETs. Keeping this in view, we have proposed a model that uses association rule, Bayesian classifier, and FCA with fuzzy proximity relation and ordering. We observed that the values in the routing information are almost identical. Hence, we have classified the routing nodes based on almost similarity using fuzzy proximity relation, and this result induces an almost-equivalence class of routing nodes. On imposing order relation on this equivalence classes, we have obtained ordered categorical classes of routing nodes, which provide further knowledge on routing nodes. We have computed the confidence level and PLFs using ordered categorical classes of routing nodes by assigning the priority order for each categorical class. We have also predicted the hidden association of routing attributes using a Bayesian classifier. The routing attributes' implications and dependence have been studied using FCA. The main observations of our analysis based on our proposed model are summarized as follows:

- The behaviors or characteristics of routing nodes can be recognized with the help of a routing information system, and the values in the routing information system are found to be almost identical.
- Since the values of a routing information system are almost identical, we have generalized Pawlak's indiscernibility relation into almost indiscernibility relation to characterize the behavior of routing nodes.
- The ordering and overall ordering of the nodes can be possible with single and multiple attribute values of a routing information system using ordering rules. That is, nodes can be ordered based on ordering rules.
- The behaviors or characteristics of routing nodes could be identified through granulation and association.
- We have used a Bayesian classifier to predict the hidden behaviors of routing nodes.
- We have used FCA to analyze the attributes of routing nodes and its implications, which provide further knowledge on routing nodes and their attributes.
- Finally, classification, analysis, and prediction of routing node behavior could lead to a proper data analysis and decision making through which an effective routing model can be developed for MANETs.

Acknowledgments

The authors are thankful to the management of Vellore Institute of Technology (VIT) University for their great support and encouragement. The research members of the Centre for Ambient Intelligence and Advanced Networking Research Lab (C-AMIR), VIT University, India, are greatly acknowledged.

References

Abolhasan, M., Wysocki, T., Dutkiewicz, E. (2004) "A review of routing protocols for mobile ad hoc networks," *Ad Hoc Networks*, Vol. 2, No. 1, pp. 1–22.

Abusalah, L., Khokhar, A., Guizani, M. (2008) "A survey of secure mobile ad hoc routing protocols," *IEEE Communications Surveys and Tutorials*, Vol. 10, No. 4, pp. 78–93.

Acharjya, D.P., Ezhilarasi, L. (2011) "A knowledge mining model for ranking institutions using rough computing with ordering rules and formal concept analysis," *International Journal of Computer Science Issues*, Vol. 8, No. 2, pp. 417–425.

Acharjya, D.P., Debasrita, R., Rahaman, Md. A. (2012) "Prediction of missing associations using rough computing and Bayesian classification," *International Journal of Intelligent Systems and Applications*, Vol. 4, No. 11, pp. 1–13.

Arora, V., Rama Krishna, C. (2010) "Performance evaluation of routing protocols for MANETs under different traffic conditions," *2nd Int. Conf. on Computer Engineering and Technology ICCET-2010*, Vol. 6, pp. 79–84.

Aswanikumar, Ch., Sumangali, K. (2012) "Performance evaluation of employees of an organization using formal concept analysis," *Int. Conf. on Pattern Recognition, Informatics and Medical Engineering, (PRIME-2012)*, pp. 94–98.

Bargiela, A., Pedrycz, W. (2006) "The roots of granular computing," *IEEE Int. Conference on Granular Computing*, pp. 806–809.

Chlamtac, I., Conti, M., Liu, J.J.N. (2003) "Mobile ad hoc networking: Imperatives and challenges," *Ad Hoc Networks*, Vol. 1, No. 1, pp. 13–64.

Cho, J.-H., Swami, A., Chen, I.-R. (2011) "A survey on trust management for mobile ad hoc networks," *IEEE Communications Surveys and Tutorials*, Vol. 13, No. 4, pp. 562–583.

Han, J., Kamber, M. (2006) *Data Mining and Concepts and Techniques*. Elsevier, New York.

Hu, Y., Perrig, A. (2004) "A survey of secure wireless ad hoc routing," *Security and Privacy, IEEE*, Vol. 2, No. 2, pp. 28–39.

Kumar, D., Srivastava, A., Gupta, S.C. (2012) "Performance comparison of pro-active and reactive routing protocols for MANET," *Int. Conf. on Computing, Communication and Applications ICCCA-2012*, pp. 1–4.

Kwon, O., Kim, J. (2009) "Concept lattices for visualizing and generating user profiles for context-aware service recommendations," *Expert Systems with Applications*, Vol. 36, pp. 1893–1902.

Liang, J.Y., Shi, Z.Z. (2004) "The information entropy, rough entropy and knowledge granulation in rough set theory," *International Journal of Uncertainty, Fuzziness and Knowledge-Based Systems*, Vol. 12, No. 1, pp. 37–46.

Lin, J.H., Haug, P.J. (2008) "Exploiting missing clinical data in Bayesian network modeling for predicting medical problems," *Journal of Biomedical Informatics*, Elsevier, Vol. 41, No. 1, pp. 1–14.

Marina, M.K., Das, S.R. (2005) "Routing in mobile ad hoc networks," *Ad Hoc Networks: Technologies and Protocols*, Chapter 3. Springer, Science+Businesss Media, Inc., Boston.

Mitchell, T.M. (1997) *Machine Learning*. McGraw Hill, New York.

Pawlak, Z. (1991) *Rough Sets: Theoretical Aspects of Reasoning about Data*. Kluwer Academic Publishers, Dordrecht, Netherlands.

Priss, U. (2006) "Formal concept analysis in information science," *Annual Review of Information Science and Technology*, Vol. 40, No. 1, pp. 521–543.

Royer, E.M., Toh, C.K. (1999) "A review of current routing protocols for ad hoc mobile wireless networks," *IEEE Personal Communications*, Vol. 6, No. 2, pp. 46–55.

Saeed, N.H., Abbod, M.F., Al-Raweshidy, H.S. (2012) "MANET routing protocols taxonomy," *Int. Conf. on Future Communication Networks (ICFCN-2012)*, pp. 123–128.

Senthilkumar, K., Acharjya, D.P., Thangavelu, A. (2013a) "Trust evaluation using fuzzy proximity relation with ordering for MANET," *International Journal of Trust Management in Computing and Communications*, Vol. 1, No. 2, pp. 105–120.

Senthilkumar, K., Thangavelu, A. (2013b) "Classification and prediction of routing nodes behavior in MANET using fuzzy proximity relation and ordering with Bayesian classifier," *IEEE Int. Conf. on Pattern Recognition, Informatics and Mobile Engineering, PRIME-2013*, pp. 454–460.

Senthilkumar, K., Thangavelu, A. (2013c) "Granular computing using association rules on routing information of MANET with fuzzy proximity relation and ordering," *Elsevier Int. Conf. on Recent Trends in Commu. and Computer Networks, ComNet-2013*, pp. 18–26.

Senthilkumar, K., Thangavelu, A. (2013d) "Classification and analysis on routing nodes in MANET using fuzzy proximity relation with ordering and formal concept analysis," *Elsevier Int. Conf. on CNC & CSEE, AIM & CCPE, CSA & SPC*, pp. 575–582.

Tripathy, B.K., Acharjya, D.P. (2011) "Association rule granulation using rough sets on intuitionistic fuzzy approximation spaces and granular computing," *Anale. Seria Informatica. Vol. IX, Fasc. 1*, pp. 125–144.

Venter, F.J., Oosthuizen, G.D., Ross, J.D. (1997) "Knowledge discovery in databases using concept lattices," *Expert Systems with Applications*, Vol. 13, No. 4, pp. 259–264.

Yao, Y.Y. (2000) "Granular computing: Basic issues and possible solutions," *Proc. of the Fifth Joint Conf. on Information Sciences*, pp. 186–189.

Yao, Y.Y. (2001) "Information granulation and rough set approximation," *International Journal of Intelligent Systems*, Vol. 6, No. 1, pp. 87–104.

Yi, L., Zhai, Y., Wang, Y., Yuan, J., You, I. (2012) "Impacts of internal network contexts on performance of MANET routing protocols: A case study," *Sixth Int. Conf. on Innovative Mobile and Internet Services in Ubiquitous Computing (IMIS-2012)*, pp. 231–236.

Chapter 22

Implication of Feature Extraction Methods to Improve Performance of Hybrid Wavelet-ANN Rainfall–Runoff Model

Vahid Nourani, Tohid Rezapour Khanghah, and Aida Hosseini Baghanam

Contents

In rainfall–runoff modeling, the wavelet-based artificial neural network (WANN) model, which links wavelet transform to an artificial neural network (ANN) in order to capture multiscale features of the process as well as to forecast the runoff values, is a beneficial method. For any hydrological process with long-term historical data, which enjoys the WANN method as a modeling tool, numerous inputs should be imposed to ANNs in order to model the process. Applying numerous inputs, without paying attention to their importance in the model, may lead to essential decline in WANN model performance. Therefore, efficient methods are needed to determine dominant data as model inputs. In this chapter, two mathematical concepts (i.e., self-organizing maps [SOMs] and entropy) were used as feature extraction methods for modeling the rainfall–runoff process of the Delaney Creek and Payne Creek Subbasins located in Florida, USA, with distinct hydrogeomorphological characteristics. Firstly, in order to handle the multifrequency characteristic of the process, both rainfall and runoff time series were decomposed into several subseries by wavelet transform. Subsequently, dominant subseries were extracted via SOM- and entropy-based criteria to be imposed into a feed-forward neural network (FFNN) model to predict runoff values in daily and monthly scales. To have better interpretation about the model efficiency, the results of two proposed models (wavelet–SOM–FFNN [WSNN] and wavelet–entropy–FFNN [WENN]) were compared with autoregressive integrated moving average with exogenous input (ARIMAX) and ad hoc FFNN methods, without any data preprocessing. The results proved that conjunction of employed feature extraction methods and the WANN approach could improve model efficiency. In monthly modeling, the WSNN and WENN showed lower performance compared with daily models. This might be due to the few numbers of subseries utilized in monthly preprocessing, which SOMs could not organize properly, and in the WENN model, this might be due to involvement of more uncertainty in the monthly data, which could be distinguished via entropy, as a measure of randomness and uncertainty.

22.1 Introduction

Rainfall–runoff modeling is one of the most important topics in hydrology, which plays an essential function in water resource engineering. To implement the projects that are defined in city planning, land uses, water resource management, and environmental engineering, precise rainfall–runoff modeling role is inevitable. Therefore, many hydrological models have been developed in order to simulate such a complex process; in this way, Nourani et al. (2007) prepared a comprehensive classification of rainfall–runoff models.

Classic time series models like autoregressive integrated moving average with exogenous input (ARIMAX) are widely used for hydrological time series forecasting (Salas et al. 1980; Nourani et al. 2011). These kinds of models, which are basically linear, fail in competence, whereas the existing hydrological processes are embedded with high complexity, dynamism, and nonlinearity in both spatial and temporal scales. However, such models still may be employed for comparison purposes and for evaluation of the efficiency of the newly developed models.

Artificial neural networks (ANNs), as a self-learning and self-adaptive approximator, have grown great ability in modeling and forecasting nonlinear hydrologic time series. The ability of ANNs in relating input and output variables in complex systems without any need of prior knowledge about the physics of the process as well as its sufficiency in representing timescale variability has led to a tremendous surge in their usage for rainfall–runoff modeling (see, e.g., Hsu et al. 1995; Maier and Dandy 2000; Dawson and Wilby 2001; Jain and Srinivasulu 2006; Iliadis and Maris 2007; Nourani et al. 2009a, 2011, 2012). A review of ANN applications in hydrology in general and in rainfall–runoff modeling in particular has been presented by the American Society of Civil Engineering (ASCE 2000a) and Abrahart et al. (2012), respectively.

Despite the fact that ANN is a flexible tool for modeling hydrological time series, it includes some drawbacks while facing a high nonstationary signal of a hydrologic process, which involved seasonalities defined as simultaneous variations of time series data in several frequencies (varying from 1 day to several decades). In such cases, ANNs may not be able to deal with nonstationary data if proper preprocessing of the input or/and output data is not performed (Cannas et al. 2006). Wavelet transform as a preprocessing technique in signal processing can be used to eliminate shortcomings that cannot be dealt with by ANNs. Potency of the wavelet transform in decomposing nonstationary time series into subseries at different scales (levels) is helpful in better interpretation of the process, and it is widely applied to time series analysis of hydrological nonstationary signals (Adamowski 2008; Nourani et al. 2012; Sang 2012, 2013). Therefore, combination of ANNs with wavelet transform as a hybrid wavelet–ANN (WANN) model, which can explain simultaneously spectral and temporal information of the signal, creates an effective execution for prediction of hydrological processes. The WANN model was firstly proposed by Aussem et al. (1998) for financial time series forecasting. Cannas et al. (2006) investigated the effect of data preprocessing on the model performance using continuous and discrete wavelet transforms and data partitioning. The results showed that networks trained on preprocessed data performed better than networks trained on undecomposed, noisy, raw signals. There are several papers that report successful applications of the WANN model to different fields of hydrology (see, e.g., Partal and Kisi 2007; Partal and Cigizoglu 2008; Nourani et al. 2009a; Adamowski and Chan 2011; Rajaee et al. 2011). In the field of rainfall–runoff modeling, Remesan et al. (2009) apply wavelet transform joint to ANNs for runoff prediction. Nourani et al. (2009b) combine the wavelet analysis with the ANN concept to model the rainfall–runoff process and investigate the effect of the mother wavelet type on the model performance. Tiwari and Chatterjee (2010) develop a hybrid wavelet–bootstrap–ANN (WBANN) model to explore the effectiveness of wavelet and bootstrapping techniques for developing an accurate and reliable ANN model for hourly flood forecasting. The results revealed that the WBANN forecasting model with confidence intervals can improve the reliability of flood forecasting. Furthermore, Nourani et al. (2011) present a rainfall–runoff model by taking advantage of the wavelet preprocessing technique to handle the seasonal features of the process. Adamowski et al. (2012) develop multivariate adaptive regression spline, WANN, and regular ANN models for runoff forecasting. More recently, Nourani et al. (2013) evaluate the efficiency of the WANN model using wavelet-based time–space preprocessing on satellite data.

In any ANN-based modeling, some of the input variables may be correlated, be noisy, or have no significant relationship with output variables and are not equally informative. Therefore, one of the essential steps in the ANN development is to determine dominant input variables that are independent, are informative, and efficiently cover the proposed input domain. Although a lot of information is included in raw data, data preprocessing magnifies dominant features of the data, and consequently, the effect of data noise is diminished. More difficult learning, divergence, obscurity, and poor model accuracy are some shortcomings that come along with application of

ANNs if it is employed without a proper data preprocessing method. Besides, high dimensionality that rainfall–runoff modeling mostly includes slows the training and simulation of the process via the ANNs. Therefore, when prediction of a process includes long time series, the time required to perform the modeling becomes expensive. Similarly, the WANN method also suffers the short-comings involved in the ANN method. Although WANNs can efficiently model hydrological processes, selection of effective inputs for such a model is still a challenge for hydrologists, especially when several subseries at different levels are obtained via the wavelet analysis and should be imposed into the ANNs. Numerous available wavelet-based subseries as input variables cause to examine several combinations of input variables (i.e., $2^u - 1$ input combinations can be selected from u input variables) and to look for a robust technique to extract dominant input combination. For this purpose and as a classic methodology, usually the computed linear correlation coefficient between input and target time series is employed (see, e.g., Partal and Kisi 2007; Rajaee et al. 2011; Maheswaran and Khosa 2012). However, as criticized by Nourani et al. (2011, 2013), in spite of a weak linear relationship, a strong nonlinear relationship may exist between input and target time series. To address this issue, in this chapter, two kinds of data preprocessing methods based on clustering and information content concepts are applied to extract important features and inputs of the WANN method for rainfall–runoff modeling.

In the content of ANN-based hydrological modeling, clustering is usually employed for classification of data, stations, zones, etc. into some homogeneous classes (see, e.g., Wu et al. 2009; Nourani and Kalantari 2010; Chang et al. 2010; Tsai et al. 2012) and optimization of the model structure by selection of dominant and relevant inputs (Bowden et al. 2005). Self-organizing maps (SOMs) are a kind of an unsupervised ANN method, which have the authority to classify, cluster, estimate, predict, and mine the data (Kalteh et al. 2008). They are an effective tool to convert complex, nonlinear, statistical relationship between high-dimensional data items into simple, geometric relationship on a low-dimensional display, where similar variables are closer to each other than the more dissimilar variables. SOMs also help to better understand data relationships due to the capability of visualization of data vectors. A main characteristic of the SOM method is nonlinearity and topological preservation of the data structure through the algorithm (ASCE 2000b). A typical characteristic of a SOM is that the desired solution or targets are not given, and the network intelligently learns to cluster the data by different recognized patterns (Kalteh et al. 2008). The SOM method was originally proposed by Kohonen et al. (1984) in speech recognition. Since Chon et al. (1996) firstly applied the SOM to pattern benthic communities in streams, the SOM was used in water resource problems. Bowden et al. (2002) divided neural network data into training, testing, and validation subsets using the SOM. Lin and Chen (2006) used the SOM for identification of homogeneous regions in regional frequency analysis of rainfall data. They compared efficiency of the SOM with regard to K-means and Ward's methods in accurately determining clusters' membership. The results showed that the SOM can identify the homogeneous regions more accurately as compared to other two clustering methods. Lin and Wu (2007) presented a SOM-based approach to estimate design hyetographs of ungauged sites. They concluded that the performance of the approach was better than methods based on conventional clustering techniques. Kalteh and Berndtsson (2007) interpolated monthly precipitation values by the SOM and a multilayer perceptron (MLP) ANN and showed that the regionalization based on the SOM performed better than the MLP. Kalteh et al. (2008) reviewed the published applications of SOM to different fields of water resource engineering, and Cereghino and Park (2009) provided some additional inputs and further perspective to their review. Nourani et al. (2013) used a two-level SOM clustering technique to identify spatially homogeneous clusters of precipitation satellite data and to choose the most operative and effective data for a feed-forward neural network (FFNN) to model the rainfall–runoff process on daily and multistep-ahead timescales.

On the other hand, entropy as a nonlinear measure of information content can be useful in obviating the selection of effective inputs among huge numbers of wavelet-based subseries. Shannon entropy-based measures are applied in this study to extract dominant inputs of the WANN model for rainfall–runoff modeling. Since the entropy measures arbitrary dependencies between random variables, it is suitable to be applied to complex classification tasks, where methods based on linear relations are prone to mistakes. Entropy can be regarded as a measure of information, disorder, chaos, and uncertainty (Shannon 1948). As a mathematical study, Ebrahimi et al. (1999) examine the role of variance and entropy in ordering distributions and random prospects and conclude that unlike variance, which measures concentration only around the mean, entropy measures diffuseness of the probability density function irrespective of the location of concentration. The theory of entropy has been applied to a great variety of problems. Examples of such applications have been reported to determine infiltration capacity (Singh 2010), movement of soil moisture (Al-hamdan and Cruise 2010), distribution of velocity in water courses (Chiu 1987), and longitude river bed profile (Cao and Chang 1988). Amorocho and Espildora (1973) were probably the first ones who employed the concept of entropy in hydrological modeling. Caselton and Husain (1980), Husain (1989), and Krstanovic and Singh (1992a,b) were the other noteworthy pioneers who utilized the information content at different fields of hydrology. Kawachi et al. (2001) measured the uncertainty of the over-a-year rainfall apportionment by entropy and constructed an isoentropy map for Japan. Mishra et al. (2009) used the entropy method to quantify variability or disorder of spatiotemporal precipitation in Texas, USA. Nourani and Zanardo (2012) utilized entropy as a filtering approach to construct wavelet-based regularized sets of locally smoother topography. Alfonso et al. (2013) presented two methodologies to design discharge monitoring networks in rivers using optimization of information theory and also ranking information theory quantities. Harmancioglu and Singh (1998) and also Singh (1997, 2011) surveyed applications of the entropy concept to environmental and water resource problems. Although most applications of entropy theory in hydrology were allocated to handle uncertainties of hydrologic quantities and to model several water resource systems, May et al. (2008) focused on an input selection algorithm for ANN models and demonstrated the superior performance of this nonlinear measure in comparison to linear correlation-based techniques. The utilization of entropy as a feature extraction method for the WANN models used in hydrological simulations is quite a novel methodology presented in the current chapter. Thus, in order to model the rainfall–runoff process of the Delaney Creek and Payne Creek Subbasins located in Florida, with almost distinct hydrogeomorphological characteristics, two robust-intelligent algorithms are proposed by conjunction of an ANN to a SOM and entropy concepts. For this purpose, firstly, the wavelet transform is used to decompose the main rainfall–runoff time series in both daily and monthly timescales into several subseries. Then two different methods (i.e., SOM- and entropy-based methods) are used in order to choose independent and effective subseries as input data to an FFNN model. The purpose of the application of SOM and entropy concepts is not only to increase the accuracy of the modeling by reducing the dimension of the input data set and complexity of the model but also to have a physical insight into the process by extracting dominant seasonalities (features) of the process, in which the classic ANN models are usually unable to provide such a physical interpretation of the process. To evaluate the performance of the models, in daily and monthly scales, the proposed wavelet–SOM–FFNN (WSNN) and wavelet–entropy–FFNN (WENN) models are compared with the ad hoc FFNN and the classic linear ARIMAX method, without data preprocessing.

22.2 Methodology

22.2.1 WANN Method and Efficiency Criteria

The combination of an FFNN with wavelet transform as the hybrid WANN model, which can explain simultaneously spectral and temporal information of the signal, creates an effective implementation for prediction of hydrological processes (see, e.g., Adamowski and Chan 2011; Nourani et al. 2011, 2013).

Artificial intelligence–based techniques can diminish time-consuming trial–error procedure in order to optimize the model. An FFNN as an artificial intelligence approach can effectively deal with nonlinearity involved in the rainfall–runoff process.

The superiority of a WANN is related to its ability to extract the seasonalities and features of a hydrological process by passing the time series of the process through the wavelet transform. Subsequently, an FFNN assigns weights due to the importance of extracted features. Based on the schematic diagram in Figure 22.1, the WANN method goes through a two-step procedure. The first step employs wavelet transform as a temporal preprocessing method. In the second step, extracted features of the main time series are imposed into an FFNN in order to model the process.

For practical applications, hydrologists do not have at their disposal a continuous-time signal process but rather a discrete-time signal. A discrete mother wavelet has the form (Addison et al. 2001)

$$g_{m,n}(t) = \frac{1}{\sqrt{a_0^m}} g\left(\frac{t - nb_0 a_0^m}{a_0^m}\right)$$

(22.1)

where m and n are integers that control the wavelet dilation and translation, respectively; a_0 is a specified dilation step greater than 1; and b_0 is the location parameter and must be greater than zero. The most common and simplest choices for parameters are $a_0 = 2$ and $b_0 = 1$.

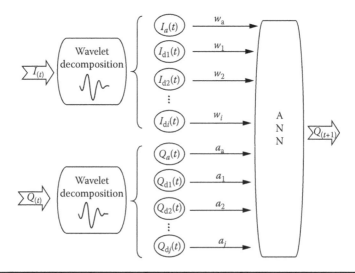

Figure 22.1 **Schematic of WANN for rainfall–runoff modeling.**

This power-of-two logarithmic scaling of the translation and dilation is known as the dyadic grid arrangement. The dyadic wavelet can be written in more compact notation as (Addison et al. 2001)

$$g_{m,n} = 2^{-m/2} g(2^{-m} i - n) \tag{22.2}$$

For a discrete time series, z_i, the dyadic wavelet transform becomes (Nourani et al. 2009a)

$$T_{m,n} = 2^{-m/2} \sum_{i=0}^{N-1} g(2^{-m} i - n) z_i \tag{22.3}$$

where $T_{m,n}$ is the wavelet coefficient for the discrete wavelet of scale $a = 2^m$ and location $b = 2^m n$. Equation 22.3 considers a finite time series, z_i, $i = 0, 1, 2,..., N-1$; and N is an integer power of 2 so that $N = 2^M$. This gives the ranges of m and n as $0 < n < 2^{M-m} - 1$ and $1 < m < M$, respectively.

The inverse discrete transform is given by (Nourani et al. 2009a)

$$z_i = \bar{T} + \sum_{m=1}^{M} \sum_{n=0}^{2^{M-m}-1} T_{m,n} 2^{-m/2} g(2^{-m} i - n) \tag{22.4}$$

or in a simple format as (Nourani et al. 2009a)

$$z_i = \bar{T} + \sum_{m=1}^{M} W_m(t) \tag{22.5}$$

in which $\bar{T}(t)$ is called the approximation subseries at level M, and $W_m(t)$ are the detailed subseries at levels $m = 1, 2,..., M$.

The wavelet coefficients, $W_m(t)$, provide the detailed series, which can capture small features of interpretational value in the data; the residual term, $\bar{T}$, represents the background information of the data. The normalized wavelet energy (E) is defined as (Mallat 1998)

$$E = \frac{|W_m(t)|^2}{\sum_{i=1}^{M} |W_i(t)|^2} \tag{22.6}$$

In the second step of modeling via a WANN (Figure 22.1), approximation and detailed subseries extracted using the wavelet transform (Equation 22.4) are imposed to an FFNN to model the process. In an FFNN, feed-forward back-propagation (FFBP) networks are common to engineers. It has been proved that the FFBP network model with three layers is satisfied for forecasting and simulating any engineering problem (Hornik et al. 1989; ASCE 2000b; Nourani et al. 2008).

As shown in Figure 22.2, three-layered FFNNs, which have been usually used in forecasting hydrologic time series, provide a general framework for representing nonlinear functional

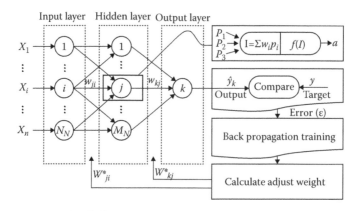

Figure 22.2 **Three-layered feed-forward neural network with BP training algorithm.**

mapping between a set of input and output variables. Three-layered FFNNs are based on a linear combination of the input variables, which are transformed by a nonlinear activation function.

In Figure 22.2, *i*, *j*, and *k* denote the input layer, hidden layer, and output layer neurons, respectively, and *w* is the applied weight by the neuron. The term "feed-forward" means that a neuron connection only exists from a neuron in the input layer to other neurons in the hidden layer or from a neuron in the hidden layer to neurons in the output layer, and the neurons within a layer are not interconnected with each other. The explicit expression for an output value of a three-layered FFNN is given by (Nourani et al. 2011)

$$\hat{y}_k = f_o\left[\sum_{j=1}^{M_N} w_{kj} \cdot f_h\left(\sum_{i=1}^{N_N} w_{ij} x_i + w_{jo}\right) + w_{ko}\right] \tag{22.7}$$

where w_{ij} is a weight in the hidden layer connecting the *i*th neuron in the input layer and the *j*th neuron in the hidden layer, w_{jo} is the bias for the *j*th hidden neuron, f_h is the activation function of the hidden neuron, w_{kj} is a weight in the output layer connecting the *j*th neuron in the hidden layer and the *k*th neuron in the output layer, w_{ko} is the bias for the *k*th output neuron, f_o is the activation function for the output neuron, x_i is the *i*th input variable for the input layer, and $\hat{y}_k$ and *y* are the computed and observed output variables, respectively. N_N and M_N are the number of the neurons in the input and hidden layers, respectively. The weights are different in the hidden and output layers, and their values can be changed during the process of the network training.

In this study, two different criteria are used to measure the network efficiency: the root mean square error (RMSE) and the coefficient of efficiency (*C*).

The error evaluation criterion, the RMSE, is a frequently used measure of the difference between values predicted by a model and the values observed in the phenomenon and is defined as (Nourani et al. 2011)

$$\text{RMSE} = \sqrt{\frac{\sum_{i=1}^{N_s}(Q_i - \hat{Q}_i)^2}{N_s}} \tag{22.8}$$

where Q_i, $\hat{Q}_i$, and $\bar{Q}$ are the observed data, predicted values, and mean of N_s observed values, respectively. On the other hand, C demonstrates the discrepancy between the computed and observed values and is used to describe the predictive accuracy of models as long as there are observed data to compare the model results to (Nourani et al. 2011):

$$C = 1 - \frac{\sum_{i=1}^{N_s}(Q_i - \hat{Q}_i)^2}{\sum_{i=1}^{N_s}(\hat{Q}_i - \bar{Q})^2}$$

(22.9)

The RMSE increases from zero for perfect forecasts to large positive values as the discrepancies between forecasts and observations become increasingly large. Obviously, a high value for C (up to 1) and a small value for RMSE indicate high efficiency of the model. Legates and McCabe (1999) indicated that a hydrological model can be sufficiently evaluated by C and RMSE.

22.2.2 Feature Extraction Methods

The increase of subseries as inputs of an FFNN may lead to essential deterioration in modeling. Therefore, application of a robust approach to extract dominant features may overcome the deficiency. In this chapter, two different methods based on clustering and information content are used to optimize the input layer of the FFNN model. Figure 22.3 shows a schematic diagram of proposed methodologies. In employed methods, the SOM as a kind of clustering-based approach

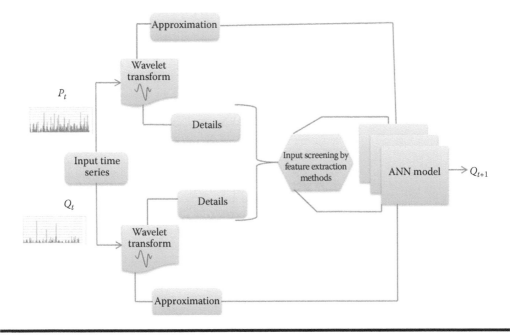

Figure 22.3 Schematic of proposed hybrid models.

and entropy as a measure of information content are applied on subseries extracted by wavelet transform to assign important features of the main time series of rainfall and runoff.

22.2.2.1 Self-Organizing Map

The way SOMs go about reducing dimensions is by producing a map of usually one or two dimensions, which plot the similarities of the data by grouping similar data items together. Thus, SOMs reduce dimensions and display similarities. The basic SOM network consists of two layers, an input layer and a Kohonen layer, which in most common applications is two-dimensional. At the input layer, one neuron is dedicated for each variable. The Kohonen layer neurons are related to every neuron of the input layer via adjustable weights. A two-level SOM neural network is a reliable approach to catch a preliminary overview on an intricate data set. It augments the conventional SOM network with an additional one-dimensional Kohonen layer in which each neuron is connected to neurons in the previous Kohonen layer. The schematic view of the two-level SOM network is shown in Figure 22.4.

The SOM is trained iteratively. Initially, the weights are randomly assigned. When the n-dimensional input vector x is sent through the network, the distance between the weight neurons of SOM (w) and the inputs is computed. The most common criterion to compute the distance is the Euclidean distance (Bowden et al. 2002):

$$\|x - w\| = \sqrt{\sum_{i=1}^{n} (x_i - w_i)^2} \tag{22.10}$$

The weight with the closest match to the presented input pattern is called winner neuron or best matching unit (BMU). The BMU and its neighboring neurons are allowed to learn by changing

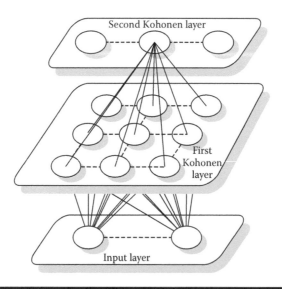

Figure 22.4 **Architecture of the two-level SOM neural network.**

the weights at each training iteration t in a manner to further reduce the distance between the weights and the input vector (Bowden et al. 2002):

$$w(t + 1) = w(t) + \alpha(t)h_{kb}(x - w(t)) \tag{22.11}$$

where α is the learning rate, in the range [0 1]; k and b are the positions of the winning neuron and its neighboring output nodes, respectively, and h_{kb} is the neighborhood function. The most commonly used neighborhood function is the Gaussian (Bowden et al. 2002):

$$h_{kb} = \exp\left(-\frac{\|k - b\|^2}{2\sigma(t)^2}\right) \tag{22.12}$$

where h_{kb} is the neighborhood function of the best matching neuron l at iteration t; $l - b$ is the distance between neurons l and b on the map grid; and σ is the width of the topological neighborhood. The training steps are repeated until convergence. After the SOM network is constructed, the homogeneous regions, that is, clusters, are defined on the map. The main privileges of the SOM method toward classic clustering algorithms are nonlinearity and not requiring the number of clusters to be assigned in advance before running the network (Nourani et al. 2013).

22.2.2.2 Shannon Entropy (Information Content)

The entropy was introduced in the context of efficiency of heat engines in the early 19th century. Shannon (1948) mathematically defined entropy in terms of its probability distribution and presented entropy as a measure of the randomness or uncertainty. For a discrete random variable X, which takes values $x_1, x_2, \ldots, x_{N_s}$ with probabilities $p_1, p_2, \ldots, p_{N_s}$, respectively, entropy is defined as (Shannon 1948)

$$H(X) = -\sum_{i=1}^{N_s} p(x_i)\log(p(x_i)) \tag{22.13}$$

where $H(X)$ is the entropy of X (also referred to entropy function) and N_s is the sample size. Different bases of the logarithm in Equation 22.13 yield entropy at different units. In this chapter, the base of the logarithm is considered as 10, which yields entropy in decibels.

The entropy of any variable always takes a positive value within limits defined as (Singh 2011)

$$0 \leq H(X) \leq \log N_s \tag{22.14}$$

The joint entropy of two variables, X and Y, is also defined as (Gao et al. 2008)

$$H(X,Y) = -\sum_{i=1}^{N_s}\sum_{j=1}^{M_s} p(x_i, y_j).\log(p(x_i, y_j)) \tag{22.15}$$

where $p(x_i, y_j)$ is the joint probability of X and Y with sample sizes of N_s and M_s, respectively. On the other hand, the mutual information (MI) measures the dependency between two random variables. It was first proposed as a registration measure in medical image registration by Viola and

Wells (1995) and by Collignon et al. (1995), independently. By definition, *MI* is the reduction in uncertainty with respect to *Y* due to observation of *X* so that *MI* can measure the statistical non-linear dependency between two random variables. It is zero when the two random variables are independent. *MI* between two random variables *X* and *Y* can be computed as (Gao et al. 2008)

$$MI(X,Y) = H(X) + H(Y) - H(X,Y) \tag{22.16}$$

For numerical calculation of *H* and *MI* using Equations 22.13 and 22.16, the probability density function for all of the variables should be specified.

MI and *H* are employed in this study as feature extraction criteria and are compared with *E* and linear correlation coefficient (*CC*)–based methods. *E*, *H*, and *MI* are calculated using Equations 22.6, 22.13, and 22.16, respectively. On the other hand, the linear *CC* value between two random variables (i.e., *X* and *Y*) is calculated as

$$CC = (\rho_{X,Y})^2 \tag{22.17}$$

in which

$$\rho_{X,Y} = \frac{\sum_{i=1}^{N_s}(x_i - \bar{x})(y_i - \bar{y})}{\sqrt{\sum_{i=1}^{N_s}(x_i - \bar{x})^2 \sum_{i=1}^{N_s}(y_i - \bar{y})^2}} \tag{22.18}$$

where $\bar{x}$ and $\bar{y}$ are the mean values of *X* and *Y*, respectively.

In order to select proper inputs of WANN models, the computed linear *CC* between the potential inputs and the output of the model has been already applied (e.g., Partal and Kisi 2007; Rajaee et al. 2011; Maheswaran and Khosa 2012). However, in a nonlinear complex hydrological process, in spite of a weak linear relationship, a strong nonlinear relationship may exist between input and output variables. Therefore, in such cases where the methods on the basis of linear relation (i.e., *CC*) may lead to unacceptable result, the information content can be a suitable choice to recognize features in complex classification tasks (such as input selecting for FFNN models in this study). *H* and *MI* are two criteria based on Shannon entropy, which are used in this study for wavelet-based feature extraction of the rainfall–runoff process. Furthermore, to evaluate the efficiency of the entropy-based feature extraction, the performance of *H* and *MI* is compared with *CC*- and *E*-based criteria. Thereinafter, *MI* and *CC* are supervised criteria calculated on the basis of the relation between input and output values (Equations 22.16 and 22.17), whereas *E* and *H* as unsupervised measures can illustrate the structural characteristics of data (Equations 22.6 and 22.15). On the other hand, *H* and *MI* are nonlinear feature extraction criteria and may be more reliable to be used in a nonlinear model such as an FFNN.

22.3 Study Area and Data

To evaluate the performance of the proposed approaches, two watersheds (i.e., the Delaney Creek and Payne Creek Subbasins) with different topological characteristics were utilized in this research. The characteristics of the watersheds are introduced in cases 1 and 2, comprehensively.

22.3.1 Case Study 1: The Delaney Creek Subbasin

The Delaney Creek Subbasin in Tampa Bay Watershed was chosen as the first study area in the current study. The basin is located at Florida State between 27°52′ and 27°56′ north latitude and 82°22′ and 82°24′ west longitude, and its drainage area is about 42 km² of open water, which drains to Tampa Bay on the Gulf of Mexico, containing the area draining from Gasparilla Pass and the watershed of Hillsborough Bay. The city of Tampa and the southern region of the metropolitan Tampa Bay Area are within the watershed (Figure 22.5).

The Tampa Bay Watershed includes some of the most productive agricultural lands of the state. This watershed is fairly flat, and its elevation varies between 10 m above and below sea level. The climate of the area is subtropical, exhibiting a transitional pattern from continental to tropical Caribbean. Long, warm, and humid summers are typical as well as mild, dry winters. The annual average temperature and the total yearly rainfall are about 23°C and 1350 mm, respectively. The observed daily and monthly stream flow and rainfall time series of the Delaney Creek Station, which is the outlet of the Delaney Creek Subbasin, were retrieved via the United States Geological Survey (USGS) website (http://waterdata.usgs.gov/usa/nwis/uv?site_no=02301750) and used in this study. Time series included 6403 daily and 210 monthly data observed from August 1993 to December 2011. The observed data from August 1993 to December 1997 were used as a verifying set, and the remaining data were employed for training the model. Rainfall and runoff time series are shown in Figure 22.6. The statistics of daily rainfall and runoff time series for the study areas are tabulated in Table 22.1.

As it can be understood from Table 22.1, the large values of maximum and standard deviation of rainfall and runoff time series appeared in the calibration data set. Such data division scheme helps the FFNN, as a data interpolator, to learn the pattern of the process much better and leads to more accurate predictions in the validation step.

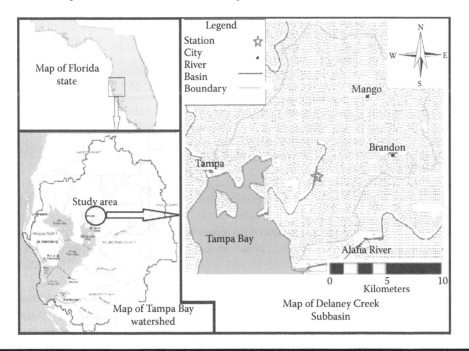

Figure 22.5 Study area (Delany Creek Subbasin).

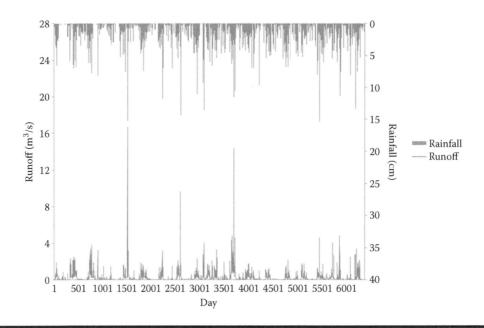

Figure 22.6 **Daily rainfall and runoff time series of the Delaney Creek Subbasin.**

Table 22.1 **Statistics of Daily Rainfall and Runoff Data for the Study Areas**

Study Area	Data Set	Rainfall Time Series (mm)				Runoff Time Series (m³/s)			
		Max	Min	Mean	Standard Deviation	Max	Min	Mean	Standard Deviation
Delaney Creek	Calibration	154.18	0	3.49	10.78	16.46	0	0.27	0.53
	Verification	81.78	0	2.49	8.90	3.75	0	0.23	0.68
Payne Creek	Calibration	158.8	0	3.60	11.2	77.84	0	3.80	6.06
	Verification	94.00	0	2.80	8.70	15.20	0	2.20	2.70

22.3.2 Case Study 2: The Payne Creek Subbasin

The Payne Creek Subbasin located in the Peace Tampa Bay Watershed in Florida State was selected as the second study area in this research. The watershed connects central Florida to the southwest coast and consists of nine subbasins. The Payne Creek Basin is the second smallest basin in the watershed located at the northwest portion of the Peace River Watershed. The Payne Creek Basin covers 322 km² areas (Figure 22.7). The Payne Creek River flows through the subbasin with an annual mean flow of 2 cms. The climate of the area is generally subtropical with an annual average temperature of about 23°C. Annual average rainfalls in or near the Payne Creek Subbasin is 1270 to 1420 mm. The observed daily stream flow values of the Payne Creek station and rainfall data of the Bartow station were used in this study. The Bartow Station is located in the upstream part of the subbasin. The location of the discharge gauge is in the middle part of the watershed where it becomes a gently sloping plain. Changes in elevation are most conspicuous along the ridges and scarps. The elevation variation between the upstream and the middle part of the watershed

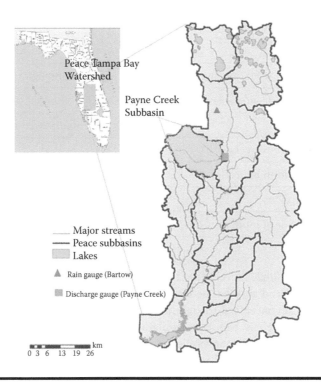

Figure 22.7 Study area (the Payne Creek Subbasin).

indicates the sloppy situation of the study area. Data used were derived from the USGS website (http://water.usgs.gov/cgi-bin/realsta.pl?station=02295420).

Rainfall and runoff time series included 5841 daily and 192 monthly data observed from July 1995 to July 2011. The observed data from July 1995 to September 2008 were used for training the model, and the remaining data were employed as a verifying set.

22.4 Results and Discussion

22.4.1 Decomposition by Wavelet Transform

Explanation of time series synchronously in both spectral and temporal terms provides a WANN for better interpretation of the process. The essential parameters of the applied FFNN (as a basic part of a WANN) are briefly presented in Table 22.2.

The optimum level of decomposition is usually obtained via trial–error procedure. In order to have a general overview on the decomposition level, initially the following formula, which offers the minimum level of decomposition, was employed (Aussem et al. 1998; Nourani et al. 2009b):

$$L = \text{int}[\log(N_s)] \tag{22.19}$$

where L and N_s are the decomposition level and the number of time series data, respectively. Due to the symmetrical relationship between values of rainfall and runoff, they were supposed to have the same seasonality level, and both were decomposed at the same level.

Table 22.2 Essential Parameters of FFNN

Parameter	Applied in Current Study
Active function for hidden layer	Tangent Sigmoid
Active function for output layer	Purelin
Training algorithm	Levenberg–Marquardt
Number of hidden layers	1
Number of hidden neurons	From n^a to $3n$
Number of epochs	From 10 to 800

[a] n is the number of input neurons in this table.

Daubechies-2 and 4 (db2, db4), Meyer, coif2, and Haar mother wavelets were applied to decompose both rainfall and runoff time series. Mallat (1998) can be referred for more information about mathematical concepts of the mother wavelets. Recent study by the authors (Nourani et al. 2009b) illustrated the effect of form similarity between a mother wavelet and the rainfall and runoff time series. Since the Haar wavelet has a pulse shape, it could properly capture the signal features of rainfall time series and may yield comparatively reliable efficiency (Nourani et al. 2009b). On the other hand, there are many jumps in the runoff time series because of sudden start and cessation of rainfall over the related watershed. Therefore, due to the shape of the db4 mother wavelet, which is similar to that of the runoff signal, it can capture the signal features, especially peak points, well, which may lead to reliable outcomes. Thus, Haar and db4 mother wavelets were also used to decompose rainfall and runoff time series, respectively. Through the current chapter, the term "Haar–db4" refers to the utilized mother wavelets that decomposed rainfall and runoff time series by Haar and db4, respectively. However, db2, coif2, and Meyer show that both rainfall and runoff time series are decomposed by the same mother wavelet.

For application of discrete wavelet transform, a code was developed in the MATLAB® environment (MathWorks 2010a). Boundary (edge) effect is one of the deficiencies in applying wavelet transform, which happens due to the application of wavelet at the beginning and end of time series (signals), where there are no data before and after. As a solution, the zero padding method was used (Addison et al. 2001). Therefore, since the time series were long enough for the current study, a suitable amount of data was neglected from the beginning and end parts of time series after wavelet application.

According to Equation 22.19 for the Delaney Creek Subbasin with daily data, $N_s = 6403$ and thus $L = 3$. The obtained level 3 was initially used to have an overview on the decomposition level. This experimental equation was derived for fully autoregressive signals, only considering time series length without paying any attention to seasonal signatures of a hydrologic process (Nourani et al. 2011). Hence, by application of decomposition level 3, only a few seasonalities of the main time series might be taken into account. Decomposition level 3 for daily data of the Delaney Creek Subbasin yields three detailed subseries (i.e., 2^1-day mode, 2^2-day mode, and 2^3-day mode, which is nearly weekly mode), but according to the hydrological base of the process, there might be other dominant seasonalities with longer periods. Therefore, other decomposition levels were also examined to obtain the optimum decomposition level. In this way, the results of two other levels for daily data of the Delaney Creek Subbasin with better performance (i.e., levels 5 and 7) were also surveyed. Decomposition level 5 contains five details: 2^1-day mode, 2^2-day mode, and 2^3-day mode, which is a nearly weekly mode, and 2^4-day mode and 2^5-day mode, which is a nearly monthly mode. Therefore, the seasonality of the process up to 1 month could be handled by the model. Decomposition in level 7 yields two more details (i.e., 2^6 days mode and 2^7 days mode). For example, Figure 22.8 shows approximation and detailed subseries of rainfall time series for the Delaney Creek Subbasin decomposed by Haar mother wavelet at level 5.

For daily data of the Payne Creek Subbasin, N_s = 5841; thus, the initial decomposition level was set as 3. To obtain the optimum decomposition level, other levels were also examined. Results of levels 5 and 7, which led to better outcomes, were compared in order to survey the effect of the decomposition level on the model performance.

To evaluate the effect of data timescale on the model performance, the proposed methodology was also applied in monthly timescale as well as daily time series. Since the monthly time series of the Delaney Creek and Payne Creek Subbasins contain 210 and 192 monthly data, respectively, only decomposition level 3 using Haar–db4 mother wavelets (i.e., Haar and db4 mother wavelets were used to decompose rainfall and runoff time series, respectively) was applied on rainfall and runoff time series of both studied areas.

The subsequent step in the WANN modeling after decomposition of time series via wavelet is the imposition of the obtained subseries (details and approximation) to the FFNN model. The increase in subseries obtained via wavelet used as inputs to the FFNN may lead to network overfitting, divergence, obscurity, and poor accuracy. Therefore, to optimize the number of inputs and improve the model training rate and efficiency, choosing the dominant subseries of the decomposed rainfall and runoff time series was tried prior to imposing into the FFNN model. In conventional trial-and-error methodology, for 10 details as potential inputs, $2^{10} - 1$ input combinations (for u inputs, $2^u - 1$ combinations can be assigned) should be examined. In a complex hydrological

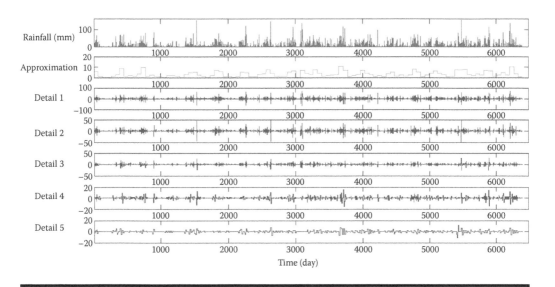

Figure 22.8 Approximation and detail subsignals of the Delaney Creek Subbasin for daily rainfall time series decomposed at level 5 by Haar mother wavelet.

system with a large value of *u*, an efficient algorithm, instead of the conventional trial-and-error method, is needed to select such dominant input variables. The problem further intensifies in time series, where appropriate lags must also be considered. In this chapter, two kinds of feature extraction methods (i.e., SOM and Shannon entropy) were applied to choose more dominant seasonalities.

22.4.2 Feature Extraction by SOM

A SOM as a feature extraction method compacts information while preserving the most important topological and metric relationships of the primary data items on display. Therefore, subseries obtained by wavelet transform were fed to the SOM to be classified into several clusters as similar subseries stood in the same cluster. Centers of clusters, which represent the cluster pattern well, were imposed into the FFNN as model inputs. For this purpose, a two-step SOM clustering method was employed to select the effective subseries and reduce the dimensionality of the input space. At the first step, a two-dimensional SOM was applied to have an overview on signal patterns and approximate number of clusters to be assigned, regarding the SOM topology. Subsequently, in the second step, in order to be ensured of the highlighted clusters, a one-dimensional SOM was applied to classify the signals with specific numbers of groups determined at the first step. Afterward, the Euclidean distance criterion was used to determine the centroid subsignal of each cluster, which was the best representative of the data pattern within the cluster. For application of the SOM on the data set, SOM Toolbox of MATLAB was used to cluster the data set (MathWorks 2010b).

Detailed subseries obtained via wavelet transform for both rainfall and runoff time series were imposed into the SOM in order to extract dominant details, which could have a significant role in attaining accurate results. The two-stage SOM approach proposed by Nourani et al. (2013) was followed in this chapter. In the following, SOM clustering results of the Delaney Creek and Payne Creek Subbasins are presented. The size of Kohonen layer for decomposed data of daily rainfall and runoff time series relevant to the Delaney Creek Subbasin was considered as a 4 × 4 via trial-and-error procedure. Since the number of detailed subseries at the decomposition level of 5 was 10 (5 rainfall detailed subseries in addition to 5 runoff detailed subseries), the mentioned size was large enough to ensure that a suitable number of clusters were formed from training data. Figure 22.9a presents the resulted neighbor weight distances of the output layer size of 4 × 4, which contains detailed subseries obtained by decomposing through Haar–db4 mother wavelets. The neighbor weight distance plan presents output neurons and their direct neighbor relationship. The regular hexagonals display the SOM output neurons, whereas the stretched hexagonals indicate the distances between neurons. The darker colors demonstrate larger distances, and the lighter colors refer to smaller distances. Figure 22.9b shows the hit plan of the output layer of size 4 × 4, which contains detailed subseries obtained by decomposing through Haar–db4 mother wavelets. The hit plan is an illustration of a SOM output layer, with each neuron showing the number of classified input vectors. The relative number of vectors for each neuron is shown via the size of a colored patch.

According to the obtained neighbor weight distances (Figure 22.9a), darker hexagonals divided Kohonen layer approximately into four parts in the two-dimensional SOM. To be ensured that the optimized clustering result was achieved, the one-dimensional SOM was also examined in the second step (i.e., 1 × 3, 1 × 4, 1 × 5, and 1 × 6 Kohonen layers). The obtained results via the FFNN sensitivity analysis proved that the output layer of size 1 × 4 could lead to better results, and four clusters was considered as the optimum number of the clusters.

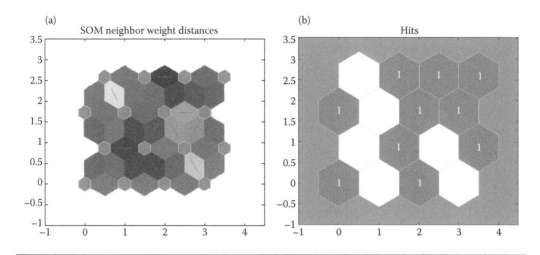

Figure 22.9 (a) Neighbor weight distances and (b) hits plan, obtained by 2D SOM for daily data of the Delaney Creek Subbasin.

The centroid of each cluster was selected using the Euclidean distance criterion and assigned as the representative of the cluster. Table 22.3 presents clustering patterns and selected subseries for each of the applied mother wavelets. In this chapter, *Qa* and *Pa* present approximation subseries of decomposed runoff and rainfall time series, respectively. *Qd1*,…, *Qd7* refer to runoff detailed subseries, and *Pd1*,…, *Pd7* refer to rainfall detailed subseries at scales (levels) 1 to 7. Detailed subseries of rainfall at levels 1 and 2 were usually grouped in a same cluster with runoff detailed subseries at same seasonalities (i.e., scales of 2^1 and 2^2 days of rainfall and runoff time series are correlated). According to the Markovian autoregressive property of runoff time series, it was expected that detailed subseries of runoff were more effective than rainfall subseries in runoff prediction. SOM-based results indicated that the dominant components of each cluster were runoff subseries, which was in agreement with the Markovian property of the process.

Two approximation subsignals and four details were chosen as the centroids of the classes in clustering daily data of the Delaney Creek Subbasin. The consequences might efficiently constitute dominant inputs of the FFNN model for the study case of the Delaney Creek Subbasin.

The same clustering procedure was employed for the subsignals of the Payne Creek Subbasin. As an instance, in using level 5 of the decomposition by all examined mother wavelets, 4 × 4 Kohonen layer was selected as the approximate optimum grid number for the two-dimensional SOM. The trial-and-error procedure on various sizes of the one-dimensional SOM (i.e., 1 × 3, 1 × 4, 1 × 5, and 1 × 6 Kohonen layers) resulted to picking the 1 × 4 grid as the appropriate size. Table 22.3 shows the results of SOM clustering for daily data of the Payne Creek Subbasin. Centroids of clusters were determined as inputs of the FFNN model.

For development of the SOM clustering approach to the monthly rainfall and runoff data of the Delaney Creek and Payne Creek Subbasins, similarly, the two-stage SOM methodology was used. Since decomposition level 3 was applied on monthly data sets, six detailed subseries were imposed to the SOM network. The trail-and-error on various clustering patterns by the SOM led to determination of two and three groups. Table 22.3 shows the results of SOM clustering for

Table 22.3 SOM Clustering for Daily and Monthly Data of Study Areas Decomposed by Haar–db4 Mother Wavelets

Timescale	Study Area	Mother Wavelet[a,b]	Cluster 1		Cluster 2		Cluster 3		Cluster 4	
			Data	*Center*	*Data*	*Center*	*Data*	*Center*	*Data*	*Center*
Daily	Delaney Creek	Haar–db4	Pd1, Pd2, Pd3, Pd4, Qd1, Qd2	Qd2	Qd3, Qd5	Qd3	Qd4	Qd4	Pd5	Pd5
		coif2	Pd1, Pd2, Pd3, Qd1, Qd2, Qd3	Qd3	Pd4, Qd4	Qd4	Qd5	Qd5	Pd5	Pd5
		db2	Pd3, Pd4, Qd1, Qd4	Qd4	Qd2, Qd3, Qd5,	Qd3	Pd1, Pd2	Pd1	Pd5	Pd5
		Meyer	Pd3, Qd2, Qd3, Qd4	Pd3	Pd1, Pd2, Qd1	Qd1	Pd5, Qd5	Qd5	Pd4	Pd4
	Payne Creek	Haar–db4	Pd3, Pd5, Qd1, Qd2, Qd4	Qd4	Pd2, Pd4, Qd5	Qd5	Pd1	Pd1	Qd3	Qd3
		coif2	Pd1, Pd2, Pd3, Qd1, Qd2, Qd3, Qd4	Qd3	Pd4	Pd4	Pd5	Pd5	Qd5	Qd5
		db2	Pd1, Pd2, Pd4, Qd1, Qd3	Qd3	Pd3, Qd2, Qd4	Qd4	Pd5	Pd5	Qd5	Qd5
		Meyer	Pd1, Pd2, Pd4, Qd1, Qd2	Pd1	Qd3, Qd4, Qd5	Qd4	Pd3	Pd3	Pd5	Pd5
Monthly	Delaney Creek	Haar–db4	Pd1, Pd2, Qd1, Qd2, Qd3	Qd2	Pd3	Pd3				
	Payne Creek	Haar–db4	Pd3, Qd1, Qd2, Qd3	Qd3	Pd1, Pd2	Pd1				

Note: Pdi, detail subseries of rainfall in level *i*; *Qdi*, detail subseries of runoff in level *i*.

[a] Except in using Haar–db4 mother wavelets, in application of other mother wavelets, both rainfall and runoff time series were decomposed by same mother wavelets (i.e., coif2, db2, or Meyer).

[b] In daily modeling, time series were decomposed at level 5, while they are decomposed at level 3 in monthly modeling.

monthly data, whereas subsignals were classified into two groups, and the group members and centroids of groups were also determined.

22.4.3 Results of WSNN Model

The proposed hybrid WSNN model contains numerous parameters such as the number of hidden neurons, the training iteration number (epoch), the number of SOM clusters, the decomposition level, and the mother wavelet type; proper determination and selection of these parameters can improve the efficiency of the model.

Two approximation subsignals and selected details of rainfall and runoff time series, as the centroids of the classes, obtained by the SOM were imposed to the FFNN models to forecast one-day and one-month-ahead runoff values resulting in daily and monthly modeling steps. As an instance, selected input variables via the SOM for decomposition level 5 as well as best structures and obtained performance criteria (i.e., C and *RMSE*) of the models according to the applied mother wavelets for daily and monthly data of both watersheds are tabulated in Table 22.4. Input variables $Qd1,..., Qd5$ and $Pd1,..., Pd5$ included wavelet details of runoff and rainfall time series, which in daily modeling indicate 2^1-day mode, 2^2-day mode, and 2^3-day mode, which is a nearly weekly mode, and 2^4-day mode and 2^5-day mode, which is a nearly monthly mode, respectively.

Table 22.4 also shows the results of proposed modeling in monthly timescale for both watersheds. Decomposition level 3 was used for monthly modeling. Input variables $Qd1$, $Qd2$, $Qd3$ and $Pd1$, $Pd2$, $Pd3$ included wavelet details of runoff and rainfall time series, which indicate 2^1-month mode and 2^2-month mode, which is near to one season and 2^3-month mode. The output variables in Table 22.4 are one-day and one-month-ahead runoff values. The network structure indicates, respectively, the number of input variables, hidden neurons, and the output variable of the selected structure. The optimal hidden neuron numbers were obtained through trial-and-error procedure. In this way, 6 to 25 and 3 to 10 hidden neurons were respectively examined for daily and monthly data sets in a single hidden layer of each FFNN structure. Table 22.4 indicates that in both study areas, decomposition of time series by Haar–db4 mother wavelets, which match patterns of the main time series, led to better performance. The results reconfirmed previous recommendation about similarity of mother wavelet formation to the main time series (Nourani et al. 2009b).

Rainfall due to its high stochastic inherence yields unpredictable effects; therefore, rainfall subseries may not be a good regressor to predict the runoff values individually. On the other hand, runoff time series, according to its Markovian inherence, shows strong relation with some of its fundamental seasonalities. Hence, runoff subseries are more effective in runoff prediction than rainfall subseries. Accordingly, models with more involved runoff subseries led to higher efficiency; in this regard, in the Delaney Creek Subbasin for preprocessed data via db2 and Meyer mother wavelets (in which both rainfall and runoff time series were decomposed by the same mother wavelet), two detailed subseries of rainfall time series took part in the modeling, which decreased C to 0.67 and 0.7, whereas in data preprocessing by coif2 and Haar–db4 mother wavelets, only one of the detailed subseries of rainfall participated in the modeling. Therefore, higher C (i.e., 0.82 and 0.86 for coif2 and Haar–db4 mother wavelets, respectively) is obtained by using two indicated mother wavelets. By comparing the data (i.e., max and standard deviation values, Table 22.1) and topologic characteristics (i.e., slope and area, see section 3) of both subbasins, it can be greatened that the Payne Creek Subbasin, with vaster area and spatially different topological features, may show more complex dynamic behavior than the Delaney Creek Subbasin. Therefore, despite the acceptable performance of the WSNN model for both subbasins, the proposed WSNN

Table 22.4 Results of Proposed WSNN Model for Daily and Monthly Modeling Decomposed at Level 5

Timescale	Case Study	Mother Wavelet[a]	Selected Input Variables[b]	FFNN Structure[c]	Calibration		Verification	
					C	RMSE (Normalized)	C	RMSE (Normalized)
Daily	Delaney Creek	Haar–db4	Qd2, Qd3, Qd4, Pd2	(6-9-1)	0.94	0.008	0.86	0.015
		coif2	Qd3, Qd4, Qd5, Pd5	(6-9-1)	0.92	0.009	0.82	0.017
		db2	Qd3, Qd4, Pd1, Pd5	(6-9-1)	0.86	0.011	0.67	0.023
		Meyer	Qd1, Qd5, Pd3, Pd4	(6-9-1)	0.86	0.012	0.70	0.022
	Payne Creek	Haar–db4	Qd3, Qd4, Qd5, Pd1	(6-11-1)	0.87	0.027	0.79	0.016
		coif2	Qd3, Qd5, Pd4, Pd5	(6-12-1)	0.86	0.031	0.75	0.022
		db2	Qd3, Qd4, Qd5, Pd5	(6-11-1)	0.88	0.029	0.76	0.019
		Meyer	Qd4, Pd1, Pd3, Pd5	(6-11-1)	0.84	0.034	0.73	0.036
Monthly	Delaney Creek	Haar–db4	Pd3, Qd2	(4-6-1)	0.84	0.054	0.71	0.063
	Payne Creek	Haar–db4	Qd3, Pd3	(4-8-1)	0.79	0.020	0.75	0.032

[a] In daily modeling, time series were decomposed at level 5, while they were decomposed at level 3 in monthly modeling.
[b] Approximation subseries of rainfall and runoff were imposed to FFNN in addition to detail subseries.
[c] The results have been presented for the best structure.

model led to lower performance for the Payne Creek Subbasin with respect to the Delaney Creek Subbasin (see Table 22.4).

To regard the effect of the decomposition level on the model efficiency in the daily modeling, two other decomposition levels of wavelet transformation (i.e., levels 3 and 7) were also examined using Haar–db4 mother wavelets. Daily data decomposition at level 3 yields three detailed subseries (i.e., 2^1-day mode, 2^2-day mode, and 2^3-day mode, which is a nearly weekly mode) and decomposition at level 7 contains four more details (i.e., 2^4-day mode and 2^5-day mode, which is a nearly monthly mode, and 2^6-day mode and 2^7-day mode). Figure 22.10 compares observed and computed data of calibration and verification time series obtained by the proposed WSNN methodology through decomposing at level 5 using Haar–db4 mother wavelets as an example for the Delaney Creek Subbasins.

22.4.4 Feature Extraction by Shannon Entropy (Information Content)

In addition to the explained clustering-based method, the concept of Shannon entropy can be also utilized as another feature extraction approach. To evaluate the efficiency of the entropy-based feature extraction criteria, performance of H and MI was illustrated and compared with CC and E-based criteria. MI and CC, as supervised measures, are calculated on the basis of the relation between input and target values (Equations 22.16 and 22.17), whereas E and H are unsupervised criteria and measure the structural characteristics of data (Equations 22.6 and 22.15). On the other hand, H and MI are nonlinear feature extraction criteria and may be more suitable to be used in a nonlinear model such FFNN. The values of H, MI, E, and CC were calculated using the Delaney Creek and Payne Creek Subbasins data considering daily subseries obtained by decomposition at levels 3, 5, and 7 as well as decomposition level of 3 for monthly data. In this way, the subseries derived from wavelet decomposition procedure were ranked according to values of CC, E, H, and MI for daily and monthly data. As an instance, general rankings of subseries for daily data at level 7 and monthly data at level 3 are respectively shown in Tables 22.5 and 22.6 for the used feature extraction criteria (CC, E, H, and MI). To rank the subseries obtained via the wavelet transform, values of E, H, MI, and CC were calculated for all subseries using Equations 22.6, 22.13, 22.16, and 22.17, and subsequently, the rank of each subseries was determined so that the first rank belonged to the maximum value (more effective input) and the last one to the minimum value.

Several results are inferred according to the ranking results presented in Tables 22.5 and 22.6 that are briefly listed in the following:

■ The type of mother wavelet has no major effect on subseries ranking, based on H and E (unsupervised criteria).
■ For the used mother wavelets, both CC- and E-based subseries rankings are almost identical (probably because of linear inherence of the criteria). However, E, as an unsupervised criterion, is calculated without any attention to the target, and consequently, the probable noise and error, contained in the target, may have no direct effect on the ranking.
■ In contrast to H-based subseries ranking, most of the prime ranks belong to Q components in ranking based on CC, MI, and E.
■ For all mother wavelets in E-based ranking (except for Meyer-based decomposition of monthly data), the first rank belongs to Qa subseries. It is notable that the energy of signal (E) is mostly distributed in the approximation subseries rather than details.

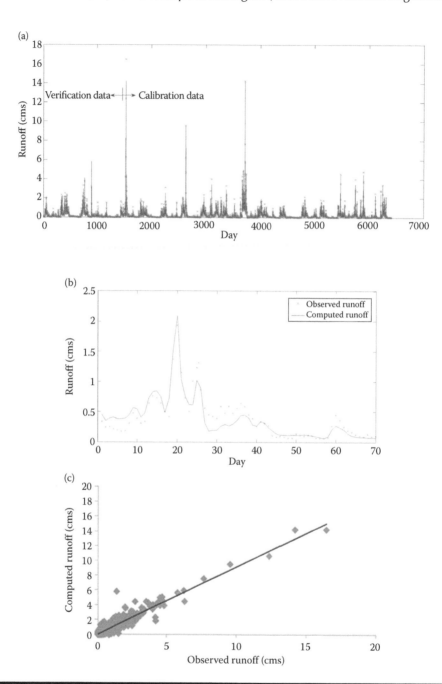

Figure 22.10 Results of daily WSNN model for decomposing by Haar–db4. (a) Computed and observed runoff, (b) detail of hydrograph, and (c) scatter plot for the Delaney Creek Subbasin.

Table 22.5 Ranking of Daily Subseries Using Different Feature Extraction Criteria and Different Mother Wavelets, Decomposed at Level 7, for Delaney Creek Subbasin

Rank	Haar–db4				db2				Coif2				Meyer			
	H	MI	CC	E	H	MI	CC	E	H	MI	CC	E	H	MI	CC	E
1	Pd7	Qd4	Qd3	Qa	Pa	Qa	Qa	Qa	Pa	Qd2	Qd3	Qa	Pa	Qd2	Qd3	Qa
2	Pa	Qd2	Qd4	Qd3	Pd7	Qd3	Qd4	Qd4	Qd7	Qd3	Qa	Qd3	Pd7	Qd3	Qa	Qd3
3	Qa	Qd3	Qd5	Qd4	Qa	Qd4	Qd3	Qd3	Pd7	Pd2	Qd1	Pd2	Qd7	Qd4	Qd5	Qd5
4	Pd6	Qd5	Qa	Qd5	Pd6	Pa	Pa	Qd2	Qd6	Qd7	Pd4	Pd3	Qa	Qa	Qd4	Qd4
5	Qd7	Qd6	Qd7	Qd7	Qd7	Qd5	Qd2	Qd7	Qa	Pd4	Pd5	Pa	Qd6	Pa	Qd7	Qd2
6	Pd5	Qa	Qd6	Qd6	Pd5	Qd2	Qd7	Qd5	Pd6	Pd7	Pd6	Pd4	Pd6	Qd1	Qd2	Qd7
7	Pd4	Pd7	Qd1	Qd1	Qd6	Qd7	Qd5	Qd1	Pd5	Qd5	Pa	Qd6	Pd5	Qd5	Pa	Qd6
8	Qd6	Qd7	Qd2	Qd2	Pd4	Qd1	Qd1	Qd6	Pd4	Qd6	Qd6	Qd1	Pd4	Qd6	Qd6	Qd1
9	Pd3	Pd4	Pa	Pd1	Qd5	Pd1	Qd6	Pd1	Qd3	Pd3	Pd7	Pd1	Pd1	Pd3	Pd7	Pd1
10	Qd5	Pa	Pd7	Pd2	Pd3	Qd6	Pd4	Pd2	Pd2	Qd4	Qd5	Qd5	Pd2	Qd2	Qd1	Pd2
11	Pd2	Pd3	Pd4	Pd3	Pd1	Pd3	Pd3	Pa	Qd1	Qa	Qd4	Qd4	Pd3	Qd7	Pd4	Pd3
12	Qd4	Pd5	Pd5	Pa	Pd2	Pd5	Pd7	Pd3	Qd4	Pa	Qd7	Qd2	Qd5	Pd4	Pd5	Pa
13	Pd1	Pd6	Pd6	Pd4	Qd4	Pd4	Pd5	Pd4	Pd1	Qd1	Qd2	Qd7	Qd4	Pd7	Pd6	Pd4
14	Qd3	Pd2	Pd3	Pd5	Qd3	Pd7	Pd6	Pd5	Qd2	Pd1	Pd3	Pd5	Qd2	Pd1	Pd3	Pd5
15	Qd2	Qd1	Pd2	Pd6	Qd2	Pd6	Pd2	Pd6	Pd3	Pd6	Pd2	Pd6	Qd3	Pd6	Pd2	Pd6
16	Qd1	Pd1	Pd1	Pd7	Qd1	Pd2	Pd1	Pd7	Qd5	Pd5	Pd1	Pd7	Qd1	Pd5	Pd1	Pd7

Table 22.6 Ranking of Monthly Subseries Using Different Feature Extraction Criteria and Different Mother Wavelets, Decomposed at Level 3, for Delaney Creek Subbasin

Rank	Haar–db4				db2				Coif2				Meyer			
	H	MI	CC	E	H	MI	CC	E	H	MI	CC	E	H	MI	CC	E
1	Pd3	Qd2	Qd2	Qa	Pa	Qd3	Qd3	Qa	Pd3	Qa	Qa	Qa	Pd3	Qd3	Qd3	Qd2
2	Pd2	Qd3	Pd2	Pd2	Pd3	Qa	Pd2	Pd2	Pa	Qd3	Pd2	Pd2	Pa	Qa	Qd2	Qa
3	Qa	Qd1	Qd3	Qd3	Pd2	Qd1	Qa	Qd3	Qa	Qd1	Qd2	Qd3	Qa	Qd2	Qa	Qd3
4	Qd3	Qa	Qd1	Qd2	Pd1	Pd2	Qd1	Qd2	Pd1	Pd2	Qd1	Qd2	Qd3	Qd1	Pd2	Pd2
5	Pd1	Pd1	Qa	Qd1	Qd3	Pd1	Qd2	Qd1	Qd1	Pd1	Qd3	Qd1	Pd1	Pa	Qd1	Pa
6	Qd2	Pd3	Pd3	Pd3	Qd2	Pd3	Pd1	Pd3	Qd2	Pd3	Pd1	Pd3	Qd2	Pd3	Pa	Qd1
7	Pa	Pd2	Pd1	Pd1	Qa	Qd2	Pd3	Pd1	Pd2	Qd2	Pd3	Pd1	Qd1	Pd2	Pd3	Pd3
8	Qd1	Pa	Pa	Pa	Qd1	Pa	Pa	Pa	Qd3	Pa	Pa	Pa	Pd2	Pd1	Pd1	Pd1

22.4.5 Results of WENN Model

To develop the WENN model, the FFNN model was fed by extracted dominant subseries in order to predict runoff values one day ahead for daily data and one month ahead for monthly data sets. Therefore, for both daily and monthly data of two case studies (the Delaney Creek and Payne Creek Subbasins), four different FFNNs were trained using the selected subseries via four feature extraction criteria (i.e., *H, MI, E,* and *CC*). In order to survey the performance of *H, CC, E,* and *MI* feature extraction criteria, the subseries of the first, second, and third ranks for daily data (see Table 22.5) and the subseries of the first and second ranks for monthly data (according to Table 22.6) were primarily considered as the inputs of the FFNN; thereinafter, the sufficient number of inputs was consequently determined using the maximum reduction rate method. Tables 22.7 and 22.8 present the results of the developed FFNN models using the selected subseries decomposed by Haar–db4, db2, coif2, and Meyer mother wavelets for daily and monthly data, respectively.

High differences between the most efficient and poor values of *C* in the verification step of both daily and monthly modeling tabulated in Tables 22.7 and 22.8 approve the sensitivity of the model to the used feature extraction criterion. Results of Tables 22.7 and 22.8 indicate that almost all models with two and three input neurons for daily data and with two neurons for monthly data could lead to acceptable outcomes except when *H* was used as the extraction criterion. Although *H* measures the information content of the subseries, it is notable that a high value of the criterion may occur due to noise or redundant information involved in the subseries, and as tabulated in Tables 22.7 and 22.8, the *H*-based feature extraction method may lead to low performance of the FFNN model. Furthermore, the results inferred from Tables 22.7 and 22.8 confirm the superiority of Haar–db4 mother wavelets in comparison with db2, coif2, and Meyer for decomposition of the main time series. The results confirm that the selected dominant inputs by the *MI* criterion tremendously lead to more accurate results. Therefore, for the rest of the current chapter, only the results of models, developed on the basis of the *MI* criterion, have been presented, and the procedure of the WENN is explained for Haar–db4–based decomposition (for other mother wavelets, the WENN models were developed by the same procedure). Reasonable values for *C* and *RMSE* guarantee the accuracy of the model with an optimum structure. The increase in input neurons led to a complex structure for the FFNN and carries out some difficulties in the training step of the model. Therewith, the input time series structurally contain some noise; thus, the increase in inputs magnifies such error and may lead to an undesirable result in the verification step. In this study, two strategies were used to arrange the input layer of the FFNN in the WENN model.

22.4.5.1 Strategy A

Subseries with maximum values of *MI* were selected and imposed to the FFNN as the inputs of the proposed model. Herein, as an example, the procedure of strategy *A* is explained for Haar–db4 mother wavelets. In order to calculate the normalized *MI* for the subseries inferred from decomposition, the value of *MI* for each subseries was divided by the maximum value of *MI*. Thus, normalized *MI* for the first rank (as presented at Tables 22.5 and 22.6) is equal to 1, and for the others, it is between 1 and 0. Figures 22.11 and 22.12 present descending orders of the subseries derived from Haar–db4 mother wavelets for daily and monthly data of the Delaney Creek Subbasin, respectively.

The maximum reduction rate of normalized *MI* separates the dominant inputs from the other subseries. Such reduction in the *MI* value is interpreted as the maximum decrease in nonlinear dependency between two random variables and presents *Qd4, Qd2, Qd3,* and *Qd5* as dominant inputs of the model for daily data and *Qd2, Qd3,* and *Qd1* for monthly data. The maximum

Table 22.7 Recognizing Best Feature Extraction Criteria (H, MI, E, or CC) for Daily Data, Decomposed at Level 7

Mother Wavelet	Ranking Base	Delaney Creek			Payne Creek		
		Input Variables[a]	Calibration C	Verification C	Input Variables	Calibration C	Verification C
Haar–db4	H	Pd7, Pa	0.23	0.02	Pd7, Qd2	0.23	0.07
	MI	Qd4, Qd2	0.79	0.68	Qd3, Qd2	0.69	0.66
	CC	Qd3, Qd4	0.73	0.66	Qd3, Qd4	0.67	0.61
	E	Qa, Qd3	0.70	0.62	Qa, Qd3	0.62	0.58
	H	Pd7, Pa, Qa	0.24	0.16	Pd7, Qd2, Qa	0.24	0.22
	MI	Qd4, Qd2, Qd3	0.83	0.79	Qd3, Qd2, Qd4	0.80	0.77
	CC	Qd3, Qd4, Qd5	0.75	0.68	Qd3, Qd4, Qd5	0.71	0.66
	E	Qa, Qd3, Qd4	0.76	0.69	Qa, Qd3, Qd5	0.70	0.64
db2	H	Pa, Pd7	0.25	0.08	Pa, Pd7	0.22	0.14
	MI	Qa, Qd3	0.66	0.46	Qa, Qd3	0.53	0.40
	CC	Qa, Qd4	0.57	0.45	Qa, Qd5	0.43	0.38
	E	Qa, Qd4	0.57	0.45	Qd3, Qa	0.53	0.40
	H	Pa, Pd7, Qa	0.36	0.10	Pa, Pd7, Qa	0.32	0.17
	MI	Qa, Qd3, Qd4	0.73	0.60	Qa, Qd3, Qd5	0.65	0.59
	CC	Qa, Qd4, Qd3	0.73	0.60	Qa, Qd5, Qd3	0.65	0.59
	E	Qa, Qd4, Qd3	0.73	0.60	Qd3, Qa, Qd4	0.59	0.52

Coif2	H	Pa, Qd7	0.28	0.12	Pa, Pd5	0.25	0.17
	MI	Qd2, Qd3	0.64	0.57	Qa, Qd3	0.60	0.51
	CC	Qd3, Qa	0.60	0.48	Qd3, Qd2	0.53	0.45
	E	Qa, Qd3	0.60	0.48	Qa, Qd3	0.60	0.51
	H	Pa, Qd7, Pd7	0.31	0.19	Pa, Pd5, Pd6	0.32	0.22
	MI	Qd2, Qd3, Pd2	0.76	0.67	Qa, Qd3, Qd2	0.77	0.66
	CC	Qd3, Qa, Qd1	0.62	0.58	Qd3, Qd2, Qd1	0.60	0.54
	E	Qa, Qd3, Pd2	0.69	0.59	Qa, Qd3, Qd2	0.77	0.66
Mayer	H	Pa, Pd7	0.30	0.13	Pd6, Pa	0.30	0.21
	MI	Qd2, Qd3	0.62	0.56	Qd2, Qd3	0.64	0.58
	CC	Qd3, Qa	0.58	0.48	Qa, Qd3	0.59	0.52
	E	Qa, Qd3	0.58	0.48	Qa, Qd5	0.59	0.48
	H	Pa, Pd7, Qa	0.29	0.22	Pd6, Pa, Qa	0.39	0.28
	MI	Qd2, Qd3, Qd4	0.75	0.68	Qd2, Qd3, Qd4	0.72	0.67
	CC	Qd3, Qa, Qd5	0.69	0.60	Qa, Qd3, Qd4	0.73	0.62
	E	Qa, Qd3, Qd5	0.69	0.60	Qa, Qd5, Pa	0.60	0.58

[a] Q_{t+1} is the output variable.

Table 22.8 Recognizing Best Feature Extraction Criteria (*H, MI, E,* or *CC*) for Monthly Data, Decomposed at Level 3

Mother Wavelet	Ranking Base	Delaney Creek			Payne Creek		
		Input Variables	Calibration C	Verification C	Input Variables	Calibration C	Verification C
Haar–db4	H	Pd3	0.44	0.32	Pd2	0.44	0.37
	MI	Qd2	0.62	0.56	Qd2	0.60	0.51
	CC	Qd2	0.52	0.46	Qa	0.53	0.48
	E	Qa	0.51	0.46	Qa	0.43	0.48
	H	Pd3, Pd2	0.53	0.41	Pd2, Pd3	0.51	0.50
	MI	Qd2, Qd3	0.75	0.71	Qd2, Qd3	0.68	0.67
	CC	Qd2, Pd2	0.58	0.51	Qa, Qd2	0.61	0.61
	E	Qa, Pd2	0.55	0.47	Qa, Qd3	0.52	0.50
db2	H	Pa	0.33	0.34	Pa	0.37	0.34
	MI	Qd3	0.56	0.49	Qa	0.49	0.45
	CC	Qd3	0.56	0.49	Qd3	0.56	0.49
	E	Qa	0.41	0.39	Qa	0.49	0.45
	H	Pa, Pd3	0.35	0.28	Pa, Pd2	0.39	0.33
	MI	Qd3, Qa	0.66	0.64	Qa, Qd2	0.66	0.50
	CC	Qd3, Pd2	0.46	0.44	Qd3, Pd2	0.49	0.47
	E	Qa, Pd2	0.46	0.40	Qa, Qd2	0.66	0.60

coif2	H	Pd3	0.34	0.32	Pd3	0.44	0.43
	MI	Qa	0.55	0.48	Qd3	0.53	0.51
	CC	Qa	0.55	0.48	Qa	0.44	0.43
	E	Qa	0.55	0.48	Qd2	0.45	0.38
	H	Pd3, Pa	0.46	0.33	Pd3, Pa	0.48	0.41
	MI	Qa, Qd3	0.69	0.62	Qd3, Qd2	0.64	0.60
	CC	Qa, Pd2	0.62	0.56	Qa, Qd2	0.58	0.54
	E	Qa, Pd2	0.62	0.56	Qd2, Qa	0.58	0.54
Meyer	H	Pd3	0.41	0.34	Pa	0.32	0.28
	MI	Qd3	0.53	0.46	Qd3	0.42	0.38
	CC	Qd3	0.53	0.46	Qd2	0.37	0.34
	E	Qd2	0.45	0.38	Qa	0.26	0.20
	H	Pd3, Pa	0.37	0.36	Pa, Pd2	0.33	0.29
	MI	Qd3, Qa	0.65	0.61	Qd3, Qa	0.57	0.53
	CC	Qd3, Qd2	0.55	0.49	Qd2, Qd1	0.53	0.51
	E	Qd2, Qa	0.48	0.45	Qa, Qd1	0.53	0.42

[a] Q_{t+1} is the output variable.

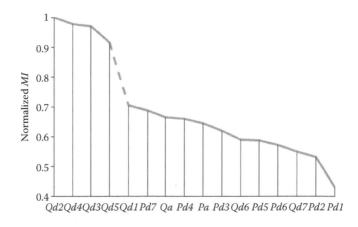

Figure 22.11 Descending order of the daily subseries derived from Haar–db4 mother wavelets in level 7 for the Delaney Creek Subbasin (normalized *MI*).

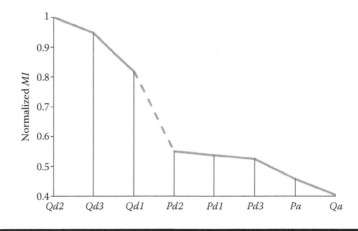

Figure 22.12 Descending order of the monthly subseries derived from Haar–db4 mother wavelets in level 3 for the Delaney Creek Subbasin (normalized *MI*).

reduction rate method also determined *Qd3*, *Qd2*, *Qd4*, and *Qa* and *Qd2*, *Qd3*, and *Qd1* as dominant subseries for daily and monthly data of the Payne Creek Subbasin, respectively. However, a shortcoming is probably associated with the maximum reduction method when no significant reduction has taken place in normalized *MI* values. In such situation, it is suggested to change the decomposition level and repeat the procedure or to utilize other input-determining methods like the presented SOM approach in Section 22.4.2.

22.4.5.2 Strategy B

According to the dyadic representation of the discrete wavelet transform, the finest scale (first level) of the daily decomposition is $2^1 = 2$ day mode. However, due to the Markovian property of the runoff process in daily timescale (Nourani et al. 2009b), a strong relation is expected between runoff values at two antecedent time steps. Thus, it seems that adding the general runoff time series with one day lag time (Q_t) as an input neuron in daily modeling, in addition to the extracted subseries considered in strategy A, may lead to more accurate results. For example, the use of strategy B for daily Haar–db4–based decomposition in the Delaney Creek Subbasin let imposing Q_t, $Qd4$, $Qd2$, $Qd3$, and $Qd5$ time series into the FFNN to predict Q_{t+1}. The results of proposed strategies for the Delaney Creek and Payne Creek Subbasins are shown in Table 22.9 using both daily and monthly data.

As presented in Table 22.9, due to the Markovian nature of runoff time series, adding the runoff time series Q_t to the dominant daily wavelet-based extracted subseries (strategy B) increased

Table 22.9   Results of *MI*-Based WENN Models for Study Areas Using Haar–db4 Mother Wavelets, Decomposed at Levels 7 and 3 in Daily and Monthly Scales, Respectively

Subbasin	Modeling Scale	Strategy	Input Variables[a]	Structure[b]	C	
					Calibration	Verification
Delaney Creek	Daily	A	$Qd4$, $Qd2$	(2,5,1)	0.79	0.68
		A	$Qd4$, $Qd2$, $Qd3$	(3,6,1)	0.83	0.79
		A	$Qd4$, $Qd2$, $Qd3$, $Qd5$	(4,8,1)	0.90	0.83
		B	$Qd4$, $Qd2$, Q_t	(3,7,1)	0.94	0.75
		B	$Qd4$, $Qd2$, $Qd3$, Q_t	(4,8,1)	0.95	0.86
		B	$Qd4$, $Qd2$, $Qd3$, $Qd5$, Q_t	(5,9,1)	0.94	0.90
	Monthly	A	$Qd2$, $Qd3$	(2,5,1)	0.75	0.71
		A	$Qd2$, $Qd3$, $Qd1$	(3,4,1)	0.81	0.79
Payne Creek	Daily	A	$Qd3$, $Qd2$	(2,5,1)	0.69	0.66
		A	$Qd3$, $Qd2$, $Qd4$	(3,6,1)	0.80	0.77
		A	$Qd3$, $Qd2$, $Qd4$, Qa	(4,7,1)	0.87	0.80
		B	$Qd3$, $Qd2$, Q_t	(3,5,1)	0.90	0.70
		B	$Qd3$, $Qd2$, $Qd4$, Q_t	(4,7,1)	0.91	0.82
		B	$Qd3$, $Qd2$, $Qd4$, Qa, Q_t	(5,8,1)	0.92	0.85
	Monthly	A	$Qd2$, $Qd3$	(2,4,1)	0.68	0.67
		A	$Qd2$, $Qd3$, $Qd1$	(3,5,1)	0.78	0.76

[a] Q_{t+1} is the output variable.
[b] Best result has been presented among several structures.

the *C* values at both calibration and verification steps up to 20%. It is also notable that the structure of the FFNN when using monthly data (the neurons of input and hidden layers of FFNN) is simpler than daily cases.

Table 22.9 presents the best structures of WENN models using different mother wavelets (Haar–db4, db2, coif2, and Meyer) for both daily and monthly data of the Delaney Creek and Payne Creek Subbasins. The results reconfirm that the similarity between the shape of the mother wavelet and the shape of study time series is the most exclusive guideline to select the proper mother wavelet. As tabulated in Table 22.10, since majority of accurate models include *Qd3*, *Qd2*, and *Qa* in their input layer, they are the most dominant subseries to develop the daily model of the process. In other words, *Qa* (trend or approximation subseries), *Qd2* (2^2 = 4 days), and *Qd3* (2^3 = 8 days, approximately weekly) modes as the dominant daily seasonalities of the process were more suitable to be used as input variables compared to other subseries. It is notable that *Qd1* (2^1 = 2 months) and *Qd3* (2^3 = 8 months) modes were recognized as the dominant monthly seasonalities of the process. It is also inferred from Table 22.10 that almost all of the dominant inputs belong to the runoff subseries.

22.4.6 *Comparison of Models*

In order to compare performance of two proposed methodologies (WSNN and WENN), obtained results are summarized in Table 22.11.

In a hybrid WSNN for daily modeling, the employed sizes of the SOM output layer for decomposing at levels 3 and 7 were 1 × 2 and 1 × 4 grids, respectively. In data preprocessing by an SOM for both study areas, the level 5 decomposition showed better results among other examined decomposition levels. When using decomposition level 3, a few seasonalities of the main time series were taken into account. Therefore, an incompetent number of timescales decreased the model performance. Model performance was greatly reduced by increasing the decomposition level up to level 7. Level 7 of decomposition contained 16 subseries (i.e., 14 detailed and 2 approximation subseries of rainfall and runoff time series), which might be too many for the SOM to handle the clustering well. Since the SOM clusters data according to similarity and does not pay attention to importance of data in modeling the process, it is possible for a cluster to completely contain insignificant data.

To determine the effect of the decomposition level in daily WENN models, two other levels (i.e., levels 3 and 5) were also examined for both subbasins. As tabulated in Table 22.11, the change of the decomposition level had no major effect on the values of *C*. The result is justifiable according to the supervised inherence of the *MI* criterion, which can accurately discern the subseries containing redundant information.

According to Table 22.11, in monthly modeling, the WSNN showed lower performance compared to the daily models. This might be due to a few numbers of subseries utilized in monthly preprocessing, which the SOM could not organize properly. It was reconfirmed via monthly WENN models, which indicated more uncertainty involved in monthly data. It should be noted that the information content is considered as a measure of randomness and uncertainty.

It is also inferred from Table 22.11 that WENN models were more accurate than WSNN models, which refers to the basic disagreement of the models. The structure of the SOM is unsupervised (similar to *E* and *H* criteria) because the method classifies the subseries with no attention to the values of the output, whereas the *MI*-based WENN is a supervised feature extraction method.

In order to evaluate the efficiency of the proposed daily and monthly models, comparison among the best results of WENN, WSNN, ad hoc FFNN (without data preprocessing), and classic ARIMAX $(p,d,q)I(t)$ models was also conducted, and the results are presented in Table 22.12. According to Section 22.1, ARIMAX and ad hoc FFNN models are reported by many researchers as

Table 22.10 Mother Wavelet Impact on Results of Proposed WENN Model for Study Areas, in Daily and Monthly Scales

Subbasin	Model Scale	Mother Wavelet	Input Variables[a]	Structure[b]	Calibration		Verification	
					C	RMSE (Normalized)	C	RMSE (Normalized)
Delaney Creek	Daily	Haar–db4	Qd4, Qd2, Qd3, Qd5,	(5,9,1)	0.94	0.008	0.90	0.011
		db2	Qa, Qd4, Qd3, Q_t	(4,8,1)	0.86	0.015	0.83	0.017
		coif2	Qd2, Qd3, Pd2, Qd7	(4,11,1)	0.86	0.014	0.81	0.018
		Meyer	Qd2, Qd3, Qd4, Qa, Q_t	(5,12,1)	0.90	0.012	0.86	0.015
	Monthly	Haar–db4	Qd2, Qd3, Qd1	(3,4,1)	0.81	0.038	0.79	0.043
		db2	Qd3, Qa, Qd1	(3,5,1)	0.80	0.038	0.75	0.042
		coif2	Qa, Qd3, Qd1, Pd2	(4,5,1)	0.77	0.040	0.74	0.043
		Meyer	Qd3, Qa	(2,4,1)	0.78	0.039	0.74	0.044
Payne Creek	Daily	Haar–db4	Qd3, Qd2, Qd4, Qa,Q_t	(5,8,1)	0.92	0.011	0.85	0.015
		db2	Qa, Qd3, Qd5, Pd2	(4,8,1)	0.85	0.016	0.80	0.019
		coif2	Qa, Qd3, Qd2,Q_t	(4,9,1)	0.84	0.017	0.79	0.020
		Meyer	Qd2, Qd3, Qd4, Qa,Q_t	(5,11,1)	0.87	0.014	0.83	0.017
	Monthly	Haar–db4	Qd2, Qd3, Qd1	(3,5,1)	0.78	0.030	0.76	0.029
		db2	Qa, Qd2, Qd1	(3,6,1)	0.76	0.031	0.71	0.034
		coif2	Qd3, Qd2, Pd2	(3,4,1)	0.72	0.033	0.71	0.033
		Meyer	Qd3, Qa, Qd1	(3,5,1)	0.72	0.034	0.70	0.034

[a] Q_{t+1} is the output variable.
[b] Best result has been presented among several structures.

Table 22.11 Comparison of WENN and WSNN Models for Daily and Monthly Modeling of Both Study Areas using Haar–db4 Mother Wavelet

Watershed	Type of Model		Level of Decomposition	Input Variables	Calibration		Verification	
					C	RMSE (Normalized)	C	RMSE (Normalized)
Delaney Creek	WENN	Daily	3	Qa, Qd1, Pa	0.89	0.012	0.82	0.019
			5	Pd2, Qd5, Qd4	0.93	0.010	0.86	0.015
			7	Qd4, Qd2, Qd3, Qd5	0.94	0.008	0.90	0.011
		Monthly	3	Qd2, Qd3, Qd1	0.81	0.038	0.79	0.043
	WSNN	Daily	3	Qa, Qd1, Pa, Pd2	0.91	0.011	0.85	0.009
			5	Qa, Qd2, Qd3, Qd4, Pa, Pd2	0.94	0.008	0.86	0.015
			7	Qa, Qd5, Qd6, Qd7, Pa, Pd7	0.62	0.020	0.54	0.028
		Monthly	3	Pa, Pd3, Qa, Qd2	0.84	0.034	0.71	0.038
Payne Creek	WENN	Daily	3	Qa, Pa, Qd2	0.92	0.011	0.83	0.023
			5	Qa, Qd3, Qd4	0.89	0.013	0.80	0.020
			7	Qd3, Qd2, Qd4, Qa	0.92	0.011	0.85	0.015
		Monthly	3	Qd2, Qd3, Qd1	0.78	0.030	0.76	0.029
	WSNN	Daily	3	Qa, Qd2, Pa, Pd2	0.82	0.025	0.75	0.059
			5	Qa, Qd4, Pa, Pd1, Pd3, Pd5	0.87	0.045	0.79	0.016
			7	Qa, Qd4, Qd6, Pa, Pd3, Pd6	0.69	0.014	0.60	0.025
		Monthly	3	Qa, Qd3, Pa, Pd3	0.79	0.020	0.75	0.032

Table 22.12 Comparison of Best Results Obtained by Different Models for Daily and Monthly Modeling of Both Study Areas

Watershed		Type of Model	C		RMSE (Normalized)	
			Calibration	Verification	Calibration	Verification
Delaney Creek	Daily	WENN	0.94	0.008	0.90	0.011
		WSNN	0.94	0.008	0.86	0.015
		Ad hoc FFNN	0.90	0.012	0.81	0.016
		ARIMAX(3, 0, 1)I(t)	0.78	0.017	0.65	0.023
	Monthly	WENN	0.81	0.038	0.79	0.043
		WSNN	0.84	0.034	0.71	0.038
		Ad hoc FFNN	0.80	0.036	0.73	0.036
		ARIMAX(3, 1, 2)I(t)	0.76	0.021	0.67	0.022
Payne Creek	Daily	WENN	0.92	0.011	0.85	0.015
		WSNN	0.87	0.045	0.79	0.016
		Ad hoc FFNN	0.94	0.015	0.73	0.016
		ARIMAX(3, 0, 1)I(t)	0.72	0.019	0.64	0.025
	Monthly	WENN	0.78	0.030	0.76	0.029
		WSNN	0.79	0.020	0.75	0.032
		Ad hoc FFNN	0.75	0.023	0.70	0.034
		ARIMAX(2, 1, 1)I(t)	0.73	0.021	0.67	0.023

the best suited conventional approaches detecting linear and nonlinear relations, respectively. The ARIMAX methodology has the ability to identify complex patterns in data and generate forecasts. It is used to predict the future according to the past input and/or output data of the process according to the linear relationships. The ARIMAX model function is represented by (p, d, q), with p representing the number of autoregressive terms, d the number of nonseasonal differences, and q the number of lagged forecast errors in the prediction equation. In this study, precipitation ($I(t)$) and antecedents of runoff data were used as exogenous inputs to predict future runoff as the output; moreover, various values were examined to the ARIMAX parameters p, q, and d. Unlike other models, the ARIMAX model was first calibrated using the training data set, and the calibrated model was then validated using the verification data set. As an example, the ARIMAX $(3, 0, 1)$ $I(t)$ refers to a model that contains three autoregressive (p) parameters and one moving average (q) parameter, which were computed for the series after it was differenced (d) 0 times. The weak performance of the ARIMAX model confirms disability of a linear model (e.g., ARIMAX) to handle a complex nonlinear hydrologic process like rainfall–runoff.

The tabulated results in Table 22.12 indicate that application of the Delany Creek data to the ARIMAX model, due to its linear inherence, was unable to completely handle the complex nonlinear rainfall–runoff process. Although ad hoc FFNN model was more efficient than the ARIMAX model, it only considered short-term autoregressive features of the process and could not capture long-term seasonality. Therefore, it obtained lower performance compared with the FFNN connected to wavelet and feature extraction concepts.

By comparing the statistics of the data (i.e., max and standard deviation values; Table 22.1) and topographic characteristics (i.e., slope and area; see Section 22.6) of both watersheds, it can be emphasized that the Payne Creek Subbasin, with a vaster area and spatially different topological features, may show more complex dynamic behavior than the Delaney Creek Subbasin. Therefore, in spite of acceptable performance of WSNN and WENN models for both watersheds, the proposed hybrid models, as well as ad hoc FFNN and ARIMAX, led to lower performance for the Payne Creek Subbasin with respect to the Delaney Creek Subbasin (see Table 22.12).

22.5 Concluding Remarks

WANN-based modeling of the rainfall–runoff process detects nonlinear relationships involved at various timescales. Despite several seasonalities, which can be found in a process, all of them are not informative or have considerable effect on the model performance. Application of a model, such as an FFNN, without proper data preprocessing can lead to decline in modeling performance, which usually becomes unveiled in the network overfitting. In this chapter, combinations of two methodologies with a WANN were applied to preprocess available rainfall–runoff time series of the Delaney Creek and Payne Creek watersheds. Wavelet transform was used to capture multiscale features of the signals by decomposing the main time series into several subseries. SOM and entropy concepts were then applied to extract the important features of the process. In the WSNN model, centers of clusters as the representative of the clusters, and in WENN model subseries diagnosed with high values of information, were determined as important and informative inputs and imposed into the FFNN in order to forecast one-day and one-month ahead values of runoff discharge. The observed rainfall and runoff data of two study areas with different topological features were used in this study. The utilized mother wavelets in order to decompose rainfall and runoff time series were db2, coif2, Meyer, and Haar–db4 mother wavelets. The results evidenced that application of mother wavelets according to the similarity of mother wavelet shape with main time series formations might lead to better results. Three decomposition levels were examined in the daily modeling (i.e., levels 3, 5, and 7). In the WSNN model, decomposing the main time series at level 5, which includes monthly seasonality, led to better performance. Model performance was drastically reduced by increasing the decomposition level up to 7. This might happen due to an increase in the subseries number, which the SOM could not cluster properly. In the WENN model, the change of the decomposition level had no major effect on the values of C and $RMSE$. The result is justifiable according to the supervised inherence of the MI criterion, which can accurately discern the subseries containing redundant information. In monthly modeling, the WSNN and WENN approaches showed lower performance compared with daily models. This might be due to a few numbers of subseries utilized in monthly preprocessing, which the SOM could not organize appropriately, and monthly WENN models because of more uncertainty involved that yielded poor consequence of modeling. Runoff subseries, according to its Markovian characteristic, showed more effect compared with rainfall subseries for rainfall–runoff modeling of the studied watersheds. To evaluate the performance of the model, the proposed methodologies were also compared with two classic models without any data preprocessing (i.e., ARIMAX method as a linear model and ad hoc FFNN as a nonlinear model). The results show that the ARIMAX model due to its linear inherence could not detect the nonlinear relationship between studied parameters. Although the ad hoc FFNN yielded better performance, it only considered short-term autoregressive features of the process and could not capture long-term seasonalities. From the point of view of uncertainty, the WSNN model was more effective than other conventional models in modeling wild watersheds (e.g., Payne Creek).

22.6 Research Plan for the Future

To complete the current study, it can be helpful to involve other effective parameters like evaporation in runoff prediction for single and multistep ahead forecasting. Furthermore, it is suggested to examine other artificial intelligence approaches to forecast runoff values. For instance, according to the capability of the fuzzy set theory, the conjunction of the fuzzy and ANN concepts as the adaptive neural-fuzzy inference system (ANFIS) may lead to a promising tool to handle the uncertainty of the hydrological process as well as its hysteretic property.

On the other hand, due to social and economic importance of the study areas, it is also suggested to couple the proposed ANN-based model to a geomorphology-based rainfall–runoff model (e.g., TOPMODEL; Nourani and Zanardo 2012) to have a comprehensive semidistributed rainfall–runoff modeling for the site.

References

Abrahart, R.J., Anctil, F., Coulibaly, P. et al. 2012. Two decades of anarchy? Emerging themes and outstanding challenges for neural network river forecasting. *Prog. Phys. Geog.* 36(4):480–513.

Adamowski, J. 2008. Development of a short-term river flood forecasting method for snowmelt driven floods based on wavelet and cross-wavelet analysis. *J. Hydrol.* 353:247–266.

Adamowski, J. and Chan, H.F. 2011. A wavelet neural network conjunction model for groundwater level forecasting. *J. Hydrol.* 407:28–40.

Adamowski, J., Chan, H.F., Prasher, S.O. and Sharda, V.N. 2012. Comparison of multivariate adaptive regression splines with coupled wavelet transform artificial neural networks for runoff forecasting in Himalayan micro-watersheds with limited data. *J. Hydroinform.* 14(3):731–744.

Addison, P.S., Murrary, K.B. and Watson, J.N. 2001. Wavelet transform analysis of open channel wake flows. *J. Eng. Mech.* 127(1):58–70.

Alfonso, L., He, L., Lobbrecht, A. and Price, R. 2013. Information theory applied to evaluate the discharge monitoring network of the Magdalena River. *J. Hydroinform.* 15(1):211–228.

Al-Hamdan, O.Z. and Cruise, J.F. 2010. Soil moisture profile development from surface observations by principle of maximum entropy. *J. Hydrol. Eng.* 15(5):327–337.

Amorocho, J. and Espildora, B. 1973. Entropy in the assessment of uncertainty in hydrologic systems and models. *Water Resour. Res.* 9(6):1551–1522.

ASCE Task Committee on the Application of ANNs in Hydrology. 2000a. Artificial neural networks in hydrology, II: Hydrologic applications. *J. Hydrol. Eng.* 5(2):115–123.

ASCE Task Committee on Application of Artificial Neural Networks in Hydrology. 2000b. Artificial neural networks in hydrology. I: Preliminary concepts. *J. Hydrol. Eng.* 5:124–137.

Aussem, A., Campbell, J. and Murtagh, F. 1998. Wavelet-based feature extraction and decomposition strategies for financial forecasting. *J. Comp. Intel. Fin.* 6(2):5–12.

Bowden, G.J., Maier, H.R. and Dandy, G.C. 2002. Optimal division of data for neural network models in water resources applications. *Water Resour. Res.* 38:1010–1011.

Bowden, G.J., Dandy, G.C. and Maier, H.R. 2005. Input determination for neural network models in water resources applications. Part 1—background and methodology. *J. Hydrol.* 301:75–92.

Cannas, B., Fanni, A., See, L. and Sias, G. 2006. Data preprocessing for river flow forecasting using neural networks: Wavelet transforms and data partitioning. *Phys. Chem. Earth.* 31(18):1164–1171.

Cao, S.Y. and Chang, H.H. 1988. Entropy as a probability concept in energy gradient distribution. Proc., 1988 National Conf. on Hydraulic Engineering, 1013–1018.

Caselton, W.F. and Husain, T. 1980. Hydrological networks: Information transmission. *J. Water Resour. Plann. Manag.* 106:503–520.

Cereghino, R. and Park, Y.S. 2009. Review of the self-organizing map (SOM) approach in water resources: Commentary. *Env. Model. Soft.* 24:945–947.

Chang, L.C., Shen, H.Y., Wang, Y.F., Huang, J.Y. and Lin, Y.T. 2010. Clustering-based hybrid inundation model for forecasting flood inundation depths. *J. Hydrol.* 385:257–268.

Chiu, C.L. 1987. Entropy and probability concepts in hydraulics. *J. Hydraul. Eng.* 113(5):583–600.

Chon, T.S., Park, Y.S., Moon, K.H. and Cha, E.Y. 1996. Patternizing communities by using an artificial neural network. *Ecol. Model.* 90:69–78.

Collignon, A., Maes, F., Delaere, D., Vandermeulen, D., Suetens, P. and Marchal, G. 1995. Automated multi-modality image registration based on information theory. Proc., Information Processing in Medical Imaging, Kluwer Academic Publishers, Dordrecht, 263–274.

Dawson, C.W. and Wilby, R.L. 2001. Hydrological modeling using artificial neural networks. *Prog. Phys. Geogr.* 25:80–108.

Ebrahimi, N., Maasoumi, E. and Soofi, E. 1999. Ordering univariate distributions by entropy and variance. *J. Econom.* 90(2):317–336.

Gao, Z., Gu, B. and Lin, J. 2008. Mono-modal image registration using mutual information based methods. *Image Vision Comput.* 26:164–173.

Harmancioglu, N.B. and Singh, V.P. 1998. Entropy in environmental and water resources. In *Encyclopedia of Hydrology and Water Resources*. Kluwer Academic Publishers, Dordrecht, 225–241.

Hornik, K., Stinchcombe, M. and White, H. 1989. Multilayer feed forward networks are universal approximators. *Neural Networks.* 2:359–366.

Hsu, K., Gupta, H.V. and Sorooshian, S. 1995. Artificial neural network modeling of rainfall-runoff process. *Water Resour. Res.* 31:2517–2530.

Husain, T. 1989. Hydrologic uncertainty measure and network design. *Water Resour. Bull.* 253:527–534.

Iliadis, L.S. and Maris, F. 2007. An artificial neural network model for mountainous water-resources management: The case of Cyprus mountainous watersheds. *Env. Model. Soft.* 22:1066–1072.

Jain, A. and Srinivasulu, S. 2006. Integrated approach to model decomposed flow hydrograph using artificial neural network and conceptual techniques. *J. Hydrol.* 317:291–306.

Kalteh, A.M. and Berndtsson, R. 2007. Interpolating monthly precipitation by self-organizing map (SOM) and multilayer perceptron (MLP). *Hydrol. Sci. J.* 52:305–317.

Kalteh, A.M., Hjorth, P. and Berndtsson, R. 2008. Review of the self-organizing map (SOM) approach in water resources: Analysis, modeling and application. *Env. Model. Soft.* 23:835–845.

Kawachi, T., Maruyama, T. and Singh, V.P. 2001. Rainfall entropy for delineation of water resources zones in Japan. *J. Hydrol.* 246:36–44.

Kohonen, T., Makisara, K. and Saramaki, T. 1984. Phonotopic maps insightful representation of phonological features for speech recognition. Proceedings of 7ICPR, International Conference on Pattern Recognition, CA, IEEE Computer Society Press, Los Alamitos, 182–185.

Krstanovic, P.F. and Singh, V.P. 1992a. Evaluation of rainfall networks using entropy I. *Water Resour. Manag.* 6:279–293.

Krstanovic, P.F. and Singh, V.P. 1992b. Evaluation of rainfall networks using entropy II. *Water Resour. Manag.* 6:295–314.

Legates, D.R. and McCabe, G.J. 1999. Evaluating the use of "goodness-of-fit" measures in hydrologic and hydroclimatic model validation. *Water Resour. Res.* 35(1):233–241.

Lin, G.F. and Chen, L.H. 2006. Identification of homogeneous regions for regional frequency analysis using the self-organizing map. *J. Hydrol.* 324:1–9.

Lin, G.F. and Wu, M.C. 2007. A SOM-based approach to estimate design hyetographs of ungauged sites. *J. Hydrol.* 339:216–226.

Maheswaran, R. and Khosa, R. 2012. Multi-scale nonlinear model for monthly stream flow forecasting: A wavelet-based approach. *J. Hydroinform.* 14:424–442.

Maier, H.R. and Dandy, G.C. 2000. Neural networks for the prediction and forecasting of water resources variables: A review of modelling issues and applications. *Env. Model. Soft.* 15:101–124.

Mallat, S.G. 1998. *A Wavelet Tour of Signal Processing*, Academic Publication, San Diego, CA.

MathWorks, Inc. 2010a. *MATLAB: User's Guide, Version 7*. The Math Works, Inc., Natick, MA.

MathWorks, Inc. 2010b. *MATLAB: SOM Toolbox (NCTOOL) User's Guide, Version 7*. The Math Works, Inc., Natick, MA.

May, R.J., Maier, H.R., Dandy, G.C. and Gayani Fernando, T.M.K. 2008. Non-linear variable selection for artificial neural networks using partial information. *Environ. Modell. Softw.* 23:1312–1326.

Mishra, A.K., Ozger, M. and Singh, V.P. 2009. An entropy-based investigation into the variability of precipitation. *J. Hydrol.* 370:139–154.

Nourani, V. and Kalantari, O. 2010. An integrated artificial neural network for spatiotemporal modeling of rainfall-runoff-sediment processes. *Environ. Eng. Sci.* 27(5):411–422.

Nourani, V. and Zanardo, S. 2012. Wavelet-based regularization of the extracted topographic index from high resolution topography for hydro-geomorphic applications. *Hydrol. Process.* Published online, doi:10.1002/hyp.9665.

Nourani, V., Monadjemi, P. and Singh, V.P. 2007. Liquid analogue model for laboratory simulation of rainfall–runoff process. *J. Hydrol. Eng.* 12:246–255.

Nourani, V., Mogaddam, A.A. and Nadiri, A. 2008. An ANN-based model for spatiotemporal groundwater level forecasting. *Hydrol. Process.* 22(26):5054–5066.

Nourani, V., Alami, M.T. and Aminfar, M.H. 2009a. A combined neural-wavelet model for prediction of Ligvanchai watershed precipitation. *Eng. Appl. Artif. Intell.* 22:466–472.

Nourani, V., Komasi, M. and Mano, A. 2009b. A multivariate ANN-Wavelet approach for rainfall runoff modelling. *Water Resour. Manag.* 23:2877–2894.

Nourani, V., Kisi, O. and Komasi, M. 2011. Two hybrid artificial intelligence approaches for modeling rainfall-runoff process. *J. Hydrol.* 402:41–59.

Nourani, V., Komasi, M. and Alami, M.T. 2012. Hybrid wavelet-genetic programming approach to optimize ANN modeling of rainfall-runoff process. *J. Hydrol. Eng.* 16:724–741.

Nourani, V., Hosseini Baghanam, A., Adamowski, J. and Gebremichael, M. 2013. Using self-organizing maps and wavelet transforms for space–time pre-processing of satellite precipitation and runoff data in neural network based rainfall–runoff modeling. *J. Hydrol.* 476:228–243.

Partal, T. and Kisi, O. 2007. Wavelet and neuro-fuzzy conjunction model for precipitation forecasting. *J. Hydrol.* 342:199–212.

Partal, T. and Cigizoglu, H.K. 2008. Estimation and forecasting of daily suspended sediment data using wavelet-neural networks. *J. Hydrol.* 358(3–4):317–331.

Rajaee, T., Nourani, V., Zounemat-Kermani, M. and Kisi, O. 2011. River suspended sediment load prediction: Application of ANN and wavelet conjunction model. *J. Hydrol. Eng.* 16(8):613–627.

Remesan, R., Shamim, M.A., Han, D. and Mathew, J. 2009. Runoff prediction using an integrated hybrid modelling scheme. *J. Hydrol.* 372:48–60.

Salas, J.D., Delleur, J.W., Yevjevich, V. and Lane, W.L. 1980. *Applied Modeling of Hydrological Time Series*. Water Resources Publications, Denver, CO.

Sang, Y.F. 2012. A practical guide to discrete wavelet decomposition of hydrologic time series. *Water Resour. Manag.* 26:3345–3365.

Sang, Y.F. 2013. A review on the applications of wavelet transform in hydrology time series analysis. *Atmos. Res.* 122:8–15.

Shannon, C.E. 1948. A mathematical theory of communications I and II. *Bell Syst. Tech. J.* 27:379–443.

Singh, V.P. 1997. The use of entropy in hydrology and water resources. *Hydrol. Process.* 11:587–626.

Singh, V.P. 2010. Entropy theory for derivation of infiltration equations. *Water Resour. Res.* 46:W03527.

Singh, V.P. 2011. Hydrologic synthesis using entropy theory: Review. *J. Hydrol. Eng.* 16:421–433.

Tiwari, M.K. and Chatterjee, C.h. 2010. Development of an accurate and reliable hourly flood forecasting model using wavelet-bootstrap-ANN (WBANN) hybrid approach. *J. Hydrol.* 394(3–4):458–470.

Tsai, C.C., Lu, M.C. and Wei, C.C. 2012. Decision tree-based classifier combined with neural-based predictor for water-stage forecasts in a river basin during typhoons: A case study in Taiwan. *Environ. Eng. Sci.* 29:108–116.

Viola, P. and Wells, W.M. 1995. Alignment by maximization of mutual information. Proc. International Conference on Computer Vision, IEEE Computer Society Press, Los Alamitos, CA, 16–23.

Wu, C.L., Chau, K.W. and Li, Y.S. 2009. Predicting monthly stream flow using data-driven models coupled with data pre-processing techniques. *Water Resour. Res.* 45:W08432.

Chapter 23

Artificial Intelligence: A Tool for Better Understanding Complex Problems in Long-Term Care

Vijay K. Mago, Ryan Woolrych,
Vahid Dabbaghian, and Andrew Sixsmith

Contents

Given the globally ageing population, governments need to prepare for the challenges of providing good-quality health care while supporting the independence and quality-of-life needs of older people. The complexity of this challenge requires novel and cross-disciplinary solutions. Current research in the area of gerontology has not fully recognized the benefits of artificial intelligence (AI)–based solutions to addressing these issues. AI and mathematical modeling techniques present the opportunity to better conceptualize and develop new insights in the area of gerontology, with the ultimate goal of designing, testing, and implementing interventions that can improve the quality of life of older people and address the challenges of an ageing population. This chapter provides an insight into five key AI and mathematical modeling techniques, namely Bayesian network, compartmental model, multiagent system, fuzzy logic, and fuzzy cognitive maps. The fundamentals of the techniques are elaborated with example scenarios chosen from long-term care (LTC) institutions. The chapter critically evaluates each of the techniques by demonstrating the strengths and weaknesses of the various approaches.

23.1 Introduction

The world population is rapidly ageing and the number of people over the age of 60 will double by the year 2050 [1]. The phenomenon of population aging is not limited to the developed world, with 64% of older people living in less developed regions, a figure that is set to rise to 80% by 2050. The pace of global ageing will have far-reaching implications on society and raises complex challenges for all levels of government in terms of how best to support the health, independence, and well-being of older people [2]. Research has attempted to address these challenges from a gerontological perspective through medical, social, and health promotion perspectives [3]. It is increasingly recognized that these perspectives may benefit from innovative, cross-disciplinary solutions in order to meet the complexities of supporting people into old age. One particular area for application is the potential of artificial intelligence (AI) and mathematical modeling techniques as a tool to help researchers and policy makers to better understand and design interventions to meet those emerging challenges. Models provide the means to (1) explain and describe real-world phenomena, (2) investigate important questions about the observed world, (3) test ideas, and (4) make predictions about the real world.

The applicability of AI and mathematical modeling techniques in the health care domain has been demonstrated in the work of the Simon Fraser University CSMG Group [4], but its potential in the more specific field of gerontology is yet to be explored. While gerontology has become a significant academic field, research is limited by disciplinary "silos" and theoretical weaknesses that undermine its applicability to applied problems and the development of effective policy and practice [1]. AI approaches may be particularly valuable in terms of addressing the inherent complexity of social problems. In this chapter, attention is given specifically to the way AI-based modeling can be used to address the delivery of care in institutional settings specifically long-term care (LTC) facilities. The numbers of older people admitted to LTC is predicted to increase in line with the ageing population, and those admitted to LTC facilities will require more intense levels of care than ever before. An LTC facility provides living accommodations for people who require continuous care and supervised support to meet their personal needs, including personal care delivery such as toileting, bathing, meal preparation, laundry, and preparing/administering medications [5]. There are a number of complex issues in the delivery of care for older people living in LTC, in the working practices of care providers, and in the organizational structure of the LTC facility, which need to be explored and better understood to ensure that older people receive the highest quality of care provision and that the needs of future older generations are met. This includes issues related to the admission of older people into LTC, the prevention of falls in LTC, reviewing medical regimes, the ongoing monitoring of residents, training, and organizing care delivery. However, there are significant variations across the Canadian provinces in the availability of services, level of public funding, eligibility criteria, and the costs of delivering services, resulting in a high degree of complexity when meeting the needs of older people.

Applying AI-based models to understanding issues in the field of gerontology and specifically in the management and delivery of care in LTC facilities is a complex and challenging task. Valuable insights gained from this relatively new, interdisciplinary approach provide the potential for policy makers to allocate funds and resources to address them effectively. Towards this end, we present some of the potential AI techniques that can be applied by researchers to better understand issues within the area of gerontology (Section 23.2). All techniques are elaborated in a concise manner and applied to examples provided from the discipline of gerontology, specifically those challenges to supporting older people who require LTC care. A critique of the techniques is provided, which highlights the relative strengths and weaknesses of each approach. Finally, we conclude our work by highlighting some of the ways in which AI-based solutions can be used in gerontology and identify some potential future directions (Section 23.3).

23.2 Modeling Approaches and Example Scenarios

In the following section, five AI and mathematical modeling approaches are described: Bayesian network (BN), compartmental model, multiagent systems (MASs), fuzzy logic (FL), and fuzzy cognitive map (FCM). Following each description, an example is provided demonstrating the potential applicability of the modeling approach to a typical and complex problem in LTC.

23.2.1 Fundamentals of Bayesian Network

Human behavior typically behaves in a random fashion due to the partial knowledge or absence/presence of certain factors. Historically, probability theory is the primary AI tool to solve the problems of randomness or uncertainty. The underlying principle of a BN lies in the interpretation of Bayes' theorem, which is stated in Equation 23.1:

$$P(h|e) = \frac{P(e|h) \times P(h)}{P(e)} \tag{23.1}$$

This is a well-defined theorem of the probability calculus. It asserts that the probability of a hypothesis h conditioned upon some evidence e is equal to its likelihood $P(e|h)$ multiplied by its probability prior to any evidence $P(h)$, normalized by dividing by $P(e)$ (so that the conditional probabilities of all hypotheses sum to 1). Further reading on Bayes' theorem can be found in the work of Spiegel and Stephens [6].

A BN is a graphical model representing probabilistic relationships among a set of variables [7]. The variables are presented as nodes in a graph and a set of directed arcs (or links) that connects pairs of the nodes, representing the direct dependencies between variables. Assuming discrete variables, the strength of the relationship among variables is quantified by conditional probability distributions associated with each node. There is a constraint on the arcs that there must not be any directed cycles, that, one cannot return to a node simply by following directed arcs. In this way, BN is constructed as a directed acyclic graph. More information concerning the construction and applicability of BN can be found in the work of Pourret et al. [8] and Mago et al. [9].

In concise terms, a BN can be seen as composed of a qualitative as well as a quantitative component. The qualitative component is an acyclic directed graph reflecting the causal structure of the domain; the quantitative part represents the joint probability distribution over its variables/nodes. Each individual variable consists of a conditional probability table (CPT) representing the probabilities of each state, given the state of the parent variable. If a variable does not have any parent variable in the graph, the CPT represents the prior probability distribution over the variable. A BN is capable of calculating the posterior probability distribution over an uncertain variable, given some evidence obtained from the related variables.

23.2.1.1 A Sample Scenario

Let us consider a sample scenario where we want to analyze a fall event within an LTC facility involving an older person. Fall incidents are the most common adverse event occurring in LTC facilities having an impact on the health and well-being of older people who can experience severe injury as a result of a fall and postfall restrictions on mobility. There is a complex interplay of factors involved in falls in the long-term with various interdependencies between them. For example, if we know that a resident of an LTC facility regularly takes medication that can increase drowsiness and reduce mental alertness, this is an established risk factor in increasing falls amongst older people [10]. At the time of the fall, if we also know that there was poor lighting in the location where the fall incident took place, this represents an environmental hazard that may have impacted on the ability of the older person to navigate his/her way around the care facility [11]. Counteracting these fall risk factors, each resident within the care facility is required to wear an accelerometer (measures movement acceleration forces), to assist in the early detection of falls amongst older people [12]. The LTC facility in question is also required to complete a fall incident at the time of the fall for monitoring and assessment purposes, which provides further information about what happened at the time of the fall. The BN for this scenario is presented in Figure 23.1.

BN is a powerful reasoning tool as it provides various reasoning mechanisms under uncertain circumstances. These are further elaborated as follows with respect to the aforementioned example.

■ *Diagnostic reasoning*: This is defined as reasoning from symptoms to cause, such as when the caregiver monitors the closed-circuit television (CCTV) footage of the fall and, by doing so, informs or updates his/her knowledge of the fall event. This may prompt the caregiver to query the apparent drowsiness of the patient or the quality of the lighting in that area of the care facility. This reasoning occurs in the opposite direction to the network arcs, bottom to top.

■ *Predictive reasoning*: This is the reasoning derived from new information about "causes" to new understandings of "effects," following the directions of the network arcs. For example,

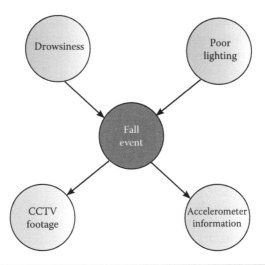

Figure 23.1   A simple Bayesian network of a fall event.

the caregiver knows the resident is taking medication that can result in drowsiness and wants to know the probability of the fall occurring and the extent to which this is heightened in the presence of poor lighting.

■ *Intercausal reasoning*: This involves reasoning about the mutual causes of a common effect; this is termed intercausal reasoning and also known as explaining away. For example, the effect of the facility having poor lighting and the resident experiencing drowsiness may have an equally contributory impact on the fall. This means that there is no connection between these two causes, that is, poor lighting and drowsiness are not related. But given that the resident has experienced a fall and that the facility has poor lighting, the causal effect of drowsiness on the fall incident reduces. So, even though the two causes are initially independent, acquiring knowledge of the presence of one explains the decreasing likelihood of the other.

■ *Combined reasoning*: Since any node may be a *query* node or *evidence* node, this type of reasoning is known as combined reasoning. The query node can be assumed as the output node or observable node, and the evidence node can be considered as the input node. Combined reasoning is a combination of diagnostic and predictive reasoning. For example, we know that the resident has fallen due to poor lighting within the LTC facility and that the caregiver has reviewed the fall incident report through CCTV footage. Now, with all this information, it is expected that the accelerometer should have recorded this event. This will help validate the accelerometer device and/or provide evidence for the manufacturer to fine-tune the functionality of the device.

23.2.1.2 Critical Appraisal

The structure of the BN and the way one can engage in a process of reasoning with BN makes it suitable in tackling uncertainty across a broad range of problems. But the principal disadvantage of BN is the amount of probabilities required to complete CPT. If a node has many parents or the parents can take a large number of states, the CPT can become overly complex and unwieldy. The size of the CPT is, in fact, exponential to the number of the parents. Thus, for the boolean networks, a variable with n parents requires a CPT with 2^{n+1} probabilities [13]. Moreover, BN does not allow feedback loops, which makes it unsuitable for some systems modeling. Nonetheless, BN is one of the most widely used techniques in modeling.

23.2.2 Basics of Compartmental Model

In order to model the progression of any phenomena in a large population, homogeneous subsystems of people are defined. These subsystems are also known as compartments, and the people in these compartments share common characteristics, such as groups of people who are susceptible to infectious disease, those who are infected with the disease, and those who have recovered from the disease, as shown in Figure 23.2.

This mathematical modeling approach has been widely used to show the progress of an epidemic of various diseases such as tuberculosis, meningitis, gonorrhea, and so forth [14] and is a popular technique amongst mathematical epidemiologists, and its impact is increasing [15]. The use of the term *SIR* defines the path from susceptible class S to the infective class I to the recovered class R. The unidirectional movement of people implies that people who are recovered from the disease cannot enter the susceptible class again. This is the simple flow diagram. Another conceivable model can be as follows:

- SIS: Susceptible to infective and then back to susceptible
- SEIS: Susceptible to exposed to infective and then back to susceptible
- SEIR: Susceptible to exposed to infective and finally to recovered
- SIRS: Susceptible to infective to recovered and then back to susceptible

The number of people in each compartment varies over a period of time. This dynamic is captured by the variable function t. If we assume that the population size, say N, is constant, then the following conditions, Equations 23.2 and 23.3, hold true:

$$S(t) + I(t) + R(t) = N \tag{23.2}$$

$$\frac{dS}{dt} + \frac{dI}{dt} + \frac{dR}{dt} = 0 \tag{23.3}$$

This simple mathematical model was first introduced by Kermack and McKendrick [16], and since then, it has been modified by various researchers by introducing new theoretical aspects from biology, clinical advancements in medicine, pathology, and so forth. Recently, Hare et al. [17] used a similar modeling approach to predict home and community care client counts in British

Figure 23.2   A schematic compartmental representation (SIR). People "move" between different categories.

Columbia (BC), Canada. This model aims to provide insight into the increasing demand of residents requiring community care over the next 20 years in BC.

23.2.2.1 A Sample Scenario

The spread of infectious disease such as MRSA or influenza is an ever-present challenge for LTC facilities, potentially compromising the health and well-being of those who work and reside in LTC. A number of environmental factors play an important role in the spread of influenza [18]. In LTC facilities, health care providers come into contact with elderly people who are frail and susceptible to contracting viruses and infections, and the risk of spreading the infection from person to person is high. A study conducted by the Norwegian Institute of Public Health highlighted the need for better infection surveillance in LTC [19].

Using the compartmental model, we can assume that the health care providers are susceptible to infection, which may result in infecting elders at the LTC. To understand the overall relationship, Grundmann and Hellriegel [20] suggested a mathematical model that utilizes a compartmental approach to address this complex health care issue. We provide a simplified model, as shown in Figure 23.3, where health care staff have some interaction with peers in addition to providing care to older people. In the flow diagram, we assume that there is an interaction of susceptible and infected people only and that the people who are recovered and reintroduced into the system behave in a more protective way, that is, by maintaining a high standard of hygiene, for example, washing hands or wearing gloves, and hence do not pose a threat of contraction again.

23.2.2.2 Critical Appraisal

This modeling approach has gained significant attention from health care professionals as it provides an insight into system dynamics. This approach describes, quantifies, and predicts the trend of a variable of interest. The main drawback of this approach is oversimplification of the process and that it requires some basic mathematical understanding of the concepts. Nevertheless, a theoretical framework and literature has emerged over the past decade or so to assist researchers in applying this mathematical modeling technique more extensively [21,22].

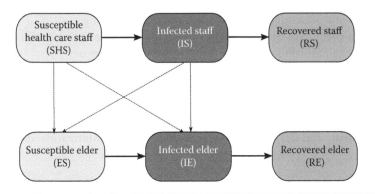

Figure 23.3   Flow diagrams for different types of health care givers at LTC who are exposed to the nosocomial infection.

23.2.3 Basics of Agent and Multiagent Systems

A large body of the research in AI is concerned with developing theories, techniques, and systems to study and understand the behavior and reasoning properties of a single cognitive entity. But with the advent of agent technology, researchers have increasingly engaged in solutions to solve complex, realistic, and large-scale problems. In concise terms, an agent is anything that perceives its environment through sensors and acts or reacts through effectors towards a designed goal. To illustrate this, assume an assistant (human agent, for example, a care assistant who has responsibility for assisting an older person in his/her everyday routine tasks). The agent recognizes that the older person will wake up in the morning and knows in advance that the person needs to visit the washroom. Prior to doing this, the human agent knows that the older persons should ensure they are fully alert and need to stabilize themselves prior to making the journey to the washroom. With his/her predefined knowledge about the tasks, the assistant can direct the old person to undertake these tasks effectively (wake–ensure alertness–stabilize–raise body–exit bed). Similarly, assume that a computer program (software agent) is able to determine (through monitoring technologies in the home) that the LTC resident has woken. This agent can mimic the behavior of the human agent and issue voice messages including prompts, encouragements, and commands such that the process can be synchronized with the activities performed by the old person. Formally, a software agent is a computer system situated within a particular environment that is capable of autonomous action in the environment in order to meet certain designed objectives. By autonomous, we mean that the system is able to act without the direct intervention of humans (or other agents). It possesses control over its own actions and internal state [23]. An agent, therefore, is a software entity that works continuously autonomously and can communicate and cooperate with other agents to demonstrate intelligence [24].

An MAS can be defined as a network of agents. These agents interact with one another in order to solve problems that are beyond the individual capacities or knowledge of each problem-solver agent. The main advantages of MAS are as follows:

- The computational resources are distributed across a network; hence, it does not suffer if one of the systems fails.
- It provides solutions in environments where expertise is distributed. The distributed expertise is a natural way of segregation of intelligence between various domain entities.
- It models the given problem in terms of autonomous interacting systems. This is a more natural way of representing task allocation and team planning.
- It enhances overall system performance, in terms of computational efficiency, reliability, robustness, maintainability, responsiveness, flexibility, and reuse.

Given these numerous merits, MAS has been employed in various health care settings [25,26] and also for monitoring Alzheimer patients in LTC facilities [27], with the aim to provide medical assistance by optimizing the visiting schedules. The MAS system also supports the decision making of the nurses' and doctors' work by providing updated information about the condition of the patient.

23.2.3.1 A Sample Scenario

Assume that in an LTC facility, we want to have a decision support system to achieve cost savings for medical supplies for residents. The requirements of each resident are unique and have to be managed individually given their unique needs and circumstances. This distributed system can be modeled by designing an MAS in which agents interact together to find the most cost-efficient medical supplies for each resident. At the highest level of abstraction, one can think of the following agents in the system:

1. A *user agent (UA)* directly interacts with the residents or representatives (such as a family member) to record their requirements. The main objective of this agent is to provide an interface to the residents through an electronic device, for example, a personal digital assistant or mobile telephone.
2. The requirements sent by the UA have to be verified before being sent to the procurement module. This can be achieved by verifying with the *nurse agent (NA)*, who is aware of the medical condition of the residents and their requirements.
3. The objective of the whole system is to optimize the medical purchase. This means that the system should have the ability to undertake negotiation capabilities with the suppliers. For this purpose, a *broker agent (BA)* needs to be designed to bargain on behalf of the UAs. This system is similar to the one used commonly to find cheaper flight tickets through an online system wherein an MAS deals with the intricacies of the complex needs of the users [28].
4. In an open market system, there are a number of different suppliers, and it is the responsibility of the BA to find the most appropriate supplier, that is, most cost effective. It means that there exist numerous *supplier agents (SAs)* in the environment with whom the BA would interact.

This example highlights the usability of the MAS in decision making from an economic perspective. There are various research papers that have been published to improve the capabilities of the decision-making aspect of agents [29,30], and other researchers have examined this from a modeling perspective [31].

23.2.3.2 Critical Appraisal

Modeling gerontological issues using MAS is a promising area of research, as there is a well-documented literature that highlights the usability of this approach in the areas of health care, and medicine. For example, there is an extensive program of research and development into ambient assistive living (AAL), which aims to create smart living environments for older people that are able to anticipate the person's needs and provide appropriate support for everyday living (e.g., providing reminders and prompts to carry out activities of daily living such as medication and personal hygiene) [32]. This modeling approach can be effectively incorporated within other modeling approaches to yield a more comprehensive systems perspective. For instance, the behavior of the BA can be modeled using FL [33] or BN [34].

23.2.4 Basics of Fuzzy Logic

The term FL was introduced by Lotfi Zadeh [35], a professor at the University of California at Berkley in 1965. He argued that when interpreting real-life scenarios, it is difficult to define whether an object (O), belongs to a *set A* or not, that is, $O \in A$ or $O \notin A$. In other words, the notion of *well-defined* boundaries of a *set* is not suitable when applied to real-life, complex cases. For example, a well-used criterion for admitting residents to LTC facilities is that the individual is "in need" of continuous care that cannot be provided at home, and this is undertaken through a need assessment. These needs invariably exist on a broad spectrum of needs, including physical, behavioral, personal, and emotional needs. While it is important to identify specifically what the needs of the individual are, it is also important to control for the vagueness that arises when these needs are subjectively evaluated. The term "need" cannot be defined by using traditional set theory concepts alone but can be managed through the use of fuzzy set. The notion of fuzzy set facilitates the possibility of handling imprecision in a more rigorous mathematical form.

One can also view FL from a problem-solving or decision-making perspective when information about the system dynamics is vague, imprecise, noisy, or ambiguous. This is similar to the way humans arrive at a particular decision without having accurate information about the system. Humans reach a decision as they are capable of finding an approximate solution without being concerned about the need for precise calculation. In computational mathematics, this has been achieved by employing FL concepts to develop inference algorithms, as proposed by Mamdani and Assilian [36], Takagi-Sugeno-Kang in [37], and Kosko [38], and other hybrid algorithms [39].

23.2.4.1 A Sample Scenario

A complex challenge when residents are admitted to LTC facilities is assessing the type and level of care that individuals require to best support their health and cognitive status. This assessment helps LTC facilities to determine the number and expertise of staff that are needed to manage that resident, for example, whether that resident needs medication administered by a trained nurse or whether the mobility of the resident is such that two care aides are needed to assist. This analysis can assist LTC in establishing how staff can be allocated to specific individuals, according to the intensity of care required for the individuals and their specific care needs, having the potential benefit of achieving efficiency outcomes within the care facility, that is, by ensuring that the right number of staff is allocated in the best possible way. However, in achieving this, there are a complexity of factors that need to be considered when making this decision, including the level of fall risk associated with that person; cognitive status (for example, levels of dementia); behavioral difficulties (for example, mood changes); and the type of personal care that needs to be delivered. It is important to consider these various factors in order to arrive at a decision about the appropriate interventions and supports needed to support the individual. It is difficult to construct a mechanism that quantifies these factors, and FL-based systems can prove to be a useful tool for analyzing the scenario. The stepwise procedure to solve this problem is described as follows, and the amalgamation of all these steps forms a fuzzy inference system (FIS):

1. *Define and design the input and output variables*: The term *define* means that the input as well as output variables are to be categorized. For the example case, the input variables are *behavioral difficulties* and *cognitive status*. The output variable is assumed to be the *level of care needed*. The term *design* means that the membership functions for the input and output variables are to be designed, using linguistics terminology, and presented in a *closed-form expression*. In simple terms, a membership function defines the degree of truth of a variable in a fuzzy set. The standard membership functions used to define fuzzy sets are triangular, trapezoidal, bell-shaped, and so forth [37]. The linguistic terms, associated with the fuzzy sets, help the domain expert perceive the whole system. For an instance, the output variable *level of care needed* is defined in Figure 23.4.

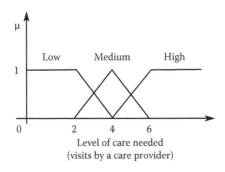

Figure 23.4 Membership functions for the variable *level of care needed*.

2. *Defining the rule base*: The core of the FL system is the set of rules that are defined by using heuristic techniques or the knowledge of domain experts [40]. For easy representation of the rules, a rule matrix is created. For instance, the input variable *behavioral difficulties* has been designed using five linguistic terms: low, low medium, medium, medium high, and high. Similarly, *cognitive status* has three linguistic definitions, no cognitive impairment (CI), somewhat impaired, and cognitively impaired, and the output variable *level of care needed* also has five fuzzy sets, the same as those of *behavioral difficulties*. A sample rule matrix is shown in Table 23.1.

3. *Deciding the inference algorithm*: In an FIS, there are number of possibilities to achieve a fuzzy solution through employing different inference algorithms. For instance, the inference system produces a fuzzy result as the *level of care needed* for a resident is *low*. This would help the LTC manager decide the number of times that the resident needs to be attended to by care aides to ensure that his/her behavior can best be managed in the context of the care facility.

4. *Converting the fuzzy solution to crisp value*: Sometimes, managers wish to know the exact value of number of visits required by the nurse for a resident. This can be achieved by defuzzifying the fuzzy solution to a crisp value, that is, rather than the fuzzy value *low*, the value can be assigned to *twice* a week, ensuring that the resident receives the appropriate intensity of care required to meet his/her needs. Interested readers may refer to the work of Ross [41] for a mathematical understanding of this concept.

Table 23.1 Rule Matrix for Deciding the *Level of Care Needed*

		Cognitive Status		
		No Cognitive Impairment	Somewhat Impaired	Cognitively Impaired
Behavioral Difficulties	Low	Low	Low	Low medium
	Low Medium	Low	Low medium	Medium
	Medium	Low medium	Medium	High medium
	Medium High	Medium	High medium	High
	High	Low high	High	High

23.2.4.2 Critical Appraisal

FL provides an alternative, unconventional approach to design a system focusing on what the system should do rather than trying to understand how it works. Even though critics suggest that FL does not apply a rigorous, robust mathematical framework, this has been challenged by research that has successfully applied FL in highly sensitive experiments such as an autonomous navigation system for robots [42], medication and diagnostic systems [43], and a missile guidance system [44]. More recently, Biswas et al. [45] discussed the application of an FL-based measure to analyze the gait stability as a causal factor in falls amongst older people in LTC.

23.2.5 Basics of Fuzzy Cognitive Map

FCM was first introduced by Kosko [46] as a modeling approach with two key advantages: it is easily understandable by human experts of a particular domain, and it is able to model the dynamics of a system [47,48]. Importantly, the approach incorporates an inference mechanism that informs the system users of how the system under consideration will evolve. More formally, FCM is a signed directed graph composed of *concepts* of a particular domain where the causality among concepts is represented on the edges of the graph. Typically, the domain experts provide opinions on the strength of the causality using linguistic terms such as "no causality," "very low causality," "low causality," "medium causality," "high causality," "very high causality," and so forth. Then, applying the FL technique, the linguistic terms are converted to a numeric value.

FCMs are particularly suitable in the modeling of social and medical systems where the uncertainty and vagueness commonly associated with expert opinion renders other modeling approaches inappropriate. The main weakness with social data sets is that they are usually recorded and inputted by human beings, and hence, they involve a degree of inaccuracy as a result of human error. The effectiveness of FCMs under such conditions has prompted researchers to use the technique extensively during the past decade in social systems [49] and in medicine [50–52]. In brief, the main advantages of FCM are that (1) it adds system understanding to the domain experts; (2) it is capable of working with qualitative variables and, hence, there is no need to have hard data; (3) it allows users to see the effects of a stimulus in the system; (4) there is no restraint on having feedback loops; and (5) the whole process is flexible enough to incorporate new concepts or causal effects.

23.2.5.1 A Sample Scenario

CI commonly afflicts people in old age and is known to progress as a person ages [53]. CI can be recognized through a general decline in the occupational, social, or day-to-day functional status of the individual [54]. In LTC, symptoms of CI can be monitored by caregivers who typically engage with the residents, and impairment can be identified by signs such as persons asking the same question repeatedly or their inability to recall recent events and so forth. Even though there are specific medical tests that can be conducted through physical examination (such as the mini medical state examination), laboratory tests, neuroimaging tests, and cognitive tests to ascertain the amount of memory deficit [55], the validity of these measures for determining the onset and progression in terms of orientation, memory, and attention have been questioned [56].

Effectively monitoring CI offers the potential for health care professionals to monitor the onset and deterioration of the condition and plan effectively for intervention. Employing FCM techniques offers the potential for managing uncertainty in complex medical problems such as

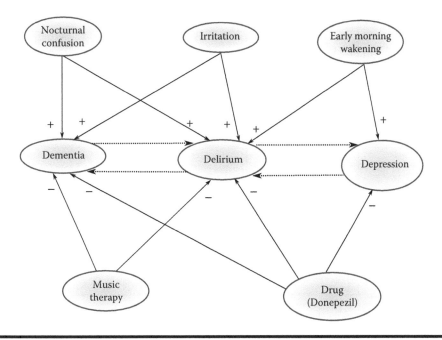

Figure 23.5 A simple FCM model for cognitive impairment among elders.

dementia. For instance, nocturnal confusion is a common symptom in dementia and delirium, but intensity varies across individuals. Early morning wakening sleep disorder is a common symptom in people suffering from depression. Furthermore, irritation and agitation are common in dementia, delirium, and depression. This information can help us build an FCM, as shown in Figure 23.5. The model can be used to simulate various possible scenarios and relate them to the progression of the disease.

23.2.5.2 Critical Appraisal

FCM modeling approach provides a mechanism to design a system in a highly participatory manner [57] by facilitating communication between stakeholders and the modelers and is particularly apt where the information is vague and imprecise. Synthesizing literature to build a model is a key feature of this approach as it allows the extraction of key information, presented using linguistic terms. The drawback of this technique is that a temporal framework is absent from the approach. In other words, the inference algorithm stops iterating when the concepts stabilize and the number of iterations has no significance. It means that the technique can help us to understand the final outcome, but the information for "how long" the outcome will take is missing.

23.2.6 Comparative Analysis of the Techniques

The main objective of this chapter is to make the reader aware of the possible AI techniques and their relative strength and weaknesses. Since there is no available data set in the public domain to compare the techniques, it is essential to understand the mathematical theories and suitability of these techniques when solving gerontology problems. Figure 23.6 summarizes the comparative analysis across four different parameters. The relative strengths of each approach are color-coded.

	Evaluation Parameters			
	Construction Mechanism	*Basis of the Theory*	*Temporal Framework*	*Predictive Capability*
Bayesian Network	Automated algorithms learn from data set or domain experts, participation	Probability theory	Present in advanced version: dynamic Bayesian network	Present
Compartmental Model	Domain experts	Differential equations and probability theory	Present	Present
Multiagent System	System specific	Cooperation among agents	Present	System specific, but historically not present
Fuzzy Logic	Automated algorithms learn from data set or domain experts, participation	Fuzzy sets	Not historically present	Present
Fuzzy Cognitive Map	Highly dependent on domain experts' participation and literature	Network theory and fuzzy logic	Not historically present	Present

Color coding representing the strength of the feature

Weak	
Medium	
Strong	

Figure 23.6   Comparative analysis of the techniques.

23.3 Future Directions

One of the major contributions of AI-based modeling is that it provides an effective framework for collaborative multidisciplinary research. Research has often been driven by a "silo mentality," an overly constrained disciplinary perspective, towards the development of information and communications technology (ICT)-based solutions [58]. This has been a major factor in limiting the practical outcomes of gerontological research, as knowledge and new interventions are often poorly aligned with the needs, preferences, and wishes of end users. Interdisciplinary and multidisciplinary approaches tend to bring different disciplines together in ways that complement each other but do not generally achieve holistic understanding, focus on problem solving, or explore methodological integration [59]. In the area of services and support for older people, complex multidimensional problems demand an innovative "transdisciplinary" approach. Transdisciplinarity is characterized by a problem focus, evolving methodology, and intense collaboration [60] whereby partnership working allows expertise, knowledge, and joint working practices to transcend disciplinary boundaries. The techniques and tools described here may be a powerful medium for a truly collaborative approach to gerontological research. For example, mathematical modeling is able to address gerontological problems and answer questions using visual representations and simulations that facilitate contributions from domain experts from different backgrounds. Modeling approaches can take seriously the inherent complexities of social problems, addressing them holistically, rather than compartmentalizing, simplifying, and/or excluding important but difficult-to-understand phenomena and data. Models can also effectively incorporate factors where the empirical evidence base may be weak or where empirical research is ambiguous or contradictory. This approach has particular relevance to understanding real-world problems and developing interventions, where all potential contributory factors need to be addressed to ensure success.

23.4 Conclusion

The modeling approaches described within this chapter allow for the development of working models that can capture the complex nature of various gerontological aspects of LTC. We argue that modeling approaches provide the opportunity to incorporate a broad range of potential factors when understanding issues affecting older people, some of which are excluded from research studies as they have only a weak empirical basis. The simulation environment provided by the different models allows stakeholders (policy makers, researchers, and care providers) to test various potential interventions or policies to optimize care delivery for older people. While this chapter identifies some of those issues impacting on long-term facilities, there is also the potential for these techniques to be applied to other settings for delivering care, for example, to better understand care delivery in hospitals or to design supports for older people living at home. More broadly, modeling approaches can be applied to other factors at the micro level (for example, understanding of the biological ageing process) and macro level (for example, forecasting health care costs for the future) and thereby offer a tool for understanding domains of gerontology in a way that can be easily understood by the various health care professionals involved in supporting older people.

Competing Interests

The authors declare that they have no competing interests.

References

1. Andrew, S., Gloria, G. Technology and the challenge of aging. In: *Technologies for Active Aging*. 2012. International Perspectives on Aging, Springer; 2013 edition (May 31, 2013), New York.
2. Public Health Agency of Canada. Canada's aging population, 2002. Available at http://www.phac-aspc.gc.ca/seniors-aines/publications/public/various-varies/papier-fed-paper/index-eng.php (accessed June 12, 2012).
3. Novak, M., Campbell, L. *Aging and Society, A Canadian Perspective*, Fifth Edition. Nelson College Indigenous; 2006. Ontario, Canada.
4. Simon Fraser University, CSMG Group. *Modelling in Healthcare*. American Mathematical Society; 2010.
5. Health Canada. Long-term facilities-based care, 2012. Available at http://www.hc-sc.gc.ca/hcs-sss/home-domicile/longdur/index-eng.php (accessed June 12, 2012).
6. Spiegel, M., Stephens, L. *Schaum's Outline of Theory and Problems of Statistics*. Schaum's Outline Series; 1999. McGraw-Hill, USA.
7. Heckerman, D. A tutorial on learning with bayesian networks. *Innovations in Bayesian Networks* 2008;**156**:33–82.
8. Pourret, O., Nam, P., Naïm, P., Marcot, B. *Bayesian Networks: A Practical Guide to Applications*, vol. 73. Wiley; 2008. New Jersey, USA.
9. Mago, V., Prasad, B., Bhatia, A., Mago, A. A decision making system for the treatment of dental caries. *Soft Computing Applications in Business* 2008;**230**:231–242.
10. Lord, S., Sherrington, C., Menz, H., Close, J.C.T. *Falls in Older People: Risk Factors and Strategies for Prevention*. Cambridge Univ Pr; 2007. Cambridge, UK.

11. Rubenstein, L. Falls in older people: Epidemiology, risk factors and strategies for prevention. *Age and Ageing* 2006;**35**(Suppl 2):ii37–ii41.
12. Li, Q., Stankovic, J., Hanson, M., Barth, A., Lach, J., Zhou, G. Accurate, fast fall detection using gyroscopes and accelerometer-derived posture information. In: *Wearable and Implantable Body Sensor Networks, 2009. BSN 2009. Sixth International Workshop on*. IEEE; 2009, pp. 138–143.
13. Korb, K., Nicholson, A. *Bayesian Artificial Intelligence*, vol. 1. CRC Press; 2004. Florida, USA.
14. Brauer, F. Compartmental models in epidemiology. *Mathematical Epidemiology* 2008;**1945**:19–79.
15. Temime, L., Hejblum, G., Setbon, M., Valleron, A. The rising impact of mathematical modelling in epidemiology: Antibiotic resistance research as a case study. *Epidemiology and Infection* 2008;**136**(3):289–298.
16. Kermack, W.O., McKendrick, A.G. A contribution to the mathematical theory of epidemics. *Proceedings of the Royal Society of London Series A, Containing Papers of a Mathematical and Physical Character* 1927;**115**(772):700–721.
17. Hare, W., Alimadad, A., Dodd, H., Ferguson, R., Rutherford, A. A deterministic model of home and community care client counts in British Columbia. *Health Care Management Science* 2009;**12**(1):80–98.
18. Lowen, A.C., Mubareka, S., Steel, J., Palese, P. Influenza virus transmission is dependent on relative humidity and temperature. *PLoS Pathogens* 2007;**3**(10):e151.
19. Eriksen, H., Iversen, B., Aavitsland, P. Prevalence of nosocomial infections and use of antibiotics in long-term care facilities in Norway, 2002 and 2003. *The Journal of Hospital Infection* 2004;**57**(4):316–320.
20. Grundmann, H., Hellriegel, B. Mathematical modelling: A tool for hospital infection control. *The Lancet Infectious Diseases* 2006;**6**(1):39–45.
21. Brauer, F., Castillo-Chavez, C. *Mathematical Models in Population Biology and Epidemiology*, vol. 40. Springer; 2011. New York, USA.
22. Heesterbeek, J. *Mathematical Epidemiology of Infectious Diseases: Model Building, Analysis, and Interpretation*, vol. 5. Wiley; 2000. West Sussex, England.
23. Jennings, N., Wooldridge, M. *Agent Technology: Foundations, Applications, and Markets*. Springer-Verlag New York Inc; 1998.
24. Bradshaw, J. An introduction to software agents. *Software Agents* 1997;**5**:3–46. California, USA.
25. Mago, V., Devi, M. A multi-agent medical system for Indian rural infant and child care. In: *Int. Joint Conference on AI*. 2007, pp. 1396–1401.
26. Su, C., Wu, C. Jade implemented mobile multi-agent based, distributed information platform for pervasive health care monitoring. *Applied Soft Computing* 2011;**11**(1):315–325.
27. Corchado, J., Bajo, J., de Paz, Y., Tapia, D. Intelligent environment for monitoring alzheimer patients, agent technology for health care. *Decision Support Systems* 2008;**44**(2):382–396.
28. Bukhari, A.C., Kim, Y.G. Integration of a secure type-2 fuzzy ontology with a multi-agent platform: A proposal to automate the personalized flight ticket booking domain. *Information Sciences* 2012;**198**:24–47.
29. Mago, V., Devi, M., Mehta, R. Decision making system: Agent diagnosing child care diseases. In: Burkhard, H.D., Lindemann, G., Verbrugge, R., Varga, L., editors. *Multi-Agent Systems and Applications V*, vol. 4696 of *Lecture Notes in Computer Science*. Springer, Berlin/Heidelberg; 2007, pp. 316–318.
30. Reig-Bolano, R., Marti-Puig, P., Bajo, J., Rodriguez, S., De Paz, J., Rubio, M. Image processing to detect and classify situations and states of elderly people. In: Corchado, E., Snasel, V., Sedano, J., Hassanien, A., Calvo, J., Slezak, D., editors. *Soft Computing Models in Industrial and Environmental Applications, 6th International Conference SOCO 2011*, vol. 87 of *Advances in Intelligent and Soft Computing*. Springer, Berlin/Heidelberg; 2011, pp. 163–172. ISBN 978-3-642-19643-0.
31. Farahbod, R., Glässer, U. The CoreASM modeling framework. *Software: Practice and Experience* 2011;**41**(2):167–178.
32. Sixsmith, A., Woolrych, R., Bierhoff, I., Mueller, S., Byrne, P. Ambient assisted living: From concept to implementation. In: Anthony P.G.D.M.K., editor. *Essential Lessons for the Success of Telehomecare—Why It's not Plug and Play*, vol. 30 of *Assistive Technology Research Series*. IOS Press; 2012, pp. 259–286.
33. Lai, K., Lin, M. Modeling agent negotiation via fuzzy constraints in e-business. *Computational Intelligence* 2004;**20**(4):624–642.

34. Zapata-Rivera, J., Greer, J. Inspectable Bayesian student modelling servers in multi-agent tutoring systems. *International Journal of Human-Computer Studies* 2004;**61**(4):535–563.
35. Zadeh, L. Fuzzy sets. *Information and Control* 1965;**8**(3):338–353.
36. Mamdani, E., Assilian, S. An experiment in linguistic synthesis with a fuzzy logic controller. *International Journal of Man-machine Studies* 1975;**7**(1):1–13.
37. Yen, J., Langari, R. *Fuzzy Logic: Intelligence, Control, and Information*. Prentice-Hall, Inc.; 1998. New Jersey, USA.
38. Kosko, B. *Fuzzy Engineering*. Prentice-Hall, Inc.; 1996. New Jersey, USA.
39. Jang, J. Anfis: Adaptive-network-based fuzzy inference system. *Systems, Man and Cybernetics, IEEE Transactions on* 1993;**23**(3):665–685.
40. Mago, V.K., Bhatia, N., Bhatia, A., Mago, A. Clinical decision support system for dental treatment. *Journal of Computational Science* 2012a;**3**(5):254–261.
41. Ross, T.J. *Fuzzy Logic with Engineering Applications*. Wiley; 2009. West Sussex, UK.
42. Saffiotti, A. The uses of fuzzy logic in autonomous robot navigation. *Soft Computing-A Fusion of Foundations, Methodologies and Applications* 1997;**1**(4):180–197.
43. Phuong, N., Kreinovich, V. Fuzzy logic and its applications in medicine. *International Journal of Medical Informatics* 2001;**62**(2–3):165–173.
44. Lin, C., Hung, H., Chen, Y., Chen, B. Development of an integrated fuzzy-logic-based missile guidance law against high speed target. *Fuzzy Systems, IEEE Transactions on* 2004;**12**(2):157–169.
45. Biswas, A., Lemaire, E., Kofman, J. Dynamic gait stability index based on plantar pressures and fuzzy logic. *Journal of Biomechanics* 2008;**41**(7):1574–1581.
46. Kosko, B. Fuzzy cognitive maps. *International Journal of Man-machine Studies* 1986;**24**(1):65–75.
47. Mago, V.K., Bakker, L., Papageorgiou, E.I., Alimadad, A., Borwein, P., Dabbaghian, V. Fuzzy cognitive maps and cellular automata: An evolutionary approach for social systems modelling. *Applied Soft Computing* 2012b;**12**(12):3771–3784.
48. Giabbanelli, P.J., Torsney-Weir, T., Mago, V.K. A fuzzy cognitive map of the psychosocial determinants of obesity. *Applied Soft Computing* 2012;**12**(12):3711–3724.
49. de Kok, J., Titus, M., Wind, H. Application of fuzzy sets and cognitive maps to incorporate social science scenarios in integrated assessment models: A case study of urbanization in Ujung Pandang, Indonesia. *Integrated Assessment* 2000;**1**(3):177–188.
50. Stylios, C., Georgopoulos, V., Malandraki, G., Chouliara, S. Fuzzy cognitive map architectures for medical decision support systems. *Applied Soft Computing* 2008;**8**(3):1243–1251.
51. Papageorgiou, E., Stylios, C., Groumpos, P. An integrated two-level hierarchical system for decision making in radiation therapy based on fuzzy cognitive maps. *Biomedical Engineering, IEEE Transactions on* 2003;**50**(12):1326–1339.
52. Georgopoulos, V., Malandraki, G., Stylios, C. A fuzzy cognitive map approach to differential diagnosis of specific language impairment. *Artificial Intelligence in Medicine* 2003;**29**(3):261–278.
53. Park, D. The basic mechanisms accounting for age-related decline in cognitive function. *Cognitive Aging: A Primer* 2000;**11**:3–19.
54. Biernacki, C. *Dementia: Metamorphosis in Care*. Wiley; 2007. West Sussex, England.
55. Ministry of Health, Canada. Cognitive impairment in the elderly—Recognition, diagnosis and management, 2007. Available at http://www.bcguidelines.ca/guideline_cognitive.html (accessed 12 June 2012).
56. Davis, K.L., Marin, D.B., Kane, R., Patrick, D., Peskind, E.R., Raskind, M.A. Puder, K.L. The caregiver activity survey (CAS): Development and validation of a new measure for caregivers of persons with Alzheimer's disease. *International Journal of Geriatric Psychiatry* 1998;**12**(10):978–988.
57. van Vliet, M., Kok, K., Veldkamp, T. Linking stakeholders and modellers in scenario studies: The use of fuzzy cognitive maps as a communication and learning tool. *Futures* 2010;**42**(1):1–14.
58. Müller, S., Sixsmith, A. User requirements for ambient assisted living: Results of the soprano project. *Gerontechnology* 2008;**7**(2):168.
59. Ramadier, T. Transdisciplinarity and its challenges: The case of urban studies. *Futures* 2004;**36**(4):423–439.
60. Wickson, F., Carew, A., Russell, A. Transdisciplinary research: Characteristics, quandaries and quality. *Futures* 2006;**38**(9):1046–1059.

Chapter 24

Combining Feature Selection and Data Classification Using Ensemble Approaches: Application to Cancer Diagnosis and Credit Scoring

Afef Ben Brahim, Waad Bouaguel, and Mohamed Limam

Contents

In this chapter, we investigate using ensemble approaches to combine feature selection and data classification for cancer diagnosis and credit scoring. First, an ensemble of feature selection techniques is used for feature selection, where each member yields a different feature set. Then, two alternatives are tested. The first one combines these feature sets to obtain a single solution on which a classifier is trained. The second alternative trains a classifier on each feature set and then combines the classifier ensemble to obtain a single classification output. We hypothesize that the reliability of prediction resulting from each ensemble combination level differs depending on the data dimensionality. Thus, in such an ensemble system, it is necessary to find out the appropriate combination level to obtain the best classification results. The proposed ensemble approaches are evaluated based on two high-dimensional data sets concerned with cancer diagnosis, as well as on two small-size data sets concerned with credit scoring. Evaluation results suggest that the ensemble approaches outperform the baseline models and that data set dimensionality can guide the choice of the aggregation level of the ensemble method.

24.1 Introduction

Selecting the set of appropriate features has always been an important issue for learning algorithms. Usually, reduced feature sets lead to reduced complexity and, in many cases, to an improvement in model accuracy. Actually, many research fields have invested in empowering feature selection tools. In the last two decades, there has been much interest in using feature selection methods for biological and financial data. Yet, in these two fields, there has been relatively little interest to selecting input features for training classifiers or clustering algorithms.

Applying feature selection in bioinformatics has shifted from being an illustrative example to becoming a real prerequisite for model building. On the other hand, most credit scoring models are constructed based on a reduced set of relevant features in order to help credit decision makers in case of abundant information.

Selecting the set of features remains the most important factor for any effective classification problem. Typically, features that are noisy, redundant, or irrelevant are ones that can never improve the predictive accuracy of a model; however, the algorithm may mistakenly include them in the learning process. For example, in the case of cancer diagnosis, our purpose is to investigate the relationship between the symptoms and their corresponding diagnosis. If the patient ID is considered by mistake as one of the input features, the learning process may come to the conclusion that the illness is determined by the ID number, which is totally irrelevant.

Another motivation for feature selection from the financial field is that the goal in banking instructions is to approximate the underlying function between the input and the target class defining the customer behavior to pay back a loan. It is reasonable and important to ignore those input features with little effect on the target class in order to keep the size of the approximate model small. Thus, removing such features reduces the dimension of the search space and speeds up the learning process.

Therefore, selecting a proper set of features is critical for a successful classification, implying the need to identify the valuable set of features and eliminate the undesired ones. The curse of dimensionality is also a big motivation to look for a reduced set of features. In fact, with too many features, the computational time of a classification algorithm increases significantly, without any significant change in the performance. With an increase in noise and dimensionality of the data, feature selection becomes an essential step.

Feature selection algorithms are designed to improve the classification performance of a single- or a multiple-classifier system by removing redundant or noisy features from the data. Typically, in order to improve the accuracy of a particular application, a feature selection technique looks for a suitable subset of features from the original set. Benefits of feature selection are to ease data understanding, reduce storage requirements, reduce training time, and deal with the curse of dimensionality. Some methods put more emphasis on one aspect than another, and this is another point of distinction between feature selection algorithms.

Feature selection algorithms can be divided into three categories: filter, wrapper, and hybrid methods (Liu and Yu 2005). Filter methods evaluate features individually and eliminate some before training a classification algorithm. Wrapper methods form a second group of feature selection methods where the prediction accuracy of a classifier directly measures the value of a feature set. While filter methods are unbiased and fast, wrapper methods give better results for a particular classifier. Although effective, the exponential number of possible subsets places computational limits for wrapper methods. Hybrid methods are a fusion of both filter and wrapper methods (Tuv et al. 2009).

Using individual feature selection algorithms may not lead to better performance since the focus will be on one particular region of the feature space. However, different algorithms will choose different feature subsets, resulting in classifiers trained on a subset that represents the whole set. The fusion of different feature selectors is a step to generate a new feature set from an individually selected set of features.

There are two possible ways to consider ensemble feature selection. First, different feature subsets, or so-called ensemble feature selection, may be used for constructing an ensemble of accurate and diverse base classifiers. A necessary condition to obtain a good performance is that individual classifiers of the ensemble should not only be accurate but also diverse, meaning that they do not all misclassify the same data examples. There are several ways of promoting diversity in an ensemble, such as using different training sets, different training parameters, and different types of classifiers or different feature sets. This creates the interesting possibility of combining classifiers trained on feature sets produced by different feature selections.

The second way of ensemble feature selection is to find a consensus between the results obtained by several feature selection methods. In this context, feature selectors' aggregation plays an important role in improving classification accuracy. In fact, there are as many candidate subsets of features as there are experts, and thus, aggregation techniques become necessary tools for combining individual results into a single one reflective of the overall preference or importance within the population (Pihur et al. 2009).

The reminder of the chapter is organized as follows. In Section 24.2, we discuss two well know application fields of feature selection, namely, cancer diagnosis and credit scoring, and their data set characteristics. In Section 24.3, we discuss ensemble feature selections and we summarize available techniques based on classifiers and feature selector aggregation. Sections 24.4 and 24.5 give experimental settings and results on four data sets. We give a discussion in Section 24.6, and we conclude this chapter with Section 24.7.

24.2 Application Fields

24.2.1 *Cancer Diagnosis*

Cancer or a malignant tumor can be seen as a disease of DNA due to gene alterations and mutations, which result in uncontrolled growth of cells or cell proliferation. That is, a tumor does not appear from nowhere and arises from mutated normal cells (Weinberg 2007; Schulz 2007). Once a cancerous cell has been created, it undergoes clonal expansion via cell division. In other words, parents of the first-generation cancerous cells are mutated and alter normal cells, while parents of the next-generation cancerous cells are the first generation of cancerous cells, and so forth.

As genes undergo changes during progression of cancer, so do gene expressions. That is, for a given gene, or a set of genes, the expression level or levels in the normal healthy state can be different from those in the cancerous state. Based on this fact, the idea of cancer classification was considered. In other words, it is assumed that by comparing microarray gene expression levels of healthy and cancerous cells, it is possible to distinguish between these two states and then diagnose cancer.

However, in some cancers and for some tumor progression states, this difference is more profound than for others. Besides, as cancerous cells originate from mutated normal cells, they may share many genes for which expression levels are almost identical. In addition, during cancer development, tumors may rapidly mutate, which affects tissue-specific gene expression values. Some cancers change their phenotype to resemble cells from a different tissue in a process called metaplasia (Schulz 2007). Also, we need to take into account the fact that different cancer types generally have different sets of tissue-specific expressed genes. Therefore, the task of assigning a patient to one of the two classes, healthy or diseased, is not as straightforward as it may seem. The very large number of genes makes this task even more challenging. This is where machine learning is typically called for help.

24.2.1.1 Biological Data and Their Characteristics

As there are thousands of gene expressions and only a few dozens of samples in a typical gene expression data set, the number of genes or rows D is on the order of 1000–10,000, while the number of biological samples or columns, N, is somewhere between 10 and 100. Such a condition makes the application of many traditional statistical methods impossible as those techniques were developed under the assumption that N is much larger than D. The problem is in an underdetermined system where there are only a few equations versus many more unknown variables (Kohane et al. 2003). Hence, the solution of such a system is not unique, and actually, multiple solutions exist. This means that multiple subsets of genes may be equally relevant to cancer classification. However, in order to reduce a chance for noisy and/or irrelevant genes to be included into one of such subsets, we need to eliminate irrelevant genes before conducting the actual classification.

But why it is impossible to increase N? The answer is that it is difficult since measuring gene expression requires a functionally relevant tissue taken under the right conditions, which is sadly rare due to the impossibility to meet all requirements at once in practice (Kohane et al. 2003; Okun 2011). So, we are left with the necessity to live and to deal with high-dimensional data.

24.2.2 Credit Scoring

Credit risk is one of the major risks that a loan institution has to manage. This risk arises when a borrower does not pay his/her debt by the fixed due date. To face this kind of risk, bank managers have to look for efficient solutions to distinguish good from bad risk applicants. Credit scoring is one of the most successful financial risk management solutions developed for lending institutions.

Over the past few years, credit scoring was a challenging research field, and there are many methods that were proposed in the literature. These methods use explanatory variables obtained from an applicant's information to estimate his/her intended performance to pay back a loan. A wide range of classification techniques have been successfully used to help lenders, to build scoring models. According to Tsai and Wu (2008), the classification accuracy of credit applicants is a crucial factor for banks in their cost control process. Then, a credit model should be able to produce fast decisions while reducing the cost of credit analysis and decreasing credit risk (Thomas 2009).

For all t classification methods used for credit scoring, the general scheme is to use the credit history of previous customers to compute the new applicant's defaulting risk. These classification techniques are only a part of the solution, and using them blindly to credit data may lead to bad results (Fernandez 2010). Available information about a credit candidate is a fundamental element for his/her credit request approval. Lack of information in credit risk valorization is suspected to lead to wrong decision making.

24.2.2.1 Financial Data and Their Characteristics

A borrower's behavior is described by a binary target variable, denoted Y, where the value taken by this last one supplies a basic element in a credit granting decision, $Y = 0$ when the borrower presents a problem and $Y = 1$ otherwise. Besides this variable, every borrower is also described by a set of description variables $(X_1, X_2,..., X_d)$ informing about the borrower and his/her accounts' functioning.

The on-hand collection of booked loans is used to build a credit scoring model that would be used to identify the associations between the applicant's characteristics and how good or bad the credit worthiness of the applicant is. Generally, portfolios used for the scoring task are voluminous, and they are in the range of several thousands. These portfolios are characterized by noise, missing values, complexity of distributions, and redundant or irrelevant features (Piramuthu 2006). High dimensionality in the feature space has advantages but also some serious disadvantages. In fact, the more the number of features grows, the more computation is required and model accuracy and scoring interpretation are reduced (Liu and Schumann 2005; Howley et al. 2006). An improving direction is to perform a dimensionality reduction on the original data by removing irrelevant features. A first approach of dimensionality reduction is to perform a feature extraction where the input data is transformed into a reduced representation set of features, so new attributes are generated from the initial ones. A second approach is feature selection, where a subset of existing features is selected without transformation. Generally, feature selection is preferred in credit scoring over feature extraction since it keeps all information about the importance of each single feature, while in feature extraction, obtained variables are usually not interpretable. Conserving the information of each feature provides much simplicity and interpretability to financial data processing. According to Rodriguez et al. (2010), three main benefits can be drawn from a successful feature selection. First, it improves the decision performance. Second, it allows scientific discovery by determining which features explain in the best way the target variable, and third, the predictive accuracy will increase while reducing overfitting risks.

24.3 Ensemble Feature Selection

24.3.1 Classifier-Based Aggregation

Feature ensemble method–based classifier combination consists in a combination of decisions from multiple classifiers. Each classifier is trained using variations of the feature representation space, obtained by means of feature selection. With this approach, relevant discriminative information contained in features neglected in a single run of a feature selection method may be recovered by the application of multiple feature set runs and contribute to the decision through the classifier combination process.

While traditional feature selection algorithms have the goal of finding the best feature subset that is relevant to both the learning task and the selected inductive learning algorithm, the task of ensemble feature selection by classifier combination has the additional goal of finding a set of feature subsets that will promote disagreement among the base classifiers. To have this disagreement, we used different feature selection algorithms to generate the feature subsets.

Opitz (1999) proposed an ensemble feature selection approach based on genetic algorithms in order to generate a set of classifiers that are accurate and diverse in their predictions. Their proposed approach works towards finding a set of feature subsets that will promote disagreement among the ensemble classifiers (Opitz 1999). Tsymbal et al. (2005) introduced also a genetic algorithm–based sequential search for ensemble feature selection (GAS-SEFS). Instead of one genetic process, it uses a series of processes, where the goal of each is to build one base classifier (Tsymbal et al. 2005).

24.3.2 Feature Selector–Based Aggregation

The concept of ensemble feature selection-based feature selector aggregation was recently introduced by Saeys et al. (2008). Ensemble feature selection techniques use an idea similar to

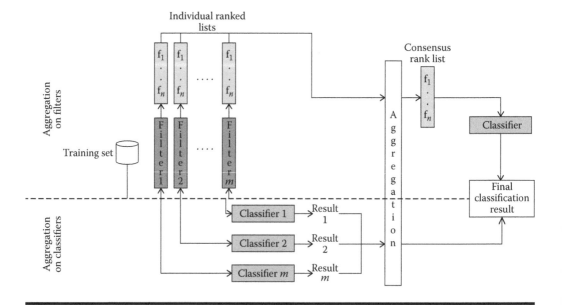

Figure 24.1 Feature selection aggregation schemas.

ensemble learning for classification (Dietterich 2000). In the first step, a number of different feature selectors are used, and in the final phase, the output of these separate selectors is aggregated and returned as the final ensemble result. Similar to the case of supervised learning, ensemble techniques might be used to improve the robustness of feature selection techniques. Different feature selection algorithms may yield feature subsets that can be considered local optima in the space of feature subsets, and ensemble feature selection might give a better approximation to the optimal subset or ranking of features. Also, the representational power of a particular feature selector might constrain its search space such that optimal subsets cannot be reached. Ensemble feature selection could help in alleviating this problem by aggregating the outputs of several feature selectors (Saeys et al. 2008). This concept was specially applied for h high-dimensional data with few samples as discussed by Saeys et al. (2008) and Schowe and Morik (2011), but it can be applied to any data dimensionality, as will be seen in our experiments. Figure 24.1 illustrates the two feature selection aggregation levels described and that can be used for ensemble feature selection.

24.4 Comparative Study

24.4.1 Data Sets

As discussed before, using too much data, in terms of the number of input variables, is not always effective. This is especially true when the problem involves unsupervised learning or supervised learning with unbalanced data with many negative observations but minimal positive observations. This chapter addresses two issues involving high-dimensional data: The first issue explores the behavior of ensemble method feature aggregation when analyzing data with hundreds or thousands of dimensions and small sample size. With such data set characteristics, experiments are conducted on two cancer diagnosis problems. The second issue deals with a huge data set with a large number of instances and where feature selection is used to extract meaningful rules from the available data. Such data sets are found typically in financial problems, and that is why we conducted experiments on two credit scoring problems.

For the first case, we evaluated our proposed approaches on the central nervous system (CNS), a large data set concerned with the prediction of CNS embryonal tumor outcome based on gene expression. This data set includes 60 samples containing 39 medulloblastoma survivors and 21 treatment failures. These samples are described by 7129 genes (Pomeroy et al. 2002). We consider also the Leukemia microarry gene expression data set that consists of 72 samples, which are all acute leukemia patients, either acute lymphoblastic leukemia (ALL; 47) or acute myelogenous leukemia (AML; 25). The total number of genes to be tested is 7129 (Golub et al. 1999).

For the second case, two credit data sets are used, the Australian and the Tunisian credit data set. The first presents an interesting mixture of attributes: six continuous, eight nominal, and a target attribute with few missing values. This data set is composed of 690 instances where 306 are creditworthy and 383 are not. All attribute names and values have been changed to meaningless symbols for confidentiality. The Tunisian data set covers a sample of 2970 instances of credit consumers where 2523 instances are creditworthy and 446 are not. Each credit applicant is described by a binary target variable and a set of 22 input variables, where 11 features are numerical and 11 are categorical. Table 24.1 displays the characteristics of the data sets that have been used for evaluation.

Table 24.1   Data Sets Summary

Names	CNS	Leukemia	Australian	Tunisian
Total instances	60	72	690	2970
Total features	7129	7129	14	22
Number of classes	2	2	2	2
Missing values	No	No	Yes	Yes

24.4.2 Feature Selection Algorithms

Our feature selection ensemble is composed of three different filter selection algorithms: relief algorithm (Kira and Rendell 1992), correlation-based feature selection (CFS) (Hall 2000), and information gain (IG) (Quinlan 1993). These algorithms are available in the Weka 3.7.0 machine learning package (Hall et al. 2009).

The relief algorithm evaluates each feature by its ability to distinguish the neighboring instances. It randomly samples the instances and checks the instances of the same and different classes that are near each other. CFS looks for feature subsets based on the degree of redundancy among the features. The objective is to find the feature subsets that are individually highly correlated with the class but have low intercorrelation. The subset evaluators use a numeric measure such as conditional entropy to guide the search iteratively and add features with the highest correlation with the class. IG measures the number of bits of information obtained for class prediction by knowing the presence or absence of a feature.

The aggregation of these filters in the feature selection level is performed by choosing the selected features shared by the three methods. We refer to the ensemble-based feature selection aggregation by ensemble feature aggregation as EFA.

24.4.3 Classifiers

We trained our approach using three well-known data mining algorithms, namely, decision trees (DTs) support vector machines (SVMs), and *K*-nearest neighbor (KNN). These algorithms are available in the Weka 3.7.0 machine learning package (Hall et al. 2009).

DT is a simple method and can be described as a set of nodes and edges, where the root node defines the first split of the credit-applicant sample. Each internal node splits the set of instances into two subsets, and each node contains individuals of a single class. The operation is repeated until the separation into subpopulations is no longer possible.

SVM is one of the most interesting machine learning techniques. The reasons behind choosing SVM, according to Burges (1998), are that it requires fewer prior assumptions about the input data and can perform on small or huge data set by doing a nonlinear mapping from an original input space to a high-dimensional feature space.

KNN is an algorithm that stores all available cases and classifies new cases based on a similarity measure (e.g., distance functions). KNN has been used in statistical estimation and pattern recognition since the early 1970s as a nonparametric technique.

The aggregation at the classifiers' level is performed by using five well-known combination rules, namely, the majority vote, the average probability, the product probability, the minimum probability, and the maximum probability combination rule. We refer to each of these ensemble-based classifier aggregations by ensemble classifier aggregation as ECA.

24.4.4 Performance Metrics

To evaluate the classification performance of each setting and perform comparisons, we used several characteristics of classification performance all derived from the confusion matrix (Okun 2011). We define briefly these evaluation metrics.

The precision is the percentage of positive predictions that are correct. The recall or sensitivity (or the TP rate) is the percentage of positive labeled instances that were predicted as positive. The *F*-measure can be interpreted as a weighted average of the precision and recall. It reaches its best value at 1 and worst score at 0.

Another characteristic of a classifier frequently used is the receiver operating characteristic (ROC) curve. It is a characteristic allowing for visual classification performance of one or several algorithms. A ROC curve is a plot of the sensitivity against one minus its specificity, as the cutoff criterion for indicating a positive test is varied. This plot depicts relative trade-offs between true positive (TP) and false positive (FP). We use the area under the ROC curve as another performance metric.

24.5 Results Analysis

We considered information retrieval measures of data sets when individual filter methods are applied using the learning algorithms by tenfold cross-validation. Then we applied the ensemble feature selection, first based on the classifier aggregation. We measured the performance of those methods and calculated the difference between them. Tables 24.2 through 24.5 show the obtained results.

In most cases, ensemble methods produced better performance than individual filter methods. In particular, the average of the probability aggregation method performed even better than other methods, especially for the Australian and the Tunisian data sets with DT and KNN learning algorithms. Also, the product of probability aggregation worked as well as the average of probability with DT and KNN learning algorithms once applied to the CNS and leukemia data sets.

We conducted the same experiments with those data sets, and we applied ensemble feature selection based on the feature set aggregation and evaluated each method by the same process. As expected, ensemble methods again give good results. In fact, for high-dimensional data sets like the CNS and leukemia data sets, ensemble methods outperform individual feature selection methods. However, the learning performance with the Australian and the Tunisian data sets did not improve that much. This could be due to the small number of features.

Histograms in Figures 24.2, 24.3, and 24.4 show the best class precision for each classifier and for each setting: after applying baseline feature selection (Individual), after ensemble classifier aggregation (ECA), and after ensemble feature selection (EFA). We can see clearly that often EFA gives the best results with CNS and leukemia data sets characterized by high-dimensional size. However, when working with small-size data sets, ECA is better than EFA, and individual setting tends to outperform the two aggregation schemes.

Based on these discussions, we conclude that if the data set size is very small and the number of features exceeds the number of instances, the best way to introduce aggregation is in the

Table 24.2   Results Summary for the Central Nervous System Data Set

	Precision	Recall	F-Measure	ROC Area
Decision Tree				
Cfs	0.676	0.641	0.658	0.512
Relief	0.600	0.538	0.568	0.399
InfoGain	0.674	0.744	0.707	0.535
Majority V	0.69	0.744	0.716	0.562
Average P	0.69	0.744	0.716	0.426
Product P	0.48	0.75	0.585	0.595
Max P	0.5	0.333	0.400	0.411
Min P	0.5	0.813	0.619	0.595
EFA	0.775	0.795	0.785	0.690
SVM				
Cfs	0.700	0.718	0.709	0.573
Relief	0.632	0.615	0.623	0.474
InfoGain	0.737	0.718	0.727	0.621
Majority V	0.737	0.718	0.727	0.621
Average P	0.737	0.718	0.727	0.58
Product P	0.737	0.718	0.727	0.58
Max P	0.704	0.487	0.576	0.542
Min P	0.704	0.760	0.731	0.553
EFA	0.9	0.923	0.911	0.866
KNN				
Cfs	0.677	0.538	0.600	0.531
Relief	0.659	0.692	0.675	0.513
InfoGain	0.727	0.615	0.667	0.593
Majority V	0.688	0.564	0.62	0.544
Average P	0.688	0.564	0.62	0.563
Product P	0.688	0.564	0.62	0.571
Max P	0.739	0.436	0.548	0.574
Min P	0.739	0.436	0.548	0.574
EFA	0.878	0.923	0.9	0.842

Table 24.3 Results Summary for the Leukemia Data Set

	Precision	Recall	F-Measure	ROC Area
Decision Tree				
Cfs	0.933	0.894	0.913	0.865
Relief	0.933	0.894	0.913	0.865
InfoGain	0.913	0.894	0.903	0.871
Majority V	0.933	0.894	0.913	0.873
Average P	0.933	0.894	0.913	0.873
Product P	0.933	0.913	0.923	0.883
Max P	0.915	0.915	0.915	0.873
Min P	0.933	0.913	0.923	0.883
EFA	0.911	0.872	0.891	0.843
SVM				
Cfs	0.958	0.979	0.968	0.949
Relief	0.979	0.979	0.979	0.969
InfoGain	0.938	0.957	0.947	0.919
Majority V	0.979	0.979	0.979	0.969
Average P	0.979	0.979	0.979	0.968
Product P	0.978	0.978	0.978	0.959
Max P	0.92	0.979	0.948	0.966
Min P	0.978	0.978	0.978	0.959
EFA	0.958	0.979	0.968	0.949
KNN				
Cfs	0.938	0.957	0.947	0.911
Relief	0.957	0.957	0.957	0.936
InfoGain	0.956	0.915	0.935	0.92
Majority V	0.957	0.957	0.957	0.939
Average P	0.957	0.957	0.957	0.958
Product P	0.957	0.957	0.957	0.958
Max P	0.92	0.979	0.948	0.956
Min P	0.92	0.979	0.948	0.956
EFA	0.978	0.936	0.957	0.947

Table 24.4   Results Summary for the Australian Data Set

	Precision	Recall	F-Measure	ROC Area
Decision Tree				
Cfs	0.906	0.833	0.868	0.882
Relief	0.878	0.849	0.863	0.889
InfoGain	0.93	0.799	0.86	0.832
Majority V	0.883	0.843	0.862	0.852
Average P	0.887	0.841	0.863	0.901
Product P	0.887	0.843	0.865	0.897
Max P	0.901	0.83	0.864	0.897
Min P	0.901	0.83	0.864	0.893
EFA	0.899	0.833	0.864	0.881
SVM				
Cfs	0.936	0.799	0.862	0.865
Relief	0.919	0.802	0.856	0.857
InfoGain	0.927	0.799	0.858	0.86
Majority V	0.921	0.794	0.853	0.855
Average P	0.921	0.794	0.853	0.863
Product P	0.935	0.799	0.862	0.861
Max P	0.914	0.802	0.854	0.864
Min P	0.935	0.799	0.862	0.861
EFA	0.925	0.802	0.859	0.86
KNN				
Cfs	0.89	0.843	0.866	0.897
Relief	0.866	0.864	0.865	0.886
InfoGain	0.853	0.896	0.874	0.892
Majority V	0.857	0.875	0.866	0.846
Average P	0.866	0.875	0.87	0.903
Product P	0.864	0.877	0.87	0.897
Max P	0.865	0.869	0.867	0.91
Min P	0.865	0.869	0.867	0.901
EFA	0.868	0.856	0.862	0.884

Table 24.5   Results Summary for the Tunisian Data Set

	Precision	Recall	F-Measure	ROC Area
Decision Tree				
Cfs	0.865	0.981	0.92	0.553
Relief	0.85	1	0.919	0.497
InfoGain	0.862	0.983	0.919	0.547
Majority V	0.865	0.985	0.921	0.557
Average P	0.85	1	0.919	0.653
Product P	0.85	0.999	0.918	0.647
Max P	0.85	0.999	0.918	0.653
Min P	0.85	0.999	0.918	0.646
EFA	0.85	1	0.919	0.497
SVM				
Cfs	0.851	0.994	0.917	0.505
Relief	0.85	1	0.919	0.5
InfoGain	0.868	0.907	0.887	0.563
Majority V	0.851	0.994	0.917	0.505
Average P	0.851	0.994	0.917	0.505
Product P	0.851	1	0.919	0.505
Max P	0.85	1	0.919	0.505
Min P	0.851	1	0.919	0.505
EFA	0.85	1	0.919	0.5
KNN				
Cfs	0.864	0.959	0.909	0.675
Relief	0.862	0.932	0.895	0.602
InfoGain	0.86	0.94	0.898	0.607
Majority V	0.86	0.967	0.91	0.539
Average P	0.86	0.957	0.906	0.67
Product P	0.86	0.937	0.897	0.658
Max P	0.86	0.937	0.897	0.67
Min P	0.86	0.937	0.897	0.643
EFA	0.861	0.931	0.895	0.596

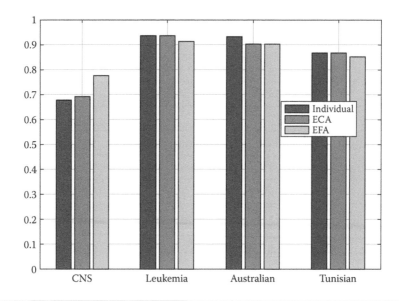

Figure 24.2   Class precision with DT classifier.

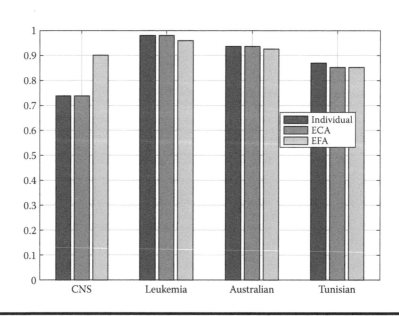

Figure 24.3   Class precision with SVM classifier.

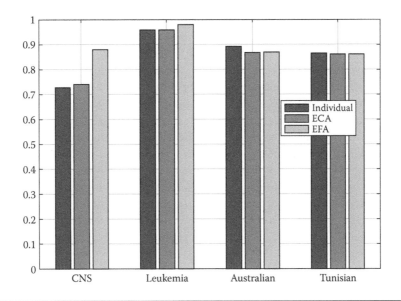

Figure 24.4 Class precision with KNN classifier.

preprocessing step before the learning process. In case the data set is big and the number of feature does not exceed the number of instances, aggregation is more beneficial once it is used on the learning algorithms trained over the reduced data by individual filters.

24.6 Discussion

In this chapter, we investigate the use of ensemble methods for classification of data sets with different sizes. The use of ensemble methods is studied on two different levels. The first is the classification level, and the second is the feature selection level. Our objective is to study the characteristics and to compare the performance of each setting but especially to search for the level in which the feature selection process is the most effective. First of all, we apply three different feature selection methods on four data sets yielding three selected feature subsets for each data set. Then, in the first setting, we apply a classification algorithm on the projection of each feature subset on the training data. We then aggregate the classification results of the ensemble. In the second setting, the three selected feature subsets obtained initially are combined in order to obtain a final individual feature subset before proceeding to the classification step. The comparison of the two settings' performances conducts to the following conclusions. On most cases, the ensemble results, obtained by either one ensemble setting or the other, outperform those obtained by the application of a single feature selection algorithm followed by a single classifier. For data sets with small dimensionality, the best performance results are obtained by classifiers' aggregation and never with feature selectors' aggregation.

For high-dimensional data sets, the best performance results are achieved by either classifiers or selector aggregation, with special high values when feature selector aggregation is applied. A possible explanation of the better performance of feature selection aggregation for high-dimensional data sets and not for small-size data sets is that with the latter, individual feature subsets, obtained by different feature selection methods, could be very similar given that the initial number of features is small. However, in the case of high-dimensional data sets, obtained feature subsets from the ensemble feature selection process could be very different since the feature space is very large. Thus, features' combination effect on classification performance is much more apparent in the case of high-dimensional data sets. Hence, the sample size is a determining factor for the choice of one or the other setting when the performance criterion taken into consideration is the classification accuracy. Stability is another important criterion for evaluating feature selection results, and in terms of this metric, we expect that feature selection algorithm ensembles will be preferred as they focus on improving classification results by strengthening feature selection results. It is not the case for classifier ensembles, which focus on strengthening classification results without special care to feature selection phase.

24.7 Conclusion and Future Directions

We proposed ensemble approaches that combine feature selection and data classification for cancer diagnosis and credit scoring. Two alternatives were tested. The first one combines feature sets obtained by applying an ensemble of feature selection techniques in order to get a single solution on which a classifier is trained. The second alternative trains a classifier on each feature set and then combines the classifier ensemble to obtain a single classification output. Our experiments on four data sets with different dimensionality and from two important fields, namely, cancer diagnosis and credit scoring, showed that sample size affects classification results obtained by one or the other setting. Thus, data dimensionality can determine which aggregation level must be chosen, classification or feature selection level, in order to have more efficient results. Stability is another performance criterion that can be used to evaluate our experiments as it becomes important to have stable feature selection results with the ever-increasing data dimensionality due to high technologies.

References

Burges, J. (1998). A tutorial on support vector machines for pattern recognition. *Data Mining and Knowledge Discovery* 2(2), 121–167.

Dietterich, T. G. (2000). Ensemble methods in machine learning. In Proceedings of the First International Workshop on Multiple Classifier Systems, London, Springer-Verlag, pp. 1–15.

Fernandez, G. (2010). *Statistical Data Mining Using SAS Applications*. Chapman & Hall/CRC: Data Mining and Knowledge Discovery, London, Taylor and Francis.

Golub, T. R., D. K. Slonim, P. Tamayo, C. Huard, M. Gaasenbeek, J. P. Mesirov, H. Coller, M. L. Loh, J. R. Downing, M. A. Caligiuri, and C. D. Bloomfield. (1999). Molecular classification of cancer: Class discovery and class prediction by gene expression monitoring. *Science* 286, 531–537.

Hall, M. A. (2000). Correlation-based feature selection for discrete and numeric class machine learning. In Proceedings of the Seventeenth International Conference on Machine Learning, Morgan Kaufmann, pp. 359–366.

Hall, M., E. Frank, G. Holmes, B. Pfahringer, P. Reutemann and I. H. Witten. (2009). The WEKA data mining software: An update. *SIGKDD Explorations* 11(1), 10–18.

Howley, T., M. G. Madden, M. L. O'Connell, and A. G. Ryder. (2006). The effect of principal component analysis on machine learning accuracy with high-dimensional spectral data. *Knowledge-Based Systems* 19, 363–370.

Kira, K. and L. Rendell. (1992). A practical approach to feature selection. In D. Sleeman and P. Edwards (Eds.), International Conference on Machine Learning, pp. 368–377.

Kohane, I. S., A. T. Kho, and A. J. Butte. (2003). *Microarrays for an Integrative Genomics*. Cambridge, MA: MIT Press.

Liu, H. and L. Yu. (2005). Toward integrating feature selection algorithms for classification and clustering. *IEEE Transactions on Knowledge and Data Engineering* 17(4), 491–502.

Liu, Y. and M. Schumann. (2005). Data mining feature selection for credit scoring models. *Journal of the Operational Research Society* 56, 1099–1108.

Okun, O. (2011). Feature Selection and Ensemble Methods for Bioinformatics: Algorithmic Classification and Implementations. Medical Information Science Reference, Hershey, PA.

Opitz, D. W. (1999). Feature selection for ensembles. In Proceedings of 16th National Conference on Artificial Intelligence (AAAI), Press, pp. 379–384.

Pihur, V., S. Datta, and S. Datta. (2009). RankAggreg, an R package for weighted rank aggregation. *BMC Bioinformatics* 10(1), 62.

Piramuthu, S. (2006). On preprocessing data for financial credit risk evaluation. *Expert Systems with Applications* 30, 489–497.

Pomeroy, S. L., P. Tamayo, M. Gaasenbeek, L. M. Sturla, M. Angelo, M. E. McLaughlin, J. Y. H. Kim, L. C. Goumnerova, P. M. Black, C. Lau, J. C. Allen, D. Zagzag, J. M. Olson, T. Curran, C. Wetmore, J. A. Biegel, T. Poggio, S. Mukherjee, R. Rifkin, A. Califano, G. Stolovitzky, D. N. Louis, J. P. Mesirov, E. S. Lander, and T. R. Golub. (2002). Prediction of central nervous system embryonal tumour outcome based on gene expression. *Nature* 415(6870), 436–442.

Quinlan, J. R. (1993). *C4.5: Programs for Machine Learning*. San Francisco, USA, Morgan Kaufmann Publishers Inc.

Rodriguez, I., R. Huerta, C. Elkan, and C. S. Cruz. (2010). Quadratic programming feature selection. *Journal of Machine Learning Research* 11, 1491–1516.

Saeys, Y., T. Abeel, and Y. Peer. (2008). Robust feature selection using ensemble feature selection techniques. In Proceedings of the European Conference on Machine Learning and Knowledge Discovery in Databases—Part II, ECML PKDD '08, Berlin, Heidelberg, Springer-Verlag, pp. 313–325.

Schowe, B. and K. Morik. (2011). Fast-ensembles of minimum redundancy feature selection. *Ensembles in Machine Learning Applications, Studies in Computational Intelligence*, pp. 373, 75–95. Berlin, Heidelberg, Springer.

Schulz, W. A. (2007). *Molecular Biology of Human Cancers: An Advanced Students Textbook*. Dordrecht, The Netherlands: Springer.

Thomas, L. (2009). *Consumer Credit Models: Pricing, Profit, and Portfolios*. New York, USA, Oxford University Press.

Tsai, C. F. and J. W. Wu. (2008). Using neural network ensembles for bankruptcy prediction and credit scoring. *Expert Systems with Applications* 34, 2639–2649.

Tsymbal, A., M. Pechenizkiy, and P. Cunningham. (2005). Sequential genetic search for ensemble feature selection. In Proceedings of the 19th International Joint Conference on Artificial Intelligence, IJCAI'05, San Francisco, Morgan Kaufmann Publishers Inc., pp. 877–882.

Tuv, E., A. Borisov, G. Runger, K. Torkkola, I. Guyon, and A. R. Saffari. (2009). Feature selection with ensembles, artificial variables, and redundancy elimination. *Journal of Machine Learning Research* 10, 1341–1366.

Weinberg, R. A. (2007). *The Biology of Cancer*. New York: Garland Science.

Chapter 25

Intelligent Grade Estimation Technique for Indian Black Tea

Amit Laddi and Neelam Rup Prakash

Contents

The physical characteristics of made black crushing, tearing, and curling (CTC) tea were investigated by machine vision, and a quality grade estimation technique was developed by the application of neuro-fuzzy algorithms. The physical characteristics such as average size, shape (aspect ratio), and surface texture of the tea granules along with infused liquor color (after tea brewing) were acquired using an image acquisition system consisting of a machine vision setup. Data analysis in the form of principal component analysis (PCA) was performed to extract the significant physical attributes. The results of PCA were further investigated to obtain the correlations among tea samples and quality grades. The most significant physical attributes were fed to intelligent grade estimation software based upon neuro-fuzzy algorithms developed in MATLAB® software by using an adaptive neuro-fuzzy inference system (ANFIS). The proposed technique showed an accuracy of about 95%. The precision and repeatability by this technique was found be closer to the tea tasters' perception, which can impart assistance to the tea tasters in a user-friendly and rapid manner, leaving aside the cumbersome chemical analysis.

25.1 Existing Scenario in Tea Quality Evaluation and Need for an Instrumentation-Based Technique: An Introduction

The black crushing, tearing, and curling (CTC) tea variety is a fermented one, and therefore, its physical characteristics are usually different from other unfermented tea varieties (Roberts 1962). The CTC tea is usually cheaper than other types of tea such as orthodox, green, and so forth but considered to be inferior in quality. However, it is the most popular tea variety in India and has maximum consumption amongst all.

The quality of black CTC tea depends upon the manufacturing process, which requires maceration and fermentation more extensively (Owuor et al. 1989). Other conditions that affect the CTC tea quality are related to the tea cultivation techniques, geographical location, atmospheric conditions, rainfall, altitude, manufacturing techniques including withering and fermentation durations, and so forth (Fernandez et al. 2002; Ashu and Ravindranath 1996; Tomlins and Mashingaidze 1997; Ravichandran and Parthiban 1998; Hazarika and Mahanta 1983; Mahanta and Baruah 1992; Emdadi et al. 2009).

Generally, tea quality assessment is done by tea auction centers through the tea taster's sensorial approach, which involves tasting and smelling the aroma of the brewed tea liquor along with its physical verification, which includes inspection of tea liquor color, surface texture, and morphological aspects (shape, size, etc.) of the tea granules. This technique of tea grading and price fixation is presently the most widely used and recognized methodology for tea quality estimation. However, tea buyers have no mediums to know the actual quality of tea as there is no authentication of the grading process, and the results may vary due to bias, which is a serious problem. Also, the human organoleptic methods may not be precise enough in discriminating different tea varieties due to subjectivity, mental state, insensitivity caused by prolonged exposure, and so forth. The error may also be involved due to different tea varieties having nearly similar color, size, shape, or odor. Such conditions may increase difficulty in classification due to limited sensitivity of human senses. Under the aforesaid circumstances, the results of the human organoleptic methods may vary from each other, resulting in confusion and doubt among tea buyers.

Researchers have tried to overcome the highly subjective nature of this technique by using instrument-based approaches that involve chemical analysis–based estimation for tea quality, but these methods are complex, laborious, expensive, and time-consuming.

Nowadays machine vision is used for the inspection of fruits and vegetables very frequently, where physical characteristics such as size, shape, and color characteristics were analyzed for quality grade estimation with advantages such as user friendliness, simplicity, quickness, low cost, and better results (Aleixos et al. 2002; Blasco et al. 2003; Leemans and Destain 2004; Leemans et al. 2002; Moreda et al. 2009; Brosnan and Sun 2002). Therefore, tea grading that involves physical evaluation of tea samples using machine vision may be more useful under current circumstances. This technique mimics the physical verification approach of tea tasters by using the advanced tools of machine vision, which are capable of classifying various black tea samples with desirable accuracy (Liang et al. 2005; Borah et al. 2007). Previous studies also showed correlations among tea samples and physical attributes and, further, their relationship with quality (Laddi et al. 2012, 2013). By taking reference from these techniques, the authors have tried to devise a novel tea grading technique, as shown in Figure 25.1, which involves acquisition of all the physical parameters using machine vision, consisting of a workstation computer attached to the machine vision setup, that is, 3CCD color camera, white LED ring light with intensity controller, aphotic housing, and so forth. Brewed liquor color along with other physical features such as surface texture, size, and shape of black tea granules were captured through machine vision in the visible spectra. To identify the significant quality attributes (which explained maximum variance in the data with good classification) among other physical characteristics, statistical analysis, that is, principal component analysis (PCA) is performed, and the significant parameters determined through PCA were trained as per the tea tasters' feedback using intelligent software techniques such as artificial neural networks (ANNs) and fuzzy logic. Recent studies suggest that ANN has the capability to imitate the human intelligence and learning. Further, the authors have tried to simplify the grading procedure through an adaptive neuro-fuzzy inference system (ANFIS). The neuro-fuzzy technique includes the data learning capabilities of ANN along with adaptability provided by fuzzy logic. The results of this technique were found to be satisfactory with very little hassle as there is no need to define new rules every time a new tea sample is added to the training database, unlike the fuzzy-based system, where rules need to be defined occasionally.

The proposed intelligent grade estimation software consists of two sections. The first section includes physical attribute acquisition from the tea samples along with the grading information gathered from the tea tasters for the respective tea sample. The second section of the system works as soft computing technique, which trains the known physical attributes of tea samples with their respective tea grades and also tests the unknown tea samples for grade estimation. The training performance was found to be very close to tea taster's results, which confirmed that the proposed system has potential to be used as commercial grade estimation technique. Also, it can be used to train tea tasters during the training sessions. The major advantage of the system is its capability for discrimination when there is some confusion between any two very similar tea samples during grade estimation. Thus, the objective of the work was to devise a methodology using machine vision and soft computing to quantify black tea quality in terms of numerical grades between 1 and 100, namely, highest to lowest qualities. The benefits of this technique are consistency, user friendliness, low cost, and instant results.

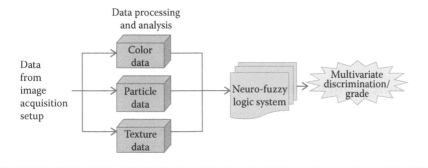

Figure 25.1   Block diagram: tea grade estimation system using physical parameters.

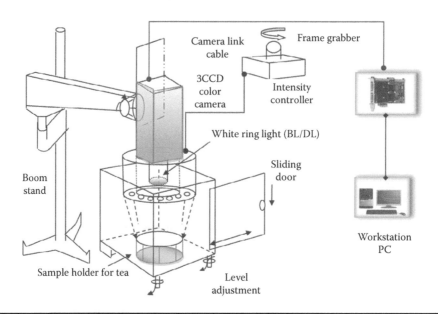

Figure 25.2   Image acquisition setup.

25.2 Imaging Setup

The image acquisition setup as shown in Figure 25.2 includes an aphotic housing built using a black acrylic sheet with a provision to hold samples for color of tea liquor, texture, and morphological features of tea granules. A 3CCD camera (Jai CV m9 CL, JAI Manufacturing, Japan) along with dual white LED ring light having an intensity controller (CS100-IC) was adjusted at the boom stand (Edmund Optics, Singapore), and both were fixed perpendicular to the sample plate in the aphotic housing. The dual ring light consists of both bright-field and dark-field illumination. The camera has an effective pixel resolution of 1024 (h) × 768 (v). The camera was connected via a Camera Link port as an interface medium to the frame grabber card mounted at the PCI express slot of the computer. The C-mount lens with 25 mm focal length was attached (KOWA LM25NC3, Kowa Optimed, Inc., USA) to the camera with a working distance of 135 mm and a field of view of 25.5 (h) × 19 (v) mm. The template plates (Edmund Optics) were used for calibrating the machine vision setup.

Multiple levels of intensity of illumination from low to high were projected at the target area of the sampler and controlled by using an intensity meter, and their effect was analyzed using the PCA technique till the maximum discrimination setting was achieved.

25.3 Sample Collection

A total of 500 Indian black tea (CTC) samples were collected from various tea auction centers across Northeastern India along with their month of harvest and place of manufacture, which includes names of tea gardens and so forth. The gathered tea samples were awarded numerical grading by the tea tasters after analyzing their aroma, taste, and physical features. The tea samples were properly labeled and filled into vacuum bottles to avoid any deterioration of quality due to the addition of the moisture.

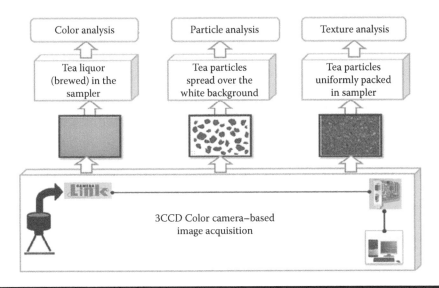

Figure 25.3   Sample preparation techniques.

25.4 Sample Preparation Procedure

The tea samples were prepared carefully to circumvent any error that may be added to the analysis part of the experiment that may affect the classification accuracy. Specialized sample preparation techniques were devised based upon the requirements to get maximum feature extraction by imaging for liquor color, texture, and particle features of the tea samples, as shown in Figure 25.3.

The procedure to prepare the tea sample to get the color information was used as per the international standards, which involves measurement of 0.500 g of each tea sample, brewed into 25 mL of fresh boiling water for about 6 min and filtered using general-purpose filter paper (Whatman No. 1) in a sampler to be used for color measurement under bright field illumination.

To prepare the sample for measurement of the textural features, the tea granules were uniformly packed into the sampler under dark-field illumination. The sample for particle analysis was prepared by spreading tea granules far away from each other over a white background such that no two granules touched each other.

25.5 Machine Vision Technique

The image acquisition began with preprocessing, which involved multisampling, geometric correction, and image calibration to minimize the errors presented into the imaging setup. The image acquisition involved color and morphological features under bright-field illumination, whereas dark-field illumination was used for texture analysis.

The three different types of images acquired from each tea sample were subjected to image processing using MATLAB version 2012 software to obtain color, texture, and particle information in terms of mean color index, textural features, average size, and shape (aspect ratio of granules) for each sample.

The color index in terms of L, a*, and b* values were obtained. The reason for choosing the International Commission for Illumination (CIE) La*b* color model over the RGB model is correct and better human perception of color identification, whereas the RGB model causes human eyes to perceive color incorrectly due to its additive and subtractive phenomenon. The color values obtained in the La*b* color model were compared with the colorimeter device, which showed identical response for all the tea samples.

The textural properties of acquired images were obtained using statistical techniques involving gray-level co-occurrence matrix (GLCM). The textural attributes such as entropy, contrast, homogeneity, correlation, and energy were calculated for each tea sample.

The first textural feature determined was "entropy," and its calculation requires conversion of a color image to a grayscale image, whereas other features were calculated from a GLCM. The GLCM is created from the grayscale image by calculating how often a pixel with gray-level (grayscale intensity) value i occurs horizontally adjacent to a pixel with the value j. Each element (i, j) in GLCM specifies the number of times that the pixel with value i occurred horizontally adjacent to a pixel with value j (Haralick et al. 1973; Haralick and Shapiro 1992).

"Entropy" is a statistical measure of randomness that can be used to characterize the texture of the input image. "Entropy" for a grayscale image is defined as follows:

$$\text{Entropy} = -\text{sum} \ (p \ [i, j] \ *\text{log2} \ (p \ [i, j]))$$

where p contains the histogram counts used for 256 bins of grayscale image (Gonzalez et al. 2003). "Entropy" is highest when all entries in $p \ [i, j]$ are of similar magnitude and is small when the entries in $p \ [i, j]$ are unequal.

GLCM is used to calculate the other four textural features. The textural feature "contrast" is a measure of the intensity contrast between a pixel and its neighbor over the whole image. The range of "contrast" lies between 0 to (size (GLCM, 1) $-1)^2$. Further, "contrast" is 0 for a constant image. The textural feature "correlation" is a measure of how correlated a pixel is to its neighbor over the whole image. Its range lies between -1 and $+1$. Also, the "correlation" is 1 or -1 for a perfectly positively or negatively correlated image. The fourth textural feature is "energy," which returns the sum of squared elements in the GLCM. The range for "energy" lies between 0 and 1, and for a constant image, its value is 1. Finally, the last textural feature calculated is "homogeneity." It is an indication of how uniformly a given region is structured. It returns a value that measures the closeness of the distribution of elements in the GLCM to the GLCM diagonal. "Homogeneity" has a range of 0 to 1. It is 1 for a diagonal GLCM.

The morphological features such as average granule size (average area and average perimeter) along with aspect ratio were obtained after image processing operations, which included image segmentation, threshold operation, binary morphological functions, and pixel measurements to get particle dimensions. The particle measurement also involved conversion of pixel values to real-world units (mm) using a calibration grid (Edmund Optics).

The color, textural, and morphological parameters of each tea sample obtained using image processing and statistical techniques were saved to the database for a data analysis procedure, which includes statistical analysis using PCA software for classification along with intelligent soft computing using ANFIS software for grade estimation.

25.6 Statistical Analysis Using PCA

The physical attributes acquired using machine vision were fed to the statistical analysis technique, that is, PCA, to reduce the dimensions of the input matrix, which consist of only significant variables to be used for the soft computing. Also, the PCA technique can be used to draw the correlations among samples as well as the variables. PCA can display an interpretable overview of the significant information in the form of multidimensional data clusters and consists of the principal components (PCs) that are the linear functions of the original variables and contain the main structured information in the data in a decreasing order. All the PCs are orthogonal to the each other. The principal components PC1, PC2, PC3, PC4, and so forth map the variance in descending order with a decrease in their significance. The plot gives clustered data showing the variability among various tea samples based upon their physical attributes in terms of calculated variance. To detect the significant physical parameters responsible for maximum discrimination, a PCA biplot is used, which is a combination of scores and loading weights that shows the relationship between samples and variables. The score vectors plotted against each other show the variance in the input data. The loading weights drawn from the origin show the significance of the corresponding variables and their contribution towards explained variance. The angles between the vectors show the relationships between the variables themselves, and the vector direction is indicative of the correlations between variables and samples. Variables close to each other, situated out towards the periphery of the plots from the PC origin, covary strongly and proportionally. If the variables lie on the same side of the origin, they have positive correlation. If they lie on opposite sides of the origin, more or less along a straight line through the PC origin, they are negatively correlated. The loading vectors that are perpendicular to each other through the origin are independent. Loadings close to the PC axis are significant only to that PC, and variables with a large loading on both the PCs are significant to them (Esbensen 2004).

25.7 Neuro-Fuzzy–Based Approach and Explanation of ANFIS Technique

Generally, a tea taster's quality explanations are based upon common language words, which are termed as linguistic terms, such as good, excellent, satisfactory, and so forth. These linguistic terms can be used to generate a fuzzy logic–based grade estimation system. It requires setting the values of physical attributes of the tea samples as per the tea taster's observations, which can vary with respect to quality of the samples, atmospheric conditions, months of harvest, and processing techniques applied. Usually, such data comes out to be unfocused due to various factors affecting the tea quality, and fuzzy logic is the convenient way of mapping an input space to an output space on such data. Therefore, the advantage of working upon nonlinear data was the reason for choosing fuzzy logic as it can model nonlinear functions of arbitrary complexity.

In the present work, tea tasters provided grading to the tea samples after evaluating their physical characteristics in terms of numbers. The designing of a fuzzy inference system (FIS) required calculation of the type, value, and number of the membership functions along with the formation of rules by using the expert advice of the tea tasters with respect to the information related to the physical attributes. Also, the number of samples under consideration was large, which required a lot of time and effort to generate rules for each sample. Therefore, to generate the rules for fuzzy logic system, a new approach was applied, known as ANFIS. In this technique, the rule generation is done automatically by using advanced learning of ANN. Moreover, it also computes and adjusts the membership function parameters associated with input/output data.

Therefore, the neuro-adaptive learning of ANFIS works similarly to that of ANN and provides a method for the fuzzy modeling procedure to learn information about any data set. Thus, the procedure of ANFIS is simplistic and efficient for training the large database of physical characteristics of tea samples with respect to their numerical grades given by tea tasters. By using a given input/output data set, the ANFIS function constructs a Sugeno-type FIS whose membership function parameters are adjusted using a backpropagation algorithm alone or in combination with a least-squares type of method. The parameters associated with the membership functions change through the learning process.

The ANFIS function is less customizable than fuzzy logic, and it has some limitations, such as it can only support Sugeno-type systems having first or zeroth order. Also, the ANFIS function generates a single output obtained using weighted average defuzzification. Its other limitations include that all output membership functions must be the same type and are either linear or constant. Also, no rule sharing is allowed, along with each rule having unity weight only. These limitations have lesser impact than its advantages, such as simplicity, ease of use, self-learning, and so forth.

The ANFIS function includes many steps, such as loading input/output data set, generation, training and validation of FIS, and so forth. The FIS is trained by loading a training data set that contains the desired input/output data of the system to be modeled, arranged in column vectors with output in the last column, and generate single-output Sugeno-type FIS by partitioning or clustering techniques such as grid partitioning, subtractive clustering, and fuzzy *c*-means (FCM) clustering, which are known as genfis1, genfis2, and genfis3, respectively. The Backpropagation or hybrid optimization methods are used to train the FIS structure. Finally, the optimization methods train the membership function parameters to emulate the training data by entering the number of training epochs or the training error tolerance to set the stopping criteria for training. The training process stops whenever the maximum epoch number is reached or the training error goal is achieved.

25.8 Results and Discussion

25.8.1 Data Analysis (PCA) and Classification of Tea Samples

Statistical analysis using PCA showed 96% variance in data involving all the physical parameters with good clustering, as shown in the biplot (Figure 25.4). It was observed that all the color values, namely, L, a*, and b*, were found to be the most significant attributes as their loading vectors were longest among all and they were found nearest to the outer ellipse. The significance of texture features such as entropy, contrast, homogeneity, correlation, and energy of the tea granules was found to intermediate between color attributes and morphological features such as average width-to-length ratio and size (area and perimeter). Amongst morphological parameters, the aspect ratio and average area have higher significance than average perimeter, which lay between inner ellipse and origin, so it was discarded for further analysis, being the least significant physical parameter. Therefore, the results obtained through PCA showed that 10 physical attributes out of the 11 were sufficient for the grade estimation procedure as insignificant parameters increase the response time and decrease the accuracy of the system.

25.8.2 ANFIS-Based Grade Estimation Algorithm

The authors have attempted to devise a novel method using a neuro-fuzzy approach to estimate grading of tea samples in terms of numbers considering only the physical characteristics.

The ANFIS-based grade estimation technique was implemented in the MATLAB programming language environment with the fuzzy logic toolbox, which consists of 10 significant physical attributes as inputs to ANFIS model and a single decision (output grade in terms of score between 1 and 100), as shown in Figure 25.5.

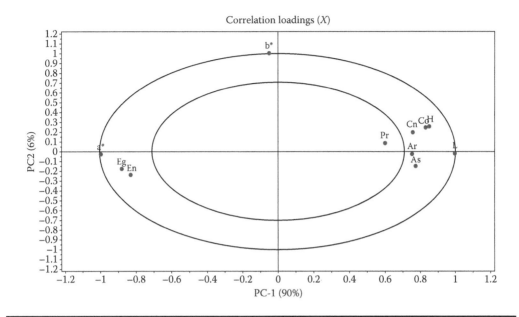

Figure 25.4   Correlation loading plot based upon all the physical parameters.

The genfis3 function was used for rule generation along with hybrid learning methodology for training fuzzy membership function parameters. The reason for using genfis3 is the fact that the tea samples are trained as per grading information, which leads to the formation of various clusters having different data points. The degree of belongingness is specified by membership grades. The data matrix consisting of physical attributes and grading information of each tea sample is fed to the genfis3, with the number of clusters fixed as 10, similar to the number of input variables. A total of 10 rules were generated, having 10 clusters for each rule.

The database was divided into 350 and 150 data points as training and testing sets, respectively. As the testing or checking data are used for testing the generalization capability of the FIS at each epoch, they have the same format as that of the training data, but their elements are different from those of the training data. The need for testing data is to avoid the overfitting problem as the model structure used for ANFIS is fixed and there is a tendency for such a model to overfit the data on which it is trained. This data set is used to cross-validate the fuzzy inference model by repeated checking.

25.8.3 PC-Based System

This ANFIS model was further used to create a PC-based system for simple user control and analysis, as shown in Figure 25.6. The graphical user interface (GUI) of the grading system was divided into three modules. The first and second modules were used for image acquisition, addition of grade information, and training the database. The third module shows the results of testing for any unknown tea sample with numerical grade as output along with an option to save it to the database as required. The results of the system were matched with tea tasters' observations with an accuracy of 95%. The system accuracy can further be improved by sufficient training on routine basis and updating the database.

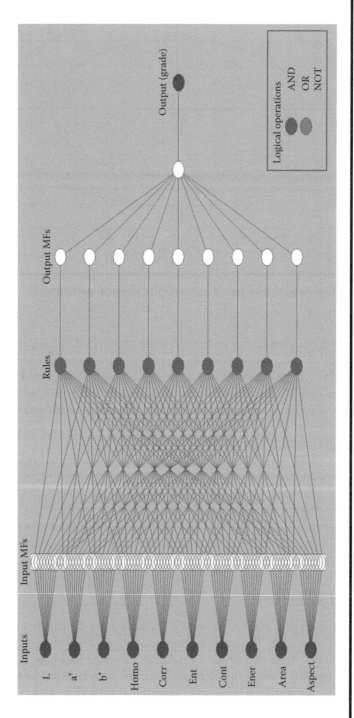

Figure 25.5   ANFIS-based grade estimation system using significant physical parameters.

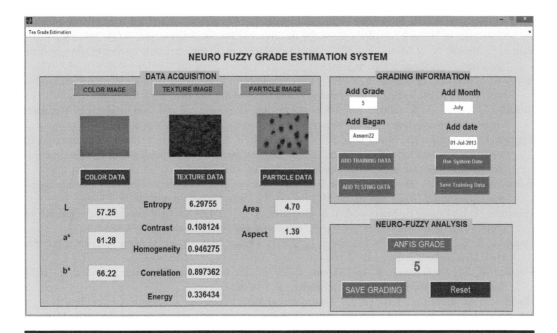

Figure 25.6   Graphical user interface for tea grade estimation instrument.

25.9 Conclusion

The PC-based system was developed along with a modified machine vision setup consisting of new sample analysis techniques for color, texture, and morphological attributes. Overall, 10 physical attributes were found to be significant using PCA. The significance of physical parameters observed by descending order is color of brewed tea liquor, textural features, and morphological aspects such as size and shape of tea granules. The average perimeter of tea granules was found to be less significant than other physical attributes; therefore, it was discarded for grade estimation. The proposed system was developed for grading based upon physical characteristics by using a combination of both ANNs and an FIS. The system was trained and tested on over 500 samples of CTC tea collected from Northeastern India. The proposed system is fast, repeatable, and hassle free with a high degree of accuracy. It is envisaged that the proposed neuro-fuzzy grade estimation (NFGE) based technique's adaptability will help tea tasters to assess tea quality more accurately along with quick verification of grading results.

Acknowledgments

The authors are thankful to the Council of Scientific & Industrial Research (CSIR) for project funding along with Dr Amod Kumar and Mrs. Shashi Sharma for their guidance and support.

References

Aleixos, N., Blasco, J., Navarrón, F. & Moltó, E. (2002). Multispectral inspection of citrus in real-time using machine vision and digital signal processors. *Computers and Electronics in Agriculture*, 33(2), 121–137.

Ashu, G. & Ravindranath, S. D. (1996). Seasonal variations in quality of Kangra Tea (Camellia sinensis (L) O Kuntze) in Himachal Pradesh. *Journal of the Science of Food and Agriculture*, 71(2), 231–236.

Blasco, J., Aleixos, N. & Moltó, E. (2003). Machine vision system for automatic quality grading of fruit. *Biosystems Engineering*, 85(4), 415–423.

Borah, S., Hines, E. L. & Bhuyan, M. (2007). Wavelet transform based image texture analysis for size estimation applied to the sorting of tea granules. *Journal of Food Engineering*, 79(2), 629–639.

Brosnan, T. & Sun, D. W. (2002). Inspection and grading of agricultural and food products by computer vision systems- a review. *Computers and Electronics in Agriculture*, 36(2–3), 193–213.

Emdadi, L., Nasernajad, B., Shokrgozar, S. T., Mehranian, M. & Vahabzadeh, F. (2009). Optimization of withering time and fermentation conditions during the manufacture of black tea using a response surface methodology. *Chemistry and Chemical Engineering*, 16(1), 61–68.

Esbensen, K. H. (2004). *Multivariate Data Analysis in Practice: An Introduction to Multivariate Data Analysis and Experimental Design*, 5th ed. CAMO Process AS, Oslo, Norway, reprint 2004, 33–40.

Fernandez, P. L., Pablos, F., Martin, M. J. & Gonzalez, A. G. (2002). Study of catechin and xanthine tea profiles as geographical tracers. *Journal of Agricultural and Food Chemistry*, 50(7), 1833–1839.

Gonzalez, R. C., Woods, R. E. & Eddins, S. L. (2003). *Digital Image Processing Using MATLAB*. Prentice Hall, New Jersey (Chapter 11).

Haralick, R. M., Shanmugam, K. & Dinstein, I. (1973). Textural features for image classification. *IEEE Transactions on Systems, Man, and Cybernetics*, (3), 610–621.

Haralick, R. M. & Shapiro, L. G. (1992). *Computer and Robot Vision*, Vol. 1. Addison-Wesley, 459.

Hazarika, M. & Mahanta, P. K. (1983). Some studies on carotenoids and their degradation in black tea manufacture. *Journal of the Science of Food and Agriculture*, 34(12), 1390–1396.

Laddi, A., Prakash, N. R., Sharma, S., Mondal, H. S., Kumar, A. & Kapur, P. (2012). Significant physical attributes affecting quality of Indian black (CTC) tea. *Journal of Food Engineering*, 113(2), 69–78.

Laddi, A., Sharma, S., Kumar, A. & Kapur, P. (2013). Classification of tea grains based upon image texture feature analysis under different illumination conditions. *Journal of Food Engineering*, 115(2), 226–231.

Leemans, V. & Destain, M. F. (2004). A real-time grading method of apples based on features extracted from defects. *Journal of Food Engineering*, 61, 83–89.

Leemans, V., Magein, H. & Destain, M. F. (2002). On-line fruit grading according to their external quality using machine vision. *Biosystems Engineering*, 83(4), 397–404.

Liang, Y., Lu, J., Zhang, L., Wu, S. & Wu, Y. (2005). Estimation of tea quality by infusion color difference analysis. *Journal of the Science of Food and Agriculture*, 85(2), 286–292.

Mahanta, P. K. & Baruah, H. K. (1992). Theaflavin pigment formation and polyphenol oxidase activity as criteria of fermentation in orthodox and CTC teas. *Journal of Agricultural and Food Chemistry*, 40(5), 860–863.

Moreda, G. P., Ortiz-Cañavate, J., García-Ramos, F. J. & Ruiz-Altisent, M. (2009). Non-destructive technologies for fruit and vegetable size determination—A Review. *Journal of Food Engineering*, 92(2), 119–136.

Owuor, P. O., Othieno, C. O. & Takeo, T. (1989). Effects of maceration method on the chemical composition and quality of clonal black. *Journal of the Science of Food and Agriculture*, 49(1), 87–94.

Ravichandran, R. & Parthiban, R. (1998). The impact of processing techniques on tea volatiles. *Food Chemistry*, 62(7), 347–353.

Roberts, E. A. H. (1962). Economic importance of flavonoid substances: Tea fermentation. In: Geissman, T. A. (Ed). *The Chemistry of Flavonoid Compounds*. Pergamon Press, Oxford, 409–512.

Tomlins, K. I. & Mashingaidze, A. (1997). Influence of withering, including leaf handling, on the manufacturing and quality of black teas-a review. *Food Chemistry*, 60(4), 573–580.

Index

Page numbers followed by f and t indicate figures and tables, respectively.